The first**writer**.com

Writers' Handbook
2014

The first**writer**.com

Writers' Handbook
2014

EDITOR
J. PAUL DYSON

Published in 2013 by JP&A Dyson
Copyright JP&A Dyson

http://www.firstwriter.com

ISBN 978-1-909935-00-6

Registered with the IP Rights Office
Copyright Registration Service
Ref: 145728779

Foreword

This directory includes hundreds of listings of **literary agents**, **book publishers**, and **magazines**, updated in **firstwriter.com**'s online databases between 2011 and 2013.

It also provides free access to the entire current databases, including over 850 literary agencies, over 1,400 book publishers, over 1,600 magazines, and constantly updated listings of current writing competitions, with typically more than 50 added each month.

For details on how to claim your free access please see the back of this book.

Included in the subscription

A subscription to the full website is not only free with this book, but comes packed with all the following features:

Advanced search features

- Save searches and save time – set up to 15 search parameters specific to your work, save them, and then access the search results with a single click whenever you log in. You can even save multiple different searches if you have different types of work you are looking to place.
- Add personal notes to listings, visible only to you and fully searchable – helping you to organise your actions.
- Set reminders on listings to notify you when to submit your work, when to follow up, when to expect a reply, or any other custom action.
- Track which listings you've viewed and when, to help you organise your search – any listings which have changed since you last viewed them will be highlighted for your attention!

Daily email updates

As a subscriber you will be able to take advantage of our email alert service, meaning you can specify your particular interests and we'll send you automatic email updates when we change or add a listing that matches them. So if you're interested in agents dealing in romantic fiction in the United States you can have us send you emails with the latest updates about them – keeping you up to date without even having to log in.

User feedback

Our agent, publisher, and magazine databases all include a user feedback feature that allows our subscribers to leave feedback on each listing – giving you not only the chance to have your say about the markets you contact, but giving a unique authors' perspective on the listings.

Save on copyright protection fees

If you're sending your work away to publishers, competitions, or literary agents, it's vital that you first protect your copyright. As a subscriber to firstwriter.com you can do this through our site and save 10% on the copyright registration fees normally payable for protecting your work internationally through the Intellectual Property Rights Office (http://www.Copyright RegistrationService.com).

firstwriter.magazine

firstwriter.magazine showcases the best in new poetry and fiction from around the world. If you're interested in writing and want to get published, the most important thing you can do is read contemporary writing that's getting into print now. Our magazine helps you do that.

Half price competitions

As well as saving money on copyright registration, subscribers to **firstwriter.com** can also make further savings by entering writing competitions at a special reduced rate. Subscribers can enter the **firstwriter.com International Poetry Competition** and **International Short Story Contest** for half price.

Monthly newsletter

When you subscribe to **firstwriter.com** you also receive our monthly email newsletter – described by one publishing company as "the best in the business" – including articles, news, and interviews for writers. And the best part is that you can continue to receive the newsletter even after you stop your paid subscription – at no cost!

For details on how to claim your free access please see the back of this book.

Contents

Magazines

Free Access

Glossary of Terms

This section explains common terms used in this handbook, and in the publishing industry more generally.

Agented

An *agented* submission is one which is submitted by a literary agent. If a publisher accepts only *agented* submissions then you will need a literary agent to submit the work on your behalf.

Author bio

A brief description of you and your life – normally in relation to your writing activity, but if intended for publication (particularly in magazines) may be broader in scope. May be similar to *Curriculum Vitae* (CV) or résumé, depending on context.

Bio

See *Author bio*.

Curriculum Vitae

A brief description of you, your qualifications, and accomplishments – normally in this context in relation to writing (any previous publications, or awards, etc.), but in the case of nonfiction proposals may also include relevant experience that qualifies you to write on the subject. Commonly abbreviated to "CV". May also be referred to as a résumé. May be similar to *Author bio*, depending on context.

CV

See *Curriculum Vitae*.

International Reply Coupon

When submitting material overseas you may be required to enclose *International Reply*

Coupons, which will enable the recipient to send a response and/or return your material at your cost. Not applicable/available in all countries, so check with your local Post Office for more information.

IRC

See *International Reply Coupon*.

Manuscript

Your complete piece of work – be it a novel, short story, or article, etc. will be referred to as your manuscript. Commonly abbreviated to "ms" (singular) or "mss" (plural).

MS

See *Manuscript*.

MSS

See *Manuscript*.

Proposal

A proposal is normally requested for nonfiction projects (where the book may not yet have been completed, or even begun). Proposals can consist of a number of components, such as an outline, table of contents, CV, marketing information, etc. but the exact requirements will vary from one publisher to another.

Query

Many agents and publishers will prefer to receive a query in the first instance, rather than your full *manuscript*. A query will typically consist of a cover letter accompanied by a *synopsis* and/or sample chapter(s). Specific requirements will vary, however, so always check on a case by case basis.

SAE

See *Stamped Addressed Envelope*. Can also be referred to as SASE.

SASE

Self-Addressed Stamped Envelope. Variation of SAE. See *Stamped Addressed Envelope*.

Stamped Addressed Envelope

Commonly abbreviated to "SAE". Can also be referred to as Self-Addressed Stamped Envelope, or SASE. When supplying an SAE, ensure that the envelope and postage is adequate for a reply or the return of your material, as required. If you are submitting overseas, remember that postage from your own country will not be accepted, and you may need to provide an *International Reply Coupon*.

Synopsis

A short outline of your story. This should cover all the main characters and events, including the ending. It is not the kind of "teaser" found on a book's back cover. The length of synopsis required can vary, but is generally between one and three pages.

TOC

Table of Contents. These are often requested as part of nonfiction proposals.

Unagented

An unagented submission is one which is not submitted through a literary agent. If a publisher accepts unagented submissions then you can approach them directly.

Unsolicited mss

A manuscript which has not been requested. Many agents and publishers will not accept unsolicited mss, but this does not necessarily mean they are closed to approaches – many will prefer to receive a short *query* in the first instance. If they like the idea, they will request the full work, which will then be a solicited manuscript.

Formatting Your Manuscript

Before submitting a manuscript to an agent, magazine, or publisher, it's important that you get the formatting right. There are industry norms covering everything from the size of your margins to the font you choose – get them wrong and you'll be marking yourself out as an amateur. Get them right, and agents and editors will be far more likely to take you seriously.

Fonts

Don't be tempted to "make your book stand out" by using fancy fonts. It *will* stand out, but not for any reason you'd want. Your entire manuscript should be in a monospaced font like Courier (not a proportional font, like Times Roman) at 12 points. (A monospaced font is one where each character takes up the same amount of space; a proportional font is where the letter "i" takes up less space than the letter "m".)

This goes for your text, your headings, your title, your name – everything. Your objective is to produce a manuscript that looks like it has been produced on a simple typewriter.

Italics / bold

Your job as the author is to indicate words that require emphasis, not to pick particular styles of font. This will be determined by the house style of the publisher in question. You indicate emphasis by underlining text; the publisher will decide whether they will use bold or italic to achieve this emphasis – you shouldn't use either in your text.

Margins

You should have a one inch (2.5 centimetre) margin around your entire page: top, bottom, left, and right.

Spacing

In terms of line spacing, your entire manuscript should be double spaced. Your word processor should provide an option for this, so you don't have to insert blank lines manually.

While line spacing should be double, spaces after punctuation should be single. If you're in the habit of putting two spaces after full stops this is the time to get out of that habit, and remove them from your manuscript. You're just creating extra work for the editor who will have to strip them all out.

Do not put blank lines between paragraphs. Start every paragraph (even those at the start of chapters) with an indent equivalent to five spaces. If you want a scene break then create a line with the "#" character centred in the middle. You don't need blank lines above or below this line.

Word count

You will need to provide an estimated word count on the front page of your manuscript. Tempting as it will be to simply use the word processor's word counting function to tell you exactly how many words there are in your manuscript, this is not what you should do. Instead, you should work out the maximum number of characters on a line, divide this number by six, and then multiply by the total number of lines in your manuscript.

Once you have got your estimated word count you need to round it to an approximate value. How you round will depend on the overall length of your manuscript:

- up to 1,500 words: round to the nearest 100;
- 1,500–10,000 words: round to the nearest 500;
- 10,000–25,000 words: round to the nearest 1,000;
- Over 25,000 words: round to the nearest 5,000.

The reason an agent or editor will need to know your word count is so that they can estimate how many pages it will make. Since actual pages include varying amounts of white space due to breaks in paragraphs, sections of speech, etc. the formula above will actually provide a better idea of how many pages will be required than an exact word count would.

And – perhaps more importantly – providing an exact word count will highlight you immediately as an amateur.

Layout of the front page

On the first page of the manuscript, place your name, address, and any other relevant contact details (such as phone number, email address, etc.) in the top left-hand corner. In the top right-hand corner write your approximate word count.

If you have registered your work for copyright protection, place the reference number two single lines (one double line) beneath your contact details. Since your manuscript will only be seen by agents or editors, not the public, this should be done as discreetly as possible, and you should refrain from using any official seal you may have been granted permissions to use. (For information on registering for copyright protection see "Protecting Your Copyright", below.)

Place your title halfway down the front page. Your title should be centred and would normally be in capital letters. You can make it bold or underlined if you want, but it should be the same size as the rest of the text.

From your title, go down two single lines (or one double line) and insert your byline. This should be centred and start with the word "By", followed by the name you are writing under. This can be your name or a pen name, but should be the name you want the work published under. However, make sure that the name in the top left-hand corner is your real, legal name.

From your byline, go down four single lines (or two double lines) and begin your manuscript.

Layout of the text

Print on only one side of the paper, even if your printer can print on both sides.

In the top right-hand corner of all pages except the first should be your running head. This should be comprised of the surname used in your byline; a keyword from your title, and the page number, e.g. "Myname / Mynovel Page 5".

Text should be left-aligned, *not* justified. This means that you should have a ragged right-hand edge to the text, with lines ending at different points. Make sure you don't have any sort of hyphenation function switched on in your word processor: if a word is too long to fit on a line it should be taken over to the next.

Start each new chapter a third of the way down the page with the centred chapter number / title, underlined. Drop down four single lines (two double lines) to the main text.

At the end of the manuscript you do not need to indicate the ending in any way: you don't need to write "The End", or "Ends", etc. The only exception to this is if your manuscript happens to end at the bottom of a page, in which case you can handwrite the word "End" at the bottom of the last page, after you have printed it out.

Protecting Your Copyright

Protecting your copyright is by no means a requirement before submitting your work, but you may feel that it is a prudent step that you would like to take before allowing strangers to see your material.

These days, you can register your work for copyright protection quickly and easily online. The Intellectual Property Rights Office operates a website called the "Copyright Registration Service" which allows you to do this:

- *http://www.CopyrightRegistrationService.com*

This website can be used for material created in any nation signed up to the Berne Convention. This includes the United States, United Kingdom, Canada, Australia, Ireland, New Zealand, and most other countries. There are around 180 countries in the world, and over 160 of them are part of the Berne Convention.

Provided you created your work in one of the Berne Convention nations, your work should be protected by copyright in all other Berne Convention nations. You can therefore protect your copyright around most of the world with a single registration, and because the process is entirely online you can have your work protected in a matter of minutes, without having to print and post a copy of your manuscript.

US Literary Agents

For the most up-to-date listings of these and hundreds of other literary agents, visit http://www.firstwriter.com/Agents

*To claim your **free** access to the site, please see the back of this book.*

A+B Works
Email: query@aplusbworks.com
Website: http://www.aplusbworks.com

Handles: Fiction; Nonfiction; *Areas:* Women's Interests; *Markets:* Adult; Children's; Youth

Specialises in young adult and middle grade fiction, women's fiction, and select narrative nonfiction. No thrillers, literary fiction, erotica, cook books, picture books, poetry, short fiction, or screenplays. Query by email only. Response not guaranteed. Accepts very few new clients.

Above the Line Agency
468 N. Camden Drive, #200, Beverly Hills, CA 90210
Tel: +1 (310) 859-6115
Fax: +1 (310) 859-6119
Website:
http://www.abovethelineagency.com

Handles: Scripts; *Areas:* Film; TV; *Markets:* Adult; Children's

Send query via online web system only. Represents writers and directors; feature films, movies of the week, animation.

Abrams Artists Agency
275 Seventh Ave, 26th Floor, New York, NY 10001

Tel: +1 (646) 486-4600
Fax: +1 (646) 486-2358
Email: literary@abramsartny.com
Website: http://www.abramsartists.com

Handles: Scripts; *Areas:* Drama; Film; Humour; Music; Mystery; Romance; Suspense; TV; *Markets:* Adult

Send query with SASE via industry professional only. Specialises in film, TV, theatre, and publishing.

Bret Adams Ltd
448 West 44th Street, New York, NY 10036
Tel: +1 (212) 765-5630
Email: bretadamsltd@bretadamsltd.net
Website: http://www.bretadamsltd.net

Handles: Scripts; *Areas:* Film; Theatre; TV; *Markets:* Adult

Handles projects for theatre, film, and TV only. No books. No unsolicited submissions. Accepts approaches by referral only.

Adams Literary
7845 Colony Road, C4 #215, Charlotte, NC 28226
Tel: +1 (704) 542-1440
Fax: +1 (704) 542-1450
Email: submissions@adamsliterary.com
Website: http://www.adamsliterary.com

Handles: Fiction; *Markets:* Children's; Youth

Handles books for children, from picture books to teen novels. No unsolicited MSS. Send query with complete ms via webform, or by email if you encounter problems with the webform. See website for full submission guidelines.

The Agency Group, Ltd
142 West 57th Street, Sixth Floor, New York, NY 10019
Tel: +1 (310) 385-2800
Fax: +1 (310) 385-1220
Email: marcgerald@theagencygroup.com
Website: http://www.theagencygroup.com

Handles: Fiction; Nonfiction; *Areas:* Anthropology; Archaeology; Architecture; Arts; Autobiography; Biography; Business; Cookery; Crime; Culture; Design; Entertainment; Finance; Health; Historical; How-to; Humour; Legal; Lifestyle; Medicine; Music; Nature; Politics; Psychology; Self-Help; Sport; *Markets:* Adult

Multimedia agency representing recording artists, celebrities, and with a literary agency operating out of the New York office. Takes on new clients by referral only.

Agency for the Performing Arts (APA)
405 S. Beverly Dr , Beverly Hills, CA 90212
Tel: +1 (310) 888-4200
Fax: +1 (310) 888-4242
Website: http://www.apa-agency.com

Handles: Fiction; Nonfiction; Scripts; *Areas:* Film; Theatre; TV; *Markets:* Adult

Handles nonfiction, novels, scripts for film, theatre, and TV, as well as musicians and other performing artists.

Aimee Entertainment Agency
15840 Ventura Blvd., Ste. 215, Encino, CA 91436
Tel: +1 (818) 783-3831
Fax: +1 (818) 783-4447

Email: info@onlinemediapublications.com
Website: http://www.aimeeentertainment.com

Handles: Fiction; Scripts; *Areas:* Film; *Markets:* Adult

Handles film scripts and book-length works.

Alive Communications, Inc
7680 Goodard Street, Suite 200, Colorado Springs, CO 80920
Tel: +1 (719) 260-7080
Fax: +1 (719) 260-8223
Email: submissions@Alivecom.com
Website: http://www.alivecom.com

Handles: Fiction; Nonfiction; *Areas:* Adventure; Autobiography; Biography; Business; Crime; Historical; How-to; Humour; Lifestyle; Mystery; Religious; Self-Help; Short Stories; Spiritual; Sport; Suspense; Thrillers; Westerns; Women's Interests; *Markets:* Adult; Children's; *Treatments:* Commercial; Literary; Mainstream; Popular

Accepts queries from published or referred authors only. Works primarily with well-established, best-selling, and career authors. Referred authors or authors with at least one commercially published book may submit query by email with bio, name of the client referring you (if applicable), and synopsis. See website for full details.

Miriam Altshuler Literary Agency
53 Old Post Road North, Red Hook, NY 12571
Tel: +1 (845) 758-9408
Fax: +1 (845) 758-3118
Website: http://www.miriamaltshuler literaryagency.com

Handles: Fiction; Nonfiction; *Areas:* Autobiography; Culture; How-to; Psychology; Self-Help; Sociology; Spiritual; *Markets:* Adult; Children's; Youth; *Treatments:* Commercial; Literary

Send query with SASE, brief author bio, and synopsis. See website for full guidelines. No

Mystery, Romance, Poetry, Fantasy, Science Fiction, Techno, Thriller, Screenplays, Horror, Western, or submissions by email or fax. Response in two weeks to queries, within three weeks to MSS. Material returned only when accompanied by SASE.

Ambassador Speakers Bureau & Literary Agency

PO Box 50358, Nashville, TN 37205
Tel: +1 (615) 370-4700
Fax: +1 (615) 661-4344
Email: info@ambassadorspeakers.com
Website:
http://www.ambassadorspeakers.com

Handles: Fiction; Nonfiction; *Areas:* Adventure; Autobiography; Biography; Culture; Current Affairs; Finance; Health; Historical; How-to; Legal; Lifestyle; Medicine; Politics; Religious; Self-Help; Women's Interests; *Markets:* Adult; *Treatments:* Contemporary; Literary; Mainstream

Represents select authors and writers who are published by religious and general market publishers in the US and Europe. No short stories, children's books, screenplays, or poetry. Send query by email with short description. Submit work on invitation only.

Anonymous Content

588 Broadway, Suite 308, New York, NY 10012
Tel: +1 (212) 925-0055
Fax: +1 (212) 925-5030
Email:
litmanagement@anonymouscontent.com
Website: http://www.anonymouscontent.com

Handles: Scripts; *Areas:* Film; TV; *Markets:* Adult

Works in the areas of film, TV, adverts, and music videos.

Arcadia

31 Lake Place North, Danbury, CT 06810
Email: arcadialit@sbcglobal.net

Handles: Fiction; Nonfiction; *Areas:*

Biography; Business; Crime; Culture; Current Affairs; Health; Historical; Music; Psychology; Science; Self-Help; Women's Interests; *Markets:* Adult; *Treatments:* Commercial; Literary

Send query with proposal or up to 50 sample pages by email (no attachments) or by post with SASE. Considers fiction by published authors only. No science fiction/fantasy, horror, humour or children's/Young Adult.

Robert Astle & Associates Literary Management, Inc.

419 Lafayette Street, New York, NY 10003
Tel: +1 (212) 277-8014
Fax: +1 (212) 228-6149
Email: robert@astleliterary.com
Website: http://www.astleliterary.com

Handles: Fiction; Nonfiction; *Areas:* Arts; Autobiography; Biography; Culture; Drama; Historical; Humour; Media; Mystery; Politics; Sport; Suspense; Theatre; Thrillers; Travel; Women's Interests; *Markets:* Adult; Children's; Youth; *Treatments:* Commercial; Literary; Mainstream

See website for submission guidelines. States that email submissions are preferred and provides details of format email should take, but also provides web form for submission and asks authors to make their approach via it. No attachments or mass emails.

Audrey A. Wolf Literary Agency

2510 Virginia Avenue NW, #702N, Washington, DC 20037
Email: audreyrwolf@gmail.com

Handles: Nonfiction; *Areas:* Autobiography; Biography; Business; Current Affairs; Finance; Health; Historical; Lifestyle; Politics; Self-Help; Sport; *Markets:* Adult

Send query by post or email, including synopsis up to two pages long showing the full structure of the book: beginning, middle, and end. Also include chapter outline.

The August Agency LLC

Email: submissions@augustagency.com
Website: http://www.augustagency.com

Handles: Fiction; Nonfiction; *Areas:* Arts;
Autobiography; Biography; Business;
Culture; Current Affairs; Entertainment;
Finance; Historical; Media; Politics;
Sociology; Technology; Women's Interests;
Markets: Adult; Family; Literary

Accepts email queries exclusively, but
essential to consult website before sending
query. No self-published works, screenplays,
children's books, cozy mysteries, genre
romance, horror, poetry, science fiction,
fantasy, short story collections, westerns, or
queries by post. No email attachments.

Avenue A Literary LLC

419 Lafayette Street, 2nd Floor, New York,
NY 10003
Tel: +1 (212) 624-5859
Fax: +1 (212) 228-6149
Email: submissions@avenuealiterary.com
Website:
http://www.avenuealiterary.com/93.html

Handles: Fiction; Nonfiction; *Markets:*
Adult; Youth; *Treatments:* Commercial;
Literary

Actively seeking new authors of fiction and
nonfiction. Send query of about 400 words
by email only, with plot synopsis and author
bio (including any publishing history). All
information must be in the body of your
email. Emails with attachments will not be
read. No hard copy submissions.

Barer Literary, LLC

20 West 20th Street, Suite 601, New York,
NY 10011
Tel: +1 (212) 691-3513
Fax: +1 (212) 691-3540
Email: submissions@barerliterary.com
Website: http://www.barerliterary.com

Handles: Fiction; Nonfiction; *Areas:*
Biography; Culture; Historical; Short
Stories; Women's Interests; *Markets:* Adult;
Treatments: Contemporary; Literary;
Mainstream

Send query with SASE and sample of the
work. Material will not be returned without
the proper postage. No reponse will be given
to queries by phone or fax. Queries by email
are accepted, provided they do not include
attachments. Handles a wide range of fiction
and nonfiction, but no Health/Fitness,
Business/Investing/Finance, Sports,
Mind/Body/Spirit, Reference,
Thrillers/Suspense, Military, Romance,
Children's Books/Picture Books,
Screenplays. No longer seeking Young
Adult.

Faye Bender Literary Agency

19 Cheever Place, Brooklyn, NY 11231
Email: info@fbliterary.com
Website: http://www.fbliterary.com

Handles: Fiction; Nonfiction; *Areas:*
Autobiography; Biography; Culture; Health;
Science; Women's Interests; *Markets:* Adult;
Youth; *Treatments:* Commercial; Literary

Send query with ten sample pages by email,
or by post with SASE. See website for
example query letter. No genre fiction
(western, romance, horror, fantasy, science
fiction).

The Bent Agency

204 Park Place, Number Two, Brooklyn, NY
11238
Email: info@thebentagency.com
Website: http://www.thebentagency.com

Handles: Fiction; Nonfiction; *Areas:* Crime;
Fantasy; Historical; Horror; Mystery;
Romance; Suspense; Thrillers; Women's
Interests; *Markets:* Adult; Children's; Youth;
Treatments: Commercial

Send query by email describing yourself,
your book, and including the first ten pages
in the body of the email. Specific email
addresses for sending adult and children's
queries available on the website.

In adult books, not considering:

Science fiction
Poetry
Picture books

Textbooks/academic books
Serious history or biography
Political science/policy
Business
Reference
Sports

In children's books, closed to:

Picture books
Poetry
Sports
Textbooks/academic books
Reference

Bidnick & Company
Email: bidnick@comcast.net

Handles: Nonfiction; *Areas:* Cookery;
Markets: Adult

Handles cookbooks and narrative nonfiction.
Send query by email only.

Vicky Bijur Literary Agency
333 West End Avenue, Apt. 5B, New York,
NY 10023
Email: queries@vickybijuragency.com
Website: http://www.vickybijuragency.com

Handles: Fiction; Nonfiction; *Areas:*
Biography; Cookery; Health; Historical;
Politics; Psychology; Science; Self-Help;
Sociology; *Markets:* Adult

Send query by email or by post with SASE.
For fiction include synopsis and first chapter
(pasted into the body of the email if
submitting electronically). For nonfiction
include proposal. No attachments or queries
by phone or fax. No children's books,
poetry, science fiction, fantasy, horror, or
romance.

David Black Literary Agency
156 Fifth Avenue, Suite 608, New York, NY
10010-7002
Tel: +1 (212) 242-5080
Fax: +1 (212) 924-6609

Handles: Fiction; Nonfiction; *Areas:*
Autobiography; Biography; Business;

Finance; Historical; Legal; Military; Politics;
Sport; *Markets:* Adult; *Treatments:*
Commercial; Literary; Mainstream

Handles mostly nonfiction. For nonfiction
works, send query with proposal including
overview, author bio, chapter outline,
marketing/publicity, competition, at least one
sample chapter, and any relevant writing
samples such as newspaper or magazine
clips. For fiction, include synopsis, author
bio, and first three chapters of the book (25-
50 pages).

Send query with SASE and outline. Accepts
simultaneous submissions, but no queries by
fax or email.

The Blumer Literary Agency, Inc.
809 West 181 Street, Suite 201, New York,
NY 10033
Tel: +1 (212) 947-3040
Email: livblumer@earthlink.net

Handles: Fiction; Nonfiction; *Areas:*
Anthropology; Archaeology; Architecture;
Arts; Autobiography; Biography; Business;
Cookery; Crafts; Crime; Criticism; Culture;
Design; Finance; Health; Historical;
Hobbies; How-to; Humour; Literature;
Medicine; Mystery; Nature; New Age;
Photography; Psychology; Religious; Self-
Help; Suspense; Thrillers; Women's
Interests; *Markets:* Adult; *Treatments:*
Contemporary; Literary; Mainstream

Send query with SASE. Particularly
interested in quality fiction and practical
nonfiction. Expect a response to queries
within two weeks and to MSS within six. No
queries by fax or email.

BookEnds, LLC
136 Long Hill Rd, Gillette, NJ 07933
Tel: +1 (908) 362-0090
Email: Editor@BookEnds-Inc.com
Website: http://www.bookends-inc.com

Handles: Fiction; Nonfiction; Reference;
Areas: Business; Crime; Culture; Current
Affairs; Fantasy; Health; Lifestyle; Mystery;

Psychology; Romance; Science; Women's Interests; *Markets:* Adult; Youth

Accepts queries from both published and unpublished authors by email only. No postal approaches. Send query directly to specific agent (see website for specific interests and email addresses). No children's books, science fiction, short fiction, poetry, screenplays, techno-thrillers, or military fiction.

Books & Such Literary Agency

52 Mission Circle, Suite 122, PMB 170, Santa Rosa, CA 95409-5370
Email: representation@booksandsuch.com
Website: http://www.booksandsuch.biz

Handles: Fiction; Nonfiction; *Areas:* Historical; Humour; Lifestyle; Religious; Romance; Women's Interests; *Markets:* Adult; Children's; Youth

Send query by email only. No attachments. Query should be up to one page detailing your book, your market, your experience, etc., as well as why you chose to contact this agency and if you are contacting others. Particularly interested in material for the Christian market. No queries by post or phone. See website for full details.

The Barbara Bova Literary Agency

3951 Gulf Shore Boulevard Unit PH 1-B, Naples, FL 34103
Tel: +1 (239) 649-7263
Fax: +1 (239) 649-7263
Email: slushpile@yahoo.com
Website:
http://www.barbarabovaliteraryagency.com

Handles: Fiction; Nonfiction; *Areas:* Adventure; Biography; Crime; Historical; Mystery; Science; Sci-Fi; Self-Help; Sociology; Suspense; Thrillers; Women's Interests; *Markets:* Adult; Youth

Send query by email or by post with SASE. Email queries should be 3-5 pages long, and include the word "Query" in the subject line.

No scripts, poetry, or children's books. See website for full details.

The Joan Brandt Agency

788 Wesley Drive, Atlanta, GA 30305-3933
Tel: +1 (404) 351-8877

Handles: Fiction; Nonfiction; *Areas:* Crime; Historical; Mystery; Short Stories; Suspense; Thrillers; Women's Interests; *Markets:* Adult; *Treatments:* Literary; Mainstream

Send query with SASE. Simultaneous submissions are accepted. No queries by fax or email.

The Helen Brann Agency, Inc.

94 Curtis Road, Bridgewater, CT 06752
Fax: +1 (860) 355-2572
Email: helenbrannagency@earthlink.net

Handles: Fiction; Nonfiction; *Markets:* Adult

Send query with SASE. Works mostly with established writers and referrals.

Barbara Braun Associates, Inc.

151 West 19th Street, 4th Floor, New York, NY 10011
Fax: +1 (212) 604-9041
Email: bbasubmissions@gmail.com
Website:
http://www.barbarabraunagency.com

Handles: Fiction; Nonfiction; *Areas:* Architecture; Arts; Beauty and Fashion; Biography; Criticism; Culture; Design; Film; Historical; Mystery; Photography; Politics; Psychology; Sociology; Thrillers; Women's Interests; *Markets:* Adult; *Treatments:* Commercial; Literary; Serious

Send query by email only, with "Query" in the subject line, including brief summary, word count, genre, any relevant publishing experience, and the first five pages pasted into the body of the email. No attachments. No poetry, science fiction, fantasy, horror, or screenplays.

Paul Bresnick Literary Agency, LLC

115 West 29th Street, 10th Floor, New York, NY 10001
Tel: +1 (212) 239-3166
Fax: +1 (212) 239-3165
Email: query@bresnickagency.com
Website: http://bresnickagency.com

Handles: Fiction; Nonfiction; *Areas:*
Autobiography; Biography; Crime; Culture;
Health; Historical; Humour; Lifestyle;
Psychology; Sport; Travel; *Markets:* Adult;
Treatments: Popular

Send query by email only, with two sample chapters (fiction) or proposal (nonfiction).

Brick House Literary Agents

80 5th Avenue, Suite 1101, New York, NY 10011
Email: submit@brickhouselit.com

Handles: Fiction; Nonfiction; *Areas:*
Autobiography; Biography; Cookery;
Culture; Historical; Lifestyle; Nature;
Science; Women's Interests; *Markets:* Adult;
Children's; *Treatments:* Commercial;
Literary

Send query by email with first page in body of the email (no attachments). Unable to respond to all queries.

Marie Brown Associates, Inc.

412 W. 154th Street, New York, NY 10032
Tel: +1 (212) 939-9725
Fax: +1 (212) 939-9728
Email: mbrownlit@aol.com

Handles: Fiction; Nonfiction; *Areas:*
Biography; Business; Historical; Music;
Religious; Women's Interests; *Markets:*
Adult; Youth; *Treatments:* Literary;
Mainstream

Send query with SASE. Particularly interested in multicultural and African-American writers. MSS should preferably not be submitted elsewhere simultaneously.

Andrea Brown Literary Agency, Inc.

1076 Eagle Drive, , Salinas, CA 93905
Email: andrea@andreabrownlit.com
Website: http://www.andreabrownlit.com

Handles: Fiction; Nonfiction; *Areas:*
Anthropology; Archaeology; Architecture;
Arts; Autobiography; Biography; Culture;
Current Affairs; Design; Drama; Fantasy;
Historical; How-to; Humour; Mystery;
Nature; Photography; Romance; Science;
Sci-Fi; Sociology; Sport; Technology;
Thrillers; Women's Interests; *Markets:*
Adult; Children's; Youth; *Treatments:*
Commercial; Literary

Send query by email only. Visit website and view individual agent profiles, then select one specific agent to send a query to at their own specific email address (given on website). Put the word "Query" in the subject line and include all material in the text of the email. No attachments.

For picture books, include full MS. For fiction send short synopsis and first three chapters. For nonfiction submit proposal and one or two sample chapters. Indicated which publishers, if any, the MS has been sent to. Historically specialises in children's books, but now also accepts specific areas of adult fiction and nonfiction. No queries by fax.

Brown Literary Agency

410 7th Street NW, Naples, FL 34120-2039
Tel: +1 (239) 455-7190
Email: broagent@aol.com
Website:
http://www.brownliteraryagency.com

Handles: Fiction; *Areas:* Erotic; Historical;
Humour; Mystery; Romance; Suspense;
Thrillers; Women's Interests; *Markets:*
Adult; Youth; *Treatments:* Contemporary

Handles romantic fiction for women only. Within these categories will consider romantic suspense, humour, contemporary, historical, and paranormal. Send query by email only with synopsis and one chapter.

Tracy Brown Literary Agency

P.O. Box 88, Scarsdale, NY 10583
Tel: +1 (914) 400-4147
Fax: +1 (914) 931-1746
Email: tracy@brownlit.com

Handles: Fiction; Nonfiction; *Areas:*
Biography; Current Affairs; Health;
Historical; Humour; Nature; Psychology;
Sport; Travel; Women's Interests; *Markets:*
Adult; *Treatments:* Contemporary; Literary;
Mainstream; Serious

Send query with author bio, outline/proposal,
synopsis, and one sample chapter. Queries
accepted by email but not by fax. No Young
Adult, Science Fiction, or Romance.

Browne & Miller Literary Associates

410 S. Michigan Avenue, Suite 460,
Chicago, IL 60605
Tel: +1 (312) 922-3063
Fax: +1 (312) 922-1905
Email: mail@browneandmiller.com
Website: http://www.browneandmiller.com

Handles: Fiction; Nonfiction; *Areas:*
Anthropology; Archaeology; Autobiography;
Biography; Business; Cookery; Crafts;
Crime; Culture; Current Affairs; Finance;
Health; Historical; Hobbies; How-to;
Humour; Lifestyle; Medicine; Mystery;
Nature; Psychology; Religious; Science;
Self-Help; Sociology; Sport; Technology;
Women's Interests; *Markets:* Adult; Youth;
Treatments: Commercial; Literary; Satirical

Send query letter only by email or by post
with SASE. Actively seeking fiction and
nonfiction that is highly commercial. No
poetry, scripts, science fiction, short stories,
articles, or unsolicited MSS.

Marcus Bryan & Associates Inc.

1500 Skokie Boulevard, Suite 310,
Northbrook, IL 60068
Tel: +1 (847) 412-9394
Fax: +1 (847) 412-9394
Email: mba3308@aol.com
Website: http://marcusbryan.com

Handles: Fiction; Scripts; *Markets:* Adult

**Note: Not accepting new clients as at July
2013. Check website for current status.**

Accepts query letters from book authors and
screenwriters.

Kelvin C. Bulger and Associates

4540 W. Washington Blvd , Chicago, IL
60624
Tel: +1 (312) 218-1943
Fax: +1 (773) 261-5950
Email: bulgerassociates@gmail.com
Website: http://bulgerandassociates.biz

Handles: Scripts; *Areas:* Adventure; Film;
Humour; Religious; TV; *Markets:* Adult

Send query by post with SASE, or by fax or
email. Include first ten pages of your
screenplay, one-page plot synopsis and one-
page logline.

Carnicelli Literary Management

7 Kipp Road, Rhinebeck, NY 12572
Email: queries@carnicellilit.com
Website: http://www.carnicellilit.com

Handles: Fiction; Nonfiction; *Areas:*
Autobiography; Biography; Business;
Culture; Current Affairs; Health; Historical;
Psychology; Science; Spiritual; Sport;
Markets: Adult; *Treatments:* Commercial;
Literary; Popular; Serious

Handles mainly nonfiction. Accepts queries
by post with SASE but prefers queries by
email. Restrict queries to one page. If
approaching by email, include the word
"Query" in the subject line and do not
include attachments. See website for full
guidelines. No poetry, plays, screenplays, or
books for children or young adults.

Cedar Grove Agency Entertainment

PO Box 1692, Issaquah, 98027-0068 WA
Tel: +1 (425) 837-1687
Email: cedargroveagency@msn.com

Handles: Scripts; *Areas:* Adventure;
Autobiography; Biography; Crime; Film;
Humour; Mystery; Romance; Science; Sport;
Suspense; Thrillers; TV; Westerns; *Markets:*
Adult; Family; Youth

Send query with one-page synopsis by post
with SASE, or by email in the body of the
email only. Handles scripts only. No books,
email attachments, or phone calls.

This agency DOES NOT handle BOOKS.
Scripts only, please.

Chalberg & Sussman
115 West 29th St, Third Floor , New York,
NY 10001
Email: rachel@chalbergsussman.com
Website: http://www.chalbergsussman.com

Handles: Fiction; Nonfiction; *Areas:*
Autobiography; Culture; Historical;
Psychology; Science; *Markets:* Adult;
Treatments: Literary; Popular

Send query by email. See website for
specific agent interests and email addresses.

Jane Chelius Literary Agency, Inc.
548 Second Street, Brooklyn, NY 11215
Tel: +1 (718) 499-0236
Fax: +1 (718) 832-7335
Email: queries@janechelius.com
Website: http://www.janechelius.com

Handles: Fiction; Nonfiction; *Areas:*
Biography; Culture; Humour; Lifestyle;
Medicine; *Markets:* Adult; *Treatments:*
Satirical

Send query letter with one-page synopsis and
SASE by post, or query email (as brief as
possible) with query letter, one-page
synopsis, and first ten pages in the body of
the email. No email attachments. Considers
all genres except children's books, poetry,
science fiction, fantasy, category romance,
stage plays or screenplays, and is always
actively seeking submissions from new and
unpublished authors. No unsolicited MSS.

Elyse Cheney Literary Associates, LLC
78 Fifth Avenue, 3rd Floor, New York, NY
10011
Tel: +1 (212) 277-8007
Fax: +1 (212) 614-0728
Email: submissions@cheneyliterary.com
Website: http://www.cheneyliterary.com

Handles: Fiction; Nonfiction; *Areas:*
Autobiography; Biography; Business;
Culture; Current Affairs; Finance; Historical;
Horror; Literature; Politics; Romance;
Science; Sport; Suspense; Thrillers;
Women's Interests; *Markets:* Adult;
Treatments: Commercial; Contemporary;
Literary

Send query only by post with SASE, or by
email (no attachments).

The Choate Agency, LLC
1320 Bolton Road, Pelham, NY 10803
Email: mickey@thechoateagency.com
Website: http://www.thechoateagency.com

Handles: Fiction; Nonfiction; *Areas:*
Biography; Cookery; Current Affairs;
Historical; Military; Mystery; Nature;
Politics; Science; *Markets:* Adult;
Treatments: Commercial

Handles commercial fiction and narrative
nonfiction. Send query with brief
synopsis/outline by post with SASE, or by
email. No genre fiction, romance, self-help,
confessional memoirs, spirituality, pop
psychology, religion, how-to, New Age
titles, children's books poetry, self-published
works or screenplays. See website for full
details.

The Chudney Agency
72 North State Road, Suite 501, Briarcliff
Manor , NY 10510
Tel: +1 (914) 488-5008
Email: mail@thechudneyagency.com
Website: http://www.thechudneyagency.com

Handles: Fiction; *Areas:* Historical;
Mystery; Suspense; *Markets:* Children's;
Youth; *Treatments:* Commercial; Literary;
Mainstream

Handles children's and young adult books. Send query only in first instance. Happy to accept queries by email. Submit material upon invitation only. See website for full guidelines.

Cine/Lit Representation

PO Box 802918, Santa Clarita, CA 91380-2918
Tel: +1 (661) 513-0268
Fax: +1 (661) 513-0915
Email: makier@msn.com

Handles: Fiction; Nonfiction; *Areas:* Adventure; Biography; Culture; Horror; Mystery; Nature; Thrillers; Travel; *Markets:* Adult; *Treatments:* Mainstream; Popular

Handles nonfiction and novels. Send query with SASE. No romance, westerns, or science fiction.

Edward B. Claflin Literary Agency, LLC

128 High Avenue, Suite #2, New York, NY 10960
Tel: +1 (845) 358-1084
Fax: +1 (845) 353-0155
Email: edclaflin@aol.com

Handles: Nonfiction; *Areas:* Business; Cookery; Current Affairs; Finance; Health; Historical; How-to; Medicine; Military; Psychology; Self-Help; Sport; *Markets:* Adult

Handles nonfiction only. Particularly interested in health, history, business, psychology, and self-help. No fiction. Send query by email or by post with SASE, synopsis, and author bio.

W.M. Clark Associates

186 Fifth Avenue, 2nd Floor, New York, NY 10010
Tel: +1 (212) 675-2784
Fax: +1 (347) 649-9262
Email: general@wmclark.com
Website: http://www.wmclark.com

Handles: Fiction; Nonfiction; *Areas:* Architecture; Arts; Autobiography;

Biography; Culture; Current Affairs; Design; Film; Historical; Music; Philosophy; Religious; Science; Sociology; Technology; Theatre; Translations; *Markets:* Adult; *Treatments:* Contemporary; Literary; Mainstream

Query through online form on website only. No simultaneous submissions or screenplays.

The Collective

8383 Wilshire Boulevard, Suite 1050, Beverly Hills, CA 90211
Tel: +1 (323) 370-1500
Website: http://www.thecollective-la.com

Handles: Scripts; *Areas:* Film; TV; *Markets:* Adult

A full-service entertainment management, media and content production company, with offices in Beverly Hills, New York, Nashville, and San Francisco. Handles scripts for film and TV.

CowlesRyan Agency

Email: katherine@cowlesryan.com
Website: http://www.cowlesryan.com

Handles: Fiction; Nonfiction; *Areas:* Arts; Autobiography; Biography; Cookery; Culture; Current Affairs; Historical; Literature; Mystery; Nature; Psychology; Science; Self-Help; Spiritual; *Markets:* Adult; Children's; *Treatments:* Commercial; Contemporary; Literary; Mainstream; Popular; Satirical

We specialise in quality fiction and non-fiction. Our primary areas of interest include literary and selected commercial fiction, history, journalism, culture, biography, memoir, science, natural history, spirituality, cooking, gardening, building and design, and young adult and children's books. We also work with institutions and organisations to develop books and book programs. We do not represent authors in a number of categories, e.g. romance and westerns, and we do not represent screenplays. See website for full submission guidelines.

The Creative Culture, Inc.

47 East 19th Street, Third Floor, New York, NY 10003
Tel: +1 (212) 680-3510
Fax: +1 (212) 680-3509
Email: submissions@thecreativeculture.com
Website: http://www.thecreativeculture.com

Handles: Fiction; Nonfiction; *Areas:*
Autobiography; Beauty and Fashion;
Cookery; Culture; Current Affairs; Health;
Humour; Lifestyle; Medicine; Music;
Psychology; Science; Self-Help; Sociology;
Spiritual; Technology; Women's Interests;
Markets: Adult; *Treatments:* Commercial;
Literary

Consult agent bios on website then contact
agent you feel will be most interested in your
work. Send query by email or post with
SASE, outline, author bio, previous writing
credits, and (for fiction) 4-7 pages of your
novel. No children's, poetry, screenplays,
science fiction, or romance.

Creative Trust, Inc.

5141 Virginia Way, Suite 320, Brentwood, TN 37027
Tel: +1 (615) 297-5010
Fax: +1 (615) 297-5020
Email: info@creativetrust.com
Website: http://www.creativetrust.com

Handles: Fiction; Scripts; *Areas:* Film;
Markets: Adult

Literary division founded in 2001 to handle
authors with particular potential in cross-
media development, including movie scripts,
graphic novels, etc. Accepts queries by email
from previously published authors only. No
attachments.

Criterion Group, Inc.

4842 Sylmar Avenue , Sherman Oaks, CA 91423
Tel: +1 (818) 995-1485
Fax: +1 (818) 995-1085
Email: info@criterion-group.com
Website: http://www.criterion-group.com

Handles: Scripts; *Areas:* Film; Theatre;
Markets: Adult

**Note: Reports that this agency is not
accepting scripts as at July 19, 2013.
Check website for current status.**

Handles film and stage scripts. Send query
by post only. No unsolicited material
accepted.

The Croce Agency

PO Box 3161, Fort Lee, NJ 07024
Tel: +1 (201) 248-3175
Email: submissions@thecroceagency.com
Website: http://www.thecroceagency.com

Handles: Fiction; Nonfiction; *Areas:*
Autobiography; Biography; Historical;
Mystery; Science; Suspense; Thrillers;
Travel; Women's Interests; *Markets:* Adult;
Treatments: Commercial; Literary;
Mainstream

**Note: not accepting submissions as at
February 2013. Check website for current
situation.**

Represents character-driven upmarket fiction
and plot-driven commercial fiction
(including chick lit). Also represents
narrative nonfiction. Searching for strong,
unique writing with commercial appeal, even
it falls outside their usual categories of work.

Actively seeking submissions, which must
be made by email and include: brief
synopsis; word count; stage of completion;
explanation of what makes your book
unique; first chapter (if written); author
credentials.

The Culinary Entertainment Agency (CEA)

53 W 36, #706, New York, NY 10018
Tel: +1 (212) 380-1264
Email: info@the-cea.com
Website: http://www.the-cea.com

Handles: Nonfiction; *Areas:* Cookery;
Lifestyle; *Markets:* Adult

Literary agency focused on the cooking and
lifestyle markets. Accepts new clients by
referral only.

Richard Curtis Associates, Inc.

171 East 74th Street, Floor 2, New York, NY 10021
Tel: +1 (212) 772-7363
Fax: +1 (212) 772-7393
Email: info@curtisagency.com
Website: http://www.curtisagency.com

Handles: Fiction; Nonfiction; *Areas:*
Autobiography; Biography; Business;
Finance; Health; Historical; Medicine;
Science; Technology; *Markets:* Adult

Accepts approaches from authors previously
published with national publishing houses
only.

Laura Dail Literary Agency

350 Seventh Avenue, Suite 2003, New York,
NY 10001
Tel: +1 (212) 239-7477
Fax: +1 (212) 947-0460
Email: queries@ldlainc.com
Website: http://www.ldlainc.com

Handles: Fiction; Nonfiction; *Areas:*
Historical; *Markets:* Adult; Youth;
Treatments: Commercial; Literary

Send query by email (preferred) with the
word "query" in the subject line, or by post
with SASE. Due to volume of submissions
cannot guarantee response to all letters and
emails. Mainly interested in commercial and
literary fiction and nonfiction, particularly
historical. Some young adult. You may
optionally include a synopsis and up to 10
pages, but if approaching by email this must
be in the body of the email, not an
attachment.

Daniel Literary Group

1701 Kingsbury Drive, Suite 100, Nashville,
TN 37215
Tel: +1 (615) 730-8207
Email:
submissions@danielliterarygroup.com
Website: http://www.danielliterarygroup.com

Handles: Nonfiction; *Markets:* Adult

Specialises in nonfiction and is closed to

submissions of fiction. No Children's
literature, Romance, Science fiction,
Screenplays, Poetry, or Short stories. Query
by email only, including brief synopsis, key
selling points, author biography, and
publishing history, all pasted into the body of
the email. No attachments, or queries by post
or telephone. Response not guranteed if
guidelines are not adhered to.

Darhansoff & Verrill Literary Agents

236 W. 26th Street, Suite 802, New York,
NY 10001
Tel: +1 (917) 305-1300
Fax: +1 (917) 305-1400
Email: submissions@dvagency.com
Website: http://www.dvagency.com

Handles: Fiction; Nonfiction; *Areas:*
Mystery; Suspense; *Markets:* Adult;
Children's; Youth; *Treatments:* Literary

Particularly interested in literary fiction,
narrative nonfiction, memoir, sophisticated
suspense, and fiction and nonfiction for
younger readers. No theatrical plays or film
scripts. Send queries by post or email. See
website for full submission guidelines.

Liza Dawson Associates

350 Seventh Avenue, Suite 2003, New York,
NY 10001
Tel: +1 (212) 465-9071
Fax: +1 (212) 947-0460
Email:
queryliza@LizaDawsonAssociates.com
Website:
http://www.lizadawsonassociates.com

Handles: Fiction; Nonfiction; *Areas:*
Autobiography; Business; Fantasy;
Historical; Lifestyle; Medicine; Military;
Mystery; Politics; Psychology; Sci-Fi; Self-
Help; Sociology; Spiritual; Suspense;
Thrillers; Women's Interests; *Markets:*
Academic; Adult; Children's; Youth;
Treatments: Literary; Mainstream

Send query letter only by email or by post
with SASE. Specialises in readable literary
fiction, mainstram historicals, women's
fiction, thrillers, academics, historians,

business, psychology and journalists. See website for specific agent interests and query appropriate agent directly.

The Jennifer DeChiara Literary Agency

31 East 32nd Street, Suite 300, New York, NY 10016
Tel: +1 (212) 481-8484 ext. 362
Fax: +1 (212) 481-9582
Email: jenndec@aol.com
Website: http://www.jdlit.com

Handles: Fiction; Nonfiction; *Areas:* Autobiography; Biography; Cookery; Crafts; Crime; Criticism; Culture; Current Affairs; Design; Fantasy; Film; Finance; Health; Historical; Hobbies; Horror; How-to; Humour; Legal; Lifestyle; Medicine; Military; Music; Mystery; Nature; Photography; Politics; Psychology; Science; Self-Help; Sociology; Sport; Suspense; Technology; Theatre; Thrillers; Women's Interests; *Markets:* Adult; Children's; Youth; *Treatments:* Contemporary; Literary; Mainstream; Popular; Satirical

Send query by email only. Posted submissions will be discarded. Put "Query" in subject line and query in the body of the email only. No attachments. Email again after two weeks if no response in case of loss of email. See website for full guidelines.

Joëlle Delbourgo Associates, Inc.

101 Park St., Montclair, Montclair, NJ 07042
Tel: +1 (973) 783-6800
Fax: +1 (973) 783-6802
Email: info@delbourgo.com
Website: http://www.delbourgo.com

Handles: Fiction; Nonfiction; Reference; *Areas:* Autobiography; Biography; Business; Culture; Current Affairs; Health; Historical; Lifestyle; Psychology; Science; *Markets:* Adult; Children's; Youth; *Treatments:* Popular

We are a highly selective agency, broad in our interests. No category romance, Westerns, science fiction, or picture books. Send query by post with SASE or by email

in first instance. See website for full guidelines.

Donadio & Olson, Inc.

121 W. 27th Street, Suite 704, New York, NY 10001
Tel: +1 (212) 691-8077
Fax: +1 (212) 633-2837
Email: mail@donadio.com
Website: http://donadio.com

Handles: Fiction; Nonfiction; *Areas:* Arts; Biography; Culture; Historical; Literature; Nature; Science; *Markets:* Adult; Youth; *Treatments:* Commercial; Literary; Mainstream

Handles literary fiction and nonfiction in a range of subjects, particularly literary history, biography, and cultural phenomenology.

Jim Donovan Literary

5635 SMU Boulevard, Suite 201, Dallas, TX 75206
Email: jdliterary@sbcglobal.net

Handles: Fiction; Nonfiction; Reference; *Areas:* Adventure; Autobiography; Biography; Business; Crime; Culture; Current Affairs; Finance; Health; Historical; How-to; Legal; Lifestyle; Medicine; Military; Music; Mystery; Nature; Politics; Sport; Suspense; Thrillers; Women's Interests; *Markets:* Adult; *Treatments:* Commercial; Contemporary; Literary; Mainstream; Popular

Send query with SASE or by email. For fiction, include first 30-50 pages and a 2-5 page outline. Handles mainly nonfiction, and specialises in commercial fiction and nonfiction. No poetry, children's, short stories, or inspirational.

Dunow, Carlson & Lerner Agency

27 West 20th Street, Suite 1107, New York, NY 10011
Tel: +1 (212) 645-7606
Email: mail@dclagency.com
Website: http://www.dclagency.com

Handles: Fiction; Nonfiction; *Areas:* Autobiography; Culture; *Markets:* Adult; Youth; *Treatments:* Commercial; Literary

Send query by post with SASE or by email. No attachments. Does not respond to all email queries.

Dupree / Miller and Associates Inc. Literary

100 Highland Park Village, Suite 350, Dallas, TX 75205
Tel: +1 (214) 559-2665
Fax: +1 (214) 559-7243
Email: editorial@dupreemiller.com
Website: http://www.dupreemiller.com

Handles: Fiction; Nonfiction; *Areas:* Adventure; Archaeology; Architecture; Arts; Autobiography; Biography; Business; Cookery; Crafts; Crime; Culture; Current Affairs; Film; Finance; Gardening; Health; Historical; How-to; Humour; Leisure; Lifestyle; Literature; Medicine; Music; Mystery; Philosophy; Photography; Politics; Psychology; Religious; Science; Self-Help; Sociology; Sport; Suspense; Technology; Theatre; Thrillers; Translations; Women's Interests; *Markets:* Adult; *Treatments:* Commercial; Experimental; Literary; Mainstream; Satirical

Send query with SASE outlining the project, providing brief author bio, and including details of marketing. No electronic queries or submissions. No juvenile, science fiction, horror, poetry, occult, romance, fantasy, or erotica. Do not send complete MS.

Dystel & Goderich Literary Management

One Union Square West, Suite 904, New York, NY 10003
Tel: +1 (212) 627-9100
Fax: +1 (212) 627-9313
Email: miriam@dystel.com
Website: http://www.dystel.com

Handles: Fiction; Nonfiction; *Areas:* Adventure; Anthropology; Archaeology; Autobiography; Biography; Business; Cookery; Crime; Culture; Current Affairs; Finance; Health; Historical; Humour;

Lifestyle; Military; Mystery; New Age; Politics; Psychology; Religious; Science; Suspense; Technology; Thrillers; Women's Interests; *Markets:* Adult; *Treatments:* Contemporary; Literary; Mainstream

Send query with brief synopsis and sample chapter by post with SASE, or by email with the cover letter in the body of the email, or attachments will not be opened. Queries should be brief, devoid of gimmicks, and professionally presented, including author details and any writing credits. See website for more details.

Eames Literary Services, LLC

4117 Hillsboro Road, Suite 251, Nashville, TN 37215
Fax: +1 (615) 463-9361
Email: info@eamesliterary.com
Website: http://www.eamesliterary.com

Handles: Fiction; Nonfiction; *Areas:* Religious; *Markets:* Adult; Youth

Handles adult and young adult fiction and nonfiction that supports a Christian perspective on life. Send query by email with book proposal; author bio (including publishing history); plot synopsis or chapter summary; and 2-3 chapters of sample content (attached as a Microsoft Word document). Incomplete enquiries will not be responded to. No queries by post.

East West Literary Agency LLC

1158 26th Street, Suite 462, Santa Monica, CA 90403
Tel: +1 (310) 573-9303
Fax: +1 (310) 453-9008
Email: rpfeffer@eastwestliteraryagency.com
Website: http://eastwestliteraryagency.com

Handles: Fiction; Nonfiction; *Markets:* Adult; Children's; Youth; *Treatments:* Niche

Specialises in children's books of all genres: from concept, novelty and picture books toh young adult literature. Represents both authors and illustrators.

Accepts queries via email only and by

referral only. See website for current details. As at June 7, 2012, website states that they will be open to queries from "the first of the year" -- however there is no indication as to which year is being referred to.

Ebeling & Associates

PO Box 790267, Pala, HI 96779
Tel: +1 (808) 579-6414
Fax: +1 (808) 579-9294
Email: ebothat@yahoo.com
Website: http://www.ebelingagency.com

Handles: Nonfiction; *Areas:* Business; Health; Self-Help; *Markets:* Adult

Accepts queries and proposals by email only. Write "Inquiry for Author Representation" in subject line and outline your book in up to 200 words in the body of the email. Attach proposal as Word or PDF document. See website for proposal requirements. Submissions by post are not accepted. No fiction, poetry, children's, illustrated books, religion, history, culture, biography, or memoir.

Judith Ehrlich Literary Management

880 Third Avenue, 8th Floor, New York, NY 10022
Tel: +1 (646) 505-1570
Email: jehrlich@judithehrlichliterary.com
Website: http://www.judithehrlichliterary.com

Handles: Fiction; Nonfiction; *Areas:* Arts; Autobiography; Biography; Business; Culture; Current Affairs; Fantasy; Health; Historical; How-to; Humour; Legal; Lifestyle; Medicine; Mystery; Politics; Psychology; Romance; Science; Self-Help; Sociology; Sport; Thrillers; Women's Interests; *Markets:* Adult; Children's; Youth; *Treatments:* Commercial; Literary; Mainstream

Send query by email only. No attachments. For nonfiction give details of your book, your qualifications for writing it, and any existing platform. For fiction include synopsis, writing credentials, and 7-10 sample pages, pasted into the body of the email. See website for full guidelines and individual agent details and email addresses. Response not guaranteed.

Einstein Thompson Agency

27 West 20th Street, Suite 1003, New York, NY 10011
Tel: +1 (212) 221-8797
Fax: +1 (212) 221-8722
Email: submissions@einsteinthompson.com
Website: http://www.einsteinthompson.com

Handles: Fiction; Nonfiction; *Areas:* Autobiography; Cookery; Crime; Culture; Health; Historical; Humour; Politics; Psychology; Science; Sport; Women's Interests; *Markets:* Adult; Children's; Youth; *Treatments:* Commercial; Literary; Popular

Accepts submissions by email only. See contact section of website for full submission guidelines.

Elaine P. English, Attorney & Literary Agent

4710 41st Street, NW, Suite D, Wahington, DC 20016
Tel: +1 (202) 362-5190
Fax: +1 (202) 362-5192
Email: queries@elaineenglish.com
Website: http://www.elaineenglish.com

Handles: Fiction; *Areas:* Erotic; Fantasy; Gothic; Historical; Humour; Mystery; Romance; Women's Interests; *Markets:* Adult; *Treatments:* Commercial; Contemporary; Dark; Light; Serious; Traditional

Handles women's fiction, mysteries, and thrillers. Handles romance ranging from historical to contemporary, funny to erotic, and paranormal. No memoirs, science fiction, fantasy (unless romance fantasy), children's, young adult, horror, thrillers, short stories, screenplays, or nonfiction. Send query by email in first instance - see website for full guidelines. No attachments or unsolicited materials.

The Epstein Literary Agency

P.O. Box 484 Kensington, Kensington, MD

Tel: +1 (781) 718-4025
Email: kate@epsteinliterary.com
Website: http://www.epsteinliterary.com

Handles: Nonfiction; Reference; *Areas:* Crafts; How-to; *Markets:* Adult; Children's; Family; Youth

My agency was founded in 2005; my expertise comes from four years as an editor at Adams Media, where I handled many of the subject areas I am currently seeking to handle as an agent.

What I look for more than anything else is distinction – how will the book grab the reader in three seconds? It's better to grab many people and only please some of them than to try to please everyone and grab no one.

I follow AAR guidelines.

Currently open to crafts titles only. See website for full details.

Felicia Eth Literary Representation
555 Bryant Street, Suite 350, Palo Alto, CA 94301
Tel: +1 (650) 375-1276
Fax: +1 (650)401-8892
Email: feliciaeth@aol.com

Handles: Fiction; Nonfiction; *Areas:* Anthropology; Autobiography; Biography; Business; Crime; Culture; Current Affairs; Finance; Health; Historical; Legal; Lifestyle; Medicine; Politics; Psychology; Science; Sociology; Technology; Women's Interests; *Markets:* Adult; *Treatments:* Commercial; Contemporary; Literary; Mainstream

Send query with SASE and outline. Particularly interested in intelligent nonfiction and quality commercial fiction. No crime fiction (true crime only).

Mary Evans, Inc.
242 East Fifth Street, New York, NY 10003
Tel: +1 (212) 979-0880
Fax: +1 (212) 979-5344
Email: info@maryevansinc.com

Website: http://www.maryevansinc.com

Handles: Fiction; Nonfiction; *Markets:* Adult; *Treatments:* Commercial; Literary

Works mainly with established authors; most new clients by referral. Send query with SASE by post only. No queries by fax.

Fairbank Literary Representation
P.O. Box 6, Hudson, NY 12534
Tel: +1 (617) 576-0030
Fax: +1 (617) 576-0030
Email: queries@fairbankliterary.com
Website: http://www.fairbankliterary.com

Handles: Fiction; Nonfiction; Reference; *Areas:* Architecture; Biography; Cookery; Crafts; Culture; Design; Humour; Lifestyle; Mystery; Science; Thrillers; *Markets:* Adult; *Treatments:* Literary

No romance, poetry, science fiction or fantasy, historical novels set before 1900, young adult, vampire or pirate stories, or children's books. Does not consider works over 100,000 words by unpublished authors. Send one-page query outlining work by post or email. If sending by post a sample chapter may be included, plus SASE if return is required. If sending by email, do not include attachments, but you may include up to the first three pages pasted into the email. No queries by fax, or phone calls.

Farris Literary Agency, Inc.
PO Box 570069, Dallas, Texas 75357-0069
Tel: +1 (972) 203-8804
Email: farris1@airmail.net
Website: http://www.farrisliterary.com

Handles: Fiction; Nonfiction; Scripts; *Areas:* Adventure; Autobiography; Biography; Business; Crime; Culture; Current Affairs; Entertainment; Finance; Health; Historical; How-to; Humour; Legal; Lifestyle; Military; Music; Mystery; Politics; Religious; Romance; Self-Help; Spiritual; Sport; Suspense; Thrillers; Travel; Women's Interests; *Markets:* Adult; *Treatments:* Mainstream; Satirical

NOTE: As at April 2, 2013, only accepting submissions by referral or writers' conferences. Check website for current status.

Send query by post with SASE, or by email. Include title, description of project, author bio, and (for fiction) the genre and word count, or (for nonfiction) the type of book and your qualifications for writing it. No science fiction, fantasy, gay and lesbian, erotica, young adult, children's, or email attachments.

Diana Finch Literary Agency

116 West 23rd Street, Suite 500, New York, NY 10011
Tel: +1 (646) 375-2081
Email: diana.finch@verizon.net
Website:
http://dianafinchliteraryagency.blogspot.com

Handles: Fiction; Nonfiction; *Areas:* Adventure; Autobiography; Biography; Business; Crime; Culture; Current Affairs; Film; Finance; Health; Historical; How-to; Humour; Legal; Lifestyle; Medicine; Military; Music; Nature; Photography; Politics; Psychology; Science; Self-Help; Sport; Technology; Theatre; Thrillers; Translations; Women's Interests; *Markets:* Academic; Adult; Youth; *Treatments:* Literary; Mainstream; Satirical

Approach using online submission system - see website for link. Particularly interested in narrative nonfiction, health, and popular science. No children's picture books, romance, or mysteries.

FinePrint Literary Management

115 West 29th Street, 3rd Floor, New York, NY 10001
Tel: +1 (212) 279-1282
Email: peter@fineprintlit.com
Website: http://www.fineprintlit.com

Handles: Fiction; Nonfiction; Reference; *Areas:* Autobiography; Beauty and Fashion; Biography; Business; Cookery; Crime; Culture; Entertainment; Fantasy; Health;

Historical; Horror; How-to; Humour; Lifestyle; Military; Music; Mystery; Nature; Religious; Romance; Science; Sci-Fi; Self-Help; Spiritual; Suspense; Technology; Thrillers; Travel; Women's Interests; *Markets:* Adult; Children's; Youth; *Treatments:* Contemporary; Dark; Literary; Serious

Consult agent profiles on website for individual interests and approach appropriate agent for your work. Send query by email (no attachments) with proposal and sample chapters for nonfiction, or synopsis and first two chapters for fiction.

The James Fitzgerald Agency

118 Waverly Pl., #1B, New York, NY 10011
Tel: +1 (212) 308-1122
Email: submissions@jfitzagency.com
Website: http://www.jfitzagency.com

Handles: Fiction; Nonfiction; *Areas:* Culture; *Markets:* Adult

Primarily represents books reflecting the popular culture of the day, in fiction, nonfiction, graphic and packaged books. No poetry or screenplays. All information must be submitted in English, even if the manuscript is in Spanish. See website for detailed submission guidelines.

Peter Fleming Agency

PO Box 458, Pacific Palisades, CA 90272
Tel: +1 (310) 454-1373
Email: peterfleming@earthlink.net

Handles: Nonfiction; *Markets:* Adult; *Treatments:* Commercial

Send query with SASE. Seeks one-of-a-kind nonfiction books that unearth innovative and uncomfortable truths, and which have bestseller potential. Must be backed up by author's expertise in given area.

The Foley Literary Agency

34 East 38th Street, New York, NY 10016-2508
Tel: +1 (212) 686-6930

Handles: Fiction; Nonfiction; *Markets:* Adult

Send query with SASE and brief outline. Represents mainly nonfiction writers (around 75 per cent) and rarely takes on new clients.

Samuel French, Inc.

45 West 25th Street, New York, NY 10010-2751
Tel: +1 (212) 206-8990
Fax: +1 (212) 206-1429
Email: info@samuelfrench.com
Website: http://www.samuelfrench.com

Handles: Scripts; *Areas:* Crime; Fantasy; Horror; Humour; Mystery; Theatre; Thrillers; *Markets:* Adult

Send query with 10-page sample via online system or by email or by post with SASE. Publishes plays and represents writers of plays. Deals in well-known plays from Broadway and London's West End. Unsolicited scripts through agents only; playwrights must query first.

Fresh Books Literary Agency

231 Diana Street, Placerville, CA 95667
Email: matt@fresh-books.com
Website: http://www.fresh-books.com

Handles: Nonfiction; Reference; *Areas:* Business; Design; Finance; Health; How-to; Humour; Lifestyle; Photography; Science; Self-Help; Technology; *Markets:* Adult

Handles narrative non-fiction, lifestyle and reference titles on subjects such as science and technology, health and fitness, computers, photography, careers, education, parenting, personal finance, recreation, cooking, gardening, etc. No fiction, children's books, screenplays, or poetry. Send query by email. No attachments. Send further material upon request only.

Sarah Jane Freymann Literary Agency

59 West 71st Street, New York, NY 10023
Tel: +1 (212) 362-9277
Fax: +1 (212) 501-8240

Email:
Submissions@SarahJaneFreymann.com
Website: http://www.sarahjanefreymann.com

Handles: Fiction; Nonfiction; *Areas:* Autobiography; Cookery; Crime; Culture; Health; Historical; Lifestyle; Nature; Psychology; Science; Self-Help; Spiritual; Thrillers; Travel; Women's Interests; *Markets:* Adult; Youth; *Treatments:* Literary; Mainstream

Prefers to receive queries by email. See website for full details.

Fredrica S. Friedman and Co. Inc.

136 East 57th Street, 14th Floor, New York, NY 10022
Tel: +1 (212) 829-9600
Fax: +1 (212) 829-9669
Email: submissions@fredricafriedman.com
Website: http://www.fredricafriedman.com

Handles: Fiction; Nonfiction; *Areas:* Arts; Autobiography; Biography; Business; Cookery; Crime; Culture; Current Affairs; Design; Film; Finance; Health; Historical; How-to; Humour; Lifestyle; Music; Photography; Politics; Psychology; Self-Help; Sociology; Women's Interests; *Markets:* Adult; *Treatments:* Literary

Send query with synopsis by email. For fiction, include one-page sample. All material must be in the body of the email - no attachments. No poetry, plays, screenplays, children's books, sci-fi/fantasy, or horror.

Full Throttle Literary Agency

P.O.Box 5, Greenwich, Ohio 44837
Tel: +1 (419) 752-0444
Email: fullthrottlelit@aol.com
Website: http://www.fullthrottleliterary.com

Handles: Fiction; Scripts; *Areas:* Adventure; Drama; Film; Horror; Humour; Mystery; Short Stories; Suspense; Thrillers; Westerns; *Markets:* Adult; Children's; Family; *Treatments:* Contemporary; Light; Mainstream; Traditional

We are an independent agency that specializes in fiction material. Accepting new clients for manuscripts,screenplays and short stories. No e-mail queries. Send query through regular mail along with S.A.S.E. and short bio.

The Gage Group
Suite 505 , 14724 Ventura Blvd, Sherman Oaks, CA 91403
Tel: +1 (818) 905-3800
Fax: +1 (818) 905-3322
Email: Literary.GageGroupLA@gmail.com

Handles: Scripts; *Areas:* Film; Theatre; TV; *Markets:* Adult

Send query by post with SASE, or by email. Prefers to receive submissions by post. Willing to consider scripts on all subjects. No queries by fax.

Nancy Gallt Literary Agency
273 Charlton Avenue, South Orange , NJ 07079
Tel: +1 (973) 761-6358
Fax: +1 (973) 761-6318
Email: nancy@nancygallt.com
Website: http://www.nancygallt.com

Handles: Fiction; *Markets:* Children's; Youth

Handles children's books only. Use submission form on website or submit by post with SASE and appropriate postage if return of material required. All online submissions must go through the submission form on the website.

The Gernert Company
136 East 57th Street, New York, NY 10022
Tel: +1 (212) 838-7777
Fax: +1 (212) 838-6020
Email: info@thegernertco.com
Website: http://www.thegernertco.com

Handles: Fiction; Nonfiction; *Areas:* Adventure; Arts; Autobiography; Biography; Crafts; Current Affairs; Fantasy; Historical; Politics; Science; Sci-Fi; Sociology; Sport; Thrillers; *Markets:* Academic; Adult;

Children's; Youth; *Treatments:* Commercial; Literary; Popular

Send query describing work by post with SASE or email with author info and sample chapter. If querying by email, send to generic email and indicate which agent you would like to query. No queries by fax. Response only if interested.

Mark Gilroy Communications, Inc.
2000 Mallory Lane, Suite 130-229, Franklin, Tennessee 37067
Email: mark@markgilroy.com
Website: http://www.markgilroy.com

Handles: Fiction; Nonfiction; *Areas:* Current Affairs; Legal; Politics; Religious; Self-Help; *Markets:* Adult

Send query with outline and two sample chapters. Particularly interested in Christian fiction aimed at a general market, Christian nonfiction, and political books focusing on conservative values. No autobiography.

Barry Goldblatt Literary Agency, Inc.
320 7th Avenue, #266, Brooklyn, NY 11215
Email: query@bgliterary.com
Website: http://www.bgliterary.com

Handles: Fiction; *Markets:* Children's; Youth

Handles books for young people; from picture books to middle grade and young adult. Send query by email including the word "Query" in the subject line and synopsis and first five pages in the body of the email. No attachments. Emails with attachments will be ignored. See website for full details.

Frances Goldin Literary Agency, Inc.
57 E. 11th Street, Suite 5B, New York, NY 10003
Tel: +1 (212) 777-0047
Fax: +1 (212) 228-1660
Email: agency@goldinlit.com

Website: http://www.goldinlit.com

Handles: Fiction; Nonfiction; *Areas:* Autobiography; Culture; Historical; Philosophy; Sociology; *Markets:* Adult; *Treatments:* Commercial; Literary; Progressive

Send query by post with SASE, or by email with project description and brief biographical information including publishing credits if any. Write "Query" in the subject line and do not send attachments. Responds in 4-6 weeks, but cannot guarantee a response to email queries due to volume received. No unsolicited MSS, or material which has previously been submitted to a publisher (including by query letter). No screenplays, illustrated books, romance, science fiction, racism, sexism, ageism, homophobia, or pornography.

The Susan Golomb Literary Agency

540 President Street, 3rd Floor, Brooklyn, NY 11215
Email: susan@sgolombagency.com

Handles: Fiction; Nonfiction; *Areas:* Anthropology; Archaeology; Autobiography; Biography; Business; Culture; Current Affairs; Finance; Health; Historical; Humour; Legal; Military; Nature; Politics; Psychology; Science; Sociology; Technology; Thrillers; Women's Interests; *Markets:* Adult; Youth; *Treatments:* Literary; Mainstream; Satirical

Send query by email or by post with SASE, including synopsis / proposal, author bio, and one sample chapter. No genre fiction.

Goodman Associates

500 West End Avenue, New York, NY 10024-4317
Tel: +1 (212) 873-4806

Handles: Fiction; Nonfiction; *Areas:* Adventure; Anthropology; Archaeology; Autobiography; Biography; Business; Cookery; Crime; Criticism; Culture; Current Affairs; Erotic; Film; Finance; Health; Historical; Legal; Leisure; Literature;

Medicine; Military; Music; Mystery; Nature; Philosophy; Politics; Psychology; Science; Sociology; Sport; Suspense; Technology; Theatre; Thrillers; Translations; Travel; Women's Interests; *Markets:* Adult; *Treatments:* Contemporary; Literary; Mainstream

Send query with SASE. Accepting new clients by recommendation only. No poetry, articles, children's, young adult, or individual stories.

Irene Goodman Literary Agency

27 W. 24 Street, Suite 700B, New York, NY 10010
Tel: +1 (212) 604-0330
Fax: +1 (212) 675-1381
Email: irene@irenegoodman.com
Website: http://www.irenegoodman.com

Handles: Fiction; Nonfiction; *Areas:* Autobiography; Cookery; Culture; Fantasy; Historical; Lifestyle; Mystery; Romance; Sociology; Suspense; Thrillers; Women's Interests; *Markets:* Adult; Youth; *Treatments:* Commercial; Literary; Popular

Select specific agent to approach based on details given on website (specific agent email addresses on website). Send query by email only with synopsis, bio, and first ten pages in the body of the email. No poetry, inspirational fiction, screenplays, or children's picture books. Response only if interested. See website for further details.

Ashley Grayson Literary Agency

1342 18th Street, San Pedro, CA 90732
Tel: +1 (310) 548-4672
Email: graysonagent@earthlink.net

Handles: Fiction; Nonfiction; *Areas:* Business; Crime; Culture; Fantasy; Finance; Health; Historical; Lifestyle; Mystery; Romance; Science; Sci-Fi; Self-Help; Spiritual; Sport; Technology; *Markets:* Adult; Children's; Youth; *Treatments:* Commercial; Literary

Accepts nonfiction proposals from authors

aho are recognised within their field, and queries from published authors. Only accepts queries from unpublished authors if they already have an offer from a reputable publisher, have an industry recommendation, or have met the agents at a conference and had an ms requested. Self-published or print on demand published does not count as published for these purposes. Send query by email. No attachments.

Kathryn Green Literary Agency, LLC

250 West 57th Street, Suite 2302, New York, NY 10107
Tel: +1 (212) 245-2445
Fax: +1 (212) 245-2040
Email: query@kgreenagency.com

Handles: Fiction; Nonfiction; *Areas:* Autobiography; Biography; Business; Cookery; Crime; Culture; Current Affairs; Design; Finance; Health; Historical; How-to; Humour; Lifestyle; Psychology; Romance; Self-Help; Sport; Suspense; Thrillers; Women's Interests; *Markets:* Adult; Youth; *Treatments:* Contemporary; Literary; Mainstream; Satirical

Send query by email. Do not send samples unless requested. No science fiction, fantasy, or queries by fax.

Greyhaus Literary Agency

3021 20th St. Pl. SW, Puyallup, WA 98373
Email: scott@greyhausagency.com
Website: http://www.greyhausagency.com

Handles: Fiction; *Areas:* Historical; Romance; Suspense; Women's Interests; *Markets:* Adult; *Treatments:* Contemporary; Traditional

ONLY focuses on traditional romance and traditional women's fiction.

Opens to submissions on May 20, 2013.

We only focus on Romance Writers in the following sub-genres: Contemporary, Mainstream Paranormal/Time Travel, Regency, Historical, Inspirational, Romantic Suspense. Send query by email or through submission form on website. Only considers writers with completed manuscript ready for publication. No Fantasy, Single Title Inspirational, YA or Middle Grade, Picture Books, Memoirs, Biographies, Erotica, Urban Fantasy, Science Fiction, Screenplays, Poetry, Authors interested in only e-publishing or self-publishing, or Works that have already been published.

Laura Gross Literary Agency

PO Box 610326, Newton Highlands, MA 02461
Tel: +1 (617) 964-2977
Fax: +1 (617) 964-3023
Email: query@lg-la.com
Website: http://lauragrossliteraryagency.com

Handles: Fiction; Nonfiction; *Areas:* Autobiography; Biography; Culture; Current Affairs; Health; Historical; Legal; Lifestyle; Medicine; Mystery; Politics; Psychology; Sport; Suspense; Thrillers; Women's Interests; *Markets:* Adult; *Treatments:* Literary; Mainstream

Submit query using online web form, including your book's genre and a synopsis or plot summary. No sample chapters in first instance.

Joy Harris Literary Agency, Inc.

381 Park Avenue South, Suite 428, New York, NY 10016
Tel: +1 (212) 924-6269
Fax: +1 (212) 725-5275
Email: submissions@jhlitagent.com
Website: http://joyharrisliterary.com

Handles: Fiction; Nonfiction; *Areas:* Culture; Historical; Humour; Media; Mystery; Short Stories; Spiritual; Suspense; Translations; Women's Interests; *Markets:* Adult; Youth; *Treatments:* Experimental; Literary; Mainstream; Satirical

Send query by post with SASE or by email, including sample chapter or outline. Response to email approaches only if interested. No poetry, screenplays, self-help, or unsolicited mss.

John Hawkins & Associates, Inc.

71 West 23rd Street, Suite 1600, New York, NY 10010
Tel: +1 (212) 807-7040
Fax: +1 (212) 807-9555
Email: jha@jhaliterary.com
Website: http://www.jhaliterary.com

Handles: Fiction; Nonfiction; *Areas:* Autobiography; Biography; Crime; Current Affairs; Gardening; Health; Historical; Lifestyle; Mystery; Nature; Psychology; Science; Short Stories; Travel; *Markets:* Adult; Youth

Send query by email. No attachments. See website for agent profiles.

The Jeff Herman Agency, LLC

PO Box 1522, Stockbridge, MA 01262
Tel: +1 (413) 298-0077
Fax: +1 (413) 298-8188
Email: submissions@jeffherman.com
Website: http://www.jeffherman.com

Handles: Nonfiction; Reference; *Areas:* Autobiography; Business; Crime; Culture; Health; Historical; How-to; Lifestyle; Psychology; Self-Help; Spiritual; *Markets:* Academic; Adult

Send query by post with SASE, or by email. With few exceptions, handles nonfiction only, with particular interest in the genres given above. No scripts or unsolicited MSS.

Hidden Value Group

1240 E. Ontario Ave, STE #102-148, Corona, CA 92881
Tel: +1 (951) 549-8891
Fax: +1 (951) 549-8891
Email: bookquery@hiddenvaluegroup.com
Website: http://www.hiddenvaluegroup.com

Handles: Fiction; Nonfiction; *Areas:* Adventure; Autobiography; Biography; Business; Crime; Criticism; Fantasy; Finance; Historical; How-to; Lifestyle; Literature; Psychology; Religious; Self-Help; Thrillers; Westerns; Women's Interests; *Markets:* Adult; Youth; *Treatments:* Literary

Represents previously published Christian authors (not including self-published authors). Send one-page summary, marketing information, author bio, and two or three sample chapters by email or by post with SASE. Cannot guarantee a response to all email queries. No poetry or short stories.

Hopkins Literary Associates

2117 Buffalo Road, Ste. 327, Rochester, NY 14624
Tel: +1 (585) 352-6268
Email: phopkin1@rochester.rr.com

Handles: Fiction; *Areas:* Historical; Romance; Women's Interests; *Markets:* Adult; *Treatments:* Contemporary; Mainstream

Send query with SASE, outline, and first three chapters up to 50 pages. Specialises in women's fiction, particularly historical and contemporary romance. No queries by fax or email.

Andrea Hurst Literary Management

PO Box 1467, Coupeville, WA 98239
Email: info@andreahurst.com
Website: http://www.andreahurst.com

Handles: Fiction; Nonfiction; *Areas:* Adventure; Autobiography; Business; Cookery; Crime; Current Affairs; Fantasy; Historical; How-to; Humour; Politics; Psychology; Religious; Romance; Science; Sci-Fi; Self-Help; Thrillers; Westerns; Women's Interests; *Markets:* Adult; Youth; *Treatments:* Commercial; Contemporary

Check website for submission guidelines. Different genres handled by different agents, so check website for correct agent to query. Query only one agent. Queries accepted by email only (email addresses for each agent available on website). Do not include any attachments, proposals, sample chapters, etc.

InkWell Management

521 Fifth Avenue, 26th Floor, New York, NY 10175
Tel: +1 (212) 922-3500

Fax: +1 (212) 922-0535
Email:
submissions@inkwellmanagement.com
Website:
http://www.inkwellmanagement.com

Handles: Fiction; Nonfiction; Business;
Crime; Current Affairs; Finance; Health;
Historical; Medicine; Mystery; Psychology;
Self-Help; Thrillers; *Markets:* Adult;
Treatments: Contemporary; Literary;
Mainstream

Send query by email or by post with SASE.
Include query letter and up to two sample
chapters. No simultaneous submissions or
unsolicited MSS.

International Transactions, Inc.
PO Box 97, Gila, NM 88038-0097
Tel: +1 (845) 373-9696
Fax: +1 (845)373-7868
Email: info@intltrans.com
Website: http://www.intltrans.com

Handles: Fiction; Nonfiction; *Areas:*
Adventure; Arts; Biography; Crime;
Historical; Medicine; Mystery; Short Stories;
Thrillers; Women's Interests; *Markets:*
Academic; Adult; Youth; *Treatments:*
Contemporary; Literary; Mainstream

Send query with outline or synopsis by
email. No fiction enquiries from unpublished
authors. No queries by fax, or material which
is too influenced by TV or other successful
novels. See website for full submission
guidelines.

Jabberwocky Literary Agency
PO Box 4558, Sunnyside, NY 11104-0558
Tel: +1 (718) 392-5985
Fax: +1 (718) 392-5985
Email: jabagent@aol.com
Website: http://awfulagent.com

Handles: Fiction; Nonfiction; *Areas:*
Adventure; Autobiography; Biography;
Business; Cookery; Crime; Culture; Current
Affairs; Finance; Health; Historical;
Humour; Legal; Literature; Medicine;
Military; Mystery; Politics; Science; Sci-Fi;

Sociology; Sport; Theatre; Women's
Interests; *Markets:* Academic; Adult; Youth;
Treatments: Contemporary; Literary;
Mainstream; Satirical

Closed to submissions as at March 2, 2011.
See website for current situation.

**DO NOT EMAIL UNLESS YOU HAVE
PRIOR PERMISSION TO DO SO**

Full-length MSS only. Looking to expand
nonfiction represented. No poetry, short
stories, articles, unsolicited MSS, or queries /
submissions by fax or email. **Unsolicited
email queries deleted on sight without
being opened.**

Jaret Entertainment
6973 Birdview Avenue, Malibu, CA 90265
Tel: +1 (310) 589-9600
Fax: +1 (310) 589-9602
Email: seth@jaretentertainment.com
Website: http://www.jaretentertainment.com

Handles: Scripts; *Areas:* Adventure; Film;
Horror; Humour; Romance; Sci-Fi; Thrillers;
TV; *Markets:* Adult

Accepts queries by post, fax, or email, from
writers who are either represented (by an
agent, manager, or lawyer) or who have been
recognised in major screen-writing
competitions. No westerns, serial killer,
black comedy, or period pieces.

Jill Grinberg Literary Management LLC
16 Court Street, Suite 3306, Brooklyn, NY
11241
Tel: +1 (212) 620-5883
Fax: +1 (212) 627-4725
Email: info@jillgrinbergliterary.com
Website: http://www.jillgrinbergliterary.com

Handles: Fiction; Nonfiction; *Areas:*
Autobiography; Biography; Business;
Culture; Current Affairs; Fantasy; Finance;
Health; Historical; Legal; Medicine; Politics;
Psychology; Romance; Science; Sci-Fi;
Spiritual; Technology; Travel; Women's
Interests; *Markets:* Adult; Children's; Youth;
Treatments: Commercial; Literary

Send query with synopsis and first 50 pages for fiction, or proposal and author bio for nonfiction. No queries by fax or email.

Virginia Kidd Agency, Inc

P.O. Box 278, Milford, PA 18337
Tel: +1 (570) 296-6205
Fax: +1 (570) 296-7266
Website: http://www.vk-agency.com

Handles: Fiction; *Areas:* Fantasy; Historical; Mystery; Sci-Fi; Suspense; Women's Interests; *Markets:* Adult; *Treatments:* Mainstream

Specialises in science fiction and fantasy. Currently accepting queries from published authors only. No approaches from unpublished authors.

Harvey Klinger, Inc

300 West 55th Street, Suite 11V, New York, NY 10019
Tel: +1 (212) 581-7068
Fax: +1 (212) 315-3823
Email: queries@harveyklinger.com
Website: http://www.harveyklinger.com

Handles: Fiction; Nonfiction; *Areas:* Adventure; Autobiography; Biography; Cookery; Crime; Culture; Fantasy; Health; How-to; Humour; Medicine; Music; Mystery; Psychology; Romance; Science; Sci-Fi; Self-Help; Spiritual; Sport; Suspense; Technology; Thrillers; Women's Interests; *Markets:* Adult; Children's; Youth; *Treatments:* Literary; Mainstream; Popular

Send query by email via submission form on website or by post with SASE. Always interested in considering new clients, whether previously published or not, but please make query as brief as possible, and under no circumstances submit a full MS unless it is requested. Details of individual agents and their preferences given on website. Address queries to specific agents or agency in general. No queries by phone or by fax. No email attachments.

Kneerim & Williams

90 Canal Street, Boston, MA 02114

Tel: +1 (617) 303-1650
Fax: +1 (617) 542-1660
Email: submissions@kwlit.com
Website: http://www.kwlit.com

Handles: Fiction; Nonfiction; *Areas:* Anthropology; Archaeology; Autobiography; Biography; Business; Culture; Current Affairs; Finance; Health; Historical; Legal; Lifestyle; Literature; Medicine; Nature; Politics; Psychology; Religious; Science; Sociology; Sport; Technology; Women's Interests; *Markets:* Adult; *Treatments:* Literary; Mainstream

Send query by email only, including cover letter outlining your book and your qualifications to write it, two-page synopsis, two sample chapters, CV and / or history of your publications. No children's literature, genre fiction (romance, western, mystery, or science fiction/fantasy), screenplays, or unsolicited MSS. No hard copy submissions.

The Knight Agency

Email: submissions@knightagency.net
Website: http://www.knightagency.net

Handles: Fiction; *Areas:* Autobiography; Business; Culture; Entertainment; Fantasy; Finance; Health; How-to; Lifestyle; Media; Mystery; Psychology; Romance; Sci-Fi; Self-Help; Suspense; Thrillers; Women's Interests; *Markets:* Adult; Youth; *Treatments:* Commercial; Literary

Send one-page query by email, providing details of your awards and affiliations, an explanation of what makes your book unique, and a synopsis. No paper or phone queries. Any unsolicited material will not be returned.

Not accepting Screen Plays, Short Story Collections, Poetry Collections, Essay Collections, Photography, Film Treatments, Picture Books (excluding graphic novels), Children's Books (excluding young adult and middle grade), Biographies, Nonfiction Historical Treatments.

Bert P. Krages

6665 S.W. Hampton Street, Suite 200,

Portland, Oregon 97223
Tel: +1 (503) 597-2525
Fax: +1 (503) 597-2549
Email: krages@onemain.com
Website: http://www.krages.com/lvaserv.htm

Handles: Nonfiction; *Areas:* Health;
Historical; Psychology; Science; *Markets:*
Adult

Send query by email, with outline, similar
books and how yours will compete with
them, and your relevant qualifications and
writing experience. Query letters should not
exceed one page. Particularly interested in
science, health, psychology, and history. Not
currently accepting fiction. Do not call or
send MS instead of query.

Edite Kroll Literary Agency, Inc.

20 Cross Street, Saco, ME 04072
Tel: +1 (207) 283-8797
Fax: +1 (207) 283-8799
Email: ekroll@maine.rr.com

Handles: Fiction; Nonfiction; *Areas:*
Autobiography; Biography; Culture; Current
Affairs; Health; Humour; Legal; Medicine;
Politics; Psychology; Religious; Self-Help;
Women's Interests; *Markets:* Academic;
Adult; Children's; Youth; *Treatments:*
Literary

Handles mainly nonfiction so very selective
about fiction. Particularly interested in
international feminists and women writers
and artists. No genre books such as
mysteries, romance, or thrillers; no diet,
cookery, etc.; no photography books, coffee
table books, or commercial fiction. Send
query by email, fax, or by post with SASE,
including synopsis, author bio, and one or
two sample chapters. For picture books, send
complete MS. No queries by phone.

KT Public Relations

1905 Cricklewood Cove, Fogelsville, PA
18051
Tel: +1 (610) 395-6298
Fax: +1 (610) 395-6299
Email: Kae@KTPublicRelations.com
Website: http://www.ktpublicrelations.com

Handles: Fiction; Nonfiction; *Areas:*
Adventure; Cookery; Crafts; Fantasy;
Gardening; Health; Historical; How-to;
Lifestyle; Medicine; Military; Mystery;
Psychology; Romance; Sci-Fi; Thrillers;
Women's Interests; *Markets:* Adult

Send query by post with SASE or by email.
No attachments. Send nothing other than a
brief query selling you, your credentials, and
your book in the first instance.

The Candace Lake Agency

P.O. Box 364, Ross, CA 94957
Tel: +1 (415) 419-5503
Email: candace@lakeliterary.com

Handles: Fiction; Scripts; *Areas:* Adventure;
Crime; Culture; Drama; Fantasy; Film;
Gothic; Historical; Horror; Humour;
Military; Mystery; New Age; Romance;
Science; Sci-Fi; Suspense; Thrillers; TV;
Westerns; *Markets:* Adult; Youth;
Treatments: Contemporary; Literary;
Mainstream

Handles mainly movie scripts and TV
scripts, but also some novels. Accepts no
unsolicited material – new clients by referral
only.

The LA Literary Agency

PO Box 46370, Los Angeles, CA 90046
Tel: +1 (323) 654-5288
Email: ann@laliteraryagency.com
Website: http://www.laliteraryagency.com

Handles: Fiction; Nonfiction; *Areas:*
Autobiography; Biography; Business;
Cookery; Health; Historical; Lifestyle;
Psychology; Science; Sport; *Markets:* Adult;
Treatments: Contemporary; Literary;
Mainstream

Send query with proposal (nonfiction) or
first 50 pages (fiction). Prefers submissions
by mail, but also welcomes submissions by
email. Response only if interested.

Peter Lampack Agency, Inc

551 Fifth Avenue, Suite 1613, New York,
NY 10176

+1 (212) 687-9106
x: +1 (212) 687-9109
mail: alampack@verizon.net

Handles: Fiction; Nonfiction; *Areas:* Adventure; Crime; Mystery; Psychology; Suspense; Thrillers; *Markets:* Adult; *Treatments:* Commercial; Literary; Mainstream

Send query by email. Particularly interested in literary and commercial fiction, suspense, thrillers, mysteries, and psychological thrillers. No horror, romance, science fiction, westerns, historical literary fiction, academic, or unsolicited MSS.

Laura Langlie, Literary Agent
63 Wyckoff Street, Brooklyn, NY 11201
Tel: +1 (718) 855-8102
Fax: +1 (718) 855-4450
Email: laura@lauralanglie.com

Handles: Fiction; Nonfiction; *Areas:* Autobiography; Biography; Crime; Culture; Current Affairs; Film; Historical; Humour; Legal; Literature; Medicine; Mystery; Nature; Politics; Psychology; Science; Short Stories; Suspense; Theatre; Thrillers; Women's Interests; *Markets:* Adult; Children's; Youth; *Treatments:* Literary; Mainstream; Satirical

Send query by post with SASE, or by fax. No poetry, children's picture books, science fiction, how-to, or erotica. Simultaneous submissions accepted.

The Steve Laube Agency
5025 N. Central Ave., #635, Phoenix, AZ 85012-1502
Email: krichards@stevelaube.com
Website: http://www.stevelaube.com

Handles: Fiction; Nonfiction; *Areas:* Religious; *Markets:* Adult; Youth

Handles quality Christian fiction and nonfiction in all genres, except poetry, personal biographies, personal stories, end-times literature (either fiction or nonfiction), and children's picture books. Handles very little young adult fiction. No queries or

submissions by email. See website for full submission guidelines.

LaunchBooks Literary Agency
566 Sweet Pea Place, Encinitas, CA 92024
Tel: +1 (760) 944-9909
Email: david@launchbooks.com
Website: http://www.launchbooks.com

Handles: Fiction; Nonfiction; *Areas:* Adventure; Business; Culture; Current Affairs; Historical; Humour; Nature; Politics; Science; Sociology; Sport; Technology; *Markets:* Adult; *Treatments:* Contemporary; Mainstream; Popular

Handles mainly nonfiction, but will also consider fun, engaging, contemporary novels that appeal to a broad audience. Send query or proposal with sample chapters by email.

Sarah Lazin Books
121 West 27th Street, Suite 704, New York, NY 10001
Tel: +1 (212) 989-5757
Fax: +1 (212) 989-1393
Email: slazin@lazinbooks.com
Website: http://lazinbooks.com

Handles: Fiction; Nonfiction; *Areas:* Autobiography; Biography; Culture; Current Affairs; Historical; Music; Politics; *Markets:* Adult

Accepting queries via referral only. No queries by email.

Lescher & Lescher
346 East 84th Street, New York, NY 10028
Tel: +1 (212) 396-1999
Fax: +1 (212) 396-1991
Email: cl@lescherltd.com

Handles: Fiction; Nonfiction; *Areas:* Autobiography; Biography; Cookery; Culture; Current Affairs; Historical; Legal; Mystery; Suspense; *Markets:* Adult; *Treatments:* Commercial; Literary

Send query by post with SASE or by email. No screenplays, science fiction, or romance.

Lippincott Massie McQuilkin

27 West 20th Street, Suite 305, New York,
NY 10011
Tel: +1 (212) 352-2055
Fax: +1 (212) 352-2059
Email: info@lmqlit.com
Website: http://www.lmqlit.com

Handles: Fiction; Nonfiction; *Areas:*
Autobiography; Biography; Crime; Culture;
Current Affairs; Historical; Humour;
Politics; Psychology; Science; Sociology;
Markets: Adult; *Treatments:* Commercial;
Literary

Send query by email only, including outline,
relevant author bio, and stating which agent
you want to review your project.

The Lisa Ekus Group, LLC

57 North Street, Hatfield, MA 01038
Tel: +1 (413) 247-9325
Fax: +1 (413) 247-9873
Email: lisaekus@lisaekus.com
Website: http://www.lisaekus.com

Handles: Nonfiction; *Areas:* Cookery;
Markets: Adult

Send query with SASE, table of contents,
summary of chapters, one complete sample
chapter, author bio, explanation of concept,
potential market, and potential competition.
Handles cookery books only. No
submissions by email or on disk. See website
for full submission guidelines.

The Literary Group

330 W 38th Street, Suite 408, New York,
NY 10018
Tel: +1 (646) 442-5896
Fax: +1 (646) 792-3969
Email: js@theliterarygroup.com
Website: http://www.theliterarygroup.com

Handles: Fiction; Nonfiction; *Areas:*
Autobiography; Biography; Cookery; Crime;
Current Affairs; Fantasy; Health; Historical;
Horror; Humour; Lifestyle; Military;
Mystery; Nature; Psychology; Religious;
Romance; Science; Sport; Suspense;
Thrillers; Women's Interests; *Markets:* Adult

Send query by email or by post with SASE,
writing credentials, 2 page synopsis, and 50-
page writing sample. Response only if
interested. Asks for a 30-day exclusivity
period, beginning from the date the material
is received.

Literary Management Group, Inc.

PO Box 40965, Nashville, TN 37204
Tel: +1 (615) 812-4445
Email: BruceBarbour@LiteraryManagement
Group.com
Website:
http://literarymanagementgroup.com

Handles: Fiction; Nonfiction; *Areas:*
Autobiography; Biography; Business;
Lifestyle; Religious; Spiritual; *Markets:*
Adult

Handles Christian books (defined as books
which are consistent with the historical,
orthodox teachings of the Christian fathers).
Handles adult nonfiction and fiction only. No
children's or illustrated books, poetry,
memoirs, YA Fiction or text/academic
books. Download proposal from website
then complete and send with sample
chapters.

Julia Lord Literary Management

38 W. Ninth Street, New York, NY 10011
Tel: +1 (212) 995-2333
Fax: +1 (212) 995-2332
Email: query@julialordliterary.com
Website: http://julialordliterary.com

Handles: Fiction; Nonfiction; Reference;
Areas: Adventure; Biography; Historical;
Humour; Lifestyle; Science; Sport; Thrillers;
Markets: Adult; Youth

Send query by post or by email. If sending
by email, include synopsis and first five
pages in the body of the email. Responds
only if interested and does not open or
respond to emails with attachments.

If sending by post include synopsis, first five
pages, and SASE for response. Responds to
all postal submissions.

Lowenstein Associates, Inc.

121 West 27th Street, Suite 601, New York, NY 10001
Tel: +1 (212) 206-1630
Email: assistant@bookhaven.com
Website:
http://www.lowensteinassociates.com

Handles: Fiction; Nonfiction; *Areas:*
Business; Crime; Fantasy; Health; Lifestyle; Literature; Psychology; Science; Sci-Fi; Sociology; Spiritual; Thrillers; Women's Interests; *Markets:* Adult; *Treatments:* Commercial; Literary

Accepts queries by email and by post. See website for details. No horror, westerns, adult science-fiction, textbooks, children's picture books, or books in need of translation.

The Jennifer Lyons Literary Agency, LLC

151 West 19th Street 3rd floor, New York, NY 10011
Tel: +1 (212) 368-2812
Email: Jenniferhlyons@earthlink.net
Website:
http://www.jenniferlyonsliteraryagency.com

Handles: Fiction; Nonfiction; *Areas:*
Adventure; Autobiography; Biography; Cookery; Culture; Current Affairs; Fantasy; Historical; Mystery; Nature; Religious; Sci-Fi; Spiritual; Sport; Thrillers; Travel; Women's Interests; *Markets:* Adult; Children's; Youth

Send query by post only. No romance, or queries by fax or email. Include SASE only if return of material is required; otherwise include email address for reply.

Lyons Literary LLC

540 President Street, Third Floor, Brooklyn, NY 11215
Tel: +1 (212) 851-8428
Fax: +1 (212) 851-8405
Email: info@lyonsliterary.com
Website: http://www.lyonsliterary.com

Handles: Fiction; Nonfiction; *Areas:*
Autobiography; Biography; Cookery; Crime;

Current Affairs; Entertainment; Fantasy; Health; Historical; Hobbies; How-to; Humour; Legal; Leisure; Lifestyle; Literature; Men's Interests; Military; Music; Mystery; Politics; Science; Sport; Suspense; Thrillers; Travel; TV; Women's Interests; *Markets:* Adult; *Treatments:* Literary

A full service literary agency in New York dedicated to providing detailed and substantive guidance to its clients throughout the publication process. The agency provides comprehensive assistance to an exclusive client list in all areas related to their intellectual property, including editorial guidance, submission and sale of works in the domestic market to both large and small publishers, contract negotiations, foreign language sales, film and television licenses, marketing and publicity strategies, and career planning.

This agency only accepts electronic queries sent electronically via the agency's website submission form. Queries sent in any other manner (including by post) will not receive a response.

Donald Maass Literary Agency

Suite 801, 121 West 27th Street, New York, NY 10001
Tel: +1 (212) 727-8383
Fax: +1 (212) 727-3271
Email: info@maassagency.com
Website: http://www.maassagency.com

Handles: Fiction; *Areas:* Crime; Fantasy; Historical; Horror; Humour; Mystery; Romance; Sci-Fi; Suspense; Westerns; Women's Interests; *Markets:* Adult; Youth; *Treatments:* Dark; Literary; Mainstream

Welcomes all genres, in particular science fiction, fantasy, mystery, suspense, horror, romance, historical, literary and mainstream novels. Send query by email with "query" in the subject line, or by post with SASE, with synopsis and first five pages. No attachments. No poetry or picture books. See website for individual agent interests and email addresses.

MacGregor Literary

2373 N.W. 185th Avenue, Suite 165,
Hillsboro, OR 97124-7076
Tel: +1 (503) 277-8308
Email: submissions@macgregorliterary.com
Website: http://www.macgregorliterary.com

Handles: Fiction; Nonfiction; *Areas:*
Autobiography; Biography; Business; Crime;
Culture; Current Affairs; Finance; Historical;
How-to; Humour; Lifestyle; Mystery;
Religious; Romance; Self-Help; Short
Stories; Sport; Suspense; Thrillers; Women's
Interests; *Markets:* Academic; Adult;
Treatments: Contemporary; Mainstream

Handles work in a variety of genres, but all
from a Christian perspective. Not accepting
unpublished authors, except through
conferences and referrals from current
clients. Unsolicited MSS will not be
returned, even if an SASE is provided.

Ricia Mainhardt Agency (RMA)

612 Argyle RD STE 5L, Brooklyn, NY
11230
Tel. +1 (718) 434 1893
Fax: +1 (347) 602-9379
Email: ricia@ricia.com
Website: http://www.ricia.com

Handles: Fiction; Nonfiction; *Areas:*
Adventure; Autobiography; Biography;
Crime; Culture; Current Affairs; Fantasy;
Gothic; Leisure; Mystery; New Age;
Romance; Sci-Fi; Self-Help; Spiritual;
Suspense; Thrillers; Women's Interests;
Markets: Adult; Children's; Family; Youth;
Treatments: Commercial; Contemporary;
Cynical; Dark; Light; Mainstream; Niche;
Popular; Progressive; Serious; Traditional

See website for full submission guidelines.
Accepts postal submissions and queries by
email to specific queries address provided on
website. No attachments or submissions on
disk.

Kirsten Manges Literary Agency, LLC

115 West 29th Street, 3rd Floor, New York,
NY 10001
Email: kirsten@mangeslit.com
Website: http://www.mangeslit.com

Handles: Fiction; Nonfiction; *Areas:*
Autobiography; Cookery; Culture; Health;
Historical; Psychology; Science; Spiritual;
Sport; Technology; Travel; Women's
Interests; *Markets:* Adult; Youth;
Treatments: Commercial; Literary

Send query by email or by post with SASE.
Particularly interested in women's issues.

March Tenth, Inc.

24 Hillside Terrace, Montvale, NJ 07645
Tel: +1 (201) 387-6551
Fax: +1 (201) 387-6552
Email: schoron@aol.com
Website: http://www.marchtenthinc.com

Handles: Fiction; Nonfiction; *Areas:*
Autobiography; Biography; Culture; Current
Affairs; Film; Health; Historical; Humour;
Literature; Medicine; Music; Theatre;
Markets: Adult; *Treatments:* Literary;
Satirical

Send query by email or by post with SASE.
In your query, include the genre of your
work, a brief description of the project, and
the approximate word count; your
qualifications and previous writing or
publishing experience or some basic
information about your background; all your
contact information; a one to two page
synopsis if you are submitting a novel as
well as the first ten pages of the first chapter
only; and state whether or not your work has
been previously shown to publishers.

For fiction, do not send entire MS until
requested. For nonfiction send entire MS and
include analysis of the market for your work.

No poetry, scripts, children's or young adult
novels.

Denise Marcil Literary Agency, Inc.

110 William Street, Suite 2202, New York,
NY 10038
Tel: +1 (212) 337-3402

Email: dmla@denisemarcilagency.com
Website:
http://www.denisemarcilagency.com

Handles: Fiction; Nonfiction; Reference;
Areas: Biography; Business; Health;
Lifestyle; Self-Help; Spiritual; Suspense;
Thrillers; Women's Interests; *Markets:*
Adult; *Treatments:* Contemporary; Popular

Send query by email or by post with SASE.
No science fiction, children's books, or
political nonfiction. No queries by fax.

Marly Russoff & Associates
PO Box 524, Bronxville, NY 10708
Tel: +1 (914) 961-7939
Email: mra_queries3@rusoffagency.com
Website: http://www.rusoffagency.com

Handles: Fiction; Nonfiction; *Markets:*
Adult

Send 1-2 page query by post or email, with
synopsis and relevant author info, plus word
or page count and email address for
response. All email queries must have the
word "query" in the subject line.

Material is never returned so do not send
return postage.

The Martell Agency
1350 Avenue of the Americas, Suite 1205,
New York, NY 10019
Tel: +1 (212) 317-2672
Email: submissions@themartellagency.com
Website: http://www.themartellagency.com

Handles: Fiction; Nonfiction; *Areas:*
Autobiography; Business; Finance; Health;
Historical; Medicine; Mystery; Psychology;
Self-Help; Suspense; Thrillers; Women's
Interests; *Markets:* Adult; *Treatments:*
Commercial

Send query by post or by email, including
summary, short bio, any information, if
appropriate, as to why you are qualified to
write on the subject of your book, any
publishing credits, the year of publication
and the publisher. No original screenplays or
poetry.

Martin Literary Management
7683 SE 27th Street, #307, Mercer Island,
WA 98040
Tel: +1 (206) 466-1773
Fax: +1 (206) 466-1774
Email:
Sharlene@martinliterarymanagement.com
Website:
http://www.martinliterarymanagement.com

Handles: Fiction; Nonfiction; *Areas:*
Autobiography; Biography; Business; Crime;
Current Affairs; Entertainment; Health;
How-to; Lifestyle; Media; Self-Help;
Women's Interests; *Markets:* Adult; Youth;
Treatments: Commercial; Literary;
Mainstream; Popular; Positive; Traditional

This agency has strong ties to film/TV.
Actively seeking nonfiction that is highly
commercial and that can be adapted to film.
Please review our website carefully to make
sure we're a good match for your work. How
to contact: Completely electronic: emails and
MS Word only. No attachments on queries.
Place letter in body of email. See submission
requirements on website. Do not send
materials unless requested. We give very
serious consideration to the material
requested. We are actively seeing new
submissions. We only ask to see materials
that we intend to offer representation for - IF
the work is saleable. Therefore, in exchange
for that close evaluation, we require a two
week exclusive consideration period,
whereby your agree if we offer
representation, you are already certain you
are willing to accept pending our contract.

The Marton Agency, Inc.
1 Union Square West, Suite 815, New York,
NY 10003-3303
Tel: +1 (212) 255-1908
Fax: +1 (212) 691-9061
Email: info@martonagency.com
Website: http://www.martonagency.com

Handles: Scripts; *Areas:* Theatre;
Translations; *Markets:* Adult

International literary rights agency,
specialising in foreign-language licensing.

Martha Millard Literary Agency

420 Central Park West, #5H, New York, NY 10025
Tel: +1 (212) 662-1030
Email: marmillink@aol.com

Handles: Fiction; Nonfiction; *Areas:* Architecture; Arts; Autobiography; Biography; Business; Cookery; Crime; Culture; Current Affairs; Design; Fantasy; Film; Finance; Health; Historical; How-to; Lifestyle; Music; Mystery; New Age; Photography; Psychology; Romance; Sci-Fi; Self-Help; Short Stories; Suspense; Theatre; Women's Interests; *Markets:* Adult; Youth

No unsolicited queries or queries by fax or email. Authors wishing to approach this agency will need to be recommended to the agent by someone else in the profession.

Monteiro Rose Dravis Agency, Inc.

4370 Tujunga AVE, Suite 145, Studio City, CA 91604
Tel: +1 (818) 501-1177
Fax: +1 (818) 501-1194
Email: monrose@monteiro-rose.com
Website: http://www.monteiro-rose.com

Handles: Scripts; *Areas:* Adventure; Crime; Drama; Film; Historical; Humour; Mystery; Romance; Sci-Fi; Suspense; Thrillers; TV; *Markets:* Adult; Children's; Family; Youth; *Treatments:* Contemporary; Mainstream

Handles for TV, film, and animation. No unsolicited mss. Accepts new clients by referral only.

Moore Literary Agency

10 State Street #309, Newburyport, MA 01950
Tel: +1 (978) 465-9015
Fax: +1 (978) 465-8817
Email: cmoore@moorelit.com

Handles: Nonfiction; *Areas:* Technology; *Markets:* Adult; Professional

Handles nonfiction books on computers and technology only. Accepts queries by email, but proposals by post with SASE only. No queries by fax.

Patricia Moosbrugger Literary Agency

Denver, CO
Email: submissions@pmagency.net
Website: http://www.pmagency.net

Handles: Fiction; Nonfiction; *Areas:* Literature; *Markets:* Adult; Youth

Send query by email with brief synopsis.

Howard Morhaim Literary Agency

30 Pierrepont Street, Brooklyn, NY 11201
Tel: +1 (718) 222-8400
Fax: +1 (718) 222-5056
Email: kmckean@morhaimliterary.com
Website: http://morhaimliterary.com

Handles: Fiction; Nonfiction; *Areas:* Culture; Fantasy; Health; Romance; Sci-Fi; Sport; Women's Interests; *Markets:* Adult; Youth; *Treatments:* Contemporary; Literary

Send query by email only with outline / proposal for nonfiction, or three sample chapters for fiction. Attachments are accepted. No thrillers, mysteries, crime, politics, true crime, mind/body/spirit, or children's picture books.

The Jean V. Naggar Literary Agency

216 East 75th Street, New York, NY 10021
Tel: +1 (212) 794-1082
Email: jvnla@jvnla.com
Website: http://www.jvnla.com

Handles: Fiction; Nonfiction; *Areas:* Adventure; Autobiography; Biography; Culture; Current Affairs; Fantasy; Gothic; Health; Historical; Horror; Humour; Lifestyle; Music; Mystery; Psychology; Romance; Science; Suspense; Thrillers; *Markets:* Adult; Children's; Youth; *Treatments:* Commercial; Dark; Literary; Mainstream; Popular

Accepts queries via online submission system only. See website for more details.

Nappaland Literary Agency

PO Box 1674, Loveland, CO 80539-1674
Fax: +1 (970) 635-9869
Email: Literary@nappaland.com
Website: http://www.nappaland.com/literary

Handles: Fiction; Nonfiction; *Areas:*
Culture; Historical; Humour; Lifestyle;
Religious; Suspense; Women's Interests;
Markets: Adult; Youth; *Treatments:* Literary

Deliberately small boutique-sized agency.
Send query letter only by email during
specific submission windows (see website).
No children's books, memoirs, screenplays,
poetry, or anything about cats.

Nelson Literary Agency, LLC

1732 Wazee Street, Suite 207, Denver, CO
80202
Tel: +1 (303) 292-2805
Email: query@nelsonagency.com
Website: http://www.nelsonagency.com

Handles: Fiction; Nonfiction; *Areas:*
Autobiography; Fantasy; Romance; Sci-Fi;
Women's Interests; *Markets:* Adult;
Children's; Youth; *Treatments:* Commercial;
Literary; Mainstream

No poetry, children's picture books,
screenplays, short story collections, horror,
mystery (unless chick lit), thrillers,
Christian/Inspirational, or any nonfiction
other than memoirs.

Submitting a query:

First, review the types of works we
represent. If fiction, does your project fall
under any of the genres? If yes, please
review how to write me an attention-getting
query. For nonfiction, if you are just starting
out, we suggest you review our tips on
submitting a good book proposal.

Please send a brief email query (we give
prefererence to email over snail mail) to
gauge our level of interest before you send
sample pages or a full proposal. Please put

the word QUERY and the title of your
project in the subject field of your email. I,
too, receive a lot of spam and following
these simple directions will ensure that your
query doesn't get accidentally deleted. No
email attachments please. Expect a quick
response to queries (three weeks).
Occasionally, it may take longer.

New Leaf Literary & Media, Inc.

110 West 40th Street, Suite 410, New York,
NY 10018
Tel: +1 (646) 248-7989
Fax: +1 (646) 861-4654
Email: query@newleafliterary.com
Website: http://www.newleafliterary.com

Handles: Fiction; Nonfiction; *Areas:*
Culture; Entertainment; Erotic; Fantasy;
Historical; Romance; Sci-Fi; Technology;
Thrillers; Women's Interests; *Markets:*
Adult; Children's; Youth; *Treatments:*
Mainstream

Send query by email only, with the word
"Query" along with the specific agent's
name in the subject line. Do not query more
than one agent. Include up to five double-
spaced sample pages in the body of the email
-- no attachments. Response only if
interested.

Niad Management

15021 Ventura Blvd. #860, Sherman Oaks,
CA 91403
Tel: +1 (818) 774-0051
Fax: +1 (818) 774-1740
Email: queries@niadmanagement.com
Website: http://www.niadmanagement.com

Handles: Fiction; Nonfiction; Scripts; *Areas:*
Adventure; Autobiography; Biography;
Crime; Culture; Drama; Film; Humour;
Mystery; Romance; Sport; Suspense;
Theatre; Thrillers; TV; *Markets:* Adult;
Youth; *Treatments:* Contemporary; Literary;
Mainstream

Manages mainly Hollywood writers, actors,
and directors, although does also handle a
very small number of books. Send query by

email or by post with SASE. Responds only if interested.

Nine Muses and Apollo, Inc.

525 Broadway, Suite 201, New York, NY 10012
Tel: +1 (212) 431-2665

Handles: Nonfiction; *Markets:* Adult

Adult nonfiction only. No children's or young adult. Send query with SASE, outline, and two sample chapters. No simultaneous submissions.

Northern Lights Literary Services

762 State Road 458, Bedford, IN 47421
Email: queries@northernlightsls.com
Website: http://www.northernlightsls.com

Handles: Fiction; Nonfiction; *Areas:* Biography; Business; Health; Historical; How-to; Lifestyle; Medicine; Mystery; New Age; Psychology; Romance; Self-Help; Suspense; Women's Interests; *Markets:* Adult

Our goal is to provide personalized service to clients and create a bond that will endure throughout your career. We seriously consider each query we receive and will accept hardworking new authors who are willing to develop their talents and skills.

Encourages email queries but responds only if interested (within 5 working days). No horror or books for children.

Objective Entertainment

609 Greenwich St. 6th Floor, New York, NY 10014
Tel: +1 (212) 431-5454
Fax: +1 (917) 464-6394
Email: IK@objectiveent.com
Website: http://www.objectiveent.com

Handles: Fiction; Nonfiction; Scripts; *Areas:* Autobiography; Biography; Business; Cookery; Culture; Current Affairs; Fantasy; Film; Lifestyle; Music; Mystery; Politics; Sci-Fi; Sport; Thrillers; TV; Women's

Interests; *Markets:* Adult; Children's; Youth; *Treatments:* Commercial; Literary

We represent over 100 celebrities, musicians, authors and bestselling writers.

Paradigm Talent and Literary Agency

360 Park Avenue South, 16th Floor, New York, NY 10010
Tel: +1 (212) 897-6400
Fax: +1 (212) 764-8941
Email: books@paradigmagency.com
Website: http://www.paradigmla.com

Handles: Fiction; Nonfiction; Scripts; *Areas:* Film; Theatre; TV; *Markets:* Adult

Talent agency with offices in Los Angeles, New York City, Monterey, California and Nashville, Tennessee, representing actors, musical artists, directors, writers and producers. Handles scripts and all areas of fiction and nonfiction. Send query by email with first ten pages of the work in the body of the email. Response only if interested.

The Park Literary Group LLC

270 Lafayette Street, Suite 1504, New York, NY 10012
Tel: +1 (212) 691-3500
Fax: +1 (212) 691-3540
Email: queries@parkliterary.com
Website: http://www.parkliterary.com

Handles: Fiction; Nonfiction; *Areas:* Adventure; Arts; Autobiography; Culture; Historical; Mystery; Politics; Science; Thrillers; Travel; *Markets:* Adult; *Treatments:* Commercial; Literary

Send query by email or by post with SASE. For fiction include short synopsis and first three chapters in the body of the email only (no attachments), and for nonfiction include proposal and sample chapter(s). No poetry or screenplays. Response only if interested.

Pavilion Literary Management

660 Massachusetts Avenue, Suite 4, Boston, MA 02118
Tel: +1 (617) 792-5218

Email: jeff@pavilionliterary.com
Website: http://www.pavilionliterary.com

Handles: Fiction; Nonfiction; *Areas:*
Adventure; Autobiography; Fantasy;
Historical; Mystery; Science; Thrillers;
Markets: Adult; Children's; Youth;
Treatments: Popular

Only accepting approaches for fiction work
by previously published authors or client
referral. Send query by email specifying
fiction or nonfiction and title of work in the
subject line. No attachments. See website for
full details.

Peregrine Whittlesey Agency
279 Central Park West, New York, NY
10024
Tel: +1 (212) 787-1802
Fax: +1 (212) 787-4985
Email: pwwagy@aol.com

Handles: Scripts; *Areas:* Film; Theatre; TV;
Markets: Adult

Handles mainly theatre scripts, plus a small
number of film/TV scripts by playwrights
who also write for screen. Send query with
SASE. No simultaneous submissions.

Barry Perelman Agency
415 Washington Boulevard, Suite 902,
Marina del Rey, CA 90292
Tel: +1 (310) 659-1122
Fax: +1 (310) 659-1122

Handles: Scripts; *Areas:* Adventure;
Biography; Drama; Film; Historical; Horror;
Mystery; Romance; Science; Thrillers; TV;
Markets: Adult; *Treatments:* Contemporary

Handles motion pictures. Send query with
SASE.

Pippin Properties, Inc
155 East 38th Street, Suite 2H, New York,
NY 10016
Tel: +1 (212) 338-9310
Fax: +1 (212) 338-9579
Email: info@pippinproperties.com
Website: http://www.pippinproperties.com

Handles: Fiction; *Markets:* Adult;
Children's; Youth

Devoted primarily to picture books, middle-
grade, and young adult novels, but also
represents adult projects on occasion. Send
query by email with synopsis,
background/publishing history, and any other
relevant details.

Alièka Pistek Literary Agency, LLC
302A West 12th St., #124, New York, NY
10014
Email: alicka@apliterary.com
Website: http://www.apliterary.com

Handles: Fiction; Nonfiction; *Areas:*
Biography; Current Affairs; Historical;
Mystery; Romance; Science; Suspense;
Thrillers; Travel; *Markets:* Adult;
Treatments: Commercial; Literary

Accepts submissions by email only. Send
query with bio and proposal/synopsis, and
for fiction first three chapters, up to 50 pages
max. Mark romance submissions as such in
the subject line as these are treated as a
special category. No fantasy, science fiction,
or westerns.

The Poynor Group
13454 Yorktown Drive, Bowie, MD 20715
Tel: +1 (301)805-6788
Email: jpoynor@aol.com

Handles: Fiction; Nonfiction; *Areas:*
Autobiography; Biography; Business;
Cookery; Culture; Finance; Health;
Medicine; Mystery; Religious; Romance;
Suspense; *Markets:* Adult; Children's; Youth

Send query by post with SASE, or by email.

Prospect Agency
551 Valley Rd., PMB 377, Upper Montclair,
NJ 07043
Tel: +1 (718) 788-3217
Fax: +1 (718) 788-3217
Email: esk@prospectagency.com
Website: http://www.prospectagency.com

Handles: Fiction; Nonfiction; *Areas:* Adventure; Autobiography; Crime; Erotic; Fantasy; Mystery; Romance; Science; Sci-Fi; Suspense; Thrillers; Westerns; Women's Interests; *Markets:* Adult; Children's; Youth; *Treatments:* Contemporary; Literary; Mainstream

Handles very little nonfiction. Specialises in romance, women's fiction, literary fiction, young adult/children's literature, and science fiction. Send submissions via website submission system **only** (no email queries – **email queries are not accepted or responded to** - or queries by post (these will be recycled). No poetry, short stories, text books, or most nonfiction.

Queen Literary Agency, Inc.

420 West End Avenue, Suite 8A, New York, NY 10024
Tel: +1 (212) 974-8333
Fax: +1 (212) 974-8347
Email: submissions@queenliterary.com
Website: http://www.queenliterary.com

Handles: Fiction; Nonfiction; *Areas:* Business; Cookery; Historical; Mystery; Psychology; Science; Sport; Thrillers; *Markets:* Adult; *Treatments:* Commercial; Literary

Founded by a former publishing executive, most recently head of IMG WORLDWIDE'S literary division. Handles a wide range of nonfiction titles, with a particular interest in business books, food writing, science and popular psychology, as well as books by well-known chefs, radio and television personalities and sports figures. Also handles commercial and literary fiction, including historical fiction, mysteries, and thrillers.

Quicksilver Books Literary Agency

508 Central Park Avenue, #5101, Scarsdale, NY 10583
Tel: +1 (914) 722-4664
Fax: +1 (914) 722-4664
Email: quicksilverbooks@hotmail.com
Website: http://www.quicksilverbooks.com

Handles: Fiction; Nonfiction; *Areas:* Adventure; Anthropology; Archaeology; Autobiography; Biography; Business; Cookery; Crime; Criticism; Culture; Current Affairs; Finance; Health; Historical; How-to; Lifestyle; Literature; Medicine; Mystery; Nature; New Age; Psychology; Religious; Science; Self-Help; Sociology; Sport; Suspense; Technology; Thrillers; Women's Interests; *Markets:* Adult; *Treatments:* Commercial; Contemporary; Literary; Mainstream; Popular

Send query by email, including: an overview of the project; your credentials and expertise on the subject; the projected market and how you can help reach it; a brief description of the competition (what makes your book special?); and a list of which publishers have already seen your manuscript, if any. Actively seeking adult mainstream trade and/or mass market fiction. Only completed full-length MSS considered. Prefers literate suspense thrillers and contemporary novels with bestseller potential. No poetry, science fiction, or explicit material.

Lynne Rabinoff Agency

72-11 Austin Street, No. 201, Forest Hills, NY 11375
Tel: +1 (718) 459-6894
Email: lynne@lynnerabinoff.com

Handles: Nonfiction; *Areas:* Anthropology; Archaeology; Autobiography; Biography; Business; Culture; Current Affairs; Finance; Historical; Legal; Military; Politics; Psychology; Religious; Science; Technology; Women's Interests; *Markets:* Adult

Particularly interested in politics, history, current affairs, and religion. Send query by email or by post with SASE, including proposal, sample chapter, and author bio. No queries by fax.

Raines & Raines

103 Kenyon Road, Medusa, NY 12120
Tel: +1 (518) 239-8311
Fax: +1 (518) 239-6029

Handles: Fiction; Nonfiction; *Areas:*

Adventure; Autobiography; Biography; Crime; Fantasy; Finance; Historical; Military; Mystery; Psychology; Sci-Fi; Suspense; Thrillers; Westerns; *Markets:* Adult

Handles nonfiction in all areas, and fiction in the areas specified above. Send query with SASE.

Redwood Agency
4300 SW 34th Avenue, Portland, OR 97239
Tel: +1 (503) 219-9019
Email: info@redwoodagency.com
Website: http://www.redwoodagency.com

Handles: Nonfiction; Reference; *Areas:* Autobiography; Business; Cookery; Culture; Gardening; Health; Humour; Lifestyle; Nature; Psychology; Self-Help; Technology; Travel; Women's Interests; *Markets:* Adult

Send query by email, or using "Quick Query" form on website. Further material will be requested if interested. With the exception of humour, no fiction.

Rees Literary Agency
14 Beacon St., Suite 710, Boston, MA 02108
Tel: +1 (617) 227-9014
Fax: +1 (617) 227-8762
Email: reesagency@reesagency.com
Website: http://www.reesagency.com

Handles: Fiction; *Areas:* Autobiography; Biography; Business; Historical; Psychology; Science; Self-Help; *Markets:* Adult; *Treatments:* Commercial; Literary

See website for specific agents' interests and submission requirements.

Regal Literary Inc.
The Capitol Building, 236 West 26th St., #801, New York, NY 10001
Tel: +1 (212) 684-7900
Fax: +1 (212) 684-7906
Email: submissions@regal-literary.com
Website: http://www.regal-literary.com

Handles: Fiction; Nonfiction; *Areas:* Biography; Historical; Photography;

Science; Short Stories; Thrillers; *Markets:* Adult; *Treatments:* Literary

Literary agency with offices in New York and London. Send one-page query by email or by post with SASE, outline, and author bio/qualifications. For fiction, include first ten pages or one story from a collection. No romance, science fiction, poetry, or screenplays. Writers based in the UK/Europe should contact the London office (see website for details).

Renee Zuckerbrot Literary Agency
115 West 29th Street, 10th floor, New York, NY 10001
Tel: +1 (212) 967-0072
Fax: +1 (212) 967-0073
Email: Submissions@rzagency.com
Website: http://rzagency.com

Handles: Fiction; Nonfiction; *Areas:* Culture; Historical; Literature; Mystery; Science; Short Stories; Thrillers; Women's Interests; *Markets:* Adult; *Treatments:* Commercial; Literary

Send query including the reason that you decided to contact this agency, synopsis, publication history, brief bio, contact information, and excerpt/sample chapter as a Word document attachment (for novels, should be the first chapter). See website for full details. No screenplays, genre romance or westerns, New Age, or how-to books. No unsolicited MSS, or queries by fax.

The Amy Rennert Agency, Inc.
1550 Tiburon Boulevard #302, Tiburon, CA 94920
Email: queries@amyrennert.com
Website: http://www.amyrennert.com

Handles: Fiction; Nonfiction; *Areas:* Autobiography; Biography; Business; Finance; Health; Historical; Lifestyle; Literature; Mystery; Spiritual; Sport; *Markets:* Adult; *Treatments:* Literary

Prefers query by email, with cover letter in body of email and a Word file attachment containing proposal and first chapter (nonfiction) or first 10-20 pages (fiction). For picture books, send cover letter in the body of the email and attach file with the text. Include phone number. Response only if interested. If querying by post do not include return postage as manuscripts will not be returned.

Riverside Literary Agency

41 Simon Keets Road, Leyden, MA 01337
Tel: +1 (413) 772-0067
Fax: +1 (413) 772-0969
Email: rivlit@sover.net

Handles: Fiction; Nonfiction; *Markets:* Adult

Send query with outline by email or by post with SASE. Usually obtains new clients by referral.

Michael D. Robins & Associates

141 Duesenberg Drive, Suite 7-B, Westlake Village, CA 91362
Tel: +1 (818) 343-1755
Fax: +1 (818) 575-9832
Email: mdr2@msn.com

Handles: Fiction; Nonfiction; Scripts; *Areas:* Film; Theatre; TV; *Markets:* Adult

Send query with SASE, or query by fax or email.

Andy Ross Agency

767 Santa Ray Avenue, Oakland, CA 94610
Tel: +1 (510) 238-8965
Email: andyrossagency@hotmail.com
Website: http://www.andyrossagency.com

Handles: Fiction; Nonfiction; *Areas:* Culture; Current Affairs; Historical; Religious; Science; *Markets:* Adult; Children's; Youth; *Treatments:* Commercial; Contemporary; Literary

We encourage queries for material in our fields of interest.

The agent has worked in the book business for 36 years, all of his working life. He was owner and general manager of Cody's Books in Berkeley, California from 1977-2006. Cody's has been recognised as one of America's great independent book stores.

During this period, the agent was the primary trade book buyer. This experience has given him a unique understanding of the retail book market, of publishing trends and, most importantly and uniquely, the hand selling of books to book buyers.

The agent is past president of the Northern California Booksellers Association, a board member and officer of the American Booksellers Association and a national spokesperson for issues concerning independent businesses. He has had signifcant profiles in the Wall Street Journal, Time Magazine, and the San Francisco Chronicle.

Queries by email only. See website for full guidelines.

The Rudy Agency

825 Wildlife Lane, Estes Park, CO 80517
Tel. +1 (970) 577-8500
Fax: +1 (970) 577-8600
Email: mak@rudyagency.com
Website: http://www.rudyagency.com

Handles: Fiction; Nonfiction; *Areas:* Autobiography; Biography; Business; Culture; Health; Historical; Medicine; Military; Science; Technology; *Markets:* Adult

Concentrates on adult nonfiction in the areas listed above. Not accepting fiction submissions, except historical fiction. No poetry, children's or young adult, religion books, parenting how-to books, or screenplays. Send query letter only in first instance, by email or by fax.

Marly Rusoff & Associates, Inc.

PO Box 524, Bronxville, NY 10708
Tel: +1 (914) 961-7939
Email: mra_queries3@rusoffagency.com
Website: http://www.rusoffagency.com

Handles: Fiction; Nonfiction; *Areas:* Architecture; Arts; Autobiography; Biography; Business; Culture; Design; Finance; Health; Historical; Medicine; Psychology; *Markets:* Adult; *Treatments:* Commercial; Literary

Send 1-2 page query by post or email, including synopsis and relevant author info and page or word count. Queries sent by email should include the word "query" in the subject line. Changes email address regularly to avoid spam, so check website before querying and notify firstwriter.com via the "Report an Error" button if address has changed from that displayed. May not respond if not interested. No PDFs, CDs, or directions to view material on websites.

Salkind Literary Agency

734 Indiana Street, Lawrence, KS 66044
Tel: +1 (785) 371-0101
Fax: +1 (516) 706-2369
Email: neil@studiob.com
Website: http://www.salkindagency.com

Handles: Fiction; Nonfiction; *Areas:* Adventure; Arts; Autobiography; Biography; Business; Cookery; Crafts; Crime; Culture; Current Affairs; Fantasy; Finance; Health; Historical; How-to; Humour; Lifestyle; Mystery; Photography; Politics; Psychology; Religious; Science; Sci-Fi; Self-Help; Spiritual; Suspense; Technology; Thrillers; Travel; Women's Interests; *Markets:* Academic; Adult

Handles general nonfiction trade, fiction, and textbook authors. Query by email or telephone.

Susan Schulman, A Literary Agency

454 West 44th Street, New York, NY 10036
Tel: +1 (212) 713-1633
Fax: +1 (212) 581-8830
Email: schulmanqueries@yahoo.com

Handles: Fiction; Nonfiction; Scripts; *Areas:* Adventure; Anthropology; Archaeology; Autobiography; Biography; Business; Cookery; Crime; Culture; Current Affairs; Finance; Health; Historical; How-to;

Humour; Legal; Lifestyle; Literature; Medicine; Music; Mystery; Politics; Psychology; Religious; Self-Help; Sociology; Sport; Suspense; Theatre; Women's Interests; *Markets:* Adult; Children's; *Treatments:* Literary; Mainstream

Send query with synopsis by email in the body of the email or by post with SASE. No poetry, TV scripts, concepts for TV, or unsolicited MSS.

Jonathan Scott, Inc

933 West Van Buren, Suite 510, Chicago, IL 60680
Tel: +1 (312) 339-7300
Email: jon_malysiak@yahoo.com
Website: http://www.jonathanscott.us

Handles: Nonfiction; *Areas:* Autobiography; Business; Cookery; Health; Historical; Sport; Travel; *Markets:* Adult

Handles nonfiction only. No fiction. Send query by email outlining your book idea and/or a proposal. Hard copy proposals will not be read.

Scribblers House LLC Literary Agency

PO Box 1007 Cooper Station, New York, NY 10276-1007
Tel: +1 (212) 714-7747
Fax: +1 (212) 714-7749
Email: query@scribblershouse.net
Website: http://www.scribblershouse.net

Handles: Fiction; Nonfiction; *Areas:* Autobiography; Biography; Business; Culture; Finance; Health; Historical; How-to; Lifestyle; Medicine; Politics; Psychology; Self-Help; Spiritual; *Markets:* Adult; *Treatments:* Literary

Represents: Mostly nonfiction and only considers novels by fiction writers who have previously published with a bona fide book publisher or have published short fiction with journals and magazines.

Considers these nonfiction areas: health, medical, diet, nutrition, the brain, psychology, self-help, how-to, business, personal finance, memoirs, biography, history, politics, writing books, language, relationships, sex, pop culture, spirituality, gender issues, and parenting.

Only considers novels classified as literary fiction.

Accepts queries by email only.

Scribe Agency LLC

5508 Joylynne Drive, Madison, WI 53716
Email: submissions@scribeagency.com
Website: http://www.scribeagency.com

Handles: Fiction; *Areas:* Fantasy; Literature; Sci-Fi; Short Stories; *Markets:* Adult; *Treatments:* Commercial; Literary; Mainstream

Handles science fiction, fantasy, and literary fiction. No nonfiction, humour, cozy mysteries, faith-based fiction, screenplays, poetry, or works based on another's ideas. Send query in body of email, with synopsis and first three chapters as Word docs, RTFs, or PDFs. No hard copy approaches. If unable to submit material electronically, send email query in first instance.

Secret Agent Man

PO Box 1078, Lake Forest, CA 92609-1078
Tel: +1 (949) 463-1638
Fax: +1 (949) 831-4648
Email: query@secretagentman.net
Website: http://www.secretagentman.net

Handles: Fiction; Nonfiction; *Areas:* Crime; Mystery; Religious; Suspense; Thrillers; Westerns; *Markets:* Adult

Send query by email only (no postal submissions) with the word "Query" in the subject line, sample consecutive chapter(s), synopsis and/or outline. No first contact by phone. Not interested in vampire; sci-fi; fantasy; horror; cold war, military or political thrillers; children's or young adult; short stories; screenplays; poetry collections; romance; or historical. Christian nonfiction should be based on Biblical theology, not speculative.

Lynn Seligman, Literary Agent

400 Highland Avenue, Upper Montclair, NJ 07043
Tel: +1 (973) 783-3631

Handles: Fiction; Nonfiction; *Areas:* Anthropology; Arts; Biography; Business; Cookery; Crime; Culture; Current Affairs; Design; Fantasy; Film; Finance; Health; Historical; Horror; How-to; Humour; Lifestyle; Music; Mystery; Nature; Photography; Politics; Psychology; Romance; Science; Sci-Fi; Self-Help; Sociology; Women's Interests; *Markets:* Adult; *Treatments:* Contemporary; Literary; Mainstream

Send query with SASE.

The Seven Bridges Group

5000 Birch Street, Suite 3000, Newport Beach, CA 92660
Tel: +1 (949) 260-2099
Fax: +1 (650) 249-1612
Email: travis.bell@sevenbridgesgroup.com
Website: http://www.sevenbridgesgroup.com

Handles: Fiction; Scripts; *Areas:* Adventure; Autobiography; Biography; Crime; Culture; Current Affairs; Drama; Entertainment; Literature; Men's Interests; Military; Music; Politics; Short Stories; Sport; Suspense; Travel; TV; Westerns; Women's Interests; *Markets:* Adult; Family; Professional; *Treatments:* Commercial; Contemporary; In-depth; Light; Literary; Mainstream; Niche; Popular; Traditional

No upfront fees will be incurred by writer (Client).

The Seymour Agency

475 Miner Street Road, Canton, NY 13617
Tel: +1 (315) 386-1831
Email: marysue@theseymouragency.com
Website: http://www.theseymouragency.com

Handles: Fiction; Nonfiction; *Areas:* Adventure; Fantasy; Mystery; Religious; Romance; Sci-Fi; Suspense; Thrillers; *Markets:* Adult; Children's; Youth

Brief email queries accepted (no

attachments). No poetry, horror or erotica. See website for full submission guidelines and specific interests of each agent.

Denise Shannon Literary Agency, Inc.

20 West 22nd Street, Suite 1603, New York, NY 10010
Tel: +1 (212) 414-2911
Fax: +1 (212) 414-2930
Email:
submissions@deniseshannonagency.com
Website: http://deniseshannonagency.com

Handles: Fiction; Nonfiction; *Areas:*
Biography; Business; Current Affairs; Health; Historical; Politics; Sociology; *Markets:* Adult; *Treatments:* Literary

Send query by email, or by post with SASE, including outline and bio listing any previous publishing credits. Notify if simultaneous submission. No unsolicited MSS, or queries for incomplete fiction MSS.

Signature Literary Agency

101 W. 23rd St, Suite 346, New York, NY 10011
Tel: +1 (201) 435-8334
Fax: +1 (202) 478-1623
Email: ellen@signaturelit.com
Website: http://www.signaturelit.com

Handles: Fiction; Nonfiction; Reference; *Areas:* Beauty and Fashion; Biography; Crime; Criticism; Culture; Current Affairs; Historical; Military; Politics; Science; Technology; Thrillers; Women's Interests; *Markets:* Adult; Children's; Youth; *Treatments:* Commercial; Literary; Popular

Agency established in Washington DC. The principal agent formerly worked at the Graybill and English Literary Agency. She has a law degree from George Washington University and extensive editorial experience.

Send query by email to specific agent (see website for individual contact details and "wishlists").

Offices in both New York and Washington DC.

SLW Literary Agency

4100 Ridgeland Avenue, Northbrook, IL 60062
Tel: +1 (847) 509-0999
Fax: +1 (847) 509-0996
Email: shariwenk@gmail.com

Handles: Nonfiction; *Areas:* Sport; *Markets:* Adult

Handles sports celebrities and sports writers only.

Valerie Smith, Literary Agent

1746 Route 44/55 RR, Box 160, Modena, NY 12548

Handles: Fiction; Nonfiction; *Areas:*
Cookery; Fantasy; Historical; How-to; Mystery; Sci-Fi; Self-Help; Suspense; Women's Interests; *Markets:* Adult; Youth; *Treatments:* Contemporary; Literary; Mainstream

Send query with SASE, synopsis, author bio, and three sample chapters, by post only. No unsolicited MSS, or queries by fax or email. Strong ties to science fiction, fantasy, and young adult.

Spectrum Literary Agency

320 Central Park West, Suite 1-D, New York, NY 10025
Tel: +1 (212) 362-4323
Fax: +1 (212) 362-4562
Email: ruddigore1@aol.com
Website:
http://www.spectrumliteraryagency.com

Handles: Fiction; Nonfiction; *Areas:*
Fantasy; Historical; Mystery; Romance; Sci-Fi; Suspense; *Markets:* Adult; *Treatments:* Contemporary; Mainstream

Send query with SASE describing your book and providing background information, publishing credits, and relevant qualifications. The first 10 pages of the work may also be included. Response within three months. No unsolicited MSS or queries by fax, email, or phone.

Spencerhill Associates

PO Box 374, Chatham, NY 12037
Tel: +1 (518) 392-9293
Fax: +1 (518) 392-9554
Email:
submission@spencerhillassociates.com
Website: http://spencerhillassociates.com

Handles: Fiction; Nonfiction; *Areas:* Erotic; Fantasy; Mystery; Romance; Thrillers; *Markets:* Adult; Youth; *Treatments:* Commercial; Literary

Handles commercial, general-interest fiction, romance including historical romance, paranormal romance, urban fantasy, erotic fiction, category romance, literary fiction, thrillers and mysteries, young adult, and nonfiction. No children's. Send query by email with synopsis and first three chapters attached in .doc / .rtf / .txt format. See website for full details.

Sternig & Byrne Literary Agency

2370 S. 107th Street, Apt 4, Milwaukee, Wisconsin 53227-2036
Tel: +1 (414) 328-8034
Fax: +1 (414) 328-8034
Email: jackbyrne@hotmail.com
Website: http://sff.net/people/jackbyrne

Handles: Fiction; Nonfiction; *Areas:* Fantasy; Horror; Mystery; Sci-Fi; Suspense; *Markets:* Adult; Youth

Send brief query by post or email in first instance (if sending by email send in the body of the mail, do not send attachments). Will request further materials if interested. Currently only considering science fiction, fantasy, and mysteries. Preference given to writers with a publishing history. No submissions by email.

Stone Manners Salners Agency

9911 West Pico Boulevard, Suite 1400, Los Angeles, CA 90048

Tel: +1 (323) 655-1313 / +1 (212) 505-1400
Email: info@smsagency.com
Website: http://www.smsagency.com

Handles: Scripts; *Areas:* Film; TV; *Markets:* Adult

Handles movie and TV scripts. Send query by email or post with SASE. No queries by fax.

Pam Strickler Author Management

134 Main Street, New Paltz, NY 12561
Email: pamstrickleragency@gmail.com

Handles: Fiction; *Areas:* Historical; Romance; Women's Interests; *Markets:* Adult

Send query by email only, including one-page letter giving brief description of plot, plus first ten pages, all pasted into the body of the email. Attachments are deleted unread. Hardcopy queries or manuscripts destroyed unread. No unsolicited MSS, children's books, or nonfiction.

Rebecca Strong International Literary Agency

235 West 108th Street, #35, New York, NY 10025
Tel: +1 (212) 865-1569
Email: info@rsila.com
Website: http://www.rsila.com

Handles: Fiction; Nonfiction; *Areas:* Autobiography; Biography; Business; Health; Historical; Science; Travel; *Markets:* Adult

Deliberately small agency focused on building careers rather than dealing with individual projects. Handles general fiction and nonfiction in the areas specified above. No poetry, screenplays, or unsolicited MSS. Generally represents writers with prior publishing experience only (for writers of fiction this includes publication in literary magazines and anthologies). Accepts query letters by email only. Include the words "Submission query" clearly in the subject line. If submitting fiction, include one or two complete chapters only.

The Strothman Agency
197 Eighth Street, Flagship Wharf - 611 , Charlestown, MA 02129
Tel: +1 (617) 742-2011
Fax: +1 (617) 742-2014
Email: strothmanagency@gmail.com
Website: http://www.strothmanagency.com

Handles: Fiction; Nonfiction; *Areas:* Arts; Autobiography; Business; Culture; Current Affairs; Historical; Nature; Science; Travel; *Markets:* Adult; Children's; Youth

Send query by email only. Postal approaches will be recycled or returned unread. Include query, details about yourself, a synopsis, and (for fiction) 2-10 sample pages. All material must be in the body of the email - no attachments. No romance, science fiction, picture books, or poetry.

The Stuart Agency
260 West 52 Street, Suite. 24-C, New York, NY 10019
Tel: +1 (212) 586-2711
Fax: +1 (212) 977-1488
Email: andrew@stuartagency.com
Website: http://www.stuartagency.com

Handles: Fiction; Nonfiction; *Areas:* Autobiography; Business; Current Affairs; Health; Historical; Lifestyle; Psychology; Religious; Science; Sport; *Markets:* Adult; *Treatments:* Commercial; Literary

Send query using submission form on website.

The Swetky Agency and Associates
2150 Balboa Way #29, St. George, Utah 84770
Tel: +1 (435) 313-8006
Email: fayeswetky@amsaw.org
Website:
http://www.amsaw.org/swetkyagency/

Handles: Fiction; Nonfiction; Scripts; *Areas:* Adventure; Anthropology; Archaeology; Architecture; Arts; Autobiography; Business; Cookery; Crime; Criticism; Culture; Current Affairs; Design; Erotic; Fantasy; Film; Finance; Gardening; Gothic; Health; Historical; How-to; Humour; Legal; Leisure; Literature; Medicine; Military; Mystery; Nature; Philosophy; Photography; Politics; Psychology; Religious; Romance; Science; Sci-Fi; Self-Help; Short Stories; Sociology; Sport; Suspense; Technology; Theatre; Thrillers; Translations; Travel; TV; Westerns; Women's Interests; *Markets:* Adult; Children's; Youth; *Treatments:* Contemporary; Experimental; Literary; Mainstream

Submit query using submission form on website only. Do not send any portion of your work until requested to do so. Follow guidelines on website precisely. Failure to do so results in automatic rejection. Willing to consider anything marketable, except short stories, poetry and children's picture books (but accepts children's fiction and nonfiction).

Talcott Notch Literary
2 Broad Street, Second Floor, Suites 1,2 & 10, Milford, Connecticut 06460
Tel: +1 (203) 876-4959
Fax: +1 (203) 876-9517
Email: editorial@talcottnotch.net
Website: http://www.talcottnotch.net

Handles: Fiction; Nonfiction; *Areas:* Autobiography; Business; Cookery; Crafts; Crime; Fantasy; Gardening; Historical; Horror; Lifestyle; Mystery; Nature; Science; Sci-Fi; Suspense; Technology; Thrillers; Women's Interests; *Markets:* Adult; Children's; Family; Youth; *Treatments:* Mainstream

Rapidly growing literary agency seeking fresh voices in fiction and expert nonfiction authors. Our President has over fifteen years in the publishing industry. Send query by email or by post with SASE, including outline or synopsis and first ten pages. No email attachments. See website for full guidelines.

Tessler Literary Agency

27 West 20th Street, Suite 1003, New York, NY 10011
Tel: +1 (212) 242-0466
Fax: +1 (212) 242-2366
Website: http://www.tessleragency.com

Handles: Fiction; Nonfiction; *Areas:* Autobiography; Biography; Business; Cookery; Historical; Psychology; Science; Travel; Women's Interests; *Markets:* Adult; *Treatments:* Commercial; Literary; Popular

Welcomes appropriate queries. Handles quality nonfiction and literary and commercial fiction. No genre fiction or children's fiction. Send query via form on website only.

Timberlake Literary Services, LLC

Email:
joantimberlake@timberlakeliterary.com
Website: http://www.timberlakeliterary.com

Handles: Fiction; Nonfiction; *Areas:* Adventure; Arts; Biography; Business; Crime; Criticism; Culture; Current Affairs; Entertainment; Film; Finance; Gardening; Health; Historical; Hobbies; Humour; Legal; Lifestyle; Literature; Medicine; Military; Music; Mystery; Nature; New Age; Politics; Psychology; Romance; Science; Self-Help; Sociology; Spiritual; Suspense; Technology; Theatre; Women's Interests; *Markets:* Academic; Adult; Professional

Offers a range of literary and contract negotiation services. We are enthusiastic and willing to work with both published and unpublished writers whose writing is high quality. We aggressively pursue our writers' goals by guiding writers through the publishing process, from determining the readiness of their manuscript to negotiating fair contracts.

Our emphasis is on print
and other traditional media, but we are committed to the new reality of publishing. Thus, we embrace new technology and new opportunities for writers in a variety of media.

Tom Lee

716 Kishwaukee Street #D, Rockford, IL 61104
Tel: +1 (815) 505-9147 or +1 (815) 708-7123
Fax: +1 (815) 964-3061
Email: chicagocatorange@yahoo.com

Handles: Fiction; Poetry; Scripts; *Areas:* Adventure; Anthropology; Antiques; Archaeology; Arts; Autobiography; Crime; Drama; Erotic; Fantasy; Film; Historical; Horror; Literature; Mystery; Religious; Sci-Fi; Short Stories; Theatre; Thrillers; *Markets:* Adult; Professional; *Treatments:* Commercial; Dark; Experimental; In-depth; Literary; Mainstream; Progressive; Serious

Want writers who have educated capability in handling their material. Meet the structural and syntactical demands of the publishers and producers, and must be easy to work with, know the industries, and not be playing the self-possessed, eccentric artiste, so to say.

TriadaUS Literary Agency, Inc.

P.O.Box 561, Sewickley, PA 15143
Tel: +1 (412) 401-3376
Email: uwe@triadaus.com
Website: http://www.triadaus.com

Handles: Fiction; Nonfiction; *Areas:* Adventure; Autobiography; Biography; Cookery; Crime; Culture; Current Affairs; Health; How-to; Mystery; Psychology; Romance; Sci-Fi; Self-Help; Sport; Thrillers; Travel; *Markets:* Adult; Children's; Youth; *Treatments:* Commercial; Literary

Actively seeking established and new writers in a wide range of genres. Will only respond to approaches following the guidelines outlined on the website. Only responds to postal queries that include an SASE. Prefers email approaches, but no attachments.

2M Literary Agency Ltd

33 West 17 Street, PH, New York, NY 10011
Tel: +1 (212) 741-1509
Fax: +1 (212) 691-4460
Email: morel@2mcommunications.com

Website:
http://www.2mcommunications.com

Handles: Nonfiction; *Areas:* Autobiography; Beauty and Fashion; Business; Cookery; Crime; Culture; Film; Health; Lifestyle; Medicine; Music; Politics; Psychology; Science; Sport; *Markets:* Adult; Family; *Treatments:* Contemporary; Mainstream; Niche; Popular; Progressive; Traditional

Only accepts queries from established ghostwriters, collaborators, and editors with experience in the fields of business; film, music and television; health and fitness; medicine and psychology; parenting; politics; science; sport; true crime; or the world of food.

Venture Literary

2683 Via de la Valle, G-714, Del Mar, CA 92014
Tel: +1 (619) 807-1887
Fax: +1 (772) 365-8321
Email: submissions@ventureliterary.com
Website: http://www.ventureliterary.com

Handles: Fiction; Nonfiction; *Areas:* Adventure; Anthropology; Antiques; Archaeology; Architecture; Arts; Autobiography; Beauty and Fashion; Biography; Business; Cookery; Crafts; Crime; Criticism; Culture; Current Affairs; Design; Drama; Entertainment; Erotic; Film; Finance; Gardening; Gothic; Health; Historical; Hobbies; Horror; How-to; Humour; Legal; Leisure; Lifestyle; Literature; Media; Medicine; Men's Interests; Military; Music; Mystery; Nature; New Age; Philosophy; Photography; Politics; Psychology; Radio; Religious; Science; Self-Help; Short Stories; Sociology; Spiritual; Sport; Suspense; Technology; Theatre; Thrillers; Translations; Travel; TV; Women's Interests; *Markets:* Adult

Willing to consider queries in all genres except fantasy, sci-fi, romance, children's picture books, and westerns. Send query letter by email only. First 50 pages will be requested by email if interested in proposal. Unsolicited queries, proposals, or manuscripts via snail mail, and all snail mail submissions will be discarded unopened.

Veritas Literary Agency

601 Van Ness Avenue, Opera Plaza Suite E, San Francisco, CA 94102
Tel: +1 (415) 647-6964
Fax: +1 (415) 647-6965
Email: submissions@veritasliterary.com
Website: http://www.veritasliterary.com

Handles: Fiction; Nonfiction; *Areas:* Business; Crime; Culture; Erotic; Fantasy; Health; Historical; Lifestyle; Mystery; Nature; Science; Sci-Fi; Self-Help; Thrillers; Women's Interests; *Markets:* Adult; Children's; Youth; *Treatments:* Commercial; Literary

Send query or proposal by email only. Submit further information on request only. For fiction, include cover letter listing previously published work, one-page summary and first two chapters. For nonfiction, include author bio, overview, chapter-by-chapter summary, and analysis of competing titles.

Beth Vesel Literary Agency

80 Fifth Avenue, Suite 1101, New York, NY 10011
Tel: +1 (212) 924-4252
Fax: +1 (212) 675-1381
Email: kezia@bvlit.com

Handles: Fiction; Nonfiction; *Areas:* Autobiography; Biography; Business; Crime; Criticism; Culture; Finance; Health; How-to; Medicine; Psychology; Thrillers; Women's Interests; *Markets:* Adult; *Treatments:* Literary; Serious

Handles serious nonfiction (sophisticated memoirs, cultural criticism, psychology, women's issues) and fiction (particularly literary psychological thrillers). Send query with SASE.

The Ward & Balkin Agency, Inc

P. O. Box 7144, Lowell, MA 01852
Tel: +1 (978) 656-8389
Email: christinawardlit@mac.com
Website: http://wardbalkin.com

Handles: Fiction; Nonfiction; *Areas:* Arts;

Autobiography; Biography; Culture; Gardening; Health; Historical; Lifestyle; Medicine; Mystery; Nature; Psychology; Sociology; Thrillers; *Markets:* Academic; Adult; *Treatments:* Contemporary; Literary

Accepts submissions and queries by email, as well as by regular post. See website for full submission guidelines. No poetry, short story collections, romance, science fiction, fantasy, or paranormal.

Irene Webb Literary

551 W. Cordova Road #238, Santa Fe, NM 87505
Tel: +1 (505) 988-1817
Email: webblit@gmail.com
Website: http://www.irenewebb.com

Handles: Fiction; Nonfiction; *Areas:* Autobiography; Crime; Culture; Health; Horror; Mystery; Nature; Self-Help; Spiritual; Thrillers; Women's Interests; *Markets:* Adult; Youth; *Treatments:* Commercial; Literary

Not accepting new clients as at June 4, 2012. Check website for current status.

Send query by email only, with the word "Query" and the title of your work in the subject field.

The Wendy Weil Agency, Inc.

232 Madison Avenue, Suite 1300, New York, NY 10016
Tel: +1 (212) 685-0030
Fax: +1 (212) 685-0765
Email: wweil@wendyweil.com
Website: http://www.wendyweil.com

Handles: Fiction; Nonfiction; *Areas:* Arts; Autobiography; Culture; Current Affairs; Health; Historical; Lifestyle; Mystery; Science; Thrillers; *Markets:* Adult; *Treatments:* Commercial; Literary

Note: The status of this agency is uncertain. The principal agent died in 2012, but the website is still up and still shows the same information as prior to her death. The two remaining agents are reported to have moved to another agency

with the intention of taking their clients with them, while the agency itself has been sold to a third party.

Send query by post (up to two pages, plus synopsis and SASE) or by email (response not guaranteed). Response in 4-6 weeks. No screenplays or textbooks.

The Weingel-Fidel Agency

310 East 46th Street, Suite 21-E, New York, NY 10017
Tel: +1 (212) 599-2959
Email: lwf@theweingel-fidelagency.com

Handles: Fiction; Nonfiction; *Areas:* Arts; Autobiography; Biography; Music; Psychology; Science; Sociology; Technology; Women's Interests; *Markets:* Adult; *Treatments:* Commercial; Literary; Mainstream

Accepts new clients by referral only - approach only via an existing client or industry contact. Specialises in commercial and literary fiction and nonfiction. Particularly interested in investigative journalism. No genre fiction, science fiction, fantasy, or self-help.

Wernick & Pratt Agency

1207 North Avenue , Beacon, NY 12508
Email: info@wernickpratt.com
Website: http://www.wernickpratt.com

Handles: Fiction; Nonfiction; *Markets:* Children's; Youth; *Treatments:* Commercial; Literary

Handles children's books of all genres, from picture books to young adult literature. Particularly interested in authors who also illustrate their picture books; humorous young chapter books; literary and commercial middle grade / young adult books.

Not interested in picture book manuscripts of more than 750 words, mood pieces, work specifically targeted to the educational market, or fiction about the American Revolution, Civil War, or World War II (unless told from a very unique perspective).

Accepts queries by email only. See website for full guidelines. Response only if interested.

Whimsy Literary Agency, LLC

310 East 12th Street, Suite 2C, New York, NY 10003
Tel: +1 (212) 674-7162
Email: whimsynyc@aol.com
Website: http://whimsyliteraryagency.com

Handles: Nonfiction; *Areas:* Beauty and Fashion; Business; Cookery; Culture; Entertainment; Health; How-to; Humour; Politics; Psychology; Religious; Self-Help; Spiritual; *Markets:* Adult; *Treatments:* Commercial

No unsolicited mss. Send query by email in first instance.

Wolfson Literary Agency

Email: query@wolfsonliterary.com
Website: http://www.wolfsonliterary.com

Handles: Fiction; Nonfiction; *Areas:* Culture; Health; How-to; Humour; Lifestyle; Medicine; Mystery; Romance; Suspense; Thrillers; Women's Interests; *Markets:* Adult; Youth; *Treatments:* Mainstream; Popular

Accepts queries by email only. Response only if interested. See website for full submission guidelines.

Wordserve Literary

10152 Knoll Circle, Highlands Ranch, CO 80130
Tel: +1 (303) 471-6675
Email: admin@wordserveliterary.com
Website: http://www.wordserveliterary.com

Handles: Fiction; Nonfiction; *Areas:* Autobiography; Biography; Culture; Current Affairs; Fantasy; Finance; Health; Historical; Legal; Military; Psychology; Religious; Romance; Sci-Fi; Self-Help; Suspense; Thrillers; Women's Interests; *Markets:* Adult; *Treatments:* Literary; Mainstream

Represents books for the general and Christian markets. Nonfiction 40,000 - 100,000 words; fiction 75,000-120,000 words. No gift books, poetry, short stories, screenplays, graphic novels, children's picture books, science fiction or fantasy for any age. Email approaches only. See website for detailed submission guidelines. Submissions that disregard the submission guidelines may themselves be disregarded.

Writers' Representatives, LLC

116 W. 14th St., 11th Fl., New York, NY 10011-7305
Tel: +1 (212) 620-0023
Fax: +1 (212) 620-0023
Email: transom@writersreps.com
Website: http://www.writersreps.com

Handles: Fiction; Nonfiction; Poetry; Reference; *Areas:* Autobiography; Biography; Business; Cookery; Criticism; Current Affairs; Finance; Historical; Humour; Legal; Literature; Mystery; Philosophy; Politics; Science; Self-Help; Thrillers; *Markets:* Adult; *Treatments:* Literary; Serious

Send email describing your project and yourself, or send proposal, outline, CV, and sample chapters, or complete unsolicited MS, with SASE. See website for submission requirements in FAQ section. Specialises in serious and literary fiction and nonfiction. No screenplays. No science fiction or children's or young adult fiction unless it aspires to serious literature.

Yates & Yates

1100 Town and Country Road, Suite 1300, Orange, CA 92868
Tel: +1 (714) 480-4000
Fax: +1 (714) 480-4001
Email: email@yates2.com
Website: http://www.yates2.com

Handles: Fiction; Nonfiction; *Areas:* Autobiography; Biography; Business; Current Affairs; Legal; Politics; Religious; Sport; Thrillers; Women's Interests; *Markets:* Adult; *Treatments:* Literary

Literary agency based in California. Takes a holistic approach, combining agency representation, expert legal advice, marketing guidance, career coaching, creative counseling, and business management consulting.

The Zack Company, Inc

PMB 525, 4653 Carmel Mountain Rd, Ste 308, San Diego, CA 92130-6650
Website: http://www.zackcompany.com

Handles: Fiction; Nonfiction; Reference; *Areas:* Adventure; Autobiography; Biography; Business; Cookery; Crime; Current Affairs; Entertainment; Erotic; Fantasy; Film; Finance; Gardening; Health; Historical; Horror; Humour; Lifestyle; Medicine; Military; Music; Mystery; Nature; Politics; Religious; Romance; Science; Sci-Fi; Self-Help; Spiritual; Sport; Suspense; Technology; Thrillers; Translations; TV; Women's Interests; *Markets:* Adult; *Treatments:* Commercial; Literary; Popular

IMPORTANT: This agency objects to being listed on firstwriter.com and has in the past threatened to reject any submission from a writer who found his details through this site. We therefore suggest that if you approach this agency you do not state where you found its contact details.

The agent has also stated that his requirements change frequently, so it is important to check the agency website before approaching. Fully consult the agency's requirements for material and queries before approaching. If you believe any of them are at odds with the information provided on this listing, please report this error using the "Report an Error" button at the top of the page. All information is correct at the time of writing.

While external reports indicate that this agency is legitimate and has made confirmed sales to royalty-paying publishers, please note that it appears to have been formerly listed as "not recommended" on another site. It no longer appears to be part of the AAR. It also offers Editorial Services, which we believe would contravene the AAR canon of ethics, which state "the practice of literary agents charging clients or potential clients for reading and evaluating literary works

(including outlines, proposals, and partial or complete manuscripts) is subject to serious abuse that reflects adversely on our profession".

See website for full guidelines on querying. Please note that approaches are not accepted to the former submissions email address (submissions@zackcompany.com). Electronic approaches must be made via the form on the website.

Karen Gantz Zahler Literary Agency

860 Fifth Ave Suite 7J, New York, NY 10021
Tel: +1 (212) 734-3619
Email: karen@karengantzlit.com
Website: http://www.karengantzlit.com

Handles: Fiction; Nonfiction; *Areas:* Autobiography; Cookery; Design; Entertainment; Historical; Lifestyle; Politics; Psychology; Religious; Sociology; Spiritual; *Markets:* Adult

Considers all genres but specialises in nonfiction. Send query and summary by email only.

Helen Zimmermann Literary Agency

3 Emmy Lane, New Paltz, NY 12561
Tel: +1 (845) 256-0977
Fax: +1 (845) 256-0979
Email: Submit@ZimmAgency.com
Website: http://www.zimmagency.com

Handles: Fiction; Nonfiction; *Areas:* Autobiography; Cookery; Culture; Health; Historical; How-to; Humour; Lifestyle; Music; Mystery; Nature; Sport; Suspense; Women's Interests; *Markets:* Adult; *Treatments:* Literary

Particularly interested in health and wellness, relationships, popular culture, women's issues, lifestyle, sports, and music. No poetry, science fiction, horror, or romance. Prefers email queries, but no attachments unless requested. Send pitch letter - for fiction include summary, bio, and first chapter in the body of the email.

UK Literary Agents

For the most up-to-date listings of these and hundreds of other literary agents, visit http://www.firstwriter.com/Agents

To claim your **free** access to the site, please see the back of this book.

Sheila Ableman Literary Agency
48-56 Bayham Place, London, NW1 0EU
Tel: +44 (0) 20 7388 7222
Email: sheila@sheilaableman.co.uk
Website: http://www.sheilaableman.com

Handles: Nonfiction; *Areas:* Autobiography; Biography; Historical; Science; *Markets:* Adult; *Treatments:* Commercial; Popular

Send query with SAE, publishing history, brief CV, one-page synopsis, and two sample chapters. Specialises in TV tie-ins and celebrity ghost writing. No poetry, children's books, gardening, or sport. Welcomes unsolicited MSS.

Aitken Alexander Associates
18–21 Cavaye Place, London, SW10 9PT
Tel: +44 (0) 20 7373 8672
Fax: +44 (0) 20 7373 6002
Email: reception@aitkenalexander.co.uk
Website: http://www.aitkenalexander.co.uk

Handles: Fiction; Nonfiction; *Markets:* Adult

Send query with return postage, synopsis up to one page, and 30 consecutive pages. No illustrated children's books, poetry or screenplays. No submissions or queries by email.

The Ampersand Agency Ltd
Ryman's Cottages, Little Tew, Chipping Norton, Oxfordshire OX7 4JJ
Tel: +44 (0) 1608 683677 / 683898
Fax: +44 (0) 1608 683449
Email: amd@theampersandagency.co.uk
Website: http://www.theampersandagency.co.uk

Handles: Fiction; Nonfiction; *Areas:* Autobiography; Biography; Crime; Current Affairs; Historical; Thrillers; Women's Interests; *Markets:* Adult; *Treatments:* Commercial; Contemporary; Literary

We handle literary and commercial fiction and non-fiction, including contemporary and historical novels, crime, thrillers, biography, women's fiction, history, and memoirs. No scripts except those by existing clients, no poetry, science fiction, fantasy, or illustrated children's books. We do not encourage unpublished American writers because in our experience British and European publishers aren't interested unless there is an American publisher on board. And we'd like to make it clear that American stamps are no use outside America!

Artellus Limited
30 Dorset House, Gloucester Place, London, NW1 5AD
Tel: +44 (0) 20 7935 6972
Fax: +44 (0) 20 8609 0347

Email: leslie@artellusltd.co.uk
Website: http://www.artellusltd.co.uk

Handles: Fiction; Nonfiction; *Areas:* Arts;
Beauty and Fashion; Biography; Crime;
Culture; Current Affairs; Entertainment;
Fantasy; Historical; Military; Science; Sci-
Fi; *Markets:* Adult; *Treatments:*
Contemporary; Literary

Supply adequate return postage with all
contact. Handles both full length and short
MSS. Will suggest revision. Works directly
in the USA and with agencies in Europe,
Japan and Russia. Also offers selective
readers' services for a fee. Welcomes
submissions from new fiction and nonfiction
writers. Send first three chapters and
synopsis in first instance. No film or TV
scripts.

Author Literary Agents
53 Talbot Road, Highgate, London, N6 4QX
Tel: +44 (0) 20 8341 0442
Fax: +44 (0) 20 8341 0442
Email: agile@authors.co.uk

Handles: Fiction; Scripts; *Markets:* Adult

Send query with SAE, one-page outline and
first chapter, scene, or writing sample.
Handles material for book publishers, screen
producers, and graphic media ideas.

AVAnti Productions & Management
Unit 6, 31 St. Aubyns, Brighton, BN3 2TH
Tel: +44 (0) 07999 193311
Email: avantiproductions@live.co.uk
Website: http://www.avantiproductions.co.uk

Handles: Fiction; Nonfiction; Poetry;
Scripts; *Areas:* Adventure; Anthropology;
Antiques; Archaeology; Arts; Business;
Crafts; Crime; Criticism; Culture; Current
Affairs; Drama; Entertainment; Fantasy;
Film; Gothic; Historical; Humour;
Literature; Media; Men's Interests; Music;
Mystery; Philosophy; Photography;
Psychology; Radio; Religious; Romance;
Sci-Fi; Short Stories; Sociology; Spiritual;
Suspense; Theatre; Thrillers; Translations;
Travel; TV; Westerns; Women's Interests;

Markets: Academic; Children's; Family;
Professional; *Treatments:* Contemporary;
Literary; Niche; Positive; Satirical;
Traditional

Talent and literary representation - also, a
film and theatre production company.

Bell Lomax Moreton Agency
Ground Floor, Watergate House, 13-15 York
Buildings, London, WC2N 6JU
Tel: +44 (0) 20 7930 4447
Fax: +44 (0) 20 7839 2667
Email: info@bell-lomax.co.uk
Website: http://www.bell-lomax.co.uk

Handles: Fiction; Nonfiction; *Areas:*
Biography; Business; Sport; *Markets:* Adult;
Children's

No unsolicited MSS without preliminary
letter. No scripts.

Lorella Belli Literary Agency (LBLA)
54 Hartford House, 35 Tavistock Crescent,
Notting Hill, London, W11 1AY
Tel: +44 (0) 20 7727 8547
Fax: +44 (0) 870 787 4194
Email: info@lorellabelliagency.com
Website: http://www.lorellabelliagency.com

Handles: Fiction; Nonfiction; *Markets:*
Adult; *Treatments:* Literary

Send query by post or by email in first
instance. No attachments. Particularly
interested in multicultural / international
writing, and books relating to Italy, or
written in Italian; first novelists, and
journalists. Welcomes queries from new
authors and will suggest revisions where
appropriate. No poetry, children's, original
scripts, academic, SF, or fantasy.

Berlin Associates
7 Tyers Gate, London , SE1 3HX
Tel: +44 (0) 20 7836 1112
Fax: +44 (0) 20 7632 5296
Email: submissions@berlinassociates.com
Website: http://www.berlinassociates.com

Handles: Scripts; *Areas:* Film; Theatre; TV;
Markets: Adult

Most clients through recommendation or
invitation, but accepts queries by email with
CV, experience, and outline of work you
would like to submit.

Blake Friedmann Literary Agency Ltd

Second Floor, 122 Arlington Road, London,
NW1 7HP
Tel: +44 (0) 20 7284 0408
Fax: +44 (0) 20 7284 0442
Email: info@blakefriedmann.co.uk
Website: http://www.blakefriedmann.co.uk

Handles: Fiction; Nonfiction; Scripts; *Areas:*
Film; Radio; Thrillers; TV; Women's
Interests; *Markets:* Adult; Youth;
Treatments: Commercial; Literary

For books, send initial letter with synopsis
and first three chapters. Letters should
contain as much information as possible on
previous writing experience, aims for future,
etc. Particularly interested in literary fiction,
commercial women's fiction, and upmarket
nonfiction. No poetry, straight science fiction
and fantasy, or children's picture books.
Prefers approaches by email. See website for
guidelines and submit to a specific agent's
email address. Do not query more than one
agent.

For films and TV, only considering writers
and directors with previous experience in the
film/television industry or in a related field,
i.e. producers/script editors.

Luigi Bonomi Associates Ltd

91 Great Russell Street, London, WC1 3PS
Tel: +44 (0) 20 7637 1234
Fax: +44 (0) 20 7637 2111
Email:
first3chapters@bonomiassociates.co.uk
Website: http://www.bonomiassociates.co.uk

Handles: Fiction; Nonfiction; *Areas:* Crime;
Health; Historical; Lifestyle; Science;
Thrillers; TV; Women's Interests; *Markets:*
Adult; Youth; *Treatments:* Commercial;
Literary

Keen to find new authors. Send query with
synopsis and first three chapters by post with
SAE (if return of material required) or email
address for response, or by email (Word or
PDF attachments only). No scripts, poetry,
children's, science fiction, or fantasy.

Bookseeker Agency

PO Box 7535, Perth, PH2 1AF
Tel: +44 (0) 1738 620688
Email: bookseeker@blueyonder.co.uk
Website: http://bookseekeragency.com

Handles: Fiction; Poetry; *Markets:* Adult

Handles poetry and general creative writing.
No nonfiction. Send query by post or email
outlining what you have written and your
current projects, along with synopsis and
sample chapter (novels) or half a dozen
poems.

Brandon & Associates

12 Repton Close, Broadstairs, Kent CT10
2UZ
Tel: +44 (0) 1843 860610
Email: john@brandon-associates.co.uk
Website: http://www.brandon-
associates.co.uk

Handles: Fiction; Nonfiction; *Areas:*
Adventure; Autobiography; Biography;
Crime; Current Affairs; Entertainment;
Historical; Legal; Military; Music; Politics;
Sport; Theatre; *Markets:* Adult; *Treatments:*
Commercial; Contemporary; Mainstream

Formed in mid 2007 to help overcome some
of the genuine frustration and feeling of
helplessness felt by so many first time
writers trying to get their book published.
We have a wide range of interests including
most fiction and non fiction, however other
agents may be better equipped to deal with
your serious poetry or short story and we are
very unlikely to get excited about hard core
sci-fi or your fantasy or horror story.
If you wish us to treat you as a serious writer
you should follow the advice given on our
website when sending us your submission.

firstwriter.com note: On May 19, 2008,
firstwriter.com received positive feedback

for this agency left by an account paid for by this agency, which is operated under the agent's name, and an email address that includes the agent's first and last names. The feedback was left under a pseudonym which differed from the name on the account, and did not make explicit any connection between the agency and the person leaving the feedback. While firstwriter.com does not suggest any impropriety, we advise users to exercise caution when approaching this agency, as the only two comparable instances in firstwriter.com's history both involved known scams, including the notorious Hill & Hill Literary Agency, which was exposed as a scam when they attempted to leave positive feedback for themselves on firstwriter.com.

Statement from John King, May 28, 2008:
"A writer John Burrett used our computor to place a postive comments about us on your site. At the time he had just agreed the final design of the cover with us and was justifibly pleased with us.
You then unfairly compare us with two scams.

We agreed to publish John Burrett's book 'One Game Too Many' at no cost to him because we believed it should be published even though it may not commercially viable. The market for this book is in New Zealand, maybe Australia and no doubt very small."

Alan Brodie Representation Ltd

Paddock Suite, The Courtyard, 55 Charterhouse Street, London, EC1M 6HA
Tel: +44 (0) 20 7253 6226
Fax: +44 (0) 20 7183 7999
Email: info@alanbrodie.com
Website: http://www.alanbrodie.com

Handles: Scripts; *Areas:* Film; Radio; Theatre; TV; *Markets:* Adult

Handles scripts only. No books. Approach with preliminary letter, recommendation from industry professional, CV, and SAE. Do not send a sample of work unless requested. No fiction, nonfiction, or poetry.

Jenny Brown Associates

33 Argyle Place, Edinburgh, Scotland EH9 1JT
Tel: +44 (0) 1312 295334
Email: jenny@jennybrownassociates.com
Website:
http://www.jennybrownassociates.com

Handles: Fiction; Nonfiction; *Areas:* Biography; Crime; Culture; Finance; Historical; Humour; Music; Romance; Science; Sport; Thrillers; Women's Interests; *Markets:* Adult; Children's; *Treatments:* Commercial; Literary; Popular

Strongly prefers queries by email. Approach by post only if not possible to do so by email. Send query with market information, bio, synopsis and first 50 pages in one document (fiction) or sample chapter and info on market and your background (nonfiction). No academic, poetry, short stories, science fiction, or fantasy. Responds only if interested. If no response in 8 weeks assume rejection. See website for individual agent interests and email addresses.

Felicity Bryan

2a North Parade Avenue, Banbury Road, Oxford, OX2 6LX
Tel: +44 (0) 1865 513816
Fax: +44 (0) 1865 310055
Email: agency@felicitybryan.com
Website: http://www.felicitybryan.com

Handles: Fiction; Nonfiction; *Areas:* Biography; Current Affairs; Historical; Science; *Markets:* Adult; Children's; Youth; *Treatments:* Commercial; Literary

Particularly interested in commercial and literary fiction and nonfiction for the adult market and children's fiction for 8+. Send query with SAE, synopsis, first three or four chapters, and CV if nonfiction, addressed to "SUBMISSIONS". No adult science fiction, horror, fantasy, light romance, self- help, memoir, film and TV scripts, plays, poetry or picture/illustrated books. Represents writers living outside the UK only in exceptional circumstances.

Brie Burkeman & Serafina Clarke Ltd

14 Neville Court, Abbey Road, London, NW8 9DD
Tel: +44 (0) 870 199 5002
Fax: +44 (0) 870 199 1029
Email: info@burkemanandclarke.com

Handles: Fiction; Nonfiction; Scripts; *Areas:* Film; Theatre; *Markets:* Adult; Children's; *Treatments:* Commercial; Literary

Not accepting unsolicited submissions as at June 26, 2012. Check website for current situation.

No academic, text, poetry, short stories, musicals or short films. For scripts, full length only. No reading fee but preliminary letter preferred. Return postage essential. Unsolicited email attachments will be deleted without opening.

Also independent film and television consultant to literary agents.

Do **not** send submissions via email – these will be deleted automatically without opening

Submissions by email with attachments will be automatically deleted. When sending material, return postage is essential.

Juliet Burton Literary Agency

2 Clifton Avenue, London, W12 9DR
Tel: +44 (0) 20 8762 0148
Fax: +44 (0) 20 8743 8765
Email: juliet.burton@btinternet.com

Handles: Fiction; Nonfiction; *Areas:* Crime; Women's Interests; *Markets:* Adult

Send query with SAE, synopsis, and two sample chapters. No poetry, plays, film scripts, children's, articles, academic material, science fiction, fantasy, unsolicited MSS, or email submissions.

Campbell Thomson & McLaughlin Ltd

50 Albemarle Street, London, W1S 4BD

Tel: +44 (0) 20 7493 4361
Fax: +44 (0) 20 7495 8961
Email: submissions@ctmcl.co.uk
Website: http://www.ctmcl.co.uk

Handles: Fiction; Nonfiction; *Markets:* Adult

Send query by post with SAE, or use online system to upload submission. Include details of any previous publishing or relevant experience, short synopsis (fiction) or summary and chapter outlines (nonfiction), three consecutive chapters up to 100 pages, and author CV. No plays, children's books, articles, film or TV scripts, short stories, or poetry. Does not represent US authors directly. See website for full details.

Capel & Land Ltd

29 Wardour Street, London, W1D 6PS
Tel: +44 (0) 20 7734 2414
Fax: +44 (0) 20 7734 8101
Email: georgina@capelland.co.uk
Website: http://www.capelland.com

Handles: Fiction; Nonfiction, *Areas:* Biography; Film; Historical; Radio; TV; *Markets:* Adult; *Treatments:* Commercial; Literary

Handles general fiction and nonfiction. Send query outlining writing history (for nonfiction, what qualifies you to write your book), with synopsis around 500 words and first three chapters, plus SAE or email address for reply. Submissions are not returned. Mark envelope for the attention of the Submissions Department. Response only if interested, normally within 6 weeks.

CardenWright Literary Agency

27 Khyber Road, London, SW11 2PZ
Tel: +44 (0) 20 7771 0012
Email: gen@cardenwright.com

Handles: Fiction; Nonfiction; Scripts; *Areas:* Theatre; *Markets:* Adult; Youth; *Treatments:* Commercial; Literary

Handles commercial and literary fiction and nonfiction, plus theatre scripts. Will consider teenage / young adult. No poetry, screenplays, or children's books. See website for submission guidelines.

Celia Catchpole

56 Gilpin Avenue, London, SW14 8QY
Tel: +44 (0) 20 8255 4835
Email:
catchpolesubmissions@googlemail.com
Website: http://www.celiacatchpole.co.uk

Handles: Fiction; *Markets:* Children's

Works on children's books with both artists and writers. Send query by email with sample pasted directly into the body of the email (no attachments). See website for full guidelines.

Mic Cheetham Literary Agency

50 Albemarle Street, London, W1S 4BD
Tel: +44 (0) 20 7495 2002
Fax: +44 (0) 20 7399 2801
Email: info@miccheetham.com
Website: http://www.miccheetham.com

Handles: Fiction; Nonfiction; *Areas:* Crime; Fantasy; Historical; Sci-Fi; Thrillers; *Markets:* Adult; *Treatments:* Commercial; Literary; Mainstream

Send query with SAE, first three chapters, and publishing history. Focuses on fiction, and is not elitist about genre or literary fiction, providing it combines good writing, great storytelling, intelligence, imagination, and (as a bonus) anarchic wit. Film and TV scripts handled for existing clients only. No poetry, children's, illustrated books, or unsolicited MSS. Do not send manuscripts by email. Approach in writing in the first instance (no email scripts accepted).

Judith Chilcote Agency

8 Wentworth Mansions, Keats Grove, London, NW3 2RL
Tel: +44 (0) 20 7794 3717
Email: judybks@aol.com

Handles: Fiction; Nonfiction; *Areas:* Autobiography; Current Affairs; TV; *Markets:* Adult; *Treatments:* Commercial

Send query with SAE, CV, synopsis, and three sample chapters. No poetry, short stories, or science fiction.

Teresa Chris Literary Agency Ltd

43 Musard Road, London, W6 8NR
Tel: +44 (0) 20 7386 0633
Email: teresachris@litagency.co.uk

Handles: Fiction; *Areas:* Crime; Women's Interests; *Markets:* Adult; *Treatments:* Commercial; Literary

Send query with SAE, first two chapters, and two-page synopsis. Specialises in crime fiction and commercial women's fiction. No poetry, short stories, scripts, academic, science fiction, fantasy, or horror.

Mary Clemmey Literary Agency

6 Dunollie Road, London, NW5 2XP
Tel: +44 (0) 20 7267 1290
Fax: +44 (0) 20 7813 9757
Email: mcwords@googlemail.com

Handles: Fiction; Nonfiction; Scripts; *Areas:* Film; Radio; Theatre; TV; *Markets:* Adult

Send query with SAE and description of work only. Handles high-quality work with an international market. No children's books, science fiction, fantasy, or unsolicited MSS or submissions by email. Scripts handled for existing clients only. Do not submit a script or idea for a script unless you are already a client.

Jonathan Clowes Ltd

10 Iron Bridge House, Bridge Approach, London, NW1 8BD
Tel: +44 (0) 20 7722 7674
Fax: +44 (0) 20 7722 7677
Email: olivia@jonathanclowes.co.uk
Website: http://www.jonathanclowes.co.uk

Handles: Fiction; Nonfiction; Scripts; *Areas:* Film; Radio; Theatre; TV; *Markets:* Adult; *Treatments:* Commercial; Literary

Send query with synopsis and three chapters

(or equivalent sample) by email. No science fiction, poetry, short stories, academic. Only considers film/TV clients with previous success in TV/film/theatre.

Rosica Colin Ltd
1 Clareville Grove Mews, London, SW7 5AH
Tel: +44 (0) 20 7370 1080
Fax: +44 (0) 20 7244 6441

Handles: Fiction; Nonfiction; Scripts; *Areas:* Autobiography; Beauty and Fashion; Biography; Cookery; Crime; Current Affairs; Erotic; Fantasy; Film; Gardening; Health; Historical; Horror; Humour; Leisure; Lifestyle; Men's Interests; Military; Mystery; Nature; Psychology; Radio; Religious; Romance; Science; Sport; Suspense; Theatre; Thrillers; Travel; TV; Women's Interests; *Markets:* Academic; Adult; Children's; *Treatments:* Literary

Send query with SAE, CV, synopsis, and list of other agents and publishers where MSS has already been sent. Considers any full-length mss (except science fiction and poetry), plus scripts, but few new writers taken on. Responds in 3-4 months to full mss – synopsis preferred in first instance.

Conville & Walsh Ltd
2 Ganton Street, London, W1F 7QL
Tel: +44 (0) 20 7287 3030
Fax: +44 (0) 20 7287 4545
Email: info@convilleandwalsh.com
Website: http://www.convilleandwalsh.com

Handles: Fiction; Nonfiction; *Areas:* Biography; Crime; Current Affairs; Historical; Humour; Leisure; Lifestyle; Men's Interests; Military; Mystery; Psychology; Science; Sport; Suspense; Thrillers; Travel; Women's Interests; *Markets:* Adult; Children's; Youth; *Treatments:* Literary

Accepts unsolicited submissions by post only. Please submit the first three sample chapters of the completed manuscript (or about 50 pages), a cover letter, a one-page synopsis and a self-addressed stamped envelope. We encourage you to approach other agencies at the same time as replies can vary from one week to three months. No poetry, screenplays, or short stories. No submissions by fax or email - these will be destroyed. See website for full guidelines.

Jane Conway-Gordon Ltd
38 Cromwell Grove, London, W6 7RG
Tel: +44 (0) 20 7371 6939
Email: jane@conway-gordon.co.uk

Handles: Fiction; Nonfiction; *Markets:* Adult

Handles fiction and general nonfiction. Send query with SAE (essential) in first instance. Associate agencies in America, Europe, and Japan. No poetry, short stories, children's, or science fiction.

Coombs Moylett Literary Agency
120 New Kings Road, London, SW6 4LZ
Email: lisa@coombsmoylett.com
Website: http://www.coombsmoylett.com

Handles: Fiction; *Areas:* Crime; Historical; Mystery; Thrillers; Women's Interests; *Markets:* Adult; *Treatments:* Commercial; Literary

Send query with synopsis and first three chapters by post. No submissions by fax, but accepts email queries. No nonfiction, poetry, plays or scripts for film and TV.

Please note that this agency also offers editorial services for which writers are charged. Caution should be exercised in relation to these services, particularly if they are pushed as a condition of representation.

The Creative Rights Agency
17 Prior Street, London, SE10 8SF
Tel: +44 (0) 20 8149 3955
Email: info@creativerightsagency.co.uk
Website: http://www.creativerightsagency.co.uk

Handles: Fiction; Nonfiction; *Areas:* Autobiography; Culture; Men's Interests; Sport; *Markets:* Adult

Specialises in men's interests. Send query by email with sample chapters, synopsis, and author bio.

Creative Authors Ltd

11A Woodlawn Street, Whitstable, Kent
CT5 1HQ
Tel: +44 (0) 01227 770947
Email: write@creativeauthors.co.uk
Website: http://www.creativeauthors.co.uk

Handles: Fiction; Nonfiction; *Areas:* Arts;
Autobiography; Biography; Business;
Cookery; Crafts; Crime; Culture; Health;
Historical; Humour; Nature; Women's
Interests; *Markets:* Adult; Children's;
Treatments: Commercial; Literary

**As at September 3, 2012, not accepting
new fiction clients. See website for current
situation.**

We are a dynamic literary agency -
established to provide an attentive and
unique platform for writers and scriptwriters
and representing a growing list of clients.
We're on the lookout for fresh talent and
books with strong commercial potential. No
unsolicited MSS, but considers queries by
email. No paper submissions. Do not
telephone regarding submissions.

Rupert Crew Ltd

6 Windsor Road, London, N3 3SS
Tel: +44 (0) 20 8346 3000
Fax: +44 (0) 20 8346 3009
Email: info@rupertcrew.co.uk
Website: http://www.rupertcrew.co.uk

Handles: Fiction; Nonfiction; *Markets:*
Adult

Send query with SAE, synopsis, and first
two or three chapters. International
representation, handling volume and
subsidiary rights in fiction and nonfiction
properties. No Short Stories, Science Fiction,
Fantasy, Horror, Poetry or original scripts for
Theatre, Television and Film. Email address
for correspondence only. No response by
post and no return of material with
insufficient return postage.

Curtis Brown Group Ltd

Haymarket House, 28/29 Haymarket,
London, SW1Y 4SP
Tel: +44 (0) 20 7393 4400
Fax: +44 (0) 20 7393 4401
Email: cb@curtisbrown.co.uk
Website: http://www.curtisbrown.co.uk

Handles: Fiction; Nonfiction; Scripts; *Areas:*
Biography; Crime; Fantasy; Film; Historical;
Radio; Science; Suspense; Theatre; Thrillers;
TV; *Markets:* Adult; Children's; Youth;
Treatments: Literary; Mainstream; Popular

Handles general fiction and nonfiction, and
scripts. Also represents directors, designers,
and presenters. Send query with SAE, CV,
and outline for nonfiction or short synopsis
and two or three sample chapters for fiction.
No email submissions.

David Luxton Associates

23 Hillcourt Avenue, London, N12 8EY
Tel: +44 (0) 20 8922 3942
Email: david@davidluxtonassociates.co.uk
Website:
http://www.davidluxtonassociates.co.uk

Handles: Nonfiction; *Areas:* Biography;
Culture; Historical; Sport; *Markets:* Adult

Send query by email with brief outline. No
unsolicited MSS or sample chapters. Handles
little in the way of fiction or children's
books. No screenplays or scripts.

Felix de Wolfe

103 Kingsway, London, WC2B 6QX
Tel: +44 (0) 20 7242 5066
Fax: +44 (0) 20 7242 8119
Email: info@felixdewolfe.com
Website: http://www.felixdewolfe.com

Handles: Fiction; Scripts; *Areas:* Film;
Theatre; TV; *Markets:* Adult

Send query letter with SAE, short synopsis,
and CV by post only, unless alternative
arrangements have been made with the
agency in advance. Quality fiction and
scripts only. No nonfiction, children's books,
or unsolicited MSS.

Dorian Literary Agency (DLA)

Upper Thornehill, 27 Church Road, St
Marychurch, Torquay, Devon TQ1 4QY
Tel: +44 (0) 1803 312095
Email: doriandot@compuserve.com

Handles: Fiction; *Areas:* Crime; Fantasy;
Historical; Horror; Romance; Sci-Fi;
Thrillers; Women's Interests; *Markets:*
Adult; *Treatments:* Popular

Concentrates on popular genre fiction. Send
SAE with outline and up to three sample
chapters. No queries or submissions by fax,
telephone, or email. No poetry, scripts, short
stories, nonfiction, children's, young adult,
or comic.

Toby Eady Associates Ltd

Third Floor, 9 Orme Court, London, W2
4RL
Tel: +44 (0) 20 7792 0092
Fax: +44 (0) 20 7792 0879
Email:
submissions@tobyeadyassociates.co.uk
Website:
http://www.tobyeadyassociates.co.uk

Handles: Fiction; Nonfiction; *Markets:*
Adult

Send first 50 pages of your fiction or
nonfiction work by email, with a synopsis,
and a letter including biographical
information. If submitting by post, include
SAE for return of material, if required. No
film / TV scripts or poetry. Particular interest
in China, Middle East, India, and Africa.

Eddison Pearson Ltd

West Hill House, 6 Swains Lane, London,
N6 6QS
Tel: +44 (0) 20 7700 7763
Fax: +44 (0) 20 7700 7866
Email: enquiries@eddisonpearson.com
Website: http://www.eddisonpearson.com

Handles: Fiction; Nonfiction; Poetry;
Markets: Children's; Youth; *Treatments:*
Literary

Send query by email only (or even blank
email) for auto-response containing up-to-

date submission guidelines and email address
for submissions. No unsolicited MSS. No
longer accepts submissions or enquiries by
post. Send query with first two chapters by
email only to address provided in auto-
response. Response in 6-10 weeks. If no
response after 10 weeks send email query.

Edwards Fuglewicz

49 Great Ormond Street, London, WC1N
3HZ
Tel: +44 (0) 20 7405 6725
Fax: +44 (0) 20 7405 6726
Email: info@efla.co.uk

Handles: Fiction; Nonfiction; *Areas:*
Biography; Culture; Historical; *Markets:*
Adult; *Treatments:* Commercial; Literary

Handles literary and commercial fiction, and
nonfiction in the areas of biography, history,
and popular culture. No children's, science
fiction, fantasy, horror, unsolicited MSS, or
email submissions.

Faith Evans Associates

27 Park Avenue North, London, N8 7RU
Tel: +44 (0) 20 8340 9920
Fax: +44 (0) 20 8340 9410
Email: faith@faith-evans.co.uk

Handles: Fiction; Nonfiction; *Markets:*
Adult

Small agency accepting new clients by
personal recommendation only. No scripts,
phone calls, or unsolicited MSS.

Film Rights Ltd in association with Laurence Fitch Ltd

Suite 306 Belsize Business Centre, 258
Belsize Road, London, NW6 4BT
Tel: +44 (0) 20 7316 1837
Fax: +44 (0) 20 7624 3629
Email: information@filmrights.ltd.uk
Website: http://filmrights.ltd.uk

Handles: Fiction; Scripts; *Areas:* Film;
Horror; Radio; Theatre; TV; *Markets:* Adult;
Children's

Represents films, plays, and novels, for adults and children.

Jill Foster Ltd (JFL)
48 Charlotte Street, London, W1T 2NS
Tel: +44 (0) 20 3137 8182
Email: agents@jflagency.com
Website: http://www.jflagency.com

Handles: Scripts; *Areas:* Drama; Film; Humour; Radio; Theatre; TV; *Markets:* Adult

Send query by post or by email giving information about your writing, what you've done, and what you want to do. Scripts for TV, drama, and comedy. No poetry, short stories, fiction, or unsolicited MSS.

Fox Mason Ltd
36-38 Glasshouse Street, London, W1B 5DL
Tel: +44 (0) 20 7287 0972
Email: info@foxmason.com
Website: http://www.foxmason.com

Handles: Fiction; Nonfiction; *Areas:* Adventure; Autobiography; Biography; Cookery; Crime; Culture; Fantasy; Historical; Horror; Mystery; Philosophy; Psychology; Sci-Fi; Suspense; Thrillers; Travel; *Markets:* Adult; *Treatments:* Commercial; Literary

Handles up-market, literary, and commercial fiction, along with narrative nonfiction. No children's authors, bog-standard genre authors, poets, playwrights, or screenwriters. See website for more details, and for online submission form. No submissions by post.

Fox & Howard Literary Agency
39 Eland Road, London, SW11 5JX
Tel: +44 (0) 20 7352 8691
Email: fandhagency@googlemail.com
Website: http://www.foxandhoward.co.uk

Handles: Nonfiction; Reference; *Areas:* Biography; Business; Culture; Health; Historical; Lifestyle; Psychology; Spiritual; *Markets:* Adult

Closed to submissions as at November 13, 2012. Check website for current status.

Send query with synopsis and SAE for response. Small agency specialising in nonfiction that works closely with its authors. No unsolicited MSS.

Fraser Ross Associates
6 Wellington Place, Edinburgh, Scotland EH6 7EQ
Tel: +44 (0) 1316 574412
Email: lindsey.fraser@tiscali.co.uk
Website: http://www.fraserross.co.uk

Handles: Fiction; *Markets:* Adult; Children's; *Treatments:* Literary; Mainstream

Send query with SAE, first three chapters, and CV. For picture books, send complete MS. No poetry, scripts, short stories, academic, or adult fantasy or science fiction. No submissions on disk or by email.

Furniss Lawton
James Grant Group Ltd, 94 Strand on the Green, Chiswick, London, W4 3NN
Tel: +44 (0) 20 8987 6804
Email: info@furnisslawton.co.uk
Website: http://furnisslawton.co.uk

Handles: Fiction; Nonfiction; *Areas:* Autobiography; Biography; Business; Cookery; Crime; Fantasy; Historical; Psychology; Science; Suspense; Thrillers; Women's Interests; *Markets:* Adult; Children's; Youth; *Treatments:* Commercial; Literary

Send query with synopsis and first 5,000 words / three chapters by post only. Include SAE if return of manuscript is required.

Eric Glass Ltd
25 Ladbroke Crescent, London, W11 1PS
Tel: +44 (0) 20 7229 9500
Fax: +44 (0) 20 7229 6220
Email: eglassltd@aol.com

Handles: Fiction; Nonfiction; Scripts; *Areas:* Film; Theatre; TV; *Markets:* Adult

Send query with SAE. No children's books, short stories, poetry, or unsolicited MSS.

David Godwin Associates

55 Monmouth Street, London, WC2H 9DG
Tel: +44 (0) 20 7240 9992
Fax: +44 (0) 20 7395 6110
Email:
assistant@davidgodwinassociates.co.uk
Website:
http://www.davidgodwinassociates.co.uk

Handles: Fiction; Nonfiction; *Areas:*
Biography; *Markets:* Adult; Children's;
Youth; *Treatments:* Literary

Handles nonfiction (including biography) and fiction (general and literary). Send query by post with SAE, brief synopsis, and first three chapters / 50 pages. Submissions without correct return postage will be recycled. Accepts submissions for children's (9+) and young adult books by email to address specified on website (see submissions page). No reference, science fiction, fantasy, self-help, poetry or collections of short stories.

Graham Maw Christie Literary Agency

19 Thornhill Crescent, London, N1 1BJ
Tel: +44 (0) 20 7609 1326
Email:
submissions@grahammawchristie.com
Website:
http://www.grahammawchristie.com

Handles: Nonfiction; Reference; *Areas:*
Autobiography; Biography; Business; Crafts;
Culture; Health; Historical; How-to;
Humour; Lifestyle; Psychology; Self-Help;
Spiritual; TV; *Markets:* Adult

Send query with one-page summary, a paragraph on the contents of each chapter, your qualifications for writing it, market analysis, and what you could do to help promote your book. Accepts approaches by email. No fiction, children's books, or poetry.

Christine Green Authors' Agent

6 Whitehorse Mews, Westminster Bridge Road, London, SE1 7QD
Tel: +44 (0) 20 7401 8844
Fax: +44 (0) 20 7401 8860
Email: info@christinegreen.co.uk
Website: http://www.christinegreen.co.uk

Handles: Fiction; Nonfiction; *Markets:*
Adult; *Treatments:* Literary

Send query with SAE/IPOs, synopsis, and first three chapters. No poetry, scripts, children's books, science fiction, fantasy, simultaneous submissions, or unsolicited MSS. No submissions by fax, email, or on disk.

Louise Greenberg Books Ltd

The End House, Church Crescent, London, N3 1BG
Tel: +44 (0) 20 8349 1179
Fax: +44 (0) 20 8343 4559
Email: louisegreenberg@msn.com

Handles: Fiction; Nonfiction; *Markets:*
Adult; *Treatments:* Literary; Serious

Handles full-length literary fiction and serious nonfiction only. All approaches must be accompanied by SAE. No approaches by telephone.

Greene & Heaton Ltd

37 Goldhawk Road, London, W12 8QQ
Tel: +44 (0) 20 8749 0315
Fax: +44 (0) 20 8749 0318
Email: submissions@greeneheaton.co.uk
Website: http://www.greeneheaton.co.uk

Handles: Fiction; Nonfiction; *Areas:* Arts;
Autobiography; Biography; Cookery; Crime;
Culture; Current Affairs; Gardening; Health;
Historical; Humour; Philosophy; Politics;
Romance; Science; Sci-Fi; Thrillers; Travel;
Markets: Adult; Children's; *Treatments:*
Commercial; Contemporary; Literary;
Traditional

Send query by email or by post with SAE, including synopsis and three chapters or approximately 50 pages. No response to unsolicited MSS with no SAE or inadequate means of return postage provided. No response to email submissions unless interested. Handles all types of fiction and nonfiction, but no scripts.

The Greenhouse Literary Agency

Stanley House, St Chad's Place, London, WC1X 9HH
Tel: +44 (0) 20 7841 3959
Email:
submissions@greenhouseliterary.com
Website: http://www.greenhouseliterary.com

Handles: Fiction; *Markets:* Children's; Youth

Transatlantic agency with offices in the US and London. Handles children's and young adult fiction only. Picture books by existing clients only. Send query by email with first chapter or first five pages (whichever is shorter) pasted into the body of the email. No attachments or hard copy submissions.

Gregory & Company, Authors' Agents

3 Barb Mews, London, W6 7PA
Tel: +44 (0) 20 7610 4676
Fax: +44 (0) 20 7610 4686
Email:
maryjones@gregoryandcompany.co.uk
Website:
http://www.gregoryandcompany.co.uk

Handles: Fiction; *Areas:* Crime; Historical; Thrillers; *Markets:* Adult; *Treatments:* Commercial

Particularly interested in Crime, Family Sagas, Historical Fiction, Thrillers and Upmarket Commercial Fiction.
Send query with CV, one-page synopsis, future writing plans, and first ten pages, by post with SAE, or by email. No unsolicited MSS, Business Books, Children's, Young Adult Fiction, Plays, Screenplays, Poetry, Science Fiction, Future Fiction, Fantasy, Self Help, Lifestyle books, Short Stories, Spiritual, New Age, Philosophy, Supernatural, Paranormal, Horror, or True Crime.

David Grossman Literary Agency Ltd

118b Holland Park Avenue, London, W11 4UA
Tel: +44 (0) 20 7221 2770
Fax: +44 (0) 20 7221 1445
Email: david@dglal.co.uk

Handles: Fiction; Nonfiction; *Markets:* Adult

Send preliminary letter before making a submission. No approaches or submissions by fax or email. Usually works with published fiction writers, but well-written and original work from beginners considered. No poetry, scripts, technical books for students, or unsolicited MSS.

Gunn Media Associates

50 Albemarle Street, London, W1S 4BD
Tel: +44 (0) 20 7529 3745
Email: ali@gunnmedia.co.uk
Website: http://www.gunnmedia.co.uk

Handles: Fiction; Nonfiction; *Markets:* Adult; *Treatments:* Commercial; Literary

Handles commercial fiction and nonfiction, including literary.

Roger Hancock Ltd

7 Broadbent Close, Highgate Village, London N6 5JW
Tel: +44 (0) 20 8341 7243
Email: info@rogerhancock.com
Website: http://www.rogerhancock.com

Handles: Scripts; *Areas:* Drama; Entertainment; Humour; *Markets:* Adult; *Treatments:* Light

Enquire by phone in first instance. Handles scripts only. Interested in comedy dramas and light entertainment. No books or unsolicited MSS.

Hardman & Swainson

4 Kelmscott Road, London, SW11 6QY
Tel: +44 (0) 20 7223 5176
Email: submissions@hardmanswainson.com
Website: http://www.hardmanswainson.com

Handles: Fiction; Nonfiction; *Areas:*
Autobiography; Crime; Philosophy; Science;
Thrillers; *Markets:* Adult; Youth;
Treatments: Commercial; Literary; Popular

Agency launched June 2012 by former
colleagues at an established agency.
Welcomes submissions of fiction across all
genres and nonfiction. Prefers email
submissions but will accept postal
submissions with SAE if return required. See
website for full submission guidelines.

Antony Harwood Limited
103 Walton Street, Oxford, OX2 6EB
Tel: +44 (0) 1865 559615
Fax: +44 (0) 1865 310660
Email: mail@antonyharwood.com
Website: http://www.antonyharwood.com

Handles: Fiction; Nonfiction; *Areas:*
Adventure; Anthropology; Antiques;
Archaeology; Architecture; Arts;
Autobiography; Beauty and Fashion;
Biography; Business; Cookery; Crafts;
Crime; Criticism; Culture; Current Affairs;
Design; Drama; Entertainment; Erotic;
Fantasy; Film; Finance; Gardening, Gothic;
Health; Historical; Hobbies; Horror; How-to;
Humour; Legal; Leisure; Lifestyle;
Literature; Media; Medicine; Men's
Interests; Military; Music; Mystery; Nature;
New Age; Philosophy; Photography;
Politics; Psychology; Radio; Religious;
Romance; Science; Sci-Fi; Self-Help; Short
Stories; Sociology; Spiritual; Sport;
Suspense; Technology; Theatre; Thrillers;
Translations; Travel; TV; Westerns;
Women's Interests; *Markets:* Adult;
Children's; Youth

Handles fiction and nonfiction in every genre
and category, except for screenwriting and
poetry. Send brief outline by email, or by
post with SASE.

A M Heath & Company Limited, Author's Agents
6 Warwick Court, Holborn, London, WC1R
5DJ
Tel: +44 (0) 20 7242 2811
Fax: +44 (0) 20 7242 2711
Email: enquiries@amheath.com

Website: http://www.amheath.com

Handles: Fiction; Nonfiction; *Areas:* Crime;
Psychology; Suspense; Thrillers; *Markets:*
Adult; Children's; *Treatments:* Commercial;
Literary

Handles general commercial and literary
fiction and nonfiction. Send query with
synopsis and first 10,000 words via online
submission system only. No paper
submissions. Aims to respond within six
weeks.

Rupert Heath Literary Agency
50 Albemarle Street, London, W1S 4BD
Tel: +44 (0) 20 7060 3385
Email: emailagency@rupertheath.com
Website: http://www.rupertheath.com

Handles: Fiction; Nonfiction; *Areas:* Arts;
Autobiography; Biography; Cookery; Crime;
Culture; Current Affairs; Historical;
Lifestyle; Nature; Politics; Science;
Thrillers; Women's Interests; *Markets:*
Adult; *Treatments:* Commercial; Literary;
Popular

Send query giving some information about
yourself and the work you would like to
submit. Prefers queries by email. Response
only if interested.

hhb agency ltd
6 Warwick Court, London, WC1R 5DJ
Tel: +44 (0) 20 7405 5525
Email: heather@hhbagency.com
Website: http://www.hhbagency.com

Handles: Fiction; Nonfiction; *Areas:*
Adventure; Autobiography; Biography;
Business; Cookery; Crime; Culture;
Entertainment; Historical; Humour; Politics;
Travel; TV; Women's Interests; *Markets:*
Adult; *Treatments:* Commercial;
Contemporary; Literary; Popular

Query by email or telephone before
submitting any material. No scripts or
unsolicited MSS. Specialises in food and
cookery.

David Higham Associates Ltd

5-8 Lower John Street, Golden Square,
London, W1F 9HA
Tel: +44 (0) 20 7434 5900
Fax: +44 (0) 20 7437 1072
Email: dha@davidhigham.co.uk
Website: http://www.davidhigham.co.uk

Handles: Fiction; Nonfiction; Scripts; *Areas:*
Biography; Current Affairs; Historical;
Markets: Adult; Children's

For adult fiction and nonfiction contact
"Adult Submissions Department" by post
only with SASE, covering letter, CV, and
synopsis (fiction)/proposal (nonfiction) and
first two or three chapters. For children's
fiction prefers submissions by email to the
specific children's submission address given
on the website, with covering letter,
synopsis, CV, and first two or three chapters
(or complete MS if a picture book). See
website for complete guidelines. Scripts by
referral only.

Hilary Churchley Literary Agent

23 Beech Road, Wheatley, Oxford OX33
1UP
Tel: +44 (0) 7768 353082
Fax: +44 (0) 1865 437496
Email: hachurchley@live.co.uk
Website: http://hilarychurchley.co.uk

Handles: Fiction; Nonfiction; *Areas:*
Biography; Historical; *Markets:* Adult;
Youth

Send query by post only with up to 50 pages
/ three chapters, synopsis, and short author
bio. No science fiction / fantasy. See website
for full submission guidelines.

Vanessa Holt Ltd

59 Crescent Road, Leigh-on-Sea, Essex
SS9 2PF
Tel: +44 (0) 1702 473787

Handles: Fiction; Nonfiction; *Areas:* Crime;
Markets: Adult; Children's; *Treatments:*
Commercial; Literary

General fiction and nonfiction. Specialises in

crime fiction and books with potential for
sales overseas and / or to TV. No scripts,
poetry, academic, technical, illustrated
children's, or unsolicited MSS. Query by
post or phone only.

Kate Hordern Literary Agency

18 Mortimer Road, Clifton, Bristol, BS8
4EY
Tel: +44 (0) 117 923 9368
Email: katehordern@blueyonder.co.uk
Website: http://www.katehordern.co.uk

Handles: Fiction; Nonfiction; Reference;
Areas: Autobiography; Business; Crime;
Culture; Current Affairs; Historical;
Sociology; Thrillers; Women's Interests;
Markets: Adult; Children's; Youth;
Treatments: Commercial; Contemporary;
Literary; Popular

Send query by email or by post with SAE
and synopsis for fiction, or proposal and
chapter breakdown for nonfiction. Send
sample chapters if requested only. Very
selective about new clients.

Valerie Hoskins Associates

20 Charlotte Street, London, W1T 2NA
Tel: +44 (0) 20 7637 4490
Fax: +44 (0) 20 7637 4493
Email: info@vhassociates.co.uk
Website: http://www.vhassociates.co.uk

Handles: Scripts; *Areas:* Film; Radio; TV;
Markets: Adult

Preliminary introductory letter essential.
Particularly interested in feature films,
animation, and TV. No unsolicited scripts.

Amanda Howard Associates Ltd

74 Clerkenwell Road, London, EC1M 5QA
Tel: +44 (0) 20 7250 1760
Email:
mail@amandahowardassociates.co.uk
Website:
http://www.amandahowardassociates.co.uk

Handles: Nonfiction; Scripts; *Areas:*
Autobiography; How-to; Humour; *Markets:*

Adult; *Treatments:* Popular

Handles actors, writers, creatives, and voice-over artsts. Send query with return postage, CV/bio, and 10-page writing sample. No poetry.

Hunter Profiles
London,
Email: info@hunterprofiles.com
Website: http://www.hunterprofiles.com

Handles: Fiction; Nonfiction; *Markets:* Adult; *Treatments:* Commercial

We specialise in commercial and narrative fiction and nonfiction. We only accept proposals by email. See website for submission guidelines.

Independent Talent Group Ltd
Oxford House, 76 Oxford Street, London, W1D 1BS
Tel: +44 (0) 20 7636 6565
Fax: +44 (0) 20 7323 0101
Email: laurarourke@independenttalent.com
Website: http://www.independenttalent.com

Handles: Scripts; *Areas:* Film; Radio; Theatre; TV; *Markets:* Adult

Specialises in scripts and works in association with agencies in Los Angeles and New York. No unsolicited MSS. Materials submitted will not be returned.

Intercontinental Literary Agency
Centric House, 390-391 Strand, London, WC2R 0LT
Tel: +44 (0) 20 7379 6611
Fax: +44 (0) 20 7379 6790
Email: ila@ila-agency.co.uk
Website: http://www.ila-agency.co.uk

Handles: Fiction; Nonfiction; *Areas:* Translations; *Markets:* Adult; Children's

Handles translation rights only for, among others, the authors of LAW Ltd, London; Harold Matson Co. Inc., New York; PFD,

London. Submissions accepted via client agencies and publishers only - no submissions from writers seeking agents.

Janet Fillingham Associates
52 Lowther Road , London, SW13 9NU
Tel: +44 (0) 20 8748 5594
Fax: +44 (0) 20 8748 7374
Email: info@janetfillingham.com
Website: http://www.janetfillingham.com

Handles: Scripts; *Areas:* Film; Theatre; TV; *Markets:* Adult; Children's; Youth

Represents writers and directors for stage, film and TV, as well as librettists, lyricists and composers in musical theatre. Does not represent books. Prospective clients may register via website.

Johnson & Alcock
Clerkenwell House, 45/47 Clerkenwell Green, London, EC1R 0HT
Tel: +44 (0) 20 7251 0125
Fax: +44 (0) 20 7251 2172
Email: info@johnsonandalcock.co.uk
Website: http://www.johnsonandalcock.com

Handles: Fiction; Nonfiction; Poetry; *Areas:* Autobiography; Biography; Culture; Current Affairs; Design; Film; Health; Historical; Lifestyle; Music; Sci-Fi; Self-Help; Sport; *Markets:* Adult; Children's; Youth; *Treatments:* Commercial; Literary

For children's fiction, ages 9+ only. Send query by post with SASE, synopsis and approximately first 50 pages. Accepts email submission, but replies only if interested. Email submissions should go to specific agents. See website for list of agents and full submission guidelines. No poetry, screenplays, children's books 0-7, or board or picture books.

Michelle Kass Associates
85 Charing Cross Road, London, WC2H 0AA
Tel: +44 (0) 20 7439 1624
Fax: +44 (0) 20 7734 3394
Email: office@michellekass.co.uk

Handles: Fiction; Scripts; *Areas:* Film; Literature; TV; *Markets:* Adult; *Treatments:* Literary

Approach by telephone in first instance.

Frances Kelly

111 Clifton Road, Kingston upon Thames, Surrey KT2 6PL
Tel: +44 (0) 20 8549 7830
Fax: +44 (0) 20 8547 0051

Handles: Nonfiction; Reference; *Areas:* Arts; Biography; Business; Cookery; Finance; Health; Historical; Lifestyle; Medicine; Self-Help; *Markets:* Academic; Adult; Professional

Send query with SAE, CV, and synopsis or brief description of work. Scripts handled for existing clients only. No unsolicited MSS.

Ki Agency Ltd

48-56 Bayham Place, London, NW1 0EU
Tel: +44 (0) 20 3214 8287
Email: meg@ki-agency.co.uk
Website: http://www.ki-agency.co.uk

Handles: Fiction; Scripts; *Areas:* Film; Theatre; TV; *Markets:* Adult

Represents novelists and scriptwriters in all media. No nonfiction, children's, or poetry. Accepts unsolicited mss by post or by email.

Kilburn Literary Agency

Belsize Road, Kilburn, London, NW6 4BT
Email: info@kilburnlit.com
Website: http://kilburnlit.com

Handles: Fiction; Nonfiction; Scripts; *Areas:* Adventure; Arts; Autobiography; Biography; Business; Health; Literature; Medicine; Mystery; Politics; Psychology; Religious; Romance; Science; Short Stories; Sociology; Spiritual; Thrillers; Women's Interests; *Markets:* Adult; Youth; *Treatments:* Commercial; Contemporary; Literary; Mainstream; Popular; Positive

We are an agency founded in 2013 and offer a window of opportunity while we

build up our list.

All submissions and queries must be by e-mail initially.

We are international in outlook.

Knight Hall Agency

Lower Ground Floor, 7 Mallow Street, London, EC1Y 8RQ
Tel: +44 (0) 20 3397 2901
Fax: +44 (0) 871 918 6068
Email: office@knighthallagency.com
Website: http://www.rodhallagency.com

Handles: Scripts; *Areas:* Drama; Film; Theatre; TV; *Markets:* Adult

Send query by post or email (no attachments). Only send sample if requested. Represents playwrights, screenwriters and writer-directors. Handles adaptation rights for novels, but does not handle books directly.

Barbara Levy Literary Agency

64 Greenhill, Hampstead High Street, London, NW3 5TZ
Tel: +44 (0) 20 7435 9046
Fax: +44 (0) 20 7431 2063
Email: blevysubmissions@gmail.com

Handles: Fiction; Nonfiction; *Markets:* Adult

Send query with synopsis by email or by post with SAE.

The Lez Barstow Agency

27 Chippendale Place, Ashton Under Lyne, Greater Manchester OL6 9HP
Tel: +44 (0) 1613 440069
Fax: +44 (0) 1613 440069
Email: lezbarstowagency@gmail.com
Website: http://web.me.com/lezbarstow/The_Lez_Barstow_Agency/Welcome.html

Handles: Fiction; Scripts; *Areas:* Adventure; Crime; Drama; Film; Gothic; Historical; Horror; Humour; Mystery; Radio; Sci-Fi; Suspense; Thrillers; Translations; TV;

Markets: Adult; Children's; Family; *Treatments:* Contemporary; Literary; Mainstream

Temporarily closed to submissions from May 5, 2011, after an overwhelming response from firstwriter.com users. Check website for current status.

The agent graduated in 1968, after studying Fine Art at Goldsmiths College. Following, he taught Art and Design.

Whilst teaching, he completed a number of courses including an advanced course in Film and Photography and in 1973 a full-time course in Film and Television at London's Honsey College of Art.

The agent found teaching rather claustrophobic and he left the profession in 1974 to take a Post Graduate Course in Vocational Guidance. In 1975, he was appointed as Information Officer- first with Salford Careers Service and from 1979 with the UK's Manpower Services Commission in London and Sheffield. During his time with the MSC, he worked as a Writer, Editor and Executive Producer on some innovative and award winning educational programmes and print projects. He was privileged to work with some outstanding writers, directors, crews and performers, many of whom such as Billy Connolly, Pamela Stephenson and Judy Finnegan were to become household names in UK broadcast television.

In 1984, the agent decided to pursue a career as an independent Writer, Producer and Director. One of his first clients was the UK Ministry of Defence and over the years, he worked with some of Europe's leading companies: British Airways, Sony Music and Central Television, to name just a few. He wrote, produced and directed around 150 programmes ranging from education and animation to music promos, commercials and corporates. In 1997, the agent decided to take time out to write and he moved to Dublin where, identifying a gap in the market, he started up a screenwriter's agency. This became his inspiration for a talent website and Internet TV channel, for which he found an investor in 2004.

Since returning to the UK, the agent has devoted himself exclusively to developing new writing talent, first through the Manchester Writers Meetup Group and more recently through this Agency.

Limelight Management
10 Filmer Mews, 75 Filmer Road , London, SW6 7JF
Tel: +44 (0) 20 7384 9950
Fax: +44 (0) 20 7384 9955
Email: mail@limelightmanagement.com
Website:
http://www.limelightmanagement.com

Handles: Fiction; Nonfiction; *Areas:* Lifestyle; *Markets:* Adult; *Treatments:* Commercial; Literary

Particularly interested in lifestyle nonfiction, and commercial and literary fiction for the adult market. For nonfiction send query with 3-4 page outline. For fiction send query with synopsis and first three or four consecutive chapters. Accepts queries by email, but no large attachments – emails with large attachments will be deleted unread. No scripts. See website for full submission guidelines.

Lindsay Literary Agency
East Worldham House, East Worldham, Alton GU34 3AT
Tel: +44 (0) 0142 083143
Email: info@lindsayliteraryagency.co.uk
Website:
http://www.lindsayliteraryagency.co.uk

Handles: Fiction; Nonfiction; *Markets:* Adult; Children's; *Treatments:* Literary; Serious

Send query by post with SASE or by email, including single-page synopsis and first three chapters.

London Independent Books
26 Chalcot Crescent, London, NW1 8YD
Tel: +44 (0) 20 7706 0486
Fax: +44 (0) 20 7724 3122

Handles: Fiction; Nonfiction; *Areas:*

Fantasy; Travel; *Markets:* Adult; Youth; *Treatments:* Commercial

Send query with synopsis, SASE, and first two chapters. All fiction and nonfiction subjects considered if treatment is strong and saleable, but no computer books, young children's, or unsolicited MSS. Particularly interested in boats, commercial fiction, fantasy, teen fiction, and travel. Scripts handled for existing clients only.

Andrew Lownie Literary Agency Ltd

36 Great Smith Street, London, SW1P 3BU
Tel: +44 (0) 20 7222 7574
Fax: +44 (0) 20 7222 7576
Email: mail@andrewlownie.co.uk
Website: http://www.andrewlownie.co.uk

Handles: Fiction; Nonfiction; Reference; *Areas:* Autobiography; Biography; Current Affairs; Entertainment; Historical; Media; Men's Interests; Military; Politics; Short Stories; *Markets:* Adult; *Treatments:* Commercial; Mainstream; Popular; Serious; Traditional

Previously focused on nonfiction, this agency has taken on a new agent through which it is actively building its fiction list. Accepts queries by email only. See website for detailed submission guidelines, and separate email addresses for fiction and nonfiction submissions. No plays, poetry, academic books, spiritual or new age philosophy, science fiction and fantasy, children's books or Young Adult or short stories.

Lucy Luck Associates

18-21 Cavaye Place, London, SW10 9PT
Tel: +44 (0) 20 7373 8672
Email: lucy@lucyluck.com
Website: http://www.lucyluck.com

Handles: Fiction; Nonfiction; *Markets:* Adult

Send query by post, email, or using form on website to provide cover letter and first 30-50 pages, plus SAE if required. No scripts, childrens books, or illustrated books.

Lutyens and Rubinstein

21 Kensington Park Road, London, W11 2EU
Tel: +44 (0) 20 7792 4855
Email: submissions@lutyensrubinstein.co.uk
Website: http://www.lutyensrubinstein.co.uk

Handles: Fiction; Nonfiction; *Markets:* Adult; *Treatments:* Commercial; Literary

Send up to 5,000 words or first three chapters by email with covering letter and short synopsis. No scripts, or unsolicited submissions by hand or by post.

Madeleine Milburn Literary Agency

42A Great Percy Street, Bloomsbury, London, WC1X 9QR
Tel: +44 (0) 20 3602 6425
Fax: +44 (0) 20 3602 6425
Email: submissions@madeleinemilburn.com
Website: http://madeleinemilburn.co.uk

Handles: Fiction; Nonfiction; Scripts; *Areas:* Autobiography; Crime; Film; Mystery; Suspense; Thrillers; TV; Women's Interests; *Markets:* Adult; Children's; Youth; *Treatments:* Literary

Send query by email only, with synopsis and first three chapters as Word or PDF attachments. See website for full submission guidelines. Film and TV scripts for established clients only.

Makepeace Towle Literary Agency

Fifth Floor, Trongate 103, Glasgow, G1 5HD
Website: http://www.makepeacetowle.com

Handles: Fiction; Nonfiction; *Areas:* Anthropology; Arts; Autobiography; Culture; Current Affairs; Fantasy; Historical; Humour; Literature; Men's Interests; Politics; Science; Sci-Fi; Translations; Travel; Women's Interests; *Markets:* Adult; Children's; Family; Professional; Youth

Please see website for latest submission details.

Andrew Mann Ltd

39 - 41 North Road, London, N7 9DP
Tel: +44 (0) 20 7609 6218
Email: info@andrewmann.co.uk
Website: http://www.andrewmann.co.uk

Handles: Fiction; Nonfiction; Scripts; *Areas:*
Film; Radio; Theatre; TV; *Markets:* Adult;
Children's

Send query by email, or by post if absolutely
necessary. No poetry, spiritual or new age
philosophy, short stories or misery memoirs.
Not currently accepting submissions for film
or theatre. See website for full submission
guidelines.

Marjacq Scripts Ltd

Box 412, 19/21 Crawford St, London, W1H
1PJ
Tel: +44 (0) 20 7935 9499
Fax: +44 (0) 20 7935 9115
Email: subs@marjacq.com
Website: http://www.marjacq.com

Handles: Fiction; Nonfiction; Scripts; *Areas:*
Film; Radio; TV; *Markets:* Adult;
Children's; *Treatments:* Commercial;
Literary

For books, send query with synopsis and
three sample chapters. For scripts, send short
treatment and entire screenplay. All queries
must include an SAE for response, if sent by
post. If sent by email send only Word or
PDF documents less than 2MB. Also handles
games developers. See website for full
details. No poetry, short stories, or stage
plays. Do not send queries without including
samples of the actual work.

The Marsh Agency

50 Albemarle Street, London, W1S 4BD
Tel: +44 (0) 20 7493 4361
Fax: +44 (0) 20 7495 8961
Email: steph@marsh-agency.co.uk
Website: http://www.marsh-agency.co.uk

Handles: Fiction; Nonfiction; *Markets:*
Adult; Youth; *Treatments:* Literary

Use online submission system to send brief
query letter with contact details, relevant

information, details of any previously
published work, and any experience which
relates to the book's subject matter; an
outline of the plot and main characters for
fiction, or a summary of the work and
chapter outlines for nonfiction. Include three
consecutive chapters up to 100 pages, and
your CV. See website for full guidelines and
online submission system. No TV, film,
radio or theatre scripts, poetry, or
children's/picture books. Does not handle
US authors as a primary English Language
Agent. Do not call or email until at least 8
weeks have elapsed from submission date.

MBA Literary Agents Ltd

62 Grafton Way, London, W1T 5DW
Tel: +44 (0) 20 7387 2076
Fax: +44 (0) 20 7387 2042
Email: submissions@mbalit.co.uk
Website: http://www.mbalit.co.uk

Handles: Fiction; Nonfiction; Scripts; *Areas:*
Arts; Biography; Crafts; Film; Health;
Historical; Lifestyle; Radio; Self-Help;
Theatre; TV; *Markets:* Adult; Children's;
Youth; *Treatments:* Commercial; Literary

For books, send query with synopsis and first
three chapters. For scripts, send query with
synopsis, CV, and finished script. Prefers
submissions by email, but will also accept
submissions by post. See website for full
submission guidelines. Works in conjunction
with agents in most countries.

MBE

21a St John's Wood High Street, London,
NW8 7NG
Tel: +44 (0) 20 7722 2313
Fax: +44 (0) 20 7722 2313

Handles: Scripts; *Areas:* Theatre; *Markets:*
Adult

Send complete ms with return postage.

Duncan McAra

28 Beresford Gardens, Edinburgh, Scotland
EH5 3ES
Tel: +44 (0) 131 552 1558
Email: duncanmcara@mac.com

Handles: Fiction; Nonfiction; *Areas:*
Archaeology; Architecture; Arts; Biography;
Historical; Military; Travel; *Markets:* Adult;
Treatments: Literary

Also interested in books of Scottish interest.
Send query letter with SAE in first instance.

McKernan Agency
Studio 50, Out of the Blue Drill Hall, 36
Dalmeny Street, Edinburgh, EH6 8RG
Tel: +44 (0) 1315 571771
Email: info@mckernanagency.co.uk
Website: http://www.mckernanagency.co.uk

Handles: Fiction; Nonfiction; *Areas:*
Autobiography; Biography; Crime; Current
Affairs; Historical; *Markets:* Adult;
Children's; Family; Youth; *Treatments:*
Literary

Handles high quality literary fiction
including historical and crime and high
quality nonfiction, including memoirs,
biography, history, current affairs etc. Also
considers fiction for older children. Submit
through online webform only. No
submissions by post or email.

Bill McLean Personal Management Ltd
23B Deodar Road, London, SW15 2NP
Tel: +44 (0) 20 8789 8191

Handles: Scripts; *Areas:* Film; Radio;
Theatre; TV; *Markets:* Adult

Query initially by letter or phone call.
Handles scripts for all media. No books or
unsolicited MSS.

The Michael Greer Literary Agency
51 Aragon Court, 8 Hotspur Street,
Kennington, London SE11 6BX
Tel: +44 (0) 777 592 0885
Email: mmichaelgreer@yahoo.co.uk
Website:
http://www.wix.com/mmichaelgreer/mgla

Handles: Fiction; Nonfiction; Scripts; *Areas:*
Business; Lifestyle; Psychology; Sport;

Markets: Adult; Children's; Professional;
Youth; *Treatments:* Commercial;
Contemporary; Literary; Mainstream;
Popular; Positive

Currently, represents writing mainly in the
Sports genre - be that covering certain
players, or covering certain games and the
philosophy of sports.

We also accept manuscripts in the Young
Adult / Teen Fiction category, and in the
Literary Fiction category - the latter with an
emphasis on work set in a City environment.

Miles Stott Children's Literary Agency
East Hook Farm, Lower Quay Road, Hook,
Haverfordwest, Pembrokeshire SA62 4LR
Tel: +44 (0) 1437 890570
Email: nancy@milesstottagency.co.uk
Website: http://www.milesstottagency.co.uk

Handles: Fiction; *Markets:* Children's

Handles picture books, novelty books, and
children's fiction. No poetry or nonfiction.
Send query with synopsis and first three or
four chapters by post (with SAE if return of
material is required) or email as Word file
attachments. Material posted from overseas
cannot be returned.

William Morris Endeavor Entertainment (UK) Ltd
Centre Point, 103 New Oxford Street,
London, WC1A 1DD
Tel: +44 (0) 20 7534 6800
Fax: +44 (0) 20 7534 6900
Email: eif@wma.com
Website: http://www.wma.com

Handles: Fiction; Nonfiction; Scripts; *Areas:*
Biography; Film; Historical; TV; *Markets:*
Adult

Worldwide theatrical and literary agency,
with offices in New York, Beverly Hills,
Nashville, Miami, and Shanghai, as well as
associates in Sydney. No unsolicited scripts
for film, TV, or theatre. No poetry or picture
books. Send query by post only with SAE,

one-page synopsis, and three chapters up to 50 pages. Submit only one title at a time.

Judith Murdoch Literary Agency

19 Chalcot Square, London, NW1 8YA
Tel: +44 (0) 20 7722 4197
Email: jmlitag@btinternet.com
Website: http://www.judithmurdoch.co.uk

Handles: Fiction; *Areas:* Crime; Women's Interests; *Markets:* Adult; *Treatments:* Commercial; Literary; Popular

Send query by post with SAE or email address for response, brief synopsis, and and two sample chapters. Provides editorial advice. No poetry, short stories, children's books, science fiction, fantasy, email submissions, or unsolicited MSS.

MNLA (Maggie Noach Literary Agency)

7 Peacock Yard, Iliffe Street, London, SE17 3LH
Tel: +44 (0) 20 7708 3073
Email: info@mnla.co.uk
Website: http://www.mnla.co.uk

Handles: Fiction; Nonfiction; *Areas:* Biography; Historical; Travel; *Markets:* Adult; Children's

Note: As at June 2013 not accepting submissions. Check website for current situation.

Deals with UK residents only. Send query with SAE, outline, and two or three sample chapters. No email attachments or fax queries. Very few new clients taken on. Deals in general adult nonfiction and non-illustrated children's books for ages 8 and upwards. No poetry, scripts, short stories, cookery, gardening, mind, body, and spirit, scientific, academic, specialist nonfiction, or unsolicited MSS.

Andrew Nurnberg Associates, Ltd

20-23 Greville Street, London, EC1N 8SS
Tel: +44 (0) 20 3327 0400
Fax: +44 (0) 20 7430 0801
Email: submissions@andrewnurnberg.com
Website: http://www.andrewnurnberg.com

Handles: Fiction; Nonfiction; *Markets:* Adult; Children's

Handles adult fiction and nonfiction, and children's fiction. No poetry, or scripts for film, TV, radio or theatre. Send query with one-page synopsis and first three chapters by post with SAE (if return required) or by email as .doc or .pdf attachments up to 3MB only.

Paterson Marsh Ltd

50 Albemarle Street, London, W1S 4BD
Tel: +44 (0) 20 7297 4311
Fax: +44 (0) 20 7495 8961
Email: paterson@patersonmarsh.co.uk
Website: http://www.patersonmarsh.co.uk

Handles: Fiction; Nonfiction; *Areas:* Psychology; *Markets:* Academic; Adult; *Treatments:* Commercial; Literary

Use online submission system, or send query with SAE, synopsis, CV, and up to three sample chapters of up to 100 pages. Handles commercial and literary fiction, general nonfiction, and some academic nonfiction, particularly in psychology and related fields. No poetry, children's picture books, film / TV scripts, or unsolicited MSS. Do not call or email regarding submission until 8 weeks have elapsed.

John Pawsey

8 Snowshill Court, Giffard Park, Milton Keynes, MK14 5QG
Tel: +44 (0) 1908 611841
Email: john.pawsey@virgin.net

Handles: Nonfiction; *Areas:* Biography; Sport; *Markets:* Adult

Send query with SAE for response. No fiction, poetry, scripts, journalism, academic, or children's books. Particularly interested in sport and biography. No email submissions.

PBJ and JBJ Management

22 Rathbone Street, London, W1T 1LA
Tel: +44 (0) 20 7287 1112
Fax: +44 (0) 20 7637 0899
Email: general@pbjmanagement.co.uk
Website: http://www.pbjmgt.co.uk

Handles: Scripts; *Areas:* Drama; Film;
Humour; Radio; Theatre; TV; *Markets:*
Adult

Handles scripts for film, TV, theatre, and
radio. Send complete MS with cover letter
and CV, if you have one. Send one script
only. No submissions by email. Particularly
interested in comedy and comedy drama.

Maggie Pearlstine Associates Ltd

31 Ashley Gardens, Ambrosden Avenue,
London, SW1P 1QE
Tel: +44 (0) 20 7828 4212
Fax: +44 (0) 20 7834 5546
Email: maggie@pearlstine.co.uk

Handles: Fiction; Nonfiction; *Areas:*
Biography; Current Affairs; Health;
Historical; *Markets:* Adult

Small, selective agency, not currently taking
on new clients.

Jonathan Pegg Literary Agency

32 Batoum Gardens, London, W6 7QD
Tel: +44 (0) 20 7603 6830
Fax: +44 (0) 20 7348 0629
Email: submissions@jonathanpegg.com
Website: http://www.jonathanpegg.com

Handles: Fiction; Nonfiction; *Areas:* Arts;
Autobiography; Biography; Culture; Current
Affairs; Historical; Lifestyle; Nature;
Psychology; Science; *Markets:* Adult;
Treatments: Commercial; Literary; Popular

Established by the agent after twelve years at
Curtis Brown. The agency's main areas of
interest are:

Fiction: literary fiction, thrillers and quality
commercial in general.

Non-Fiction: current affairs, memoir and
biography, history, popular science, nature,
arts and culture, lifestyle, popular
psychology.

Rights:
Aside from the UK market, the agency will
work in association with translation, US, TV
& film agents according to each client's best
interests.

If you're looking for an agent:
I accept submissions by email. Please
include a 1-page mini-synopsis, a half-page
cv, a longer synopsis (for non-fiction) and
the first three chapters, or around 50 pages to
a natural break. Please ensure it is via 'word
document' attachments, 1.5 line spacing.

See website for full submission guidelines.

The Peters Fraser & Dunlop Group Ltd (PFD)

Drury House, 34-43 Russell Street, London,
WC2B 5HA
Tel: +44 (0) 20 7344 1000
Fax: +44 (0) 20 7836 9523
Email: info@pfd.co.uk
Website: http://www.pfd.co.uk

Handles: Fiction; Nonfiction; Scripts; *Areas:*
Film; Radio; Theatre; TV; *Markets:* Adult;
Children's

Send query with SAE, CV, synopsis and
three sample chapters. Currently not
accepting children's and illustrators
submissions, or fantasy or science fiction.
Submissions by post only. No fax or email
submissions. Film, stage, and TV department
is accepting new writers by referral only. No
unsolicited scripts or pitches.

Shelley Power Literary Agency Ltd

35 Rutland Court, New Church Road, Hove,
BN3 4AF
Tel: +44 (0) 1273 728730
Email: sp@shelleypower.co.uk

Handles: Fiction; Nonfiction; *Markets:*
Adult

Send query by email or by post with return postage. No attachments. No poetry, short stories, scripts, or children's books.

Redhammer

186 Bickenhall Mansions, Bickenhall Street, London, W1U 6BX
Tel: +44 (0) 20 7486 3465
Fax: +44 (0) 20 7000 1249
Email: info@redhammer.biz
Website: http://www.redhammer.info

Handles: Nonfiction; *Areas:* Autobiography; Current Affairs; Health; Lifestyle; Science; *Markets:* Adult

Specialises in mid-list authors who are already experienced in the mainstream publishing world. No radio scripts, theatre scripts, or unsolicited MSS.

Previously published authors may send query via form on website. Unpublished authors are advised that this is probably not the best initial agency for novice writers to approach. Does not encourage writers to send unsolicited submissions, but if you do you are advised to keep a copy as submissions will not be returned, nor correspondence entered into.

Regal Literary

6 Steeles Mews North, London, NW3 4RJ
Email: uk@regal-literary.com
Website: http://www.regal-literary.com

Handles: Fiction; Nonfiction; *Areas:* Biography; Historical; Photography; Science; Thrillers; *Markets:* Adult; *Treatments:* Literary

Literary agency with offices in New York and London. Handles literary fiction, thrillers, narrative nonfiction (history, biography, science, etc.) and photography. No romance, science fiction, poetry, or screenplays. Send query by email or by post with SASE and details of the book and author. For fiction, include first ten pages or one short story from a collection. See website for full details.

Robert Dudley Agency

50 Rannoch Road, London , W6 9SR
Email: info@robertdudleyagency.co.uk
Website:
http://www.robertdudleyagency.co.uk

Handles: Fiction; Nonfiction; *Areas:* Biography; Business; Current Affairs; Historical; Military; Politics; Sport; *Markets:* Adult

Specialises in nonfiction. Represents a select group of novelists but not accepting fiction submissions. Send query outlining your idea by post or by email in first instance. See website for full guidelines.

Robin Jones Literary Agency

6b Marmora Road, London, SE22 0RX
Tel: +44 (0) 20 8693 6062
Email: robijones@gmail.com

Handles: Fiction; Nonfiction; *Markets:* Adult; *Treatments:* Commercial; Literary

London-based literary agency founded in 2007 by an agent who has previously worked at four other agencies, and was the UK scout for international publishers in 11 countries.

Rocking Chair Books

2 Rudgwick Terrace, London, NW8 6BR
Tel: +44 (0) 7809 461342
Email: samar@rockingchairbooks.com
Website: http://www.rockingchairbooks.com

Handles: Fiction; Nonfiction; *Areas:* Adventure; Arts; Crime; Culture; Current Affairs; Entertainment; Historical; Horror; Lifestyle; Literature; Mystery; Nature; Romance; Thrillers; Translations; Travel; Women's Interests; *Markets:* Adult; *Treatments:* Commercial; Contemporary; Cynical; Dark; Experimental; In-depth; Light; Literary; Mainstream; Popular; Positive; Progressive; Satirical; Serious; Traditional

Founded in 2011 after the founder worked for five years as a Director at an established London literary agency.

Uli Rushby-Smith Literary Agency

72 Plimsoll Road, London, N4 2EE
Tel: +44 (0) 20 7354 2718
Fax: +44 (0) 20 7354 2718

Handles: Fiction; Nonfiction; *Markets:*
Adult; Children's; *Treatments:* Commercial;
Literary

Send query with SAE, outline, and two or
three sample chapters. Film and TV rights
handled in conjunction with a sub-agent. No
disks, poetry or plays.

The Sayle Literary Agency

1 Petersfield, Cambridge, CB1 1BB
Tel: +44 (0) 1223 303035
Fax: +44 (0) 1223 301638
Email: info@sayleliteraryagency.com
Website:
http://www.sayleliteraryagency.com

Handles: Fiction; Nonfiction; *Areas:*
Biography; Crime; Current Affairs;
Historical; Music; Science; Travel; *Markets:*
Adult; *Treatments:* Literary

Send query with CV, synopsis, and three
sample chapters. No text books, technical,
legal, medical, children's, plays, poetry,
unsolicited MSS, or approaches by email. Do
not include SAE as all material submitted is
recycled. If no response after three months
assume rejection.

Sayle Screen Ltd

11 Jubilee Place, London, SW3 3TD
Tel: +44 (0) 20 7823 3883
Fax: +44 (0) 20 7823 3363
Email: info@saylescreen.com
Website: http://www.saylescreen.com

Handles: Scripts; *Areas:* Film; Radio;
Theatre; TV; *Markets:* Adult

Send query by post with CV and showreel or
script. No submissions by email. Specialises
in writers and directors for film and TV.

The Science Factory

Scheideweg 34C, Hamburg, Germany 20253

Tel: +44 (0) 20 7193 7296
Email: info@sciencefactory.co.uk
Website: http://www.sciencefactory.co.uk
Handles: Fiction; Nonfiction; *Areas:*
Autobiography; Biography; Current Affairs;
Historical; Medicine; Politics; Science;
Technology; Travel; *Markets:* Adult

Specialises in science, technology, medicine,
and natural history, but will also consider
other areas of nonfiction. Novelists handled
only occasionally, and if there is some
special relevance to the agency (e.g. a thriller
about scientists, or a novel of ideas). See
website for full submission guidelines.

Please note that the agency address is in
Germany, but the country is listed as United
Kingdom, as the company is registered in the
United Kingdom.

Linda Seifert Management

48-56 Bayham Place, London, NW1 0EU
Tel: +44 (0) 20 3214 8293
Email: contact@lindaseifert.com
Website: http://www.lindaseifert.com

Handles: Scripts; *Areas:* Film; TV; *Markets:*
Adult; Children's

A London-based management company
representing screenwriters and directors for
film and television. Our outstanding client
list ranges from the highly established to the
new and exciting emerging talent of
tomorrow. Represents UK-based writers and
directors only. Accepts submissions by post
only. No novels or short stories. See website
for full submission guidelines.

Sheil Land Associates Ltd

52 Doughty Street, London, WC1N 2LS
Tel: +44 (0) 20 7405 9351
Fax: +44 (0) 20 7831 2127
Email: info@sheilland.co.uk
Website: http://www.sheilland.co.uk

Handles: Fiction; Nonfiction; Scripts; *Areas:*
Autobiography; Biography; Cookery; Crime;
Drama; Fantasy; Film; Gardening;
Historical; Humour; Lifestyle; Military;
Mystery; Politics; Psychology; Romance;
Science; Sci-Fi; Self-Help; Theatre;

Thrillers; Travel; TV; Women's Interests;
Markets: Adult; Children's; Youth;
Treatments: Commercial; Contemporary;
Literary

Send query with SAE, synopsis, CV, and
first three chapters, addressed to "The
Submissions Dept". Welcome approaches
from new clients either to start or develop
their careers.

Dorie Simmonds Agency
Riverbank House, 1 Putney Bridge
Approach, London, SW6 3JD
Tel: +44 (0) 20 7736 0002
Fax: +44 (0) 20 7736 0010
Email: dorie@doriesimmonds.com

Handles: Fiction; Nonfiction; *Areas:*
Biography; Historical; Women's Interests;
Markets: Adult; Children's; *Treatments:*
Commercial; Contemporary

Send query with SAE, CV of writing /
publishing history, and outline for nonfiction
or short synopsis with 2-3 sample chapters
for fiction. Particularly interested in
contemporary personalities, women's fiction,
children's books, and historical biographies.

Jeffrey Simmons
15 Penn House, Mallory Street, London,
NW8 8SX
Tel: +44 (0) 20 7224 8917
Email: jasimmons@unicombox.co.uk

Handles: Fiction; Nonfiction; *Areas:*
Autobiography; Biography; Crime; Current
Affairs; Film; Historical; Legal; Politics;
Psychology; Sport; Theatre; *Markets:* Adult;
Treatments: Commercial; Literary

Send query with brief bio, synopsis, history
of any prior publication, and list of any
publishers or agents to have already seen the
MSS. Particularly interested in personality
books of all kinds and fiction from young
writers (under 40) with a future. No
children's books, science fiction, fantasy,
cookery, crafts, gardening, or hobbies. Film
scripts handled for existing book clients
only.

Sinclair-Stevenson
3 South Terrace, London, SW7 2TB
Tel: +44 (0) 20 7581 2550
Fax: +44 (0) 20 7581 2550

Handles: Fiction; Nonfiction; *Areas:* Arts;
Biography; Current Affairs; Historical;
Travel; *Markets:* Adult

Send query with synopsis and SAE. No
children's books, scripts, academic, science
fiction, or fantasy.

Robert Smith Literary Agency Ltd
12 Bridge Wharf, 156 Caledonian Road,
London, N1 9UU
Tel: +44 (0) 20 7278 2444
Fax: +44 (0) 20 7833 5680
Email:
robertsmith.literaryagency@virgin.net

Handles: Nonfiction; *Areas:* Autobiography;
Biography; Crime; Culture; Entertainment;
Health; Historical; Lifestyle; Sport; *Markets:*
Adult

Send query with synopsis initially. No
poetry, fiction, scripts, children's books,
academic, or unsolicited MSS. Will suggest
revision.

South West Artists
Silver Street, Milverton, Somerset TA4 1LA
Tel: +44 (0) 844 3755265
Email: nick@southwestartists.co.uk
Website: http://www.southwestartists.co.uk

Handles: Scripts; *Areas:* Crime; Drama;
Entertainment; Fantasy; Film; Horror;
Music; Mystery; Romance; Sci-Fi; Theatre;
Thrillers; TV; Westerns; *Markets:* Adult;
Children's; Family; Youth; *Treatments:*
Contemporary; Dark; Experimental;
Mainstream

Represents writers, filmmakers and
musicians based in Somerset, Devon and
Cornwall.

Standen Literary Agency
53 Hardwicke Road , London, N13 4SL

Tel: +44 (0) 20 8889 1167
Fax: +44 (0) 20 8889 1167
Email:
submissions@standenliteraryagency.com
Website:
http://www.standenliteraryagency.com

Handles: Fiction; Nonfiction; *Markets:*
Adult; Children's; Youth; *Treatments:*
Commercial; Literary

Based in London. For fiction, send synopsis
and first three chapters by email only.
Responds if interested only. If no response in
12 weeks assume rejection. For nonfiction,
query in first instance.

Elaine Steel

110 Gloucester Avenue, London, NW1 8HX
Tel: +44 (0) 20 8348 0918
Fax: +44 (0) 20 8341 9807
Email: ecmsteel@aol.com

Handles: Fiction; Nonfiction; Scripts;
Markets: Adult

Phone in first instance. Represents
screenwriters and book writers. No technical
or academic.

Abner Stein

10 Roland Gardens, London, SW7 3PH
Tel: +44 (0) 20 7373 0456
Fax: +44 (0) 20 7370 6316
Email: arabella@abnerstein.co.uk

Handles: Fiction; Nonfiction; *Markets:*
Adult

Send query with outline. No scripts,
scientific, technical, or unsolicited MSS.
Mainly represents US agents and authors.

Susanna Lea Associates (UK)

34 Lexington Street, London, W1F 0LH
Tel: +44 (0) 20 7287 7757
Fax: +44 (0) 20 7287 7775
Email: uk-submission@susannalea.com
Website: http://www.susannalea.com

Handles: Fiction; Nonfiction; *Markets:*
Adult

Literary agency with offices in Paris,
London, and New York. Always on the
lookout for exciting new talent. No poetry,
plays, screen plays, science fiction,
educational text books, short stories or
illustrated works. Accepts queries by email
only. Include cover letter, synopsis, and first
three chapters or proposal. Response not
guaranteed.

The Susijn Agency

3rd Floor, 64 Great Titchfield Street,
London, W1W 7QH
Tel: +44 (0) 20 7580 6341
Fax: +44 (0) 20 7580 8626
Email: info@thesusijnagency.com
Website: http://www.thesusijnagency.com

Handles: Fiction; Nonfiction; *Markets:*
Adult; *Treatments:* Literary

Send query with synopsis and first two
chapters only by post or by email. Include
SASE if return of material required.
Response in 6-8 weeks. Specialises in selling
rights worldwide and also represents non-
English language authors and publishers for
US, UK, and translation rights worldwide.
No self-help, science-fiction, fantasy,
romance, sagas, computer, illustrated,
business, or screenplays.

SYLA - Susan Yearwood Literary Agency

2 Knebworth House, Londesborough Road,
Stoke Newington, London N16 8RL
Tel: +44 (0) 20 7503 0954
Email: susan@susanyearwood.com
Website: http://www.susanyearwood.com

Handles: Fiction; Nonfiction; *Areas:* Crime;
Thrillers; Women's Interests; *Markets:*
Adult; Children's; Youth; *Treatments:*
Commercial; Literary

Send query by email, including synopsis and
first thirty pages in one Word file
attachment. No poetry or screenwriting.

The Tennyson Agency

10 Cleveland Avenue, Wimbledon Chase,
London, SW20 9EW

Tel: +44 (0) 20 8543 5939
Email: submissions@tenagy.co.uk
Website: http://www.tenagy.co.uk

Handles: Scripts; *Areas:* Drama; Film;
Literature; Radio; Theatre; TV; *Markets:*
Adult

Mainly deals in scripts for film, TV, theatre,
and radio, along with related material on an
ad-hoc basis. Handles writers in the
European Union only. Send query with CV
and outline of work. No Poetry, Short
Stories, S. F., Fantasy, Children's Writing, or
unsolicited MSS.

Thomas Moore Literary Agency

London,
Email: thomasj.moore@me.com

Handles: Fiction; Nonfiction; Poetry;
Reference; Scripts; *Areas:* Arts; Cookery;
Crafts; Culture; Design; Drama;
Entertainment; Film; Gardening; Historical;
How-to; Lifestyle; Literature; Media; Music;
Nature; Philosophy; Photography; Radio;
Romance; Short Stories; Theatre;
Translations; Travel; TV; *Markets:*
Academic; Adult; Children's; Family;
Professional; Youth; *Treatments:*
Commercial; Contemporary; Cynical; Dark;
Experimental; In-depth; Light; Literary;
Mainstream; Niche; Popular; Positive;
Progressive; Satirical; Serious; Traditional

Discovering, fostering and promoting
talented writers. We currently have an open
submissions and are looking to work with
writers who are breaking new ground and
challenging what modern literature is.

We will only read manuscripts that are
accompanied by a short synopsis and an in
depth biography of the Client. Clients must
be based in the UK.

Jane Turnbull

Barn Cottage, Veryan, Truro TR2 5QA
Tel: +44 (0) 20 7727 9409 / +44 (0) 1872
501317
Email: jane@janeturnbull.co.uk
Website: http://www.janeturnbull.co.uk

Handles: Fiction; Nonfiction; *Areas:*
Biography; Current Affairs; Gardening;
Historical; Humour; Lifestyle; Nature;
Markets: Adult

Agency with offices in London and
Cornwall. New clients always welcome and
a few taken on every year. Send query by
post to Cornwall office with short
description of your book or idea. No
unsolicited MSS.

United Agents

12–26 Lexington Street, London, W1F 0LE
Tel: +44 (0) 20 3214 0800
Fax: +44 (0) 20 3214 0801
Email: info@unitedagents.co.uk
Website: http://unitedagents.co.uk

Handles: Fiction; Nonfiction; Scripts; *Areas:*
Biography; Film; Radio; Theatre; TV;
Markets: Adult; Children's

Do not approach the book department
generally. Consult website and view details
of each agent before selecting a specific
agent to approach personally.

Ed Victor Ltd

6 Bayley Street, Bedford Square, London,
WC1B 3HE
Tel: +44 (0) 20 7304 4100
Fax: +44 (0) 20 7304 4111
Email: ed@edvictor.com
Website: http://www.edvictor.com

Handles: Fiction; Nonfiction; *Markets:*
Adult; Children's; *Treatments:* Commercial

Wide range of material but prefers
commercial end of market. Takes on very
few new writers. No poetry, scripts,
academic, or unsolicited MSS. Send query
with outline and up to two sample chapters
by post only.

Wade & Doherty Literary Agency

33 Cormorant Lodge, Thomas More Street,
London, E1W 1AU
Tel: +44 (0) 20 7488 4171
Fax: +44 (0) 20 7488 4172

Email: rw@rwla.com
Website: http://www.rwla.com

Handles: Fiction; Nonfiction; *Markets:* Adult; Youth

New full-length proposals for adult and young adult fiction and nonfiction always welcome. Send query with detailed 1–6 page synopsis, brief biography, and first 10,000 words via email as Word documents (.doc) or PDF; or by post with SAE if return required. We much prefer to correspond by email. Actively seeking new writers across the literary spectrum. No poetry, children's, short stories, scripts or plays.

Watson, Little Ltd

48-56 Bayham Place , London, NW1 0EU
Tel: +44 (0) 20 7388 7529
Fax: +44 (0) 20 7388 8501
Email: office@watsonlittle.com
Website: http://www.watsonlittle.com

Handles: Fiction; Nonfiction; *Areas:* Business; Crime; Historical; Leisure; Psychology; Science; Self-Help; Women's Interests; *Markets:* Adult; Children's; Youth; *Treatments:* Commercial; Literary

Send query with synopsis, sample chapters, and return postage if return / response by post required; otherwise response is by email. No scripts, poetry, short stories, purely academic writers, emails, or unsolicited MSS.

A.P. Watt Ltd

20 John Street, London, WC1N 2DR
Tel: +44 (0) 20 7405 6774
Fax: +44 (0) 20 7831 2154
Email: apw@apwatt.co.uk
Website: http://www.apwatt.co.uk

Handles: Fiction; Nonfiction; Scripts; *Areas:* Biography; Film; Historical; TV; *Markets:* Adult; Children's

No poetry, academic, specialist, or unsolicited MSS. Send query letter by post or by email in first instance, giving full plot synopsis.

Whispering Buffalo Literary Agency Ltd

97 Chesson Road, London, W14 9QS
Tel: +44 (0) 20 7565 4737
Email: info@whisperingbuffalo.com
Website: http://www.whisperingbuffalo.com

Handles: Fiction; Nonfiction; *Areas:* Adventure; Anthropology; Arts; Autobiography; Beauty and Fashion; Design; Entertainment; Film; Health; Humour; Lifestyle; Music; Nature; Politics; Romance; Sci-Fi; Self-Help; Thrillers; *Markets:* Adult; Children's; Youth; *Treatments:* Commercial; Literary

Handles commercial/literary fiction/nonfiction and children's/YA fiction with special interest in book to film adaptations. No TV, film, radio or theatre scripts, or poetry or academic. Send query with SAE, CV, synopsis, and three sample chapters. Also accepts email submissions in .doc format only, but prefers hard-copy approaches.

Eve White: Literary Agent

54 Gloucester Street, London, SW1V 4EG
Tel: +44 (0) 20 7630 1155
Email: eve@evewhite.co.uk
Website: http://www.evewhite.co.uk

Handles: Fiction; Nonfiction; *Areas:* Adventure; Anthropology; Antiques; Archaeology; Architecture; Arts; Autobiography; Beauty and Fashion; Biography; Business; Cookery; Crafts; Crime; Criticism; Culture; Current Affairs; Design; Drama; Entertainment; Erotic; Fantasy; Film; Finance; Gardening; Gothic; Health; Historical; Hobbies; Horror; How-to; Humour; Legal; Leisure; Lifestyle; Literature; Media; Medicine; Men's Interests; Military; Music; Mystery; Nature; New Age; Philosophy; Photography; Politics; Psychology; Radio; Religious; Romance; Science; Sci-Fi; Self-Help; Sociology; Spiritual; Sport; Suspense; Technology; Theatre; Thrillers; Translations; Travel; TV; Westerns; Women's Interests; *Markets:* Adult; Children's; Family; Professional; Youth; *Treatments:* Commercial; Contemporary; Cynical; Dark;

Experimental; In-depth; Light; Literary; Mainstream; Niche; Popular; Positive; Progressive; Satirical; Serious; Traditional

Important! Check and follow website submission guidelines before contacting!

DO NOT send submissions to email address below – see website for submission email addresses.

QUERIES ONLY to the email address below.

This agency requests that you go to their website for up-to-date submission procedure.

Commercial and literary fiction, nonfiction, children's fiction ages 7+ (home 15%, overseas 20%). No reading fee. See website for detailed submission guidelines. Submission by email only.

The Wylie Agency (UK) Ltd
17 Bedford Square, London, WC2B 3JA
Tel: +44 (0) 20 7908 5900
Fax: +44 (0) 20 7908 5901
Email: mail@wylieagency.co.uk
Website: http://www.wylieagency.co.uk

Handles: Fiction; Nonfiction; *Markets:* Adult

Send query by post or email before submitting. All submissions must include adequate return postage. No scripts, children's books, or unsolicited MSS.

Canadian Literary Agents

For the most up-to-date listings of these and hundreds of other literary agents, visit http://www.firstwriter.com/Agents

*To claim your **free** access to the site, please see the back of this book.*

Abela Literature

39 King St, Box 20039 Brunswick Square, Saint John, New Brunswick E2L 5B2
Email: submissions@abela-lit.com
Website: http://www.abela-lit.com

Handles: Fiction; *Areas:* Adventure; Crime; Drama; Fantasy; Gothic; Historical; Horror; Literature; Mystery; Sci-Fi; Suspense, Thrillers, Westerns; *Markets:* Adult; Family; *Treatments:* Literary; Popular; Traditional

Happy to work with both first time and previously published authors. We are not currently looking for any nonfiction projects, but would be interested in queries for manuscripts in a variety of fiction categories.

Rick Broadhead & Associates Literary Agency

47 St. Clair Avenue West, Suite 501, Toronto, Ontario M4V 3A5
Tel: +1 (416) 929-0516
Fax: +1 (416) 927-8732
Email: submissions@rbaliterary.com
Website: http://www.rbaliterary.com

Handles: Nonfiction; *Areas:* Biography; Business; Culture; Current Affairs; Health; Historical; Humour; Lifestyle; Medicine; Military; Nature; Politics; Science; Self-Help; *Markets:* Adult

Prefers queries by email. Send brief query outlining your project and your credentials. Responds only if interested. No screenplays, poetry, children's books, or fiction.

The Characters Talent Agency

8 Elm Street, Toronto, Ontario M3H 1Y9
Tel: +1 (416) 964-8522
Fax: +1 (416) 964-8206
Email: classistant@canadafilm.com
Website: http://www.thecharacters.com

Handles: Scripts; *Areas:* Biography; Drama; Erotic; Fantasy; Film; Historical; Horror; Humour; Mystery; Romance; Science; Sport; Thrillers; TV; Westerns; Women's Interests; *Markets:* Adult; Children's; Youth; *Treatments:* Contemporary; Mainstream

Send query by post with SASE with CV, 30-word loglin, and a one page synopsis or a resume and demo reel or portfolio. Handles scripts for film and TV features, as well as series and miniseries. Particularly interested in comedy, romantic comedy, and movie thrillers with strong female leads. Handles scripts only - no books. Submissions not returned.

The Cooke Agency

278 Bloor St. East, Suite 305, Toronto, Ontario M4W 3M4
Tel: +1 (416) 406-3390
Fax: +1 (416) 406-3389
Email: egriffin@cookeagency.ca

Website: http://www.cookeagency.ca

Handles: Fiction; Nonfiction; *Areas:* Culture; Fantasy; Historical; Nature; Politics; Romance; Science; Sci-Fi; *Markets:* Adult; Children's; Youth; *Treatments:* Commercial; Literary

Send query by email with "Author Query" in the subject line (no attachments). No illustrated, photographic or children's picture books, US political thrillers, or poetry. No queries or submissions by post. Consult website before making contact.

The Core Group Talent Agency, Inc.

89 Bloor Street West, Suite #300, Toronto, ON M5S 1M1
Tel: +1 (416) 955-0819
Fax: +1 (416) 955-0825
Email: info@coregroupta.com
Website: http://www.coregroupta.com

Handles: Scripts; *Areas:* Biography; Crime; Drama; Erotic; Fantasy; Film; Historical; Horror; Humour; Mystery; Romance; Sport; Theatre; Thrillers; TV; Westerns; *Markets:* Adult; Children's; Family; Youth; *Treatments:* Contemporary; Experimental; Mainstream

Send query by email, or by post with SASE. Particularly interested in writers who have had material produced already, and are established within Canada. No international writers not established within Canada.

The Helen Heller Agency

4-216 Heath Street West, Toronto, ON M5P 1N7
Tel: +1 (416) 489-0396
Email: info@helenhelleragency.com
Website: http://www.helenhelleragency.com

Handles: Fiction; Nonfiction; *Markets:* Adult; Youth

Handles adult and young adult nonfiction and fiction. No children's, screenplays, or genre fiction (sci-fi / fantasy etc.). Send query by email or by post with SASE,

including brief synopsis and any relevant publishing history.

Charlene Kay Agency

901 Beaudry Street, Suite 6,
St.Jean/Richelieu, QC J3A 1C6

Handles: Scripts; *Areas:* Adventure; Biography; Drama; Fantasy; Film; Humour; Romance; Science; TV; *Markets:* Adult; Family

Send query with SASE and outline. Handles teleplays and screenplays only. Seeks unusual stories presented in a well-crafted script. No barbaric or erotic films, thrillers, books, or unsolicited MSS. Submitted materials are not returned.

Robert Lecker Agency

4055 Melrose Avenue, Montréal, Québec H4A 2S5
Tel: +1 (514) 830-4818
Fax: +1 (514) 483-1644
Email: leckerlink@aol.com
Website: http://www.leckeragency.com

Handles: Fiction; Nonfiction; *Areas:* Adventure; Autobiography; Biography; Cookery; Crime; Culture; Entertainment; Erotic; Film; Historical; How-to; Literature; Music; Mystery; Science; Suspense; Theatre; Thrillers; Travel; *Markets:* Academic; Adult; *Treatments:* Contemporary; Literary; Mainstream

Specialises in books about entertainment, music, popular culture, popular science, intellectual and cultural history, food, and travel, but willing to consider any original and well presented material. Particularly interested in books written by academics that can attract a broad range of readers. Send query by email before sending any other material.

Seventh Avenue Literary Agency

2052 - 124th Street , South Surrey, BC V4A 9K3
Tel: +1 (604) 538-7252
Fax: +1 (604) 538-7252

Email: info@seventhavenuelit.com
Website: http://www.seventhavenuelit.com

Handles: Nonfiction; *Markets:* Adult

Handles nonfiction only and takes on few new clients. Send by mail or by email a query; brief description of work and its category; outline; potential market; table of contents with short description of each chapter; one sample chapter; and author bio, including previously published material, and your qualifications on the subject you have written on.

Include adequate return postage for return of material. No fiction, poetry, screenplays, children's books, young adult titles, or genre writing such as science fiction, fantasy or erotica, or telephone queries.

P. Stathonikos Agency
146 Springbluff Heights SW, Calgary, Alberta T3H 5E5
Tel: +1 (403) 245-2087
Fax: +1 (403) 245-2087
Email: pastath@telus.net

Handles: Fiction; Nonfiction; *Markets:* Children's; Youth

Handles children's books and some young adult. Send query by email or by post with SASE. No romance, fantasy, historical fiction, plays, movie scripts, poetry, or queries by fax.

Westwood Creative Artists
94 Harbord Street, Toronto , Ontario M5S 1G6
Tel: +1 (416) 964-3302
Fax: +1 (416) 975-9209
Email: wca_office@wcaltd.com
Website: http://www.wcaltd.com

Handles: Fiction; Nonfiction; *Areas:* Autobiography; Biography; Current Affairs; Historical; Mystery; Science; Thrillers; *Markets:* Adult; Children's; Youth; *Treatments:* Commercial; Literary

Send query by email with your credentials, a synopsis, and short sample up to ten pages in the body of the email. No attachments.

Irish Literary Agents

For the most up-to-date listings of these and hundreds of other literary agents, visit http://www.firstwriter.com/Agents

*To claim your **free** access to the site, please see the back of this book.*

Author Rights Agency

20 Victoria Road, Rathgar,
Dublin, 6
Tel: +353 1 4922112
Email:
submissions@authorrightsagency.com
Website:
http://www.authorrightsagency.com

Handles: Fiction; Nonfiction; Areas: Crime;
Fantasy; Historical; Sci-Fi; Women's
Interests; Markets: Adult; Children's; Youth;
Treatments: Contemporary; Literary

Welcomes submissions in English,
particularly from Irish and American writers.
Send query by email only with synopsis,
ideally one page long, and writing sample up
to 10 pages or about 3,000 words, as a Word
or RTF attachment. Do not include in the
body of the email, or send full manuscripts.
See website for full guidelines. No phone
calls.

Marianne Gunn O'Connor Literary Agency

Morrison Chambers, Suite 17, 32 Nassau
Street,, Dublin, 2
Tel: 353 1 677 9100
Fax: 353 1 677 9101
Email: mgoclitagency@eircom.net

Handles: Fiction; Nonfiction; *Areas:*
Biography; Health; *Markets:* Adult;

Children's; *Treatments:* Commercial;
Literary

Send query with half-page synopsis by
email.

Jonathan Williams Literary Agency

Upper Glenagary Road, Glenageary, Co.
Dublin
Tel: +353 (0) 1-280-3482
Fax: +353 (0) 1-280-3482

Handles: Fiction; Nonfiction; *Markets:*
Adult; *Treatments:* Literary

Agency also has agents in Holland, Italy,
France, Spain, and Japan. Send SASE with
IRCs if outside of Ireland. Charges a reading
fee if a very fast decision is required.

The Lisa Richards Agency

108 Upper Leeson Street, Dublin, 4
Tel: +353 1 637 5000
Fax: +353 1 667 1256
Email: info@lisarichards.ie
Website: http://www.lisarichards.ie

Handles: Fiction; Nonfiction; Scripts; *Areas:*
Autobiography; Biography; Culture;
Historical; Humour; Lifestyle; Self-Help;
Sport; Theatre; *Markets:* Adult; Children's;
Treatments: Commercial; Literary; Popular

Send query by email or by post with SASE, including three or four sample chapters in the case of fiction, or proposal and sample chapter for nonfiction. No horror, science fiction, screenplays, or children's picture books.

Australian Literary Agents

For the most up-to-date listings of these and hundreds of other literary agents, visit http://www.firstwriter.com/Agents

*To claim your **free** access to the site, please see the back of this book.*

Cameron Creswell Agency

Level 7 61 Marlborough Street, Surry Hills,
New South Wales 2010
Tel: +61 (0) 2 9319 7199
Fax: +61 (0) 2 9319 6866
Email:
submissions@cameronsmanagement.com.au
Website:
http://www.cameronsmanagement.com.au

Handles: Fiction; Nonfiction; Scripts; Areas:
Film; Theatre; TV; Markets: Adult;
Children's; Youth; Treatments: Commercial;
Literary

Describes itself as the first independent
literary agency established in Australia.
Handles commercial and literary fiction and
nonfiction for adults and children, plus
scripts for TV, film, and theatre. Fiction list
is closed to submissions as at January 6,
2011 - check website for current information.

Nonfiction list open to all but specialist
professional titles, including business. Send
queries by email only, including synopsis
and first 3,000 words in the body of the text.
No attachments.

The Mary Cunnane Agency Pty Ltd

PO Box 336, Bermagui, NSW 2546
Tel: +61 (0) 2 6493 3880
Fax: +61 (0) 2 6493 3881
Email: mary@cunnaneagency.com
Website: http://www.cunnaneagency.com

Handles: Fiction; Nonfiction; Markets: Adult

Make initial query by post, phone, or email.
If querying by email, copy in both agents.
Does not handle North American writers. No
science fiction, fantasy, romance novels, new
age/spiritual books, or children's books.

Literary Agents Subject Index

This section lists literary agents by their subject matter, with directions to the section of the book where the full listing can be found.

You can create your own customised lists of literary agents using different combinations of these subject areas, plus over a dozen other criteria, instantly online at http://www.firstwriter.com.

*To claim your **free** access to the site, please see the back of this book.*

Adventure
Abela Literature (*Can*)
Alive Communications, Inc (*US*)
Ambassador Speakers Bureau & Literary Agency (*US*)
AVAnti Productions & Management (*UK*)
The Barbara Bova Literary Agency (*US*)
Brandon & Associates (*UK*)
Kelvin C. Bulger and Associates (*US*)
Cedar Grove Agency Entertainment (*US*)
Cine/Lit Representation (*US*)
Jim Donovan Literary (*US*)
Dupree / Miller and Associates Inc. Literary (*US*)
Dystel & Goderich Literary Management (*US*)
Farris Literary Agency, Inc. (*US*)
Diana Finch Literary Agency (*US*)
Fox Mason Ltd (*UK*)
Full Throttle Literary Agency (*US*)
The Gernert Company (*US*)
Goodman Associates (*US*)
Antony Harwood Limited (*UK*)
hhb agency ltd (*UK*)
Hidden Value Group (*US*)
Andrea Hurst Literary Management (*US*)
International Transactions, Inc. (*US*)
Jabberwocky Literary Agency (*US*)
Jaret Entertainment (*US*)
Charlene Kay Agency (*Can*)
Kilburn Literary Agency (*UK*)
Harvey Klinger, Inc (*US*)
KT Public Relations (*US*)
The Candace Lake Agency (*US*)
Peter Lampack Agency, Inc (*US*)
LaunchBooks Literary Agency (*US*)
Robert Lecker Agency (*Can*)
The Lez Barstow Agency (*UK*)
Julia Lord Literary Management (*US*)
The Jennifer Lyons Literary Agency, LLC (*US*)
Ricia Mainhardt Agency (RMA) (*US*)
Monteiro Rose Dravis Agency, Inc. (*US*)
The Jean V. Naggar Literary Agency (*US*)
Niad Management (*US*)
The Park Literary Group LLC (*US*)
Pavilion Literary Management (*US*)
Barry Perelman Agency (*US*)
Prospect Agency (*US*)
Quicksilver Books Literary Agency (*US*)
Raines & Raines (*US*)
Rocking Chair Books (*UK*)
Salkind Literary Agency (*US*)
Susan Schulman, A Literary Agency (*US*)
The Seven Bridges Group (*US*)
The Seymour Agency (*US*)
The Swetky Agency and Associates (*US*)
Timberlake Literary Services, LLC (*US*)
Tom Lee (*US*)
TriadaUS Literary Agency, Inc. (*US*)
Venture Literary (*US*)
Whispering Buffalo Literary Agency Ltd (*UK*)
Eve White: Literary Agent (*UK*)
The Zack Company, Inc (*US*)
Anthropology
The Agency Group, Ltd (*US*)
AVAnti Productions & Management (*UK*)
The Blumer Literary Agency, Inc. (*US*)
Andrea Brown Literary Agency, Inc. (*US*)
Browne & Miller Literary Associates (*US*)
Dystel & Goderich Literary Management (*US*)

Felicia Eth Literary Representation (*US*)
The Susan Golomb Literary Agency (*US*)
Goodman Associates (*US*)
Antony Harwood Limited (*UK*)
Kneerim & Williams (*US*)
Makepeace Towle Literary Agency (*UK*)
Quicksilver Books Literary Agency (*US*)
Lynne Rabinoff Agency (*US*)
Susan Schulman, A Literary Agency (*US*)
Lynn Seligman, Literary Agent (*US*)
The Swetky Agency and Associates (*US*)
Tom Lee (*US*)
Venture Literary (*US*)
Whispering Buffalo Literary Agency Ltd (*UK*)
Eve White: Literary Agent (*UK*)
Antiques
AVAnti Productions & Management (*UK*)
Antony Harwood Limited (*UK*)
Tom Lee (*US*)
Venture Literary (*US*)
Eve White: Literary Agent (*UK*)
Archaeology
The Agency Group, Ltd (*US*)
AVAnti Productions & Management (*UK*)
The Blumer Literary Agency, Inc. (*US*)
Andrea Brown Literary Agency, Inc. (*US*)
Browne & Miller Literary Associates (*US*)
Dupree / Miller and Associates Inc. Literary (*US*)
Dystel & Goderich Literary Management (*US*)
The Susan Golomb Literary Agency (*US*)
Goodman Associates (*US*)
Antony Harwood Limited (*UK*)
Kneerim & Williams (*US*)
Duncan McAra (*UK*)
Quicksilver Books Literary Agency (*US*)
Lynne Rabinoff Agency (*US*)
Susan Schulman, A Literary Agency (*US*)
The Swetky Agency and Associates (*US*)
Tom Lee (*US*)
Venture Literary (*US*)
Eve White: Literary Agent (*UK*)
Architecture
The Agency Group, Ltd (*US*)
The Blumer Literary Agency, Inc. (*US*)
Barbara Braun Associates, Inc. (*US*)
Andrea Brown Literary Agency, Inc. (*US*)
W.M. Clark Associates (*US*)
Dupree / Miller and Associates Inc. Literary (*US*)
Fairbank Literary Representation (*US*)
Antony Harwood Limited (*UK*)
Duncan McAra (*UK*)
Martha Millard Literary Agency (*US*)
Marly Rusoff & Associates, Inc. (*US*)
The Swetky Agency and Associates (*US*)
Venture Literary (*US*)
Eve White: Literary Agent (*UK*)
Arts
The Agency Group, Ltd (*US*)
Artellus Limited (*UK*)
Robert Astle & Associates Literary Management, Inc. (*US*)
The August Agency LLC (*US*)
AVAnti Productions & Management (*UK*)

The Blumer Literary Agency, Inc. (*US*)
Barbara Braun Associates, Inc. (*US*)
Andrea Brown Literary Agency, Inc. (*US*)
W.M. Clark Associates (*US*)
CowlesRyan Agency (*US*)
Creative Authors Ltd (*UK*)
Donadio & Olson, Inc. (*US*)
Dupree / Miller and Associates Inc. Literary (*US*)
Judith Ehrlich Literary Management (*US*)
Fredrica S. Friedman and Co. Inc. (*US*)
The Gernert Company (*US*)
Greene & Heaton Ltd (*UK*)
Antony Harwood Limited (*UK*)
Rupert Heath Literary Agency (*UK*)
International Transactions, Inc. (*US*)
Frances Kelly (*UK*)
Kilburn Literary Agency (*UK*)
Makepeace Towle Literary Agency (*UK*)
MBA Literary Agents Ltd (*UK*)
Duncan McAra (*UK*)
Martha Millard Literary Agency (*US*)
The Park Literary Group LLC (*US*)
Jonathan Pegg Literary Agency (*UK*)
Rocking Chair Books (*UK*)
Marly Rusoff & Associates, Inc. (*US*)
Salkind Literary Agency (*US*)
Lynn Seligman, Literary Agent (*US*)
Sinclair-Stevenson (*UK*)
The Strothman Agency (*US*)
The Swetky Agency and Associates (*US*)
Thomas Moore Literary Agency (*UK*)
Timberlake Literary Services, LLC (*US*)
Tom Lee (*US*)
Venture Literary (*US*)
The Ward & Balkin Agency, Inc (*US*)
The Wendy Weil Agency, Inc. (*US*)
The Weingel-Fidel Agency (*US*)
Whispering Buffalo Literary Agency Ltd (*UK*)
Eve White: Literary Agent (*UK*)
Autobiography
Sheila Ableman Literary Agency (*UK*)
The Agency Group, Ltd (*US*)
Alive Communications, Inc (*US*)
Miriam Altshuler Literary Agency (*US*)
Ambassador Speakers Bureau & Literary Agency (*US*)
The Ampersand Agency Ltd (*UK*)
Robert Astle & Associates Literary Management, Inc. (*US*)
Audrey A. Wolf Literary Agency (*US*)
The August Agency LLC (*US*)
Faye Bender Literary Agency (*US*)
David Black Literary Agency (*US*)
The Blumer Literary Agency, Inc. (*US*)
Brandon & Associates (*UK*)
Paul Bresnick Literary Agency, LLC (*US*)
Brick House Literary Agents (*US*)
Andrea Brown Literary Agency, Inc. (*US*)
Browne & Miller Literary Associates (*US*)
Carnicelli Literary Management (*US*)
Cedar Grove Agency Entertainment (*US*)
Chalberg & Sussman (*US*)
Elyse Cheney Literary Associates, LLC (*US*)

Judith Chilcote Agency (*UK*)
W.M. Clark Associates (*US*)
Rosica Colin Ltd (*UK*)
CowlesRyan Agency (*US*)
The Creative Rights Agency (*UK*)
The Creative Culture, Inc. (*US*)
Creative Authors Ltd (*UK*)
The Croce Agency (*US*)
Richard Curtis Associates, Inc. (*US*)
Liza Dawson Associates (*US*)
The Jennifer DeChiara Literary Agency (*US*)
Joëlle Delbourgo Associates, Inc. (*US*)
Jim Donovan Literary (*US*)
Dunow, Carlson & Lerner Agency (*US*)
Dupree / Miller and Associates Inc. Literary (*US*)
Dystel & Goderich Literary Management (*US*)
Judith Ehrlich Literary Management (*US*)
Einstein Thompson Agency (*US*)
Felicia Eth Literary Representation (*US*)
Farris Literary Agency, Inc. (*US*)
Diana Finch Literary Agency (*US*)
FinePrint Literary Management (*US*)
Fox Mason Ltd (*UK*)
Sarah Jane Freymann Literary Agency (*US*)
Fredrica S. Friedman and Co. Inc. (*US*)
Furniss Lawton (*UK*)
The Gernert Company (*US*)
Frances Goldin Literary Agency, Inc. (*US*)
The Susan Golomb Literary Agency (*US*)
Goodman Associates (*US*)
Irene Goodman Literary Agency (*US*)
Graham Maw Christie Literary Agency (*UK*)
Kathryn Green Literary Agency, LLC (*US*)
Greene & Heaton Ltd (*UK*)
Laura Gross Literary Agency (*US*)
Hardman & Swainson (*UK*)
Antony Harwood Limited (*UK*)
John Hawkins & Associates, Inc. (*US*)
Rupert Heath Literary Agency (*UK*)
The Jeff Herman Agency, LLC (*US*)
hhb agency ltd (*UK*)
Hidden Value Group (*US*)
Kate Hordern Literary Agency (*UK*)
Amanda Howard Associates Ltd (*UK*)
Andrea Hurst Literary Management (*US*)
Jabberwocky Literary Agency (*US*)
Jill Grinberg Literary Management LLC (*US*)
Johnson & Alcock (*UK*)
Kilburn Literary Agency (*UK*)
Harvey Klinger, Inc (*US*)
Kneerim & Williams (*US*)
The Knight Agency (*US*)
Edite Kroll Literary Agency, Inc. (*US*)
The LA Literary Agency (*US*)
Laura Langlie, Literary Agent (*US*)
Sarah Lazin Books (*US*)
Robert Lecker Agency (*Can*)
Lescher & Lescher (*US*)
Lippincott Massie McQuilkin (*US*)
The Literary Group (*US*)
Literary Management Group, Inc. (*US*)
Andrew Lownie Literary Agency Ltd (*UK*)
The Jennifer Lyons Literary Agency, LLC (*US*)

Lyons Literary LLC (*US*)
MacGregor Literary (*US*)
Madeleine Milburn Literary Agency (*UK*)
Ricia Mainhardt Agency (RMA) (*US*)
Makepeace Towle Literary Agency (*UK*)
Kirsten Manges Literary Agency, LLC (*US*)
March Tenth, Inc. (*US*)
The Martell Agency (*US*)
Martin Literary Management (*US*)
McKernan Agency (*UK*)
Martha Millard Literary Agency (*US*)
The Jean V. Naggar Literary Agency (*US*)
Nelson Literary Agency, LLC (*US*)
Niad Management (*US*)
Objective Entertainment (*US*)
The Park Literary Group LLC (*US*)
Pavilion Literary Management (*US*)
Jonathan Pegg Literary Agency (*UK*)
The Poynor Group (*US*)
Prospect Agency (*US*)
Quicksilver Books Literary Agency (*US*)
Lynne Rabinoff Agency (*US*)
Raines & Raines (*US*)
Redhammer (*UK*)
Redwood Agency (*US*)
Rees Literary Agency (*US*)
The Amy Rennert Agency, Inc. (*US*)
The Lisa Richards Agency (*Ire*)
The Rudy Agency (*US*)
Marly Rusoff & Associates, Inc. (*US*)
Salkind Literary Agency (*US*)
Susan Schulman, A Literary Agency (*US*)
The Science Factory (*UK*)
Jonathan Scott, Inc (*US*)
Scribblers House LLC Literary Agency (*US*)
The Seven Bridges Group (*US*)
Sheil Land Associates Ltd (*UK*)
Jeffrey Simmons (*UK*)
Robert Smith Literary Agency Ltd (*UK*)
Rebecca Strong International Literary Agency (*US*)
The Strothman Agency (*US*)
The Stuart Agency (*US*)
The Swetky Agency and Associates (*US*)
Talcott Notch Literary (*US*)
Tessler Literary Agency (*US*)
Tom Lee (*US*)
TriadaUS Literary Agency, Inc. (*US*)
2M Literary Agency Ltd (*US*)
Venture Literary (*US*)
Beth Vesel Literary Agency (*US*)
The Ward & Balkin Agency, Inc (*US*)
Irene Webb Literary (*US*)
The Wendy Weil Agency, Inc. (*US*)
The Weingel-Fidel Agency (*US*)
Westwood Creative Artists (*Can*)
Whispering Buffalo Literary Agency Ltd (*UK*)
Eve White: Literary Agent (*UK*)
Wordserve Literary (*US*)
Writers' Representatives, LLC (*US*)
Yates & Yates (*US*)
The Zack Company, Inc (*US*)
Karen Gantz Zahler Literary Agency (*US*)

Helen Zimmermann Literary Agency (*US*)
Beauty and Fashion
Artellus Limited (*UK*)
Barbara Braun Associates, Inc. (*US*)
Rosica Colin Ltd (*UK*)
The Creative Culture, Inc. (*US*)
FinePrint Literary Management (*US*)
Antony Harwood Limited (*UK*)
Signature Literary Agency (*US*)
2M Literary Agency Ltd (*US*)
Venture Literary (*US*)
Whimsy Literary Agency, LLC (*US*)
Whispering Buffalo Literary Agency Ltd (*UK*)
Eve White: Literary Agent (*UK*)
Biography
Sheila Ableman Literary Agency (*UK*)
The Agency Group, Ltd (*US*)
Alive Communications, Inc (*US*)
Ambassador Speakers Bureau & Literary Agency (*US*)
The Ampersand Agency Ltd (*UK*)
Arcadia (*US*)
Artellus Limited (*UK*)
Robert Astle & Associates Literary Management, Inc. (*US*)
Audrey A. Wolf Literary Agency (*US*)
The August Agency LLC (*US*)
Barer Literary, LLC (*US*)
Bell Lomax Moreton Agency (*UK*)
Faye Bender Literary Agency (*US*)
Vicky Bijur Literary Agency (*US*)
David Black Literary Agency (*US*)
The Blumer Literary Agency, Inc. (*US*)
The Barbara Bova Literary Agency (*US*)
Brandon & Associates (*UK*)
Barbara Braun Associates, Inc. (*US*)
Paul Bresnick Literary Agency, LLC (*US*)
Brick House Literary Agents (*US*)
Rick Broadhead & Associates Literary Agency (*Can*)
Jenny Brown Associates (*UK*)
Marie Brown Associates, Inc. (*US*)
Andrea Brown Literary Agency, Inc. (*US*)
Tracy Brown Literary Agency (*US*)
Browne & Miller Literary Associates (*US*)
Felicity Bryan (*UK*)
Capel & Land Ltd (*UK*)
Carnicelli Literary Management (*US*)
Cedar Grove Agency Entertainment (*US*)
The Characters Talent Agency (*Can*)
Jane Chelius Literary Agency, Inc. (*US*)
Elyse Cheney Literary Associates, LLC (*US*)
The Choate Agency, LLC (*US*)
Cine/Lit Representation (*US*)
W.M. Clark Associates (*US*)
Rosica Colin Ltd (*UK*)
Conville & Walsh Ltd (*UK*)
The Core Group Talent Agency, Inc. (*Can*)
CowlesRyan Agency (*US*)
Creative Authors Ltd (*UK*)
The Croce Agency (*US*)
Curtis Brown Group Ltd (*UK*)
Richard Curtis Associates, Inc. (*US*)

David Luxton Associates (*UK*)
The Jennifer DeChiara Literary Agency (*US*)
Joëlle Delbourgo Associates, Inc. (*US*)
Donadio & Olson, Inc. (*US*)
Jim Donovan Literary (*US*)
Dupree / Miller and Associates Inc. Literary (*US*)
Dystel & Goderich Literary Management (*US*)
Edwards Fuglewicz (*UK*)
Judith Ehrlich Literary Management (*US*)
Felicia Eth Literary Representation (*US*)
Fairbank Literary Representation (*US*)
Farris Literary Agency, Inc. (*US*)
Diana Finch Literary Agency (*US*)
FinePrint Literary Management (*US*)
Fox Mason Ltd (*UK*)
Fox & Howard Literary Agency (*UK*)
Fredrica S. Friedman and Co. Inc. (*US*)
Furniss Lawton (*UK*)
The Gernert Company (*US*)
David Godwin Associates (*UK*)
The Susan Golomb Literary Agency (*US*)
Goodman Associates (*US*)
Graham Maw Christie Literary Agency (*UK*)
Kathryn Green Literary Agency, LLC (*US*)
Greene & Heaton Ltd (*UK*)
Laura Gross Literary Agency (*US*)
Marianne Gunn O'Connor Literary Agency (*Ire*)
Antony Harwood Limited (*UK*)
John Hawkins & Associates, Inc. (*US*)
Rupert Heath Literary Agency (*UK*)
hhb agency ltd (*UK*)
Hidden Value Group (*US*)
David Higham Associates Ltd (*UK*)
Hilary Churchley Literary Agent (*UK*)
International Transactions, Inc. (*US*)
Jabberwocky Literary Agency (*US*)
Jill Grinberg Literary Management LLC (*US*)
Johnson & Alcock (*UK*)
Charlene Kay Agency (*Can*)
Frances Kelly (*UK*)
Kilburn Literary Agency (*UK*)
Harvey Klinger, Inc (*US*)
Kneerim & Williams (*US*)
Edite Kroll Literary Agency, Inc. (*US*)
The LA Literary Agency (*US*)
Laura Langlie, Literary Agent (*US*)
Sarah Lazin Books (*US*)
Robert Lecker Agency (*Can*)
Lescher & Lescher (*US*)
Lippincott Massie McQuilkin (*US*)
The Literary Group (*US*)
Literary Management Group, Inc. (*US*)
Julia Lord Literary Management (*US*)
Andrew Lownie Literary Agency Ltd (*UK*)
The Jennifer Lyons Literary Agency, LLC (*US*)
Lyons Literary LLC (*US*)
MacGregor Literary (*US*)
Ricia Mainhardt Agency (RMA) (*US*)
March Tenth, Inc. (*US*)
Denise Marcil Literary Agency, Inc. (*US*)
Martin Literary Management (*US*)
MBA Literary Agents Ltd (*UK*)
Duncan McAra (*UK*)

McKernan Agency (*UK*)
Martha Millard Literary Agency (*US*)
William Morris Endeavor Entertainment (UK)
Ltd (*UK*)
The Jean V. Naggar Literary Agency (*US*)
Niad Management (*US*)
MNLA (Maggie Noach Literary Agency) (*UK*)
Northern Lights Literary Services (*US*)
Objective Entertainment (*US*)
John Pawsey (*UK*)
Maggie Pearlstine Associates Ltd (*UK*)
Jonathan Pegg Literary Agency (*UK*)
Barry Perelman Agency (*US*)
Alièka Pistek Literary Agency, LLC (*US*)
The Poynor Group (*US*)
Quicksilver Books Literary Agency (*US*)
Lynne Rabinoff Agency (*US*)
Raines & Raines (*US*)
Rees Literary Agency (*US*)
Regal Literary (*UK*)
Regal Literary Inc. (*US*)
The Amy Rennert Agency, Inc. (*US*)
The Lisa Richards Agency (*Ire*)
Robert Dudley Agency (*UK*)
The Rudy Agency (*US*)
Marly Rusoff & Associates, Inc. (*US*)
Salkind Literary Agency (*US*)
The Sayle Literary Agency (*UK*)
Susan Schulman, A Literary Agency (*US*)
The Science Factory (*UK*)
Scribblers House LLC Literary Agency (*US*)
Lynn Seligman, Literary Agent (*US*)
The Seven Bridges Group (*US*)
Denise Shannon Literary Agency, Inc. (*US*)
Sheil Land Associates Ltd (*UK*)
Signature Literary Agency (*US*)
Dorie Simmonds Agency (*UK*)
Jeffrey Simmons (*UK*)
Sinclair-Stevenson (*UK*)
Robert Smith Literary Agency Ltd (*UK*)
Rebecca Strong International Literary Agency
(*US*)
Tessler Literary Agency (*US*)
Timberlake Literary Services, LLC (*US*)
TriadaUS Literary Agency, Inc. (*US*)
Jane Turnbull (*UK*)
United Agents (*UK*)
Venture Literary (*US*)
Beth Vesel Literary Agency (*US*)
The Ward & Balkin Agency, Inc (*US*)
A.P. Watt Ltd (*UK*)
The Weingel-Fidel Agency (*US*)
Westwood Creative Artists (*Can*)
Eve White: Literary Agent (*UK*)
Wordserve Literary (*US*)
Writers' Representatives, LLC (*US*)
Yates & Yates (*US*)
The Zack Company, Inc (*US*)
Business
The Agency Group, Ltd (*US*)
Alive Communications, Inc (*US*)
Arcadia (*US*)
Audrey A. Wolf Literary Agency (*US*)

The August Agency LLC (*US*)
AVAnti Productions & Management (*UK*)
Bell Lomax Moreton Agency (*UK*)
David Black Literary Agency (*US*)
The Blumer Literary Agency, Inc. (*US*)
BookEnds, LLC (*US*)
Rick Broadhead & Associates Literary Agency
(*Can*)
Marie Brown Associates, Inc. (*US*)
Browne & Miller Literary Associates (*US*)
Carnicelli Literary Management (*US*)
Elyse Cheney Literary Associates, LLC (*US*)
Edward B. Claflin Literary Agency, LLC (*US*)
Creative Authors Ltd (*UK*)
Richard Curtis Associates, Inc. (*US*)
Liza Dawson Associates (*US*)
Joëlle Delbourgo Associates, Inc. (*US*)
Jim Donovan Literary (*US*)
Dupree / Miller and Associates Inc. Literary (*US*)
Dystel & Goderich Literary Management (*US*)
Ebeling & Associates (*US*)
Judith Ehrlich Literary Management (*US*)
Felicia Eth Literary Representation (*US*)
Farris Literary Agency, Inc. (*US*)
Diana Finch Literary Agency (*US*)
FinePrint Literary Management (*US*)
Fox & Howard Literary Agency (*UK*)
Fresh Books Literary Agency (*US*)
Fredrica S. Friedman and Co. Inc. (*US*)
Furniss Lawton (*UK*)
The Susan Golomb Literary Agency (*US*)
Goodman Associates (*US*)
Graham Maw Christie Literary Agency (*UK*)
Ashley Grayson Literary Agency (*US*)
Kathryn Green Literary Agency, LLC (*US*)
Antony Harwood Limited (*UK*)
The Jeff Herman Agency, LLC (*US*)
hhb agency ltd (*UK*)
Hidden Value Group (*US*)
Kate Hordern Literary Agency (*UK*)
Andrea Hurst Literary Management (*US*)
InkWell Management (*US*)
Jabberwocky Literary Agency (*US*)
Jill Grinberg Literary Management LLC (*US*)
Frances Kelly (*UK*)
Kilburn Literary Agency (*UK*)
Kneerim & Williams (*US*)
The Knight Agency (*US*)
The LA Literary Agency (*US*)
LaunchBooks Literary Agency (*US*)
Literary Management Group, Inc. (*US*)
Lowenstein Associates, Inc. (*US*)
MacGregor Literary (*US*)
Denise Marcil Literary Agency, Inc. (*US*)
The Martell Agency (*US*)
Martin Literary Management (*US*)
The Michael Greer Literary Agency (*UK*)
Martha Millard Literary Agency (*US*)
Northern Lights Literary Services (*US*)
Objective Entertainment (*US*)
The Poynor Group (*US*)
Queen Literary Agency, Inc. (*US*)
Quicksilver Books Literary Agency (*US*)

Lynne Rabinoff Agency (*US*)
Redwood Agency (*US*)
Rees Literary Agency (*US*)
The Amy Rennert Agency, Inc. (*US*)
Robert Dudley Agency (*UK*)
The Rudy Agency (*US*)
Marly Rusoff & Associates, Inc. (*US*)
Salkind Literary Agency (*US*)
Susan Schulman, A Literary Agency (*US*)
Jonathan Scott, Inc (*US*)
Scribblers House LLC Literary Agency (*US*)
Lynn Seligman, Literary Agent (*US*)
Denise Shannon Literary Agency, Inc. (*US*)
Rebecca Strong International Literary Agency
(*US*)
The Strothman Agency (*US*)
The Stuart Agency (*US*)
The Swetky Agency and Associates (*US*)
Talcott Notch Literary (*US*)
Tessler Literary Agency (*US*)
Timberlake Literary Services, LLC (*US*)
2M Literary Agency Ltd (*US*)
Venture Literary (*US*)
Veritas Literary Agency (*US*)
Beth Vesel Literary Agency (*US*)
Watson, Little Ltd (*UK*)
Whimsy Literary Agency, LLC (*US*)
Eve White: Literary Agent (*UK*)
Writers' Representatives, LLC (*US*)
Yates & Yates (*US*)
The Zack Company, Inc (*US*)
Cookery
The Agency Group, Ltd (*US*)
Bidnick & Company (*US*)
Vicky Bijur Literary Agency (*US*)
The Blumer Literary Agency, Inc. (*US*)
Brick House Literary Agents (*US*)
Browne & Miller Literary Associates (*US*)
The Choate Agency, LLC (*US*)
Edward B. Claflin Literary Agency, LLC (*US*)
Rosica Colin Ltd (*UK*)
CowlesRyan Agency (*US*)
The Creative Culture, Inc. (*US*)
Creative Authors Ltd (*UK*)
The Culinary Entertainment Agency (CEA) (*US*)
The Jennifer DeChiara Literary Agency (*US*)
Dupree / Miller and Associates Inc. Literary (*US*)
Dystel & Goderich Literary Management (*US*)
Einstein Thompson Agency (*US*)
Fairbank Literary Representation (*US*)
FinePrint Literary Management (*US*)
Fox Mason Ltd (*UK*)
Sarah Jane Freymann Literary Agency (*US*)
Fredrica S. Friedman and Co. Inc. (*US*)
Furniss Lawton (*UK*)
Goodman Associates (*US*)
Irene Goodman Literary Agency (*US*)
Kathryn Green Literary Agency, LLC (*US*)
Greene & Heaton Ltd (*UK*)
Antony Harwood Limited (*UK*)
Rupert Heath Literary Agency (*UK*)
hhb agency ltd (*UK*)
Andrea Hurst Literary Management (*US*)

Jabberwocky Literary Agency (*US*)
Frances Kelly (*UK*)
Harvey Klinger, Inc (*US*)
KT Public Relations (*US*)
The LA Literary Agency (*US*)
Robert Lecker Agency (*Can*)
Lescher & Lescher (*US*)
The Lisa Ekus Group, LLC (*US*)
The Literary Group (*US*)
The Jennifer Lyons Literary Agency, LLC (*US*)
Lyons Literary LLC (*US*)
Kirsten Manges Literary Agency, LLC (*US*)
Martha Millard Literary Agency (*US*)
Objective Entertainment (*US*)
The Poynor Group (*US*)
Queen Literary Agency, Inc. (*US*)
Quicksilver Books Literary Agency (*US*)
Redwood Agency (*US*)
Salkind Literary Agency (*US*)
Susan Schulman, A Literary Agency (*US*)
Jonathan Scott, Inc (*US*)
Lynn Seligman, Literary Agent (*US*)
Sheil Land Associates Ltd (*UK*)
Valerie Smith, Literary Agent (*US*)
The Swetky Agency and Associates (*US*)
Talcott Notch Literary (*US*)
Tessler Literary Agency (*US*)
Thomas Moore Literary Agency (*UK*)
TriadaUS Literary Agency, Inc. (*US*)
2M Literary Agency Ltd (*US*)
Venture Literary (*US*)
Whimsy Literary Agency, LLC (*US*)
Eve White: Literary Agent (*UK*)
Writers' Representatives, LLC (*US*)
The Zack Company, Inc (*US*)
Karen Gantz Zahler Literary Agency (*US*)
Helen Zimmermann Literary Agency (*US*)
Crafts
AVAnti Productions & Management (*UK*)
The Blumer Literary Agency, Inc. (*US*)
Browne & Miller Literary Associates (*US*)
Creative Authors Ltd (*UK*)
The Jennifer DeChiara Literary Agency (*US*)
Dupree / Miller and Associates Inc. Literary (*US*)
The Epstein Literary Agency (*US*)
Fairbank Literary Representation (*US*)
The Gernert Company (*US*)
Graham Maw Christie Literary Agency (*UK*)
Antony Harwood Limited (*UK*)
KT Public Relations (*US*)
MBA Literary Agents Ltd (*UK*)
Salkind Literary Agency (*US*)
Talcott Notch Literary (*US*)
Thomas Moore Literary Agency (*UK*)
Venture Literary (*US*)
Eve White: Literary Agent (*UK*)
Crime
Abela Literature (*Can*)
The Agency Group, Ltd (*US*)
Alive Communications, Inc (*US*)
The Ampersand Agency Ltd (*UK*)
Arcadia (*US*)
Artellus Limited (*UK*)

Author Rights Agency (*Ire*)
AVAnti Productions & Management (*UK*)
The Bent Agency (*US*)
The Blumer Literary Agency, Inc. (*US*)
Luigi Bonomi Associates Ltd (*UK*)
BookEnds, LLC (*US*)
The Barbara Bova Literary Agency (*US*)
Brandon & Associates (*UK*)
The Joan Brandt Agency (*US*)
Paul Bresnick Literary Agency, LLC (*US*)
Jenny Brown Associates (*UK*)
Browne & Miller Literary Associates (*US*)
Juliet Burton Literary Agency (*UK*)
Cedar Grove Agency Entertainment (*US*)
Mic Cheetham Literary Agency (*UK*)
Teresa Chris Literary Agency Ltd (*UK*)
Rosica Colin Ltd (*UK*)
Conville & Walsh Ltd (*UK*)
Coombs Moylett Literary Agency (*UK*)
The Core Group Talent Agency, Inc. (*Can*)
Creative Authors Ltd (*UK*)
Curtis Brown Group Ltd (*UK*)
The Jennifer DeChiara Literary Agency (*US*)
Jim Donovan Literary (*US*)
Dorian Literary Agency (DLA) (*UK*)
Dupree / Miller and Associates Inc. Literary (*US*)
Dystel & Goderich Literary Management (*US*)
Einstein Thompson Agency (*US*)
Felicia Eth Literary Representation (*US*)
Farris Literary Agency, Inc. (*US*)
Diana Finch Literary Agency (*US*)
FinePrint Literary Management (*US*)
Fox Mason Ltd (*UK*)
Samuel French, Inc. (*US*)
Sarah Jane Freymann Literary Agency (*US*)
Fredrica S. Friedman and Co. Inc. (*US*)
Furniss Lawton (*UK*)
Goodman Associates (*US*)
Ashley Grayson Literary Agency (*US*)
Kathryn Green Literary Agency, LLC (*US*)
Greene & Heaton Ltd (*UK*)
Gregory & Company, Authors' Agents (*UK*)
Hardman & Swainson (*UK*)
Antony Harwood Limited (*UK*)
John Hawkins & Associates, Inc. (*US*)
A M Heath & Company Limited, Author's
Agents (*UK*)
Rupert Heath Literary Agency (*UK*)
The Jeff Herman Agency, LLC (*US*)
hhb agency ltd (*UK*)
Hidden Value Group (*US*)
Vanessa Holt Ltd (*UK*)
Kate Hordern Literary Agency (*UK*)
Andrea Hurst Literary Management (*US*)
InkWell Management (*US*)
International Transactions, Inc. (*US*)
Jabberwocky Literary Agency (*US*)
Harvey Klinger, Inc (*US*)
The Candace Lake Agency (*US*)
Peter Lampack Agency, Inc (*US*)
Laura Langlie, Literary Agent (*US*)
Robert Lecker Agency (*Can*)
The Lez Barstow Agency (*UK*)

Lippincott Massie McQuilkin (*US*)
The Literary Group (*US*)
Lowenstein Associates, Inc. (*US*)
Lyons Literary LLC (*US*)
Donald Maass Literary Agency (*US*)
MacGregor Literary (*US*)
Madeleine Milburn Literary Agency (*UK*)
Ricia Mainhardt Agency (RMA) (*US*)
Martin Literary Management (*US*)
McKernan Agency (*UK*)
Martha Millard Literary Agency (*US*)
Monteiro Rose Dravis Agency, Inc. (*US*)
Judith Murdoch Literary Agency (*UK*)
Niad Management (*US*)
Prospect Agency (*US*)
Quicksilver Books Literary Agency (*US*)
Raines & Raines (*US*)
Rocking Chair Books (*UK*)
Salkind Literary Agency (*US*)
The Sayle Literary Agency (*UK*)
Susan Schulman, A Literary Agency (*US*)
Secret Agent Man (*US*)
Lynn Seligman, Literary Agent (*US*)
The Seven Bridges Group (*US*)
Sheil Land Associates Ltd (*UK*)
Signature Literary Agency (*US*)
Jeffrey Simmons (*UK*)
Robert Smith Literary Agency Ltd (*UK*)
South West Artists (*UK*)
The Swetky Agency and Associates (*US*)
SYLA - Susan Yearwood Literary Agency (*UK*)
Talcott Notch Literary (*US*)
Timberlake Literary Services, LLC (*US*)
Tom Lee (*US*)
TriadaUS Literary Agency, Inc. (*US*)
2M Literary Agency Ltd (*US*)
Venture Literary (*US*)
Veritas Literary Agency (*US*)
Beth Vesel Literary Agency (*US*)
Watson, Little Ltd (*UK*)
Irene Webb Literary (*US*)
Eve White: Literary Agent (*UK*)
The Zack Company, Inc (*US*)
Criticism
AVAnti Productions & Management (*UK*)
The Blumer Literary Agency, Inc. (*US*)
Barbara Braun Associates, Inc. (*US*)
The Jennifer DeChiara Literary Agency (*US*)
Goodman Associates (*US*)
Antony Harwood Limited (*UK*)
Hidden Value Group (*US*)
Quicksilver Books Literary Agency (*US*)
Signature Literary Agency (*US*)
The Swetky Agency and Associates (*US*)
Timberlake Literary Services, LLC (*US*)
Venture Literary (*US*)
Beth Vesel Literary Agency (*US*)
Eve White: Literary Agent (*UK*)
Writers' Representatives, LLC (*US*)
Culture
The Agency Group, Ltd (*US*)
Miriam Altshuler Literary Agency (*US*)

Ambassador Speakers Bureau & Literary Agency (*US*)
Arcadia (*US*)
Artellus Limited (*UK*)
Robert Astle & Associates Literary Management, Inc. (*US*)
The August Agency LLC (*US*)
AVAnti Productions & Management (*UK*)
Barer Literary, LLC (*US*)
Faye Bender Literary Agency (*US*)
The Blumer Literary Agency, Inc. (*US*)
BookEnds, LLC (*US*)
Barbara Braun Associates, Inc. (*US*)
Paul Bresnick Literary Agency, LLC (*US*)
Brick House Literary Agents (*US*)
Rick Broadhead & Associates Literary Agency (*Can*)
Jenny Brown Associates (*UK*)
Andrea Brown Literary Agency, Inc. (*US*)
Browne & Miller Literary Associates (*US*)
Carnicelli Literary Management (*US*)
Chalberg & Sussman (*US*)
Jane Chelius Literary Agency, Inc. (*US*)
Elyse Cheney Literary Associates, LLC (*US*)
Cine/Lit Representation (*US*)
W.M. Clark Associates (*US*)
The Cooke Agency (*Can*)
CowlesRyan Agency (*US*)
The Creative Rights Agency (*UK*)
The Creative Culture, Inc. (*US*)
Creative Authors Ltd (*UK*)
David Luxton Associates (*UK*)
The Jennifer DeChiara Literary Agency (*US*)
Joëlle Delbourgo Associates, Inc. (*US*)
Donadio & Olson, Inc. (*US*)
Jim Donovan Literary (*US*)
Dunow, Carlson & Lerner Agency (*US*)
Dupree / Miller and Associates Inc. Literary (*US*)
Dystel & Goderich Literary Management (*US*)
Edwards Fuglewicz (*UK*)
Judith Ehrlich Literary Management (*US*)
Einstein Thompson Agency (*US*)
Felicia Eth Literary Representation (*US*)
Fairbank Literary Representation (*US*)
Farris Literary Agency, Inc. (*US*)
Diana Finch Literary Agency (*US*)
FinePrint Literary Management (*US*)
The James Fitzgerald Agency (*US*)
Fox Mason Ltd (*UK*)
Fox & Howard Literary Agency (*UK*)
Sarah Jane Freymann Literary Agency (*US*)
Fredrica S. Friedman and Co. Inc. (*US*)
Frances Goldin Literary Agency, Inc. (*US*)
The Susan Golomb Literary Agency (*US*)
Goodman Associates (*US*)
Irene Goodman Literary Agency (*US*)
Graham Maw Christie Literary Agency (*UK*)
Ashley Grayson Literary Agency (*US*)
Kathryn Green Literary Agency, LLC (*US*)
Greene & Heaton Ltd (*UK*)
Laura Gross Literary Agency (*US*)
Joy Harris Literary Agency, Inc. (*US*)
Antony Harwood Limited (*UK*)

Rupert Heath Literary Agency (*UK*)
The Jeff Herman Agency, LLC (*US*)
hhb agency ltd (*UK*)
Kate Hordern Literary Agency (*UK*)
Jabberwocky Literary Agency (*US*)
Jill Grinberg Literary Management LLC (*US*)
Johnson & Alcock (*UK*)
Harvey Klinger, Inc (*US*)
Kneerim & Williams (*US*)
The Knight Agency (*US*)
Edite Kroll Literary Agency, Inc. (*US*)
The Candace Lake Agency (*US*)
Laura Langlie, Literary Agent (*US*)
LaunchBooks Literary Agency (*US*)
Sarah Lazin Books (*US*)
Robert Lecker Agency (*Can*)
Lescher & Lescher (*US*)
Lippincott Massie McQuilkin (*US*)
The Jennifer Lyons Literary Agency, LLC (*US*)
MacGregor Literary (*US*)
Ricia Mainhardt Agency (RMA) (*US*)
Makepeace Towle Literary Agency (*UK*)
Kirsten Manges Literary Agency, LLC (*US*)
March Tenth, Inc. (*US*)
Martha Millard Literary Agency (*US*)
Howard Morhaim Literary Agency (*US*)
The Jean V. Naggar Literary Agency (*US*)
Nappaland Literary Agency (*US*)
New Leaf Literary & Media, Inc. (*US*)
Niad Management (*US*)
Objective Entertainment (*US*)
The Park Literary Group LLC (*US*)
Jonathan Pegg Literary Agency (*UK*)
The Poynor Group (*US*)
Quicksilver Books Literary Agency (*US*)
Lynne Rabinoff Agency (*US*)
Redwood Agency (*US*)
Renee Zuckerbrot Literary Agency (*US*)
The Lisa Richards Agency (*Ire*)
Rocking Chair Books (*UK*)
Andy Ross Agency (*US*)
The Rudy Agency (*US*)
Marly Rusoff & Associates, Inc. (*US*)
Salkind Literary Agency (*US*)
Susan Schulman, A Literary Agency (*US*)
Scribblers House LLC Literary Agency (*US*)
Lynn Seligman, Literary Agent (*US*)
The Seven Bridges Group (*US*)
Signature Literary Agency (*US*)
Robert Smith Literary Agency Ltd (*UK*)
The Strothman Agency (*US*)
The Swetky Agency and Associates (*US*)
Thomas Moore Literary Agency (*UK*)
Timberlake Literary Services, LLC (*US*)
TriadaUS Literary Agency, Inc. (*US*)
2M Literary Agency Ltd (*US*)
Venture Literary (*US*)
Veritas Literary Agency (*US*)
Beth Vesel Literary Agency (*US*)
The Ward & Balkin Agency, Inc (*US*)
Irene Webb Literary (*US*)
The Wendy Weil Agency, Inc. (*US*)
Whimsy Literary Agency, LLC (*US*)

Literary Agents Subject Index   101

Eve White: Literary Agent (*UK*)
Wolfson Literary Agency (*US*)
Wordserve Literary (*US*)
Helen Zimmermann Literary Agency (*US*)
Current Affairs
Ambassador Speakers Bureau & Literary Agency (*US*)
The Ampersand Agency Ltd (*UK*)
Arcadia (*US*)
Artellus Limited (*UK*)
Audrey A. Wolf Literary Agency (*US*)
The August Agency LLC (*US*)
AVAnti Productions & Management (*UK*)
BookEnds, LLC (*US*)
Brandon & Associates (*UK*)
Rick Broadhead & Associates Literary Agency (*Can*)
Andrea Brown Literary Agency, Inc. (*US*)
Tracy Brown Literary Agency (*US*)
Browne & Miller Literary Associates (*US*)
Felicity Bryan (*UK*)
Carnicelli Literary Management (*US*)
Elyse Cheney Literary Associates, LLC (*US*)
Judith Chilcote Agency (*UK*)
The Choate Agency, LLC (*US*)
Edward B. Claflin Literary Agency, LLC (*US*)
W.M. Clark Associates (*US*)
Rosica Colin Ltd (*UK*)
Conville & Walsh Ltd (*UK*)
CowlesRyan Agency (*US*)
The Creative Culture, Inc. (*US*)
The Jennifer DeChiara Literary Agency (*US*)
Joëlle Delbourgo Associates, Inc. (*US*)
Jim Donovan Literary (*US*)
Dupree / Miller and Associates Inc. Literary (*US*)
Dystel & Goderich Literary Management (*US*)
Judith Ehrlich Literary Management (*US*)
Felicia Eth Literary Representation (*US*)
Farris Literary Agency, Inc. (*US*)
Diana Finch Literary Agency (*US*)
Fredrica S. Friedman and Co. Inc. (*US*)
The Gernert Company (*US*)
Mark Gilroy Communications, Inc. (*US*)
The Susan Golomb Literary Agency (*US*)
Goodman Associates (*US*)
Kathryn Green Literary Agency, LLC (*US*)
Greene & Heaton Ltd (*UK*)
Laura Gross Literary Agency (*US*)
Antony Harwood Limited (*UK*)
John Hawkins & Associates, Inc. (*US*)
Rupert Heath Literary Agency (*UK*)
David Higham Associates Ltd (*UK*)
Kate Hordern Literary Agency (*UK*)
Andrea Hurst Literary Management (*US*)
InkWell Management (*US*)
Jabberwocky Literary Agency (*US*)
Jill Grinberg Literary Management LLC (*US*)
Johnson & Alcock (*UK*)
Kneerim & Williams (*US*)
Edite Kroll Literary Agency, Inc. (*US*)
Laura Langlie, Literary Agent (*US*)
LaunchBooks Literary Agency (*US*)
Sarah Lazin Books (*US*)

Lescher & Lescher (*US*)
Lippincott Massie McQuilkin (*US*)
The Literary Group (*US*)
Andrew Lownie Literary Agency Ltd (*UK*)
The Jennifer Lyons Literary Agency, LLC (*US*)
Lyons Literary LLC (*US*)
MacGregor Literary (*US*)
Ricia Mainhardt Agency (RMA) (*US*)
Makepeace Towle Literary Agency (*UK*)
March Tenth, Inc. (*US*)
Martin Literary Management (*US*)
McKernan Agency (*UK*)
Martha Millard Literary Agency (*US*)
The Jean V. Naggar Literary Agency (*US*)
Objective Entertainment (*US*)
Maggie Pearlstine Associates Ltd (*UK*)
Jonathan Pegg Literary Agency (*UK*)
Alièka Pistek Literary Agency, LLC (*US*)
Quicksilver Books Literary Agency (*US*)
Lynne Rabinoff Agency (*US*)
Redhammer (*UK*)
Robert Dudley Agency (*UK*)
Rocking Chair Books (*UK*)
Andy Ross Agency (*US*)
Salkind Literary Agency (*US*)
The Sayle Literary Agency (*UK*)
Susan Schulman, A Literary Agency (*US*)
The Science Factory (*UK*)
Lynn Seligman, Literary Agent (*US*)
The Seven Bridges Group (*US*)
Denise Shannon Literary Agency, Inc. (*US*)
Signature Literary Agency (*US*)
Jeffrey Simmons (*UK*)
Sinclair-Stevenson (*UK*)
The Strothman Agency (*US*)
The Stuart Agency (*US*)
The Swetky Agency and Associates (*US*)
Timberlake Literary Services, LLC (*US*)
TriadaUS Literary Agency, Inc. (*US*)
Jane Turnbull (*UK*)
Venture Literary (*US*)
The Wendy Weil Agency, Inc. (*US*)
Westwood Creative Artists (*Can*)
Eve White: Literary Agent (*UK*)
Wordserve Literary (*US*)
Writers' Representatives, LLC (*US*)
Yates & Yates (*US*)
The Zack Company, Inc (*US*)
Design
The Agency Group, Ltd (*US*)
The Blumer Literary Agency, Inc. (*US*)
Barbara Braun Associates, Inc. (*US*)
Andrea Brown Literary Agency, Inc. (*US*)
W.M. Clark Associates (*US*)
The Jennifer DeChiara Literary Agency (*US*)
Fairbank Literary Representation (*US*)
Fresh Books Literary Agency (*US*)
Fredrica S. Friedman and Co. Inc. (*US*)
Kathryn Green Literary Agency, LLC (*US*)
Antony Harwood Limited (*UK*)
Johnson & Alcock (*UK*)
Martha Millard Literary Agency (*US*)
Marly Rusoff & Associates, Inc. (*US*)

Lynn Seligman, Literary Agent (*US*)
The Swetky Agency and Associates (*US*)
Thomas Moore Literary Agency (*UK*)
Venture Literary (*US*)
Whispering Buffalo Literary Agency Ltd (*UK*)
Eve White: Literary Agent (*UK*)
Karen Gantz Zahler Literary Agency (*US*)
Drama
Abela Literature (*Can*)
Abrams Artists Agency (*US*)
Robert Astle & Associates Literary Management, Inc. (*US*)
AVAnti Productions & Management (*UK*)
Andrea Brown Literary Agency, Inc. (*US*)
The Characters Talent Agency (*Can*)
The Core Group Talent Agency, Inc. (*Can*)
Jill Foster Ltd (JFL) (*UK*)
Full Throttle Literary Agency (*US*)
Roger Hancock Ltd (*UK*)
Antony Harwood Limited (*UK*)
Charlene Kay Agency (*Can*)
Knight Hall Agency (*UK*)
The Candace Lake Agency (*US*)
The Lez Barstow Agency (*UK*)
Monteiro Rose Dravis Agency, Inc. (*US*)
Niad Management (*US*)
PBJ and JBJ Management (*UK*)
Barry Perelman Agency (*US*)
The Seven Bridges Group (*US*)
Sheil Land Associates Ltd (*UK*)
South West Artists (*UK*)
The Tennyson Agency (*UK*)
Thomas Moore Literary Agency (*UK*)
Tom Lee (*US*)
Venture Literary (*US*)
Eve White: Literary Agent (*UK*)
Entertainment
The Agency Group, Ltd (*US*)
Artellus Limited (*UK*)
The August Agency LLC (*US*)
AVAnti Productions & Management (*UK*)
Brandon & Associates (*UK*)
Farris Literary Agency, Inc. (*US*)
FinePrint Literary Management (*US*)
Roger Hancock Ltd (*UK*)
Antony Harwood Limited (*UK*)
hhb agency ltd (*UK*)
The Knight Agency (*US*)
Robert Lecker Agency (*Can*)
Andrew Lownie Literary Agency Ltd (*UK*)
Lyons Literary LLC (*US*)
Martin Literary Management (*US*)
New Leaf Literary & Media, Inc. (*US*)
Rocking Chair Books (*UK*)
The Seven Bridges Group (*US*)
Robert Smith Literary Agency Ltd (*UK*)
South West Artists (*UK*)
Thomas Moore Literary Agency (*UK*)
Timberlake Literary Services, LLC (*US*)
Venture Literary (*US*)
Whimsy Literary Agency, LLC (*US*)
Whispering Buffalo Literary Agency Ltd (*UK*)
Eve White: Literary Agent (*UK*)

The Zack Company, Inc (*US*)
Karen Gantz Zahler Literary Agency (*US*)
Erotic
Brown Literary Agency (*US*)
The Characters Talent Agency (*Can*)
Rosica Colin Ltd (*UK*)
The Core Group Talent Agency, Inc. (*Can*)
Elaine P. English, Attorney & Literary Agent (*US*)
Goodman Associates (*US*)
Antony Harwood Limited (*UK*)
Robert Lecker Agency (*Can*)
New Leaf Literary & Media, Inc. (*US*)
Prospect Agency (*US*)
Spencerhill Associates (*US*)
The Swetky Agency and Associates (*US*)
Tom Lee (*US*)
Venture Literary (*US*)
Veritas Literary Agency (*US*)
Eve White: Literary Agent (*UK*)
The Zack Company, Inc (*US*)
Fantasy
Abela Literature (*Can*)
Artellus Limited (*UK*)
Author Rights Agency (*Ire*)
AVAnti Productions & Management (*UK*)
The Bent Agency (*US*)
BookEnds, LLC (*US*)
Andrea Brown Literary Agency, Inc. (*US*)
The Characters Talent Agency (*Can*)
Mic Cheetham Literary Agency (*UK*)
Rosica Colin Ltd (*UK*)
The Cooke Agency (*Can*)
The Core Group Talent Agency, Inc. (*Can*)
Curtis Brown Group Ltd (*UK*)
Liza Dawson Associates (*US*)
The Jennifer DeChiara Literary Agency (*US*)
Dorian Literary Agency (DLA) (*UK*)
Judith Ehrlich Literary Management (*US*)
Elaine P. English, Attorney & Literary Agent (*US*)
FinePrint Literary Management (*US*)
Fox Mason Ltd (*UK*)
Samuel French, Inc. (*US*)
Furniss Lawton (*UK*)
The Gernert Company (*US*)
Irene Goodman Literary Agency (*US*)
Ashley Grayson Literary Agency (*US*)
Antony Harwood Limited (*UK*)
Hidden Value Group (*US*)
Andrea Hurst Literary Management (*US*)
Jill Grinberg Literary Management LLC (*US*)
Charlene Kay Agency (*Can*)
Virginia Kidd Agency, Inc (*US*)
Harvey Klinger, Inc (*US*)
The Knight Agency (*US*)
KT Public Relations (*US*)
The Candace Lake Agency (*US*)
The Literary Group (*US*)
London Independent Books (*UK*)
Lowenstein Associates, Inc. (*US*)
The Jennifer Lyons Literary Agency, LLC (*US*)
Lyons Literary LLC (*US*)

Donald Maass Literary Agency (*US*)
Ricia Mainhardt Agency (RMA) (*US*)
Makepeace Towle Literary Agency (*UK*)
Martha Millard Literary Agency (*US*)
Howard Morhaim Literary Agency (*US*)
The Jean V. Naggar Literary Agency (*US*)
Nelson Literary Agency, LLC (*US*)
New Leaf Literary & Media, Inc. (*US*)
Objective Entertainment (*US*)
Pavilion Literary Management (*US*)
Prospect Agency (*US*)
Raines & Raines (*US*)
Salkind Literary Agency (*US*)
Scribe Agency LLC (*US*)
Lynn Seligman, Literary Agent (*US*)
The Seymour Agency (*US*)
Sheil Land Associates Ltd (*UK*)
Valerie Smith, Literary Agent (*US*)
South West Artists (*UK*)
Spectrum Literary Agency (*US*)
Spencerhill Associates (*US*)
Sternig & Byrne Literary Agency (*US*)
The Swetky Agency and Associates (*US*)
Talcott Notch Literary (*US*)
Tom Lee (*US*)
Veritas Literary Agency (*US*)
Eve White: Literary Agent (*UK*)
Wordserve Literary (*US*)
The Zack Company, Inc (*US*)
Fiction
A+B Works (*US*)
Abela Literature (*Can*)
Adams Literary (*US*)
The Agency Group, Ltd (*US*)
Agency for the Performing Arts (APA) (*US*)
Aimee Entertainment Agency (*US*)
Aitken Alexander Associates (*UK*)
Alive Communications, Inc (*US*)
Miriam Altshuler Literary Agency (*US*)
Ambassador Speakers Bureau & Literary Agency (*US*)
The Ampersand Agency Ltd (*UK*)
Arcadia (*US*)
Artellus Limited (*UK*)
Robert Astle & Associates Literary Management, Inc. (*US*)
The August Agency LLC (*US*)
Author Literary Agents (*UK*)
Author Rights Agency (*Ire*)
AVAnti Productions & Management (*UK*)
Avenue A Literary LLC (*US*)
Barer Literary, LLC (*US*)
Bell Lomax Moreton Agency (*UK*)
Lorella Belli Literary Agency (LBLA) (*UK*)
Faye Bender Literary Agency (*US*)
The Bent Agency (*US*)
Vicky Bijur Literary Agency (*US*)
David Black Literary Agency (*US*)
Blake Friedmann Literary Agency Ltd (*UK*)
The Blumer Literary Agency, Inc. (*US*)
Luigi Bonomi Associates Ltd (*UK*)
BookEnds, LLC (*US*)
Books & Such Literary Agency (*US*)

Bookseeker Agency (*UK*)
The Barbara Bova Literary Agency (*US*)
Brandon & Associates (*UK*)
The Joan Brandt Agency (*US*)
The Helen Brann Agency, Inc. (*US*)
Barbara Braun Associates, Inc. (*US*)
Paul Bresnick Literary Agency, LLC (*US*)
Brick House Literary Agents (*US*)
Jenny Brown Associates (*UK*)
Marie Brown Associates, Inc. (*US*)
Andrea Brown Literary Agency, Inc. (*US*)
Brown Literary Agency (*US*)
Tracy Brown Literary Agency (*US*)
Browne & Miller Literary Associates (*US*)
Felicity Bryan (*UK*)
Marcus Bryan & Associates Inc. (*US*)
Brie Burkeman & Serafina Clarke Ltd (*UK*)
Juliet Burton Literary Agency (*UK*)
Cameron Creswell Agency (*Aus*)
Campbell Thomson & McLaughlin Ltd (*UK*)
Capel & Land Ltd (*UK*)
CardenWright Literary Agency (*UK*)
Carnicelli Literary Management (*US*)
Celia Catchpole (*UK*)
Chalberg & Sussman (*US*)
Mic Cheetham Literary Agency (*UK*)
Jane Chelius Literary Agency, Inc. (*US*)
Elyse Cheney Literary Associates, LLC (*US*)
Judith Chilcote Agency (*UK*)
The Choate Agency, LLC (*US*)
Teresa Chris Literary Agency Ltd (*UK*)
The Chudney Agency (*US*)
Cine/Lit Representation (*US*)
W.M. Clark Associates (*US*)
Mary Clemmey Literary Agency (*UK*)
Jonathan Clowes Ltd (*UK*)
Rosica Colin Ltd (*UK*)
Conville & Walsh Ltd (*UK*)
Jane Conway-Gordon Ltd (*UK*)
The Cooke Agency (*Can*)
Coombs Moylett Literary Agency (*UK*)
CowlesRyan Agency (*US*)
The Creative Rights Agency (*UK*)
The Creative Culture, Inc. (*US*)
Creative Authors Ltd (*UK*)
Creative Trust, Inc. (*US*)
Rupert Crew Ltd (*UK*)
The Croce Agency (*US*)
The Mary Cunnane Agency Pty Ltd (*Aus*)
Curtis Brown Group Ltd (*UK*)
Richard Curtis Associates, Inc. (*US*)
Laura Dail Literary Agency (*US*)
Darhansoff & Verrill Literary Agents (*US*)
Liza Dawson Associates (*US*)
The Jennifer DeChiara Literary Agency (*US*)
Joëlle Delbourgo Associates, Inc. (*US*)
Felix de Wolfe (*US*)
Donadio & Olson, Inc. (*US*)
Jim Donovan Literary (*US*)
Dorian Literary Agency (DLA) (*UK*)
Dunow, Carlson & Lerner Agency (*US*)
Dupree / Miller and Associates Inc. Literary (*US*)
Dystel & Goderich Literary Management (*US*)

Toby Eady Associates Ltd (*UK*)
Eames Literary Services, LLC (*US*)
East West Literary Agency LLC (*US*)
Eddison Pearson Ltd (*UK*)
Edwards Fuglewicz (*UK*)
Judith Ehrlich Literary Management (*US*)
Einstein Thompson Agency (*US*)
Elaine P. English, Attorney & Literary Agent (*US*)
Felicia Eth Literary Representation (*US*)
Faith Evans Associates (*UK*)
Mary Evans, Inc. (*US*)
Fairbank Literary Representation (*US*)
Farris Literary Agency, Inc. (*US*)
Film Rights Ltd in association with Laurence Fitch Ltd (*UK*)
Diana Finch Literary Agency (*US*)
FinePrint Literary Management (*US*)
The James Fitzgerald Agency (*US*)
The Foley Literary Agency (*US*)
Fox Mason Ltd (*UK*)
Fraser Ross Associates (*UK*)
Sarah Jane Freymann Literary Agency (*US*)
Fredrica S. Friedman and Co. Inc. (*US*)
Full Throttle Literary Agency (*US*)
Furniss Lawton (*UK*)
Nancy Gallt Literary Agency (*US*)
The Gernert Company (*US*)
Mark Gilroy Communications, Inc. (*US*)
Eric Glass Ltd (*UK*)
David Godwin Associates (*UK*)
Barry Goldblatt Literary Agency, Inc. (*US*)
Frances Goldin Literary Agency, Inc. (*US*)
The Susan Golomb Literary Agency (*US*)
Goodman Associates (*US*)
Irene Goodman Literary Agency (*US*)
Ashley Grayson Literary Agency (*US*)
Christine Green Authors' Agent (*UK*)
Kathryn Green Literary Agency, LLC (*US*)
Louise Greenberg Books Ltd (*UK*)
Greene & Heaton Ltd (*UK*)
The Greenhouse Literary Agency (*UK*)
Gregory & Company, Authors' Agents (*UK*)
Greyhaus Literary Agency (*UK*)
Laura Gross Literary Agency (*US*)
David Grossman Literary Agency Ltd (*UK*)
Marianne Gunn O'Connor Literary Agency (*Ire*)
Gunn Media Associates (*UK*)
Hardman & Swainson (*UK*)
Joy Harris Literary Agency, Inc. (*US*)
Antony Harwood Limited (*UK*)
John Hawkins & Associates, Inc. (*US*)
A M Heath & Company Limited, Author's Agents (*UK*)
Rupert Heath Literary Agency (*UK*)
The Helen Heller Agency (*Can*)
hhb agency ltd (*UK*)
Hidden Value Group (*US*)
David Higham Associates Ltd (*UK*)
Hilary Churchley Literary Agent (*UK*)
Vanessa Holt Ltd (*UK*)
Hopkins Literary Associates (*US*)
Kate Hordern Literary Agency (*UK*)

Hunter Profiles (*UK*)
Andrea Hurst Literary Management (*US*)
InkWell Management (*US*)
Intercontinental Literary Agency (*UK*)
International Transactions, Inc. (*US*)
Jabberwocky Literary Agency (*US*)
Jill Grinberg Literary Management LLC (*US*)
Johnson & Alcock (*UK*)
Jonathan Williams Literary Agency (*Ire*)
Michelle Kass Associates (*UK*)
Ki Agency Ltd (*UK*)
Virginia Kidd Agency, Inc (*US*)
Kilburn Literary Agency (*UK*)
Harvey Klinger, Inc (*US*)
Kneerim & Williams (*US*)
The Knight Agency (*US*)
Edite Kroll Literary Agency, Inc. (*US*)
KT Public Relations (*US*)
The Candace Lake Agency (*US*)
The LA Literary Agency (*US*)
Peter Lampack Agency, Inc (*US*)
Laura Langlie, Literary Agent (*US*)
The Steve Laube Agency (*US*)
LaunchBooks Literary Agency (*US*)
Sarah Lazin Books (*US*)
Robert Lecker Agency (*Can*)
Lescher & Lescher (*US*)
Barbara Levy Literary Agency (*UK*)
The Lez Barstow Agency (*UK*)
Limelight Management (*UK*)
Lindsay Literary Agency (*UK*)
Lippincott Massie McQuilkin (*US*)
The Literary Group (*US*)
Literary Management Group, Inc. (*US*)
London Independent Books (*UK*)
Julia Lord Literary Management (*US*)
Lowenstein Associates, Inc. (*US*)
Andrew Lownie Literary Agency Ltd (*UK*)
Lucy Luck Associates (*UK*)
Lutyens and Rubinstein (*UK*)
The Jennifer Lyons Literary Agency, LLC (*US*)
Lyons Literary LLC (*US*)
Donald Maass Literary Agency (*US*)
MacGregor Literary (*US*)
Madeleine Milburn Literary Agency (*UK*)
Ricia Mainhardt Agency (RMA) (*US*)
Makepeace Towle Literary Agency (*UK*)
Kirsten Manges Literary Agency, LLC (*US*)
Andrew Mann Ltd (*UK*)
March Tenth, Inc. (*US*)
Denise Marcil Literary Agency, Inc. (*US*)
Marjacq Scripts Ltd (*UK*)
Marly Russoff & Associates (*US*)
The Marsh Agency (*UK*)
The Martell Agency (*US*)
Martin Literary Management (*US*)
MBA Literary Agents Ltd (*UK*)
Duncan McAra (*UK*)
McKernan Agency (*UK*)
The Michael Greer Literary Agency (*UK*)
Miles Stott Children's Literary Agency (*UK*)
Martha Millard Literary Agency (*US*)
Patricia Moosbrugger Literary Agency (*US*)

Howard Morhaim Literary Agency (*US*)
William Morris Endeavor Entertainment (UK)
Ltd (*UK*)
Judith Murdoch Literary Agency (*UK*)
The Jean V. Naggar Literary Agency (*US*)
Nappaland Literary Agency (*US*)
Nelson Literary Agency, LLC (*US*)
New Leaf Literary & Media, Inc. (*US*)
Niad Management (*US*)
MNLA (Maggie Noach Literary Agency) (*UK*)
Northern Lights Literary Services (*US*)
Andrew Nurnberg Associates, Ltd (*UK*)
Objective Entertainment (*US*)
Paradigm Talent and Literary Agency (*US*)
The Park Literary Group LLC (*US*)
Paterson Marsh Ltd (*UK*)
Pavilion Literary Management (*US*)
Maggie Pearlstine Associates Ltd (*UK*)
Jonathan Pegg Literary Agency (*UK*)
The Peters Fraser & Dunlop Group Ltd (PFD)
(*UK*)
Pippin Properties, Inc (*US*)
Alièka Pistek Literary Agency, LLC (*US*)
Shelley Power Literary Agency Ltd (*UK*)
The Poynor Group (*US*)
Prospect Agency (*US*)
Queen Literary Agency, Inc. (*US*)
Quicksilver Books Literary Agency (*US*)
Raines & Raines (*US*)
Rees Literary Agency (*US*)
Regal Literary (*UK*)
Regal Literary Inc. (*US*)
Renee Zuckerbrot Literary Agency (*US*)
The Amy Rennert Agency, Inc. (*US*)
The Lisa Richards Agency (*Ire*)
Riverside Literary Agency (*US*)
Robert Dudley Agency (*UK*)
Robin Jones Literary Agency (*UK*)
Michael D. Robins & Associates (*US*)
Rocking Chair Books (*UK*)
Andy Ross Agency (*US*)
The Rudy Agency (*US*)
Uli Rushby-Smith Literary Agency (*UK*)
Marly Rusoff & Associates, Inc. (*US*)
Salkind Literary Agency (*US*)
The Sayle Literary Agency (*UK*)
Susan Schulman, A Literary Agency (*US*)
The Science Factory (*UK*)
Scribblers House LLC Literary Agency (*US*)
Scribe Agency LLC (*US*)
Secret Agent Man (*US*)
Lynn Seligman, Literary Agent (*US*)
The Seven Bridges Group (*US*)
The Seymour Agency (*US*)
Denise Shannon Literary Agency, Inc. (*US*)
Sheil Land Associates Ltd (*UK*)
Signature Literary Agency (*US*)
Dorie Simmonds Agency (*UK*)
Jeffrey Simmons (*UK*)
Sinclair-Stevenson (*UK*)
Valerie Smith, Literary Agent (*US*)
Spectrum Literary Agency (*US*)
Spencerhill Associates (*US*)

Standen Literary Agency (*UK*)
P. Stathonikos Agency (*Can*)
Elaine Steel (*UK*)
Abner Stein (*UK*)
Sternig & Byrne Literary Agency (*US*)
Pam Strickler Author Management (*US*)
Rebecca Strong International Literary Agency
(*US*)
The Strothman Agency (*US*)
The Stuart Agency (*US*)
Susanna Lea Associates (UK) (*UK*)
The Susijn Agency (*UK*)
The Swetky Agency and Associates (*US*)
SYLA - Susan Yearwood Literary Agency (*UK*)
Talcott Notch Literary (*US*)
Tessler Literary Agency (*US*)
Thomas Moore Literary Agency (*UK*)
Timberlake Literary Services, LLC (*US*)
Tom Lee (*US*)
TriadaUS Literary Agency, Inc. (*US*)
Jane Turnbull (*UK*)
United Agents (*UK*)
Venture Literary (*US*)
Veritas Literary Agency (*US*)
Beth Vesel Literary Agency (*US*)
Ed Victor Ltd (*UK*)
Wade & Doherty Literary Agency (*UK*)
The Ward & Balkin Agency, Inc (*US*)
Watson, Little Ltd (*UK*)
A.P. Watt Ltd (*UK*)
Irene Webb Literary (*US*)
The Wendy Weil Agency, Inc. (*US*)
The Weingel-Fidel Agency (*US*)
Wernick & Pratt Agency (*US*)
Westwood Creative Artists (*Can*)
Whispering Buffalo Literary Agency Ltd (*UK*)
Eve White: Literary Agent (*UK*)
Wolfson Literary Agency (*US*)
Wordserve Literary (*US*)
Writers' Representatives, LLC (*US*)
The Wylie Agency (UK) Ltd (*UK*)
Yates & Yates (*US*)
The Zack Company, Inc (*US*)
Karen Gantz Zahler Literary Agency (*US*)
Helen Zimmermann Literary Agency (*US*)
Film
Above the Line Agency (*US*)
Abrams Artists Agency (*US*)
Bret Adams Ltd (*US*)
Agency for the Performing Arts (APA) (*US*)
Aimee Entertainment Agency (*US*)
Anonymous Content (*US*)
AVAnti Productions & Management (*UK*)
Berlin Associates (*UK*)
Blake Friedmann Literary Agency Ltd (*UK*)
Barbara Braun Associates, Inc. (*US*)
Alan Brodie Representation Ltd (*UK*)
Kelvin C. Bulger and Associates (*US*)
Brie Burkeman & Serafina Clarke Ltd (*UK*)
Cameron Creswell Agency (*Aus*)
Capel & Land Ltd (*UK*)
Cedar Grove Agency Entertainment (*US*)
The Characters Talent Agency (*Can*)

W.M. Clark Associates (*US*)
Mary Clemmey Literary Agency (*UK*)
Jonathan Clowes Ltd (*UK*)
Rosica Colin Ltd (*UK*)
The Collective (*US*)
The Core Group Talent Agency, Inc. (*Can*)
Creative Trust, Inc. (*US*)
Criterion Group, Inc. (*US*)
Curtis Brown Group Ltd (*UK*)
The Jennifer DeChiara Literary Agency (*US*)
Felix de Wolfe (*UK*)
Dupree / Miller and Associates Inc. Literary (*US*)
Film Rights Ltd in association with Laurence Fitch Ltd (*UK*)
Diana Finch Literary Agency (*US*)
Jill Foster Ltd (JFL) (*UK*)
Fredrica S. Friedman and Co. Inc. (*US*)
Full Throttle Literary Agency (*US*)
The Gage Group (*US*)
Eric Glass Ltd (*UK*)
Goodman Associates (*US*)
Antony Harwood Limited (*UK*)
Valerie Hoskins Associates (*UK*)
Independent Talent Group Ltd (*UK*)
Janet Fillingham Associates (*UK*)
Jaret Entertainment (*US*)
Johnson & Alcock (*UK*)
Michelle Kass Associates (*UK*)
Charlene Kay Agency (*Can*)
Ki Agency Ltd (*UK*)
Knight Hall Agency (*UK*)
The Candace Lake Agency (*US*)
Laura Langlie, Literary Agent (*US*)
Robert Lecker Agency (*Can*)
The Lez Barstow Agency (*UK*)
Madeleine Milburn Literary Agency (*UK*)
Andrew Mann Ltd (*UK*)
March Tenth, Inc. (*US*)
Marjacq Scripts Ltd (*UK*)
MBA Literary Agents Ltd (*UK*)
Bill McLean Personal Management Ltd (*UK*)
Martha Millard Literary Agency (*US*)
Monteiro Rose Dravis Agency, Inc. (*US*)
William Morris Endeavor Entertainment (UK) Ltd (*UK*)
Niad Management (*US*)
Objective Entertainment (*US*)
Paradigm Talent and Literary Agency (*US*)
PBJ and JBJ Management (*UK*)
Peregrine Whittlesey Agency (*US*)
Barry Perelman Agency (*US*)
The Peters Fraser & Dunlop Group Ltd (PFD) (*UK*)
Michael D. Robins & Associates (*US*)
Sayle Screen Ltd (*UK*)
Linda Seifert Management (*UK*)
Lynn Seligman, Literary Agent (*US*)
Sheil Land Associates Ltd (*UK*)
Jeffrey Simmons (*UK*)
South West Artists (*UK*)
Stone Manners Salners Agency (*US*)
The Swetky Agency and Associates (*US*)
The Tennyson Agency (*UK*)

Thomas Moore Literary Agency (*UK*)
Timberlake Literary Services, LLC (*US*)
Tom Lee (*US*)
2M Literary Agency Ltd (*US*)
United Agents (*UK*)
Venture Literary (*US*)
A.P. Watt Ltd (*UK*)
Whispering Buffalo Literary Agency Ltd (*UK*)
Eve White: Literary Agent (*UK*)
The Zack Company, Inc (*US*)

Finance
The Agency Group, Ltd (*US*)
Ambassador Speakers Bureau & Literary Agency (*US*)
Audrey A. Wolf Literary Agency (*US*)
The August Agency LLC (*US*)
David Black Literary Agency (*US*)
The Blumer Literary Agency, Inc. (*US*)
Jenny Brown Associates (*UK*)
Browne & Miller Literary Associates (*US*)
Elyse Cheney Literary Associates, LLC (*US*)
Edward B. Claflin Literary Agency, LLC (*US*)
Richard Curtis Associates, Inc. (*US*)
The Jennifer DeChiara Literary Agency (*US*)
Jim Donovan Literary (*US*)
Dupree / Miller and Associates Inc. Literary (*US*)
Dystel & Goderich Literary Management (*US*)
Felicia Eth Literary Representation (*US*)
Farris Literary Agency, Inc. (*US*)
Diana Finch Literary Agency (*US*)
Fresh Books Literary Agency (*US*)
Fredrica S. Friedman and Co. Inc. (*US*)
The Susan Golomb Literary Agency (*US*)
Goodman Associates (*US*)
Ashley Grayson Literary Agency (*US*)
Kathryn Green Literary Agency, LLC (*US*)
Antony Harwood Limited (*UK*)
Hidden Value Group (*US*)
InkWell Management (*US*)
Jabberwocky Literary Agency (*US*)
Jill Grinberg Literary Management LLC (*US*)
Frances Kelly (*UK*)
Kneerim & Williams (*US*)
The Knight Agency (*US*)
MacGregor Literary (*US*)
The Martell Agency (*US*)
Martha Millard Literary Agency (*US*)
The Poynor Group (*US*)
Quicksilver Books Literary Agency (*US*)
Lynne Rabinoff Agency (*US*)
Raines & Raines (*US*)
The Amy Rennert Agency, Inc. (*US*)
Marly Rusoff & Associates, Inc. (*US*)
Salkind Literary Agency (*US*)
Susan Schulman, A Literary Agency (*US*)
Scribblers House LLC Literary Agency (*US*)
Lynn Seligman, Literary Agent (*US*)
The Swetky Agency and Associates (*US*)
Timberlake Literary Services, LLC (*US*)
Venture Literary (*US*)
Beth Vesel Literary Agency (*US*)
Eve White: Literary Agent (*UK*)
Wordserve Literary (*US*)

Writers' Representatives, LLC (*US*)
The Zack Company, Inc (*US*)
Gardening
Rosica Colin Ltd (*UK*)
Dupree / Miller and Associates Inc. Literary (*US*)
Greene & Heaton Ltd (*UK*)
Antony Harwood Limited (*UK*)
John Hawkins & Associates, Inc. (*US*)
KT Public Relations (*US*)
Redwood Agency (*US*)
Sheil Land Associates Ltd (*UK*)
The Swetky Agency and Associates (*US*)
Talcott Notch Literary (*US*)
Thomas Moore Literary Agency (*UK*)
Timberlake Literary Services, LLC (*US*)
Jane Turnbull (*UK*)
Venture Literary (*US*)
The Ward & Balkin Agency, Inc (*US*)
Eve White: Literary Agent (*UK*)
The Zack Company, Inc (*US*)
Gothic
Abela Literature (*Can*)
AVAnti Productions & Management (*UK*)
Elaine P. English, Attorney & Literary Agent (*US*)
Antony Harwood Limited (*UK*)
The Candace Lake Agency (*US*)
The Lez Barstow Agency (*UK*)
Ricia Mainhardt Agency (RMA) (*US*)
The Jean V. Naggar Literary Agency (*US*)
The Swetky Agency and Associates (*US*)
Venture Literary (*US*)
Eve White: Literary Agent (*UK*)
Health
The Agency Group, Ltd (*US*)
Ambassador Speakers Bureau & Literary Agency (*US*)
Arcadia (*US*)
Audrey A. Wolf Literary Agency (*US*)
Faye Bender Literary Agency (*US*)
Vicky Bijur Literary Agency (*US*)
The Blumer Literary Agency, Inc. (*US*)
Luigi Bonomi Associates Ltd (*UK*)
BookEnds, LLC (*US*)
Paul Bresnick Literary Agency, LLC (*US*)
Rick Broadhead & Associates Literary Agency (*Can*)
Tracy Brown Literary Agency (*US*)
Browne & Miller Literary Associates (*US*)
Carnicelli Literary Management (*US*)
Edward B. Claflin Literary Agency, LLC (*US*)
Rosica Colin Ltd (*UK*)
The Creative Culture, Inc. (*US*)
Creative Authors Ltd (*UK*)
Richard Curtis Associates, Inc. (*US*)
The Jennifer DeChiara Literary Agency (*US*)
Joëlle Delbourgo Associates, Inc. (*US*)
Jim Donovan Literary (*US*)
Dupree / Miller and Associates Inc. Literary (*US*)
Dystel & Goderich Literary Management (*US*)
Ebeling & Associates (*US*)
Judith Ehrlich Literary Management (*US*)
Einstein Thompson Agency (*US*)

Felicia Eth Literary Representation (*US*)
Farris Literary Agency, Inc. (*US*)
Diana Finch Literary Agency (*US*)
FinePrint Literary Management (*US*)
Fox & Howard Literary Agency (*UK*)
Fresh Books Literary Agency (*US*)
Sarah Jane Freymann Literary Agency (*US*)
Fredrica S. Friedman and Co. Inc. (*US*)
The Susan Golomb Literary Agency (*US*)
Goodman Associates (*US*)
Graham Maw Christie Literary Agency (*UK*)
Ashley Grayson Literary Agency (*US*)
Kathryn Green Literary Agency, LLC (*US*)
Greene & Heaton Ltd (*UK*)
Laura Gross Literary Agency (*US*)
Marianne Gunn O'Connor Literary Agency (*Ire*)
Antony Harwood Limited (*UK*)
John Hawkins & Associates, Inc. (*US*)
The Jeff Herman Agency, LLC (*US*)
InkWell Management (*US*)
Jabberwocky Literary Agency (*US*)
Jill Grinberg Literary Management LLC (*US*)
Johnson & Alcock (*UK*)
Frances Kelly (*UK*)
Kilburn Literary Agency (*UK*)
Harvey Klinger, Inc (*US*)
Kneerim & Williams (*US*)
The Knight Agency (*US*)
Bert P. Krages (*US*)
Edite Kroll Literary Agency, Inc. (*US*)
KT Public Relations (*US*)
The LA Literary Agency (*US*)
The Literary Group (*US*)
Lowenstein Associates, Inc. (*US*)
Lyons Literary LLC (*US*)
Kirsten Manges Literary Agency, LLC (*US*)
March Tenth, Inc. (*US*)
Denise Marcil Literary Agency, Inc. (*US*)
The Martell Agency (*US*)
Martin Literary Management (*US*)
MBA Literary Agents Ltd (*UK*)
Martha Millard Literary Agency (*US*)
Howard Morhaim Literary Agency (*US*)
The Jean V. Naggar Literary Agency (*US*)
Northern Lights Literary Services (*US*)
Maggie Pearlstine Associates Ltd (*UK*)
The Poynor Group (*US*)
Quicksilver Books Literary Agency (*US*)
Redhammer (*UK*)
Redwood Agency (*US*)
The Amy Rennert Agency, Inc. (*US*)
The Rudy Agency (*US*)
Marly Rusoff & Associates, Inc. (*US*)
Salkind Literary Agency (*US*)
Susan Schulman, A Literary Agency (*US*)
Jonathan Scott, Inc (*US*)
Scribblers House LLC Literary Agency (*US*)
Lynn Seligman, Literary Agent (*US*)
Denise Shannon Literary Agency, Inc. (*US*)
Robert Smith Literary Agency Ltd (*UK*)
Rebecca Strong International Literary Agency (*US*)
The Stuart Agency (*US*)

The Swetky Agency and Associates (*US*)
Timberlake Literary Services, LLC (*US*)
TriadaUS Literary Agency, Inc. (*US*)
2M Literary Agency Ltd (*US*)
Venture Literary (*US*)
Veritas Literary Agency (*US*)
Beth Vesel Literary Agency (*US*)
The Ward & Balkin Agency, Inc (*US*)
Irene Webb Literary (*US*)
The Wendy Weil Agency, Inc. (*US*)
Whimsy Literary Agency, LLC (*US*)
Whispering Buffalo Literary Agency Ltd (*UK*)
Eve White: Literary Agent (*UK*)
Wolfson Literary Agency (*US*)
Wordserve Literary (*US*)
The Zack Company, Inc (*US*)
Helen Zimmermann Literary Agency (*US*)

Historical
Abela Literature (*Can*)
Sheila Ableman Literary Agency (*UK*)
The Agency Group, Ltd (*US*)
Alive Communications, Inc (*US*)
Ambassador Speakers Bureau & Literary Agency (*US*)
The Ampersand Agency Ltd (*UK*)
Arcadia (*US*)
Artellus Limited (*UK*)
Robert Astle & Associates Literary Management, Inc. (*US*)
Audrey A. Wolf Literary Agency (*US*)
The August Agency LLC (*US*)
Author Rights Agency (*Ire*)
AVAnti Productions & Management (*UK*)
Barer Literary, LLC (*US*)
The Bent Agency (*US*)
Vicky Bijur Literary Agency (*US*)
David Black Literary Agency (*US*)
The Blumer Literary Agency, Inc. (*US*)
Luigi Bonomi Associates Ltd (*UK*)
Books & Such Literary Agency (*US*)
The Barbara Bova Literary Agency (*US*)
Brandon & Associates (*UK*)
The Joan Brandt Agency (*US*)
Barbara Braun Associates, Inc. (*US*)
Paul Bresnick Literary Agency, LLC (*US*)
Brick House Literary Agents (*US*)
Rick Broadhead & Associates Literary Agency (*Can*)
Jenny Brown Associates (*UK*)
Marie Brown Associates, Inc. (*US*)
Andrea Brown Literary Agency, Inc. (*US*)
Brown Literary Agency (*US*)
Tracy Brown Literary Agency (*US*)
Browne & Miller Literary Associates (*US*)
Felicity Bryan (*UK*)
Capel & Land Ltd (*UK*)
Carnicelli Literary Management (*US*)
Chalberg & Sussman (*US*)
The Characters Talent Agency (*Can*)
Mic Cheetham Literary Agency (*UK*)
Elyse Cheney Literary Associates, LLC (*US*)
The Choate Agency, LLC (*US*)
The Chudney Agency (*US*)

Edward B. Claflin Literary Agency, LLC (*US*)
W.M. Clark Associates (*US*)
Rosica Colin Ltd (*UK*)
Conville & Walsh Ltd (*UK*)
The Cooke Agency (*Can*)
Coombs Moylett Literary Agency (*UK*)
The Core Group Talent Agency, Inc. (*Can*)
CowlesRyan Agency (*US*)
Creative Authors Ltd (*UK*)
The Croce Agency (*US*)
Curtis Brown Group Ltd (*UK*)
Richard Curtis Associates, Inc. (*US*)
Laura Dail Literary Agency (*US*)
David Luxton Associates (*UK*)
Liza Dawson Associates (*US*)
The Jennifer DeChiara Literary Agency (*US*)
Joëlle Delbourgo Associates, Inc. (*US*)
Donadio & Olson, Inc. (*US*)
Jim Donovan Literary (*US*)
Dorian Literary Agency (DLA) (*UK*)
Dupree / Miller and Associates Inc. Literary (*US*)
Dystel & Goderich Literary Management (*US*)
Edwards Fuglewicz (*UK*)
Judith Ehrlich Literary Management (*US*)
Einstein Thompson Agency (*US*)
Elaine P. English, Attorney & Literary Agent (*US*)
Felicia Eth Literary Representation (*US*)
Farris Literary Agency, Inc. (*US*)
Diana Finch Literary Agency (*US*)
FinePrint Literary Management (*US*)
Fox Mason Ltd (*UK*)
Fox & Howard Literary Agency (*UK*)
Sarah Jane Freymann Literary Agency (*US*)
Fredrica S. Friedman and Co. Inc. (*US*)
Furniss Lawton (*UK*)
The Gernert Company (*US*)
Frances Goldin Literary Agency, Inc. (*US*)
The Susan Golomb Literary Agency (*US*)
Goodman Associates (*US*)
Irene Goodman Literary Agency (*US*)
Graham Maw Christie Literary Agency (*UK*)
Ashley Grayson Literary Agency (*US*)
Kathryn Green Literary Agency, LLC (*US*)
Greene & Heaton Ltd (*UK*)
Gregory & Company, Authors' Agents (*UK*)
Greyhaus Literary Agency (*US*)
Laura Gross Literary Agency (*US*)
Joy Harris Literary Agency, Inc. (*US*)
Antony Harwood Limited (*UK*)
John Hawkins & Associates, Inc. (*US*)
Rupert Heath Literary Agency (*UK*)
The Jeff Herman Agency, LLC (*US*)
hhb agency ltd (*UK*)
Hidden Value Group (*US*)
David Higham Associates Ltd (*UK*)
Hilary Churchley Literary Agent (*UK*)
Hopkins Literary Associates (*US*)
Kate Hordern Literary Agency (*UK*)
Andrea Hurst Literary Management (*US*)
InkWell Management (*US*)
International Transactions, Inc. (*US*)
Jabberwocky Literary Agency (*US*)

Jill Grinberg Literary Management LLC (*US*)
Johnson & Alcock (*UK*)
Frances Kelly (*UK*)
Virginia Kidd Agency, Inc (*US*)
Kneerim & Williams (*US*)
Bert P. Krages (*US*)
KT Public Relations (*US*)
The Candace Lake Agency (*US*)
The LA Literary Agency (*US*)
Laura Langlie, Literary Agent (*US*)
LaunchBooks Literary Agency (*US*)
Sarah Lazin Books (*US*)
Robert Lecker Agency (*Can*)
Lescher & Lescher (*US*)
The Lez Barstow Agency (*UK*)
Lippincott Massie McQuilkin (*US*)
The Literary Group (*US*)
Julia Lord Literary Management (*US*)
Andrew Lownie Literary Agency Ltd (*UK*)
The Jennifer Lyons Literary Agency, LLC (*US*)
Lyons Literary LLC (*US*)
Donald Maass Literary Agency (*US*)
MacGregor Literary (*US*)
Makepeace Towle Literary Agency (*UK*)
Kirsten Manges Literary Agency, LLC (*US*)
March Tenth, Inc. (*US*)
The Martell Agency (*US*)
MBA Literary Agents Ltd (*UK*)
Duncan McAra (*UK*)
McKernan Agency (*UK*)
Martha Millard Literary Agency (*US*)
Monteiro Rose Dravis Agency, Inc. (*US*)
William Morris Endeavor Entertainment (UK)
Ltd (*UK*)
The Jean V. Naggar Literary Agency (*US*)
Nappaland Literary Agency (*US*)
New Leaf Literary & Media, Inc. (*US*)
MNLA (Maggie Noach Literary Agency) (*UK*)
Northern Lights Literary Services (*US*)
The Park Literary Group LLC (*US*)
Pavilion Literary Management (*US*)
Maggie Pearlstine Associates Ltd (*UK*)
Jonathan Pegg Literary Agency (*UK*)
Barry Perelman Agency (*US*)
Alièka Pistek Literary Agency, LLC (*US*)
Queen Literary Agency, Inc. (*US*)
Quicksilver Books Literary Agency (*US*)
Lynne Rabinoff Agency (*US*)
Raines & Raines (*US*)
Rees Literary Agency (*US*)
Regal Literary (*UK*)
Regal Literary Inc. (*US*)
Renee Zuckerbrot Literary Agency (*US*)
The Amy Rennert Agency, Inc. (*US*)
The Lisa Richards Agency (*Ire*)
Robert Dudley Agency (*UK*)
Rocking Chair Books (*UK*)
Andy Ross Agency (*US*)
The Rudy Agency (*US*)
Marly Rusoff & Associates, Inc. (*US*)
Salkind Literary Agency (*US*)
The Sayle Literary Agency (*UK*)
Susan Schulman, A Literary Agency (*US*)

The Science Factory (*UK*)
Jonathan Scott, Inc (*US*)
Scribblers House LLC Literary Agency (*US*)
Lynn Seligman, Literary Agent (*US*)
Denise Shannon Literary Agency, Inc. (*US*)
Sheil Land Associates Ltd (*UK*)
Signature Literary Agency (*US*)
Dorie Simmonds Agency (*UK*)
Jeffrey Simmons (*UK*)
Sinclair-Stevenson (*UK*)
Robert Smith Literary Agency Ltd (*UK*)
Valerie Smith, Literary Agent (*US*)
Spectrum Literary Agency (*US*)
Pam Strickler Author Management (*US*)
Rebecca Strong International Literary Agency
(*US*)
The Strothman Agency (*US*)
The Stuart Agency (*US*)
The Swetky Agency and Associates (*US*)
Talcott Notch Literary (*US*)
Tessler Literary Agency (*US*)
Thomas Moore Literary Agency (*UK*)
Timberlake Literary Services, LLC (*US*)
Tom Lee (*US*)
Jane Turnbull (*UK*)
Venture Literary (*US*)
Veritas Literary Agency (*US*)
The Ward & Balkin Agency, Inc (*US*)
Watson, Little Ltd (*UK*)
A.P. Watt Ltd (*UK*)
The Wendy Weil Agency, Inc. (*US*)
Westwood Creative Artists (*Can*)
Eve White, Literary Agent (*UK*)
Wordserve Literary (*US*)
Writers' Representatives, LLC (*US*)
The Zack Company, Inc (*US*)
Karen Gantz Zahler Literary Agency (*US*)
Helen Zimmermann Literary Agency (*US*)
Hobbies
The Blumer Literary Agency, Inc. (*US*)
Browne & Miller Literary Associates (*US*)
The Jennifer DeChiara Literary Agency (*US*)
Antony Harwood Limited (*UK*)
Lyons Literary LLC (*US*)
Timberlake Literary Services, LLC (*US*)
Venture Literary (*US*)
Eve White: Literary Agent (*UK*)
Horror
Abela Literature (*Can*)
The Bent Agency (*US*)
The Characters Talent Agency (*Can*)
Elyse Cheney Literary Associates, LLC (*US*)
Cine/Lit Representation (*US*)
Rosica Colin Ltd (*UK*)
The Core Group Talent Agency, Inc. (*Can*)
The Jennifer DeChiara Literary Agency (*US*)
Dorian Literary Agency (DLA) (*UK*)
Film Rights Ltd in association with Laurence
Fitch Ltd (*UK*)
FinePrint Literary Management (*US*)
Fox Mason Ltd (*UK*)
Samuel French, Inc. (*US*)
Full Throttle Literary Agency (*US*)

Antony Harwood Limited (*UK*)
Jaret Entertainment (*US*)
The Candace Lake Agency (*US*)
The Lez Barstow Agency (*UK*)
The Literary Group (*US*)
Donald Maass Literary Agency (*US*)
The Jean V. Naggar Literary Agency (*US*)
Barry Perelman Agency (*US*)
Rocking Chair Books (*UK*)
Lynn Seligman, Literary Agent (*US*)
South West Artists (*UK*)
Sternig & Byrne Literary Agency (*US*)
Talcott Notch Literary (*US*)
Tom Lee (*US*)
Venture Literary (*US*)
Irene Webb Literary (*US*)
Eve White: Literary Agent (*UK*)
The Zack Company, Inc (*US*)
How-to
The Agency Group, Ltd (*US*)
Alive Communications, Inc (*US*)
Miriam Altshuler Literary Agency (*US*)
Ambassador Speakers Bureau & Literary Agency (*US*)
The Blumer Literary Agency, Inc. (*US*)
Andrea Brown Literary Agency, Inc. (*US*)
Browne & Miller Literary Associates (*US*)
Edward B. Claflin Literary Agency, LLC (*US*)
The Jennifer DeChiara Literary Agency (*US*)
Jim Donovan Literary (*US*)
Dupree / Miller and Associates Inc. Literary (*US*)
Judith Ehrlich Literary Management (*US*)
The Epstein Literary Agency (*US*)
Farris Literary Agency, Inc. (*US*)
Diana Finch Literary Agency (*US*)
FinePrint Literary Management (*US*)
Fresh Books Literary Agency (*US*)
Fredrica S. Friedman and Co. Inc. (*US*)
Graham Maw Christie Literary Agency (*UK*)
Kathryn Green Literary Agency, LLC (*US*)
Antony Harwood Limited (*UK*)
The Jeff Herman Agency, LLC (*US*)
Hidden Value Group (*US*)
Amanda Howard Associates Ltd (*UK*)
Andrea Hurst Literary Management (*US*)
Harvey Klinger, Inc (*US*)
The Knight Agency (*US*)
KT Public Relations (*US*)
Robert Lecker Agency (*Can*)
Lyons Literary LLC (*US*)
MacGregor Literary (*US*)
Martin Literary Management (*US*)
Martha Millard Literary Agency (*US*)
Northern Lights Literary Services (*US*)
Quicksilver Books Literary Agency (*US*)
Salkind Literary Agency (*US*)
Susan Schulman, A Literary Agency (*US*)
Scribblers House LLC Literary Agency (*US*)
Lynn Seligman, Literary Agent (*US*)
Valerie Smith, Literary Agent (*US*)
The Swetky Agency and Associates (*US*)
Thomas Moore Literary Agency (*UK*)
TriadaUS Literary Agency, Inc. (*US*)

Venture Literary (*US*)
Beth Vesel Literary Agency (*US*)
Whimsy Literary Agency, LLC (*US*)
Eve White: Literary Agent (*UK*)
Wolfson Literary Agency (*US*)
Helen Zimmermann Literary Agency (*US*)
Humour
Abrams Artists Agency (*US*)
The Agency Group, Ltd (*US*)
Alive Communications, Inc (*US*)
Robert Astle & Associates Literary Management, Inc. (*US*)
AVAnti Productions & Management (*UK*)
The Blumer Literary Agency, Inc. (*US*)
Books & Such Literary Agency (*US*)
Paul Bresnick Literary Agency, LLC (*US*)
Rick Broadhead & Associates Literary Agency (*Can*)
Jenny Brown Associates (*UK*)
Andrea Brown Literary Agency, Inc. (*US*)
Brown Literary Agency (*US*)
Tracy Brown Literary Agency (*US*)
Browne & Miller Literary Associates (*US*)
Kelvin C. Bulger and Associates (*US*)
Cedar Grove Agency Entertainment (*US*)
The Characters Talent Agency (*Can*)
Jane Chelius Literary Agency, Inc. (*US*)
Rosica Colin Ltd (*UK*)
Conville & Walsh Ltd (*UK*)
The Core Group Talent Agency, Inc. (*Can*)
The Creative Culture, Inc. (*US*)
Creative Authors Ltd (*UK*)
The Jennifer DeChiara Literary Agency (*US*)
Dupree / Miller and Associates Inc. Literary (*US*)
Dystel & Goderich Literary Management (*US*)
Judith Ehrlich Literary Management (*US*)
Einstein Thompson Agency (*US*)
Elaine P. English, Attorney & Literary Agent (*US*)
Fairbank Literary Representation (*US*)
Farris Literary Agency, Inc. (*US*)
Diana Finch Literary Agency (*US*)
FinePrint Literary Management (*US*)
Jill Foster Ltd (JFL) (*UK*)
Samuel French, Inc. (*US*)
Fresh Books Literary Agency (*US*)
Fredrica S. Friedman and Co. Inc. (*US*)
Full Throttle Literary Agency (*US*)
The Susan Golomb Literary Agency (*US*)
Graham Maw Christie Literary Agency (*UK*)
Kathryn Green Literary Agency, LLC (*US*)
Greene & Heaton Ltd (*UK*)
Roger Hancock Ltd (*UK*)
Joy Harris Literary Agency, Inc. (*US*)
Antony Harwood Limited (*UK*)
hhb agency ltd (*UK*)
Amanda Howard Associates Ltd (*UK*)
Andrea Hurst Literary Management (*US*)
Jabberwocky Literary Agency (*US*)
Jaret Entertainment (*US*)
Charlene Kay Agency (*Can*)
Harvey Klinger, Inc (*US*)
Edite Kroll Literary Agency, Inc. (*US*)

The Candace Lake Agency (*US*)
Laura Langlie, Literary Agent (*US*)
LaunchBooks Literary Agency (*US*)
The Lez Barstow Agency (*UK*)
Lippincott Massie McQuilkin (*US*)
The Literary Group (*US*)
Julia Lord Literary Management (*US*)
Lyons Literary LLC (*US*)
Donald Maass Literary Agency (*US*)
MacGregor Literary (*US*)
Makepeace Towle Literary Agency (*UK*)
March Tenth, Inc. (*US*)
Monteiro Rose Dravis Agency, Inc. (*US*)
The Jean V. Naggar Literary Agency (*US*)
Nappaland Literary Agency (*US*)
Niad Management (*US*)
PBJ and JBJ Management (*UK*)
Redwood Agency (*US*)
The Lisa Richards Agency (*Ire*)
Salkind Literary Agency (*US*)
Susan Schulman, A Literary Agency (*US*)
Lynn Seligman, Literary Agent (*US*)
Sheil Land Associates Ltd (*UK*)
The Swetky Agency and Associates (*US*)
Timberlake Literary Services, LLC (*US*)
Jane Turnbull (*UK*)
Venture Literary (*US*)
Whimsy Literary Agency, LLC (*US*)
Whispering Buffalo Literary Agency Ltd (*UK*)
Eve White: Literary Agent (*UK*)
Wolfson Literary Agency (*US*)
Writers' Representatives, LLC (*US*)
The Zack Company, Inc (*US*)
Helen Zimmermann Literary Agency (*US*)

Legal
The Agency Group, Ltd (*US*)
Ambassador Speakers Bureau & Literary Agency (*US*)
David Black Literary Agency (*US*)
Brandon & Associates (*UK*)
The Jennifer DeChiara Literary Agency (*US*)
Jim Donovan Literary (*US*)
Judith Ehrlich Literary Management (*US*)
Felicia Eth Literary Representation (*US*)
Farris Literary Agency, Inc. (*US*)
Diana Finch Literary Agency (*US*)
Mark Gilroy Communications, Inc. (*US*)
The Susan Golomb Literary Agency (*US*)
Goodman Associates (*US*)
Laura Gross Literary Agency (*US*)
Antony Harwood Limited (*UK*)
Jabberwocky Literary Agency (*US*)
Jill Grinberg Literary Management LLC (*US*)
Kneerim & Williams (*US*)
Edite Kroll Literary Agency, Inc. (*US*)
Laura Langlie, Literary Agent (*US*)
Lescher & Lescher (*US*)
Lyons Literary LLC (*US*)
Lynne Rabinoff Agency (*US*)
Susan Schulman, A Literary Agency (*US*)
Jeffrey Simmons (*UK*)
The Swetky Agency and Associates (*US*)
Timberlake Literary Services, LLC (*US*)

Venture Literary (*US*)
Eve White: Literary Agent (*UK*)
Wordserve Literary (*US*)
Writers' Representatives, LLC (*US*)
Yates & Yates (*US*)

Leisure
Rosica Colin Ltd (*UK*)
Conville & Walsh Ltd (*UK*)
Dupree / Miller and Associates Inc. Literary (*US*)
Goodman Associates (*US*)
Antony Harwood Limited (*UK*)
Lyons Literary LLC (*US*)
Ricia Mainhardt Agency (RMA) (*US*)
The Swetky Agency and Associates (*US*)
Venture Literary (*US*)
Watson, Little Ltd (*UK*)
Eve White: Literary Agent (*UK*)

Lifestyle
The Agency Group, Ltd (*US*)
Alive Communications, Inc (*US*)
Ambassador Speakers Bureau & Literary Agency (*US*)
Audrey A. Wolf Literary Agency (*US*)
Luigi Bonomi Associates Ltd (*UK*)
BookEnds, LLC (*US*)
Books & Such Literary Agency (*US*)
Paul Bresnick Literary Agency, LLC (*US*)
Brick House Literary Agents (*US*)
Rick Broadhead & Associates Literary Agency (*Can*)
Browne & Miller Literary Associates (*US*)
Jane Chelius Literary Agency, Inc. (*US*)
Rosica Colin Ltd (*UK*)
Conville & Walsh Ltd (*UK*)
The Creative Culture, Inc. (*US*)
The Culinary Entertainment Agency (CEA) (*US*)
Liza Dawson Associates (*US*)
The Jennifer DeChiara Literary Agency (*US*)
Joëlle Delbourgo Associates, Inc. (*US*)
Jim Donovan Literary (*US*)
Dupree / Miller and Associates Inc. Literary (*US*)
Dystel & Goderich Literary Management (*US*)
Judith Ehrlich Literary Management (*US*)
Felicia Eth Literary Representation (*US*)
Fairbank Literary Representation (*US*)
Farris Literary Agency, Inc. (*US*)
Diana Finch Literary Agency (*US*)
FinePrint Literary Management (*US*)
Fox & Howard Literary Agency (*UK*)
Fresh Books Literary Agency (*US*)
Sarah Jane Freymann Literary Agency (*US*)
Fredrica S. Friedman and Co. Inc. (*US*)
Irene Goodman Literary Agency (*US*)
Graham Maw Christie Literary Agency (*UK*)
Ashley Grayson Literary Agency (*US*)
Kathryn Green Literary Agency, LLC (*US*)
Laura Gross Literary Agency (*US*)
Antony Harwood Limited (*UK*)
John Hawkins & Associates, Inc. (*US*)
Rupert Heath Literary Agency (*UK*)
The Jeff Herman Agency, LLC (*US*)
Hidden Value Group (*US*)
Johnson & Alcock (*UK*)

Frances Kelly (*UK*)
Kneerim & Williams (*US*)
The Knight Agency (*US*)
KT Public Relations (*US*)
The LA Literary Agency (*US*)
Limelight Management (*UK*)
The Literary Group (*US*)
Literary Management Group, Inc. (*US*)
Julia Lord Literary Management (*US*)
Lowenstein Associates, Inc. (*US*)
Lyons Literary LLC (*US*)
MacGregor Literary (*US*)
Denise Marcil Literary Agency, Inc. (*US*)
Martin Literary Management (*US*)
MBA Literary Agents Ltd (*UK*)
The Michael Greer Literary Agency (*UK*)
Martha Millard Literary Agency (*US*)
The Jean V. Naggar Literary Agency (*US*)
Nappaland Literary Agency (*US*)
Northern Lights Literary Services (*US*)
Objective Entertainment (*US*)
Jonathan Pegg Literary Agency (*UK*)
Quicksilver Books Literary Agency (*US*)
Redhammer (*UK*)
Redwood Agency (*US*)
The Amy Rennert Agency, Inc. (*US*)
The Lisa Richards Agency (*Ire*)
Rocking Chair Books (*UK*)
Salkind Literary Agency (*US*)
Susan Schulman, A Literary Agency (*US*)
Scribblers House LLC Literary Agency (*US*)
Lynn Seligman, Literary Agent (*US*)
Sheil Land Associates Ltd (*UK*)
Robert Smith Literary Agency Ltd (*UK*)
The Stuart Agency (*US*)
Talcott Notch Literary (*US*)
Thomas Moore Literary Agency (*UK*)
Timberlake Literary Services, LLC (*US*)
Jane Turnbull (*UK*)
2M Literary Agency Ltd (*US*)
Venture Literary (*US*)
Veritas Literary Agency (*US*)
The Ward & Balkin Agency, Inc (*US*)
The Wendy Weil Agency, Inc. (*US*)
Whispering Buffalo Literary Agency Ltd (*UK*)
Eve White: Literary Agent (*UK*)
Wolfson Literary Agency (*US*)
The Zack Company, Inc (*US*)
Karen Gantz Zahler Literary Agency (*US*)
Helen Zimmermann Literary Agency (*US*)
Literature
Abela Literature (*Can*)
AVAnti Productions & Management (*UK*)
The Blumer Literary Agency, Inc. (*US*)
Elyse Cheney Literary Associates, LLC (*US*)
CowlesRyan Agency (*US*)
Donadio & Olson, Inc. (*US*)
Dupree / Miller and Associates Inc. Literary (*US*)
Goodman Associates (*US*)
Antony Harwood Limited (*UK*)
Hidden Value Group (*US*)
Jabberwocky Literary Agency (*US*)
Michelle Kass Associates (*UK*)

Kilburn Literary Agency (*UK*)
Kneerim & Williams (*US*)
Laura Langlie, Literary Agent (*US*)
Robert Lecker Agency (*Can*)
Lowenstein Associates, Inc. (*US*)
Lyons Literary LLC (*US*)
Makepeace Towle Literary Agency (*UK*)
March Tenth, Inc. (*US*)
Patricia Moosbrugger Literary Agency (*US*)
Quicksilver Books Literary Agency (*US*)
Renee Zuckerbrot Literary Agency (*US*)
The Amy Rennert Agency, Inc. (*US*)
Rocking Chair Books (*UK*)
Susan Schulman, A Literary Agency (*US*)
Scribe Agency LLC (*US*)
The Seven Bridges Group (*US*)
The Swetky Agency and Associates (*US*)
The Tennyson Agency (*UK*)
Thomas Moore Literary Agency (*UK*)
Timberlake Literary Services, LLC (*US*)
Tom Lee (*US*)
Venture Literary (*US*)
Eve White: Literary Agent (*UK*)
Writers' Representatives, LLC (*US*)
Media
Robert Astle & Associates Literary Management, Inc. (*US*)
The August Agency LLC (*US*)
AVAnti Productions & Management (*UK*)
Joy Harris Literary Agency, Inc. (*US*)
Antony Harwood Limited (*UK*)
The Knight Agency (*US*)
Andrew Lownie Literary Agency Ltd (*UK*)
Martin Literary Management (*US*)
Thomas Moore Literary Agency (*UK*)
Venture Literary (*US*)
Eve White: Literary Agent (*UK*)
Medicine
The Agency Group, Ltd (*US*)
Ambassador Speakers Bureau & Literary Agency (*US*)
The Blumer Literary Agency, Inc. (*US*)
Rick Broadhead & Associates Literary Agency (*Can*)
Browne & Miller Literary Associates (*US*)
Jane Chelius Literary Agency, Inc. (*US*)
Edward B. Claflin Literary Agency, LLC (*US*)
The Creative Culture, Inc. (*US*)
Richard Curtis Associates, Inc. (*US*)
Liza Dawson Associates (*US*)
The Jennifer DeChiara Literary Agency (*US*)
Jim Donovan Literary (*US*)
Dupree / Miller and Associates Inc. Literary (*US*)
Judith Ehrlich Literary Management (*US*)
Felicia Eth Literary Representation (*US*)
Diana Finch Literary Agency (*US*)
Goodman Associates (*US*)
Laura Gross Literary Agency (*US*)
Antony Harwood Limited (*UK*)
InkWell Management (*US*)
International Transactions, Inc. (*US*)
Jabberwocky Literary Agency (*US*)
Jill Grinberg Literary Management LLC (*US*)

Frances Kelly (*UK*)
Kilburn Literary Agency (*UK*)
Harvey Klinger, Inc (*US*)
Kneerim & Williams (*US*)
Edite Kroll Literary Agency, Inc. (*US*)
KT Public Relations (*US*)
Laura Langlie, Literary Agent (*US*)
March Tenth, Inc. (*US*)
The Martell Agency (*US*)
Northern Lights Literary Services (*US*)
The Poynor Group (*US*)
Quicksilver Books Literary Agency (*US*)
The Rudy Agency (*US*)
Marly Rusoff & Associates, Inc. (*US*)
Susan Schulman, A Literary Agency (*US*)
The Science Factory (*UK*)
Scribblers House LLC Literary Agency (*US*)
The Swetky Agency and Associates (*US*)
Timberlake Literary Services, LLC (*US*)
2M Literary Agency Ltd (*US*)
Venture Literary (*US*)
Beth Vesel Literary Agency (*US*)
The Ward & Balkin Agency, Inc (*US*)
Eve White: Literary Agent (*UK*)
Wolfson Literary Agency (*US*)
The Zack Company, Inc (*US*)

Men's Interests
AVAnti Productions & Management (*UK*)
Rosica Colin Ltd (*UK*)
Conville & Walsh Ltd (*UK*)
The Creative Rights Agency (*UK*)
Antony Harwood Limited (*UK*)
Andrew Lownie Literary Agency Ltd (*UK*)
Lyons Literary LLC (*US*)
Makepeace Towle Literary Agency (*UK*)
The Seven Bridges Group (*US*)
Venture Literary (*US*)
Eve White: Literary Agent (*UK*)

Military
Artellus Limited (*UK*)
David Black Literary Agency (*US*)
Brandon & Associates (*UK*)
Rick Broadhead & Associates Literary Agency (*Can*)
The Choate Agency, LLC (*US*)
Edward B. Claflin Literary Agency, LLC (*US*)
Rosica Colin Ltd (*UK*)
Conville & Walsh Ltd (*UK*)
Liza Dawson Associates (*US*)
The Jennifer DeChiara Literary Agency (*US*)
Jim Donovan Literary (*US*)
Dystel & Goderich Literary Management (*US*)
Farris Literary Agency, Inc. (*US*)
Diana Finch Literary Agency (*US*)
FinePrint Literary Management (*US*)
The Susan Golomb Literary Agency (*US*)
Goodman Associates (*US*)
Antony Harwood Limited (*UK*)
Jabberwocky Literary Agency (*US*)
KT Public Relations (*US*)
The Candace Lake Agency (*US*)
The Literary Group (*US*)
Andrew Lownie Literary Agency Ltd (*UK*)

Lyons Literary LLC (*US*)
Duncan McAra (*UK*)
Lynne Rabinoff Agency (*US*)
Raines & Raines (*US*)
Robert Dudley Agency (*UK*)
The Rudy Agency (*US*)
The Seven Bridges Group (*US*)
Sheil Land Associates Ltd (*UK*)
Signature Literary Agency (*US*)
The Swetky Agency and Associates (*US*)
Timberlake Literary Services, LLC (*US*)
Venture Literary (*US*)
Eve White: Literary Agent (*UK*)
Wordserve Literary (*US*)
The Zack Company, Inc (*US*)

Music
Abrams Artists Agency (*US*)
The Agency Group, Ltd (*US*)
Arcadia (*US*)
AVAnti Productions & Management (*UK*)
Brandon & Associates (*UK*)
Jenny Brown Associates (*UK*)
Marie Brown Associates, Inc. (*US*)
W.M. Clark Associates (*US*)
The Creative Culture, Inc. (*US*)
The Jennifer DeChiara Literary Agency (*US*)
Jim Donovan Literary (*US*)
Dupree / Miller and Associates Inc. Literary (*US*)
Farris Literary Agency, Inc. (*US*)
Diana Finch Literary Agency (*US*)
FinePrint Literary Management (*US*)
Fredrica S. Friedman and Co. Inc. (*US*)
Goodman Associates (*US*)
Antony Harwood Limited (*UK*)
Johnson & Alcock (*UK*)
Harvey Klinger, Inc (*US*)
Sarah Lazin Books (*US*)
Robert Lecker Agency (*Can*)
Lyons Literary LLC (*US*)
March Tenth, Inc. (*US*)
Martha Millard Literary Agency (*US*)
The Jean V. Naggar Literary Agency (*US*)
Objective Entertainment (*US*)
The Sayle Literary Agency (*UK*)
Susan Schulman, A Literary Agency (*US*)
Lynn Seligman, Literary Agent (*US*)
The Seven Bridges Group (*US*)
South West Artists (*UK*)
Thomas Moore Literary Agency (*UK*)
Timberlake Literary Services, LLC (*US*)
2M Literary Agency Ltd (*US*)
Venture Literary (*US*)
The Weingel-Fidel Agency (*US*)
Whispering Buffalo Literary Agency Ltd (*UK*)
Eve White: Literary Agent (*UK*)
The Zack Company, Inc (*US*)
Helen Zimmermann Literary Agency (*US*)

Mystery
Abela Literature (*Can*)
Abrams Artists Agency (*US*)
Alive Communications, Inc (*US*)
Robert Astle & Associates Literary Management, Inc. (*US*)

AVAnti Productions & Management (*UK*)
The Bent Agency (*US*)
The Blumer Literary Agency, Inc. (*US*)
BookEnds, LLC (*US*)
The Barbara Bova Literary Agency (*US*)
The Joan Brandt Agency (*US*)
Barbara Braun Associates, Inc. (*US*)
Andrea Brown Literary Agency, Inc. (*US*)
Brown Literary Agency (*US*)
Browne & Miller Literary Associates (*US*)
Cedar Grove Agency Entertainment (*US*)
The Characters Talent Agency (*Can*)
The Choate Agency, LLC (*US*)
The Chudney Agency (*US*)
Cine/Lit Representation (*US*)
Rosica Colin Ltd (*UK*)
Conville & Walsh Ltd (*UK*)
Coombs Moylett Literary Agency (*UK*)
The Core Group Talent Agency, Inc. (*Can*)
CowlesRyan Agency (*US*)
The Croce Agency (*US*)
Darhansoff & Verrill Literary Agents (*US*)
Liza Dawson Associates (*US*)
The Jennifer DeChiara Literary Agency (*US*)
Jim Donovan Literary (*US*)
Dupree / Miller and Associates Inc. Literary (*US*)
Dystel & Goderich Literary Management (*US*)
Judith Ehrlich Literary Management (*US*)
Elaine P. English, Attorney & Literary Agent (*US*)
Fairbank Literary Representation (*US*)
Farris Literary Agency, Inc. (*US*)
FinePrint Literary Management (*US*)
Fox Mason Ltd (*UK*)
Samuel French, Inc. (*US*)
Full Throttle Literary Agency (*US*)
Goodman Associates (*US*)
Irene Goodman Literary Agency (*US*)
Ashley Grayson Literary Agency (*US*)
Laura Gross Literary Agency (*US*)
Joy Harris Literary Agency, Inc. (*US*)
Antony Harwood Limited (*UK*)
John Hawkins & Associates, Inc. (*US*)
InkWell Management (*US*)
International Transactions, Inc. (*US*)
Jabberwocky Literary Agency (*US*)
Virginia Kidd Agency, Inc (*US*)
Kilburn Literary Agency (*UK*)
Harvey Klinger, Inc (*US*)
The Knight Agency (*US*)
KT Public Relations (*US*)
The Candace Lake Agency (*US*)
Peter Lampack Agency, Inc (*US*)
Laura Langlie, Literary Agent (*US*)
Robert Lecker Agency (*Can*)
Lescher & Lescher (*US*)
The Lez Barstow Agency (*UK*)
The Literary Group (*US*)
The Jennifer Lyons Literary Agency, LLC (*US*)
Lyons Literary LLC (*US*)
Donald Maass Literary Agency (*US*)
MacGregor Literary (*US*)
Madeleine Milburn Literary Agency (*UK*)

Ricia Mainhardt Agency (RMA) (*US*)
The Martell Agency (*US*)
Martha Millard Literary Agency (*US*)
Monteiro Rose Dravis Agency, Inc. (*US*)
The Jean V. Naggar Literary Agency (*US*)
Niad Management (*US*)
Northern Lights Literary Services (*US*)
Objective Entertainment (*US*)
The Park Literary Group LLC (*US*)
Pavilion Literary Management (*US*)
Barry Perelman Agency (*US*)
Alièka Pistek Literary Agency, LLC (*US*)
The Poynor Group (*US*)
Prospect Agency (*US*)
Queen Literary Agency, Inc. (*US*)
Quicksilver Books Literary Agency (*US*)
Raines & Raines (*US*)
Renee Zuckerbrot Literary Agency (*US*)
The Amy Rennert Agency, Inc. (*US*)
Rocking Chair Books (*UK*)
Salkind Literary Agency (*US*)
Susan Schulman, A Literary Agency (*US*)
Secret Agent Man (*US*)
Lynn Seligman, Literary Agent (*US*)
The Seymour Agency (*US*)
Sheil Land Associates Ltd (*UK*)
Valerie Smith, Literary Agent (*US*)
South West Artists (*UK*)
Spectrum Literary Agency (*US*)
Spencerhill Associates (*US*)
Sternig & Byrne Literary Agency (*US*)
The Swetky Agency and Associates (*US*)
Talcott Notch Literary (*US*)
Timberlake Literary Services, LLC (*US*)
Tom Lee (*US*)
TriadaUS Literary Agency, Inc. (*US*)
Venture Literary (*US*)
Veritas Literary Agency (*US*)
The Ward & Balkin Agency, Inc (*US*)
Irene Webb Literary (*US*)
The Wendy Weil Agency, Inc. (*US*)
Westwood Creative Artists (*Can*)
Eve White: Literary Agent (*UK*)
Wolfson Literary Agency (*US*)
Writers' Representatives, LLC (*US*)
The Zack Company, Inc (*US*)
Helen Zimmermann Literary Agency (*US*)
Nature
The Agency Group, Ltd (*US*)
The Blumer Literary Agency, Inc. (*US*)
Brick House Literary Agents (*US*)
Rick Broadhead & Associates Literary Agency (*Can*)
Andrea Brown Literary Agency, Inc. (*US*)
Tracy Brown Literary Agency (*US*)
Browne & Miller Literary Associates (*US*)
The Choate Agency, LLC (*US*)
Cine/Lit Representation (*US*)
Rosica Colin Ltd (*UK*)
The Cooke Agency (*Can*)
CowlesRyan Agency (*US*)
Creative Authors Ltd (*UK*)
The Jennifer DeChiara Literary Agency (*US*)

Donadio & Olson, Inc. (*US*)
Jim Donovan Literary (*US*)
Diana Finch Literary Agency (*US*)
FinePrint Literary Management (*US*)
Sarah Jane Freymann Literary Agency (*US*)
The Susan Golomb Literary Agency (*US*)
Goodman Associates (*US*)
Antony Harwood Limited (*UK*)
John Hawkins & Associates, Inc. (*US*)
Rupert Heath Literary Agency (*UK*)
Kneerim & Williams (*US*)
Laura Langlie, Literary Agent (*US*)
LaunchBooks Literary Agency (*US*)
The Literary Group (*US*)
The Jennifer Lyons Literary Agency, LLC (*US*)
Jonathan Pegg Literary Agency (*UK*)
Quicksilver Books Literary Agency (*US*)
Redwood Agency (*US*)
Rocking Chair Books (*UK*)
Lynn Seligman, Literary Agent (*US*)
The Strothman Agency (*US*)
The Swetky Agency and Associates (*US*)
Talcott Notch Literary (*US*)
Thomas Moore Literary Agency (*UK*)
Timberlake Literary Services, LLC (*US*)
Jane Turnbull (*UK*)
Venture Literary (*US*)
Veritas Literary Agency (*US*)
The Ward & Balkin Agency, Inc (*US*)
Irene Webb Literary (*US*)
Whispering Buffalo Literary Agency Ltd (*UK*)
Eve White: Literary Agent (*UK*)
The Zack Company, Inc (*US*)
Helen Zimmermann Literary Agency (*US*)
New Age
The Blumer Literary Agency, Inc. (*US*)
Dystel & Goderich Literary Management (*US*)
Antony Harwood Limited (*UK*)
The Candace Lake Agency (*US*)
Ricia Mainhardt Agency (RMA) (*US*)
Martha Millard Literary Agency (*US*)
Northern Lights Literary Services (*US*)
Quicksilver Books Literary Agency (*US*)
Timberlake Literary Services, LLC (*US*)
Venture Literary (*US*)
Eve White: Literary Agent (*UK*)
Nonfiction
A+B Works (*US*)
Sheila Ableman Literary Agency (*UK*)
The Agency Group, Ltd (*US*)
Agency for the Performing Arts (APA) (*US*)
Aitken Alexander Associates (*UK*)
Alive Communications, Inc (*US*)
Miriam Altshuler Literary Agency (*US*)
Ambassador Speakers Bureau & Literary Agency (*US*)
The Ampersand Agency Ltd (*UK*)
Arcadia (*US*)
Artellus Limited (*UK*)
Robert Astle & Associates Literary Management, Inc. (*US*)
Audrey A. Wolf Literary Agency (*US*)
The August Agency LLC (*US*)

Author Rights Agency (*Ire*)
AVAnti Productions & Management (*UK*)
Avenue A Literary LLC (*US*)
Barer Literary, LLC (*US*)
Bell Lomax Moreton Agency (*UK*)
Lorella Belli Literary Agency (LBLA) (*UK*)
Faye Bender Literary Agency (*US*)
The Bent Agency (*US*)
Bidnick & Company (*US*)
Vicky Bijur Literary Agency (*US*)
David Black Literary Agency (*US*)
Blake Friedmann Literary Agency Ltd (*UK*)
The Blumer Literary Agency, Inc. (*US*)
Luigi Bonomi Associates Ltd (*UK*)
BookEnds, LLC (*US*)
Books & Such Literary Agency (*US*)
The Barbara Bova Literary Agency (*US*)
Brandon & Associates (*UK*)
The Joan Brandt Agency (*US*)
The Helen Brann Agency, Inc. (*US*)
Barbara Braun Associates, Inc. (*US*)
Paul Bresnick Literary Agency, LLC (*US*)
Brick House Literary Agents (*US*)
Rick Broadhead & Associates Literary Agency (*Can*)
Jenny Brown Associates (*UK*)
Marie Brown Associates, Inc. (*US*)
Andrea Brown Literary Agency, Inc. (*US*)
Tracy Brown Literary Agency (*US*)
Browne & Miller Literary Associates (*US*)
Felicity Bryan (*UK*)
Brie Burkeman & Serafina Clarke Ltd (*UK*)
Juliet Burton Literary Agency (*UK*)
Cameron Creswell Agency (*Aus*)
Campbell Thomson & McLaughlin Ltd (*UK*)
Capel & Land Ltd (*UK*)
CardenWright Literary Agency (*UK*)
Carnicelli Literary Management (*US*)
Chalberg & Sussman (*US*)
Mic Cheetham Literary Agency (*UK*)
Jane Chelius Literary Agency, Inc. (*US*)
Elyse Cheney Literary Associates, LLC (*US*)
Judith Chilcote Agency (*UK*)
The Choate Agency, LLC (*US*)
Cine/Lit Representation (*US*)
Edward B. Claflin Literary Agency, LLC (*US*)
W.M. Clark Associates (*US*)
Mary Clemmey Literary Agency (*UK*)
Jonathan Clowes Ltd (*UK*)
Rosica Colin Ltd (*UK*)
Conville & Walsh Ltd (*UK*)
Jane Conway-Gordon Ltd (*UK*)
The Cooke Agency (*Can*)
CowlesRyan Agency (*US*)
The Creative Rights Agency (*UK*)
The Creative Culture, Inc. (*US*)
Creative Authors Ltd (*UK*)
Rupert Crew Ltd (*UK*)
The Croce Agency (*US*)
The Culinary Entertainment Agency (CEA) (*US*)
The Mary Cunnane Agency Pty Ltd (*Aus*)
Curtis Brown Group Ltd (*UK*)
Richard Curtis Associates, Inc. (*US*)

The Michael Greer Literary Agency (*UK*)
Martha Millard Literary Agency (*US*)
Moore Literary Agency (*US*)
Patricia Moosbrugger Literary Agency (*US*)
Howard Morhaim Literary Agency (*US*)
William Morris Endeavor Entertainment (UK)
Ltd (*UK*)
The Jean V. Naggar Literary Agency (*US*)
Nappaland Literary Agency (*US*)
Nelson Literary Agency, LLC (*US*)
New Leaf Literary & Media, Inc. (*US*)
Niad Management (*US*)
Nine Muses and Apollo, Inc. (*US*)
MNLA (Maggie Noach Literary Agency) (*UK*)
Northern Lights Literary Services (*US*)
Andrew Nurnberg Associates, Ltd (*UK*)
Objective Entertainment (*US*)
Paradigm Talent and Literary Agency (*US*)
The Park Literary Group LLC (*US*)
Paterson Marsh Ltd (*UK*)
Pavilion Literary Management (*US*)
John Pawsey (*UK*)
Maggie Pearlstine Associates Ltd (*UK*)
Jonathan Pegg Literary Agency (*UK*)
The Peters Fraser & Dunlop Group Ltd (PFD)
(*UK*)
Alièka Pistek Literary Agency, LLC (*US*)
Shelley Power Literary Agency Ltd (*UK*)
The Poynor Group (*US*)
Prospect Agency (*US*)
Queen Literary Agency, Inc. (*US*)
Quicksilver Books Literary Agency (*US*)
Lynne Rabinoff Agency (*US*)
Raines & Raines (*US*)
Redhammer (*UK*)
Redwood Agency (*US*)
Regal Literary (*UK*)
Regal Literary Inc. (*US*)
Renee Zuckerbrot Literary Agency (*US*)
The Amy Rennert Agency, Inc. (*US*)
The Lisa Richards Agency (*Ire*)
Riverside Literary Agency (*US*)
Robert Dudley Agency (*UK*)
Robin Jones Literary Agency (*UK*)
Michael D. Robins & Associates (*US*)
Rocking Chair Books (*UK*)
Andy Ross Agency (*US*)
The Rudy Agency (*US*)
Uli Rushby-Smith Literary Agency (*UK*)
Marly Rusoff & Associates, Inc. (*US*)
Salkind Literary Agency (*US*)
The Sayle Literary Agency (*UK*)
Susan Schulman, A Literary Agency (*US*)
The Science Factory (*UK*)
Jonathan Scott, Inc (*US*)
Scribblers House LLC Literary Agency (*US*)
Secret Agent Man (*US*)
Lynn Seligman, Literary Agent (*US*)
Seventh Avenue Literary Agency (*Can*)
The Seymour Agency (*US*)
Denise Shannon Literary Agency, Inc. (*US*)
Sheil Land Associates Ltd (*UK*)
Signature Literary Agency (*US*)

Dorie Simmonds Agency (*UK*)
Jeffrey Simmons (*UK*)
Sinclair-Stevenson (*UK*)
SLW Literary Agency (*US*)
Robert Smith Literary Agency Ltd (*UK*)
Valerie Smith, Literary Agent (*US*)
Spectrum Literary Agency (*US*)
Spencerhill Associates (*US*)
Standen Literary Agency (*UK*)
P. Stathonikos Agency (*Can*)
Elaine Steel (*UK*)
Abner Stein (*UK*)
Sternig & Byrne Literary Agency (*US*)
Rebecca Strong International Literary Agency
(*US*)
The Strothman Agency (*US*)
The Stuart Agency (*US*)
Susanna Lea Associates (UK) (*UK*)
The Susijn Agency (*UK*)
The Swetky Agency and Associates (*US*)
SYLA - Susan Yearwood Literary Agency (*UK*)
Talcott Notch Literary (*US*)
Tessler Literary Agency (*US*)
Thomas Moore Literary Agency (*UK*)
Timberlake Literary Services, LLC (*US*)
TriadaUS Literary Agency, Inc. (*US*)
Jane Turnbull (*UK*)
2M Literary Agency Ltd (*US*)
United Agents (*UK*)
Venture Literary (*US*)
Veritas Literary Agency (*US*)
Beth Vesel Literary Agency (*US*)
Ed Victor Ltd (*UK*)
Wade & Doherty Literary Agency (*UK*)
The Ward & Balkin Agency, Inc (*US*)
Watson, Little Ltd (*UK*)
A.P. Watt Ltd (*UK*)
Irene Webb Literary (*US*)
The Wendy Weil Agency, Inc. (*US*)
The Weingel-Fidel Agency (*US*)
Wernick & Pratt Agency (*US*)
Westwood Creative Artists (*Can*)
Whimsy Literary Agency, LLC (*US*)
Whispering Buffalo Literary Agency Ltd (*UK*)
Eve White: Literary Agent (*UK*)
Wolfson Literary Agency (*US*)
Wordserve Literary (*US*)
Writers' Representatives, LLC (*US*)
The Wylie Agency (UK) Ltd (*UK*)
Yates & Yates (*US*)
The Zack Company, Inc (*US*)
Karen Gantz Zahler Literary Agency (*US*)
Helen Zimmermann Literary Agency (*US*)
Philosophy
AVAnti Productions & Management (*UK*)
W.M. Clark Associates (*US*)
Dupree / Miller and Associates Inc. Literary (*US*)
Fox Mason Ltd (*UK*)
Frances Goldin Literary Agency, Inc. (*US*)
Goodman Associates (*US*)
Greene & Heaton Ltd (*UK*)
Hardman & Swainson (*UK*)
Antony Harwood Limited (*UK*)

The Swetky Agency and Associates (*US*)
Thomas Moore Literary Agency (*UK*)
Venture Literary (*US*)
Eve White: Literary Agent (*UK*)
Writers' Representatives, LLC (*US*)

Photography
AVAnti Productions & Management (*UK*)
The Blumer Literary Agency, Inc. (*US*)
Barbara Braun Associates, Inc. (*US*)
Andrea Brown Literary Agency, Inc. (*US*)
The Jennifer DeChiara Literary Agency (*US*)
Dupree / Miller and Associates Inc. Literary (*US*)
Diana Finch Literary Agency (*US*)
Fresh Books Literary Agency (*US*)
Fredrica S. Friedman and Co. Inc. (*US*)
Antony Harwood Limited (*UK*)
Martha Millard Literary Agency (*US*)
Regal Literary (*UK*)
Regal Literary Inc. (*US*)
Salkind Literary Agency (*US*)
Lynn Seligman, Literary Agent (*US*)
The Swetky Agency and Associates (*US*)
Thomas Moore Literary Agency (*UK*)
Venture Literary (*US*)
Eve White: Literary Agent (*UK*)

Poetry
AVAnti Productions & Management (*UK*)
Bookseeker Agency (*UK*)
Eddison Pearson Ltd (*UK*)
Johnson & Alcock (*UK*)
Thomas Moore Literary Agency (*UK*)
Tom Lee (*US*)
Writers' Representatives, LLC (*US*)

Politics
The Agency Group, Ltd (*US*)
Ambassador Speakers Bureau & Literary Agency (*US*)
Robert Astle & Associates Literary Management, Inc. (*US*)
Audrey A. Wolf Literary Agency (*US*)
The August Agency LLC (*US*)
Vicky Bijur Literary Agency (*US*)
David Black Literary Agency (*US*)
Brandon & Associates (*UK*)
Barbara Braun Associates, Inc. (*US*)
Rick Broadhead & Associates Literary Agency (*Can*)
Elyse Cheney Literary Associates, LLC (*US*)
The Choate Agency, LLC (*US*)
The Cooke Agency (*Can*)
Liza Dawson Associates (*US*)
The Jennifer DeChiara Literary Agency (*US*)
Jim Donovan Literary (*US*)
Dupree / Miller and Associates Inc. Literary (*US*)
Dystel & Goderich Literary Management (*US*)
Judith Ehrlich Literary Management (*US*)
Einstein Thompson Agency (*US*)
Felicia Eth Literary Representation (*US*)
Farris Literary Agency, Inc. (*US*)
Diana Finch Literary Agency (*US*)
Fredrica S. Friedman and Co. Inc. (*US*)
The Gernert Company (*US*)
Mark Gilroy Communications, Inc. (*US*)

The Susan Golomb Literary Agency (*US*)
Goodman Associates (*US*)
Greene & Heaton Ltd (*UK*)
Laura Gross Literary Agency (*US*)
Antony Harwood Limited (*UK*)
Rupert Heath Literary Agency (*UK*)
hhb agency ltd (*UK*)
Andrea Hurst Literary Management (*US*)
Jabberwocky Literary Agency (*US*)
Jill Grinberg Literary Management LLC (*US*)
Kilburn Literary Agency (*UK*)
Kneerim & Williams (*US*)
Edite Kroll Literary Agency, Inc. (*US*)
Laura Langlie, Literary Agent (*US*)
LaunchBooks Literary Agency (*US*)
Sarah Lazin Books (*US*)
Lippincott Massie McQuilkin (*US*)
Andrew Lownie Literary Agency Ltd (*UK*)
Lyons Literary LLC (*US*)
Makepeace Towle Literary Agency (*UK*)
Objective Entertainment (*US*)
The Park Literary Group LLC (*US*)
Lynne Rabinoff Agency (*US*)
Robert Dudley Agency (*UK*)
Salkind Literary Agency (*US*)
Susan Schulman, A Literary Agency (*US*)
The Science Factory (*UK*)
Scribblers House LLC Literary Agency (*US*)
Lynn Seligman, Literary Agent (*US*)
The Seven Bridges Group (*US*)
Denise Shannon Literary Agency, Inc. (*US*)
Sheil Land Associates Ltd (*UK*)
Signature Literary Agency (*US*)
Jeffrey Simmons (*UK*)
The Swetky Agency and Associates (*US*)
Timberlake Literary Services, LLC (*US*)
2M Literary Agency Ltd (*US*)
Venture Literary (*US*)
Whimsy Literary Agency, LLC (*US*)
Whispering Buffalo Literary Agency Ltd (*UK*)
Eve White: Literary Agent (*UK*)
Writers' Representatives, LLC (*US*)
Yates & Yates (*US*)
The Zack Company, Inc (*US*)
Karen Gantz Zahler Literary Agency (*US*)

Psychology
The Agency Group, Ltd (*US*)
Miriam Altshuler Literary Agency (*US*)
Arcadia (*US*)
AVAnti Productions & Management (*UK*)
Vicky Bijur Literary Agency (*US*)
The Blumer Literary Agency, Inc. (*US*)
BookEnds, LLC (*US*)
Barbara Braun Associates, Inc. (*US*)
Paul Bresnick Literary Agency, LLC (*US*)
Tracy Brown Literary Agency (*US*)
Browne & Miller Literary Associates (*US*)
Carnicelli Literary Management (*US*)
Chalberg & Sussman (*US*)
Edward B. Claflin Literary Agency, LLC (*US*)
Rosica Colin Ltd (*UK*)
Conville & Walsh Ltd (*UK*)
CowlesRyan Agency (*US*)

The Creative Culture, Inc. (*US*)
Liza Dawson Associates (*US*)
The Jennifer DeChiara Literary Agency (*US*)
Joëlle Delbourgo Associates, Inc. (*US*)
Dupree / Miller and Associates Inc. Literary (*US*)
Dystel & Goderich Literary Management (*US*)
Judith Ehrlich Literary Management (*US*)
Einstein Thompson Agency (*US*)
Felicia Eth Literary Representation (*US*)
Diana Finch Literary Agency (*US*)
Fox Mason Ltd (*UK*)
Fox & Howard Literary Agency (*UK*)
Sarah Jane Freymann Literary Agency (*US*)
Fredrica S. Friedman and Co. Inc. (*US*)
Furniss Lawton (*UK*)
The Susan Golomb Literary Agency (*US*)
Goodman Associates (*US*)
Graham Maw Christie Literary Agency (*UK*)
Kathryn Green Literary Agency, LLC (*US*)
Laura Gross Literary Agency (*US*)
Antony Harwood Limited (*UK*)
John Hawkins & Associates, Inc. (*US*)
A M Heath & Company Limited, Author's
Agents (*UK*)
The Jeff Herman Agency, LLC (*US*)
Hidden Value Group (*US*)
Andrea Hurst Literary Management (*US*)
InkWell Management (*US*)
Jill Grinberg Literary Management LLC (*US*)
Kilburn Literary Agency (*UK*)
Harvey Klinger, Inc (*US*)
Kneerim & Williams (*US*)
The Knight Agency (*US*)
Bert P. Krages (*US*)
Edite Kroll Literary Agency, Inc (*US*)
KT Public Relations (*US*)
The LA Literary Agency (*US*)
Peter Lampack Agency, Inc (*US*)
Laura Langlie, Literary Agent (*US*)
Lippincott Massie McQuilkin (*US*)
The Literary Group (*US*)
Lowenstein Associates, Inc. (*US*)
Kirsten Manges Literary Agency, LLC (*US*)
The Martell Agency (*US*)
The Michael Greer Literary Agency (*UK*)
Martha Millard Literary Agency (*US*)
The Jean V. Naggar Literary Agency (*US*)
Northern Lights Literary Services (*US*)
Paterson Marsh Ltd (*UK*)
Jonathan Pegg Literary Agency (*UK*)
Queen Literary Agency, Inc. (*US*)
Quicksilver Books Literary Agency (*US*)
Lynne Rabinoff Agency (*US*)
Raines & Raines (*US*)
Redwood Agency (*US*)
Rees Literary Agency (*US*)
Marly Rusoff & Associates, Inc. (*US*)
Salkind Literary Agency (*US*)
Susan Schulman, A Literary Agency (*US*)
Scribblers House LLC Literary Agency (*US*)
Lynn Seligman, Literary Agent (*US*)
Sheil Land Associates Ltd (*UK*)
Jeffrey Simmons (*UK*)

The Stuart Agency (*US*)
The Swetky Agency and Associates (*US*)
Tessler Literary Agency (*US*)
Timberlake Literary Services, LLC (*US*)
TriadaUS Literary Agency, Inc. (*US*)
2M Literary Agency Ltd (*US*)
Venture Literary (*US*)
Beth Vesel Literary Agency (*US*)
The Ward & Balkin Agency, Inc (*US*)
Watson, Little Ltd (*UK*)
The Weingel-Fidel Agency (*US*)
Whimsy Literary Agency, LLC (*US*)
Eve White: Literary Agent (*UK*)
Wordserve Literary (*US*)
Karen Gantz Zahler Literary Agency (*US*)
Radio
AVAnti Productions & Management (*UK*)
Blake Friedmann Literary Agency Ltd (*UK*)
Alan Brodie Representation Ltd (*UK*)
Capel & Land Ltd (*UK*)
Mary Clemmey Literary Agency (*UK*)
Jonathan Clowes Ltd (*UK*)
Rosica Colin Ltd (*UK*)
Curtis Brown Group Ltd (*UK*)
Film Rights Ltd in association with Laurence
Fitch Ltd (*UK*)
Jill Foster Ltd (JFL) (*UK*)
Antony Harwood Limited (*UK*)
Valerie Hoskins Associates (*UK*)
Independent Talent Group Ltd (*UK*)
The Lez Barstow Agency (*UK*)
Andrew Mann Ltd (*UK*)
Marjacq Scripts Ltd (*UK*)
MBA Literary Agents Ltd (*UK*)
Bill McLean Personal Management Ltd (*UK*)
PBJ and JBJ Management (*UK*)
The Peters Fraser & Dunlop Group Ltd (PFD)
(*UK*)
Sayle Screen Ltd (*UK*)
The Tennyson Agency (*UK*)
Thomas Moore Literary Agency (*UK*)
United Agents (*UK*)
Venture Literary (*US*)
Eve White: Literary Agent (*UK*)
Reference
BookEnds, LLC (*US*)
Joëlle Delbourgo Associates, Inc. (*US*)
Jim Donovan Literary (*US*)
The Epstein Literary Agency (*US*)
Fairbank Literary Representation (*US*)
FinePrint Literary Management (*US*)
Fox & Howard Literary Agency (*UK*)
Fresh Books Literary Agency (*US*)
Graham Maw Christie Literary Agency (*UK*)
The Jeff Herman Agency, LLC (*US*)
Kate Hordern Literary Agency (*UK*)
Frances Kelly (*UK*)
Julia Lord Literary Management (*US*)
Andrew Lownie Literary Agency Ltd (*UK*)
Denise Marcil Literary Agency, Inc. (*US*)
Redwood Agency (*US*)
Signature Literary Agency (*US*)
Thomas Moore Literary Agency (*UK*)

Writers' Representatives, LLC (*US*)
The Zack Company, Inc (*US*)
Religious
Alive Communications, Inc (*US*)
Ambassador Speakers Bureau & Literary Agency (*US*)
AVAnti Productions & Management (*UK*)
The Blumer Literary Agency, Inc. (*US*)
Books & Such Literary Agency (*US*)
Marie Brown Associates, Inc. (*US*)
Browne & Miller Literary Associates (*US*)
Kelvin C. Bulger and Associates (*US*)
W.M. Clark Associates (*US*)
Rosica Colin Ltd (*UK*)
Dupree / Miller and Associates Inc. Literary (*US*)
Dystel & Goderich Literary Management (*US*)
Eames Literary Services, LLC (*US*)
Farris Literary Agency, Inc. (*US*)
FinePrint Literary Management (*US*)
Mark Gilroy Communications, Inc. (*US*)
Antony Harwood Limited (*UK*)
Hidden Value Group (*US*)
Andrea Hurst Literary Management (*US*)
Kilburn Literary Agency (*UK*)
Kneerim & Williams (*US*)
Edite Kroll Literary Agency, Inc. (*US*)
The Steve Laube Agency (*US*)
The Literary Group (*US*)
Literary Management Group, Inc. (*US*)
The Jennifer Lyons Literary Agency, LLC (*US*)
MacGregor Literary (*US*)
Nappaland Literary Agency (*US*)
The Poynor Group (*US*)
Quicksilver Books Literary Agency (*US*)
Lynne Rabinoff Agency (*US*)
Andy Ross Agency (*US*)
Salkind Literary Agency (*US*)
Susan Schulman, A Literary Agency (*US*)
Secret Agent Man (*US*)
The Seymour Agency (*US*)
The Stuart Agency (*US*)
The Swetky Agency and Associates (*US*)
Tom Lee (*US*)
Venture Literary (*US*)
Whimsy Literary Agency, LLC (*US*)
Eve White: Literary Agent (*UK*)
Wordserve Literary (*US*)
Yates & Yates (*US*)
The Zack Company, Inc (*US*)
Karen Gantz Zahler Literary Agency (*US*)
Romance
Abrams Artists Agency (*US*)
AVAnti Productions & Management (*UK*)
The Bent Agency (*US*)
BookEnds, LLC (*US*)
Books & Such Literary Agency (*US*)
Jenny Brown Associates (*UK*)
Andrea Brown Literary Agency, Inc. (*US*)
Brown Literary Agency (*US*)
Cedar Grove Agency Entertainment (*US*)
The Characters Talent Agency (*Can*)
Elyse Cheney Literary Associates, LLC (*US*)
Rosica Colin Ltd (*UK*)

The Cooke Agency (*Can*)
The Core Group Talent Agency, Inc. (*Can*)
Dorian Literary Agency (DLA) (*UK*)
Judith Ehrlich Literary Management (*US*)
Elaine P. English, Attorney & Literary Agent (*US*)
Farris Literary Agency, Inc. (*US*)
FinePrint Literary Management (*US*)
Irene Goodman Literary Agency (*US*)
Ashley Grayson Literary Agency (*US*)
Kathryn Green Literary Agency, LLC (*US*)
Greene & Heaton Ltd (*UK*)
Greyhaus Literary Agency (*US*)
Antony Harwood Limited (*UK*)
Hopkins Literary Associates (*US*)
Andrea Hurst Literary Management (*US*)
Jaret Entertainment (*US*)
Jill Grinberg Literary Management LLC (*US*)
Charlene Kay Agency (*Can*)
Kilburn Literary Agency (*UK*)
Harvey Klinger, Inc (*US*)
The Knight Agency (*US*)
KT Public Relations (*US*)
The Candace Lake Agency (*US*)
The Literary Group (*US*)
Donald Maass Literary Agency (*US*)
MacGregor Literary (*US*)
Ricia Mainhardt Agency (RMA) (*US*)
Martha Millard Literary Agency (*US*)
Monteiro Rose Dravis Agency, Inc. (*US*)
Howard Morhaim Literary Agency (*US*)
The Jean V. Naggar Literary Agency (*US*)
Nelson Literary Agency, LLC (*US*)
New Leaf Literary & Media, Inc. (*US*)
Niad Management (*US*)
Northern Lights Literary Services (*US*)
Barry Perelman Agency (*US*)
Alièka Pistek Literary Agency, LLC (*US*)
The Poynor Group (*US*)
Prospect Agency (*US*)
Rocking Chair Books (*UK*)
Lynn Seligman, Literary Agent (*US*)
The Seymour Agency (*US*)
Sheil Land Associates Ltd (*UK*)
South West Artists (*UK*)
Spectrum Literary Agency (*US*)
Spencerhill Associates (*US*)
Pam Strickler Author Management (*US*)
The Swetky Agency and Associates (*US*)
Thomas Moore Literary Agency (*UK*)
Timberlake Literary Services, LLC (*US*)
TriadaUS Literary Agency, Inc. (*US*)
Whispering Buffalo Literary Agency Ltd (*UK*)
Eve White: Literary Agent (*UK*)
Wolfson Literary Agency (*US*)
Wordserve Literary (*US*)
The Zack Company, Inc (*US*)
Science
Sheila Ableman Literary Agency (*UK*)
Arcadia (*US*)
Artellus Limited (*UK*)
Faye Bender Literary Agency (*US*)
Vicky Bijur Literary Agency (*US*)

Luigi Bonomi Associates Ltd (*UK*)
BookEnds, LLC (*US*)
The Barbara Bova Literary Agency (*US*)
Brick House Literary Agents (*US*)
Rick Broadhead & Associates Literary Agency (*Can*)
Jenny Brown Associates (*UK*)
Andrea Brown Literary Agency, Inc. (*US*)
Browne & Miller Literary Associates (*US*)
Felicity Bryan (*UK*)
Carnicelli Literary Management (*US*)
Cedar Grove Agency Entertainment (*US*)
Chalberg & Sussman (*US*)
The Characters Talent Agency (*Can*)
Elyse Cheney Literary Associates, LLC (*US*)
The Choate Agency, LLC (*US*)
W.M. Clark Associates (*US*)
Rosica Colin Ltd (*UK*)
Conville & Walsh Ltd (*UK*)
The Cooke Agency (*Can*)
CowlesRyan Agency (*US*)
The Creative Culture, Inc. (*US*)
The Croce Agency (*US*)
Curtis Brown Group Ltd (*UK*)
Richard Curtis Associates, Inc. (*US*)
The Jennifer DeChiara Literary Agency (*US*)
Joëlle Delbourgo Associates, Inc. (*US*)
Donadio & Olson, Inc. (*US*)
Dupree / Miller and Associates Inc. Literary (*US*)
Dystel & Goderich Literary Management (*US*)
Judith Ehrlich Literary Management (*US*)
Einstein Thompson Agency (*US*)
Felicia Eth Literary Representation (*US*)
Fairbank Literary Representation (*US*)
Diana Finch Literary Agency (*US*)
FinePrint Literary Management (*US*)
Fresh Books Literary Agency (*US*)
Sarah Jane Freymann Literary Agency (*US*)
Furniss Lawton (*UK*)
The Gernert Company (*US*)
The Susan Golomb Literary Agency (*US*)
Goodman Associates (*US*)
Ashley Grayson Literary Agency (*US*)
Greene & Heaton Ltd (*UK*)
Hardman & Swainson (*UK*)
Antony Harwood Limited (*UK*)
John Hawkins & Associates, Inc. (*US*)
Rupert Heath Literary Agency (*UK*)
Andrea Hurst Literary Management (*US*)
Jabberwocky Literary Agency (*US*)
Jill Grinberg Literary Management LLC (*US*)
Charlene Kay Agency (*Can*)
Kilburn Literary Agency (*UK*)
Harvey Klinger, Inc (*US*)
Kneerim & Williams (*US*)
Bert P. Krages (*US*)
The Candace Lake Agency (*US*)
The LA Literary Agency (*US*)
Laura Langlie, Literary Agent (*US*)
LaunchBooks Literary Agency (*US*)
Robert Lecker Agency (*Can*)
Lippincott Massie McQuilkin (*US*)
The Literary Group (*US*)

Julia Lord Literary Management (*US*)
Lowenstein Associates, Inc. (*US*)
Lyons Literary LLC (*US*)
Makepeace Towle Literary Agency (*UK*)
Kirsten Manges Literary Agency, LLC (*US*)
The Jean V. Naggar Literary Agency (*US*)
The Park Literary Group LLC (*US*)
Pavilion Literary Management (*US*)
Jonathan Pegg Literary Agency (*UK*)
Barry Perelman Agency (*US*)
Alièka Pistek Literary Agency, LLC (*US*)
Prospect Agency (*US*)
Queen Literary Agency, Inc. (*US*)
Quicksilver Books Literary Agency (*US*)
Lynne Rabinoff Agency (*US*)
Redhammer (*UK*)
Rees Literary Agency (*US*)
Regal Literary (*UK*)
Regal Literary Inc. (*US*)
Renee Zuckerbrot Literary Agency (*US*)
Andy Ross Agency (*US*)
The Rudy Agency (*US*)
Salkind Literary Agency (*US*)
The Sayle Literary Agency (*UK*)
The Science Factory (*UK*)
Lynn Seligman, Literary Agent (*US*)
Sheil Land Associates Ltd (*UK*)
Signature Literary Agency (*US*)
Rebecca Strong International Literary Agency (*US*)
The Strothman Agency (*US*)
The Stuart Agency (*US*)
The Swetky Agency and Associates (*US*)
Talcott Notch Literary (*US*)
Tessler Literary Agency (*US*)
Timberlake Literary Services, LLC (*US*)
2M Literary Agency Ltd (*US*)
Venture Literary (*US*)
Veritas Literary Agency (*US*)
Watson, Little Ltd (*UK*)
The Wendy Weil Agency, Inc. (*US*)
The Weingel-Fidel Agency (*US*)
Westwood Creative Artists (*Can*)
Eve White: Literary Agent (*UK*)
Writers' Representatives, LLC (*US*)
The Zack Company, Inc (*US*)

Sci-Fi
Abela Literature (*Can*)
Artellus Limited (*UK*)
Author Rights Agency (*Ire*)
AVAnti Productions & Management (*UK*)
The Barbara Bova Literary Agency (*US*)
Andrea Brown Literary Agency, Inc. (*US*)
Mic Cheetham Literary Agency (*UK*)
The Cooke Agency (*Can*)
Liza Dawson Associates (*US*)
Dorian Literary Agency (DLA) (*UK*)
FinePrint Literary Management (*US*)
Fox Mason Ltd (*UK*)
The Gernert Company (*US*)
Ashley Grayson Literary Agency (*US*)
Greene & Heaton Ltd (*UK*)
Antony Harwood Limited (*UK*)

Andrea Hurst Literary Management (*US*)
Jabberwocky Literary Agency (*US*)
Jaret Entertainment (*US*)
Jill Grinberg Literary Management LLC (*US*)
Johnson & Alcock (*UK*)
Virginia Kidd Agency, Inc (*US*)
Harvey Klinger, Inc (*US*)
The Knight Agency (*US*)
KT Public Relations (*US*)
The Candace Lake Agency (*US*)
The Lez Barstow Agency (*UK*)
Lowenstein Associates, Inc. (*US*)
The Jennifer Lyons Literary Agency, LLC (*US*)
Donald Maass Literary Agency (*US*)
Ricia Mainhardt Agency (RMA) (*US*)
Makepeace Towle Literary Agency (*UK*)
Martha Millard Literary Agency (*US*)
Monteiro Rose Dravis Agency, Inc. (*US*)
Howard Morhaim Literary Agency (*US*)
Nelson Literary Agency, LLC (*US*)
New Leaf Literary & Media, Inc. (*US*)
Objective Entertainment (*US*)
Prospect Agency (*US*)
Raines & Raines (*US*)
Salkind Literary Agency (*US*)
Scribe Agency LLC (*US*)
Lynn Seligman, Literary Agent (*US*)
The Seymour Agency (*US*)
Sheil Land Associates Ltd (*UK*)
Valerie Smith, Literary Agent (*US*)
South West Artists (*UK*)
Spectrum Literary Agency (*US*)
Sternig & Byrne Literary Agency (*US*)
The Swetky Agency and Associates (*US*)
Talcott Notch Literary (*US*)
Tom Lee (*US*)
TriadaUS Literary Agency, Inc. (*US*)
Veritas Literary Agency (*US*)
Whispering Buffalo Literary Agency Ltd (*UK*)
Eve White: Literary Agent (*UK*)
Wordserve Literary (*US*)
The Zack Company, Inc (*US*)
Scripts
Above the Line Agency (*US*)
Abrams Artists Agency (*US*)
Bret Adams Ltd (*US*)
Agency for the Performing Arts (APA) (*US*)
Aimee Entertainment Agency (*US*)
Anonymous Content (*US*)
Author Literary Agents (*UK*)
AVAnti Productions & Management (*UK*)
Berlin Associates (*UK*)
Blake Friedmann Literary Agency Ltd (*UK*)
Alan Brodie Representation Ltd (*UK*)
Marcus Bryan & Associates Inc. (*US*)
Kelvin C. Bulger and Associates (*US*)
Brie Burkeman & Serafina Clarke Ltd (*UK*)
Cameron Creswell Agency (*Aus*)
CardenWright Literary Agency (*UK*)
Cedar Grove Agency Entertainment (*US*)
The Characters Talent Agency (*Can*)
Mary Clemmey Literary Agency (*UK*)
Jonathan Clowes Ltd (*UK*)

Rosica Colin Ltd (*UK*)
The Collective (*US*)
The Core Group Talent Agency, Inc. (*Can*)
Creative Trust, Inc. (*US*)
Criterion Group, Inc. (*US*)
Curtis Brown Group Ltd (*UK*)
Felix de Wolfe (*UK*)
Farris Literary Agency, Inc. (*US*)
Film Rights Ltd in association with Laurence
Fitch Ltd (*UK*)
Jill Foster Ltd (JFL) (*UK*)
Samuel French, Inc. (*US*)
Full Throttle Literary Agency (*US*)
The Gage Group (*US*)
Eric Glass Ltd (*UK*)
Roger Hancock Ltd (*UK*)
David Higham Associates Ltd (*UK*)
Valerie Hoskins Associates (*UK*)
Amanda Howard Associates Ltd (*UK*)
Independent Talent Group Ltd (*UK*)
Janet Fillingham Associates (*UK*)
Jaret Entertainment (*US*)
Michelle Kass Associates (*UK*)
Charlene Kay Agency (*Can*)
Ki Agency Ltd (*UK*)
Kilburn Literary Agency (*UK*)
Knight Hall Agency (*UK*)
The Candace Lake Agency (*US*)
The Lez Barstow Agency (*UK*)
Madeleine Milburn Literary Agency (*UK*)
Andrew Mann Ltd (*UK*)
Marjacq Scripts Ltd (*UK*)
The Marton Agency, Inc. (*US*)
MBA Literary Agents Ltd (*UK*)
MBE (*UK*)
Bill McLean Personal Management Ltd (*UK*)
The Michael Greer Literary Agency (*UK*)
Monteiro Rose Dravis Agency, Inc. (*US*)
William Morris Endeavor Entertainment (UK)
Ltd (*UK*)
Niad Management (*US*)
Objective Entertainment (*US*)
Paradigm Talent and Literary Agency (*US*)
PBJ and JBJ Management (*UK*)
Peregrine Whittlesey Agency (*US*)
Barry Perelman Agency (*US*)
The Peters Fraser & Dunlop Group Ltd (PFD)
(*UK*)
The Lisa Richards Agency (*Ire*)
Michael D. Robins & Associates (*US*)
Sayle Screen Ltd (*UK*)
Susan Schulman, A Literary Agency (*US*)
Linda Seifert Management (*UK*)
The Seven Bridges Group (*US*)
Sheil Land Associates Ltd (*UK*)
South West Artists (*UK*)
Elaine Steel (*UK*)
Stone Manners Salners Agency (*US*)
The Swetky Agency and Associates (*US*)
The Tennyson Agency (*UK*)
Thomas Moore Literary Agency (*UK*)
Tom Lee (*US*)
United Agents (*UK*)

A.P. Watt Ltd (*UK*)
Self-Help
The Agency Group, Ltd (*US*)
Alive Communications, Inc (*US*)
Miriam Altshuler Literary Agency (*US*)
Ambassador Speakers Bureau & Literary Agency
  (*US*)
Arcadia (*US*)
Audrey A. Wolf Literary Agency (*US*)
Vicky Bijur Literary Agency (*US*)
The Blumer Literary Agency, Inc. (*US*)
The Barbara Bova Literary Agency (*US*)
Rick Broadhead & Associates Literary Agency
  (*Can*)
Browne & Miller Literary Associates (*US*)
Edward B. Claflin Literary Agency, LLC (*US*)
CowlesRyan Agency (*US*)
The Creative Culture, Inc. (*US*)
Liza Dawson Associates (*US*)
The Jennifer DeChiara Literary Agency (*US*)
Dupree / Miller and Associates Inc. Literary (*US*)
Ebeling & Associates (*US*)
Judith Ehrlich Literary Management (*US*)
Farris Literary Agency, Inc. (*US*)
Diana Finch Literary Agency (*US*)
FinePrint Literary Management (*US*)
Fresh Books Literary Agency (*US*)
Sarah Jane Freymann Literary Agency (*US*)
Fredrica S. Friedman and Co. Inc. (*US*)
Mark Gilroy Communications, Inc. (*US*)
Graham Maw Christie Literary Agency (*UK*)
Ashley Grayson Literary Agency (*US*)
Kathryn Green Literary Agency, LLC (*US*)
Antony Harwood Limited (*UK*)
The Jeff Herman Agency, LLC (*US*)
Hidden Value Group (*US*)
Andrea Hurst Literary Management (*US*)
InkWell Management (*US*)
Johnson & Alcock (*UK*)
Frances Kelly (*UK*)
Harvey Klinger, Inc (*US*)
The Knight Agency (*US*)
Edite Kroll Literary Agency, Inc. (*US*)
MacGregor Literary (*US*)
Ricia Mainhardt Agency (RMA) (*US*)
Denise Marcil Literary Agency, Inc. (*US*)
The Martell Agency (*US*)
Martin Literary Management (*US*)
MBA Literary Agents Ltd (*UK*)
Martha Millard Literary Agency (*US*)
Northern Lights Literary Services (*US*)
Quicksilver Books Literary Agency (*US*)
Redwood Agency (*US*)
Rees Literary Agency (*US*)
The Lisa Richards Agency (*Ire*)
Salkind Literary Agency (*US*)
Susan Schulman, A Literary Agency (*US*)
Scribblers House LLC Literary Agency (*US*)
Lynn Seligman, Literary Agent (*US*)
Sheil Land Associates Ltd (*UK*)
Valerie Smith, Literary Agent (*US*)
The Swetky Agency and Associates (*US*)
Timberlake Literary Services, LLC (*US*)

TriadaUS Literary Agency, Inc. (*US*)
Venture Literary (*US*)
Veritas Literary Agency (*US*)
Watson, Little Ltd (*UK*)
Irene Webb Literary (*US*)
Whimsy Literary Agency, LLC (*US*)
Whispering Buffalo Literary Agency Ltd (*UK*)
Eve White: Literary Agent (*UK*)
Wordserve Literary (*US*)
Writers' Representatives, LLC (*US*)
The Zack Company, Inc (*US*)
Short Stories
Alive Communications, Inc (*US*)
AVAnti Productions & Management (*UK*)
Barer Literary, LLC (*US*)
The Joan Brandt Agency (*US*)
Full Throttle Literary Agency (*US*)
Joy Harris Literary Agency, Inc. (*US*)
Antony Harwood Limited (*UK*)
John Hawkins & Associates, Inc. (*US*)
International Transactions, Inc. (*US*)
Kilburn Literary Agency (*UK*)
Laura Langlie, Literary Agent (*US*)
Andrew Lownie Literary Agency Ltd (*UK*)
MacGregor Literary (*US*)
Martha Millard Literary Agency (*US*)
Regal Literary Inc. (*US*)
Renee Zuckerbrot Literary Agency (*US*)
Scribe Agency LLC (*US*)
The Seven Bridges Group (*US*)
The Swetky Agency and Associates (*US*)
Thomas Moore Literary Agency (*UK*)
Tom Lee (*US*)
Venture Literary (*US*)
Sociology
Miriam Altshuler Literary Agency (*US*)
The August Agency LLC (*US*)
AVAnti Productions & Management (*UK*)
Vicky Bijur Literary Agency (*US*)
The Barbara Bova Literary Agency (*US*)
Barbara Braun Associates, Inc. (*US*)
Andrea Brown Literary Agency, Inc. (*US*)
Browne & Miller Literary Associates (*US*)
W.M. Clark Associates (*US*)
The Creative Culture, Inc. (*US*)
Liza Dawson Associates (*US*)
The Jennifer DeChiara Literary Agency (*US*)
Dupree / Miller and Associates Inc. Literary (*US*)
Judith Ehrlich Literary Management (*US*)
Felicia Eth Literary Representation (*US*)
Fredrica S. Friedman and Co. Inc. (*US*)
The Gernert Company (*US*)
Frances Goldin Literary Agency, Inc. (*US*)
The Susan Golomb Literary Agency (*US*)
Goodman Associates (*US*)
Irene Goodman Literary Agency (*US*)
Antony Harwood Limited (*UK*)
Kate Hordern Literary Agency (*UK*)
Jabberwocky Literary Agency (*US*)
Kilburn Literary Agency (*UK*)
Kneerim & Williams (*US*)
LaunchBooks Literary Agency (*US*)
Lippincott Massie McQuilkin (*US*)

Lowenstein Associates, Inc. (*US*)
Quicksilver Books Literary Agency (*US*)
Susan Schulman, A Literary Agency (*US*)
Lynn Seligman, Literary Agent (*US*)
Denise Shannon Literary Agency, Inc. (*US*)
The Swetky Agency and Associates (*US*)
Timberlake Literary Services, LLC (*US*)
Venture Literary (*US*)
The Ward & Balkin Agency, Inc (*US*)
The Weingel-Fidel Agency (*US*)
Eve White: Literary Agent (*UK*)
Karen Gantz Zahler Literary Agency (*US*)
Spiritual
Alive Communications, Inc (*US*)
Miriam Altshuler Literary Agency (*US*)
AVAnti Productions & Management (*UK*)
Carnicelli Literary Management (*US*)
CowlesRyan Agency (*US*)
The Creative Culture, Inc. (*US*)
Liza Dawson Associates (*US*)
Farris Literary Agency, Inc. (*US*)
FinePrint Literary Management (*US*)
Fox & Howard Literary Agency (*UK*)
Sarah Jane Freymann Literary Agency (*US*)
Graham Maw Christie Literary Agency (*UK*)
Ashley Grayson Literary Agency (*US*)
Joy Harris Literary Agency, Inc. (*US*)
Antony Harwood Limited (*UK*)
The Jeff Herman Agency, LLC (*US*)
Jill Grinberg Literary Management LLC (*US*)
Kilburn Literary Agency (*UK*)
Harvey Klinger, Inc (*US*)
Literary Management Group, Inc. (*US*)
Lowenstein Associates, Inc. (*US*)
The Jennifer Lyons Literary Agency, LLC (*US*)
Ricia Mainhardt Agency (RMA) (*US*)
Kirsten Manges Literary Agency, LLC (*US*)
Denise Marcil Literary Agency, Inc. (*US*)
The Amy Rennert Agency, Inc. (*US*)
Salkind Literary Agency (*US*)
Scribblers House LLC Literary Agency (*US*)
Timberlake Literary Services, LLC (*US*)
Venture Literary (*US*)
Irene Webb Literary (*US*)
Whimsy Literary Agency, LLC (*US*)
Eve White: Literary Agent (*UK*)
The Zack Company, Inc (*US*)
Karen Gantz Zahler Literary Agency (*US*)
Sport
The Agency Group, Ltd (*US*)
Alive Communications, Inc (*US*)
Robert Astle & Associates Literary Management, Inc. (*US*)
Audrey A. Wolf Literary Agency (*US*)
Bell Lomax Moreton Agency (*UK*)
David Black Literary Agency (*US*)
Brandon & Associates (*UK*)
Paul Bresnick Literary Agency, LLC (*US*)
Jenny Brown Associates (*UK*)
Andrea Brown Literary Agency, Inc. (*US*)
Tracy Brown Literary Agency (*US*)
Browne & Miller Literary Associates (*US*)
Carnicelli Literary Management (*US*)

Cedar Grove Agency Entertainment (*US*)
The Characters Talent Agency (*Can*)
Elyse Cheney Literary Associates, LLC (*US*)
Edward B. Claflin Literary Agency, LLC (*US*)
Rosica Colin Ltd (*UK*)
Conville & Walsh Ltd (*UK*)
The Core Group Talent Agency, Inc. (*Can*)
The Creative Rights Agency (*UK*)
David Luxton Associates (*UK*)
The Jennifer DeChiara Literary Agency (*US*)
Jim Donovan Literary (*US*)
Dupree / Miller and Associates Inc. Literary (*US*)
Judith Ehrlich Literary Management (*US*)
Einstein Thompson Agency (*US*)
Farris Literary Agency, Inc. (*US*)
Diana Finch Literary Agency (*US*)
The Gernert Company (*US*)
Goodman Associates (*US*)
Ashley Grayson Literary Agency (*US*)
Kathryn Green Literary Agency, LLC (*US*)
Laura Gross Literary Agency (*US*)
Antony Harwood Limited (*UK*)
Jabberwocky Literary Agency (*US*)
Johnson & Alcock (*UK*)
Harvey Klinger, Inc (*US*)
Kneerim & Williams (*US*)
The LA Literary Agency (*US*)
LaunchBooks Literary Agency (*US*)
The Literary Group (*US*)
Julia Lord Literary Management (*US*)
The Jennifer Lyons Literary Agency, LLC (*US*)
Lyons Literary LLC (*US*)
MacGregor Literary (*US*)
Kirsten Manges Literary Agency, LLC (*US*)
The Michael Greer Literary Agency (*UK*)
Howard Morhaim Literary Agency (*US*)
Niad Management (*US*)
Objective Entertainment (*US*)
John Pawsey (*UK*)
Queen Literary Agency, Inc. (*US*)
Quicksilver Books Literary Agency (*US*)
The Amy Rennert Agency, Inc. (*US*)
The Lisa Richards Agency (*Ire*)
Robert Dudley Agency (*UK*)
Susan Schulman, A Literary Agency (*US*)
Jonathan Scott, Inc (*US*)
The Seven Bridges Group (*US*)
Jeffrey Simmons (*UK*)
SLW Literary Agency (*US*)
Robert Smith Literary Agency Ltd (*UK*)
The Stuart Agency (*US*)
The Swetky Agency and Associates (*US*)
TriadaUS Literary Agency, Inc. (*US*)
2M Literary Agency Ltd (*US*)
Venture Literary (*US*)
Eve White: Literary Agent (*UK*)
Yates & Yates (*US*)
The Zack Company, Inc (*US*)
Helen Zimmermann Literary Agency (*US*)
Suspense
Abela Literature (*Can*)
Abrams Artists Agency (*US*)
Alive Communications, Inc (*US*)

Robert Astle & Associates Literary Management, Inc. (*US*)
AVAnti Productions & Management (*UK*)
The Bent Agency (*US*)
The Blumer Literary Agency, Inc. (*US*)
The Barbara Bova Literary Agency (*US*)
The Joan Brandt Agency (*US*)
Brown Literary Agency (*US*)
Cedar Grove Agency Entertainment (*US*)
Elyse Cheney Literary Associates, LLC (*US*)
The Chudney Agency (*US*)
Rosica Colin Ltd (*UK*)
Conville & Walsh Ltd (*UK*)
The Croce Agency (*US*)
Curtis Brown Group Ltd (*UK*)
Darhansoff & Verrill Literary Agents (*US*)
Liza Dawson Associates (*US*)
The Jennifer DeChiara Literary Agency (*US*)
Jim Donovan Literary (*US*)
Dupree / Miller and Associates Inc. Literary (*US*)
Dystel & Goderich Literary Management (*US*)
Farris Literary Agency, Inc. (*US*)
FinePrint Literary Management (*US*)
Fox Mason Ltd (*UK*)
Full Throttle Literary Agency (*US*)
Furniss Lawton (*UK*)
Goodman Associates (*US*)
Irene Goodman Literary Agency (*US*)
Kathryn Green Literary Agency, LLC (*US*)
Greyhaus Literary Agency (*US*)
Laura Gross Literary Agency (*US*)
Joy Harris Literary Agency, Inc. (*US*)
Antony Harwood Limited (*UK*)
A M Heath & Company Limited, Author's Agents (*UK*)
Virginia Kidd Agency, Inc (*US*)
Harvey Klinger, Inc (*US*)
The Knight Agency (*US*)
The Candace Lake Agency (*US*)
Peter Lampack Agency, Inc (*US*)
Laura Langlie, Literary Agent (*US*)
Robert Lecker Agency (*Can*)
Lescher & Lescher (*US*)
The Lez Barstow Agency (*UK*)
The Literary Group (*US*)
Lyons Literary LLC (*US*)
Donald Maass Literary Agency (*US*)
MacGregor Literary (*US*)
Madeleine Milburn Literary Agency (*UK*)
Ricia Mainhardt Agency (RMA) (*US*)
Denise Marcil Literary Agency, Inc. (*US*)
The Martell Agency (*US*)
Martha Millard Literary Agency (*US*)
Monteiro Rose Dravis Agency, Inc. (*US*)
The Jean V. Naggar Literary Agency (*US*)
Nappaland Literary Agency (*US*)
Niad Management (*US*)
Northern Lights Literary Services (*US*)
Alièka Pistek Literary Agency, LLC (*US*)
The Poynor Group (*US*)
Prospect Agency (*US*)
Quicksilver Books Literary Agency (*US*)
Raines & Raines (*US*)

Salkind Literary Agency (*US*)
Susan Schulman, A Literary Agency (*US*)
Secret Agent Man (*US*)
The Seven Bridges Group (*US*)
The Seymour Agency (*US*)
Valerie Smith, Literary Agent (*US*)
Spectrum Literary Agency (*US*)
Sternig & Byrne Literary Agency (*US*)
The Swetky Agency and Associates (*US*)
Talcott Notch Literary (*US*)
Timberlake Literary Services, LLC (*US*)
Venture Literary (*US*)
Eve White: Literary Agent (*UK*)
Wolfson Literary Agency (*US*)
Wordserve Literary (*US*)
The Zack Company, Inc (*US*)
Helen Zimmermann Literary Agency (*US*)

Technology
The August Agency LLC (*US*)
Andrea Brown Literary Agency, Inc. (*US*)
Browne & Miller Literary Associates (*US*)
W.M. Clark Associates (*US*)
The Creative Culture, Inc. (*US*)
Richard Curtis Associates, Inc. (*US*)
The Jennifer DeChiara Literary Agency (*US*)
Dupree / Miller and Associates Inc. Literary (*US*)
Dystel & Goderich Literary Management (*US*)
Felicia Eth Literary Representation (*US*)
Diana Finch Literary Agency (*US*)
FinePrint Literary Management (*US*)
Fresh Books Literary Agency (*US*)
The Susan Golomb Literary Agency (*US*)
Goodman Associates (*US*)
Ashley Grayson Literary Agency (*US*)
Antony Harwood Limited (*UK*)
Jill Grinberg Literary Management LLC (*US*)
Harvey Klinger, Inc (*US*)
Kneerim & Williams (*US*)
LaunchBooks Literary Agency (*US*)
Kirsten Manges Literary Agency, LLC (*US*)
Moore Literary Agency (*US*)
New Leaf Literary & Media, Inc. (*US*)
Quicksilver Books Literary Agency (*US*)
Lynne Rabinoff Agency (*US*)
Redwood Agency (*US*)
The Rudy Agency (*US*)
Salkind Literary Agency (*US*)
The Science Factory (*UK*)
Signature Literary Agency (*US*)
The Swetky Agency and Associates (*US*)
Talcott Notch Literary (*US*)
Timberlake Literary Services, LLC (*US*)
Venture Literary (*US*)
The Weingel-Fidel Agency (*US*)
Eve White: Literary Agent (*UK*)
The Zack Company, Inc (*US*)

Theatre
Bret Adams Ltd (*US*)
Agency for the Performing Arts (APA) (*US*)
Robert Astle & Associates Literary Management, Inc. (*US*)
AVAnti Productions & Management (*UK*)
Berlin Associates (*UK*)

Brandon & Associates (*UK*)
Alan Brodie Representation Ltd (*UK*)
Brie Burkeman & Serafina Clarke Ltd (*UK*)
Cameron Creswell Agency (*Aus*)
CardenWright Literary Agency (*UK*)
W.M. Clark Associates (*US*)
Mary Clemmey Literary Agency (*UK*)
Jonathan Clowes Ltd (*UK*)
Rosica Colin Ltd (*UK*)
The Core Group Talent Agency, Inc. (*Can*)
Criterion Group, Inc. (*US*)
Curtis Brown Group Ltd (*UK*)
The Jennifer DeChiara Literary Agency (*US*)
Felix de Wolfe (*UK*)
Dupree / Miller and Associates Inc. Literary (*US*)
Film Rights Ltd in association with Laurence
Fitch Ltd (*UK*)
Diana Finch Literary Agency (*US*)
Jill Foster Ltd (JFL) (*UK*)
Samuel French, Inc. (*US*)
The Gage Group (*US*)
Eric Glass Ltd (*UK*)
Goodman Associates (*US*)
Antony Harwood Limited (*UK*)
Independent Talent Group Ltd (*UK*)
Jabberwocky Literary Agency (*US*)
Janet Fillingham Associates (*UK*)
Ki Agency Ltd (*UK*)
Knight Hall Agency (*UK*)
Laura Langlie, Literary Agent (*US*)
Robert Lecker Agency (*Can*)
Andrew Mann Ltd (*UK*)
March Tenth, Inc. (*US*)
The Marton Agency, Inc. (*US*)
MBA Literary Agents Ltd (*UK*)
MBE (*UK*)
Bill McLean Personal Management Ltd (*UK*)
Martha Millard Literary Agency (*US*)
Niad Management (*US*)
Paradigm Talent and Literary Agency (*US*)
PBJ and JBJ Management (*UK*)
Peregrine Whittlesey Agency (*US*)
The Peters Fraser & Dunlop Group Ltd (PFD)
(*UK*)
The Lisa Richards Agency (*Ire*)
Michael D. Robins & Associates (*US*)
Sayle Screen Ltd (*UK*)
Susan Schulman, A Literary Agency (*US*)
Sheil Land Associates Ltd (*UK*)
Jeffrey Simmons (*UK*)
South West Artists (*UK*)
The Swetky Agency and Associates (*US*)
The Tennyson Agency (*UK*)
Thomas Moore Literary Agency (*UK*)
Timberlake Literary Services, LLC (*US*)
Tom Lee (*US*)
United Agents (*UK*)
Venture Literary (*US*)
Eve White: Literary Agent (*UK*)
Thrillers
Abela Literature (*Can*)
Alive Communications, Inc (*US*)
The Ampersand Agency Ltd (*UK*)

Robert Astle & Associates Literary Management,
Inc. (*US*)
AVAnti Productions & Management (*UK*)
The Bent Agency (*US*)
Blake Friedmann Literary Agency Ltd (*UK*)
The Blumer Literary Agency, Inc. (*US*)
Luigi Bonomi Associates Ltd (*UK*)
The Barbara Bova Literary Agency (*US*)
The Joan Brandt Agency (*US*)
Barbara Braun Associates, Inc. (*US*)
Jenny Brown Associates (*UK*)
Andrea Brown Literary Agency, Inc. (*US*)
Brown Literary Agency (*US*)
Cedar Grove Agency Entertainment (*US*)
The Characters Talent Agency (*Can*)
Mic Cheetham Literary Agency (*UK*)
Elyse Cheney Literary Associates, LLC (*US*)
Cine/Lit Representation (*US*)
Rosica Colin Ltd (*UK*)
Conville & Walsh Ltd (*UK*)
Coombs Moylett Literary Agency (*UK*)
The Core Group Talent Agency, Inc. (*Can*)
The Croce Agency (*US*)
Curtis Brown Group Ltd (*UK*)
Liza Dawson Associates (*US*)
The Jennifer DeChiara Literary Agency (*US*)
Jim Donovan Literary (*US*)
Dorian Literary Agency (DLA) (*UK*)
Dupree / Miller and Associates Inc. Literary (*US*)
Dystel & Goderich Literary Management (*US*)
Judith Ehrlich Literary Management (*US*)
Fairbank Literary Representation (*US*)
Farris Literary Agency, Inc. (*US*)
Diana Finch Literary Agency (*US*)
FinePrint Literary Management (*US*)
Fox Mason Ltd (*UK*)
Samuel French, Inc. (*US*)
Sarah Jane Freymann Literary Agency (*US*)
Full Throttle Literary Agency (*US*)
Furniss Lawton (*UK*)
The Gernert Company (*US*)
The Susan Golomb Literary Agency (*US*)
Goodman Associates (*US*)
Irene Goodman Literary Agency (*US*)
Kathryn Green Literary Agency, LLC (*US*)
Greene & Heaton Ltd (*UK*)
Gregory & Company, Authors' Agents (*UK*)
Laura Gross Literary Agency (*US*)
Hardman & Swainson (*UK*)
Antony Harwood Limited (*UK*)
A M Heath & Company Limited, Author's
Agents (*UK*)
Rupert Heath Literary Agency (*UK*)
Hidden Value Group (*US*)
Kate Hordern Literary Agency (*UK*)
Andrea Hurst Literary Management (*US*)
InkWell Management (*US*)
International Transactions, Inc. (*US*)
Jaret Entertainment (*US*)
Kilburn Literary Agency (*UK*)
Harvey Klinger, Inc (*US*)
The Knight Agency (*US*)
KT Public Relations (*US*)

The Candace Lake Agency (*US*)
Peter Lampack Agency, Inc (*US*)
Laura Langlie, Literary Agent (*US*)
Robert Lecker Agency (*Can*)
The Lez Barstow Agency (*UK*)
The Literary Group (*US*)
Julia Lord Literary Management (*US*)
Lowenstein Associates, Inc. (*US*)
The Jennifer Lyons Literary Agency, LLC (*US*)
Lyons Literary LLC (*US*)
MacGregor Literary (*US*)
Madeleine Milburn Literary Agency (*UK*)
Ricia Mainhardt Agency (RMA) (*US*)
Denise Marcil Literary Agency, Inc. (*US*)
The Martell Agency (*US*)
Monteiro Rose Dravis Agency, Inc. (*US*)
The Jean V. Naggar Literary Agency (*US*)
New Leaf Literary & Media, Inc. (*US*)
Niad Management (*US*)
Objective Entertainment (*US*)
The Park Literary Group LLC (*US*)
Pavilion Literary Management (*US*)
Barry Perelman Agency (*US*)
Alièka Pistek Literary Agency, LLC (*US*)
Prospect Agency (*US*)
Queen Literary Agency, Inc. (*US*)
Quicksilver Books Literary Agency (*US*)
Raines & Raines (*US*)
Regal Literary (*UK*)
Regal Literary Inc. (*US*)
Renee Zuckerbrot Literary Agency (*US*)
Rocking Chair Books (*UK*)
Salkind Literary Agency (*US*)
Secret Agent Man (*US*)
The Seymour Agency (*US*)
Sheil Land Associates Ltd (*UK*)
Signature Literary Agency (*US*)
South West Artists (*UK*)
Spencerhill Associates (*US*)
The Swetky Agency and Associates (*US*)
SYLA - Susan Yearwood Literary Agency (*UK*)
Talcott Notch Literary (*US*)
Tom Lee (*US*)
TriadaUS Literary Agency, Inc. (*US*)
Venture Literary (*US*)
Veritas Literary Agency (*US*)
Beth Vesel Literary Agency (*US*)
The Ward & Balkin Agency, Inc (*US*)
Irene Webb Literary (*US*)
The Wendy Weil Agency, Inc. (*US*)
Westwood Creative Artists (*Can*)
Whispering Buffalo Literary Agency Ltd (*UK*)
Eve White: Literary Agent (*UK*)
Wolfson Literary Agency (*US*)
Wordserve Literary (*US*)
Writers' Representatives, LLC (*US*)
Yates & Yates (*US*)
The Zack Company, Inc (*US*)
Translations
AVAnti Productions & Management (*UK*)
W.M. Clark Associates (*US*)
Dupree / Miller and Associates Inc. Literary (*US*)
Diana Finch Literary Agency (*US*)

Goodman Associates (*US*)
Joy Harris Literary Agency, Inc. (*US*)
Antony Harwood Limited (*UK*)
Intercontinental Literary Agency (*UK*)
The Lez Barstow Agency (*UK*)
Makepeace Towle Literary Agency (*UK*)
The Marton Agency, Inc. (*US*)
Rocking Chair Books (*UK*)
The Swetky Agency and Associates (*US*)
Thomas Moore Literary Agency (*UK*)
Venture Literary (*US*)
Eve White: Literary Agent (*UK*)
The Zack Company, Inc (*US*)
Travel
Robert Astle & Associates Literary Management,
   Inc. (*US*)
AVAnti Productions & Management (*UK*)
Paul Bresnick Literary Agency, LLC (*US*)
Tracy Brown Literary Agency (*US*)
Cine/Lit Representation (*US*)
Rosica Colin Ltd (*UK*)
Conville & Walsh Ltd (*UK*)
The Croce Agency (*US*)
Farris Literary Agency, Inc. (*US*)
FinePrint Literary Management (*US*)
Fox Mason Ltd (*UK*)
Sarah Jane Freymann Literary Agency (*US*)
Goodman Associates (*US*)
Greene & Heaton Ltd (*UK*)
Antony Harwood Limited (*UK*)
John Hawkins & Associates, Inc. (*US*)
hhb agency ltd (*UK*)
Jill Grinberg Literary Management LLC (*US*)
Robert Lecker Agency (*Can*)
London Independent Books (*UK*)
The Jennifer Lyons Literary Agency, LLC (*US*)
Lyons Literary LLC (*US*)
Makepeace Towle Literary Agency (*UK*)
Kirsten Manges Literary Agency, LLC (*US*)
Duncan McAra (*UK*)
MNLA (Maggie Noach Literary Agency) (*UK*)
The Park Literary Group LLC (*US*)
Alièka Pistek Literary Agency, LLC (*US*)
Redwood Agency (*US*)
Rocking Chair Books (*UK*)
Salkind Literary Agency (*US*)
The Sayle Literary Agency (*UK*)
The Science Factory (*UK*)
Jonathan Scott, Inc (*US*)
The Seven Bridges Group (*US*)
Sheil Land Associates Ltd (*UK*)
Sinclair-Stevenson (*UK*)
Rebecca Strong International Literary Agency
   (*US*)
The Strothman Agency (*US*)
The Swetky Agency and Associates (*US*)
Tessler Literary Agency (*US*)
Thomas Moore Literary Agency (*UK*)
TriadaUS Literary Agency, Inc. (*US*)
Venture Literary (*US*)
Eve White: Literary Agent (*UK*)
TV
Above the Line Agency (*US*)

Abrams Artists Agency (*US*)
Bret Adams Ltd (*US*)
Agency for the Performing Arts (APA) (*US*)
Anonymous Content (*US*)
AVAnti Productions & Management (*UK*)
Berlin Associates (*UK*)
Blake Friedmann Literary Agency Ltd (*UK*)
Luigi Bonomi Associates Ltd (*UK*)
Alan Brodie Representation Ltd (*UK*)
Kelvin C. Bulger and Associates (*US*)
Cameron Creswell Agency (*Aus*)
Capel & Land Ltd (*UK*)
Cedar Grove Agency Entertainment (*US*)
The Characters Talent Agency (*Can*)
Judith Chilcote Agency (*UK*)
Mary Clemmey Literary Agency (*UK*)
Jonathan Clowes Ltd (*UK*)
Rosica Colin Ltd (*UK*)
The Collective (*US*)
The Core Group Talent Agency, Inc. (*Can*)
Curtis Brown Group Ltd (*UK*)
Felix de Wolfe (*UK*)
Film Rights Ltd in association with Laurence
Fitch Ltd (*UK*)
Jill Foster Ltd (JFL) (*UK*)
The Gage Group (*US*)
Eric Glass Ltd (*UK*)
Graham Maw Christie Literary Agency (*UK*)
Antony Harwood Limited (*UK*)
hhb agency ltd (*UK*)
Valerie Hoskins Associates (*UK*)
Independent Talent Group Ltd (*UK*)
Janet Fillingham Associates (*UK*)
Jaret Entertainment (*US*)
Michelle Kass Associates (*UK*)
Charlene Kay Agency (*Can*)
Ki Agency Ltd (*UK*)
Knight Hall Agency (*UK*)
The Candace Lake Agency (*US*)
The Lez Barstow Agency (*UK*)
Lyons Literary LLC (*US*)
Madeleine Milburn Literary Agency (*UK*)
Andrew Mann Ltd (*UK*)
Marjacq Scripts Ltd (*UK*)
MBA Literary Agents Ltd (*UK*)
Bill McLean Personal Management Ltd (*UK*)
Monteiro Rose Dravis Agency, Inc. (*US*)
William Morris Endeavor Entertainment (UK)
Ltd (*UK*)
Niad Management (*US*)
Objective Entertainment (*US*)
Paradigm Talent and Literary Agency (*US*)
PBJ and JBJ Management (*UK*)
Peregrine Whittlesey Agency (*US*)
Barry Perelman Agency (*US*)
The Peters Fraser & Dunlop Group Ltd (PFD)
(*UK*)
Michael D. Robins & Associates (*US*)
Sayle Screen Ltd (*UK*)
Linda Seifert Management (*UK*)
The Seven Bridges Group (*US*)
Sheil Land Associates Ltd (*UK*)
South West Artists (*UK*)

Stone Manners Salners Agency (*US*)
The Swetky Agency and Associates (*US*)
The Tennyson Agency (*UK*)
Thomas Moore Literary Agency (*UK*)
United Agents (*UK*)
Venture Literary (*US*)
A.P. Watt Ltd (*UK*)
Eve White: Literary Agent (*UK*)
The Zack Company, Inc (*US*)
Westerns
Abela Literature (*Can*)
Alive Communications, Inc (*US*)
AVAnti Productions & Management (*UK*)
Cedar Grove Agency Entertainment (*US*)
The Characters Talent Agency (*Can*)
The Core Group Talent Agency, Inc. (*Can*)
Full Throttle Literary Agency (*US*)
Antony Harwood Limited (*UK*)
Hidden Value Group (*US*)
Andrea Hurst Literary Management (*US*)
The Candace Lake Agency (*US*)
Donald Maass Literary Agency (*US*)
Prospect Agency (*US*)
Raines & Raines (*US*)
Secret Agent Man (*US*)
The Seven Bridges Group (*US*)
South West Artists (*UK*)
The Swetky Agency and Associates (*US*)
Eve White: Literary Agent (*UK*)
Women's Interests
A+B Works (*US*)
Alive Communications, Inc (*US*)
Ambassador Speakers Bureau & Literary Agency
(*US*)
The Ampersand Agency Ltd (*UK*)
Arcadia (*US*)
Robert Astle & Associates Literary Management,
Inc. (*US*)
The August Agency LLC (*US*)
Author Rights Agency (*Ire*)
AVAnti Productions & Management (*UK*)
Barer Literary, LLC (*US*)
Faye Bender Literary Agency (*US*)
The Bent Agency (*US*)
Blake Friedmann Literary Agency Ltd (*UK*)
The Blumer Literary Agency, Inc. (*US*)
Luigi Bonomi Associates Ltd (*UK*)
BookEnds, LLC (*US*)
Books & Such Literary Agency (*US*)
The Barbara Bova Literary Agency (*US*)
The Joan Brandt Agency (*US*)
Barbara Braun Associates, Inc. (*US*)
Brick House Literary Agents (*US*)
Jenny Brown Associates (*UK*)
Marie Brown Associates, Inc. (*US*)
Andrea Brown Literary Agency, Inc. (*US*)
Brown Literary Agency (*US*)
Tracy Brown Literary Agency (*US*)
Browne & Miller Literary Associates (*US*)
Juliet Burton Literary Agency (*UK*)
The Characters Talent Agency (*Can*)
Elyse Cheney Literary Associates, LLC (*US*)
Teresa Chris Literary Agency Ltd (*UK*)

Rosica Colin Ltd (*UK*)
Conville & Walsh Ltd (*UK*)
Coombs Moylett Literary Agency (*UK*)
The Creative Culture, Inc. (*US*)
Creative Authors Ltd (*UK*)
The Croce Agency (*US*)
Liza Dawson Associates (*US*)
The Jennifer DeChiara Literary Agency (*US*)
Jim Donovan Literary (*US*)
Dorian Literary Agency (DLA) (*UK*)
Dupree / Miller and Associates Inc. Literary (*US*)
Dystel & Goderich Literary Management (*US*)
Judith Ehrlich Literary Management (*US*)
Einstein Thompson Agency (*US*)
Elaine P. English, Attorney & Literary Agent (*US*)
Felicia Eth Literary Representation (*US*)
Farris Literary Agency, Inc. (*US*)
Diana Finch Literary Agency (*US*)
FinePrint Literary Management (*US*)
Sarah Jane Freymann Literary Agency (*US*)
Fredrica S. Friedman and Co. Inc. (*US*)
Furniss Lawton (*UK*)
The Susan Golomb Literary Agency (*US*)
Goodman Associates (*US*)
Irene Goodman Literary Agency (*US*)
Kathryn Green Literary Agency, LLC (*US*)
Greyhaus Literary Agency (*US*)
Laura Gross Literary Agency (*US*)
Joy Harris Literary Agency, Inc. (*US*)
Antony Harwood Limited (*UK*)
Rupert Heath Literary Agency (*UK*)
hhb agency ltd (*UK*)
Hidden Value Group (*US*)
Hopkins Literary Associates (*US*)
Kate Hordern Literary Agency (*UK*)
Andrea Hurst Literary Management (*US*)
International Transactions, Inc. (*US*)
Jabberwocky Literary Agency (*US*)
Jill Grinberg Literary Management LLC (*US*)
Virginia Kidd Agency, Inc (*US*)
Kilburn Literary Agency (*UK*)
Harvey Klinger, Inc (*US*)
Kneerim & Williams (*US*)
The Knight Agency (*US*)
Edite Kroll Literary Agency, Inc. (*US*)
KT Public Relations (*US*)
Laura Langlie, Literary Agent (*US*)
The Literary Group (*US*)
Lowenstein Associates, Inc. (*US*)
The Jennifer Lyons Literary Agency, LLC (*US*)

Lyons Literary LLC (*US*)
Donald Maass Literary Agency (*US*)
MacGregor Literary (*US*)
Madeleine Milburn Literary Agency (*UK*)
Ricia Mainhardt Agency (RMA) (*US*)
Makepeace Towle Literary Agency (*UK*)
Kirsten Manges Literary Agency, LLC (*US*)
Denise Marcil Literary Agency, Inc. (*US*)
The Martell Agency (*US*)
Martin Literary Management (*US*)
Martha Millard Literary Agency (*US*)
Howard Morhaim Literary Agency (*US*)
Judith Murdoch Literary Agency (*UK*)
Nappaland Literary Agency (*US*)
Nelson Literary Agency, LLC (*US*)
New Leaf Literary & Media, Inc. (*US*)
Northern Lights Literary Services (*US*)
Objective Entertainment (*US*)
Prospect Agency (*US*)
Quicksilver Books Literary Agency (*US*)
Lynne Rabinoff Agency (*US*)
Redwood Agency (*US*)
Renee Zuckerbrot Literary Agency (*US*)
Rocking Chair Books (*UK*)
Salkind Literary Agency (*US*)
Susan Schulman, A Literary Agency (*US*)
Lynn Seligman, Literary Agent (*US*)
The Seven Bridges Group (*US*)
Sheil Land Associates Ltd (*UK*)
Signature Literary Agency (*US*)
Dorie Simmonds Agency (*UK*)
Valerie Smith, Literary Agent (*US*)
Pam Strickler Author Management (*US*)
The Swetky Agency and Associates (*US*)
SYLA - Susan Yearwood Literary Agency (*UK*)
Talcott Notch Literary (*US*)
Tessler Literary Agency (*US*)
Timberlake Literary Services, LLC (*US*)
Venture Literary (*US*)
Veritas Literary Agency (*US*)
Beth Vesel Literary Agency (*US*)
Watson, Little Ltd (*UK*)
Irene Webb Literary (*US*)
The Weingel-Fidel Agency (*US*)
Eve White: Literary Agent (*UK*)
Wolfson Literary Agency (*US*)
Wordserve Literary (*US*)
Yates & Yates (*US*)
The Zack Company, Inc (*US*)
Helen Zimmermann Literary Agency (*US*)

US Publishers

For the most up-to-date listings of these and hundreds of other publishers, visit http://www.firstwriter.com/publishers

*To claim your **free** access to the site, please see the back of this book.*

ABC-CLIO / Greenwood
Acquisitions Department/Greenwood
ABC-CLIO
PO Box 1911
Santa Barbara, CA 93116-1911
Tel: +1 (800) 368-6868
Email: ccasey@abc-clio.com
Website: http://www.abc-clio.com

Publishes: Nonfiction; Reference; *Areas:* Biography; Historical; Military; Religious; Sociology; *Markets:* Academic; Adult

Contact: Cathleen Casey

Publisher of general nonfiction and reference covering history, humanities, and general interest topics across the secondary and higher education curriculum. No fiction, poetry, or drama. Welcomes proposals in appropriate areas. See website for specific imprint / editor contact details.

Able Muse Press
467 Saratoga Avenue #602
San Jose, CA 95129
Email: submission@ablemuse.com
Website: http://www.ablemusepress.com

Publishes: Fiction; Poetry; *Markets:* Adult

Publishes fiction and poetry. Prefers submissions via online form, but will also accept submissions by email with ms attached as a separate document. Do not paste material in the body of the email. See website for full details.

Addicus Books
PO Box 45327
Omaha, NE 68145
Tel: +1 (402) 330-7493
Fax: +1 (402) 330-1707
Email: info@addicusbooks.com
Website: http://www.addicusbooks.com

Publishes: Nonfiction; *Areas:* Business; Crime; Finance; Health; Psychology; Self-Help; *Markets:* Adult

Send one-page query by email (non attachments) or by post, including synopsis, two or three chapters, outline, and information on author background, completion date, illustrations, word count, target audience / market info. See website for full guidelines.

Affluent Publishing Corporation
Acquisition Department
231 North Ave., West, Suite #317
Westfield, NJ 07090
Website: http://www.affluent-publishing.com

Publishes: Fiction; *Areas:* Adventure; Mystery; Romance; Suspense; *Markets:*

Adult; Youth; *Treatments:* Contemporary;
Literary; Mainstream

Send query only in first instance. Further
material should be submitted upon request
only. No submissions by email.

Alexander Hamilton Institute

Business Management Daily
PO Box 9070
McLean, VA 22102-0070
Tel: +1 (800) 543-2055
Fax: +1 (703) 905-8040
Email:
Editor@BusinessManagementDaily.com
Website: http://www.legalworkplace.com

Publishes: Nonfiction; *Areas:* Business;
Legal; *Markets:* Professional

Publishes material for executives, upper
management, and HR managers.

Alice James Books

238 Main St.
Farmington, ME 04936
Tel: +1 (207) 778-7071
Fax: +1 (207) 778-7766
Email: info@alicejamesbooks.org
Website: http://alicejamesbooks.org

Publishes: Poetry; *Markets:* Adult

Poetry press accepting submissions through
its various competitions only. Competitions
include large cash prizes and reasonable
entry fees.

American Atheists

PO Box 5733
Parsippany, NJ 07054-6733
Tel: +1 (908) 276-7300
Fax: +1 (908) 276-7402
Email: editor@americanatheists.org
Website: http://www.atheists.org

Publishes: Nonfiction; *Areas:* Historical;
Legal; Lifestyle; Philosophy; Politics;
Markets: Adult

Publishes books promoting an atheist
viewpoint. Send outline and sample chapters.

American Correctional Association (ACA)

206 N. Washington St., Suite 200
Alexandria, VA 22314
Tel: +1 (703) 224-0194
Fax: +1 (703) 224-0179
Email: aliceh@aca.org
Website: https://www.aca.org

Publishes: Nonfiction; *Areas:* How-to;
Markets: Academic; Professional

Contact: Alice Heiserman, Publications and
Research Manager

Publishes practical books on jails and other
correctional facilities, aimed at correctional
practitioners and students studying related
subjects. Send query by post or by email in
first instance.

American Psychological Association (APA) Books

750 First Street, NE
Washington, DC 20002-4242
Tel: +1 (800) 374-2721
Email: books@apa.org
Website: http://www.apa.org/pubs/books

Publishes: Nonfiction; *Areas:* Psychology;
Science; Sociology; *Markets:* Academic;
Professional

Publishes books on psychology for
academics and professionals. Submit
proposal with table of contents and market
information in first instance.

Amherst Media

175 Rano Street, Suite 200
Buffalo, NY 14207
Tel: +1 (716) 874-4450
Fax: +1 (716) 874-4508
Email: submissions@AmherstMedia.com
Website: http://www.amherstmedia.com

Publishes: Nonfiction; *Areas:* How-to;
Photography; *Markets:* Adult; Professional

Publishes instructional books on
photography for beginners to advanced
photographers. Most titles run up to 128

pages, with 15,000 to 30,000 words and anywhere from 25 to 300 images. Send outline, small sample of your photographic work and contact information (including email address) by post or by email.

Ampichellis Ebooks

Email: editor@ampichellisebooks.com
Website: http://www.ampichellisebooks.com

Publishes: Fiction; *Areas:* Crime; Mystery; Sci-Fi; Thrillers; *Markets:* Adult; Children's

Former literary agency turned eBook publisher. Send query by email.

Angoor Press LLC

2734 Bruchez Pkwy, Unit 103
Denver, CO 80234
Email: angoorpress@gmail.com
Website: http://angoorpress.com

Publishes: Poetry; *Markets:* Adult

Publishes poetry volumes of at least 100 poems. Submit by email only with your work as an Word file attachment, including short poet bio. Any material sent by post will not be considered or replied to. See website for full guidelines.

Antarctic Press

7272 Wurzbach #204
San Antonio, TX 78240
Email: davidjhutchison@yahoo.com
Website: http://www.antarctic-press.com

Publishes: Fiction; *Areas:* Adventure; *Markets:* Adult; Children's; Family; Youth

Contact: David Hutchison

Publishes comics and graphic novels. If you can illustrate as well as write then this will be to your benefit, but you can team up with an illustrator if necessary. This will mean you have to share the payments, though. See website for full guidelines.

Archaia

1680 N. Vine Street
Hollywood, CA 90028
Email: editorial@archaia.com
Website: http://www.archaia.com

Publishes: Fiction; *Areas:* Adventure; Fantasy; Horror; Sci-Fi; *Markets:* Adult; Children's; Youth

Publishes graphic novels and prose novels. Though has tended to specialise in the genres above, is willing to consider works in any genre. Submit query via submission form on website.

Arctos Press

PO Box 401
Sausalito, CA 94966-0401
Tel: +1 (415) 331-2503
Email: runes@aol.com
Website: http://www.arctospress.com

Publishes: Poetry; *Markets:* Adult

Publishes a few quality poetry books every year. Send query by email in first instance.

Arkansas Research, Inc.

PO Box 303
Conway, AR 72033
Tel: +1 (501) 470-1120
Email: sales@ArkansasResearch.com
Website: http://www.arkansasresearch.com

Publishes: Nonfiction; *Areas:* Historical; Hobbies; Military; *Markets:* Adult

Publishes books for those interested in the history of Arkansas, particularly genealogists. No autobiographies or genealogies of single families. Send query with SASE in first instance.

Artemis Press

236 West Portal Avenue #525
San Francisco, CA 94127
Tel: +1 (866) 216-7333
Email: artemispressdigital-info@yahoo.com
Website: http://www.artemispress.com

Publishes: Fiction; *Areas:* Crime; Erotic;

Mystery; Romance; Sci-Fi; Short Stories; Women's Interests; *Markets:* Adult

Publishes novellas, flash fiction, short fiction of interest to women of all backgrounds, sexual orientations and ethnicities. Particularly interested in lesbian romance and erotica, lesbian and female detective fiction, and lesbian erotica. Will also consider short fiction featuring strong, dynamic female characters in other genres. Send query only by email. No unsolicited mss. See website for full guidelines.

Aunt Lute Books

PO Box 410687
San Francisco, CA 94141
Tel: +1 (415) 826-1300
Fax: +1 (415) 826-8300
Email: books@auntlute.com
Website: http://auntlute.com

Publishes: Fiction; Nonfiction; Poetry; *Areas:* Women's Interests; *Markets:* Adult

Contact: Acquisitions Editor

A multicultural women's press. Particularly interested in works by women of colour. No therapy or self-help. Poetry only considered as part of a larger work. Send query by post only, with table of contents and two sample chapters (or approximately 50 pages), plus SASE if return of work is required. See website for full submission guidelines.

Aurora Publishing, Inc

3655 Torrance Blvd., Suite 430
Torrance, CA 90503
Tel: +1 (310) 540-2800
Email: info@aurora-publishing.com
Website: http://www.aurora-publishing.com

Publishes: Fiction; *Areas:* Adventure; Translations; *Markets:* Adult; Children's; Youth

Publishes Japanese manga graphic novels translated into English, and also original American manga for US and worldwide consumption. Keen to develop manga for a more mature audience.

Aviation Supplies & Academics, Inc.

7005 132nd Place SE
Newcastle, WA 98059
Tel: +1 (800) 272-2359
Fax: +1 (425) 235-0128
Email: feedback@asa2fly.com
Website: http://www.asa2fly.com

Publishes: Nonfiction; *Areas:* Technology; Travel; *Markets:* Academic; Professional

Publishes books on aviation, specialising in educational titles. Send query with outline.

Azro Press

PMB 342
1704 Llano St B
Santa Fe, NM 87505
Tel: +1 (505) 989-3272
Fax: +1 (505) 989-3832
Email: books@azropress.com
Website: http://www.azropress.com

Publishes: Fiction; Nonfiction; *Markets:* Children's

Publishes picture books and illustrated easy reader books for young children. Currently focusing on books written and illustrated by residents of the Southwest. Books need not be about the Southwest, but may be at an advantage if they are. See website for full guidelines.

Baywood Publishing Company, Inc.

26 Austin Avenue
PO Box 337
Amityville, NY 11701
Tel: +1 (631) 691-1270
Fax: +1 (631) 691-1770
Email: info@baywood.com
Website: http://www.baywood.com

Publishes: Nonfiction; *Areas:* Anthropology; Archaeology; Health; Nature; Psychology; Science; Sociology; Technology; Women's Interests; *Markets:* Academic; Professional

Scholarly professional publisher accepting proposals for publications in counseling, death & bereavement, psychology, and gerontology, health policy and technical communication. See website for full instructions on submitting a proposal.

Behrman House

11 Edison Place
Springfield, NJ 07081
Tel: +1 (973) 379-7200
Fax: +1 (973) 379-7280
Email:
customersupport@behrmanhouse.com
Website: http://www.behrmanhouse.com

Publishes: Nonfiction; *Areas:* Historical; Philosophy; Religious; *Markets:* Academic; Adult

Publishes books of Jewish content for the classroom and general readership. Send query with SASE, two sample chapters, table of contents, and market info. No submissions by email.

Betterway Home Books

4700 East Galbraith Road
Cincinnati, OH 45236
Website: http://www.betterwaybooks.com

Publishes: Nonfiction; *Areas:* Architecture; Design; How-to; Lifestyle; *Markets:* Adult

Publishes books on homemaking: repair, improvement, organisation, etc. Send query with SASE, proposal package, outline, and one sample chapter.

Birdsong Books

1322 Bayview Road
Middletown, DE 19709
Tel: +1 (302) 378-7274
Fax: +1 (302) 378-0339
Email: birdsong@birdsongbooks.com
Website: http://www.birdsongbooks.com

Publishes: Nonfiction; *Areas:* Nature; Science; *Markets:* Children's

Publishes natural science picture books for children, concentrating on North American animals and habitats. See website for manuscript submission guidelines.

Blind Eye Books

1141 Grant Street
Bellingham, WA 98225
Email: editor@blindeyebooks.com
Website: http://www.blindeyebooks.com

Publishes: Fiction; *Areas:* Fantasy; Romance; Sci-Fi; *Markets:* Adult

Contact: Nicole Kimberling, Editor

Publishes science fiction, fantasy and paranormal romance novels featuring gay or lesbian protagonists. No short story collections, poetry, erotica, horror or nonfiction. Manuscripts should generally be between 70,000 and 150,000 words. Send complete ms by post, unless from overseas, in which case email editor for electronic submission guidelines. See website for full details.

Blue Dolphin Publishing

P.O. Box 8
Nevada City, CA 95959
Tel: +1 (530) 477-1503
Fax: +1 (530) 477-8342
Email.
bdolphin@bluedolphinpublishing.com
Website:
http://www.bluedolphinpublishing.com

Publishes: Fiction; Nonfiction; Poetry; *Areas:* Biography; Health; Lifestyle; Philosophy; Politics; Psychology; Religious; Self-Help; Sociology; Spiritual; Women's Interests; *Markets:* Adult; Children's; Youth

Contact: Paul and Nancy Clemens

Include cover letter, synopsis, table of contents, sample chapters, author resume, and SASE. See website for full guidelines. Response in 3-6 months.

BlueBridge

BlueBridge / United Tribes Media Inc.
PO Box 601
Katonah, NY 10536
Tel: +1 (914) 301-5901
Email: janguerth@bluebridgebooks.com
Website: http://www.bluebridgebooks.com

Publishes: Nonfiction; *Areas:* Biography; Culture; Current Affairs; Historical; Self-Help; Spiritual; Travel; Markets

Send query by email (preferred), or by post with SASE.

The Bold Strummer Ltd

110-C Imperial Avenue
PO Box 2037
Westport, CT 06880
Tel: +1 (203) 227-8588
Fax: +1 (203) 227-8775
Email: theboldstrummer@msn.com
Website: http://www.boldstrummerltd.com

Publishes: Nonfiction; *Areas:* How-to; Music; *Markets:* Adult

Publishes books and music for and about the guitar.

Books For All Times

Post Office Box 202
Warrenton, Virginia 20188
Tel: +1 (540) 428-3175
Email: staff@bfat.com
Website: http://www.bfat.com

Publishes: Fiction; *Areas:* Short Stories; *Markets:* Adult; *Treatments:* Contemporary; Literary; Mainstream

Contact: Joe David

Publishes literary fiction only. Not interested in popular fiction or entertainment. Think along the lines of Victor Hugo, Fyodor Dostoyevsky and Sinclair Lewis. More likely to publish a collection of short stories than a novel at the moment. Send query with SASE.

Bottom Dog Press

PO Box 425
Huron, OH 44839
Tel: +1 (419) 433-5560
Fax: +1 (419) 616-3966
Email: Lsmithdog@smithdocs.net
Website: http://smithdocs.net

Publishes: Fiction; Nonfiction; Poetry; *Areas:* Short Stories; *Markets:* Adult

Small press publishing collections of poetry, stories, and essays. Does not accept submissions of single stories / poems / essays, however. Focuses on the following themes: Sense of Place (ie. the Midwest) -- Working-Class Culture and Values-- American Zen Writing--African-American Writing from the Midwest--Literary Biography--Family and Spirit--Peace and Justice. Send query by post or email.

Writers should note that if a full ms is requested there is a reading fee of $20 charged.

Bracket Books

PO Box 286098
New York, NY 10128-9991
Email: info@bracketbooks.com
Website: http://bracketbooks.com

Publishes: Fiction; Nonfiction; *Areas:* Culture; Photography; *Markets:* Adult; Family; *Treatments:* Commercial; Contemporary; Literary; Mainstream

Contact: Sam Majors

Based in New York, New York. The company was established to fill a niche, a publishing void that grows larger as traditional print publishers continue to consolidate, struggle to maintain their narrow profit margins, and hold onto outmoded methods of distribution and old-fashioned book marketing techniques. Our business model embraces digital distribution and online marketing, and although we love to design and devour books that are produced in a printed form, we understand that the key to succeeding in the book industry in the coming decades won't be price points or corporate alliances; the key will be, as it always has been, matching the right author with the right audience, and doing so in an efficient, intelligent way.

Although we publish fiction, our focus is non-fiction, and we'll be releasing approximately four non-fiction titles for each fiction title we publish. At this time, we do not publish coffee table books, art books, or children's books, and we cannot imagine ever being interested in publishing poetry or plays. We are primarily interested in books about the art of photography or about photographers, but we will also publish fiction that is connected, in an important way, to pop culture, particularly to movements in film or genres of popular music (think, for instance, of Michael Chabon's The Amazing Adventures of Kavalier & Clay).

Brick Road Poetry Press
PO Box 751
Columbus, GA 31902-0751
Email: editor@brickroadpoetrypress.com
Website:
http://www.brickroadpoetrypress.com

Publishes: Poetry; *Markets:* Adult

Publishes collections of poetry 50-100 pages long. Accepts general submissions February to August, and competition entries ($25 fee) August to November. Submit by post or using online submission system. See website for more details.

Bridge Burner's Publishing
PO Box 5255
Mankato, MN 56002
Email: CEO@bridgeburners.com
Website: http://www.bridgeburners.com

Publishes: Poetry; *Markets:* Adult

Poetry press. Send query with author bio and sample poems.

Bright Mountain Books, Inc.
206 Riva Ridge Drive
Fairview, NC 28730
Tel: +1 (800) 437-3959
Fax: +1 (828) 628-1755
Email: booksbmb@charter.net
Website:
http://www.brightmountainbooks.com

Publishes: Nonfiction; *Markets:* Adult

Contact: Cynthia Bright; Carol Bruckner

Publishes adult, nonfiction manuscripts with Southern Appalachian or North and South Carolina content. Particularly interested in writers from the area. Also publishes creative nonfiction, but no fiction or poetry. See website for full guidelines.

Bristol Publishing Enterprises
2714 McCone Avenue
Hayward, CA 94545
Tel: +1 (800) 346-4889
Fax: +1 (800) 346-7064
Email: orders@bristolpublishing.com
Website: http://www.bristolpublishing.com

Publishes: Nonfiction; *Areas:* Cookery; Hobbies; *Markets:* Adult

Publishes books on cookery. Send query with outline, author CV, and sample chapter or other writing sample.

BSTSLLR
Email: bstsllr.com@gmail.com
Website: http://bstsllr.com

Publishes: Fiction; *Markets:* Adult

Digital publisher of both original fiction and digital editions of fiction by established authors and talented newcomers. See website for more details.

Burford Books
101 E State Street #301
Ithaca, NY 14850
Tel: +1 (607) 319-4373
Fax: +1 (866) 212-7750
Email: info@burfordbooks.com
Website: http://www.burfordbooks.com

Publishes: Nonfiction; *Areas:* Adventure; Cookery; Gardening; Leisure; Military; Nature; Sport; Travel; *Markets:* Adult

Publishes books on the outdoors, in the widest sense. Send query by email in the first instance. See website for full guidelines.

Cadence Jazz Books
Cadence Building
Redwood, NY 13679
Tel: +1 (315) 287-2852
Email: orders@cadencebuilding.com

Website: http://www.cadencejazzbooks.com

Publishes: Nonfiction; Reference; *Areas:* Autobiography; Biography; Music; *Markets:* Academic; Adult

Publisher of jazz discographies, reference works, biographies and autobiographies. Send query with SASE, outline, and sample chapters.

Cardoza Publishing

5473 S. Eastern Ave
Las Vegas, NV 89119
Tel: +1 (702) 870-7200
Fax: +1 (702) 822-6500
Email: info@cardozabooks.com
Website: http://www.cardozapub.com

Publishes: Nonfiction; *Areas:* Hobbies; Leisure; *Markets:* Adult; Professional

Publishes books on games, gambling, chess and backgammon. Send proposal by post with SASE or by email with entire manuscript if available. Include suggested table of contents, overview, comparison of similar titles, and reasons why the book is unique and should be published. Also include list qualifications and credentials relevant to the writing of the proposed book.

Carolrhoda Books, Inc.

241 First Avenue North
Minneapolis, MN 55401
Tel: +1 (612) 332-3344
Fax: +1 (612) 332-7615

Publishes: Fiction; Nonfiction; *Areas:* Biography; Historical; *Markets:* Children's

Contact: Rebecca Poole, Submissions Editor

No submissions.

Carstens Publications, Inc.

108 Phil Hardin Road
Newton, NJ 07860
Tel: +1 (973) 383-3355
Fax: +1 (973) 383-4064
Email: carstens@carstens-publications.com
Website: http://www.carstens-publications.com

Publishes: Nonfiction; *Areas:* Hobbies; How-to; Photography; *Markets:* Adult

Publishes books for model train and plane enthusiasts. Send query with SASE.

Cedar Fort

2373 W. 700
S. Springville, UT 84663
Tel: +1 (801) 489-4084
Email: submissions@cedarfort.com
Website: http://www.cedarfort.com

Publishes: Fiction; Nonfiction; *Areas:* Historical; Religious; Self-Help; Short Stories; Spiritual; *Markets:* Adult; Children's; Youth; *Treatments:* Positive

Publishes books with strong moral or religious values that inspire readers to be better people. No poetry. Rarely publishes biographies, autobiographies, or memoirs, and is very selective about children's books. See website for full submission guidelines.

Changeling Press LLC

PO Box 1046
Martinsburg, WV 25402
Email: Submissions@ChangelingPress.com
Website: http://www.changelingpress.com

Publishes: Fiction; *Areas:* Adventure; Erotic; Fantasy; Romance; Sci-Fi; *Markets:* Adult; *Treatments:* Dark; Positive

Contact: Margaret Riley

Publishes Paranormal, Dark Fantasy, Urban Fantasy, Sci-Fi, Futuristic, BDSM, and Action/Adventure romantic love stories in print and as ebooks. Accepts multiple submissions but not simultaneous submissions. Stories should be between 10,000 and 28,000 words and have a happy ending. Submit by email only. See website for full submission guidelines.

Channel Lake, Inc.

P.O. Box 1771

New York, NY 10156-1771
Tel: +1 (347) 329-5576
Fax: +1 (866) 794-5507
Email: info@channellake.com
Website: http://www.channellake.com

Publishes: Nonfiction; *Areas:* Travel;
Markets: Adult

Publishes travel guides and books of local
interest, mainly for sale in the specific local
area to tourists and holidaymakers. Send
query for full guidelines in first instance.

Chapultepec Press
4222 Chambers
Cincinnati, Ohio 45223
Email: ChapultepecPress@hotmail.com
Website: http://www.tokyoroserecords.com

Publishes: Fiction; Nonfiction; Poetry;
Areas: Arts; Autobiography; Criticism;
Culture; Drama; Historical; Legal; Leisure;
Literature; Music; Nature; Philosophy;
Photography; Politics; Short Stories;
Translations; *Markets:* Adult; *Treatments:*
Experimental

Specialises in shorter publications of 100
pages or fewer. For prose send proposal with
outline and 2-3 sample chapters. For poetry,
send query with sample poems or complete
ms, with author bio and details of any
publishing history.

Chemical Publishing Company
PO Box 676
Revere, MA, 02151
Tel: +1 (888) 439-3976
Email: info@chemical-publishing.com
Website: http://www.chemical-publishing.com

Publishes: Nonfiction; Reference; *Areas:*
Business; Medicine; Science; Technology;
Markets: Academic; Professional

Publishes technical chemistry titles for
professionals and academics on graduate
courses. See website for more details.
Considers both proposals and completed
mss.

Church Growth Institute
PO Box 7
Elkton, MD 21922-0007
Tel: +1 (434) 525-0022
Fax: +1 (434) 525-0608
Email: info@churchgrowth.org
Website: http://www.churchgrowth.org

Publishes: Nonfiction; *Areas:* How-to;
Religious; *Markets:* Adult; Professional

Publishes how-to books for religious
professionals and individuals. Send query by
post or by email.

City Lights Publishers
Editorial Department
261 Columbus Avenue
San Francisco, CA 94133
Tel: +1 (415) 362-1901
Email: staff@citylights.com
Website:
http://www.citylights.com/publishing

Publishes: Fiction; Nonfiction; Poetry;
Areas: Autobiography; Politics; Sociology;
Translations; *Markets:* Adult

Independent publisher of fiction, essays,
memoirs, translations, poetry, and books on
social and political issues. No New Age,
self-help, children's literature, how-to
guides, or genre works such as romance,
westerns, or science fiction. Send query by
post only with SASE, including a description
of you and your book, a sample of 10-20
pages, and also an outline and table of
contents for nonfiction. See website for full
guidelines. No unsolicited mss, or queries by
email or in person.

Clear Light Books
823 Don Diego
Santa Fe, NM 87505
Tel: +1 (505) 989-9590
Fax: +1 (505) 989-9519
Email: market@clearlightbooks.com
Website: http://clearlightbooks.com

Publishes: Nonfiction; *Areas:* Cookery;
Culture; Historical; Philosophy; Religious;
Markets: Adult; Children's

Publishes books on American Indian culture, religion, and history; Southwestern Americana; and Eastern philosophy and religion. Also publishes cookbooks and children's books relevant to these areas. See website for full submission guidelines.

Coffee House Press
79 Thirteenth Ave NE, Suite 110
Minneapolis, MN 55413
Tel: +1 (612) 338-0125
Fax: +1 (612) 338-4004
Email: info@coffeehousepress.org
Website: http://www.coffeehousepress.org

Publishes: Fiction; Nonfiction; Poetry;
Areas: Autobiography; Short Stories;
Markets: Adult; *Treatments:* Literary

Contact: Anitra Budd, Managing Editor

Publishes literary novels, full-length short story collections, poetry, and a small number of essay collections and memoirs. No submissions for anthologies, or genre fiction such as mysteries, Gothic romances, Westerns, science fiction, or books for children. Not accepting poetry as at June 6, 2012 (see website for current situation). Strongly discourages approaches by post - unless you are unable to, use the online submission system available via website. Reading periods are March 1 – April 30 and September 1 – October 31 annually. See website for full details.

The College Board
The College Board National Office
45 Columbus Avenue
New York, NY 10023-6917
Tel: +1 (212) 713-8000
Website: http://www.collegeboard.com

Publishes: Nonfiction; *Areas:* How-to;
Markets: Academic

Publishes books aimed at providing guidance to students who are about to make the move to college. Send query with SASE, sample chapters, and outline.

Consortium Publishing
640 Weaver Hill Road
West Greenwich, Rhode Island 02817-2261
Tel: +1 (401) 387-9838
Fax: +1 (401) 392-1926
Email: ConsortiumPub@msn.com
Website: http://consortiumpublishing.tripod.com

Publishes: Nonfiction; *Areas:* Music; Psychology; Science; Self-Help; *Markets:* Academic; Children's

Publishes university and college text books, laboratory manuals, workbooks and other items used in college courses in various subject matter areas, including Chemistry, Counseling and Self-Help, Child Development and Early Childhood Education, English and Technical Writing, and Music. See website for more details. Send query with SASE, proposal, outline, table of contents, and sample chapter.

Corwin
2455 Teller Road
Thousand Oaks, CA 91320
Tel: +1 (800) 233-9936
Fax: +1 (805) 499-9734
Email: lisa.shaw@corwin.com
Website: http://www.corwin.com

Publishes: Nonfiction; *Areas:* Literature; Science; Technology; *Markets:* Professional

Publishes books for educational professionals. See website for full guidelines and specific editor email addresses.

The Countryman Press
PO Box 748
Woodstock, VT 05091
Tel: +1 (802) 457-4826
Email: countrymanpress@wwnorton.com
Website: http://www.countrymanpress.com

Publishes: Nonfiction; *Areas:* Autobiography; Cookery; Crafts; Culture; Historical; Hobbies; Leisure; Lifestyle; Mystery; Nature; Photography; Travel; *Markets:* Adult

Sends query with SASE, outlining you and

your work, and including a book proposal. See website for full guidelines.

The Creative Company
PO Box 227
Mankato, MN 56002
Tel: +1 (800) 445-6209
Fax: +1 (507) 388-2746
Email: info@thecreativecompany.us
Website: http://www.thecreativecompany.us

Publishes: Fiction; Nonfiction; *Areas:* Arts; Biography; Crafts; Culture; Health; Historical; Hobbies; Music; Nature; Religious; Science; Sociology; Sport; *Markets:* Children's; Youth

Publishes picture books and nonfiction aimed at children and young adults. Accepts nonfiction submissions only - no fiction. Send query with synopsis and two sample chapters.

Cross-Cultural Communications Publications
239 Wynsum Avenue
Merrick, NY 11566-4725
Tel: +1 (516) 868-5635
Email: info@cross-culturalcommunications.com
Website: http://www.cross-culturalcommunications.com

Publishes: Fiction; Nonfiction; Poetry; *Areas:* Autobiography; Culture; Historical; Literature; Translations; *Markets:* Adult

Publishes cross-culture fiction, nonfiction, and poetry. Most interested in poetry in translation. Send query with SASE, or for bilingual poetry submit a sample of 3-6 short poems in their original language accompanied by translation, with brief bio of author and translator.

Crossway
1300 Crescent Street
Wheaton, IL 60187
Tel: +1 (630) 682-4300
Fax: +1 (630) 682-4785
Email: info@crossway.org
Website: http://www.crossway.org

Publishes: Nonfiction; *Areas:* Religious; *Markets:* Adult

Publishes books written from an evangelical Christian perspective. Send query by email in the first instance.

Cycle Publishing / Van der Plas Publications
1282 7th Avenue
San Francisco, CA 94122
Tel: +1 (415) 665-8214
Fax: +1 (415) 753-8572
Email: rvdp@cyclepublishing.com
Website: http://www.cyclepublishing.com

Publishes: Nonfiction; *Areas:* Hobbies; Leisure; Sport; *Markets:* Adult

Mainly focuses on books on cycling, but has also published books on other sports, such as golf and baseball.

Demarche Publishing
Address P.O. Box 36
Mohegan Lake NY 10547-9998
Tel: +1 (914) 413-6264
Email: info@demarchepublishing.com
Website: http://www.demarchepublishing.com

Publishes: Fiction; Nonfiction; Reference; *Areas:* Adventure; Autobiography; Crime; Culture; Current Affairs; Drama; Fantasy; Finance; Health; Historical; Hobbies; Horror; How-to; Humour; Leisure; Lifestyle; Literature; Military; Mystery; Nature; Politics; Psychology; Radio; Religious; Romance; Science; Sci-Fi; Self-Help; Short Stories; Sociology; Spiritual; Sport; Suspense; Technology; Thrillers; Women's Interests; *Markets:* Academic; Adult; Children's; Family; Professional; Youth; *Treatments:* Contemporary; Literary; Mainstream; Popular; Traditional

Contact: Faith Smith

A traditional book publisher. We pays the production costs associated with bringing their authors' work to market and they do not charge reading fees.

We are a growing company and we are aggressively seeking to launch as many titles as possible. We are looking for published and unpublished authors who are committed to their work and their writing and want to build a close relationship with their publisher.

We accept a wide variety of works, including adventure/action, detective/police/crime, fantasy/science fiction, general fiction, horror, mainstream/contemporary, mystery/suspense, religion/inspirational, romance. We also publish limited non-fiction. We prefer email queries and multicultural books

Demontreville Press, Inc.
BOX 835
Lake Elmo, Minnesota 55042-0835
Email: publisher@demontrevillepress.com
Website: http://www.demontrevillepress.com

Publishes: Fiction; Nonfiction; *Areas:* Adventure; Current Affairs; Historical; Mystery; Nature; Short Stories; Technology; Travel; *Markets:* Adult; Children's; Youth

Contact: Kevin Clemens

Publishes fiction and nonfiction books with an automotive or adventure travel theme only. These may be full-length or collections of short fiction/nonfiction. Automotive-themed mystery is fine, but no science fiction, fantasy, romance, gothic, gore, or horror. Has also recently branched out to include books dealing with current affairs and environmental, energy, and infrastructure concerns. Send query by email only, with description of the book, why you are the person to write it, and brief bio. No paper approaches.

Digital Manga, Inc.
ATTN: SUBMISSIONS
1487 West 178th Street, Suite 300
Gardena, CA 90248
Tel: +1 (310) 817-8010
Fax: +1 (310) 817-8018
Email: contact@emanga.com
Website: http://www.emanga.com

Publishes: Fiction; *Markets:* Adult

Accepts submissions of completed manga works only. Does not publish literary books or Western-style comics. Unable to match writers with artists at this time. Completed works must contain at least 90 pages of material and may be black and white or full colour. Send material by post or provide link to place of publication online. See website for full guidelines.

Diversion Books
80 5th Ave, Suite 1101
New York, NY 10011
Tel: +1 (212) 961-6390
Email: info@DiversionBooks.com
Website: http://www.diversionbooks.com

Publishes: Fiction; Nonfiction; *Markets:* Adult

eBook publisher dealing in fiction and nonfiction, in particular those areas not suited to traditional publishing (niche markets or low page extents, for instance). Submit proposal using online submission form on website.

Divertir Publishing LLC
PO Box 232
North Salem, NH 03073
Email: query@divertirpublishing.com
Website: http://divertirpublishing.com

Publishes: Fiction; Nonfiction; Poetry; *Areas:* Crafts; Current Affairs; Fantasy; Historical; Hobbies; Humour; Mystery; Politics; Religious; Romance; Sci-Fi; Self-Help; Short Stories; Spiritual; Suspense; *Markets:* Adult; *Treatments:* Contemporary; Satirical

Publishes full-length fiction, short fiction, poetry, and nonfiction. No erotica or material which is disrespectful to the opinions of others. Accepts queries and submissions by email only. See website for full guidelines.

DK Publishing
375 Hudson Street
New York, NY 10014

Tel: +1 (646) 674-4000
Email: ecommerce@us.penguingroup.com
Website: http://www.dk.com

Publishes: Nonfiction; *Markets:* Children's

Publishes highly visual nonfiction for children. Assumes no responsibility for unsolicited mss and prefers approaches through an established literary agent.

Dover Publications, Inc.

Attn: Editorial Department
31 East 2nd Street
Mineola, NY 11501
Tel: +1 (516) 294-7000
Fax: +1 (516) 873-1401
Website: http://store.doverpublications.com

Publishes: Nonfiction; *Areas:* Antiques; Architecture; Arts; Crafts; Literature; Music; Science; *Markets:* Adult; Children's

No original fiction, music, or poetry. Welcomes submissions in other areas, but cannot return material and responds only if interested. Send query by post with outline, table of contents, and one sample chapter, if available.

Down East Books

ATTN: Books
PO Box 679
Camden, ME 04843
Email: submissions@downeast.com
Website: http://www.downeast.com

Publishes: Fiction; Nonfiction; *Areas:* Culture; Historical; Leisure; Nature; Sport; *Markets:* Adult; Children's; Family; Youth; *Treatments:* Contemporary; Mainstream

Publishes regional books focusing on New England, and in particular Maine. Publishes mainly nonfiction, but also publishes a handful of adult and juvenile fiction titles per year. Accepts queries by post or by email, but prefers email queries. Send one-page letter describing you and your project, and optionally the first two pages (up to 1,000 words). No unsolicited mss. See website for full guidelines.

Down The Shore Publishing

Attn: Acquisitions Editor
PO Box 100
West Creek, NJ 08092
Fax: +1 (609) 597-0422
Email: info@down-the-shore.com
Website: http://www.down-the-shore.com

Publishes: Fiction; Nonfiction; Poetry; *Areas:* Historical; Nature; Short Stories; *Markets:* Adult

Small regional publisher focusing on New Jersey, the Jersey Shore, the mid-Atlantic, and seashore and coastal subjects. Specialises in regional histories; pictorial, coffee table books; literary anthologies; and natural history titles appropriate to the market. Rarely publishes fiction, and does not generally publish poetry unless as part of an anthology. Willing to consider any exceptional work appropriate to the market, however. See website for more details.

Dragonfairy Press

Email: info@dragonfairypress.com
Website: http://www.dragonfairypress.com

Publishes: Fiction; *Areas:* Fantasy; Romance; Sci-Fi; *Markets:* Adult; Youth

Please follow submission instructions on website. We want manuscripts that stretch beyond the world as we know it. That means fantasy and science fiction, including their various subgenres, such as urban fantasy, paranormal romance/erotica, cyberpunk, supernatural horror, and others. Don't worry about sex, gore, or foul language. While we certainly do not require these, we don't shy away from them either. Although we don't expect manuscripts to be publication-ready, we strongly recommend that your manuscript be clean enough (and in our manuscript format) to minimize distractions as we read. We look for strong writing and well-paced stories.

Dzanc Books

1334 Woodbourne Street
Westland, MI 48186
Email: info@dzancbooks.org
Website: http://www.dzancbooks.org

Publishes: Fiction; *Areas:* Literature; Short Stories; *Markets:* Adult; *Treatments:* Literary

Non-profit publisher of literary fiction that need not fill a particular market niche. No young adult fiction or literary nonfiction. For novels, send first one or two chapters up to 35 pages maximum via online submission manager. Accepts short stories through short story contest only ($20 entry fee). See website for more details.

Eastland Press
PO Box 99749
Seattle, WA 98139
Tel: +1 (206) 217-0204
Fax: +1 (206) 217-0205
Email: info@eastlandpress.com
Website: http://www.eastlandpress.com

Publishes: Nonfiction; *Areas:* Health; Medicine; *Markets:* Professional

Publishes textbooks for practitioners of Chinese medicine, osteopathy, and other forms of bodywork.

EDCON Publishing Group
30 Montauk Boulevard
Oakdale, NY 11769-1399
Tel: +1 (631) 567-7227
Fax: +1 (631) 567-8745
Email: edcon@EDCONPublishing.com
Website: https://www.edconpublishing.com

Publishes: Fiction; Nonfiction; *Markets:* Children's

Publishes educational nonfiction, fiction, and puzzles for children. Particularly maths, science, reading and social studies. For fiction, send query with SASE, synopsis, and one sample chapter.

Edupress, Inc.
PO Box 8610
Madison, WI 53708-8610
Tel: +1 (800) 694-5827
Email: lbowie@highsmith.com
Website: http://www.edupressinc.com

Publishes: Nonfiction; *Markets:* Professional

Publishes original curriculum resources for PreK through to eighth grade, designed to aid teachers in helping students reach current assessment standards. Mostly written by authors in the educational field. See website for full guidelines.

EMIS Inc. Medical Publishers
PO Box 270666
Fort Collins, CO 80527-0666
Tel: +1 (214) 349-0077
Fax: +1 (970) 672-8606
Website: http://www.emispub.com

Publishes: Nonfiction; Reference; *Areas:* Health; Medicine; Psychology; *Markets:* Professional

Publishes medical books for physicians. Send query with three sample chapters and SASE.

ETC Publications
1456 Rodeo Road
Palm Springs, CA 92262
Tel: +1 (760) 316-9695
Fax: +1 (760) 316-9681
Website: http://www.etcpublications.com

Publishes: Nonfiction; *Areas:* Business; Historical; Military; Religious; Sociology; Sport; Travel; *Markets:* Academic; Adult; Professional

Primarily concerned with publishing nonfiction works that are interesting and useful to the reader. Prefers books for schools (students, teachers, staff, and administrators) but will consider and publish other nonfiction types as well. Send complete ms with SASE.

Faery Rose
Email: queryus@thewildrosepress.com
Website: http://wildrosepress.us

Publishes: Fiction; *Areas:* Fantasy; Romance; Sci-Fi; *Markets:* Adult

Publisher of fantasy romance. Stories may

include fantasticaly creatures (dragons, elves, etc.), time travel, futuristic worlds, etc. but must be primarily romances. Send queries by email only, with synopsis, personal information, and word count in the body of the email. No attachments. See website for full details.

Farcountry Press

Acquisitions
Farcountry Press
PO Box 5630
Helena, MT 59604
Email: editor@farcountrypress.com
Website: http://www.farcountrypress.com

Publishes: Nonfiction; *Areas:* Cookery; Historical; Nature; Photography; *Markets:* Adult; Children's

Publishes photography, nature, and history books for adults and children, as well as guidebooks and cookery titles. No fiction or poetry. Send query with SASE, sample chapters, and sample table of contents. See website for full submission guidelines.

Florida Academic Press

PO Box 357425
Gainesville, FL 32635
Tel: +1 (352) 332-5104
Fax: +1 (352) 331-6003
Email: FAPress@gmail.com
Website:
http://www.floridaacademicpress.com

Publishes: Fiction; Nonfiction; *Areas:* Historical; Politics; Sociology; *Markets:* Academic; Adult

Publishes mainly nonfiction and scholarly books, however also publishes fiction. Particularly interested in the history and politics of the Third World (Africa, Middle East, Asia) and books on the social sciences in general. Do not send query letter. Send complete ms with SASE. See website for full guidelines.

48fourteen

Email: query@48fourteen.com
Website: http://www.48fourteen.com

Publishes: Fiction; *Areas:* Fantasy; Horror; Humour; Romance; Sci-Fi; Thrillers; Women's Interests; *Markets:* Adult; Children's; Youth

Publishes all genres, including science fiction, fantasy, urban fantasy, cyber/steam punk, thrillers, horror, romance, women's fiction, comedy, young adult/children's, and graphic novels/comics. Send query with synopsis, bio, and first three chapters in the body of an email (no attachments). Alternatively, send query and synopsis only using online form. See website for full details.

Four Way Books

P.O. Box 535, Village Station
New York, NY 10014
Tel: +1 (212) 334-5430
Email: editors@fourwaybooks.com
Website: http://www.fourwaybooks.com

Publishes: Fiction; Poetry; *Areas:* Short Stories; *Markets:* Adult

Not-for-profit literary press publishing poetry and short fiction by both established and emerging writers. Prefers to receive contributions during specific reading periods (see website), but may consider work outside of these periods - send query by email to ask if this is acceptable. See website for full details.

Fox Chapel Publishing

1970 Broad Street
East Petersburg, PA 17520
Tel: +1 (800) 457-9112
Fax: +1 (717) 560-4702
Email:
acquisitions@foxchapelpublishing.com
Website:
http://www.foxchapelpublishing.com

Publishes: Nonfiction; Reference; *Areas:* Arts; Cookery; Crafts; Design; Gardening; How-to; Nature; Photography; Sport; Travel; *Markets:* Adult; Professional

Contact: Book Acquisition Editor

Publishes books on woodworking, crafting,

gardening, do-it-yourself projects, cooking, and other similar topics. See website for full submission guidelines and FAQ.

Freelance Writer's Resource
36523 Water Street
Highland, CA 92346

Tel: +1 (909) 798-2269
Email:
submit@freelancewritersresource.com
Website:
http://www.freelancewritersresource.com

Publishes: Nonfiction; *Areas:* Arts; Business; Current Affairs; Entertainment; Finance; Health; How-to; Legal; Leisure; Lifestyle; Media; Medicine; Military; Nature; Psychology; Science; Sci-Fi; Sociology; Spiritual; Technology; Travel; *Markets:* Family; Professional; Commercial; In-depth; Mainstream; Niche; Popular; Positive; Progressive; Serious; Traditional

Contact: Kevin Kan

Seeking articles, blog posts and web content between 300 – 1,500 words for publication on a variety of online niche publications. The homepage of the website states what articles are currently open for submission. Read the Terms of Service page first before submitting any material.

Freya's Bower
PO Box 4897
Culver City, CA 90231-4897
Tel: +1 (424) 258-0897
Email: submit@freyasbower.com
Website: http://www.freyasbower.com

Publishes: Fiction; *Areas:* Erotic; Romance; Short Stories; *Markets:* Adult

Publishes romance and erotica. Send query with synopsis and first chapter in the body of an email, including details about the book and a marketing plan. See website for full details.

Fulcrum Publishing
4690 Table Mountain Drive, Suite 100

Golden, Colorado 80403
Tel: +1 (800) 992-2908
Fax: +1 (800) 726-7112
Email: acquisitions@fulcrumbooks.com
Website: http://www.fulcrum-books.com

Publishes: Nonfiction; *Areas:* Culture; Gardening; Historical; Nature; Politics; *Markets:* Adult; Children's

Publishes nonfiction exploring Western Culture and History (adult and children's), Native American Culture and History (adult and children's), Environment and Nature (adult and children's), Public Policy, and Western Gardening. No fiction or memoirs. Accepts queries by email only. See website for full guidelines.

Gauthier Publications
PO Box 806241
Saint Clair Shores, MI 48080
Email:
Submissions@Gauthierpublications.com
Website:
http://www.gauthierpublications.com

Publishes: Fiction; Nonfiction; *Areas:* Adventure; Culture; Fantasy; Historical; Horror; Humour; Military; Mystery; Photography; Religious; Romance; Self-Help; Short Stories; Suspense; Thrillers; Translations; *Markets:* Adult; Children's; Youth; *Treatments:* Contemporary; Literary; Mainstream

No unsolicited mss. Send query by post with SASE or by email. Send outline and sample chapters only if requested. Postal queries without SASE will be destroyed without reply if not interested. See website for more information.

Gem Guides Book Co.
1275 West 9th Street
Upland, CA 91786
Email: info@gemguidesbooks.com
Website: http://www.gemguidesbooks.com

Publishes: Nonfiction; *Areas:* Crafts; How-to; New Age; Science; Travel; *Markets:* Adult

Publishes how-to and where-to books on Rocks, Minerals, Gems; Field Guides for Rock and Fossil Collectors; Lapidary Work or Jewellery Crafts; New Age Related to Crystals and Gems; Gold Prospecting / Treasure Hunting; Travel, Hiking, and Outdoor Guides of the West/Southwest. Accepts submissions of proposals or unsolicited mss by post. Include SASE if return of material required. See website for full details.

Glass Page Books

PO Box 333
Signal Mountain, TN 37377
Email: glasspage@epbfi.com
Website: http://www.glasspagebooks.com

Publishes: Fiction; *Areas:* Drama; Short Stories; *Markets:* Adult

Accepts submissions for dramatic literature via literary agents only. No agent is required for submissions of short stories for anthologies. See submissions section of website for current calls and details on submitting.

Glenbridge Publishing Ltd

19923 East Long Avenue
Centennial, CO 80016
Tel: +1 (800) 986-4135
Email: glenbridge@qwestoffice.net
Website:
http://www.glenbridgepublishing.com

Publishes: Fiction; Nonfiction; *Areas:* Business; Cookery; Film; Finance; Historical; Humour; Lifestyle; Literature; Medicine; Music; Nature; Politics; Self-Help; Theatre; *Markets:* Adult

Send query by email, including outline or synopsis and sample chapters.

The Glencannon Press

P.O. Box 1428
El Cerrito, CA 94530
Tel: +1 (510) 528-4216
Fax: +1 (510) 528-3194
Email: info@glencannon.com
Website: http://www.glencannon.com

Publishes: Fiction; Nonfiction; *Areas:* Adventure; Military; Travel; *Markets:* Adult; Children's

Publishes nonfiction and fiction about ships and the sea; including World War I and II, steamships, battleships, sailing ships, and true adventure.

Golden West Books

PO Box 80250
San Marino CA 91118
Tel: +1 (626) 458-8148
Fax: +1 (626) 458-8148
Email: trainbook@earthlink.net
Website: http://www.goldenwestbooks.com

Publishes: Nonfiction; *Areas:* Historical; Travel; *Markets:* Adult

Publishes books on railroad history. Send query in first instance, via online form on website or by post with SASE.

Grand Canyon Association

PO Box 399
Grand Canyon, AZ 86023
Tel: +1 (928) 638-2481
Fax: +1 (928) 638-2484
Email: gcassociation@grandcanyon.org
Website: http://www.grandcanyon.org

Publishes: Fiction; Nonfiction; *Areas:* Anthropology; Archaeology; Architecture; Historical; Leisure; Nature; Photography; Science; Sport; Travel; *Markets:* Adult; Children's

Publishes nonfiction and children's fiction and nonfiction relating to the Grand Canyon only. Send query with SASE, outline, details of previous publishing credits, and either 3-4 sample chapters or complete ms.

Gulf Publishing Company

2 Greenway Plaza, Suite 1020
Houston, Texas 77046
Tel: +1 (713) 529-4301
Fax: +1 (713) 520-4433
Email: store@gulfpub.com
Website: http://www.gulfpub.com

Publishes: Nonfiction; *Areas:* Design; Science; Technology; *Markets:* Academic; Professional

Oil and gas industry publisher, producing books for engineers, students, well managers, academics, etc. Submit outline with 1-2 sample chapters, or complete ms.

Heritage Books, Inc.
5810 Ruatan Street
Berwyn Heights, MD 20740
Tel: +1 (800) 876-6103
Fax: +1 (410) 558-6574
Email: submissions@HeritageBooks.com
Website: http://www.heritagebooks.com

Publishes: Fiction; Nonfiction; Reference; *Areas:* Autobiography; Historical; Military; *Markets:* Academic; Adult

Publishes nonfiction in genealogy, history, military history, historical fiction, and memoirs. Also some fact-rich historical novels. Send query with SASE or submit outline by email.

The Habit of Rainy Nights Press
Oregon
Email: editors@rainynightspress.org
Website: http://rainynightspress.org

Publishes: Fiction; Nonfiction; Poetry; *Markets:* Adult; *Treatments:* Literary

Contact: Duane Poncy, Fiction Editor; Patricia McLean, Nonfiction Editor; Ger Killeen, Poetry Editor

A very small micro-press publishing 2-3 print books and half a dozen ebooks a year. Accepts submissions for ebooks all year, but submission window for print books is January 1 - May 31 only. Emphasises unknown or under-appreciated authors whose work has depth and social importance, as well as under-represented voices: immigrants, persons of colour, and Native American voices, in particular. Looks for strong narrative in both fiction and poetry. No romance, erotica, Christian, New Age, vampires, zombies, or superheroes. Submit

via online submission system only (see website).

Hadley Rille Books
PO Box 25466
Overland Park KS 66225
Email: subs@hadleyrillebooks.com
Website: http://www.hadleyrillebooks.com

Publishes: Fiction; *Areas:* Archaeology; Fantasy; Historical; Sci-Fi; *Markets:* Adult

Contact: Eric T. Reynolds, Editor/Publisher

Publishes Science Fiction stories with an emphasis on space, archaeology, climate and other science-related topics. Opens to submissions in specific months. See website for details.

The Harvard Common Press
535 Albany Street
Boston, MA 02118
Tel: +1 (617) 423-5803
Fax: +1 (617) 695-9794
Email: editorial@harvardcommonpress.com
Website:
http://www.harvardcommonpress.com

Publishes: Nonfiction; *Areas:* Cookery; Lifestyle; *Markets:* Adult

Independent publisher of books on cookery and parenting. See website for full guidelines on submitting a proposal. No phone calls. Postal submissions cannot be returned.

Hayes School Publishing Co., Inc.
321 Pennwood Avenue
Pittsburgh, PA 15221

Tel: +1 (800) 245-6234
Email: chayes@hayespub.com
Website: http://www.hayespub.com

Publishes: Nonfiction; *Markets:* Academic; Children's

Publishes school books for children. Welcomes manuscripts and ideas for new products. Send query by email to receive a copy of the author's guide.

High-Lonesome
P. O. Box 878
Silver City, NM 88062
Tel: +1 (575) 388-3763
Fax: +1 (575) 388-5705
Email: Orders@High-LonesomeBooks.com
Website: http://www.high-lonesomebooks.com/cgi-bin/hlb/index.html

Publishes: Fiction; Nonfiction; *Areas:* Adventure; Anthropology; Archaeology; Biography; Crime; Historical; Westerns; *Markets:* Academic; Adult; *Treatments:* Experimental; Niche; Traditional

Contact: Cherie and M. H. Salmon

Specializes in topics dealing with NM, AZ, TX, wilderness, history, fishing, environment, western americana.

Founded by a writer, publisher, former newspaperman in 1986.

Query by email.

Highland Press
Submissions Department
PO Box 2292
High Springs, FL 32655
Email: Submissions.hp@gmail.com
Website: http://www.highlandpress.org

Publishes: Fiction; Nonfiction; Reference; *Areas:* Fantasy; Historical; Mystery; Romance; Suspense; *Markets:* Adult; Children's; Youth; *Treatments:* Contemporary

Has previously focused on publishing historical fictions, but currently open to all genres except erotic. Particularly interested in both contemporary and historical Christian / Inspirational / family. Accepts queries by post and email, but any approaches not adhering to the submission guidelines will be discarded. See website for full submission guidelines.

Homestead Publishing
Acquisitions
Box 193
Moose, Wyoming 83012
Tel: +1 (307) 733-6248
Fax: +1 (307) 733-6248
Email: homesteadpublishing@mac.com
Website: http://www.homesteadpublishing.net

Publishes: Fiction; Nonfiction; *Areas:* Architecture; Arts; Biography; Cookery; Design; Literature; Nature; Photography; Travel; *Markets:* Adult; *Treatments:* Literary

Publishes fine art, design, photography, and architecture; full-color nature books; national park guide books: cookbooks; biographies and literary fiction; Western Americana; regional and international travel guides, including Yellowstone, Grand Teton, Glacier-Waterton and Banff-Jasper national parks. Particularly interested in outdoor guide—hiking, climbing, bicycling, canoeing, mountaineering—and travel books. Accepts queries with samples. See website for full submission guidelines.

Hopewell Publications
PO Box 11
Titusville, NJ 08560-0011
Tel: +1 (609) 818-1049
Fax: +1 (609) 964-1718
Email: submissions@hopepubs.com
Website: http://www.hopepubs.com

Publishes: Fiction; Nonfiction; *Markets:* Adult; Youth

Publishes fiction and nonfiction. Specialises in classic reprints but also considers new titles. See website for submission guidelines. Queries which do not follow them will be deleted unread.

Humanics Publishing Group
12 S. Dixie Hwy, Ste. 203
Lake Worth, FL 33460
Tel: +1 (800) 874-8844
Fax: +1 (888) 874-8844
Email: humanics@mindspring.com
Website: http://www.humanicspub.com

Publishes: Nonfiction; Finance; How-to; New Age; Religious; Science; Self-Help; *Markets:* Adult; Children's

Contact: W. Arthur Bligh, Acquisitions Editor

Started in 1969, in response to the need from the education community for quality classroom materials to support parents as the prime educators of their children. In 1984 launched a New Age imprint. Accepts unsolicited mss by post with SASE. See website for full submission guidelines.

Hyperink

333 Bryant Street, Suite 330
San Francisco, CA 94107
Tel: +1 (650) 395-7596
Email: contact@hyperink.com
Website: http://www.hyperink.com

Publishes: Nonfiction; *Markets:* Adult

Publishes nonfiction by experts - primarily as eBooks but also print. Specialises in having journalists work with busy experts to interview and write the books for them, but experts can also write the books themselves. Apply online via website.

Ideals Publications

2630 Elm Hill Pike, Suite 100
Nashville, TN 37214
Tel: +1 (615) 781-1451
Email: kwest@guideposts.org
Website: http://www.idealsbooks.com

Publishes: Fiction; Nonfiction; *Markets:* Children's

Publishes fiction and nonfiction picture books for children aged 4-8 (up to 800 words), and board and novelty books for children 2-5 (up to 250 words). Subjects include holiday, inspirational, and patriotic themes; relationships and values; and general fiction. Submit complete mss only - no queries or proposals. No submissions by email or computer disk. See website for full guidelines.

Ignatius Press

1348 10th Avenue
San Francisco, CA 94122
Email: info@ignatius.com
Website: http://www.ignatius.com

Publishes: Nonfiction; *Areas:* Religious; *Markets:* Adult

Christian publisher. Submit complete ms. No phone calls or emails. See webite for full submission guidelines.

The Ilium Press

Tel: +1 (509) 928-7950
Email: submissions@iliumpress.com
Website: http://www.iliumpress.com

Publishes: Fiction; Nonfiction; Poetry; *Areas:* Biography; Crime; Historical; Music; *Markets:* Adult; *Treatments:* Literary

Contact: John Lemon

Publishes epic poetry, literary fiction, books on music (both fiction and nonfiction), crime novels, historical fiction, and dystopian speculative fiction. Send query by email with summary, two or three sample chapters (up to 50 pages), bio and list of previous publications, and contact information. See website for full guidelines.

Image Comics

Submissions
c/o Image Comics
2134 Allston Way, 2nd Floor
Berkeley, CA 94704
Email: submissions@imagecomics.com
Website: http://www.imagecomics.com

Publishes: Fiction; *Markets:* Adult; Youth

Third largest comic book publisher in the United States. Publishes comics and graphic novels. Only interested in creator-owned comics. Does not acquire any rights. Looking for comics that are well written and well drawn, by people who are dedicated and can meet deadlines, not any specific genre or type of comic book. See website for full submission guidelines.

ImaJinn Books

Tel: +1 (623) 236-3361
Email: editors@imajinnbooks.com
Website: http://www.imajinnbooks.com

Publishes: Fiction; *Areas:* Erotic; Fantasy;
Horror; Mystery; Romance; Sci-Fi; *Markets:*
Adult

Print-on-demand publisher also offering
ebooks. No unsolicited mss. Send query in
first instance by email only, including
synopsis up to six double-spaced pages long.
Prefers shorter works (as small as 30,000
words) and does not publish books over
90,000 words. See website for more details.

Immedium

PO Box 31846
San Francisco, CA 94131

Email: submissions@immedium.com
Website: http://www.immedium.com

Publishes: Fiction; Nonfiction; *Areas:* Arts;
Culture; *Markets:* Children's

Publishes children's picture books, Asian-
America, and Arts and Culture. Send query
with SASE, CV, and full manuscript (picture
books) or one-page summary and two
sample chapters (50 pages total). See website
for full guidelines.

Impact Books

F+W Media, Inc.
10151 Carver Road, Suite 200
Blue Ash, OH 45242
Email: Pam.wissman@fwpubs.com
Website: http://www.impact-books.com

Publishes: Nonfiction; Reference; *Areas:*
Arts; How-to; *Markets:* Adult

Contact: Pamela Wissman, Acquisitions
Editor

Publishes books to assist artists drawing
comics, superheroes, Japanese-style manga,
fantasy, creatures, action, caricature, anime,
etc.

Ingalls Publishing Group, Inc.

PO Box 2500
Banner Elk, NC 28604
Tel: +1 (828) 297-6884
Fax: +1 (828) 297-6880
Email: editor@ingallspublishinggroup.com
Website:
http://www.ingallspublishinggroup.com

Publishes: Fiction; Nonfiction; *Areas:*
Adventure; Autobiography; Crime;
Historical; Humour; Mystery; Romance;
Markets: Adult

Publishes memoirs and fiction with authors
and settings in North Carolina, South
Carolina, Virginia, Florida, Tennessee or
Georgia. Fiction must involve adventure,
murder, mystery, humour, romance, or
historical events. 50,000 - 100,000 words.
Prefers queries by email, with synopsis up to
a maximum of two pages. Include link to
your website if available.

International Press

PO Box 43502
Somerville, MA 02143
Tel: +1 (617) 623-3855
Fax: +1 (617) 623-3101
Email: ipb-info@intlpress.com
Website: http://www.intlpress.com

Publishes: Nonfiction; Science; *Markets:*
Academic

Contact: Mr Lixin Qin

Academic publisher of high-level
mathematics and mathematical physics book
titles, including monographs, textbooks, and
more.

Ion Imagination Entertainment, Inc.

PO Box 210943
Nashville, TN 37221-0943
Tel: +1 (615) 646-6276
Email: ionimagin@aol.com
Website: http://www.flumpa.com

Publishes: Fiction; *Areas:* Science; *Markets:*
Children's

Publishes science-related fiction for children. Send query with SASE, bio, and publishing history. No unsolicited mss.

Itoh Press

535 Moats Lane
Bowling Green, KY 42103
Fax: +1 (270) 783-0888
Email: carolitoh@itohpress.com
Website: http://www.itohpress.com

Publishes: Fiction; Nonfiction; *Areas:* Adventure; Autobiography; Beauty and Fashion; Crime; Culture; Current Affairs; Drama; Entertainment; Erotic; Fantasy; Film; Gothic; Historical; Horror; Humour; Leisure; Lifestyle; Literature; Music; New Age; Philosophy; Politics; Religious; Romance; Sci-Fi; Sociology; Spiritual; Suspense; Theatre; TV; Westerns; Women's Interests; *Markets:* Adult; Youth; *Treatments:* Contemporary; Dark; Light; Literary; Mainstream; Niche; Popular; Positive; Satirical

Contact: Carol Itoh

We are dedicated to women writers and the southern voice. We welcome all submissions and we never charge authors any fees. We are committed to providing the highest standard in literaure to our readers. In an effort to green we only accept electronic queries and submissions.

Jewish Lights Publishing

Sunset Farm Offices
Route 4, PO Box 237
Woodstock, VT 05091
Tel: +1 (802) 457-4000
Fax: +1 (802) 457-4004
Email: editorial@jewishlights.com
Website: http://jewishlights.com

Publishes: Fiction; Nonfiction; *Areas:* Crime; Historical; Men's Interests; Mystery; Philosophy; Religious; Sci-Fi; Spiritual; Women's Interests; *Markets:* Adult; Children's; Youth

Publishes books for people of all faiths and backgrounds, drawing on the Jewish wisdom tradition. Books are almost exclusively nonfiction, covering topics such as religion, Jewish life cycle, theology, philosophy, history, and spirituality, however does publish some fiction, including children's books and graphic novels. No biography, haggadot, or poetry. Send proposal by post only - no email submissions or unsolicited mss. See website for full details.

John F. Blair, Publisher

1406 Plaza Drive
Winston-Salem, NC 27103
Tel: +1 (800) 222-9796
Fax: +1 (336) 768-9194
Email: kirk@blairpub.com
Website: http://www.blairpub.com

Publishes: Fiction; Nonfiction; *Areas:* Biography; Historical; Travel; *Markets:* Adult

Contact: Steve Kirk, Editor-in-Chief

Publishes regional books relating to the Southeast of the United States. Publishes mainly nonfiction in areas such as history, travel, folklore, and biography, but also one or two works of fiction each year which are connected to the Southeast either by setting or by the author's background. No children's books, poetry, or category fiction such as romances, science fiction, or spy thrillers; collections of short stories, essays, or newspaper columns. No electronic or fax proposals. SASE required for response / return of materials. See website for full submission guidelines.

Jonathan David Publishers, Inc.

68-22 Eliot Avenue
Middle Village, NY 11379-1194
Email: submissions@JDBooks.com
Website: http://www.jdbooks.com

Publishes: Nonfiction; Reference; *Areas:* Cookery; Culture; Humour; Religious; Sport; *Markets:* Adult; *Treatments:* Popular

New York-based nonfiction trade book publisher specialising in sports, biography, reference, and popular Judaica. Send query by post only with SASE, brief synopsis, table of contents, sample chapter, and résumé. No multiple submissions, or submissions by email.

Jones & Bartlett Learning
5 Wall Street
Burlington, MA 01803
Tel: +1 (978) 443-5000
Fax: +1 (978) 443-8000
Email: info@jblearning.com
Website: http://www.jblearning.com

Publishes: Nonfiction; *Areas:* Health; Legal; Medicine; Science; Technology; *Markets:* Academic; Professional

Publisher of educational and professional material. See website for full list of editorial contacts.

Jupiter Gardens Press
Email: submissions@jupitergardens.com
Website: http://jupitergardenspress.com

Publishes: Fiction; Nonfiction; *Areas:* Erotic; Fantasy; New Age; Romance; Sci-Fi; Short Stories; *Markets:* Adult; Children's; Youth

Send query by email with 2-4 pages synopsis, author bio, and first three chapters as .DOC or .RTF attachments.

Just Us Books
Submissions Manager
Just Us Books
356 Glenwood Avenue
East Orange, NJ 07017
Tel: +1 (973) 672-7701
Fax: +1 (973) 677-7570
Email: cheryl_hudson@justusbooks.com
Website: http://justusbooks.com

Publishes: Fiction; Nonfiction; Poetry; *Markets:* Children's; Youth

Publishes Black-interest books for young people, including picture books, chapter books for middle readers, poetry, nonfiction series, biographies and young adult fiction. Currently accepting queries for young adult titles only. Send query with SAE, author bio,

1-2 page synopsis, and 3-5 page sample. See website for full submission guidelines.

Kalmbach Publishing Co.
21027 Crossroads Circle
PO Box 1612
Waukesha, WI 53187-1612
Tel: +1 (262) 796-8776 Ext. 421
Fax: +1 (262) 796-1615
Email: books@kalmbach.com
Website: http://www.kalmbach.com

Publishes: Nonfiction; Reference; *Areas:* Crafts; Hobbies; How-to; *Markets:* Adult

Publishes books on arts and crafts, model-making, jewellery-making, toy trains, etc. Send query with 2-3 page outline, plus sample chapter with photos.

Kamehameha Publishing
567 South King Street, Suite 118
Honolulu, HI 96813
Tel: +1 (808) 523-6200
Email: publishing@ksbe.edu
Website:
http://www.kamehamehapublishing.org

Publishes: Fiction; Nonfiction; *Areas:* Biography; Culture; Historical; *Markets:* Academic; Adult; Children's; Youth

Publishes books on Hawaiian language, culture, history, and community, for children, young people, and adults. See website for full details and submission guidelines.

Kane Miller Books
4901 Morena Boulevard, Ste 213
San Diego, CA 92117
Tel: +1 (800) 475-4522
Email: submissions@kanemiller.com
Website: http://www.kanemiller.com

Publishes: Fiction; *Areas:* Adventure; Fantasy; Historical; Mystery; *Markets:* Children's; Youth

This publisher is committed to expanding their picture book, chapter book, and middle-grade fiction lists. Particularly interested in engaging characters and American subjects. Send query by email with complete ms (picture books) or synopsis and two sample chapters in the body of the email. No attachments or links to websites.

Kearney Street Books
PO Box 2021
Bellingham, WA 98227
Tel: +1 (360) 738-1355
Email: garyrmc@mac.com
Website: http://kearneystreetbooks.com

Publishes: Fiction; *Areas:* Music; *Markets:* Adult; *Treatments:* Niche

Publishes fiction by or about musicians or music. Publishes very few titles a year. Send query by email or send complete ms by post with SASE for reply only.

Kelly Point Publishing LLC
Martin Sisters Publishing LLC
PO Box 1154
Barbourville, KY 40906
Email:
submissions@kellypointpublishing.com
Website:
http://www.kellypointpublishing.com

Publishes: Fiction; *Areas:* Adventure; Fantasy; Historical; Humour; Mystery; Religious; Romance; Sci-Fi; Short Stories; Spiritual; Sport; Westerns; Women's Interests; *Markets:* Adult; Children's; Youth; *Treatments:* Contemporary; Literary; Mainstream

Open to all genres of fiction. No nonfiction or poetry. Send query by email, with marketing plan and first three chapters pasted into the body of the email. No attachments. See website for full guidelines.

Kitsune Books
P.O. Box 1154
Crawfordville, FL 32326-1154
Email: contact@kitsunebooks.com
Website: http://www.kitsunebooks.com

Publishes: Fiction; Nonfiction; Poetry; *Areas:* Autobiography; Criticism; Fantasy;

Literature; New Age; Short Stories; *Markets:* Academic; Adult; *Treatments:* Dark; Literary

Contact: Lynn Holschuh

Open to submissions January-June only.

1. Before submitting, always check our website for updates
2. We prefer fiction/nonfiction ms. of 70,000-100,000 words; poetry ms. of 100 pages or more. No chapbooks, no novellas.
3. No hardcopy submissions - email only. Send email query that includes the book title, genre, word count (if fiction or nonfiction), and intended audience. You can also include a paragraph summary of the plot, and any details about yourself that you feel are relevant.
4. Attach the complete ms. in MS Word format to your query - no partial submissions.
5. You will receive an acknowledgement that your submission has been logged in.

Response time for ms. review is typically 150 days (you may ask about the status of your ms. if you haven't heard from us after 150 days).

Knox Robinson Publishing (US)
244 5th Avenue, Suite 1861
New York, NY 10001
Tel: +1 (646) 652-6980
Email: subs@knoxrobinsonpublishing.com
Website:
http://www.knoxrobinsonpublishing.com

Publishes: Fiction; *Areas:* Fantasy; Historical; Romance; *Markets:* Adult

Publishes historical fiction, historical romance (pre-1960), and medieval fantasy. No science fiction, time travel, or fantasy with children and/or animal protagonists. Send query by email only, with detailed synopsis and the first three chapters. No approaches by fax or post. See website for full details.

Legacy Press

Rainbow Publishers
PO Box 261129
San Diego, CA 92196
Tel: +1 (800) 638-4428
Fax: +1 (800) 331-0297
Email:
john.gregory@rainbowpublishers.com
Website: http://www.legacypresskids.com

Publishes: Fiction; Nonfiction; *Areas:*
Religious; *Markets:* Children's

Publishes devotions, instructional books, and
faith-based fiction for kids. See website for
submission guidelines.

Lawyers & Judges Publishing Co.

917 N Swan, Suite 300
Tucson, AZ 85711
Tel: +1 (520) 323-1500
Fax: +1 (520) 323-0055
Email: steve@lawyersandjudges.com
Website: http://www.lawyersandjudges.com

Publishes: Nonfiction; Reference; *Areas:*
Legal; Medicine; *Markets:* Professional

Contact: Steve Weintraub

Publishes legal and medical books for
professionals. See website for submission
guidelines.

Leapfrog Press

PO Box 505
Fredonia, NY 14063
Email: acquisitions@leapfrogpress.com
Website: http://www.leapfrogpress.com

Publishes: Fiction; Nonfiction; Poetry;
Markets: Adult; Children's; *Treatments:*
Literary

Publisher with an eclectic list of fiction,
poetry, and nonfiction, including paperback
originals of adult and middle-grade fiction
and nonfiction. Closed to submissions
between January 15 and May each year.
Accepts queries by email only: send query
letter and short sample within the email

itself. No attachments. See website for full
guidelines.

Ledge Hill Publishing

PO Box 337
Alton, NH 03809
Tel: +1 (603) 998-6801
Email: info@ledgehillpublishing.com
Website:
http://www.ledgehillpublishing.com

Publishes: Fiction; Nonfiction; Poetry;
Areas: Short Stories; *Markets:* Adult

Publishes short fiction, poetry, and creative
nonfiction. Electronic approaches only. Send
short query via webform on website, or send
complete ms with covering letter by email.
See website for full details.

Les Figues Press

PO Box 7736
Los Angeles, CA 90007
Tel: +1 (323) 734-4732
Email: info@lesfigues.com
Website: http://www.lesfigues.com

Publishes. Fiction; Poetry; *Areas:* Short
Stories; *Markets:* Adult

Publishes fiction and poetry. Accepts
submissions through its annual contest only
($25 entry fee). Accepts poetry, novellas,
innovative novels, anti-novels, short story
collections, lyric essays, hybrids, and all
forms not otherwise specified. Submit via
form on website.

Linden Publishing

2006 South Mary
Fresno, CA 93721
Tel: +1 (559) 233-6633
Fax: +1 (559) 233-6933
Email: richard@lindenpub.com
Website: http://www.lindenpub.com

Publishes: Nonfiction; *Areas:* Arts; Crafts;
Historical; Hobbies; How-to; *Markets:* Adult

Publishes books on woodworking. Send
email for full submission guidelines.

Local Gems Poetry Press

Email: localgemspoetrypress@gmail.com
Website:
http://www.localgemspoetrypress.com

Publishes: Poetry; *Areas:* Humour; *Markets:*
Family; Professional; Youth; *Treatments:*
Contemporary; Experimental; Mainstream;
Niche

Contact: Ishwa

A Long Island based poetry press
specializing in anthologies with creative
themes. Best method of approach for authors
looking to publish full length books with us
is to submit to our anthologies first so we
become familiar with their material. We are
open to all forms of poetry and like to use
poetry for social change.

Loose Id

Email: submissions@loose-id.com
Website: http://www.loose-id.com

Publishes: Fiction; *Areas:* Erotic; Fantasy;
Historical; Mystery; Romance; Sci-Fi;
Suspense; Westerns; *Markets:* Adult;
Treatments: Contemporary

Publisher of erotic romance ebooks, which
are occasionally also released in print. Send
query by email with synopsis and first three
chapters as RTF attachments only (no .doc
files or submissions in the body of the
email). See website for full guidelines.

Lucent Books

Attn: Publisher – Lucent Books
27500 Drake Road
Farmington Hills, MI 48331
Email: betz.deschenes@cengage.com
Website:
http://www.gale.cengage.com/greenhaven

Publishes: Nonfiction; *Markets:* Academic;
Children's

Publishes educational, nonfiction books that
support middle school curriculum and
national standards. Send query by email with
CV and list of previous publications.

M P Publishing USA

6 Petaluma Blvd N, Suite 6
Petaluma, CA
94952
Email: msatris@mppublishingusa.com
Website: http://mppublishingusa.com

Publishes: Fiction; Nonfiction; *Areas:*
Adventure; Crime; Fantasy; Gothic;
Literature; Mystery; Romance; Sci-Fi; Short
Stories; Suspense; Thrillers; Women's
Interests; *Markets:* Adult; Youth;
Treatments: Commercial; Contemporary;
Dark; Experimental; In-depth; Light;
Literary; Mainstream; Niche; Popular;
Progressive; Satirical; Serious; Traditional

Contact: Marthine Satris

Founded on the Isle of Man in 2008 as an
aggregator to small and mid-size publishers
wishing to enter the world of electronic
books. After acquiring and distributing more
than four hundred e-book titles, the publisher
decided to turn an eye to launching original
titles both in electronic format and by
conventional means. In 2010, released its
first original title, a SIBA award finalist.
Following in its wake, 2011 marks the
company's first full list of original titles and
paperback reprints. With offices and
distribution both in the U.S. and U.K., the
publishing house is rapidly expanding and
looking forward to launching great new
books throughout the world for years to
come.

Looking for a range of genres -- the only
thing we insist on is excellent, fresh writing.
We publish thriller and mystery novels,
young adult novels, experimental fiction, and
literary fiction. We believe in publishing the
author, not just the manuscript, and in
building a close and fruitful relationship
between our authors and our editors. Because
agents reject books for the wrong reasons,
we encourage authors to submit manuscripts
directly to our editors for review, and we will
deliver thoughtful, substantive responses to
all submissions within 30 days.

Submit via form on website.

Malachite Quills Publishing

655 Choteau Circle
Rancho Cordova, CA 95671
Email: malachitequills@gmail.com
Website: http://www.malachitequills.com

Publishes: Fiction; *Areas:* Fantasy; Sci-Fi;
Markets: Adult; Family; Youth; *Treatments:*
Commercial; Contemporary; Cynical; Dark;
Experimental; In-depth; Light; Literary;
Mainstream; Niche; Popular; Positive;
Progressive; Satirical; Serious; Traditional

Contact: Jeremy Trimble

We are a sci-fi/fantasy publisher interested in
working with new and previously published
writers. We accept all subgenres of sci-fi and
fantasy. Please see our submission guidelines
for additional information.

Master Books

PO Box 726
Green Forest, AR 72638
Tel: +1 (800) 999-3777
Email: nlp@newleafpress.net
Website: http://www.masterbooks.net

Publishes: Nonfiction; *Areas:* Religious,
Markets: Adult; Children's; Family; Youth

Publishes Christian and creation-based
books.

Medallion Media Group

100 S. River Street
Aurora, IL 60506
Tel: +1 (630) 513-8316
Fax: +1 (630) 513-8362
Email:
submissions@medallionmediagroup.com
Website: http://medallionmediagroup.com

Publishes: Fiction; Nonfiction; *Areas:* Arts;
Autobiography; Biography; Design; Fantasy;
Health; Historical; Horror; Mystery;
Religious; Romance; Sci-Fi; Suspense;
Thrillers; *Markets:* Adult; Youth;
Treatments: Literary; Mainstream

Contact: Emily Steele

Publishes fiction and nonfiction for adults

and young adults. No children's books, short
stories, or erotica. Accepts nonfiction
proposals through agents only. Submit via
submission form on website. No hard copy
submissions.

Medical Group Management Association (MGMA)

104 Inverness Terrace East
Englewood, CO 80112-5306
Tel: +1 (303) 799-1111
Email: support@mgma.com
Website: http://www.mgma.com

Publishes: Nonfiction; *Areas:* Business;
Medicine; *Markets:* Professional

Publishes books for professionals, aimed at
the business side of medicine. Submit
complete ms, or proposal including outline
and three sample chapters.

Messianic Jewish Publishers

6120 Day Long Lane
Clarksville, MD 21029
Tel: +1 (410) 531-6644
Email: editor@messianicjewish.net
Website: http://www.messianicjewish.net

Publishes: Fiction; Nonfiction; *Areas:*
Religious; *Markets:* Adult

Publishes books which address Jewish
evangelism; the Jewish roots of Christianity;
Messianic Judaism; Israel; the Jewish
People. Publishes mainly nonfiction, but
some fiction. See website for full submission
guidelines.

Michael Wiese Books

12400 Ventura Blvd., #1111
Studio City, CA 91604
Tel: +1 (800) 833-5738
Fax: +1 (818) 986-3408
Email: kenlee@mwp.com
Website: http://www.mwp.com

Publishes: Nonfiction; *Areas:* Film; How-to;
Markets: Professional

Contact: Ken Lee, Vice President

Publishes instructional books for film-makers. Before approaching, see factsheet for authors on website.

Moon Tide Press
PO Box 27182
Anaheim, CA 92809
Website: http://www.moontidepress.com

Publishes: Poetry; *Markets:* Adult

Publisher dedicated to showcasing the finest poets in Southern California. Send query with sample poems, bio, and details of any previous publishing credits.

Moonshadow Press
Email: submissions@wakestonepress.com
Website: http://www.wakestonepress.com

Publishes: Fiction; *Areas:* Adventure; Fantasy; Horror; *Markets:* Children's; Youth

Imprint publishing fiction, fantasy, young adult stories, and stories for boys. Send submissions by email. See website for more information.

Morgan Kaufmann Publishers
30 Corporate Drive, Suite 400
Burlington, MA 01803-4252
Tel: +1 (781) 663-5200
Email: a.dierna@elsevier.com
Website: http://mkp.com

Publishes: Nonfiction; *Areas:* Science; Technology; *Markets:* Professional

Publishes books for the computer science community. Complete New Book Proposal Questionnaire (available on website) and send it by email to the appropriate editor (list available on website).

Mountain Press Publishing Company
PO Box 2399
Missoula, MT 59806
Tel: +1 (406) 728-1900
Email: Info@mtnpress.com
Website: http://mountain-press.com

Publishes: Nonfiction; *Areas:* Historical; Nature; Science; *Markets:* Adult; Children's

Publishes books on natural history, western US history, and earth science. Send query by post only, with proposal including outline or table of contents and sample (one or two chapters). See website for full submission guidelines.

My Pouty Lips
Email: angelicka@mypoutylips.com
Website: http://www.mypoutylips.com

Publishes: Fiction; Nonfiction; Reference; *Areas:* Erotic; How-to; Men's Interests; Romance; Self-Help; Short Stories; Women's Interests; *Markets:* Adult; *Treatments:* Contemporary; Dark; Experimental; In-depth; Light; Literary; Mainstream; Niche; Popular; Positive; Progressive; Traditional

Contact: Angelicka Wallows

Publishing Erotica Authors.

I am happy to announce that I have started publishing erotica authors to help them make their name out there, or widen their distribution network. Basically what I do is editing and publishing (entirely free of charge) erotica stories, novels, anthologies, guides and how-tos both in eBook and paperback formats. EBooks are distributed via the major online retailers such as Apple, Sony, Barnes & Noble, Amazon, Kobo and more. Paperback versions are distributed via Amazon. An author contract is signed between us and you will be getting royalties on the profits made with the books.

If you are interested, please use the submission form at the bottom of the page to send us your text to publish. Please note that we will need more than just your text though, so get everything ready before submitting it to us. Here is what we will need:

Your complete manuscript (in word format – .doc – please do not format your text with bold, italic, tabs, colors or anything like that. We need to remove all formatting before we can start publishing and reformatting it in our

system. Make sure you have your text checked again for typos, grammar, style, spelling, punctuation. Your minimum word count should be 10,000 or above. The best size for erotica eBooks is around 60,000 words. Please note that we publish only text, so don't send photos to illustrate your pages!)
A photo of you (it could be a drawing, an illustration, a picture. Just make sure it is high resolution, clear, and clean)
Your biography (in less than half a page, tell us about you as an author, your background and inspiration, if you have published books already, etc). Feel free to include some links like social media, your blog, twitter, etc.
A short description of your work (It will be used to market your book on our site, and shared with some retailers. Please no email, hyperlink, or promotion. Your description should be a single paragraph in complete sentences, limited to 400 characters or less).
A long presentation of your work (An extended version of the above, needed for promotion purpose. Again, no email, hyperlink, or promotion. Try to raise the curiosity of the reader and want to learn more about your book. Minimum 600 characters, maximum 4,000)
Your Paypal email (we need to update our files with your payment info. Also you will be automatically opted in to our Authors newsletter to keep you in the loop about what is going on on our side. Please do not opt out as this method will be used to send you important information)

Once you have all these files ready, please do double check them again for typos, grammar, style, spelling, punctuation... The better the files you send, the better your final book will be. If you are 100% confident that they are OK, visit the website to start the submission of your files.

New Libri

Email: query@newlibri.com
Website: http://www.newlibri.com

Publishes: Fiction; Nonfiction; *Areas:* Fantasy; Literature; Sci-Fi; Technology; *Markets:* Adult; *Treatments:* Literary

Contact: Stanislav Fritz; Michael Muller

Send query by email with complete ms or at least 50 pages as Word or PDF format file. Include synopsis, word count, and genre/target market. No vampire stories. See website for full guidelines.

NavPress

PO Box 35002
Colorado Springs, CO 80935
Tel: +1 (800) 366-7788
Fax: +1 (800) 343-3902
Email: CustomerService@NavPress.com
Website: http://www.navpress.com

Publishes: Nonfiction; *Areas:* Culture; How-to; Lifestyle; Religious; Sociology; Spiritual; *Markets:* Adult

Christian publisher based in Colorado Springs. Aims to publish products that are biblically rooted, culturally relevant, and highly practical.

New Native Press

Post Office Box 661
Cullowhee, North Carolina 28723
Tel: +1 (828) 293-9237
Email: NewNativePress@hotmail.com
Website: http://www.newnativepress.com

Publishes: Poetry; *Areas:* Translations; *Markets:* Adult

Contact: Thomas Rain Crowe

Publishes bilingual books by authors writing poetry in marginalised languages, translated into English. Send query with bio, publishing credits, and ten sample poems.

New Rivers Press

Minnesota State University Moorhead
1104 7th Ave South
Moorhead, MN 56563
Tel: +1 (800) 593-7246
Email: davisa@mnstate.edu
Website: http://www.newriverspress.com

Publishes: Fiction; Nonfiction; Poetry; *Areas:* Autobiography; Short Stories; *Markets:* Adult; *Treatments:* Literary

Contact: Alan Davis; Suzzanne Kelley

Reads general book-length submissions in April and May. Also runs fiction and poetry contests at other times of the year. See website for full details.

New Victoria Publishers

P.O. Box 13173
Chicago, IL 60613-0173
Tel: +1 (773) 793-2244
Email: newvictoriapub@att.net
Website: http://www.newvictoria.com

Publishes: Fiction; Nonfiction; Poetry; Reference; *Areas:* Biography; Cookery; Crime; Fantasy; Humour; Mystery; New Age; Politics; Religious; Romance; Sci-Fi; Short Stories; Thrillers; Travel; Women's Interests; *Markets:* Adult

Publishes lesbian feminist fiction, nonfiction, and poetry. Accepts unsolicited mss, but prefers query in first instance with synopsis and sample up to 50 pages. No queries by email.

Nicolas Hays Publishers

PO Box 540206
Lake Worth, FL 33454-0206
Email: info@nicolas hays.com
Website: http://www.nicolashays.com

Publishes: Nonfiction; *Areas:* Biography; Health; Historical; Mystery; Politics; Psychology; Religious; Self-Help; *Markets:* Adult

Publishes books on topics such as Eastern and Western mysteries, magick and occultism, alchemy, astrology, etc. See website for more details.

Nortia Press

Tel: +1 (800) 283-3572
Fax: +1 (800) 351-5073
Email: acquisitions@nortiapress.com
Website: http://nortiapress.com

Publishes: Fiction; Nonfiction; *Areas:* Current Affairs; *Markets:* Adult; *Treatments:* Literary

Publishes literary fiction and nonfiction with a global affairs bent. Send queries for fiction and proposals for nonfiction by email. See website for more details.

Nova Press

9058 Lloyd P,ace
West Hollywood CA 90069
Email: sales@novapress.net
Website: http://novapress.net

Publishes: Nonfiction; Reference; *Markets:* Academic

Publishes test prep books for college entrance exams, and related reference books.

Open Court Publishing Company

Attn: Acquisitions Editor
70 East Lake Street, Suite 300
Chicago, IL 60601
Tel: +1 (800) 815-2280
Fax: +1 (312) 701-1728
Email: opencourt@caruspub.com
Website: http://www.opencourtbooks.com

Publishes: Nonfiction; *Areas:* Culture; Philosophy; *Markets:* Adult; *Treatments:* Popular

Accepts approaches for its Popular Culture and Philosophy series only. Send query by post only, with SASE, outline, and sample chapter. No approaches by fax or email. See website for full guidelines.

Open Idea Publishing, LLC

PO Box 1060
Owings Mills, MD 21117
Tel: +1 (410) 356-7014
Email: editors@openideapublishing.com
Website:
http://www.openideapublishing.com

Publishes: Fiction; Poetry; *Areas:* Adventure; Arts; Drama; Erotic; Fantasy; Leisure; Literature; Mystery; Romance; Short Stories; Theatre; *Markets:* Adult; Family; Youth; *Treatments:* Contemporary; Literary; Popular; Positive; Progressive; Satirical; Traditional

Contact: K Jones

Publishing company founded in 2012 whose mission is to get talented writers successfully published. There is no specialty at this time. Mainly interested in true life emotions and events.

P&R Publishing

PO Box 817
Phillipsburg, NJ 08865-0817
Tel: +1 (908) 454-0505
Fax: +1 (908) 859-2390
Email: editorial@prpbooks.com
Website: http://www.prpbooks.com

Publishes: Fiction; Nonfiction; *Areas:* Biography; Historical; Lifestyle; Religious; Women's Interests; *Markets:* Academic; Adult; Children's; Youth; *Treatments:* Popular

Publishes books that promote biblical understanding and godly living, ranging from books aimed at the popular market to academic works that advance biblical and theological scholarship. Submit 2-3 chapters as Word or .rtf files by email, along with completed submission form (available from website).

Pants On Fire Press

13750 West Colonial Dr., Suite 350
Winter Garden, FL 34787
Tel: +1 (863) 546-0760
Email: editor@pantsonfirepress.com
Website: http://www.pantsonfirepress.com

Publishes: Fiction; Nonfiction; *Areas:* Adventure; Crime; Culture; Drama; Entertainment; Fantasy; Health; Historical; Horror; Military; Nature; Romance; Sci-Fi; Sport; Suspense; Technology; Thrillers; Westerns; *Markets:* Children's; Youth; *Treatments:* Commercial; Mainstream; Popular; Traditional

Contact: Becca Goldman

A children's book publisher. We publish popular genre fiction and select nonfiction children's books, picture books and young adult books for children and discerning adults. We are carefully building the brand. Being deeply entrenched in Disney values, as it is our heritage, we strive to follow a high standard of excellence while maintaining high-quality standards. Titles we publish will tell timeless and engaging stories that delight and inspire. At this press, entertainment is about hope, aspiration and positive resolutions. We seek our audiences trust. Our fun is about laughing at our experiences and ourselves.

Manuscript Submissions

Attention picture book authors: Thank you for all the picture book submissions. We have enjoyed reading them. Please note that we have selected the picture books for our 2013 catalog, hence we are no longer accepting unsolicited picture book queries. We are still open to YA and Middle Grade submissions.

We are one of a few children's book publishers accepting unsolicited manuscripts. Please note that we are not interested in evaluating scripts simultaneously submitted to, or under consideration by, another publisher unless you are prepared to accept an offer from us within eight weeks. We are acquiring Children's Picture Books, Chapter Books, Middle-grade and Young Adult fiction. We are looking for strong writers who are excited about marketing their stories and building a following of readers. For novels, the body of the email should include your query and the first three chapters along with:

A synopsis
The genre of the book
Approximate word count
A short pitch
Writing credentials
Your contact info
If the work is agented, agent info
Complete bio
List of any and all previous titles with sales history

For illustrations, send three sample illustrations. Paste the query letter and chapters in the body of the e-mail and send by email. Text attachments will be deleted. Art may be attached.

Quick Guide

0-2,000 words for picture books
10,000-35,000 for middle-grade fiction
40,000-80,000 for young adult
always include a synopsis which includes the ending
allow 8-12 weeks for response

Picture Books
We're looking for author/illustrators who have the ability to use language and art to inspire the imagination, and:

0-2,000 words
a clear and fantastic theme
strong storytelling
beautiful artwork

Middle-grade Fiction
Our readers want to relate to the characters and the world they live in, so we're looking of authors who have:

10,000-35,000 words
an exciting plot
strong voices and edited scripts
developed characters
strong storytelling

Young Adult Fiction
We are looking for strong writers whose books have something fresh to offer the growing Young Adult audience.

40,000-80,000 words
A real voice for the readers
A new premise with a marketing hook that can be conveyed in 2-3 sentences
Protagonists who are 15-19
Powerful, believable world-building
An age-appropriate romantic element is a plus even if it's not the center of the story
Memorable characters readers care about and can relate to one way or another

Please allow 8-12 weeks for a response.

Note that we do not accept unsolicited novel-length manuscripts. So do not send them! And never send us your original work or art. And finally, we will contact you if we are interested.

We do not assume responsibility for any unsolicited manuscripts which we may receive. Further, in receiving a submission, we do not assume any duty not to publish a book based on a similar idea, concept or story. All submissions are recycled.

One more thing to note. We actively blog. In sending your submission you acknowledge that we may post any or all of your correspondence with us on our blog.

Peachtree Publishers
1700 Chattahoochee Avenue
Atlanta, GA 30318-2112
Tel: +1 (404) 876-8761
Fax: +1 (404) 875-2578
Email: hello@peachtree-online.com
Website: http://peachtree-online.com

Publishes: Fiction; Nonfiction; *Areas:* Autobiography; Biography; Health; Historical; Lifestyle; Nature; Science; Self-Help; Sport; *Markets:* Adult; Children's; Youth

Contact: Helen Harriss, Acquisitions Editor

Publishes children's fiction and nonfiction picture books, chapter books, middle readers, and young adult books, as well as education, parenting, self-help, and health books of interest to the general trade. All submissions must include complete ms or sample chapters, and must be made by post. No submissions by fax or email. See website for full guidelines.

PennWell Books
1421 South Sheridan
Tulsa, OK 74112
Tel: +1 (918) 831-9421
Fax: +1 (918) 831-9555
Email: BookProposals@pennwell.com
Website: http://www.pennwellbooks.com

Publishes: Nonfiction; *Areas:* How-to; Technology; *Markets:* Professional

Publishes practical books that would be of immediate use to practitioners in the following industries:

Petroleum

Energy
Electric Utility
Fire Service and Training
Controls and Instrumentation

Accepts proposals by email. See website for full guidelines.

Penny-Farthing Press

2000 West Sam Houston Parkway South, Suite 550
Houston, Texas 77042
Tel: +1 (713) 780-0300
Fax: +1 (713) 780-4004
Email: corp@pfpress.com
Website: http://www.pfpress.com

Publishes: Fiction; *Markets:* Adult; Children's

Award-winning publisher of comics and children's books. Send query with synopsis by post only. If submitting one single-issue story (standard 32 pp.), include full script. If submitting a story for a series or graphic novel send only first chapter. No submissions by fax or email. See website for full guidelines.

Perugia Press

PO Box 60364
Florence, MA 01062
Tel: +1 (413) 348-6635
Email: susan@perugiapress.com
Website: http://www.perugiapress.com

Publishes: Poetry; *Markets:* Adult

Contact: Susan Kan

Publishes one book of poetry by a female US resident each year. Accepts submissions through annual competition running August 1 - November 15 annually ($25 entry fee).

Peter Lang Publishing, Inc.

29 Broadway
New York, NY 10006
Tel: +1 (212) 647-7706
Fax: +1 (212) 647-7707
Email: CustomerService@plang.com
Website: http://www.peterlang.com

Publishes: Nonfiction; *Markets:* Academic

International academic publisher. Submit query via web form.

Pressgang

4600 Sunset Ave
Jordan Hall, Eng. Dept.
Indianapolis, IN 46208
Email: pressgang@butler.edu
Website: http://blogs.butler.edu/pressgang

Publishes: Fiction; Nonfiction; *Areas:* Autobiography; Drama; Horror; Humour; Literature; Mystery; Short Stories; Suspense; *Markets:* Academic; Adult; *Treatments:* Commercial; Contemporary; Literary; Popular; Satirical

Contact: Bryan Furuness

Who We Are

A small press affiliated with the MFA Program in Creative Writing at a University. Founded in 2012, our mission is to publish full-length books of fiction, creative nonfiction, graphic novels, and, in the future, poetry.

What We Like

Literary heft and helium. Seriousness of purpose, surprising execution, the well-wrought joke, the well-crafted sentence. The blurring of boundaries. Think Vonnegut meets Saunders meets Poe. Think Byron meets Bulgakov, Gogol, Nabokov. Think Kafka and Beckett. Think Lorrie Moore, think Laurie Anderson, think Lemony Snickett. Think Dorothy Parker mixed with Edward Gorey meets Steven Millhauser meets Dickens with a word limit.

PUBSLUSH Press

Website: http://www.pubslush.com

Publishes: Fiction; Nonfiction; Poetry; Reference; Scripts; *Markets:* Academic; Adult; Children's; Family; Professional; Youth

A new publishing model where writers can

upload the first ten pages of their novel for
other users to read, and (if they wish), pre-
order. If 2,000 pre-orders are received then
that book is automatically selected for
publication.

Pureplay Press

350 Judah Street, Suite 302
San Francisco, CA 94122
Email: info@pureplaypress.com
Website: http://www.pureplaypress.com

Publishes: Fiction; Nonfiction; Poetry;
Areas: Culture; Historical; Politics; *Markets:*
Adult

Publishes books with Cuban themes only, in
English and Spanish. No unsolicited MSS.
Send query of up to 250 words, similar to the
book blurb you would expect on the back of
a book.

Que Publishing

Pearson Education
800 East 96th Street
Indianapolis, IN 46240
Tel: +1 (317) 581-3500
Email: proposals@quepublishing.com
Website: http://www.quepublishing.com

Publishes: Nonfiction; *Areas:* Technology;
Markets: Adult

Publishes books on computers and
electronics. Submit proposal including CV,
writing sample, and market details.

Quite Specific Media Group

7373 Pyramid Place
Hollywood, CA 90046
Tel: +1 (323) 851-5797
Fax: +1 (323) 851-5798
Email: info@quitespecificmedia.com
Website: http://www.quitespecificmedia.com

Publishes: Nonfiction; Scripts; *Areas:*
Beauty and Fashion; Design; Drama;
Entertainment; Music; Theatre; *Markets:*
Adult; Professional

Publishes books in the design and
entertainment field.

Rattapallax Press

217 Thompson Street, Suite 353
New York, NY 10012
Email: info@rattapallax.com
Website: http://www.rattapallax.com

Publishes: Poetry; *Markets:* Adult;
Treatments: Contemporary

Publisher of contemporary poetry. Send
query with SASE and sample poems.

Razorbill

345 Hudson Street
New York, NY 10014
Website: http://www.razorbillbooks.com

Publishes: Fiction; Nonfiction; *Areas:*
Adventure; Culture; Fantasy; Humour;
Romance; Sci-Fi; Suspense; *Markets:*
Children's; Youth; *Treatments:*
Contemporary; Literary

Publishes mainly fiction for middle grade
and young adult. Send query with SASE,
outline, target group, publishing credits (if
any), and up to 30 pages. No picture books.
Response only if interested.

Red Moon Press

P.0. Box 2461
Winchester, VA 22604-1661
Tel: +1 (540) 722-2156
Email: jim.kacian@redmoonpress.com
Website: http://www.redmoonpress.com

Publishes: Fiction; Nonfiction; Poetry;
Areas: Biography; Criticism; Literature;
Translations; *Markets:* Adult

Publishes anthologies of haiku, Haibun, and
related forms, plus relevant works of fiction,
collections of essays, translations, criticism,
etc. Send query with outline and first
chapter, or 30-40 poems.

Red Rock Press

Suite 114
459 Columbus Avenue
New York, NY 10024
Tel: +1 (212) 362-8304
Fax: +1 (212) 362-6216

Email: info@redrockpress.com
Website: http://www.redrockpress.com

Publishes: Nonfiction; *Areas:* Humour; Self-Help; *Markets:* Adult; Children's

Contact: Ilene Barth

Independent publisher of books on a variety of subjects. All books are pegged to a gift-giving holiday. Prefers approaches through agents, but will consider proposals for appropriate books, if accompanied by SASE and marketing plan. No proposals by email.

Renaissance House
465 Westview Avenue
Englewood, NY 07631
Tel: +1 (201) 408-4048
Email: info@renaissancehouse.net
Website: http://renaissancehouse.net

Publishes: Fiction; Nonfiction; *Markets:* Adult; Children's

Creates books in English and in Spanish. Offers c-publishing. Send ideas by email.

Richard C. Owen Publishers, Inc.
PO Box 585
Katonah, NY 10536
Tel: +1 (914) 232-3903
Fax: +1 (914) 232-3977
Email: richardowen@rcowen.com
Website: http://www.rcowen.com

Publishes: Nonfiction; *Markets:* Academic; Children's; Professional

Publishes books on literacy education, including classroom materials for for grades PK-8, and books for teachers and administrators.

Riverhead Books
Penguin Putnam
375 Hudson Street, Office #4079
New York, NY 10014
Email:
riverhead.web@us.penguingroup.com
Website: http://www.riverheadbooks.com

Publishes: Fiction; Nonfiction; *Markets:* Adult; *Treatments:* Contemporary; Literary; Mainstream

Contact: Megan Lynch

Publisher of bestselling literary fiction and quality nonfiction. Approach via literary agent only.

Robert D. Reed Publishers
POB 1992
Bandon, OR 97411
Tel: +1 (541) 347-9882
Email: 4bobreed@msn.com
Website: http://www.rdrpublishers.com

Publishes: Fiction; Nonfiction; *Areas:* Business; Finance; Health; Humour; Psychology; Self-Help; Spiritual; *Markets:* Adult; Children's

Send query by post with SASE or by email, or via online submission form.

Rolenta Press
P O Box 1365
Springfield, NJ 07081-5365
Tel: +1 (973) 564-7252
Email: info@rolentapress.com
Website: http://www.rolentapress.com

Publishes: Nonfiction; *Areas:* Technology; *Markets:* Adult

Publishes books on video games and their history only. No strategy books or books on how to break into the business. Send query with SASE and proposal.

Rose Alley Press
4203 Brooklyn Avenue NE, #103A, Seattle, WA 98105-5911
Tel: +1 (206) 633-2725
Email: roselleypress@juno.com
Website: http://www.roselleypress.com

Publishes: Poetry; *Markets:* Adult

Contact: David D. Horowitz, Publisher

Publisher contacts authors whose work he

wants to publish. Does not accept or consider unsolicited mss.

Rowman & Littlefield Publishing Group

4501 Forbes Boulevard, Suite 200
Lanham, MD 20706
Tel: +1 (301) 459-3366
Fax: +1 (301) 429-5748
Email: jsisk@rowmanlittlefield.com
Website: https://rowman.com

Publishes: Nonfiction; *Areas:* Crime; Health; Historical; Legal; Nature; Philosophy; Politics; Psychology; Religious; Sociology; *Markets:* Academic; Adult; Professional

Publishes books on subjects throughout the humanities and social sciences, both for general readers and professional and scholarly titles. See website for submission guidelines.

Sun Books / Sun Publishing Company

P.O. BOX 5588
Santa Fe, New Mexico 87502-5588
Tel: +1 (505) 471-5177
Fax: +1 (505) 473-4458
Email: info@sunbooks.com
Website: http://www.sunbooks.com

Publishes: Nonfiction; *Areas:* Self-Help; *Markets:* Adult

Publishes inspirational, motivational, self-help, and leadership titles. Send queries by email only.

Saint Mary's Press

702 Terrace Heights
Winona, MN 55987
Tel: +1 (507) 457-7900
Fax: +1 (507) 457-7990
Email: submissions@smp.org
Website: http://www.smp.org

Publishes: Nonfiction; *Areas:* Religious; Spiritual; *Markets:* Children's; Youth

Contact: Submissions Editor

Publisher of Catholic religious resources for young people and those who minister to adolescents. See website for full submission guidelines.

Sam's Dot Publishing

P.O. Box 782
Cedar Rapids, Iowa 52406-0782
Email: samsdot@samsdotpublishing.com
Website: http://www.samsdotpublishing.com

Publishes: Fiction; Poetry; *Areas:* Horror; Sci-Fi; Short Stories; *Markets:* Adult

Contact: Tyree Campbell

Publishes magazines and anthologies of genre fiction and poetry. See website for full details and different submission guidelines.

Samhain Publishing

577 Mulberry Street, Suite 1520
Macon, GA 31201
Tel: +1 (478) 314-5144
Fax: +1 (478) 314-5148
Email: editor@samhainpublishing.com
Website: http://www.samhainpublishing.com

Publishes: Fiction; *Areas:* Erotic; Horror; Romance; *Markets:* Adult

Primarily an e-publisher, but also works in print. Submissions by email only. See website for submission guidelines and specific email addresses for submissions of different genres.

Santa Monica Press

P.O. Box 850
Solana Beach, CA 92075
Tel: +1 (858) 793-1890
Fax: +1 (858) 777-0444
Email: books@santamonicapress.com
Website: http://www.santamonicapress.com

Publishes: Nonfiction; Reference; *Areas:* Architecture; Arts; Biography; Culture; Entertainment; Film; Historical; Humour; Literature; Photography; Sport; Travel; *Markets:* Adult

Send query with SASE, outline, 2–3 sample

chapters, author bio, marketing and publicity plans, and analysis of competing titles.

Search Institute Press

615 First Avenue NE
Minneapolis, MN 55413
Tel: +1 (612) 399-0200
Fax: +1 (612) 692-5553
Email: acquisitions@search-institute.org
Website: http://www.search-institute.org

Publishes: Nonfiction; Reference; *Areas:*
How-to; Lifestyle; Self-Help; Sociology;
Markets: Adult; Professional

Publishes books aimed at educators, youth program leaders, mentors, and parents. Send query with SASE.

Self-Counsel Press

1704 North State Street
Bellingham, WA 92225
Tel: +1 (360) 676-4530
Website: http://www.self-counsel.com

Publishes: Nonfiction; *Areas:* Business;
Finance; Legal; Self-Help; *Markets:* Adult

Publishes self-help books for lay-people. Send query with outline, CV, and two sample chapters.

Sheed & Ward

4501 Forbes Blvd., Suite 200
Lanham, MD 20706
Tel: +1 (301) 459-3366, ext. 5634
Fax: +1 (301) 429-5747
Email: sstanton@rowman.com
Website: http://www.sheedandward.com

Publishes: Nonfiction; *Areas:* Biography;
Historical; Religious; Spiritual; *Markets:*
Adult

Contact: Sarah Stanton, Acquisitions Editor

Publisher of Catholic / Christian books. Send query with CV, prospectus, detailed table of contents, one or two sample chapters, and list of 4–7 potential peer reviewers. See website for full guidelines.

Shelfstealers

220 N. Zapata Hwy, #11
Laredo, TX 78043
Tel: +1 (210) 399-9013
Email: shelfstealers@shelfstealers.com
Website: http://www.shelfstealers.com

Publishes: Fiction; Nonfiction; *Areas:*
Adventure; Anthropology; Architecture;
Arts; Autobiography; Beauty and Fashion;
Biography; Business; Cookery; Crime;
Criticism; Culture; Current Affairs; Fantasy;
Finance; Health; Historical; Hobbies;
Horror; How-to; Humour; Legal; Leisure;
Lifestyle; Literature; Men's Interests;
Military; Mystery; Nature; Philosophy;
Politics; Psychology; Romance; Science;
Sci-Fi; Self-Help; Short Stories; Sociology;
Spiritual; Suspense; Technology; Thrillers;
Travel; Westerns; Women's Interests;
Markets: Adult; Children's; Family;
Professional; Youth

Contact: Sheryl J. Dunn

A royalty publisher, not a self-publisher. We edit, produce the covers and do all the layout work, market our books and help our authors to market them, and we care about quality writing beyond any other factor.

Best to submit using the online form.

We don't pay advances, but we offer a 50/50 split on ebooks, POD books, and audio books.

Our existing authors would be pleased to be contacted about us.

Silman-James Press

3624 Shannon Road
Los Angeles, CA 90027
Tel: +1 (323) 661-9922
Fax: +1 (323) 661-9933
Email: info@silmanjamespress.com
Website: http://www.silmanjamespress.com

Publishes: Nonfiction; *Areas:* Arts; Film;
Hobbies; Media; *Markets:* Adult

Publishes books on films, film-making, performing arts, the movie industry, and chess. Send proposal package with outline and sample chapter, or query by phone.

SLACK Incorporated

ATTN: Acquisitions Department
Health Care Books and Journals
SLACK Incorporated
6900 Grove Road
Thorofare, NJ 08086
Tel: +1 (856) 848-1000
Fax: +1 (856) 848-6091
Email: bookspublishing@slackinc.com
Website: http://www.slackbooks.com

Publishes: Nonfiction; Reference; *Areas:* Health; Medicine; *Markets:* Academic; Professional

Publisher of professional and academic books and journals on healthcare. See website for full submission guidelines.

Speak Up Press

PO Box 100506
Denver, CO 80250
Tel: +1 (303) 715-0837
Fax: +1 (303) 715-0793
Email: submit@speakuppress.org
Website: http://speakuppress.org

Publishes: Nonfiction; *Markets:* Youth

Publishes young adult nonfiction only. Send query by email only, in the body of the email (no attachments). If additional material is included then your query will be ignored. See website for full submission guidelines.

Spire Press, Inc.

217 Thompson St. #298,
New York, NY 10012
Email: info@spirepress.org
Website: http://www.spirepress.org

Publishes: Fiction; Nonfiction; Poetry; *Markets:* Adult; *Treatments:* Literary

During August only accepts up to 20 sample pages of poetry, literary fiction, or creative nonfiction for consideration for chapbook publication. See website for full guidelines.

Spout Press

PO Box 581067
Minneapolis, MN 55458-1067
Email: editors@spoutpress.org
Website: http://www.spoutpress.org

Publishes: Fiction; Poetry; *Areas:* Short Stories; *Markets:* Adult; *Treatments:* Contemporary; Experimental; Literary

Originally a magazine publisher, has in addition been publishing paperbacks with print runs of about 1,000 since 1997. Send query with SASE, estimated word count, brief bio, and list of publishing credits. Aims to publish and promote the finest in contemporary experimental writing.

Square One Publishers, Inc.

ATT: Acquisitions Editor
Square One Publishers, Inc.
115 Herricks Road
Garden City Park, NY 11040
Tel: +1 (516) 535-2010
Fax: +1 (516) 535-2014
Email: sq1publish@aol.com
Website:
http://www.squareonepublishers.com

Publishes: Nonfiction; *Areas:* Cookery; Finance; Health; How-to; Lifestyle; Self-Help; *Markets:* Adult

Send query with outline, table of contents, biographical information and SASE. See website for full guidelines.

Starcherone Books

P.O. Box 303
Buffalo, NY 14201-0303
Tel: +1 (716) 885-2726
Email: starcherone@gmail.com
Website: http://www.starcherone.com

Publishes: Fiction; *Markets:* Adult; *Treatments:* Experimental; Literary

Small press accepting queries for experimental and literary fiction only during late summer / early fall (autumn). See website for details.

Stenhouse Publishers

480 Congress Street
Portland, ME 04101-3400
Tel: +1 (800) 988-9812
Fax: +1 (800) 833-9164
Email: customerservice@stenhouse.com
Website: http://www.stenhouse.com

Publishes: Nonfiction; *Markets:* Professional

Publishes books for teachers on education, particularly literacy. No books for students. Send query with SASE.

Trafalgar Square Books

Box 257, Howe Hill Road
N. Pomfret, VT 05053
Tel: +1 (802) 457-1911
Fax: +1 (802) 457-1913
Email: rdidier@sover.net
Website:
http://www.horseandriderbooks.com

Publishes: Nonfiction; Reference; *Areas:* How-to; *Markets:* Adult

Contact: Rebecca Didier

Publishes instructional books for horse riders. Send query by post or by email outlining your experience and qualifications for writing the book, audience info, three sample chapters, details of illustrations, promotional plan, and whether submitted elsewhere simultaneously. See website for full guidelines.

Texas Western Press

500 W. University Avenue
El Paso, TX 79968-0582
Tel: +1 (915) 747-5688
Website: http://twp.utep.edu

Publishes: Nonfiction; *Areas:* Arts; Criticism; Historical; Literature; Photography; Sociology; *Markets:* Adult

Publishes nonfiction related to the El Paso Borderlands and the immediate surrounding area in Texas, New Mexico, and Mexico. Send query qith sample chapters in first instance. See website for full guidelines.

Tilbury House, Publishers

103 Brunswick Avenue
Gardiner, Maine 04345
Tel: +1 (800) 582-1899
Email: tilbury@tilburyhouse.com
Website: http://www.tilburyhouse.com

Publishes: Fiction; Nonfiction; *Areas:* Culture; Historical; Nature; *Markets:* Adult

Publishes children's fiction and nonfiction; mainly aimed at ages 7–12 and on the subjects of cultural diversity, nature, or the environment. Also adult nonfiction about Maine or the Northeast, particularly books that are documentary or about Maine's history. Send query by post with SASE or by email with "Book Query" in the subject line (no attachments). Alternatively send partial and outline, or full ms in the case of children's books. See website for full guidelines. No fiction, short stories, memoirs, or poetry.

Timberline Press Books

5710 South Kimbark #3
Chicago, IL 60637-1615
Email: steven_schroeder@earthlink.net
Website: http://vacpoetry.org/timberline-press-books/

Publishes: Fiction; Poetry; *Markets:* Adult

Contact: Steven Schroeder

Publishes poetry chapbooks, usually 20–30 pages, hand bound, limited editions of 50–100. Will also consider fiction if deemed suitable. Submit using online submission system available via website.

Tor/Forge

Tom Doherty Associates, LLC
175 Fifth Avenue
New York, NY 10010
Website:
http://us.macmillan.com/TorForge.aspx

Publishes: Fiction; Nonfiction; *Areas:* Fantasy; Historical; Horror; Mystery; Sci-Fi; Suspense; Women's Interests; *Markets:* Adult

Particular emphasis on science fiction, fantasy, and horror. Open submissions policy. Send query with synopsis, first three chapters, and SASE for response. See website for full submission guidelines.

Torrey House Press, LLC

P.O. Box 750196
Torrey, UT 84775
Email: mail@torreyhouse.com
Website: http://torreyhouse.com

Publishes: Fiction; Nonfiction; Poetry; *Areas:* Culture; Historical; Nature; *Markets:* Adult; *Treatments:* Literary

Contact: Mark Bailey; Kirsten Johanna Allen

Publishes fiction, creative nonfiction, and poetry relating to the landscape of the Colorado Plateau and the American West; its people, nature, and history. Prefers email submissions but also accepts postal approaches. See website for full guidelines.

The Trinity Foundation

PO Box 68
Unicoi, TN 37692
Tel: +1 (423) 743-0199
Fax: +1 (423) 743-2005
Email: jrob1517@aol.com
Website: http://www.trinityfoundation.org

Publishes: Nonfiction; *Areas:* Business; Finance; Historical; Philosophy; Politics; Religious; Science; *Markets:* Adult

Publishes books on a number of subjects, but all must be compatible with the theology of the publisher. Send query with SASE in the first instance.

Unbridled Books

29834 N. Cave Creek Rd., Ste. 118-139
Cave Creek, AZ 85331

FOR SUBMISSIONS:
Greg Michalson
Co-Publisher
200 N. 9th Street, Ste A
Columbia, MO 65201

-OR-

Fred Ramey
Co-Publisher
2000 Wadsworth Blvd., #195
Lakewood, CO 80214
Email: contact@unbridledbooks.com
Website: http://unbridledbooks.com

Publishes: Fiction; Nonfiction; *Areas:* Autobiography; Historical; *Markets:* Adult; *Treatments:* Literary

Contact: Greg Michalson; Fred Ramey

Publishes literary fiction, nonfiction, and creative nonfiction. Send query by email in the first instance to one (but not both) of the co-publishers. See website for specific email addresses and full guidelines.

Union Square Publishing

Sterling Publishing Co., Inc.
387 Park Avenue South, 11th floor
New York, NY 10016-8810
Email: editorial@sterlingpublishing.com

Publishes: Nonfiction; *Areas:* Adventure; Biography; Culture; Current Affairs; Nature; Politics; Sociology; *Markets:* Adult

Send query with outline, sample chapter, and details about yourself including publishing history and your qualifications for writing the book. No email submissions. See website for full guidelines.

University of North Carolina Press

116 South Boundary Street
Chapel Hill, NC 27514-3808
Tel: +1 (919) 966-3829
Email: uncpress@unc.edu
Website: http://www.uncpress.unc.edu

Publishes: Nonfiction; *Areas:* Business; Cookery; Crafts; Finance; Historical; Legal; Military; Nature; Religious; Sociology; *Markets:* Academic; Adult

Published for academic and general audiences. Consult website for appropriate acquisitions editor then send query with description, table of contents, and author CV. No unsolicited mss. No original fiction, poetry, drama, memoir, or festschriften.

The University Press of Kentucky

663 South Limestone Street
Lexington, KY 40508-4008
Tel: +1 (859) 257-8434
Fax: +1 (859) 257-1873
Email: adwatk0@email.uky.edu
Website: http://www.kentuckypress.com

Publishes: Nonfiction; *Areas:* Culture; Film; Historical; Military; Philosophy; Politics; *Markets:* Academic; Professional

Contact: STEPHEN M. WRINN; ANNE DEAN WATKINS; ASHLEY RUNYON

Academic and professional publisher. No fiction, drama, poetry, translations, children's books, or memoirs. Send query in first instance. See website for full details and appropriate editor to contact.

Upstart Books

P.O. Box 7820
Madison, WI 53707-7820
Tel: +1 (800) 448-4887
Fax: +1 (800) 448-5828
Email: m.mulder@highsmith.com
Website:
http://www.highsmith.com/upstartbooks

Publishes: Fiction; Nonfiction; *Areas:* Literature; Short Stories; *Markets:* Children's; Professional

Contact: Matt Mulder, Publications Manager

Publishes fiction and nonfiction to support teachers and librarians in promoting reading and library skills amongst children. For manuscripts under 100 pages, submit complete MS. For longer manuscripts send proposal. See website for full guidelines.

The Urban Land Institute (ULI)

1025 Thomas Jefferson Street, N.W., Suite 500 West
Washington, DC 20007

Tel: +1 (202) 624-7000
Fax: +1 (202) 624-7140
Email: customerservice@uli.org
Website: http://www.uli.org

Publishes: Nonfiction; *Areas:* Business; Finance; *Markets:* Professional

Publishes books on land development and real estate planning. Send query with SASE in first instance.

Velazquez Press

9682 Telstar Ave Suite 110
El Monte, CA 91731
Tel: +1 (626) 448-3448
Fax: +1 (626) 602-3817
Email: info@academiclearningcompany.com
Website: http://velazquezpress.com

Publishes: Nonfiction; Reference; *Markets:* Academic; Adult

Bilingual publisher. Publishes Spanish and English dictionaries and interested in bilingual educational materials. Send query letter with proposal and two sample chapters, or submit complete mis.

Vitesse Press

PMB 367
45 State Street
Montpelier, VT 05601-2100
Tel: +1 (802) 229-4243
Fax: +1 (802) 229-6939
Email: dick@vitessepress.com
Website: http://vitessepress.com

Publishes: Nonfiction; *Areas:* Health; Leisure; Medicine; Sport; *Markets:* Adult

Contact: Richard H. Mansfield

Publishes books on fitness, cycling, etc. Send query by email with enough information to judge whether further consideration is worthwhile. See website for full details.

Woodbine House

6510 Bells Mill Road
Bethesda, MD 20817
Tel: +1 (800) 843-7323

Email: info@woodbinehouse.com
Website: http://www.woodbinehouse.com

Publishes: Fiction; Nonfiction; *Areas:*
Health; How-to; Psychology; *Markets:*
Adult; Children's; Professional; Youth

Contact: Nancy Gray Paul

Publishes books for and about children with
disabilities. No adult fiction, poetry, or books
expressing a religious viewpoint. See
website for full submission guidelines.

Washington Writers' Publishing House
PO Box 15271
Washington, DC 20003
Email: wwphpress@gmail.com
Website: http://www.washingtonwriters.org

Publishes: Fiction; Poetry; *Markets:* Adult

Contact: Patric Pepper

Publishes poetry and fiction. Accepts
submissions from Washington and Baltimore
areas via annual competitions only, for
which an entry fee is charged. See website
for more details.

Wellness Institute/Self-Help Books, LLC
97444 Diamondhead Drive West
Diamondhead, MS 39525
Email: Publisher@SelfHelpBooks.com
Website: http://www.selfhelpbooks.com

Publishes: Nonfiction; *Areas:* Health;
Medicine; Psychology; Self-Help;
Sociology; *Markets:* Adult

Publishes self-help books. Send proposal
with outline.

Westholme Publishing
904 Edgewood Road
Yardley, PA 19067
Tel: 1-800-621-2736
Fax: 215-321-6104
Email: editorial@westholmepublishing.com
Website:

http://www.westholmepublishing.com/
contact.html

Publishes: Nonfiction; *Areas:* Archaeology;
Biography; Historical; Military; Science;
Sport; Westerns; *Markets:* Academic; Adult;
Family; Professional; *Treatments:* In-depth;
Mainstream; Niche

Contact: Bruce H. Franklin

Book proposals in American history, military
history, ancient studies, biography, European
and world history, sports, natural history, and
science are welcome. Please email a brief
description of the project or submit a
proposal in writing to the address above.
Posted material will not be returned unless
requested and accompanied by a SASE.

White Eagle Coffee Store Press
PO Box 383
Fox River Grove, IL 60021
Email: WECSPress@aol.com
Website:
http://whiteeaglecoffeestorepress.com

Publishes: Poetry; *Markets:* Adult

Publishes poetry chapbooks submitted
through solicitation or via poetry chapbook
competition ($15 entry fee). See website for
more details.

White Mane Kids
Attn: Acquisitions Department
White Mane Publishing Co., Inc.
73 W. Burd St.
P.O. Box 708
Shippensburg, PA 17257
Email: marketing@whitemane.com
Website: http://www.whitemane.com

Publishes: Fiction; *Areas:* Historical;
Markets: Children's; Youth

Publishes historical fiction for middle grade
and young adults. Books should contain
accurate historical information while at the
same time captivating readers. See website
for submission guidelines.

White Mane Publishing Co., Inc.
73 W. Burd St.
P.O. Box 708
Shippensburg, PA 17257
Tel: +1 (717) 532-2237
Fax: +1 (717) 532-6110
Email: marketing@whitemane.com
Website: http://www.whitemane.com

Publishes: Nonfiction; *Areas:* Historical;
Military; *Markets:* Adult

Contact: Attn: Acquisitions Department

Download proposal form from website and
submit along with required materials by post.

The Wild Rose Press
PO Box 708
Adam's Basin NY 14410
Email: queryus@thewildrosepress.com
Website: http://www.thewildrosepress.com

Publishes: Fiction; *Areas:* Romance;
Markets: Adult

Publishes romance only. Send query by
email with synopsis in the body of the email.
No attachments. See website for full
submission guidelines.

WindRiver Publishing
72 N WindRiver Rd
Silverton ID 83867-0446
Tel: +1 (208) 752-1836
Fax: +1 (208) 752-1876
Email: Info@WindRiverPublishing.com
Website:
http://www.windriverpublishing.com

Publishes: Fiction; Nonfiction; *Areas:*
Autobiography; Historical; How-to;
Lifestyle; Mystery; Politics; Religious;
Romance; Sci-Fi; Self-Help; Suspense;
Thrillers; *Markets:* Adult; Children's; Youth

**Note: Only publishing works by their
current authors as at July 1, 2012. See
website for current status.**

Accepts submissions in the specified genres
only – any other submissions will be rejected

automatically. Submit via online submission
system, or by hard copy in the post, but not
by email. See website for full details.

Windswept House Publishers
Mt. Desert
ME 04660-0159
Tel: +1 (207) 244-5027
Fax: +1 (207) 244-3369
Email: windswt@acadia.net
Website: http://www.musarts.net/windswept

Publishes: Fiction; Nonfiction; *Markets:*
Adult; Children's; Youth

Small independent publisher based in Mount
Desert, Maine.

Windward Publishing
8075 215th Street West
Lakeville, Minn. 55044
Tel: +1 (952) 469-6699
Fax: +1 (952) 469-1968
Email: info@finneyco.com
Website: http://www.finney-hobar.com

Publishes: Fiction; Nonfiction; *Areas:*
Leisure; Nature; Science; *Markets:* Adult;
Children's

Publishes natural history and science,
outdoor recreation, and children's literature.
Generally publishes nonfiction only, but will
consider fiction if of educational value. See
website for full submission guidelines.

Wizards of the Coast
c/o Book Publishing
P.O. Box 707
Renton, WA 98057-0707
Website: http://www.wizards.com

Publishes: Fiction; *Areas:* Fantasy; Sci-Fi;
Markets: Adult; Children's; Youth

Publishes shared world fantasy and science
fiction novels for adults, young adults, and
children. Not accepting stand-alone novels,
but will consider queries from writers who
wish to be considered to write on one of the
existing series. Send query with 30-page
(10,000 word) writing sample, along with

legal agreement (available on website). See website for full details.

The Zharmae Publishing Press

1827 W Shannon Ave
Spokane, WA 99205
Email: questions@zharmae.com
Website: http://www.zharmae.com

Publishes: Fiction; *Areas:* Adventure; Erotic; Fantasy; Horror; Humour; Mystery; Romance; Sci-Fi; Suspense; Thrillers; *Markets:* Adult; Youth; *Treatments:* Commercial; Contemporary; Cynical; Dark; Experimental; In-depth; Light; Literary; Mainstream; Niche; Popular; Positive; Progressive; Satirical; Serious; Traditional

Contact: Travis Grundy

Focuses on category fiction with a heavy emphasis on artistry through prose, while staying true to the formulaic, sensationalistic, melodramatic, and sentimental nature normally exhibited in such types of fiction. We are committed to producing work featuring elevated, poetic, and idiosyncratic prose that defy reader expectations, or which go beyond the normal plot scope associated with genre fiction. While Zharmae accepts all types of fiction, our emphasis is heavily weighted towards Science Fiction and Fantasy.

Due to our belief in the environment and sustainability, we actively seek ways to reduce the waste of paper and other pollutants. As such, we require all subbmissions to be sent electronically, please visit our website for more information about submissions.

We are a new book publisher based in the Pacific Northwest, as such, we are currently seeking new writers to join our team.

UK Publishers

For the most up-to-date listings of these and hundreds of other publishers, visit http://www.firstwriter.com/publishers

*To claim your **free** access to the site, please see the back of this book.*

AA Publishing

The Automobile Association
Fanum House
Basingstoke
RG21 4EA
Tel: +44 (0) 1256 491524
Fax: +44 (0) 1614 887544
Email: AAPublish@TheAA.com
Website: http://www.theAA.com

Publishes: Nonfiction; Reference; *Areas:* Leisure; Travel; *Markets:* Adult

Contact: David Watchus

Publishes motoring and travel books including maps, guidebooks and atlases etc.

Absolute Press

Scarborough House
29 James Street West
Bath
BA1 2BT
Tel: +44 (0) 1225 316013
Fax: +44 (0) 1225 445836
Email: info@absolutepress.co.uk
Website: http://www.absolutepress.co.uk

Publishes: Nonfiction; *Areas:* Cookery; *Markets:* Adult

Contact: Jon Croft (Managing Director); Meg Avent (Commissioning Editor)

Publishes book relating to food and wine. No unsolicited MSS, but accepts synopses and ideas.

Alastair Sawday Publishing Co. Ltd

The Old Farmyard
Yanley Lane
Long Ashton
Bristol
BS41 9LR
Tel: +44 (0) 1275 395430
Email: specialplaces@sawdays.co.uk
Website: http://www.sawdays.co.uk

Publishes: Nonfiction; *Areas:* Nature; Travel; *Markets:* Adult

Publishes guidebooks and books on environmental topics.

Ian Allan Publishing Ltd

Riverdene Business Park
Molesey Road
Hersham
KT12 4RG
Tel: +44 (0) 1932 266600
Fax: +44 (0) 1932 266601
Email: info@ianallanpublishing.co.uk
Website: http://www.ianallanpublishing.com

Publishes: Nonfiction; Reference; *Areas:* Historical; Hobbies; Military; Travel; *Markets:* Adult

Publishes nonfiction and reference books relating to transport, including aviation, military, road, rail, maps, and atalases. Also modelling, including railway modelling. Send query with SAE, synopsis, and sample chapter.

J.A. Allen

Clerkenwell House
45–47 Clerkenwell Green
London
EC1R 0HT
Tel: +44 (0) 20 7251 2661
Fax: +44 (0) 20 7490 4958
Email: allen@halebooks.com
Website: http://www.halebooks.com

Publishes: Nonfiction; *Areas:* How-to; *Markets:* Adult

Contact: Lesley Gowers

Publishes books on horses and horsemanship. Send proposal with SASE, outline, aim, background and market, detailed synopsis, and three sample chapters.

Allison & Busby Ltd

13 Charlotte Mews
London
W1T 4EJ
Tel: +44 (0) 20 7580 1080
Fax: +44 (0) 20 7580 1180
Email: susie@allisonandbusby.com
Website: http://www.allisonandbusby.com

Publishes: Fiction; Nonfiction; *Areas:* Autobiography; Biography; Crime; Culture; Fantasy; Historical; Military; Mystery; Sci-Fi; Self-Help; Short Stories; Thrillers; Travel; Women's Interests; *Markets:* Adult; Youth; *Treatments:* Contemporary; Literary

Contact: Susie Dunlop, Publishing Director

Accepts approaches via a literary agent only. No unsolicited MSS or queries from authors. In field of nonfiction publishes guides for writers. No horror, romance, spirituality, short stories, self-help, poetry or plays.

Alma Books Ltd

London House
243-253 Lower Mortlake Road
Richmond
Surrey
TW9 2LL
Tel: +44 (0) 20 8948 9550
Fax: +44 (0) 20 8948 5599
Email: info@almabooks.com
Website: http://www.almabooks.co.uk

Publishes: Fiction; Nonfiction; *Areas:* Historical; Literature; *Markets:* Adult; *Treatments:* Contemporary; Literary

Publishes literary fiction and a small number of nonfiction titles with a strong literary or historical connotation. No children's books, poetry, academic works, science fiction, horror, or fantasy. Accepts unsolicited MSS by post with synopsis, two sample chapters, and SAE if return of material required. No submissions by email.

Amberley Publishing

The Hill
Stroud
Gloucestershire
GL5 4EP
Tel: +44 (0) 1453 847800
Fax: +44 (0) 1453 847820
Email: submissions@amberley-books.com
Website: http://www.amberleybooks.com

Publishes: Nonfiction; *Areas:* Archaeology; Biography; Crime; Historical; Military; Sociology; Sport; Travel; *Markets:* Adult

Publishes local interest and niche history. Send query by email or by post, with one-page proposal describing the book; reason for writing the book; proposed word count; proposed number of images; and any other relevant information.

Ammonite Press

166 High Street
Lewes
East Sussex
BN7 1XU
Tel: +44 (0) 1273 488006
Fax: +44 (0) 1273 472418
Email: richard.wiles@ammonitepress.com

Website: http://www.ammonitepress.com

Publishes: Nonfiction; *Areas:* Historical; Photography; Sociology; *Markets:* Adult

Contact: Richard Wiles (Managing Editor)

Publishes books on photography, social history, and also gift books.

Anarchy Books
PO BOX 40
SPILSBY
PE23 9AR
Email: anarchy-books@hotmail.co.uk
Website: http://anarchy-books.com

Publishes: Fiction; *Markets:* Adult

Online submissions only (no postal approaches). Send one attached document (preferably .doc, .pdf or .rtf) including shot bio, blurb, and complete ms. No short stories or nonfiction. See website for full details.

Andrews UK Limited
The Hat Factory
65-67 Bute Street
Luton
Bedfordshire
LU1 2EY
Email: Info@andrewsuk.com
Website: http://www.andrewsuk.com

Publishes: Fiction; Nonfiction; Poetry; Reference; *Areas:* Adventure; Anthropology; Antiques; Archaeology; Architecture; Arts; Autobiography; Beauty and Fashion; Biography; Business; Cookery; Crafts; Crime; Criticism; Culture; Current Affairs; Design; Drama; Entertainment; Erotic; Fantasy; Film; Finance; Gardening; Gothic; Health; Historical; Hobbies; Horror; How-to; Humour; Legal; Leisure; Lifestyle; Literature; Media; Medicine; Men's Interests; Military; Music; Mystery; Nature; New Age; Philosophy; Photography; Politics; Psychology; Radio; Religious; Romance; Science; Sci-Fi; Self-Help; Short Stories; Sociology; Spiritual; Sport; Suspense; Technology; Theatre; Thrillers; Translations; Travel; TV; Westerns; Women's Interests; *Markets:* Academic;

Adult; Children's; Family; Professional; Youth; *Treatments:* Commercial; Contemporary; Experimental; Mainstream; Niche; Popular

Contact: Paul Andrews - ceo

This is the new breed of publisher, but from an established company, with both digital and print books, we are becoming a world leader in publishing. We welcome contact from authors and agents.

Anova Books
The Old Magistrates Court
10 Southcombe Street
London
W14 0RA
Tel: +44 (0) 20 7314 1400
Fax: +44 (0) 20 7605 1401
Email: customerservices@anovabooks.com
Website: http://www.anovabooks.com

Publishes: Fiction; Nonfiction; Reference; *Areas:* Architecture; Arts; Beauty and Fashion; Biography; Cookery; Crafts; Entertainment; Film; Gardening; Historical; Hobbies; Humour; Leisure; Lifestyle; Military; Music; Photography; Sport; Technology; Travel; *Markets:* Adult; Children's

Specialises in books of illustrated nonfiction. Happy to receive unsolicited submissions, but cannot acknowledge receipt. Send query including your name, address and other contact details, with SAE, proposed outline, chapter outline and sample chapter if available. Address material to specific imprint.

Arabia Books
70 Cadogan Place
London
SW1X 9AH
Tel: +44 (0) 20 7838 9055
Email: harry@hauspublishing.com
Website: http://www.arabiabooks.co.uk

Publishes: Fiction; *Areas:* Translations; *Markets:* Adult; *Treatments:* Contemporary

Contact: Harry Hall

Publisher of English translations of contemporary Arabic fiction.

Arcturus Publishing Ltd

26/27 Bickels Yard
151-153 Bermondsey Street
London
SE1 3HA
Tel: +44 (0) 20 7407 9400
Fax: +44 (0) 20 7407 9444
Email: info@arcturuspublishing.com
Website: http://www.arcturuspublishing.com

Publishes: Fiction; Nonfiction; Reference; *Areas:* Autobiography; Crime; Erotic; Health; Historical; Hobbies; Horror; Humour; Leisure; Military; New Age; Philosophy; Religious; Science; Sport; *Markets:* Adult; Children's

Send query with SAE, outline, and sample chapter, or submit complete MS. In nonfiction, particularly interested in history and military. No adult fiction, modern children's fiction, or erotica.

The Armchair Traveller at the bookHaus

Editorial Submissions
Haus Publishing Ltd
70 Cadogan Place
London
SW1X 9AH
Tel: +44 (0) 20 7838 9055
Email: info@hauspublishing.com
Website:
http://www.thearmchairtraveller.com

Publishes: Nonfiction; *Areas:* Travel; *Markets:* Adult

Publishes travel writing. Send query with book proposal, sample three chapters if book has already been written, and SAE if return of manuscript is required. No submissions by email.

Arris Publishing Ltd

12 Main Street
Adlestrop
Moreton in Marsh
Gloucestershire

GL56 OYN
Tel: +44 (0) 1608 658758
Fax: +44 (0) 1608 659345
Email: victoriama.huxley@btinternet.com
Website: http://arrisbooks.com

Publishes: Fiction; Nonfiction; *Areas:* Historical; Politics; Translations; Travel; *Markets:* Adult

Contact: The Commissioning Editor

Publishes nonfiction books on travel, history, and politics; and translations of fiction, generally from non-European languages. No poetry, original fiction in English, or unsolicited MSS. Email or telephone in the first instance.

Ashmolean Museum Publications

Ashmolean Museum
Beaumont Street
Oxford
OX1 2PH
Tel: +44 (0) 1865 278010
Fax: +44 (0) 1865 278018
Email: publications@ashmus.ox.ac.uk
Website: http://www.ashmolean.org

Publishes: Nonfiction; *Areas:* Archaeology; Arts; Historical; *Markets:* Adult; Children's

Contact: Declan McCarthy

Publications mainly based on in-house collections. Publishes both adult and Children's on the subjects of European archeology and ancient history, European and Oriental arts, Egyptology and numismatics. No fiction, African / American / modern art, post-medieval history, ethnography, or unsolicited MSS.

AudioGO Ltd

St James House
The Square
Lower Bristol Road
Bath
BA2 3BH
Tel: +44 (0) 1225 443400
Fax: +44 (0) 1225 448005
Email: info@audiogo.co.uk

Publishes: Fiction; *Markets:* Adult; Children's; Family; Youth

Publishes audio books and large print versions of existing titles. No original books.

Aurora Metro Press

67 Grove Avenue
Twickenham
TW1 4HX
Tel: +44 (0) 20 3261 0000
Fax: +44 (0) 20 8898 0735
Email: info@aurorametro.com
Website: http://www.aurorametro.com

Publishes: Fiction; Nonfiction; Scripts; *Areas:* Biography; Cookery; Drama; Translations; Women's Interests; *Markets:* Adult; Children's

Contact: Neil Gregory (Submissions Manager)

Publisher set up to promote new writing by women. Specialises in anthologising new drama, fiction, and work in translation. Send synopsis and three chapters of the finished book by post. No unsolicited MSS or submissions by email. For play submissions, if a production is scheduled then the full script must be sent at least 6 weeks before opening night.

Aurum Press Ltd

74-77 White Lion Street
London
N1 9PF
Tel: +44 (0) 20 7284 9300
Fax: +44 (0) 20 7485 0490
Email: sales@aurumpress.co.uk
Website: http://www.aurumpress.co.uk

Publishes: Nonfiction; *Areas:* Arts; Biography; Crafts; Current Affairs; Film; Historical; Lifestyle; Military; Music; Photography; Sport; Travel; *Markets:* Adult

Publishes adult nonfiction in the above areas, both illustrated and not.

Award Publications Limited

The Old Riding School

The Welbeck Estate
Worksop
Nottinghamshire
S80 3LR
Tel: +44 (0) 1909 478170
Fax: +44 (0) 1909 484632
Email: info@awardpublications.co.uk
Website:
http://www.awardpublications.co.uk

Publishes: Fiction; Nonfiction; Reference; *Markets:* Children's

Publishes children's fiction, nonfiction, and reference. Not currently accepting unsolicited mss, but always on the lookout for illustrators and designers. Send samples by email.

Barefoot Books Ltd

294 Banbury Road
Oxford
OX2 7ED
Tel: +44 (0) 1865 311100
Fax: +44 (0) 1865 514965
Email: info@barefootbooks.co.uk
Website: http://www.barefootbooks.com

Publishes: Fiction; *Markets:* Children's

Publishing program currently full as at September 29, 2011. Check website for current status.

Publishes high-quality picture-books for children. Particularly interested in both new and traditional stories from a variety of cultures. Submit material via submission form on website.

Belvedere Publishing

Mirador
Wearne Lane
Langport
Somerset
TA10 9HB
Tel: 44 (0) 845 519 7471
Email: sarah@belvederepublishing.com
Website:
http://www.belvederepublishing.com

Publishes: Fiction; *Areas:* Adventure; Crime; Drama; Erotic; Fantasy; Gothic;

Horror; Humour; Legal; Men's Interests;
Military; Mystery; New Age; Romance;
Science; Sci-Fi; Suspense; Thrillers;
Westerns; Women's Interests; *Markets:*
Adult; Family; Youth; *Treatments:*
Contemporary; Dark; Light; Literary;
Mainstream; Niche; Positive; Progressive;
Satirical; Serious; Traditional

Contact: Sarah Luddington

Looking for new writers. Especially
interested in Sci-fi, fantasy, horror, thrillers,
erotica, short story collections. Preferred
word count is under 100k for previously
unpublished authors.
Submissions should be email as an
attachment in Word or RTF and consist of
Synopsis and three chapters.

Birlinn Ltd

West Newington House
10 Newington Road
Edinburgh
EH9 1QS
Tel: +44 (0) 131 668 4371
Fax: +44 (0) 131 668 4466
Email: submissions@birlinn.co.uk
Website: http://www.birlinn.co.uk

Publishes: Fiction; Nonfiction; Poetry;
Reference; *Areas:* Adventure; Architecture;
Arts; Autobiography; Biography; Culture;
Current Affairs; Finance; Historical;
Humour; Legal; Medicine; Military; Nature;
Politics; Sociology; Sport; Travel; *Markets:*
Adult; Children's

Focuses on Scottish material: local, military,
and Highland history; humour, adventure;
reference, guidebooks, and folklore. No
unsolicited MSS. Not currently accepting
unsolicited children's books, fiction, poetry,
or short stories. Accepts nonfiction by post
or by email. See website for full details.

Black & White Publishing Ltd

29 Ocean Drive
Edinburgh
EH6 6JL
Tel: +44 (0) 01316 254500
Email: mail@blackandwhitepublishing.com
Website:

http://www.blackandwhitepublishing.com

Publishes: Fiction; Nonfiction; *Areas:*
Biography; Cookery; Crime; Humour;
Romance; Sport; *Markets:* Academic; Adult;
Children's

Contact: Campbell Brown (Director)

Publisher of general fiction and nonfiction.
See website for an idea of the kind of books
normally published. Send query with brief
synopsis and sample chapters up to 30 pages,
in a single Word file using online submission
system, or by email.

Black Coffey Publishing

23 Cromwell rd
Warley
Brentwood
Essex
CM14 5DT
Email: Paul@blackcoffeypublishing.com
Website:
http://www.blackcoffeypublishing.com

Publishes: Fiction; *Areas:* Adventure;
Crime; Drama; Fantasy; Humour; Mystery;
Sci-Fi; Short Stories; Suspense; Thrillers;
Westerns; *Markets:* Adult; Family; Youth;
Treatments: Commercial; Contemporary;
Popular; Progressive; Satirical

Contact: Paul Coffey

Specialist digital publisher actively looking
for short stories in our 2012 release schedule.
We scheduled to publish humorous short
story collections on:

+ 'Office life'
+ 'Growing up in the 1970s'
+ 'Leaving home for the first time'

Submissions can be made via our website.

Black Dog Publishing London UK

10A Acton Street
London
WC1X 9NG
Tel: +44 (0) 20 7713 5097
Fax: +44 (0) 20 7713 8682

Email: editorial@blackdogonline.com
Website: http://blackdogonline.com

Publishes: Nonfiction; *Areas:* Architecture;
Arts; Beauty and Fashion; Culture; Design;
Music; Nature; Photography; *Markets:*
Adult; *Treatments:* Contemporary

Publishes illustrated books with a fresh,
eclectic take on contemporary culture.
Originally focused on art and architecture,
but now includes subjects as varied as
design, fashion, music and environmental
concerns.

Blackline Press

15 Lister Road
Ipswich
IP1 5EQ
Email: author@blacklinepress.com
Website: http://www.blacklinepress.com

Publishes: Nonfiction; *Areas:* Sport;
Markets: Adult

Publishes books about football. Particularly
interested in groundhopping tours and
challenges, club histories and non-league
autobiographies, but welcomes all ideas.
Actively seeking new authors. Send query by
email.

Blackstaff Press Ltd

4c Heron Wharf
Sydenham Business Park
Belfast
BT3 9LE
Tel: +44 (0) 28 9045 5006
Fax: +44 (0) 28 9046 6237
Email: info@blackstaffpress.com
Website: http://www.blackstaffpress.com

Publishes: Fiction; Nonfiction; Poetry;
Areas: Autobiography; Biography; Cookery;
Historical; Humour; Nature; Politics; Short
Stories; Sport; Travel; *Markets:* Adult

Contact: Patsy Horton

Not currently accepting poetry or short story
collections as all slots have been filled for
the foreseeable future. For full length fiction
and nonfiction, send query with SAE,

synopsis, and three sample chapters in first
instance. For nonfiction, include market
information. No unsolicited MSS or
electronic submissions. Concentrates on, but
is not limited to, books or Irish interest.
Queries or submissions without SAE will not
be considered.

Bloodaxe Books Ltd

Highgreen
Tarset
Northumberland
NE48 1RP
Tel: +44 (0) 1434 240500
Fax: +44 (0) 1434 240505
Email: editor@bloodaxebooks.com
Website: http://www.bloodaxebooks.com

Publishes: Nonfiction; Poetry; *Areas:*
Criticism; Literature; *Markets:* Adult

Contact: Neil Astley, Managing/Editorial
Director

Submit poetry only if you have a track
record of publication in magazines. If so,
send sample of up to a dozen poems with
SAE or IRCs. No submissions by email or
on disk. Poems sent without return postage
will be recycled unread.

Bloomsbury Academic

50 Bedford Square
London
WC1B 3DP
Tel: +44 (0) 20 7631 5600
Email:
caroline.wintersgill@bloomsbury.com
Website:
http://www.bloomsburyacademic.com

Publishes: Nonfiction; Reference; *Areas:*
Anthropology; Archaeology; Business;
Crime; Culture; Drama; Film; Finance;
Historical; Legal; Literature; Media; Music;
Philosophy; Politics; Sociology;
Technology; *Markets:* Academic

Contact: See website for list of Editorial
contacts, and contact appropriate Editor.

Download publishing proposal form from
website, then submit by email to appropriate

editor (see website for list of editors, areas, and email addresses).

Bloomsbury Professional

41-43 Boltro Road
Haywards Heath
West Sussex
RH16 1BJ
Tel: +44 (0) 1444 416119
Email: martin.casimir@bloomsbury
professional.com
Website:
http://www.bloomsburyprofessional.com

Publishes: Nonfiction; Reference; *Areas:* Business; Finance; Legal; *Markets:* Professional

Contact: Martin Casimir

Publisher of books aimed at lawyers, accountants, and business people. Send query by email in first instance.

Blue Guides Limited

27 John Street
London
WC1N 2BX
Email: editorial@blueguides.com
Website: http://blueguides.com

Publishes: Nonfiction; *Areas:* Travel; *Markets:* Adult

Publishes travel guides. Always on the lookout for new authors. Contact by email in first instance, giving an indication of your areas of interest.

Boathook Books

Email: query@boathookbooks.com

Publishes: Fiction; Nonfiction; Reference; *Areas:* Adventure; Entertainment; Hobbies; How-to; Literature; Nature; Short Stories; Sport; Travel; *Markets:* Adult; Children's; Family; Youth

Imprint designed to serve the boating community - from blue water sailing to canal boats, barges, riverboats, etc.

We are a small traditional publisher, but because it's our money we're putting out there, we have to truly love your book to take it on for our list. And because boating books are a niche market, we will discuss with you the best sort of print runs to produce, depending on the book itself. If we love your book but can't take it on in the traditional way, we'll talk to you about alternatives.

bookouture

23 Sussex Road
Uxbridge
UB10 8PN
Email: oliver@bookouture.com
Website: http://www.bookouture.com

Publishes: Fiction; *Areas:* Crime; Erotic; Fantasy; Historical; Mystery; Romance; Sci-Fi; Suspense; Thrillers; *Markets:* Adult; *Treatments:* Commercial; Contemporary; Light; Mainstream; Popular; Positive

Contact: Oliver Rhodes

A digital first publisher of entertaining women's fiction - anything from contemporary romance to paranormal.

For most authors outside the bestseller lists, traditional publishers simply aren't adding enough value to justify low royalty rates. And because authors aren't all experts in editing, design, or marketing, self-publishing doesn't get the most out of their books or time. Digital publishing offers incredible opportunities to connect with readers all over the world – but finding the help you need to make the most of them can be tricky.

That's why we bring both big publisher experience and small team creativity. We genuinely understand and invest in brands – developing long-term strategies, marketing plans and websites for each of our authors.

And we work with the most brilliant editorial, design and marketing professionals in the business to make sure that everything we do is perfectly tailored to you and ridiculously good.

Combine all of that with an incredible 45%

royalty rate we think we're simply the perfect combination of high returns and inspirational publishing.

Booth-Clibborn Editions

Studio 83
235 Earls Court Road
London
SW5 9FE
Tel: +44 (0) 20 7565 0688
Fax: +44 (0) 20 7244 1018
Email: info@booth-clibborn.com
Website: http://www.booth-clibborn.com

Publishes: Nonfiction; *Areas:* Arts; Culture; Design; Media; Photography; *Markets:* Adult

Publishes books on the fine, media, and decorative arts.

Canongate Books

14 High Street
Edinburgh
EH1 1TE
Tel: +44 (0) 1315 575111
Fax: 144 (0) 1315 575211
Email: info@canongate.co.uk
Website: http://www.canongate.net

Publishes: Fiction; Nonfiction; *Areas:* Autobiography; Biography; Culture; Historical; Humour; Politics; Science; Translations; Travel; *Markets:* Adult; *Treatments:* Literary

Contact: Jamie Byng, Publisher

Publisher of a wide range of literary fiction and nonfiction, with a traditionally Scottish slant but becoming increasingly international. Publishes fiction in translation under its international imprint. No children's books, poetry, or drama. Send synopsis with three sample chapters and info about yourself.

Carcanet Press Ltd

4th Floor
Alliance House
Cross Street
Manchester
M2 7AP
Tel: +44 (0) 161 834 8730
Fax: +44 (0) 161 832 0084
Email: info@carcanet.co.uk
Website: http://www.carcanet.co.uk

Publishes: Nonfiction; Poetry; *Areas:* Biography; Literature; Translations; *Markets:* Academic; Adult; *Treatments:* Literary

Award-winning small press, publishing mainly poetry and academic material. Authors should familiarise themselves with the publisher's list, then, if appropriate, submit 6-10 pages of poetry or translations, with SAE. For other projects, send a full synopsis and covering letter, with sample pages, having first ascertained from the website that the kind of book proposed is suitable. No phone calls. No short stories, childrens prose/poetry or non-poetry related titles.

Child's Play (International) Ltd

Ashworth Road
Bridgemead
Swindon
Wiltshire
SN5 7YD
Tel: +44 (0) 1793 616286
Fax: +44 (0) 1793 512795
Email: office@childs-play.com
Website: http://www.childs-play.com

Publishes: Fiction; *Markets:* Children's

Contact: Sue Baker, Editor

Unsolicited MSS welcome, but SAE required for response. Specialises in publishing books that allow children to learn through play. No novels.

Christian Focus Publications

Geanies House
Fearn by Tain
Ross-shire
IV20 1TW
Tel: +44 (0) 1862 871011
Fax: +44 (0) 1862 871699
Email: info@christianfocus.com
Website: http://www.christianfocus.com

Publishes: Fiction; Nonfiction; *Areas:* Biography; Current Affairs; Historical; Lifestyle; Religious; *Markets:* Academic; Adult; Children's; Professional

Send query with a synopsis, contents page, two sample chapters, your CV, detailing your own religious background, a completed Author Information Sheet and a completed Book Information Sheet (both available at website). For children's fiction send synopsis, chapter headings, three sameple chapters, and Author Information Sheet. Publishes religious fiction and nonfiction for children, and nonfiction for adults. No poetry or adult fiction. See website for full details.

James Clarke & Co.
PO Box 60
Cambridge
CB1 2NT
Tel: +44 (0) 1223 350865
Fax: +44 (0) 1223 366951
Email: publishing@jamesclarke.co.uk
Website: http://www.jamesclarke.co

Publishes: Nonfiction; Reference; *Areas:* Religious; *Markets:* Academic

Publishes nonfiction and reference for the academic market on mainly theological subject matter. No fiction, cookery, drama, or poetry. Send query by email or by post with SAE, synopsis, detailed contents list, and one or two sample chapters.

Colin Smythe Ltd
38 Mill Lane
Gerrards Cross
Buckinghamshire
SL9 8BA
Tel: +44 (0) 1753 886000
Fax: +44 (0) 1753 886469
Email: cpsmythe@aol.com
Website: http://www.colinsmythe.co.uk

Publishes: Fiction; Nonfiction; Poetry; Scripts; *Areas:* Biography; Criticism; Drama; Fantasy; Historical; Hobbies; Literature; Sci-Fi; Theatre; *Markets:* Adult

Contact: Colin Smythe

Publishes fiction, nonfiction, drama, and poetry. Particular interest in Irish literature. No unsolicited MSS.

Compelling Books
Compelling Ideas Ltd
Basepoint Centre
Metcalf Way
RH11 7XX
Email: info@compellingbooks.com
Website: http://www.compellingbooks

Publishes: Fiction; Nonfiction; *Areas:* Adventure; Autobiography; Biography; Crime; Culture; Fantasy; Gothic; Historical; Horror; How-to; Humour; Literature; Mystery; Philosophy; Psychology; Science; Sci-Fi; Short Stories; Technology; Translations; *Markets:* Adult; Youth; *Treatments:* Commercial; Contemporary; Cynical; Dark; Light; Literary; Mainstream; Niche; Popular; Progressive; Serious; Traditional

Contact: Peter J Allen

Innovative independent publisher of compelling new fiction and non-fiction across all genres. Offers groundbreaking support for authors, with creative marketing, international scope, excellent royalty rates and uniquely ethical contracts.

We welcome new material - send a synopsis and first chapter via the submissions page of our website. (Hardcopy/print mss are NOT accepted.)

Constable & Robinson Ltd
55-56 Russell Square
London
WC1B 4HP
Tel: +44 (0) 20 7268 9700
Email: enquiries@constablerobinson.com
Website: http://www.constablerobinson.com

Publishes: Fiction; Nonfiction; Reference; *Areas:* Autobiography; Biography; Cookery; Crime; Current Affairs; Erotic; Fantasy; Gardening; Health; Historical; Horror; Humour; Leisure; Lifestyle; Military; Photography; Psychology; Sci-Fi; Self-Help;

Sport; Travel; *Markets:* Adult; Children's; *Treatments:* Commercial; Literary

Welcomes synopses and ideas for books by post with SASE only. Send query outlining targetted readership, previous experience, expertise, etc. plus one-page synopsis and one sample chapter. No unsolicited MSS or email or fax submissions.

Cressrelles Publishing Co. Ltd

10 Station Road Industrial Estate
Colwall
Malvern
WR13 6RN
Tel: +44 (0) 1684 540154
Fax: +44 (0) 1684 540154
Email: simon@cressrelles.co.uk

Publishes: Nonfiction; Scripts; *Areas:* Drama; *Markets:* Academic; Adult

Welcomes submissions. Publishes plays, theatre and drama textbooks, and local interest books.

James Currey Publishers

Box 242
266 Banbury Road
Oxford
OX2 7DL
Tel: +44 (0) 1865 559200
Fax: +44 (0) 1865 559200
Email: djohnson@boydell.co.uk
Website: http://www.jamescurrey.co.uk

Publishes: Nonfiction; *Areas:* Anthropology; Archaeology; Criticism; Film; Finance; Historical; Literature; Politics; Sociology; Theatre; *Markets:* Academic

Contact: Douglas H. Johnson, General Editor

Publishes books relating to Africa only. Send query by post or email, with 5-6 page proposal, including brief synopsis, outline, readership details, etc. Full details on website. No email attachments or full MSS.

Dagda Publishing

Email: dagdapublishing@hotmail.co.uk

Website:
http://www.dagdapublishing.wordpress.com

Publishes: Poetry; *Areas:* Criticism; Culture; Current Affairs; Drama; Entertainment; Fantasy; Gothic; Horror; Humour; Philosophy; Psychology; Sci-Fi; Suspense; *Markets:* Adult; *Treatments:* Contemporary; Dark; Experimental; Literary; Niche; Progressive; Satirical

Contact: R Davey

Poetry site actively seeking new writers and unsolicited MSS. We put out a few anthologies a year, and will feature new writers on the site on a regular frequency (every 1-2 weeks).

Please send submissions/ MSS in either the body of an email or as an attachment (.Doc .txt or .odt preferred).

Sorry, we cannot enter into correspondence with unsuccessful authors or provide criticism if unsuccessful.

Dedalus Ltd

Langford Lodge
St Judith's Lane
Sawtry
PE28 5XE
Tel: +44 (0) 1487 832382
Fax: +44 (0) 1487 832382
Email: info@dedalusbooks.com
Website: http://www.dedalusbooks.com

Publishes: Fiction; *Areas:* Literature; Translations; *Markets:* Adult; *Treatments:* Contemporary; Literary

Send query letter describing yourself along with SAE, synopsis, three sample chapters, and explanation of why you think this publisher in particular is right for you – essential to be familiar with and have read other books on this publisher's list before submitting, as most material received is entirely inappropriate. Welcomes submissions of suitable original fiction and is particularly interested in intellectually clever and unusual fiction. No email or disk submissions, or collections of short stories by unknown authors. Novels should be over 40,000 words – ideally over 50,000.

Duckworth Publishers

Editorial Submissions
Duckworth General
Duckworth Publishers
First Floor, East Wing
90-93 Cowcross Street
London
EC1M 6BF
Tel: +44 (0) 20 7490 7300
Fax: +44 (0) 20 7490 0080
Email: info@duckworth-publishers.co.uk
Website: http://www.ducknet.co.uk

Publishes: Fiction; Nonfiction; *Areas:* Archaeology; Biography; Historical; Philosophy; Translations; *Markets:* Academic; Adult; *Treatments:* Commercial; Literary

Independent publisher with a general trade and academic list. Publishes literary and commercial fiction and nonfiction, including history, biography and memoir. Academic imprint features important new scholarly monographs and series in Archaeology, Classics, Ancient History and Ancient Philosophy. Backlist includes school and student texts in Latin, Greek, Russian, French, German and Spanish language and literature. Also has a list of Russian literature in translation.

Not accepting fiction queries. Send nonfiction queries with SASE and three sample chapters by post only. No response without SASE. For academic submissions, approaches are preferred by email to address given on website. See website for full submission guidelines.

Egmont UK Ltd

3rd Floor, Beaumont House
Kensington Village
Avonmore Road
London
W14 6TS
Tel: +44 (0) 20 7605 6600
Fax: +44 (0) 20 7605 6601
Email: childrensreader@euk.egmont.com
Website: http://www.egmont.co.uk

Publishes: Fiction; *Markets:* Children's

Publishes picture books and children's fiction. Submit by email only; any hard copy submissions will be recycled. Send query with synopsis and first three chapters as attachments, or for picture books submit complete MS.

Eleusinian Press

34A Norton Terrace
Newhaven
BN9 0BT
Email: alastair.kemp@yahoo.co.uk
Website: http://www.eleusinianpress.co.uk

Publishes: Fiction; Nonfiction; Poetry; Reference; *Areas:* Anthropology; Archaeology; Architecture; Arts; Autobiography; Biography; Criticism; Culture; Current Affairs; Drama; Fantasy; Film; Health; Historical; Horror; Legal; Literature; Media; Medicine; Men's Interests; Music; Philosophy; Photography; Politics; Psychology; Science; Sci-Fi; Self-Help; Short Stories; Sociology; Spiritual; Theatre; Thrillers; Translations; Travel; Women's Interests; *Markets:* Academic; Adult; Professional; *Treatments:* Contemporary; Cynical; Dark; Experimental; In-depth; Literary; Niche; Progressive; Satirical; Serious

Contact: Alastair Kemp

A small publisher specialising in madness, music and radical politics. It has a flagship series of edited volumes, for which we accept fiction and non-fiction of 4000 words plus.
We also are looking for longer book-length monologues for 2013 and 2014.

Elliott & Thompson

27 John Street
London
WC1N 2BX
Tel: +44 (0) 20 7831 5013
Fax: +44 (0) 20 7831 5011
Email: ellen@eandtbooks.com
Website: http://www.eandtbooks.com

Publishes: Fiction; Nonfiction; *Areas:*

Biography; Historical; Music; Sport; *Markets:* Adult; *Treatments:* Literary

Currently accepting new nonfiction only. No new fiction. Send query by email with one-page synopsis and sample chapters up to 5,000 words. No postal submissions.

Emissary Publishing

PO Box 33
Bicester
OX26 2BU
Tel: +44 (0) 1869 323447
Fax: +44 (0) 1869 322552
Email: books@emissary-publishing.com
Website: http://www.emissary-publishing.com

Publishes: Fiction; Nonfiction; *Areas:* Humour; Thrillers; *Markets:* Adult

Contact: Val Miller

Publisher based in Bicester, originally set up to reprint a range of humour books only available in hardback from libraries as new paperbacks. Now also diversifying into other genres such as nonfiction and thrillers.

Enitharmon Press

26B Caversham Road
London
NW5 2DU
Tel: +44 (0) 20 7482 5967
Fax: +44 (0) 20 7284 1787
Email: info@enitharmon.co.uk
Website: http://www.enitharmon.co.uk

Publishes: Fiction; Poetry; *Areas:* Arts; Criticism; Photography; *Markets:* Adult; *Treatments:* Literary

One of Britain's leading literary publishers, specialising in poetry and in high-quality artists' books and original prints. It is divided into two companies: the press, which publishes poetry and general literature in small-format volumes and anthologies, and the editions, which produces de luxe artists' books in the tradition of the livre d'artiste. Send a preliminary enquiry to the editor before submitting material.

Erotic Review (ER) Books

Email: submissions@erbooks.org
Website: http://erbooks.org

Publishes: Fiction; Nonfiction; *Areas:* Arts; Erotic; Literature; Photography; Short Stories; *Markets:* Adult

Send query including biographical information by email with synopsis and two sample chapters / stories. See website for more details.

Evans Brothers Ltd

2A Portman Mansions
Chiltern Street
London
W1U 6NR
Tel: +44 (0) 20 7487 0920
Fax: +44 (0) 20 7487 0921
Email: sales@evansbrothers.co.uk
Website: http://www.evansbooks.co.uk

Publishes: Fiction; Nonfiction; Poetry; *Areas:* Arts; Design; Drama; Historical; Media; Music; Religious; Science; Sociology; Technology; *Markets:* Children's; Professional

Publishes children's fiction, poetry, and nonfiction; educational books; as well as teacher resources, etc. Strong connections in Africa. Welcomes submissions but no response unless interested.

Everyman Chess

Northburgh House
10 Northburgh Street
London
EC1V 0AT
Tel: +44 (0) 20 7253 7887
Fax: +44 (0) 20 7490 3708
Email: editor@everymanchess.com
Website: http://www.everymanchess.com

Publishes: Nonfiction; *Areas:* Hobbies; Leisure; *Markets:* Academic; Adult

Describes itself as the world's leading chess book publisher.

Faber & Faber Ltd

Bloomsbury House
74-77 Great Russell Street
London
WC1B 3DA
Tel: +44 (0) 20 7927 3800
Fax: +44 (0) 20 7927 3801
Website: http://www.faber.co.uk

Publishes: Fiction; Nonfiction; Poetry;
Scripts; *Areas:* Biography; Drama; Film;
Music; Politics; Theatre; *Markets:* Adult;
Children's

Originally published poetry and plays but
has expanded into other areas. Has published
some of the most prominent writers of the
twentieth century, including several poet
laureates. No longer accepting unsolicited
MSS in any areas other than poetry. Submit
6 poems in first instance, with adequate
return postage. Submissions of material other
than poetry will neither be read nor returned.
No submissions by email, fax, or on disk.

Facet Publishing

7 Ridgmount Street
London
WC1E 7AE
Tel: +44 (0) 20 7255 0590
Fax: +44 (0) 20 7255 0591
Email: sarah.busby@facetpublishing.co.uk
Website: http://www.facetpublishing.co.uk

Publishes: Nonfiction; Reference; *Areas:*
Technology; *Markets:* Professional

Contact: Sarah Busby (Commissioning
Editor)

Send query with synopsis, overview, word
count, estimated completion date, one or two
sample chapters, author bio, and market /
competition information. Queries may be
sent by post or by email. Publishes
nonfiction and reference books for library
and information professionals.

Findhorn Press Ltd

Delft Cottage
Dyke
Forres
IV36 2TF
Tel: +44 (0) 1309 690582
Email: submissions@findhornpress.com
Website: http://www.findhornpress.com

Publishes: Nonfiction; *Areas:* Health; New
Age; Spiritual; *Markets:* Adult

Publishes books on mind, body, spirit, New
Age and healing. Approach by email only.
Send 1-2 page synopsis, word count, number
of illustrations, table of contents, page
describing intended readership, brief
personal bio including any previous
publications, and details on ways you can
help promote your book. See website for
more information.

Fingerpress UK

Email: firstwriter@fingerpress.co.uk
Website: http://www.fingerpress.co.uk

Publishes: Fiction; Nonfiction; *Areas:*
Adventure; Crime; Culture; Entertainment;
Erotic; Fantasy; Gothic; Historical; Horror;
How-to; Humour; Men's Interests; Military;
Photography; Science; Sci-Fi; Suspense;
Technology; Thrillers; Travel; Women's
Interests; *Markets:* Adult; Youth;
Treatments: Commercial; Contemporary;
Cynical; Dark; Experimental; Mainstream;
Niche; Popular; Positive; Progressive;
Satirical; Serious; Traditional

We're an independent publisher based in
London. We're building a range of savvy,
entertaining titles that are both thought-
provoking and a good read. The ideal novel
will have memorable characters with good
plot development and pacing.

We are actively looking for:

* high-quality travel writing for inclusion in
iBooks-based travel guides

* books on IT/software development

* submissions of completed, professionally
edited, commercial-grade novels

Please read the submissions page on the
website before submitting anything.

First & Best in Education Ltd
Hamilton House Mailings plc
Editorial Dept
Earlstrees Ct
Earlstrees Rd
Corby
Northants
NN17 4HH
Tel: +44 (0) 1536 399005
Fax: +44 (0) 1536 399012
Email: editorial@firstandbest.co.uk
Website: http://www.firstandbest.co.uk

Publishes: Nonfiction; *Markets:* Academic

Contact: Anne Cockburn

Check website or send SAE for details of requirements and current projects in first instance. Publishes educational books for children of all ages, teachers and parents. Always looking for new authors of educational books. No fiction.

Flame Lily Books
13 Stapleton Road
Meole Brace
Shrewsbury
Shropshire
SY3 9LY
Tel: +44 (0) 1743 245969
Email: timpagden@flamelilybooks.co.uk
Website: http://www.flamelilybooks.co.uk

Publishes: Fiction; Nonfiction; *Areas:* Adventure; Archaeology; Biography; Business; Cookery; Crafts; Crime; Design; Drama; Fantasy; Film; Gardening; Historical; Hobbies; How-to; Humour; Leisure; Literature; Military; Music; Mystery; Nature; Religious; Romance; Science; Sci-Fi; Short Stories; Suspense; Technology; Thrillers; Travel; Westerns; *Markets:* Adult; Children's; Youth; *Treatments:* Commercial; In-depth; Light; Literary; Mainstream; Niche; Popular; Positive; Traditional

Contact: Tim Pagden

We accept submissions from unpublished writers.

Of particular interest are new and different books aimed at children and early teens, especially science fiction and fantasy, but not exclusively. We will, however, read submissions in almost any genre and aimed at any age group.

We are also interested in non-fiction books on any subject. For example "How to ..." books again aimed at the younger generation. And finally we would welcome books with a Christian theme.

There are some subjects and genres which we will not publish and we don't accept printed manuscripts. For these reasons, and so as not too waste our time and yours, please read the submissions page before sending any work to us.

Floris Books
15 Harrison Gardens
Edinburgh
EH11 1SH
Tel: +44 (0) 1313 372372
Fax: +44 (0) 1313 479919
Email: floris@florisbooks.co.uk
Website: http://www.florisbooks.co.uk

Publishes: Fiction; Nonfiction; *Areas:* Architecture; Arts; Biography; Crafts; Health; Historical; Literature; Philosophy; Religious; Science; Self-Help; Sociology; Spiritual; *Markets:* Adult; Children's; Youth

Publishes a range of books connected to the Steiner movement, including children's fiction and picture books with a Scottish theme (no general children's fiction or adult fiction). No autobiography, adult fiction, children's fiction over 12, or poetry. See website for full details of areas covered and submission guidelines.

Fountain Press
Newpro UK Ltd
Old Sawmills Road
Faringdon
Oxon
SN7 7DS
Tel: +44 (0) 1367 242411
Fax: +44 (0) 1367 241124
Email: sales@newprouk.co.uk
Website: http://www.newprouk.co.uk

Publishes: Nonfiction; *Areas:* Nature;
Photography; *Markets:* Adult

Contact: C.J. Coleman

Publisher of books on photography and
natural history. Welcomes synopses and
unsolicited MSS.

Frontline Books
The Editorial Department,
Frontline Books
5A Accommodation Road
Golders Green
London
NW11 8ED
Email: michael@frontline-books.com
Website: http://www.frontline-books.com

Publishes: Nonfiction; *Areas:* Historical;
Military; *Markets:* Adult

Military history publisher. Send synopsis and
if available a sample chapter, but no
complete MSS. See website for full
submission guidelines.

George Ronald Publisher
3 Rosecroft Lane
Welwyn
Herts
AL6 0UB
Tel: +44 (0) 1438 716062
Email: sales@grbooks.com
Website: http://grbooks.com

Publishes: Nonfiction; *Areas:* Religious;
Markets: Adult

Religious publisher, concentrating solely on
books of interest to Bahá'ís. Send email for
copy of submission guidelines.

Galore Park Publishing Ltd
19/21 Sayers Lane
Tenterden
Kent
TN30 6BW
Tel: +44 (0) 1580 764242
Fax: +44 (0) 1580 764142
Email: info@galorepark.co.uk
Website: http://www.galorepark.co.uk

Publishes: Nonfiction; *Markets:* Academic;
Children's

Publisher of school textbooks and revision
resources. Welcomes synopses and ideas, but
no unsolicited MSS. Send query by email.

Geddes & Grosset
144 Port Dundas Road
Glasgow
G4 0HZ
Tel: +44 (0) 1415 672830
Fax: +44 (0) 1415 672831
Website: http://www.geddesandgrosset.co.uk

Publishes: Fiction; Nonfiction; Reference;
Areas: Cookery; Historical; Humour;
Markets: Adult; Children's

Contact: Ron Grosset; R. Michael Miller

Publishes Children's and reference books.
Unsolicited MSS, and synopses and ideas for
books are welcomed, but adult fiction is not
accepted.

Gibson Square Books Ltd
15 Gibson Square
London
N1 0RD
Tel: +44 (0) 20 7096 1100
Fax: +44 (0) 20 7993 2214
Email: info@gibsonsquare.com
Website: http://www.gibsonsquare.com

Publishes: Nonfiction; *Areas:* Arts;
Biography; Criticism; Culture; Current
Affairs; Historical; Philosophy; Politics;
Psychology; Travel; *Markets:* Adult

Synopses, and ideas welcomed. Send query
by email only. Publishes books which
contribute to a general debate. No fiction.
See website for full guidelines.

Giles de la Mare Publishers Ltd
PO Box 25351
London
NW5 1ZT
Tel: +44 (0) 20 7485 2533
Fax: +44 (0) 20 7485 2534

Email: gilesdelamare@dial.pipex.com
Website: http://www.gilesdelamare.co.uk

Publishes: Nonfiction; *Areas:* Architecture;
Arts; Biography; Historical; Music; Travel;
Markets: Adult

Contact: Giles de la Mare

Welcomes unsolicited MSS, synopses, and
ideas, after initial telephone query.

Glastonbury Publishing
Mirador
Wearne Lane
Langport
TA109HB
Tel: +44 (0) 845 519 7471
Email: sarah@glastonburypublishing.com
Website:
http://www.glastonburypublishing.com

Publishes: Fiction; *Areas:* Adventure;
Crime; Drama; Erotic; Fantasy; Gothic;
Historical; Horror; Humour; Men's Interests;
Mystery; New Age; Romance; Sci-Fi;
Suspense; Thrillers; Women's Interests;
Markets: Adult; *Treatments:* Contemporary;
Dark; Mainstream; Niche; Popular

Contact: Sarah Luddington

After many years as a successful author I
have decided to give something back and
help a few new writers on the road to
success.

I select a very few titles each year with
which I feel I can work. I will then guide
you, the author, to polish your work up to the
required standard and together we will bring
your book to the market.

Gomer Press
Llandysul
Ceredigion
SA44 4JL
Tel: +44 (0) 1559 362371
Fax: +44 (0) 1559 363758
Email: gwasg@gomer.co.uk
Website: http://www.gomer.co.uk

Publishes: Fiction; Nonfiction; Poetry;

Reference; Scripts; *Areas:* Arts;
Autobiography; Biography; Culture; Drama;
Historical; Leisure; Literature; Music;
Nature; Religious; Sport; Theatre; Travel;
Markets: Academic; Adult; Children's

Publishes fiction, nonfiction, plays, poetry,
language books, and educational material,
for adults and children, in English and in
Welsh. See website for contact details of
editors and query appropriate editor with
sample chapter, synopsis, CV, and sales
strengths of your proposal. Do not send
complete MS in first instance.

Green Books
Dartington Space
Dartington Hall
Totnes
TQ9 6EN
Tel: +44 (0) 1803 863260
Fax: +44 (0) 1803 863843
Email: edit@greenbooks.co.uk
Website: http://www.greenbooks.co.uk

Publishes: Nonfiction; *Areas:* Biography;
Business; Gardening; How-to; Humour;
Lifestyle; Literature; Nature; Politics;
Markets: Adult

Publishes books on environmental issues,
including politics, lifestyle, and practical
books. No fiction or children's books.

Potential authors should first familiarise
themselves with the website and the type of
material published, then send email query
including all six elements listed on website.
No unsolicited MSS. See website for full
guidelines.

Gresham Books Ltd
19/21 Sayers Lane
Tenterden
Kent
TN30 6BW
Tel: +44 (0) 1580 767596
Fax: +44 (0) 1580 764142
Email: info@gresham-books.co.uk
Website: http://www.gresham-books.co.uk

Publishes: Nonfiction; *Areas:* Religious;
Markets: Academic; Adult; Children's

Contact: Paul Lewis

Publishes hymn and service books for churches and schools, plus school histories and literary works with a special school interest. Also produces choir, orchestral, report and record of achievement folders. Ideas welcome, but no unsolicited MSS.

Grey Hen Press
PO Box 450
Keighley
West Yorkshire
BD22 9WS
Email: contact@greyhenpress.com
Website: http://www.greyhenpress.com

Publishes: Poetry; *Markets:* Adult

Publishes anthologies of poetry by women over 60. Aims to give less well-known poets the opportunity of having their work published alongside that of established writers.

Grub Street Publishing
4 Rainham Close
London
SW11 6SS
Tel: +44 (0) 20 7924 3966 / 20 7738 1008
Fax: +44 (0) 20 7738 1009
Email: post@grubstreet.co.uk
Website: http://www.grubstreet.co.uk

Publishes: Nonfiction; *Areas:* Cookery; Health; Historical; Military; *Markets:* Adult

Contact: John Davies (Military); Anne Dolamore (Cookery)

Publishes books on cookery and military/aviation history only. No fiction or poetry. Accepts synopses and unsolicited MSS by post only with SASE. No email queries or submissions. See website for full submission guidelines.

Guild of Master Craftsman (GMC) Publications Ltd
166 High Street
Lewes
BN7 1XU

Tel: +44 (0) 1273 477374
Fax: +44 (0) 1273 402866
Email: pubs@thegmcgroup.com

Publishes: Nonfiction; Reference; *Areas:* Architecture; Arts; Cookery; Crafts; Film; Gardening; Hobbies; How-to; Humour; Photography; TV; *Markets:* Adult; Children's

Welcomes ideas, synopses, and unsolicited MSS. Publishes books on the above topics, plus woodworking, dolls houses, and miniatures. Also publishes magazines and videos. No fiction.

Gullane Children's Books
185 Fleet Street
London
EC4A 2HS
Tel: +44 (0) 20 7400 1037
Fax: +44 (0) 20 7400 1084
Email: stories@gullanebooks.com
Website: http://www.gullanebooks.com

Publishes: Fiction; *Markets:* Children's

Contact: Submissions Editor

Publishes picture books for children up to 500 words. Send submissions by post or email. Response only if interested. Include SAE if return of manuscript required. Submissions from outside the UK cannot be returned under any circumstances.

Gwasg Carreg Gwalch
12 Iard yr Orsaf
Llanrwst
Conwy
LL26 0EH
Tel: +44 (0) 1492 642031
Fax: +44 (0) 1492 641502
Email: llanrwst@carreg-gwalch.com
Website: http://www.carreg-gwalch.co.uk

Publishes: Nonfiction; Reference; *Areas:* Historical; Travel; *Markets:* Adult

Publishes Welsh language books, and books in English of Welsh interest, such as history and folklore. Also publishes Welsh guides and walks. Unsolicited MSS welcome if on topics of Welsh interest.

Hachette Children's Books

338 Euston Road
London
NW1 3BH
Tel: +44 (0) 20 7873 6000
Fax: +44 (0) 20 7873 6024
Email: ad@hachettechildrens.co.uk
Website: http://www.hachettechildrens.co.uk

Publishes: Fiction; Nonfiction; Reference; *Markets:* Children's

Large publisher of fiction, nonfiction, reference, picture books, audio books, and novelty books, for children. No unsolicited mss.

Hachette UK

338 Euston Road
London
NW1 3BH
Tel: +44 (0) 20 7873 6000
Fax: +44 (0) 20 7873 6024
Website: http://www.hachette.co.uk

Publishes: Fiction; Nonfiction; *Markets:* Adult

Describes itself as the largest and one of the most diversified book publishers in the UK. Accepts submissions via literary agents only.

Halban Publishers

22 Golden Square
London
W1F 9JW
Tel: +44 (0) 20 7437 9300
Fax: +44 (0) 20 7437 9512
Email: books@halbanpublishers.com
Website: http://www.halbanpublishers.com

Publishes: Fiction; Nonfiction; *Areas:* Autobiography; Biography; Criticism; Historical; Literature; Philosophy; Politics; Religious; *Markets:* Adult

Contact: Peter Halban; Martine Halban

Independent publisher of fiction, memoirs,

history, biography, and books of Jewish interest. Send query by post. No unsolicited MSS. Unsolicited emails deleted unread.

Halsgrove

Halsgrove House
Ryelands Business Park
Bagley Road
Wellington
Somerset
TA21 9PZ
Tel: +44 (0) 1823 653777
Fax: +44 (0) 1823 216796
Email: sales@halsgrove.com
Website: http://www.halsgrove.com

Publishes: Nonfiction; *Areas:* Arts; Biography; Historical; Photography; *Markets:* Adult

Unsolicited MSS, ideas and synopses welcomed. Publishes regional material covering various regions in the areas of history, biography, photography, and art. No fiction or poetry.

Hammersmith Press Ltd

14 Greville Street
London
EC1N 8SB
Email: gmb@hammersmithpress.co.uk
Website:
http://www.hammersmithpress.co.uk

Publishes: Nonfiction; *Areas:* Health; Medicine; *Markets:* Academic; Adult; Professional

Contact: Georgina Bentliff

Publisher of health, medicine, and nutrition books for the general public, health professionals, and academic markets. No unsolicited MSS but queries / synopses / ideas welcome.

Harriman House Ltd

3A Penns Road
Petersfield
Hampshire
GU32 2EW
Tel: +44 (0) 1730 233870

Fax: +44 (0) 1730 233880
Email: commissioning@harriman-house.com
Website: http://www.harriman-house.com

Publishes: Nonfiction; *Areas:* Business; Finance; How-to; Lifestyle; Politics; *Markets:* Adult; Professional

Publisher concentrating on finance, investing and politics, but willing to consider other nonfiction in other, peripheral areas. Download proposal form from website and submit via email.

Hart Publishing Ltd

16c Worcester Place
Oxford
OX1 2JW
Tel: +44 (0) 1865 517530
Fax: +44 (0) 1865 510710
Email: richard@hartpub.co.uk
Website: http://www.hartpub.co.uk

Publishes: Nonfiction; *Areas:* Legal; *Markets:* Academic; Professional

Publisher or legal books and journals for the professional and academic markets. See website for submission guidelines.

Hay House Publishers

Submissions
292B Kensal Road
London
W10 5BE
Tel: +44 (0) 20 8962 1230
Fax: +44 (0) 20 8962 1239
Email: submissions@hayhouse.co.uk
Website: http://www.hayhouse.co.uk

Publishes: Nonfiction; *Areas:* Biography; Business; Current Affairs; Finance; Health; Lifestyle; Medicine; Men's Interests; Nature; Philosophy; Psychology; Religious; Self-Help; Sociology; Spiritual; Women's Interests; *Markets:* Adult; *Treatments:* Positive

Describes itself as the world's leading mind body and spirit publisher. Accepts proposals as hard copy by post or by email, but prefers email approaches. See website for full submission guidelines.

Haynes Publishing

Sparkford
Near Yeovil
Somerset
BA22 7JJ
Tel: +44 (0) 1963 440635
Fax: +44 (0) 1963 440023
Email: bookseditorial@haynes.co.uk
Website: http://www.haynes.co.uk

Publishes: Nonfiction; Reference; *Areas:* How-to; Leisure; Military; Sport; Technology

Contact: John H. Haynes OBE (Chairman)

Mostly publishes motoring and transport titles, including DIY service and repair manuals for cars and motorbikes, motoring in general (including Motor Sports), but also home, DIY, and leisure titles. Unsolicited MSS welcome, if on one of the above areas of interest.

Headland Publications

38 York Avenue
West Kirby
Wirral
CH48 3JF
Tel: +44 (0) 01516 259128
Email: headlandpublications@hotmail.co.uk
Website: http://www.headlandpublications.co.uk

Publishes: Fiction; Nonfiction; Poetry; *Areas:* Biography; Short Stories; *Markets:* Adult

Specialises in poetry, but has expanded scope to include short stories and biography.

High Stakes Publishing

Oldcastle Books
P O Box 394
Harpenden
AL5 1XJ
Tel: +44 (0) 1582 766348
Fax: +44 (0) 1582 766348

Website:
http://www.highstakespublishing.co.uk

Publishes: Nonfiction; *Areas:* Hobbies;
Markets: Adult

Imprint publishing books on gambling.

Hilmarton Manor Press
Calne
Wiltshire
SN11 8SB
Tel: +44 (0) 1249 760208
Fax: +44 (0) 1249 760379
Email: mailorder@hilmartonpress.co.uk

Publishes: Nonfiction; *Areas:* Antiques;
Arts; *Markets:* Adult

Publishes books on visual arts, fine art,
antiques, and wine.

Hodder Education
338 Euston Road
London
NW1 3BH
Tel: +44 (0) 20 7873 6000
Fax: +44 (0) 20 7873 6299
Email: educationenquiries@hodder.co.uk
Website: http://www.hoddereducation.co.uk

Publishes: Nonfiction; Reference; *Areas:*
Health; Medicine; Science; Self-Help;
Markets: Academic; Adult

Publishes educational and reference books
including home learning and school
textbooks. See website for more details and
for specific submission addresses for
different types of books.

Hogs Back Books
The Stables
Down Place
Hogs Back
Guildford
GU3 1DE
Email: enquiries@hogsbackbooks.com
Website: http://www.hogsbackbooks.com

Publishes: Fiction; *Markets:* Children's

Publishes illustrated books for children up to
the age of 10. Welcomes texts direct from
authors, or through literary agents.

Honno Welsh Women's Press
Honno
Unit 14, Creative Units
Aberystwyth Arts Centre
Aberystwyth
Ceredigion
SY23 3GL
Tel: +44 (0) 1970 623150
Fax: +44 (0) 1970 623150
Email: post@honno.co.uk
Website: http://www.honno.co.uk

Publishes: Fiction; Nonfiction; Poetry;
Areas: Autobiography; Short Stories;
Women's Interests; *Markets:* Adult;
Children's; Youth

Contact: Caroline Oakley

Welcomes MSS and ideas for books from
women born in, living in, or significantly
connected to Wales, only. Publishes fiction,
autobiographical writing and reprints of
classic titles in English and Welsh, as well as
anthologies of poetry and short stories. All
submissions must be sent as hard copy; no
email submissions. Send query with synopsis
and first 50 pages. Not currently accepting
children/teenage novels or poetry or short
story collections by a single author.

Hopscotch
St Jude's Church
Dulwich Road
Herne Hill
London
SE24 0PB
Tel: +44 (0) 1722 716 935
Email: sales@hopscotchbooks.com
Website: http://www.hopscotchbooks.com

Publishes: Nonfiction; *Markets:* Professional

Publishes teaching resources for primary
school teachers. Happy to hear from authors
both new and established, with completed
mss or just ideas. Contact editorial
department by phone or submit complete ms.

House of Lochar

Isle of Colonsay
PA61 7YR
Tel: +44 (0) 1951 200232
Fax: +44 (0) 1951 200232
Email: Lochar@colonsay.org.uk
Website: http://www.houseoflochar.com

Publishes: Fiction; Nonfiction; *Areas:*
Biography; Historical; Literature; Travel;
Markets: Adult; Children's

Welcomes unsolicited MSS for fiction and
nonfiction related to Scotland and / or Celtic
themes, including history, fiction, transport,
maritime, genealogy, Gaelic, and books for
children. No poetry or books unrelated to
Scottish or Celtic themes.

How to Books Ltd

Spring Hill House
Spring Hill Road
Begbroke
Oxford
OX5 1RX
Tel: +44 (0) 1865 375794
Fax: +44 (0) 1865 379162
Email: read@howtobooks.co.uk
Website: http://www.howtobooks.co.uk

Publishes: Nonfiction; Reference; *Areas:*
Business; How-to; Leisure; Lifestyle; Self-
Help; Travel; *Markets:* Adult

Contact: Nikki Read

Publishes "how-to" books on areas such as
management, career development, self-
employment, education, living and working
overseas, etc. Potential authors should have
first-hand experience of the area they are
wanting to write about.

ICSA Information & Training Ltd

16 Park Crescent
London
W1B 1AH
Tel: +44 (0) 20 7612 7020
Fax: +44 (0) 20 7612 7034
Email: publishing@icsa.co.uk
Website: http://www.icsabookshop.co.uk

Publishes: Nonfiction; Reference; *Areas:*
Legal; *Markets:* Professional

Publishes books aimed at secretaries and
administrators, providing guidance on legal
and regulatory compliance.

Igloo Books Limited

Cottage Farm
Mears Ashby Road
Sywell
Northants
NN6 0BJ
Tel: +44 (0) 1604 741116
Fax: +44 (0) 1604 670495
Email: customerservice@igloobooks.com
Website: http://igloobooks.com

Publishes: Fiction; Nonfiction; Reference;
Areas: Cookery; Hobbies; *Markets:* Adult;
Children's

Publishes nonfiction and gift and puzzle
books for adults, and fiction, nonfiction, and
novelty books for children.

Impress Books Limited

Innovation Centre
Rennes Drive
University of Exeter
Devon
EX4 4RN
Tel: +44 (0) 1392 262301
Fax: +44 (0) 1392 262303
Email: enquiries@impress-books.co.uk
Website: http://www.impress-books.co.uk

Publishes: Fiction; Nonfiction; *Markets:*
Adult

Interested in quality, thought-provoking titles
for the enquiring general reader. Send query
by post or by email, or via form on website.

Indigo Dreams Publishing

132 Hinckley Road
Stoney Stanton
Leics
LE9 4LN
Tel: +44 (0) 1455 272861
Email: publishing@indigodreams.co.uk
Website: http://www.indigodreams.co.uk

Publishes: Fiction; Nonfiction; Poetry; *Areas:* Adventure; Antiques; Arts; Autobiography; Biography; Crime; Entertainment; Erotic; Fantasy; Film; Gothic; Historical; Hobbies; Horror; How-to; Humour; Leisure; Lifestyle; Literature; Media; Men's Interests; Music; Mystery; Nature; New Age; Photography; Romance; Science; Sci-Fi; Spiritual; Sport; Suspense; Theatre; Thrillers; Translations; Travel; Westerns; Women's Interests; *Markets:* Adult; Family; Professional; *Treatments:* Commercial; Contemporary; Cynical; Dark; Experimental; In-depth; Light; Literary; Mainstream; Niche; Popular; Positive; Progressive; Satirical; Serious; Traditional

Contact: Ronnie Goodyer

Note: Closed to poetry submissions until 2013. Check website for latest information.

IDP are an independant publisher of fiction and poetry but are also looking to the non-fiction market. They have a speedy decision process through frequent Acquisition Meetings and an established method of approach, initially via a form on their website. Interesting proposals are then contacted for complete manuscripts in a second stage process and these are read and considered at the relevant Acquisitions Meetings. Books are distributed through Central Books, London. IDP are free to choose whatever material they wish as they have independant finance and no restrictions other than those which are self-imposed.

Inter-Varsity Press
Book Proposals
FAO Eleanor Trotter
IVP UK
Norton Street
Nottingham
NG7 3HR
Tel: +44 (0) 115 978 1054
Fax: +44 (0) 115 942 2694
Email: bookproposals@ivpbooks.com
Website: http://www.ivpbooks.com

Publishes: Nonfiction; Reference; *Areas:* Lifestyle; Religious; *Markets:* Adult

Contact: Eleanor Trotter

Publishes bible commentaries and reference works, as well as material on Christian beliefs and lifestyles. All material must empathise with orthodox Protestant Christianity. No secular material, booklets, PhDs, fiction, poetry, or children's books. Send query by email or by post including overview, contents list, one or two sample chapters, readership, competing titles, info about the author, and any other relevant information.

Jo Fletcher Books
55 Baker Street
7th Floor
South Block
London
W1U 8EW
Tel: +44 (0) 20 7291 7200
Email: submissions@jofletcherbooks.co.uk
Website: http://www.jofletcherbooks.com

Publishes: Fiction; *Areas:* Fantasy; Horror; Sci-Fi; *Markets:* Adult

Contact: Nicola Budd

Specialist science fiction, fantasy and horror imprint. Send query by email with synopsis and first three chapters or first 10,000 words.

Jolly Learning Ltd
Tailours House
High Road
Chigwell
Essex
IG7 6DL
Tel: +44 (0) 20 8501 0405
Fax: +44 (0) 20 8500 1696
Email: info@jollylearning.co.uk
Website: http://jollylearning.co.uk

Publishes: Fiction; *Markets:* Academic; Children's

Publishes books for children to help with reading, using the synthetic phonics method of teaching the letter sounds in a way that aims to be fun and multi-sensory.

Jessica Kingsley Publishers
116 Pentonville Road

London
N1 9JB
Tel: +44 (0) 20 7833 2307
Fax: +44 (0) 20 7837 2917
Email: post@jkp.com
Website: http://www.jkp.com

Publishes: Nonfiction; *Areas:* Arts;
Psychology; Religious; Sociology; *Markets:*
Academic; Professional

Contact: Jessica Kingsley

Send query with author CV, and book
proposal form (available on website), by post
or email. Publishes books for academics and
professionals on subjects connected to
behavioural and social sciences: art therapy;
child psychology; psychotherapy and
forensic psychotherapy; practical theology;
social work; special needs, etc.

Knox Robinson Publishing (UK)

34 New House
67-68 Hatton Garden
London
EC1N 8JY
Tel: +44 (0) 20 8816 8630
Fax: +44 (0) 20 8711 2334
Email: subs@knoxrobinsonpublishing.com
Website:
http://www.knoxrobinsonpublishing.com

Publishes: Fiction; *Areas:* Fantasy;
Historical; Romance; *Markets:* Adult

Publishes historical fiction, historical
romance (pre-1960), and medieval fantasy.
No science fiction, time travel, or fantasy
with children and/or animal protagonists.
Send query by email only, with detailed
synopsis and the first three chapters. No
approaches by fax or post. See website for
full details.

Legend Press

2 London Wall Buildings
London
EC2M 5UU
Tel: +44 (0) 20 7448 5137
Email: submissions@legend-
paperbooks.co.uk

Website: http://www.legendpress.co.uk

Publishes: Fiction; *Markets:* Adult;
Treatments: Contemporary; Mainstream

Contact: Tom Chalmers

Publishes a diverse list of contemporary
adult novels. Send query by email, including
synopsis, and first three chapters as
attachments. No hard copy submissions.

Frances Lincoln Ltd

4 Torriano Mews
Torriano Avenue
London
NW5 2RZ
Tel: +44 (0) 20 7284 4009
Fax: +44 (0) 20 7485 0490
Email: fl@frances-lincoln.com
Website: http://www.franceslincoln.com

Publishes: Fiction; Nonfiction; *Areas:*
Architecture; Arts; Design; Gardening;
Leisure; Lifestyle; Travel; *Markets:* Adult;
Children's

Publishers of illustrated nonfiction books for
adults, particularly on gardening, walking
and the outdoors, art, architecture, design
and landscape. In the area of children's
fiction, accepts picture books only. See
website for full submission guidelines and
specific email addresses for adult/children
submissions.

Lion Hudson Plc

Wilkinson House
Jordan Hill Road
Oxford
OX2 8DR
Tel: +44 (0) 1865 302750
Fax: +44 (0) 1865 302757
Email: info@lionhudson.com
Website: http://www.lionhudson.com

Publishes: Fiction; Nonfiction; Reference;
Areas: Autobiography; Biography; Health;
Religious; Spiritual; *Markets:* Adult;
Children's; *Treatments:* Positive

Publishes books that reflect Christian values
or are inspired by a Christian world view,

---

including adult nonfiction / reference, and children's fiction and nonfiction. See website for specific submission guidelines for different imprints.

Little Tiger Press

1 The Coda Centre
189 Munster Road
London
SW6 6AW
Tel: +44 (0) 20 7385 6333
Fax: +44 (0) 20 7385 7333
Email: info@littletiger.co.uk
Website: http://www.littletigerpress.com

Publishes: Fiction; *Markets:* Children's

Contact: Mara Alperin, Submissions Editor

Accepts unsolicited MSS up to 750 words. If inside UK include SAE for response (no postage vouchers/coupons); if from outside the UK include email address for response (no material returned). See website for full guidelines. No submissions by email or on disc.

Little, Brown Book Group

100 Victoria Embankment
London
EC4Y 0DY
Tel: +44 (0) 20 7911 8000
Fax: +44 (0) 20 7911 8100
Email: uk@littlebrown.co.uk
Website: http://www.littlebrown.co.uk

Publishes: Fiction; Nonfiction; *Areas:* Autobiography; Biography; Crime; Entertainment; Fantasy; Historical; Humour; Literature; Sci-Fi; Thrillers; *Markets:* Adult; Youth; *Treatments:* Literary; Popular

Accepts submissions via agents only. No proposals by email.

Liverpool University Press

4 Cambridge Street
Liverpool
L69 7ZU
Tel: +44 (0) 1517 942233
Fax: +44 (0) 1517 942235
Email: lup@liv.ac.uk

Website: http://www.liverpool-unipress.co.uk

Publishes: Nonfiction; *Areas:* Archaeology; Architecture; Arts; Culture; Historical; Literature; Music; Politics; Sci-Fi; Sociology; *Markets:* Academic

Contact: Robin Bloxsidge

Send proposal by email in first instance, including provisional title and a description of the purpose and scope of the proposed book; an analysis of the structure, together with a breakdown of (sections and) chapters showing the detailed scope of each chapter; a copy of the Introduction if available; a commentary on your research experience in the field of your proposed book; CV; consideration of the relationship of your work in the field to the work of others in the same field, bearing particularly on the distinctiveness of your proposed book in relation to other published works; the intended readership level (e.g. undergraduate, graduate, general); the intended market (e.g. library, scholars, students); potential geographical sales area (e.g. UK, continental Europe, North America); and provisional timetable for completion of the book or its revision.

Lost Tower Publications

Email: rainbowme@rocketmail.com
Website:
http://losttowerpublications.jigsy.com

Publishes: Fiction; Poetry; *Areas:* Adventure; Autobiography; Crime; Fantasy; Gothic; Horror; Leisure; Lifestyle; Mystery; Sci-Fi; Spiritual; Suspense; Thrillers; Women's Interests; *Markets:* Adult; Children's; Family; Youth; *Treatments:* Contemporary; Dark; Experimental; Niche; Positive; Progressive

Contact: Harry Yang

Formed in 2011 as part of a poetry book publishing campaign to promote poetry world wide as an attractive and entertaining art form for the twenty first century. We print 3-4 books a year collecting the best photographs and poetry from around the world, to produce high quality books for people to enjoy. Our books are available to buy worldwide either from Amazon or to order through your local bookshop.

In March 2013 we published a journey of hope through poems and photographs which have been collected from around the world. The work in this anthology has been collected from every continent of our planet and illustrates ideas of hope from many of the world religions; looks at the different forms hope can take and how hope can always be found if you look carefully into the world which surrounds you.

Luath Press Ltd

543/2 Castlehill
The Royal Mile
Edinburgh
EH1 2ND
Tel: +44 (0) 131 225 4326
Fax: +44 (0) 131 225 4324
Email: submissions@luath.co.uk
Website: http://www.luath.co.uk

Publishes: Fiction; Nonfiction; Poetry; *Areas:* Arts; Beauty and Fashion; Biography; Crime; Current Affairs; Drama; Historical; Leisure; Lifestyle; Nature; Photography; Politics; Sociology; Sport; Thrillers; Travel; *Markets:* Adult; Children's; Youth

Contact: G.H. MacDougall, Managing Editor

Publishes a range of books, usually with a Scottish connection. Check upcoming publishing schedule on website, and - if you think your book fits - send query with SAE, synopsis, manuscript or sample chapters, author bio, and any other relevant material. See website FAQ for full submission guidelines.

Lund Humphries Limited

140-142 St John Street
London
EC1V 4UB
Tel: +44 (0) 20 7440 7530
Fax: +44 (0) 20 7440 7545
Email: lclark@lundhumphries.com
Website: http://www.lundhumphries.com

Publishes: Nonfiction; *Areas:* Architecture; Arts; Design; Historical; *Markets:* Adult

Contact: Lucy Clark

Publishes books on art, art history, and design. See website for guidelines on submitting a proposal.

The Lutterworth Press

PO Box 60
Cambridge
CB1 2NT
Tel: +44 (0) 1223 350865
Fax: +44 (0) 1223 366951
Email: publishing@lutterworth.com
Website: http://www.lutterworth.com

Publishes: Fiction; Nonfiction; *Areas:* Religious; *Markets:* Adult; Children's

Publisher of religious books. Handles nonfiction for adults, and fiction and nonfiction for children. Send query with ideas in first instance. No adult fiction, cookery books, or drama or poetry. Email queries accepted.

Not accepting children's books as at December 2, 2011. Check submission guidelines on website for current status.

Macmillan New Writing

Pan Macmillan Publishers
20 New Wharf Road
London
N1 9RR
Tel: +44 (0) 20 7014 6000
Fax: +44 (0) 20 7014 6001
Email: newwriting@macmillan.co.uk
Website: http://www.macmillannewwriting.com

Publishes: Fiction; *Markets:* Adult

Contact: Maria Rejt (Publishing Editor); Will Atkins (Commissioning Editor)

Initiative by a large publisher to offer an opportunity for more new authors to achieve publication through a streamlined business model. Accepts fiction for adults in all genres, between 60,000 and 130,000 words.

Send complete novel as standard word processor file (Microsoft Word preferred) as an email attachment, with synopsis and author details in body of email. Do not send multiple files or zip files. Subject line must include title of novel. No nonfiction, children's, illustrated, or previously published books (unless self-published or vanity published). State if other work has been previously published. No hardcopy submissions. Response only if interested.

Mainstream Publishing Co. (Edinburgh) Ltd
7 Albany Street
Edinburgh
EH1 3UG
Tel: +44 (0) 131 557 2959
Fax: +44 (0) 131 556 8720
Email: seonaid.macleod@mainstream publishing.com
Website:
http://www.mainstreampublishing.com

Publishes: Nonfiction; *Areas:*
Autobiography; Biography; Crime;
Historical; Politics; Sport; *Markets:* Adult

Send query letter and synopsis with SASE or return postage in first instance.

Management Books 2000 Ltd
Forge House
Limes Road
Kemble
Cirencester
Gloucestershire
GL7 6AD
Tel: +44 (0) 1285 771 441
Fax: +44 (0) 1285 771 055
Email: info@mb2000.com
Website: http://www.mb2000.com

Publishes: Nonfiction; *Areas:* Business;
Finance; Lifestyle; Self-Help; *Markets:*
Adult

Send outline of book, including why it was written, where it would be sold and read, etc. synopsis or detailed contents page, and a couple of sample chapters. Publishes books on management, business, finance, and related topics. Welcomes new ideas.

Mandrake of Oxford
PO Box 250
Oxford
OX1 1AP
Email: mandrake@mandrake.uk.net
Website: http://mandrake.uk.net

Publishes: Fiction; Nonfiction; *Areas:* Arts;
Crime; Culture; Erotic; Health; Horror;
Lifestyle; Mystery; Philosophy; Self-Help;
Spiritual; *Markets:* Adult

Send query by post or by email. May also include synopsis. See website for full guidelines, and for examples of the kind of material published.

Mango Publishing
PO Box 13378
London
SE27 0ZN
Tel: +44 (0) 20 8480 7771
Fax: +44 (0) 20 8480 7771
Email: info@mangoprint.com
Website: http://www.mangoprint.com

Publishes: Fiction; Nonfiction; Poetry;
Areas: Autobiography; Literature; Short
Stories; Translations; *Markets:* Adult;
Treatments: Literary

Small press publishing literary works by writers from British, Caribbean, and Latin American literary traditions, including short story anthologies, poetry, novels, autobiographical work, and translations into English.

Mantra Lingua Ltd
Global House
303 Ballards Lane
London
N12 8NP
Tel: +44 (0) 20 8445 5123
Fax: +44 (0) 20 8446 7745
Email: editor@mantralingua.com
Website: http://www.mantralingua.com

Publishes: Fiction; Nonfiction; *Areas:*
Translations; *Markets:* Children's

Multilingual educational publishers of nonfiction and picture books for children up to 12 years. 1,400 words maximum (800 for children up to 7). Send submissions by email. See website for more details.

Kevin Mayhew Publishers
Buxhall
Stowmarket
Suffolk
IP14 3BW
Tel: +44 (0) 845 3881634
Fax: +44 (0) 1449 737834
Email: info@kevinmayhew.com
Website: http://www.kevinmayhew.com

Publishes: Nonfiction; *Areas:* Music; Religious; Spiritual; *Markets:* Academic; Adult; Children's

Contact: Manuscript Submissions Department

Publishes books relating to Christiantity and music, for adults, children, schools, etc. Send query with synopsis and one or two sample chapters. No approaches by telephone. See website for full guidelines.

McGraw-Hill Education EMEA
Shoppenhangers Road
Maidenhead
Berkshire
SL6 2QL
Tel: +44 (0) 1628 502720
Fax: +44 (0) 1628 635895
Email: emea_queries@mcgraw-hill.com
Website: http://www.mcgraw-hill.co.uk

Publishes: Nonfiction; *Areas:* Business; Finance; Sociology; *Markets:* Academic; Professional

Publisher of books for the professional and academic markets, particularly accounting, business, finance, and social sciences.

Meadowside Children's Books
185 Fleet Street
London
EC4A 2HS
Tel: +44 (0) 20 7400 1084
Fax: +44 (0) 20 7400 1037
Email: queries@dctbooks.co.uk

Website: http://www.meadowsidebooks.com

Publishes: Fiction; *Markets:* Children's; Youth

Contact: Submissions Editor

Publishes picture and novelty books, and junior fiction. Send complete MS with cover letter, and SAE if return of samples required. Prefers to receive material digitally, but do also send a printed copy of the story. Only replies to successful submissions.

The Merlin Press
99b Wallis Road
London
E9 5LN
Tel: +44 (0) 20 8533 5800
Email: info@merlinpress.co.uk
Website: http://www.merlinpress.co.uk

Publishes: Nonfiction; *Areas:* Historical; Philosophy; Politics; *Markets:* Adult

Publisher based in London specialising in history, philosophy, and politics.

Methuen Publishing Ltd
35 Hospital Fields Road
York
YO10 4DZ
Tel: +44 (0) 1904 624730
Fax: +44 (0) 1904 624733
Email: editorial@methuen.co.uk
Website: http://www.methuen.co.uk

Publishes: Fiction; Nonfiction; Poetry; Scripts; *Areas:* Architecture; Autobiography; Biography; Culture; Current Affairs; Film; Historical; Hobbies; How-to; Humour; Literature; Military; Philosophy; Politics; Sport; Theatre; Travel; *Markets:* Adult

No unsolicited submissions. Send query by email for information about manuscript submission policy. No children's books.

Monarch Books
Lion Hudson Plc.
Wilkinson House
Jordan Hill Road

Oxford
OX2 8DR
Tel: +44 (0) 1865 302750
Fax: +44 (0) 1865 302757
Email: info@lionhudson.com
Website: http://www.lionhudson.com/
divisions.php?division=monarch

Publishes: Fiction; Nonfiction; *Areas:*
Politics; Psychology; Religious; Spiritual;
Markets: Adult

Contact: Tony Collins, Editorial Director

Publishes a wide range of Christian books.
Welcomes unsolicited MSS, synopses, and
ideas. Accepts submissions by email.

Motor Racing Publications

PO Box 1318
Croydon
CR9 5YP
Tel: +44 (0) 20 8654 2711
Fax: +44 (0) 20 8407 0339
Email: john@mrpbooks.co.uk
Website:
http://www.motorracingpublications.co.uk

Publishes: Nonfiction; *Areas:* Historical;
Sport; *Markets:* Adult

Contact: John Blunsden (Chairman /
Editorial Head)

Send synopses and ideas for books on motor
sport history, race track driving, off-road
driving, collection and restoration of classic
and performance cars, etc.

Myriad Editions

59 Lansdowne Place
Brighton
BN3 1FL
Tel: +44 (0) 1273 720000
Fax: +44 (0) 1273 720000
Email: info@MyriadEditions.com
Website: http://www.myriadeditions.com

Publishes: Fiction; Nonfiction; Reference;
Markets: Adult

Contact: Vicky Blunden

Publishes atlases, works or graphical
nonfiction, and fiction. Send synopsis and
first three chapters by post only. No email
approaches. Include SASE if return required.
No short stories, poetry, plays, children's
books, teenage/young adult fiction or general
nonfiction.

Myrmidon Books Ltd

Submissions Dept
Myrmidon Books Ltd
Rotterdam House
116 Quayside
Newcastle upon Tyne
NE1 3DY
Tel: +44 (0) 191 2064005
Fax: +44 (0) 191 2064001
Email: enquiries@myrmidonbooks.com
Website: http://www.myrmidonbooks.com

Publishes: Fiction; *Markets:* Adult;
Treatments: Contemporary; Literary

Send query with author bio, and first two or
three chapters. Rarely reads synopses. If
including a plot synopsis restrict to two A4
pages. No approaches by email. Include SAE
and appropriate return postage from the UK.
No nonfiction, children's books, short stories
or novellas.

New Dawn Publishers Ltd

292 Rochfords Gardens
Slough, Berkshire
SL2 5XW
Tel: +44 (0) 1753 822557
Email: newdawnpublishersltd@gmail.com
Website:
http://www.newdawnpublishersltd.co.uk

Publishes: Fiction; *Areas:* Adventure;
Crime; Current Affairs; Drama;
Entertainment; Fantasy; Gothic; Horror;
Humour; Literature; Mystery; Romance; Sci-
Fi; Short Stories; Suspense; Thrillers;
Westerns; *Markets:* Adult; Children's;
Family; Youth; *Treatments:* Commercial;
Contemporary; Dark; Light; Literary;
Mainstream; Popular; Progressive; Satirical;
Serious

Contact: Sundeep S. Parhar

A young fiction publishing house which focuses on giving student and graduate authors the opportunity they deserve.

Here it isn't the soliciting of a manuscript by literary agents that matters to us. Instead, we only accept submissions from those who have the qualifications, or those working towards acquiring them. As the only publisher in the UK to implement such a policy, we believe that the investment of time and effort to further one's self and improve the standard of one's work deserves to be rewarded.

After all, Creative Writing degrees have been offered at several institutions across the UK for so long now, but when it comes down to it, the wider publishing industry still seems to perceive these qualifications to be barely worth the paper that the award certificates are printed on. Not any more. Here we give these qualifications the credit they deserve.

So, whether you're a university student or graduate with ambitions of becoming a professional fiction author, an institute of higher education or book retailer who may be interested in getting involved, or just someone who wants to take a look at what today's emerging literary talent has to offer, then --- is here for YOU.

We accept fiction of all genres and all lengths- full length novels, novellas and short stories*. In responding to submissions we make an effort to supply constructive feedback whenever possible, citing the key reasons for our decision and outlining the strengths and weaknesses of your work. And if we do decide to take your work on, we'll be here for you, ready to give you our support and guidance whenever you need it, working closely with you at every stage of the editing process to make your work the best it can can be.

To submit your work to us, simply send up to three sample chapters and a one - paragraph blurb, together with a brief section (no more than 600 word s long) outlining your credentials and explaining why you and your work deserve to get published, to us by email. And until the 13th May 2012, unless you let us know that you don't want them to be, any submissions will also be entered into our competition, with the opportunity to get your work published in an anthology and win a cash prize!

*-those submitting short stories will need to send the entirety of the work, along with a full synopsis instead of a blurb.

Neil Wilson Publishing Ltd
G/R 19 Netherton Avenue
Glasgow
G13 1BQ
Tel: +44 (0) 1419 548007
Fax: +44 (0) 5601 504806
Email: submissions@nwp.co.uk
Website: http://www.nwp.co.uk

Publishes: Nonfiction; Reference; *Areas:* Biography; Cookery; Crime; Culture; Historical; Humour; Music; Nature; Travel; *Markets:* Adult

Welcomes approaches by email only. Publishes books of Scottish interest through a variety of imprints, including history, hill-walking, humour, food and drink (including whisky), biography, true crime, and reference. Has published fiction in the past, but longer does so. No academic, political, fiction, or technical. See website for full guidelines.

Netherworld Books
Wearne Lane
Langport
Tel: +44 (0) 845 519 7471
Email: claire@netherworldbooks.com
Website: http://www.netherworldbooks.com

Publishes: Fiction; *Areas:* Adventure; Erotic; Fantasy; Gothic; Horror; Humour; Mystery; New Age; Religious; Romance; Science; Sci-Fi; Spiritual; Suspense; Thrillers; *Markets:* Adult; Family; *Treatments:* Commercial; Contemporary; Dark; Light; Mainstream; Niche; Popular; Satirical

Contact: Claire Edwards

We are a traditional publisher looking to support new talent in the specific genres of

Horror, Science Fiction, Fantasy, Supernatural Romance and Historical Fantasy. We prefer email submissions and will not accept novels of over 100k words for first time novelists.

New Beacon Books, Ltd
76 Stroud Green Road
Finsbury Park
London
N4 3EN
Tel: +44 (0) 20 7272 4889
Fax: +44 (0) 20 7281 4662
Email: newbeaconbooks@btconnect.com

Publishes: Fiction; Nonfiction; Poetry; *Areas:* Culture; Historical; Politics; *Markets:* Adult

Publishes a range of fiction, nonfiction, and poetry, all concerning black people. No unsolicited MSS.

Northumbria University Press
Trinity Building
Northumbria University
Newcastle upon Tyne
NE1 8ST
Tel: +44 (0) 1912 274603
Email: andrew.peden-smith@northumbria.ac.uk
Website: http://www.northumbria.ac.uk/sd/central/its/uni_press/

Publishes: Nonfiction; *Areas:* Arts; Biography; Culture; Leisure; Music; Nature; Photography; Sport; *Markets:* Adult

Contact: Andrew Peden Smith

Emphasis on popular culture. Send query with up up to three sample chapters and completed Initial Author Questionnaire (available to download from website).

Nosy Crow
The Crow's Nest
11 The Chandlery
50 Westminster Bridge Road
London
SE1 7QY
Tel: +44 (0) 20 7953 7677

Fax: +44 (0) 20 7953 7673
Email: adrian@nosycrow.com
Website: http://nosycrow.com

Publishes: Fiction; Nonfiction; *Markets:* Children's

Contact: Adrian Soar

Publishes fiction and nonfiction for children aged 0-14, plus Apps. For short works (picture/novelty books) send complete text; otherwise send query by email or post with synopsis and first chapter. See website for full guidelines.

O Books/John Hunt Publishing Ltd
Laurel House
Station Approach
Alresford
Hampshire
SO24 9JH
Email: trevor.greenfield@o-books.net
Website: http://www.o-books.com

Publishes: Fiction; Nonfiction; Poetry; Reference; *Areas:* Antiques; Architecture; Arts; Autobiography; Biography; Business; Cookery; Crafts; Criticism; Finance; Health; Historical; Hobbies; Humour; Lifestyle; Medicine; Music; Nature; Philosophy; Photography; Politics; Psychology; Religious; Science; Self-Help; Sociology; Spiritual; Sport; Technology; Travel; *Markets:* Adult; Children's

Contact: Trevor Greenfield

Send query by email with info about you and the work, and as much text as you have, as a Microsoft Word attachment. Do not send from a Mac, in rich text, or as a zip file. See website for full details.

Michael O'Mara Books Ltd
9 Lion Yard
Tremadoc Road
London
SW4 7NQ
Tel: +44 (0) 20 7720 8643
Fax: +44 (0) 20 7627 4900
Email: enquiries@mombooks.com

Website: http://www.mombooks.com

Publishes: Nonfiction; *Areas:* Biography; Historical; Humour; *Markets:* Adult; Children's

Independent publisher dealing in general nonfiction, royal and celebrity biographies, humour, and anthologies, and books for children through its imprint (including quirky nonfiction, humour, novelty, picture, and board books). Welcomes ideas, and prefers synopses and sample text to unsolicited mss. No fiction. See website for full details.

Oberon Books
521 Caledonian Road
London
N7 9RH
Tel: +44 (0) 20 7607 3637
Fax: +44 (0) 20 7607 3629
Email: andrew@oberonbooks.com
Website: http://www.oberonbooks.com

Publishes: Nonfiction; Scripts; *Areas:* Drama; Theatre; *Markets:* Adult

Contact: Andrew Walby, Senior Editor

Publishes play texts, and books on dance and theatre. Specialises in translations of European classics and contemporary plays, though also publishes edited performance versions of classics including Shakespeare. Play texts are usually published in conjunction with a production.

Octagon Press Ltd
78 York Street
London
W1H 1DP
Tel: +44 (0) 20 7193 6456
Fax: +44 (0) 20 7117 3955
Email: admin@octagonpress.com
Website: http://www.octagonpress.com

Publishes: Fiction; Nonfiction; *Areas:* Biography; Literature; Philosophy; Psychology; Travel; *Markets:* Adult

Enquire in writing only. Interested in Eastern culture. Publishes Eastern religion, translation of Eastern classics, philosophy, travel, psychology, and research monographs in series. No unsolicted MSS.

Octopus Publishing Group Limited
Endeavour House
189 Shaftesbury Avenue
London
WC2H 8JY
Tel: +44 (0) 20 7632 5400
Fax: +44 (0) 20 7632 5405
Email: publisher@octopus-publishing.co.uk
Website: http://www.octopus-publishing.co.uk

Publishes: Nonfiction; Reference; *Areas:* Antiques; Architecture; Arts; Cookery; Crafts; Culture; Design; Film; Gardening; Health; Historical; Humour; Lifestyle; Music; Psychology; Spiritual; Sport; Travel; *Markets:* Adult

Publisher with wide range of imprints dealing with a variety of nonfiction and reference subjects. See website for specific email addresses dedicated to each individual imprint.

Old Street Publishing Ltd
Trebinshun House
Bwlch
Brecon
Powys
LD3
Tel: +44 (0) 1884 861765
Email: info@oldstreetpublishing.co.uk
Website: http://www.oldstreetpublishing.co.uk

Publishes: Fiction; Nonfiction; *Areas:* Crime; Humour; Thrillers; Translations; *Markets:* Adult; *Treatments:* Commercial; Literary; Mainstream

Contact: David Reynolds (Chairman); Ben Yarde-Buller (Managing Director)

Publisher of fiction, nonfiction, and the "better sort" of humour. No poetry, children's, or technical. No unsolicited MSS, but welcomes synopses and ideas by email.

Omnibus Press

14/15 Berners Street
London
W1T 3LJ
Tel: +44 (0) 20 7612 7400
Fax: +44 (0) 20 7612 7545
Email: info@omnibuspress.com
Website: http://www.omnibuspress.com

Publishes: Nonfiction; *Areas:* Biography;
Music; *Markets:* Adult

Contact: Chris Charlesworth

Publisher of music books, including song
sheets and rock and pop biographies.
Welcomes ideas, synopses, and unsolicited
MSS for appropriate books.

Oneworld Publications

10 Bloomsbury Street
London
WC1B 3SR
Tel: +44 (0) 20 7307 8900
Email: submissions@oneworld-
publications.com
Website: http://www.oneworld-
publications.com

Publishes: Fiction; Nonfiction; *Areas:*
Biography; Business; Current Affairs;
Historical; Philosophy; Politics; Psychology;
Religious; Science; Self-Help; *Markets:*
Adult; *Treatments:* Commercial; Literary

Nonfiction authors must be academics and/or
experts in their field. Approaches for fiction
must provide a clear and concise synopsis,
outlining the novel's main themes. See
website for full submission guidelines, and
forms for fiction and nonfiction, which may
be submitted by email.

Onlywomen Press Ltd

40d St Lawrence Terrace
London
W10 5ST
Tel: +44 (0) 20 8354 0796
Fax: +44 (0) 20 8960 2817
Email: onlywomenpress@btconnect.com
Website: http://onlywomenpress.com

Publishes: Fiction; Nonfiction; Poetry;
Areas: Women's Interests; *Markets:* Adult;
Treatments: Literary

Send query with SASE, author bio, intended
market, and synopsis. Not currently
accepting poetry. Prose writers should send
only the first 60 pages of novels or of nonfiction. Queries accepted by email, but no
electronic submissions, by email, disk, or
other (hard copy MSS only).

Publishes consistent with a feminist
perpective: feminist fiction, nonfiction and
poetry. Priority given to lesbian authors.

Open Gate Press

51 Achilles Road
London
NW6 1DZ
Tel: +44 (0) 20 7431 4391
Fax: +44 (0) 20 7431 5129
Email: books@opengatepress.co.uk
Website: http://www.opengatepress.co.uk

Publishes: Nonfiction; *Areas:* Culture;
Literature; Nature; Philosophy; Politics;
Psychology; Religious; Sociology; *Markets:*
Adult

Aims to provide a forum for psychoanalytic
social studies. Publishes books on
psychoanalysis, philosophy, social sciences,
politics, literature, religion, and environment.

The Orion Publishing Group Limited

Orion House
5 Upper Saint Martin's Lane
London
WC2H 9EA
Tel: +44 (0) 20 7240 3444
Fax: +44 (0) 20 7240 4822
Website: http://www.orionbooks.co.uk

Publishes: Fiction; Nonfiction; Reference;
Areas: Adventure; Archaeology; Arts;
Autobiography; Beauty and Fashion;
Biography; Cookery; Culture; Current
Affairs; Design; Fantasy; Gardening; Health;
Historical; Lifestyle; Literature; Military;
Nature; Sci-Fi; Sport; Travel; *Markets:*
Adult; Children's; Youth; *Treatments:*
Commercial

One of the UK's leading commercial publishers. Accepts approaches through agents only.

Oversteps Books

6 Halwell House
South Pool
Nr Kingsbridge
Devon
TQ7 2RX
Email: alwynmarriage@overstepsbooks.com
Website: http://www.overstepsbooks.com

Publishes: Poetry; *Markets:* Adult

Poetry publisher. Send email with copies of three poems that have been published in magazines or won competitions, along with details of dates or issue numbers and email addresses of the editors. Include poems and information in the body of your email.

Peter Owen Publishers

20 Holland Park Avenue
London
W11 3QU
Tel: +44 (0) 20 8350 1775
Fax: +44 (0) 20 8340 9488
Email: admin@peterowen.com
Website: http://www.peterowen.com

Publishes: Fiction; Nonfiction; *Areas:* Arts; Biography; Criticism; Historical; Literature; Translations; *Markets:* Adult; *Treatments:* Literary

Contact: Antonia Owen (Editorial Director)

Publishes general nonfiction and international literary fiction. No first novels, short stories, poetry, plays, sport, spirituality, self-help, or children's or genre fiction. Prefers query by email or alternatively by post with return postage, including cover letter, synopsis, and one or two sample chapters. Prefers fiction to come from an agent or translator as appropriate.

Oxford University Press

Great Clarendon Street
Oxford
OX2 6DP

Tel: +44 (0) 1865 556767
Fax: +44 (0) 1865 556646
Email: webenquiry.uk@oup.com
Website: http://www.oup.com

Publishes: Fiction; Nonfiction; Reference; *Areas:* Current Affairs; Drama; Finance; Historical; Legal; Literature; Medicine; Music; Philosophy; Politics; Religious; Science; Sociology; *Markets:* Academic; Adult; Children's; Professional

Publishes academic works including journals, schoolbooks, dictionaries, reference works, classics, and children's fiction, and nonfiction. Email addresses for editorial available on website.

PaperBooks Ltd.

2 London Wall Buildings
London
EC2M 5UU
Tel: +44 (0) 20 7448 5137
Email: submissions@legend-paperbooks.co.uk
Website: http://www.paperbooks.co.uk

Publishes: Fiction; *Markets:* Adult; *Treatments:* Contemporary

Acquired by fellow independent publisher in 2008. Send query by email with synopsis and three chapters.

Parthian Books

426 Grove Extension
Swansea University
Singleton Park
Swansea
SA2 8PP
Tel: +44 (0) 1792 606605
Email: Lucy@parthianbooks.co.uk
Website: http://www.parthianbooks.co.uk

Publishes: Fiction; Poetry; Scripts; *Areas:* Drama; Short Stories; Translations; *Markets:* Adult

Contact: Lucy Llewellyn

Publisher of poetry, drama, and fiction, of Welsh origin, in the English language. Also publishes English language translations of

Welsh language work. Send query with SAE, one-page synopsis, and first 30 pages. No email submissions. See website for full submission guidelines.

Pavilion Publishing

Rayford House
School Road
Hove
East Sussex
BN3 5HX
Tel: +44 (0) 1273 434943
Fax: +44 (0) 1273 227308
Email: info@pavpub.com
Website: http://www.pavpub.com

Publishes: Nonfiction; Reference; *Areas:* Health; Sociology; *Markets:* Professional

Publishes books and resources for public, private and voluntary workers in the health, social care, education and community safety sectors.

Pen & Sword Books Ltd

47 Church Street
Barnsley
South Yorkshire
S70 2AS
Tel: +44 (0) 1226 734555
Fax: +44 (0) 1226 734438
Email: editorialoffice@pen-and-sword.co.uk
Website: http://www.pen-and-sword.co.uk

Publishes: Fiction; Nonfiction; *Areas:* Adventure; Archaeology; Autobiography; Biography; Crime; Historical; Military; Sociology; Travel; *Markets:* Adult

Submissions of unsolicited synopses and ideas welcomed, but no unsolicited MSS. Publishes across a number of areas including military, aviation, maritime, family, local, true crime and transport history. Also launching historical fiction, adventure and discovery, archaeology and social history imprints. Send query by email with synopsis and sample chapter.

Pennant Books Ltd

PO Box 5675
London

W1A 3FB
Tel: +44 (0) 20 7387 6400
Email: editor@pennantbooks.com
Website: http://www.pennantbooks.com

Publishes: Nonfiction; *Areas:* Biography; Crime; Culture; Sport; *Markets:* Adult

Contact: Paul A Woods, Editor

Send initial query by email. No fiction, unsolicited MSS, or books for children. See website for full submission guidelines.

Phaidon Press Limited

Regent's Wharf
All Saints Street
London
N1 9PA
Tel: +44 (0) 20 7843 1000
Fax: +44 (0) 20 7843 1010
Email: submissions@phaidon.com
Website: http://www.phaidon.com

Publishes: Nonfiction; *Areas:* Architecture; Arts; Beauty and Fashion; Cookery; Culture; Design; Film; Historical; Music; Photography; Travel, *Markets:* Academic; Adult; Children's

Publishes books in the areas of art, architecture, design, photography, film, fashion, contemporary culture, decorative arts, music, performing arts, cultural history, food and cookery, travel and books for children. No fiction or approaches by post. Send query by email only, with CV and short description of the project.

Phoenix Yard Books

65 King's Cross Road
London
WC1X 9LW
Tel: +44 (0) 20 7239 4968
Email: submissions@phoenixyardbooks.com
Website: http://www.phoenixyardbooks.com

Publishes: Fiction; Nonfiction; Poetry; *Markets:* Children's; Youth; *Treatments:* Literary

Contact: Emma Langley

Publishes picture books, fiction, poetry, nonfiction and illustration for children aged around three to thirteen. Considers books of all genres, but leans more towards the literary and of the fiction spectrum. Particularly interested in character-based series, and fiction appealing to boys aged 6-9. Does not concentrate on young adult fiction, but will consider older fiction as part of epic series, sagas or trilogies. Send query by post with SAE or by email, with synopsis and three sample chapters. See website for full submission guidelines. Replies to email queries only if interested.

Piatkus Books
Piatkus Submissions
Little, Brown Book Group
100 Victoria Embankment
London
EC4Y 0DY
Tel: +44 (0) 20 7911 8030
Fax: +44 (0) 20 7911 8100
Email: info@littlebrown.co.uk
Website: http://www.piatkus.co.uk

Publishes: Fiction; Nonfiction; *Areas:* Autobiography; Biography; Business; Crime; Health; Historical; Humour; Lifestyle; Psychology; Self-Help; Spiritual; Thrillers; *Markets:* Adult; *Treatments:* Light; Popular; Serious

Contact: Gill Bailey (Nonfiction); Emma Beswetherick (Fiction)

No longer accepts unsolicited submissions. Accepts material through a literary agent only.

Piccadilly Press
5 Castle Road
London
NW1 8PR
Tel: +44 (0) 20 7267 4492
Fax: +44 (0) 20 7267 4493
Email: books@piccadillypress.co.uk
Website: http://www.piccadillypress.co.uk

Publishes: Fiction; Nonfiction; *Areas:* Humour; *Markets:* Children's; Youth; *Treatments:* Contemporary; Light

Publishes a range of titles, including parental books, but for new titles focuses on three main areas: picture books for children aged 2 to 5; teen fiction; and teen nonfiction.

Picture books should be character led and between 500 and 1,000 words. No novelty books. Prefers authors to be familiar with other books published before submitting – a catalogue is available upon request.

Publishes teen fiction and nonfiction which is contemporary, humorous, and deals with the issues faced by teenagers. Usually 25,000-35,000 words.

Send letter with SAE and entire MS for picture books, or synopsis and a couple of chapters for longer books, double-spaced. Do not send disks. No submissions by email.

Plexus Publishing Limited
25 Mallinson Road
London
SW11 1BW
Tel: +44 (0) 20 7924 4662
Fax: +44 (0) 20 7924 5096
Email: info@plexusuk.demon.co.uk
Website: http://www.plexusbooks.com

Publishes: Nonfiction; *Areas:* Biography; Culture; Film; Music; *Markets:* Adult; *Treatments:* Popular

Publishes illustrated nonfiction books specialising in biography, popular culture, movies and music.

Pluto Publishing Ltd
345 Archway Road
London
N6 5AA
Tel: +44 (0) 20 8348 2724
Fax: +44 (0) 20 8348 9133
Email: pluto@plutobooks.com
Website: http://www.plutobooks.com

Publishes: Nonfiction; *Areas:* Anthropology; Culture; Current Affairs; Finance; Historical; Legal; Media; Nature; Politics; Sociology; *Markets:* Academic

Contact: Anne Beech; David Castle; Roger van Zwanenberg

Academic press publishing books for students and academics in higher education. Consult website for appropriate commissioning editor to submit your proposal to, then contact by email giving outline of book, synopsis and table of contents, format and delivery estimate, plus market info (see website for more information).

Pocket Mountains
Jenny Wren
Holm Street
Moffat
Dumfries and Gallloway
DG10 9EB
Tel: +44 (0) 1683 221641
Email: info@pocketmountains.com
Website: http://www.pocketmountains.com

Publishes: Nonfiction; *Areas:* Adventure; Leisure; Nature; Travel; *Markets:* Adult

Contact: Robbie Porteous; April Simmons

Publisher of outdoor books, including guides on mountaineering, walking, and cycling in Scotland and Europe, plus wildlife books. Send query by email or by post with SAE, including outline, draft couple of pages (up to about 1,000 words), and author info and experience.

The Policy Press
University of Bristol
Fourth Floor
Beacon House
Queen's Road
Bristol
BS8 1QU
Tel: +44 (0) 117 331 4054
Fax: +44 (0) 117 331 4093
Email: tpp-info@bristol.ac.uk
Website: http://www.policypress.co.uk

Publishes: Nonfiction; *Areas:* Sociology; *Markets:* Academic; Professional

Publishes monographs, texts and journals for scholars internationally; reports for policy makers, professionals and researchers; and practice guides for practitioners and user groups. Aims to publish the latest policy research for the whole policy studies community, including academics, policy makers, practitioners and students. Welcomes proposals for books, reports, guides or journals. Author guidelines available on website.

Portland Press Ltd
Third floor
Charles Darwin House
12 Roger Street
London
WC1N 2JU
Tel: +44 (0) 20 7685 2410
Fax: +44 (0) 20 7685 2469
Email: editorial@portlandpress.com
Website: http://www.portlandpress.com

Publishes: Nonfiction; *Areas:* Medicine; Science; *Markets:* Academic; Adult

Publisher of books on biochemistry and medicine, mainly for graduate, post-graduate, and research students, but increasingly also for schools and general readership. Welcomes synopses, ideas, and unsolicited MSS. No fiction.

Prestel Publishing Ltd
4 Bloomsbury Place
London
WC1A 2QA
Tel: +44 (0) 20 7323 5004
Fax: +44 (0) 20 7636 8004
Email: sales@prestel-uk.co.uk
Website: http://www.prestel.com

Publishes: Nonfiction; *Areas:* Architecture; Arts; Beauty and Fashion; Design; Photography; *Markets:* Adult; Children's

German publisher of art, architecture, photography, design, cultural history, and ethnography, with offices in the UK and USA. Welcomes unsolicited MSS and synopses by post or email.

Profile Books
3A Exmouth House

Pine Street
Exmouth Market
London
EC1R OJH
Tel: +44 (0) 20 7841 6300
Fax: +44 (0) 20 7833 3969
Email: info@profilebooks.co.uk
Website: http://www.profilebooks.co.uk

Publishes: Nonfiction; *Areas:* Biography;
Business; Culture; Current Affairs; Finance;
Historical; Humour; Politics; Psychology;
Science; *Markets:* Adult

Award-winning small publisher noted for
author-friendly relations. Published the
number-one Christmas bestseller in 2003.
Recommends approaches be through a
literary agent.

Psychology Press
27 Church Road
Hove
East Sussex
BN3 2FA
Tel: +44 (0) 20 7017 7747
Fax: +44 (0) 20 7017 6717
Website: http://www.psypress.com

Publishes: Nonfiction; *Areas:* Psychology;
Markets: Academic; Professional

Publishes academic and professional books
and journals on psychology. Use book
proposal submission form on website, or
send hard copy submission following
guidelines on website.

Quercus Books
55 Baker Street, 7th Floor
South Block
London
W1U 8EW
Tel: +44 (0) 20 7291 7200
Email: enquiries@quercusbooks.co.uk
Website: http://www.quercusbooks.co.uk

Publishes: Fiction; Nonfiction; *Areas:*
Crime; Fantasy; Sci-Fi; *Markets:* Adult;
Children's

Publishes fiction and nonfiction. Does not
accept unsolicited submissions at this time.

Quiller Publishing Ltd
Wykey House
Wykey
Shrewsbury
Shropshire
SY4 1JA
Tel: +44 (0) 1939 261616
Fax: +44 (0) 1939 261606
Email: admin@quillerbooks.com
Website:
http://www.countrybooksdirect.com

Publishes: Nonfiction; Reference; *Areas:*
Architecture; Biography; Business; Cookery;
Gardening; Humour; Sport; Travel; *Markets:*
Adult

Contact: John Beaton

Publishes books for all lovers of fishing,
shooting, equestrian and country pursuits.
Accepts unsolicited MSS from authors. Send
submissions as hard copy only, with email
address for reply or SAE if return of ms is
required.

Radcliffe Publishing Ltd
Unit C5, Sunningdale House,
Caldecotte Lake Business Park,
43 Caldecotte Lake Drive,
Milton Keynes
MK7 8LF
Tel: +44 (0) 1908 277177
Fax: +44 (0) 1908 278297
Email:
gillian.nineham@radcliffepublishing.com
Website: http://www.radcliffe-oxford.com

Publishes: Nonfiction; *Areas:* Health;
Medicine; *Markets:* Professional

Contact: Gillian Nineham (Editorial
Director)

Publishes books on medicine, including
health care policy and management, and also
training materials. Welcomes synopses,
ideas, and unsolicited MSS.

Ragged Bears Limited
Unit 14A
Bennett's Field Trading Estate
Southgate Road

Wincanton
Somerset
BA9 9DT
Tel: +44 (0) 1963 34300
Email: info@raggedbears.co.uk
Website: http://www.raggedbears.co.uk

Publishes: Fiction; *Markets:* Children's;
Youth

Publishes picture books and novelty books,
up to young teen fiction. Accepts
submissions by post with SAE (no original
artwork), but prefers submissions by email.

Ramsay Publishing

17 Castle Heather Drive
Inverness
Email: submissions@ramsaypublishing.com

Publishes: Fiction; *Areas:* Adventure;
Entertainment; Humour; Sci-Fi; Short
Stories; *Markets:* Children's; Family;
Treatments: Mainstream; Popular

Contact: Aaron Ramsay

Brand new publisher starting up dealing
solely with electronic media. Please note, we
do not publish printed books in any form.

Specifically looking for new children's
books, pictures books and any books rich in
graphics and media. Our new cutting edge
service turns standard print books into fully
interactive digital products which can be sold
for laptops/computer, android phones and
pads, iPhones and iPads, Meego, Blackberry
and more.

All conversion is done by us - submission
need only be artwork with accompanying
stories. Full voice over service available.
Complete projects are fully interactive and
read aloud the book with rich graphics,
interactive animation, sounds and even
questions/activities about page content.

Books will never die, but we aim to help
bring them back into the current generation.

Note, you must own all the rights to your
work for publication, however existing print

publications are acceptable if this criteria is
met.

Ransom Publishing Ltd

Radley House
8 St Cross Road
Winchester
Hampshire
SO23 9HX
Tel: +44 (0) 1962 862307
Fax: +44 (0) 5601 148881
Email: ransom@ransom.co.uk
Website: http://www.ransom.co.uk

Publishes: Fiction; Nonfiction; *Markets:*
Adult; Children's; Professional; Youth

An independent specialist publisher of high
quality, inspirational books that encourage
and help children, young adults, and adults to
develop their reading skills. Books are
intended to have content which is age
appropriate and engaging, but reading levels
that would normally be appropriate for
younger readers. Also publishes resources
for both the library and classroom. Will
consider unsolicited mss. Email in first
instance.

Reed Business Information (RBI)

Tel: +44 (0) 20 8652 3500
Email: webmaster@rbi.co.uk
Website: http://www.reedbusiness.com

Publishes: Nonfiction; *Areas:* Business;
Culture; Current Affairs; Entertainment;
Finance; Media; Politics; Science; Travel;
Markets: Professional

Publishes a range of information and data
services for professionals in a range of
sectors.

Rivers Oram Press

144 Hemingford Road
London
N1 1DE
Tel: +44 (0) 20 7607 0823
Fax: +44 (0) 20 7609 2776
Email: ro@riversoram.com
Website: http://www.riversoram.com

Publishes: Nonfiction; *Areas:* Culture; Current Affairs; Historical; Politics; Sociology; Women's Interests; *Markets:* Adult

Publisher of social and political sciences, including sexual politics, gender studies, social history, cultural studies, and current affairs.

Robert Hale Publishers

Clerkenwell House
45-47 Clerkenwell Green
London
EC1R 0HT
Tel: +44 (0) 20 7251 2661
Fax: +44 (0) 20 7490 4958
Email: submissions@halebooks.com
Website: http://www.halebooks.com

Publishes: Fiction; Nonfiction; Reference; *Areas:* Arts; Autobiography; Biography; Cookery; Crime; Historical; Humour; Leisure; Military; Spiritual; Westerns; *Markets:* Adult

Currently considering General Fiction, Crime, Westerns, Equestrian books, and Nonfiction titles. See website for list of material NOT currently accepted. Send query with synopsis and three sample chapters.

Sage Publications

1 Oliver's Yard
55 City Road
London
EC1Y 1SP
Tel: +44 (0) 20 7324 8500
Fax: +44 (0) 20 7324 8600
Email: info@sagepub.co.uk
Website: http://www.sagepub.co.uk

Publishes: Nonfiction; *Areas:* Anthropology; Archaeology; Arts; Business; Crime; Finance; Health; Historical; Media; Medicine; Politics; Psychology; Religious; Science; Sociology; Technology; *Markets:* Academic; Professional

Publishes academic books and journals. See website for guides for authors and making submissions, etc.

SalGad Publishing Group

Redditch
Worcestershire
Email: info@salgad.com
Website: http://www.salgadpublishing.com

Publishes: Fiction; *Areas:* Crime; Drama; Horror; Mystery; Romance; Thrillers; *Markets:* Adult; Youth; *Treatments:* Commercial; Contemporary; Dark; Light; Mainstream; Popular

Contact: Sally Stote

A publisher dedicated to 'helping writers make a living'.

We are a group of young and enthusiastic people that understand the current generation's reliance upon technology and "social media". While older publishers are struggling to adapt their old ways and outdated methods, we are fully prepared for the digital revolution of the book industry.

One of our founding members is an already-established writer that has found great success himself through the sale of his ebooks and by exploiting social media's marketing prowess. Our other members include a world-class artist, a successful businesswoman, and several other people directly involved in publishing.

Please see our why choose us page on our website.

Salt Publishing Ltd

12 Norwich Road
CROMER
Norfolk
NR27 0AX
Tel: +44 (0) 1263 511011
Email: submissions@saltpublishing.com
Website: http://www.saltpublishing.com

Publishes: Fiction; *Areas:* Crime; Gothic; Literature; Thrillers; *Markets:* Adult; *Treatments:* Dark; Literary; Mainstream; Traditional

Must be in English and aimed at a British market, and should be under 80,000 words. Not currently accepting short stories, poetry, fantasy or memoirs. Send query by email with biographical note up to 80 words, exciting 250 word description, and six bullet points up to 15 words each explaining why British booksellers would want to sell your novel. Full submission guidelines on website.

Science Navigation Group
Middlesex House
34-42 Cleveland Street
London
W1T 4LB
Tel: +44 (0) 20 7323 0323
Fax: +44 (0) 20 7580 1938
Email: info@sciencenavigation.com
Website: http://www.sciencenavigation.com

Publishes: Nonfiction; *Areas:* Medicine; Science; *Markets:* Academic; Adult; Professional

Publishes material for the biomedical community, aimed at physicians, scientists, pharmaceutical companies, patients, students and the general public.

SCM-Canterbury Press
Hymns Ancient and Modern Ltd
3rd Floor
Invicta House
108-114 Golden Lane
London
EC1Y 0TG
Tel: +44 (0) 20 7776 7540
Fax: +44 (0) 20 7776 7556
Email: christine@hymnsam.co.uk
Website: http://www.canterburypress.co.uk

Publishes: Nonfiction; Reference; *Areas:* Philosophy; Religious; Spiritual; *Markets:* Adult

Publisher of religious nonfiction and reference. No dissertations, fiction, poetry, drama, children's books, books of specialist local interest, or (as a general rule) multi-authored collections of essays or symposium papers.

Seafarer Books
102 Redwald Road
Rendlesham
Woodbridge
Suffolk
IP12 2TE
Tel: +44 (0) 1394 420789
Fax: +44 (0) 1394 461314
Email: info@seafarerbooks.com
Website: http://www.seafarerbooks.com

Publishes: Fiction; Nonfiction; *Areas:* Arts; Crafts; Historical; How-to; Military; Music; Travel; *Markets:* Adult; *Treatments:* Traditional

Contact: Patricia Eve

Publishes fiction and nonfiction books on sailing, including maritime history, practical seamanship and boatbuilding, etc. Also music CDs, cards, and calendars. No unsolicited MSS. Send query in first instance.

Seren
57 Nolton Street
Bridgend
Wales
CF31 3AE
Tel: +44 (0) 1656 663018
Fax: +44 (0) 1656 649226
Email: Info@SerenBooks.com
Website: http://www.serenbooks.com

Publishes: Fiction; Nonfiction; Poetry; *Areas:* Anthropology; Arts; Biography; Criticism; Current Affairs; Drama; Historical; Music; Photography; Politics; Sport; Translations; Travel; *Markets:* Adult; Children's; *Treatments:* Literary

Unsolicited MSS, synopses, and ideas welcomed. Specialises in English-language writing from Wales and aims to bring Welsh culture, art, literature, and politics to a wider audience. Accepts nonfiction submissions only by email; no poetry or fiction submissions by email. See website for complete submission guidelines.

Shearsman Books
50 Westons Hill Drive
Emersons Green
Bristol

BS16 7DF
Tel: +44 (0) 1179 572957
Email: editor@shearsman.com
Website: http://www.shearsman.com

Publishes: Nonfiction; Poetry; *Areas:*
Autobiography; Criticism; Literature;
Translations; *Markets:* Adult

Contact: Tony Frazer

Publishes poetry books of 70-72 A5 pages.
Publishes mainly poetry by British, Irish,
North American and Australian/New
Zealand poets, plus poetry in translation
from any language—although particular
interest in German, Spanish and Latin
American poetry.

Submit only if MS is of appropriate length
and most of it has already appeared in UK or
US magazines of some repute. Send
selection of 10 poems or 10 pages
(whichever is shorter) by post with SASE or
by email with material embedded in the text
or as PDF attachment. No other kind of
attachments accepted.

Also sometimes publishes literary criticism
on poetry, and essays or memoirs by poets.

Sheldrake Press

188 Cavendish Road
London
SW12 0DA
Tel: +44 (0) 20 8675 1767
Fax: +44 (0) 20 8675 7736
Email: enquiries@sheldrakepress.co.uk
Website: http://www.sheldrakepress.co.uk

Publishes: Nonfiction; *Areas:* Architecture;
Cookery; Design; Historical; Travel;
Markets: Adult

Contact: Simon Rigge, Publisher

Publisher of illustrated nonfiction titles
covering travel, history, cookery, and
stationery. Ideas and synopses welcome. No
fiction.

Shepheard-Walwyn (Publishers) Ltd

107 Parkway House
Sheen Lane
London
SW14 8LS
Tel: +44 (0) 20 8241 5927
Email: books@shepheard-walwyn.co.uk
Website: http://www.shepheard-walwyn.co.uk

Publishes: Nonfiction; Poetry; *Areas:*
Biography; Finance; Historical; Philosophy;
Politics; *Markets:* Adult

Publishes mainly nonfiction, particularly the
areas listed above and also books of Scottish
interest, and gift books in calligraphy and /
or illustrated. Also some poetry.

Short Books

3A Exmouth House
Pine St
London
EC1R OJH
Tel: +44 (0) 20 7833 9429
Email: info@shortbooks.co.uk
Website: http://shortbooks.co.uk

Publishes: Fiction; Nonfiction; *Markets:*
Adult

Cannot guarantee that all unsolicited
submissions will be read, so recommends
approach via literary agent. Will accept
direct submissions, however. Send cover
letter with synopsis and first three chapters /
roughly 30 pages by post. Include email
address or SAE for response, however
response not guaranteed.

Society of Genealogists

14 Charterhouse Buildings
Goswell Road
London
EC1M 7BA
Tel: +44 (0) 20 7251 8799
Fax: +44 (0) 20 7250 1800
Email: sales@sog.org.uk
Website: http://sog.org.uk

Publishes: Nonfiction; *Areas:* Historical;
Markets: Adult

Publishes books, magazines, and software on local and family history.

SportsBooks Limited
1 Evelyn Court
Malvern Road
Cheltenham
GL50 2JR
Tel: +44 (0) 1242 256755
Fax: +44 (0) 0560 310 8126
Email: info@sportsbooks.ltd.uk
Website: http://www.sportsbooks.ltd.uk

Publishes: Nonfiction; *Areas:* Biography; Sport; *Markets:* Adult

Welcomes submissions by hard copy or email as .txt or .rtf attachments. Send query with synopsis and up to three sample chapters, plus information on market and marketing. No fiction.

Sunberry Books
10 Aspen Close
Harriseahead
Staffordshire
ST5 9PL
Tel: +44 (0) 1692 678832
Email: query@sunpenny.com
Website: http://www.sunberrybooks.com

Publishes: Fiction; *Areas:* Adventure; Entertainment; Literature; Mystery; Religious; *Markets:* Children's; Youth; *Treatments:* Literary

We believe that while we are going to be spending a lot of time and effort getting your book into shape for publication, and on follow-through afterwards, it's still your book - you provide the manuscript, we publish at our expense, and do what marketing we can while you do your bit too.

Sunflower Books
Commissioning Editor
Sunflower Books
PO Box 36160
London
SW7 3HG
Email: mail@sunflowerbooks.co.uk
Website: http://www.sunflowerbooks.co.uk

Publishes: Nonfiction; *Areas:* Leisure; Travel; *Markets:* Adult

Publishes walking guides only. Authors are advised to submit a proposal (hard copy by post only) before starting work on a book, as the format must match that of existing titles. No proposals by email.

Sussex Academic Press
PO Box 139
Eastbourne
East Sussex
BN24 9BP
Tel: +44 (0) 1323 479220
Fax: +44 (0) 1323 478185
Email: edit@sussex-academic.com
Website: http://www.sussex-academic.com

Publishes: Nonfiction; *Areas:* Anthropology; Archaeology; Arts; Biography; Criticism; Culture; Drama; Finance; Historical; Literature; Media; Music; Nature; Philosophy; Politics; Psychology; Religious; Sociology; Theatre; Women's Interests; *Markets:* Academic

Contact: Anthony V, P, Grahame, Editorial Director

Academic publisher. Send query by post. Book proposal form available on website. No unsolicited MSS.

TSO (The Stationery Office)
St Crispins
Duke Street
Norwich
NR3 1PD
Tel: +44 (0) 1603 622211
Email: customer.services@tso.co.uk
Website: http://www.tso.co.uk

Publishes: Nonfiction; Reference; *Areas:* Business; Current Affairs; Medicine; *Markets:* Professional

One of the largest publishers by volume in the UK, publishing more than 9,000 titles a year in print and digital formats.

Taylor & Francis Books
4 Park Square
Milton Park
Abingdon
Oxfordshire
OX14 4RN
Tel: +44 (0) 20 7017 6000
Fax: +44 (0) 20 7017 6336
Email: info@tandf.co.uk
Website:
http://www.taylorandfrancisgroup.com

Publishes: Nonfiction; *Markets:* Academic

Publishes everything from core text books to research monographs, mainly at university level.

Thames and Hudson Ltd
181A High Holborn
London
WC1V 7QX
Tel: +44 (0) 20 7845 5000
Fax: +44 (0) 20 7845 5050
Email: editorial@thameshudson.co.uk
Website: http://www.thamesandhudson.com

Publishes: Nonfiction; Reference; *Areas:* Archaeology; Architecture; Arts; Beauty and Fashion; Biography; Culture; Design; Gardening; Historical; Photography; Religious; Travel; *Markets:* Adult

Publishes illustrated nonfiction only. No fiction. Send query by email with short outline and CV in the body of the email. No attachments.

Tiger of the Stripe
50 Albert Road
Richmond
Surrey
TW10 6DP
Tel: +44 (0) 20 8940 8087
Email: peter@tigerofthestripe.co.uk
Website: http://www.tigerofthestripe.co.uk

Publishes: Fiction; Nonfiction; Poetry; *Areas:* Antiques; Archaeology; Architecture; Arts; Autobiography; Biography; Business; Cookery; Crafts; Crime; Criticism; Culture; Current Affairs; Design; Drama; Entertainment; Film; Finance; Gardening;

Health; Historical; Hobbies; How-to; Humour; Legal; Leisure; Lifestyle; Literature; Media; Medicine; Military; Music; Mystery; Nature; Photography; Politics; Psychology; Radio; Religious; Romance; Science; Self-Help; Short Stories; Suspense; Technology; Theatre; Thrillers; Translations; Travel; *Markets:* Academic; Adult; Professional; *Treatments:* In-depth; Literary; Popular; Serious; Traditional

Contact: Peter Danckwerts

Eclectic but with an emphasis on well-researched academic or semi-academic works. Also interested in biographies, history, language textbooks, cookbooks, typography.

Trentham Books Limited
28 Hillside Gardens
Highgate
London
N6 5ST
Tel: +44 (0) 1782 745567
Fax: +44 (0) 1782 745553
Email: Gillian@trentham-books.co.uk
Website: http://www.trentham-books.co.uk

Publishes: Nonfiction; *Areas:* Culture; Humour; Legal; Sociology; Women's Interests; *Markets:* Academic; Professional

Contact: Dr Gillian Klein

Publishes academic and professional books. No fiction, biography, or poetry. No unsolicited MSS, but accepts queries by post with SASE, or by email with your name in the subject line. See website for full guidelines.

Two Ravens Press Ltd
Taigh nam Fitheach
26 Breanish
Uig
Isle of Lewis
HS 9HB
Email: info@tworavenspress.com
Website: http://www.tworavenspress.com

Publishes: Fiction; Nonfiction; Poetry; *Markets:* Adult; *Treatments:* Contemporary;

Experimental; Progressive

Contact: Sharon Blackie (fiction / nonfiction); David Knowles (poetry)

Small independent publisher of fiction, nonfiction, and poetry, which is contemporary, cutting-edge, innovative, risk-taking, and challenging. Accepts queries by email only – see website for full guidelines.

Ulric Publishing
PO Box 55
Church Stretton
Shropshire
SY6 6WR
Tel: +44 (0) 1694 781354
Email: enquiries@ulricpublishing.com
Website: http://www.ulricpublishing.com

Publishes: Nonfiction; *Areas:* Military; Technology; Travel; *Markets:* Adult

Publishes military and motoring history.

Unicorn Press Ltd
66 Charlotte Street
LONDON
W1T 4QE
Tel: +44 (0) 7836 633377
Email: ian@unicornpress.org
Website: http://unicornpress.org

Publishes: Nonfiction; Reference; *Areas:* Architecture; Arts; Biography; Historical; *Markets:* Adult

Contact: Ian Strathcarron (Publisher)

Works with artists, authors, museums, and galleries to publish high-quality fine and decorative art reference books, guides and monographs.

University of Wales Press
10 Columbus Walk
Brigantine Place
Cardiff
CF10 4UP
Tel: +44 (0) 29 2049 6899
Fax: +44 (0) 29 2049 6108
Email: press@press.wales.ac.uk

Website: http://www.uwp.co.uk

Publishes: Nonfiction; *Areas:* Culture; Historical; Literature; Media; Nature; Philosophy; Politics; Religious; Sociology; *Markets:* Academic

Submit proposal by email at an early stage – preferably before book is written.

Wooden Books
8A Market Place
Glastonbury
BA6 8LT
Email: info@woodenbooks.com
Website: http://www.woodenbooks.com

Publishes: Nonfiction; *Areas:* Historical; Science; Spiritual; *Markets:* Adult

Publishes illustration-heavy books on such topics as ancient sciences, magic, mathematics, etc. Prospective authors will need to provide high quality illustrations. Essential to query before commencing work. Send query by email or by post. See website for full details.

Wallflower Press
4 Eastern Terrace Mews
Brighton
BN2 1EP
Email: yoram@wallflowerpress.co.uk
Website: http://www.wallflowerpress.co.uk

Publishes: Nonfiction; *Areas:* Culture; Entertainment; Film; Media; *Markets:* Academic; Adult

Contact: Yoram Allon, Consulting Editor to Columbia

Publisher of books relating to film, plus related media and culture, for both popular and academic markets. Contact by email in first instance. No fiction, or academic nonfiction which is not related to the moving image.

Acquired by a US publisher in 2011, the previous editorial and pre-production team continue to work directly with authors as an imprint of the US firm.

Welsh Academic Press

PO Box 733,
Caerdydd
Cardiff
CF14 7ZY
Tel: +44 (0) 29 2021 8187
Email: post@welsh-academic-press.com
Website: http://www.welsh-academic-press.com

Publishes: Nonfiction; *Areas:* Historical; Politics; *Markets:* Academic

Publishes academic monographs, reference works, text books and popular scholarly titles in the fields of education, history, political studies, Scandinavian and Baltic studies, contemporary work and employment, and medieval Wales. Complete questionnaire available on website.

Which? Books

2 Marylebone Road
London
NW1 4DF
Tel: +44 (0) 20 7770 7000
Fax: +44 (0) 20 7770 7600
Email: which@which.co.uk
Website: http://www.which.net

Publishes: Nonfiction; Reference; *Areas:* Finance; Gardening; Health; Legal; Lifestyle; Technology; *Markets:* Adult

Publishes books on consumer issues. Send query with outline of idea or synopsis. No unsolicited MSS.

Whittet Books Ltd

1 St John's Lane
Stansted
Essex
CM24 8JU
Tel: +44 (0) 1279 815871
Fax: +44 (0) 1279 647564
Email: mail@whittetbooks.com
Website: http://www.whittetbooks.com

Publishes: Nonfiction; *Areas:* Nature; *Markets:* Adult

Publishes books of rural interest, including horses, pets, poultry, livestock, horticulture,

natural history, etc. Send query with outline in first instance; preferably by email.

William Reed Business Media

Broadfield Park
Crawley
West Sussex
RH11 9RT
Tel: +44 (0) 1293 613400
Website: http://www.william-reed.com

Publishes: Nonfiction; Reference; *Areas:* Business; *Markets:* Professional

Publishes business to business directories and reports.

Wolters Kluwer (UK) Ltd

145 London Road
Kingston upon Thames
Surrey
KT2 6SR
Tel: +44 (0) 20 8547 3333
Fax: +44 (0) 20 8547 2637
Email: info@croner.co.uk
Website: http://www.wolterskluwer.co.uk

Publishes: Nonfiction; Reference; *Areas:* Business; Finance; Legal; *Markets:* Professional

Publishes books, looseleafs, and online services for professionals. Areas of expertise include: Human Resources, Health and Safety, Tax and Accountancy, Education and Healthcare, Manufacturing and Construction.

Woodhead Publishing Ltd

80 High Street
Sawston
Cambridge
CB22 3HJ
Tel: +44 (0) 1223 499140
Fax: +44 (0) 1223 832819
Email: wp@woodheadpublishing.com
Website: http://www.woodheadpublishing.com

Publishes: Nonfiction; *Areas:* Finance; Nature; Science; Technology; *Markets:* Adult

Publishes books on engineering, finance, environmental science, and the technologies of materials, textiles, and food. Welcomes unsolicited MSS.

Zero to Ten Limited
327 High Street
Slough
Berkshire
SL1 1TX
Tel: +44 (0) 1753 578 499
Email: annamcquinn@zerototen.co.uk

Publishes: Nonfiction; *Markets:* Children's

Contact: Anna McQuinn

Publishes nonfiction for children up to 10 years old, including board books and toddler books. Welcomes submissions, but responds only if interested.

ZigZag Education
Unit 3
Greenway Business Centre
Doncaster Road
Bristol
BS10 5PY
Tel: +44 (0) 1179 503199
Fax: +44 (0) 1179 591695
Email: support@PublishMeNow.co.uk
Website: http://www.zigzageducation.co.uk

Publishes: Nonfiction; *Areas:* Arts; Business; Design; Drama; Finance; Health; Historical; Legal; Leisure; Media; Music; Philosophy; Politics; Psychology; Religious; Science; Sociology; Sport; Technology; Travel; *Markets:* Academic; Children's; Professional; Youth

Educational publisher publishing photocopiable and digital teaching resources for schools and colleges. Register on publisher's author support website if interested in writing or contributing to resources.

Canadian Publishers

For the most up-to-date listings of these and hundreds of other publishers, visit http://www.firstwriter.com/publishers

*To claim your **free** access to the site, please see the back of this book.*

Borealis Press

8 Mohawk Crescent
Ottawa
Ontario
K2H 7G6
Tel: +1 (613) 829-0150
Fax: +1 (613) 829-7783
Email: drt@borealispress.com
Website: http://www.borealispress.com

Publishes: Fiction; Nonfiction; Poetry; Scripts; *Areas:* Adventure; Historical; Legal; Literature; Politics; Romance; Short Stories; *Markets:* Adult; Children's; Youth; *Treatments:* Contemporary; Literary; Mainstream

Publishes most genres, but specialises in Canadian authored or oriented material. Send query with SASE, synopsis/outline and sample chapter or equivalent. Material without return postage is disposed of unread.

Brighter Books Publishing House

4825 Fairbrook Cresc.
Nanaimo, B.C. V9T 6M6
Tel: +1 (250) 585-7372
Email: info@brighterbooks.com
Website: http://www.brighterbooks.com

Publishes: Fiction; Nonfiction; *Areas:* Fantasy; How-to; Sci-Fi; *Markets:* Children's; Youth

Canadian publisher with a focus on children's books and educational books. See website for full guidelines and online submission system.

Central Avenue Publishing

Delta, British Columbia
Email:
meghan@centralavenuepublishing.com
Website:
http://www.centralavenuepublishing.com

Publishes: Fiction; Poetry; *Areas:* Adventure; Arts; Autobiography; Beauty and Fashion; Biography; Crime; Culture; Current Affairs; Drama; Entertainment; Erotic; Fantasy; Gothic; Historical; Horror; Humour; Leisure; Lifestyle; Literature; Media; Men's Interests; Military; Music; Mystery; Nature; New Age; Philosophy; Photography; Politics; Psychology; Religious; Romance; Science; Sci-Fi; Self-Help; Short Stories; Sociology; Spiritual; Sport; Suspense; Technology; Theatre; Thrillers; Translations; Travel; Westerns; Women's Interests; *Markets:* Adult; Children's; Family; Youth; *Treatments:* Commercial; Contemporary; Cynical; Dark; Experimental; In-depth; Light; Literary; Mainstream; Niche; Popular; Positive; Progressive; Satirical; Serious; Traditional

Contact: Michelle Halket

Press specialising in electronic books (with

select books going into print). Fiction, poetry, short stories. Email with query, agent not necessary.

Coastal West Publishing

324-1755 Robson Street
Vancouver, British Columbia
Fax: +1 (604) 677-6651
Email: info@coastalwest.ca
Website: http://coastalwest.ca

Publishes: Nonfiction; *Areas:* Biography; Crime; Culture; Historical; Legal; Media; Short Stories; Spiritual; *Markets:* Adult; Family; Professional; *Treatments:* In-depth; Literary; Niche; Positive; Progressive; Serious

It is our goal to both educate and entertain our readers with stories that have an emphasis in and around the justice system and all of its participants. Was founded on and for the purpose of truth, encouragement, education through books.

If you have a manuscript and would like us to review it, make sure it falls into one of the following categories:

Organized Crime
Law and Policing
The Criminal Court System
The Prison System
The Parole System
Youth Gangs
Testimonials of change in any of these systems

Accepts manuscripts by snail mail, email and fax.

Has won an award of Excellence Graphic Design.

We do not accept books that are fictional or that glorify crime, criminal behaviour or illegal activities.

Submissions do not have a length required, and do not need to be passed though a literary agent.

Our staff is happy to answer any questions you may have.

Everheart Books

Email:
meghan@centralavenuepublishing.com
Website: http://www.everheartbooks.com

Publishes: Fiction; Poetry; *Areas:* Erotic; Romance; *Markets:* Adult; Family; *Treatments:* Commercial; Contemporary; Cynical; Dark; Experimental; In-depth; Light; Literary; Mainstream; Niche; Popular; Positive; Progressive; Satirical; Serious; Traditional

Contact: Meg

We publish erotica and all subgenres of romance. Send us your query and first three chapters of your story. We pay royalties quarterly. We handle everything from cover design to distribution. We'd love to take a look at your romance or erotic novel.

Fifth House Publishers

Fitzhenry & Whiteside Limited
195 Allstate Parkway
Markham, Ontario L3R 4T8
Tel: +1 (800) 387-9776
Fax: +1 (800) 260-9777
Email: stewart@fifthhousepublishers.ca
Website: http://www.fifthhousepublishers.ca

Publishes: Nonfiction; *Areas:* Culture; Historical; Nature; *Markets:* Adult

Contact: Tracey Dettman

Publishes books on Canadian history, culture, and environment, particularly focusing on the west. See website for more details.

House of Anansi Press

110 Spadina Ave., Suite 801
Toronto, ON
M5V 2K4
Tel: +1 (416) 363-4343
Fax: +1 (416) 363-1017
Email: customerservice@houseofanansi.com
Website: http://www.houseofanansi.com

Publishes: Fiction; Nonfiction; Poetry; *Markets:* Adult; *Treatments:* Literary; Serious

Publishes literary fiction, poetry, and serious nonfiction. Particular interest in Canadian writers; attitude towards international writers seems potentially contradictory:

"publishes Canadian and international writers..."

Yet further down the same page of their website:

"does not accept unsolicited materials from non-Canadian writers."

Kindred Productions

1310 Taylor Avenue
Winnipeg, MB R3M 3Z6
Tel: +1 (204) 669-6575
Fax: +1 (204) 654-1865
Email: custserv@kindredproductions.com
Website:
https://www.kindredproductions.com

Publishes: Nonfiction; *Areas:* Historical; Religious; *Markets:* Adult; Children's; Youth

Religious book publisher. Send query by email for a copy of the full submission guidelines. See website for more details.

Kids Can Press

Corus Quay
25 Dockside Drive
Toronto, Ontario
M5A 0B5
Tel: +1 (416) 479-7000
Fax: +1 (416) 960-5437
Email: customerservice@kidscan.com
Website: http://www.kidscanpress.com

Publishes: Fiction; Nonfiction; *Markets:* Children's

Publishes quality picture books and nonfiction manuscripts for children, as well as chapter books for ages 7–10. No young adult fiction or fantasy novels for any age. No unsolicited manuscripts from children or teenagers, or from authors outside of Canada. No submissions by disk, fax, or email.

Magenta Publishing for the Arts

151 Winchester Street
Toronto, Ontario
M4X 1B5
Email: info@magentafoundation.org
Website: http://www.magentafoundation.org

Publishes: Nonfiction; *Areas:* Arts; Photography; *Markets:* Adult

Established to publish works of art by Canadian and International artists.

MBooks of BC (Multicultural Books of British Columbia)

307 Birchwood Court
6311 Gilbert Road
Richmond, B.C.
V7C 3V7
Tel: +1 (604) 447-0979
Email: jrmbooks@hotmail.com
Website: http://www.mbooksofbc.com

Publishes: Fiction; Nonfiction; Poetry; *Markets:* Adult; Children's; *Treatments:* Literary

Contact: Joe M. Ruggier B.A.; Mr. Basil Nainan

Small press publishing mainly poetry and related literature. Also offers publishing services. Send query with sample or complete ms in first instance. See website for more information.

Moose Hide Books

684 Walls Road
Sault Ste. Marie
Ontario
P6A 5K6
Tel: +1 (705) 779-3331
Fax: +1 (705) 779-3331
Email: ealcid@moosehidebooks.com
Website: http://www.moosehidebooks.com

Publishes: Fiction; Nonfiction; Poetry; *Areas:* Adventure; Biography; Culture; Drama; Fantasy; Historical; Humour; Mystery; Short Stories; Suspense; Theatre; *Markets:* Adult; Children's; Youth

Contact: Edmond Alcid (Editor)

Publishes novels, short story collections, nonfiction, narrative verse, and theatrical plays for age groups children to adult. Query in first instance. See website for full details.

NeWest Press
Attn: Acquisitions
#201 8540 - 109 Street
Edmonton, Alberta T6G 1E6
Website: http://www.newestpress.com

Publishes: Fiction; Nonfiction; Poetry; Scripts; *Areas:* Drama; Historical; Literature; Nature; Politics; *Markets:* Adult; *Treatments:* Literary

Publishes fiction, poetry, drama, and nonfiction works with literary merit by established and emerging Canadian authors. Not considering poetry, mystery, or short fiction manuscripts as at May 2012 (check website for latest information). See website for submission guidelines.

Tightrope Books
602 Markham Street
Toronto, ON
M6G 2L8
Email: shirarose@tightropebooks.com
Website: http://tightropebooks.com

Publishes: Fiction; *Areas:* Short Stories; *Markets:* Adult; Youth

Contact: Shirarose Wilensky

Publishes adult and YA fiction, short fiction, creative nonfiction, and anthologies. Send queries by email only with bio and sample 10 pages. Postal submissions will not be read. No children's books, self-help books, religious books, or genre fiction (fantasy, sci-fi, mystery, crime, thriller). No simultaneous submissions. See website for full details.

TouchWood Editions
340 - 1105 Pandora Avenue
Victoria, BC, V8V 3P9

Email: info@touchwoodeditions.com
Website: http://www.touchwoodeditions.com

Publishes: Fiction; Nonfiction; *Areas:* Arts; Biography; Cookery; Culture; Gardening; Historical; Mystery; Nature; Suspense; Travel; *Markets:* Adult

Accepts submissions as hard copy by post and digitally by email. Publishes Canadian authors only. See website for full guidelines.

Tradewind Books
202-1807 Maritime Mews
Vancouver, BC
V6H 3W7
Email: tradewindbooks@mail.lycos.com
Website: http://www.tradewindbooks.com

Publishes: Fiction; Poetry; *Markets:* Children's; Youth

Writers must be able to prove that they have read at least three books from this publisher. Accepts young adult fiction from Canadian authors only, but accepts chapter books, picture books, and poetry from Canadians and non-Canadians. Send complete MS with cover letter, author bio, and SASE.

University of Ottawa Press
542 King Edward Avenue
Ottawa, ON K1N 6N5
Tel: +1 (613) 562-5800 ext. 3065
Email: enelson@uottawa.ca
Website: http://www.press.uottawa.ca

Publishes: Nonfiction; Reference; *Areas:* Arts; Autobiography; Crime; Culture; Current Affairs; Finance; Health; Historical; Legal; Literature; Media; Military; Philosophy; Politics; Psychology; Religious; Sociology; Technology; Translations; Women's Interests; *Markets:* Academic; Adult; *Treatments:* Serious

Contact: Eric Nelson, Acquisitions Editor

Publishes books for the academic market and serious general readership. Committed to bilingual publishing French/English. See website for full details.

Irish Publishers

For the most up-to-date listings of these and hundreds of other publishers, visit http://www.firstwriter.com/publishers

To claim your free access to the site, please see the back of this book.

Irish Academic Press

2 Brookside
Dundrum Road
Dublin 14
Tel: +353 (0) 1 298 9937
Fax: +353 (0) 1 298 2783
Email: info@iap.ie
Website:
http://www.irishacademicireland.com

Publishes: Nonfiction; Areas: Culture; Historical; Literature; Markets: Academic

Academic publisher based in Dublin, focusing on 19th and 20th century history, literature, heritage and culture.

John Lynch Digital Publishing House

Email:
sian@johnlynchdigitalpublishinghouse.com
Website:
http://www.johnlynchdigitalpublishinghouse.com

Publishes: Fiction; Areas: Romance; Sci-Fi; Markets: Adult; Treatments: Contemporary; Literary

Looking for novel-length literary or contemporary fiction (between 70,000 and 120,000 words). Will consider sub-genres within contemporary fiction (e.g. contemporary romance or science fiction), provided that they provide a compelling storyline and strong characters. Send query by email with synopsis and first three chapters. See website for full guidelines.

The Lilliput Press

62-63 Sitric Road
Arbour Hill
Dublin 7
Tel: +353 (01) 671 16 47
Fax: +353 (01) 671 12 33
Email: info@lilliputpress.ie
Website: http://www.lilliputpress.ie

Publishes: Fiction; Nonfiction; Poetry; Reference; Scripts; Areas: Architecture; Arts; Autobiography; Biography; Business; Cookery; Criticism; Culture; Current Affairs; Drama; Historical; Literature; Music; Nature; Philosophy; Photography; Politics; Sociology; Sport; Travel; Markets: Adult; Treatments: Literary; Popular

Publishes books broadly focused on Irish themes.

Mercier Press

Unit 3b
Oak House
Bessboro Road
Blackrock
Cork
Tel: +353 21-4614700
Email: commissioning@mercierpress.ie

Website: http://www.mercierpress.ie

Publishes: Fiction; Nonfiction; Areas:
Autobiography; Biography; Business;
Cookery; Current Affairs; Health; Historical;
Humour; Lifestyle; Military; Politics;
Religious; Sport; Markets: Adult; Children's

Contact: Mary Feehan

Publishes Irish-interest fiction and nonfiction
for adults and children. Prefers approaches
by email. See website for full submission
guidelines.

New Island

New Island
2 Brookside
Dundrum Road
Dublin 14
Tel: 00 353 1 2989937 / 2983411
Fax: 00 353 1 2982783
Email: editor@newisland.ie
Website: http://www.newisland.ie

Publishes: Fiction; Nonfiction; Poetry;
Scripts; Areas: Biography; Criticism;
Current Affairs; Drama; Historical; Humour;
Literature; Politics; Sociology; Travel;
Women's Interests; Markets: Adult;
Treatments: Literary; Popular

Contact: Editorial Manager

Committed to literature and literary
publishing. Publishes in all literary areas,
from fiction to drama to poetry. Also
publishes nonfiction of Irish interest,
especially social affairs and biographies. No
children's books. Accepts submissions by
email only. Send query with one-page
synopsis and sample of the text as Word .doc
or .docx attachments. Include details of any
previous publications. No submissions by
post. See website for full details.

The O'Brien Press

12 Terenure Road East
Rathgar
Dublin 6
Tel: +353-1-4923333
Fax: +353-1-4922777
Email: books@obrien.ie

Website: http://www.obrien.ie

Publishes: Fiction; Nonfiction; Poetry;
Reference; Areas: Architecture; Arts;
Autobiography; Biography; Business;
Cookery; Crafts; Crime; Drama; Historical;
Humour; Lifestyle; Literature; Music;
Nature; Photography; Politics; Religious;
Sport; Travel; Markets: Adult; Children's;
Youth

Mainly publishes children's fiction,
children's nonfiction and adult nonfiction.
Generally doesn't publish poetry, academic
works or adult fiction. Send synopsis and
two or three sample chapters. If fewer than
1,000 words, send complete ms. See website
for full guidelines.

Onstream Publications Ltd

Currabaha
Cloghroe
Blarney
Co. Cork
Tel: +353 21 4385798
Email: info@onstream.ie
Website: http://www.onstream.ie

Publishes: Fiction; Nonfiction; Areas:
Cookery; Historical; Travel; Markets:
Academic; Adult

Publisher of mainly nonfiction, although
some fiction published. Also offers services
to authors.

Poolbeg

123 Grange Hill
Baldoyle Industrial Estate
Baldoyle
Dublin 13
Tel: +353 1 832 1477
Email: info@poolbeg.com
Website: http://www.poolbeg.com

Publishes: Fiction; Nonfiction; Areas:
Cookery; Gardening; Travel; Markets:
Adult; Children's

Contact: Paula Campbell, publisher

Accepts submissions of nonfiction, and
fiction up to 100,000 words. Send query by

post with SASE, CV, short bio, first six chapters in hard copy, and full ms as Word file on CD. See website for full submission guidelines.

Somerville Press

Dromore
Bantry
Co. Cork
Tel: 353 (0) 28 32873
Fax: 353 (0) 28 328
Email: somervillepress@eircom.net
Website: http://www.somervillepress.com

Publishes: Fiction; Nonfiction; Markets: Adult

Publishes fiction and nonfiction of Irish interest.

Tirgearr Publishing

Email: info@tirgearrpublishing.com

Website: http://www.tirgearrpublishing.com

Publishes: Fiction; Areas: Adventure; Anthropology; Biography; Business; Cookery; Crafts; Crime; Culture; Current Affairs; Drama; Entertainment; Erotic; Fantasy; Film; Gothic; Health; Historical; Hobbies; Horror; How-to; Humour; Legal; Leisure; Lifestyle; Literature; Media; Men's Interests; Military; Nature; New Age; Romance; Science; Sci-Fi; Self-Help; Suspense; Technology; Thrillers; Westerns; Women's Interests; Markets: Adult; Family; Commercial; Contemporary; Popular

Contact: Kemberlee Shortland

A small independently-owned digital-only publishing company of adult genre fiction.

They offer full-circle services, working with authors on a one-on-one basis to ensure each book we publish is of the highest quality.

Australian Publishers

For the most up-to-date listings of these and hundreds of other publishers, visit http://www.firstwriter.com/publishers

*To claim your **free** access to the site, please see the back of this book.*

Hinkler Books

45-55 Fairchild Street
Heatherton
Victoria 3202
Tel: +61 (0) 3 9552 1333
Fax: +61 (0) 3 9558 2566
Email: editor@hinkler.com.au
Website: http://www.hinklerbooks.com

Publishes: Nonfiction; Reference; Areas: Cookery; Crafts, Health; Humour; Lifestyle; Music; Spiritual; Sport; Markets: Adult; Children's; Family

Book publisher and packager - creates and produces books for publishers and consumers around the world. Specialises in nonfiction for adults and children. Send one-page query by fax, post, or email in first instance. No unsolicited mss. See website for full details.

Primordial Traditions

Email: info@primordialtraditions.com
Website:
http://www.primordialtraditions.com

Publishes: Nonfiction; Areas: Anthropology; Archaeology; Culture; Historical; Lifestyle; New Age; Philosophy; Politics; Religious; Spiritual; Translations; Markets: Academic; Adult; Treatments: Cynical; Dark; Experimental; Niche; Serious; Traditional

Contact: Gwendolyn Toynton

Specialises in semi-academic content on spirituality, mythology, culture, philosophy, religion, and esoteric/occult. In 2011 we are expanding into new areas so all submissions are welcome.

Publishers Subject Index

This section lists publishers by their subject matter, with directions to the section of the book where the full listing can be found.

You can create your own customised lists of publishers using different combinations of these subject areas, plus over a dozen other criteria, instantly online at http://www.firstwriter.com.

*To claim your **free** access to the site, please see the back of this book.*

Tiger of the Stripe (*UK*)
Archaeology
Amberley Publishing (*UK*)
Andrews UK Limited (*UK*)
Ashmolean Museum Publications (*UK*)
Baywood Publishing Company, Inc. (*US*)
Bloomsbury Academic (*UK*)
James Currey Publishers (*UK*)
Duckworth Publishers (*UK*)
Eleusinian Press (*UK*)
Flame Lily Books (*UK*)
Grand Canyon Association (*US*)
Hadley Rille Books (*US*)
High-Lonesome (*US*)
Liverpool University Press (*UK*)
The Orion Publishing Group Limited (*UK*)
Pen & Sword Books Ltd (*UK*)
Primordial Traditions (*Aus*)
Sage Publications (*UK*)
Sussex Academic Press (*UK*)
Thames and Hudson Ltd (*UK*)
Tiger of the Stripe (*UK*)
Westholme Publishing (*US*)
Architecture
Andrews UK Limited (*UK*)
Anova Books (*UK*)
Betterway Home Books (*US*)
Birlinn Ltd (*UK*)
Black Dog Publishing London UK (*UK*)
Dover Publications, Inc. (*US*)
Eleusinian Press (*UK*)
Floris Books (*UK*)
Giles de la Mare Publishers Ltd (*UK*)
Grand Canyon Association (*US*)
Guild of Master Craftsman (GMC) Publications Ltd (*UK*)
Homestead Publishing (*US*)
The Lilliput Press (*Ire*)
Frances Lincoln Ltd (*UK*)
Liverpool University Press (*UK*)
Lund Humphries Limited (*UK*)
Methuen Publishing Ltd (*UK*)
O Books/John Hunt Publishing Ltd (*UK*)
The O'Brien Press (*Ire*)
Octopus Publishing Group Limited (*UK*)
Phaidon Press Limited (*UK*)
Prestel Publishing Ltd (*UK*)
Quiller Publishing Ltd (*UK*)
Santa Monica Press (*US*)
Sheldrake Press (*UK*)
Shelfstealers (*US*)
Thames and Hudson Ltd (*UK*)
Tiger of the Stripe (*UK*)
Unicorn Press Ltd (*UK*)
Arts
Andrews UK Limited (*UK*)
Anova Books (*UK*)
Ashmolean Museum Publications (*UK*)
Aurum Press Ltd (*UK*)
Birlinn Ltd (*UK*)
Black Dog Publishing London UK (*UK*)
Booth-Clibborn Editions (*UK*)
Central Avenue Publishing (*Can*)

Chapultepec Press (*US*)
The Creative Company (*US*)
Dover Publications, Inc. (*US*)
Eleusinian Press (*UK*)
Enitharmon Press (*UK*)
Erotic Review (ER) Books (*UK*)
Evans Brothers Ltd (*UK*)
Floris Books (*UK*)
Fox Chapel Publishing (*US*)
Freelance Writer's Resource (*US*)
Gibson Square Books Ltd (*UK*)
Giles de la Mare Publishers Ltd (*UK*)
Gomer Press (*UK*)
Guild of Master Craftsman (GMC) Publications Ltd (*UK*)
Halsgrove (*UK*)
Hilmarton Manor Press (*UK*)
Homestead Publishing (*US*)
Immedium (*US*)
Impact Books (*US*)
Indigo Dreams Publishing (*UK*)
Jessica Kingsley Publishers (*UK*)
The Lilliput Press (*Ire*)
Frances Lincoln Ltd (*UK*)
Linden Publishing (*US*)
Liverpool University Press (*UK*)
Luath Press Ltd (*UK*)
Lund Humphries Limited (*UK*)
Magenta Publishing for the Arts (*Can*)
Mandrake of Oxford (*UK*)
Medallion Media Group (*US*)
Northumbria University Press (*UK*)
O Books/John Hunt Publishing Ltd (*UK*)
The O'Brien Press (*Ire*)
Octopus Publishing Group Limited (*UK*)
Open Idea Publishing, LLC (*US*)
The Orion Publishing Group Limited (*UK*)
Peter Owen Publishers (*UK*)
Phaidon Press Limited (*UK*)
Prestel Publishing Ltd (*UK*)
Robert Hale Publishers (*UK*)
Sage Publications (*UK*)
Santa Monica Press (*US*)
Seafarer Books (*UK*)
Seren (*UK*)
Shelfstealers (*US*)
Silman-James Press (*US*)
Sussex Academic Press (*UK*)
Texas Western Press (*US*)
Thames and Hudson Ltd (*UK*)
Tiger of the Stripe (*UK*)
TouchWood Editions (*Can*)
Unicorn Press Ltd (*UK*)
University of Ottawa Press (*Can*)
ZigZag Education (*UK*)
Autobiography
Allison & Busby Ltd (*UK*)
Andrews UK Limited (*UK*)
Arcturus Publishing Ltd (*UK*)
Birlinn Ltd (*UK*)
Blackstaff Press Ltd (*UK*)
Cadence Jazz Books (*US*)
Canongate Books (*UK*)

Central Avenue Publishing (*Can*)
Chapultepec Press (*US*)
City Lights Publishers (*US*)
Coffee House Press (*US*)
Compelling Books (*UK*)
Constable & Robinson Ltd (*UK*)
The Countryman Press (*US*)
Cross-Cultural Communications Publications
(*US*)
Demarche Publishing (*US*)
Eleusinian Press (*UK*)
Gomer Press (*UK*)
Heritage Books, Inc. (*US*)
Halban Publishers (*UK*)
Honno Welsh Women's Press (*UK*)
Indigo Dreams Publishing (*UK*)
Ingalls Publishing Group, Inc. (*US*)
Itoh Press (*US*)
Kitsune Books (*US*)
The Lilliput Press (*Ire*)
Lion Hudson Plc (*UK*)
Little, Brown Book Group (*UK*)
Lost Tower Publications (*UK*)
Mainstream Publishing Co. (Edinburgh) Ltd
(*UK*)
Mango Publishing (*UK*)
Medallion Media Group (*US*)
Mercier Press (*Ire*)
Methuen Publishing Ltd (*UK*)
New Rivers Press (*US*)
O Books/John Hunt Publishing Ltd (*UK*)
The O'Brien Press (*Ire*)
The Orion Publishing Group Limited (*UK*)
Peachtree Publishers (*US*)
Pen & Sword Books Ltd (*UK*)
Piatkus Books (*UK*)
Pressgang (*US*)
Robert Hale Publishers (*UK*)
Shearsman Books (*UK*)
Shelfstealers (*US*)
Tiger of the Stripe (*UK*)
Unbridled Books (*US*)
University of Ottawa Press (*Can*)
WindRiver Publishing (*US*)
Beauty and Fashion
Andrews UK Limited (*UK*)
Anova Books (*UK*)
Black Dog Publishing London UK (*UK*)
Central Avenue Publishing (*Can*)
Itoh Press (*US*)
Luath Press Ltd (*UK*)
The Orion Publishing Group Limited (*UK*)
Phaidon Press Limited (*UK*)
Prestel Publishing Ltd (*UK*)
Quite Specific Media Group (*US*)
Shelfstealers (*US*)
Thames and Hudson Ltd (*UK*)
Biography
ABC-CLIO / Greenwood (*US*)
Allison & Busby Ltd (*UK*)
Amberley Publishing (*UK*)
Andrews UK Limited (*UK*)
Anova Books (*UK*)

Aurora Metro Press (*UK*)
Aurum Press Ltd (*UK*)
Birlinn Ltd (*UK*)
Black & White Publishing Ltd (*UK*)
Blackstaff Press Ltd (*UK*)
Blue Dolphin Publishing (*US*)
BlueBridge (*US*)
Cadence Jazz Books (*US*)
Canongate Books (*UK*)
Carcanet Press Ltd (*UK*)
Carolrhoda Books, Inc. (*US*)
Central Avenue Publishing (*Can*)
Christian Focus Publications (*UK*)
Coastal West Publishing (*Can*)
Colin Smythe Ltd (*UK*)
Compelling Books (*UK*)
Constable & Robinson Ltd (*UK*)
The Creative Company (*US*)
Duckworth Publishers (*UK*)
Eleusinian Press (*UK*)
Elliott & Thompson (*UK*)
Faber & Faber Ltd (*UK*)
Flame Lily Books (*UK*)
Floris Books (*UK*)
Gibson Square Books Ltd (*UK*)
Giles de la Mare Publishers Ltd (*UK*)
Gomer Press (*UK*)
Green Books (*UK*)
Halban Publishers (*UK*)
Halsgrove (*UK*)
Hay House Publishers (*UK*)
Headland Publications (*UK*)
High-Lonesome (*US*)
Homestead Publishing (*US*)
House of Lochar (*UK*)
The Ilium Press (*US*)
Indigo Dreams Publishing (*UK*)
John F. Blair, Publisher (*US*)
Kamehameha Publishing (*US*)
The Lilliput Press (*Ire*)
Lion Hudson Plc (*UK*)
Little, Brown Book Group (*UK*)
Luath Press Ltd (*UK*)
Mainstream Publishing Co. (Edinburgh) Ltd
(*UK*)
Medallion Media Group (*US*)
Mercier Press (*Ire*)
Methuen Publishing Ltd (*UK*)
Moose Hide Books (*Can*)
Neil Wilson Publishing Ltd (*UK*)
New Island (*Ire*)
New Victoria Publishers (*US*)
Nicolas Hays Publishers (*US*)
Northumbria University Press (*UK*)
O Books/John Hunt Publishing Ltd (*UK*)
The O'Brien Press (*Ire*)
Michael O'Mara Books Ltd (*UK*)
Octagon Press Ltd (*UK*)
Omnibus Press (*UK*)
Oneworld Publications (*UK*)
The Orion Publishing Group Limited (*UK*)
Peter Owen Publishers (*UK*)
P&R Publishing (*US*)

Peachtree Publishers (*US*)
Pen & Sword Books Ltd (*UK*)
Pennant Books Ltd (*UK*)
Piatkus Books (*UK*)
Plexus Publishing Limited (*UK*)
Profile Books (*UK*)
Quiller Publishing Ltd (*UK*)
Red Moon Press (*US*)
Robert Hale Publishers (*UK*)
Santa Monica Press (*US*)
Seren (*UK*)
Sheed & Ward (*US*)
Shelfstealers (*US*)
Shepheard-Walwyn (Publishers) Ltd (*UK*)
SportsBooks Limited (*UK*)
Sussex Academic Press (*UK*)
Tirgearr Publishing (*Ire*)
Thames and Hudson Ltd (*UK*)
Tiger of the Stripe (*UK*)
TouchWood Editions (*Can*)
Unicorn Press Ltd (*UK*)
Union Square Publishing (*US*)
Westholme Publishing (*US*)

Business
Addicus Books (*US*)
Alexander Hamilton Institute (*US*)
Andrews UK Limited (*UK*)
Bloomsbury Academic (*UK*)
Bloomsbury Professional (*UK*)
Chemical Publishing Company (*US*)
ETC Publications (*US*)
Flame Lily Books (*UK*)
Freelance Writer's Resource (*US*)
Glenbridge Publishing Ltd (*US*)
Green Books (*UK*)
Harriman House Ltd (*UK*)
Hay House Publishers (*UK*)
How to Books Ltd (*UK*)
The Lilliput Press (*Ire*)
Management Books 2000 Ltd (*UK*)
McGraw-Hill Education EMEA (*UK*)
Medical Group Management Association (MGMA) (*US*)
Mercier Press (*Ire*)
O Books/John Hunt Publishing Ltd (*UK*)
The O'Brien Press (*Ire*)
Oneworld Publications (*UK*)
Piatkus Books (*UK*)
Profile Books (*UK*)
Quiller Publishing Ltd (*UK*)
Reed Business Information (RBI) (*UK*)
Robert D. Reed Publishers (*US*)
Sage Publications (*UK*)
Self-Counsel Press (*US*)
Shelfstealers (*US*)
TSO (The Stationery Office) (*UK*)
Tirgearr Publishing (*Ire*)
Tiger of the Stripe (*UK*)
The Trinity Foundation (*US*)
University of North Carolina Press (*US*)
The Urban Land Institute (ULI) (*US*)
William Reed Business Media (*UK*)
Wolters Kluwer (UK) Ltd (*UK*)

ZigZag Education (*UK*)
Cookery
Absolute Press (*UK*)
Andrews UK Limited (*UK*)
Anova Books (*UK*)
Aurora Metro Press (*UK*)
Black & White Publishing Ltd (*UK*)
Blackstaff Press Ltd (*UK*)
Bristol Publishing Enterprises (*US*)
Burford Books (*US*)
Clear Light Books (*US*)
Constable & Robinson Ltd (*UK*)
The Countryman Press (*US*)
Farcountry Press (*US*)
Flame Lily Books (*UK*)
Fox Chapel Publishing (*US*)
Geddes & Grosset (*UK*)
Glenbridge Publishing Ltd (*US*)
Grub Street Publishing (*UK*)
Guild of Master Craftsman (GMC) Publications Ltd (*UK*)
The Harvard Common Press (*US*)
Hinkler Books (*Aus*)
Homestead Publishing (*US*)
Igloo Books Limited (*UK*)
Jonathan David Publishers, Inc. (*US*)
The Lilliput Press (*Ire*)
Mercier Press (*Ire*)
Neil Wilson Publishing Ltd (*UK*)
New Victoria Publishers (*US*)
O Books/John Hunt Publishing Ltd (*UK*)
The O'Brien Press (*Ire*)
Octopus Publishing Group Limited (*UK*)
Onstream Publications Ltd (*Ire*)
The Orion Publishing Group Limited (*UK*)
Phaidon Press Limited (*UK*)
Poolbeg (*Ire*)
Quiller Publishing Ltd (*UK*)
Robert Hale Publishers (*UK*)
Sheldrake Press (*UK*)
Shelfstealers (*US*)
Square One Publishers, Inc. (*US*)
Tirgearr Publishing (*Ire*)
Tiger of the Stripe (*UK*)
TouchWood Editions (*Can*)
University of North Carolina Press (*US*)
Crafts
Andrews UK Limited (*UK*)
Anova Books (*UK*)
Aurum Press Ltd (*UK*)
The Countryman Press (*US*)
The Creative Company (*US*)
Divertir Publishing LLC (*US*)
Dover Publications, Inc. (*US*)
Flame Lily Books (*UK*)
Floris Books (*UK*)
Fox Chapel Publishing (*US*)
Gem Guides Book Co. (*US*)
Guild of Master Craftsman (GMC) Publications Ltd (*UK*)
Hinkler Books (*Aus*)
Kalmbach Publishing Co. (*US*)
Linden Publishing (*US*)

O Books/John Hunt Publishing Ltd (*UK*)
The O'Brien Press (*Ire*)
Octopus Publishing Group Limited (*UK*)
Seafarer Books (*UK*)
Tirgearr Publishing (*Ire*)
Tiger of the Stripe (*UK*)
University of North Carolina Press (*US*)
Crime
Addicus Books (*US*)
Allison & Busby Ltd (*UK*)
Amberley Publishing (*UK*)
Ampichellis Ebooks (*US*)
Andrews UK Limited (*UK*)
Arcturus Publishing Ltd (*UK*)
Artemis Press (*US*)
Belvedere Publishing (*UK*)
Black & White Publishing Ltd (*UK*)
Black Coffey Publishing (*UK*)
Bloomsbury Academic (*UK*)
bookouture (*UK*)
Central Avenue Publishing (*Can*)
Coastal West Publishing (*Can*)
Compelling Books (*UK*)
Constable & Robinson Ltd (*UK*)
Demarche Publishing (*US*)
Fingerpress UK (*UK*)
Flame Lily Books (*UK*)
Glastonbury Publishing (*UK*)
High-Lonesome (*US*)
The Ilium Press (*US*)
Indigo Dreams Publishing (*UK*)
Ingalls Publishing Group, Inc. (*US*)
Itoh Press (*US*)
Jewish Lights Publishing (*US*)
Little, Brown Book Group (*UK*)
Lost Tower Publications (*UK*)
Luath Press Ltd (*UK*)
M P Publishing USA (*US*)
Mainstream Publishing Co. (Edinburgh) Ltd (*UK*)
Mandrake of Oxford (*UK*)
New Dawn Publishers Ltd (*UK*)
Neil Wilson Publishing Ltd (*UK*)
New Victoria Publishers (*US*)
The O'Brien Press (*Ire*)
Old Street Publishing Ltd (*UK*)
Pants On Fire Press (*US*)
Pen & Sword Books Ltd (*UK*)
Pennant Books Ltd (*UK*)
Piatkus Books (*UK*)
Quercus Books (*UK*)
Robert Hale Publishers (*UK*)
Rowman & Littlefield Publishing Group (*US*)
Sage Publications (*UK*)
SalGad Publishing Group (*UK*)
Salt Publishing Ltd (*UK*)
Shelfstealers (*US*)
Tirgearr Publishing (*Ire*)
Tiger of the Stripe (*UK*)
University of Ottawa Press (*Can*)
Criticism
Andrews UK Limited (*UK*)
Bloodaxe Books Ltd (*UK*)

Chapultepec Press (*US*)
Colin Smythe Ltd (*UK*)
James Currey Publishers (*UK*)
Dagda Publishing (*UK*)
Eleusinian Press (*UK*)
Enitharmon Press (*UK*)
Gibson Square Books Ltd (*UK*)
Halban Publishers (*UK*)
Kitsune Books (*US*)
The Lilliput Press (*Ire*)
New Island (*Ire*)
O Books/John Hunt Publishing Ltd (*UK*)
Peter Owen Publishers (*UK*)
Red Moon Press (*US*)
Seren (*UK*)
Shearsman Books (*UK*)
Shelfstealers (*US*)
Sussex Academic Press (*UK*)
Texas Western Press (*US*)
Tiger of the Stripe (*UK*)
Culture
Allison & Busby Ltd (*UK*)
Andrews UK Limited (*UK*)
Birlinn Ltd (*UK*)
Black Dog Publishing London UK (*UK*)
Bloomsbury Academic (*UK*)
BlueBridge (*US*)
Booth-Clibborn Editions (*UK*)
Bracket Books (*US*)
Canongate Books (*UK*)
Central Avenue Publishing (*Can*)
Chapultepec Press (*US*)
Clear Light Books (*US*)
Coastal West Publishing (*Can*)
Compelling Books (*UK*)
The Countryman Press (*US*)
The Creative Company (*US*)
Cross-Cultural Communications Publications (*US*)
Dagda Publishing (*UK*)
Demarche Publishing (*US*)
Down East Books (*US*)
Eleusinian Press (*UK*)
Fifth House Publishers (*Can*)
Fingerpress UK (*UK*)
Fulcrum Publishing (*US*)
Gauthier Publications (*US*)
Gibson Square Books Ltd (*UK*)
Gomer Press (*UK*)
Immedium (*US*)
Irish Academic Press (*Ire*)
Itoh Press (*US*)
Jonathan David Publishers, Inc. (*US*)
Kamehameha Publishing (*US*)
The Lilliput Press (*Ire*)
Liverpool University Press (*UK*)
Mandrake of Oxford (*UK*)
Methuen Publishing Ltd (*UK*)
Moose Hide Books (*Can*)
NavPress (*US*)
Neil Wilson Publishing Ltd (*UK*)
New Beacon Books, Ltd (*UK*)
Northumbria University Press (*UK*)

Octopus Publishing Group Limited (*UK*)
Open Court Publishing Company (*US*)
Open Gate Press (*UK*)
The Orion Publishing Group Limited (*UK*)
Pants On Fire Press (*US*)
Pennant Books Ltd (*UK*)
Phaidon Press Limited (*UK*)
Plexus Publishing Limited (*UK*)
Pluto Publishing Ltd (*UK*)
Primordial Traditions (*Aus*)
Profile Books (*UK*)
Pureplay Press (*US*)
Razorbill (*US*)
Reed Business Information (RBI) (*UK*)
Rivers Oram Press (*UK*)
Santa Monica Press (*US*)
Shelfstealers (*US*)
Sussex Academic Press (*UK*)
Tirgearr Publishing (*Ire*)
Thames and Hudson Ltd (*UK*)
Tiger of the Stripe (*UK*)
Tilbury House, Publishers (*US*)
Torrey House Press, LLC (*US*)
TouchWood Editions (*Can*)
Trentham Books Limited (*UK*)
Union Square Publishing (*US*)
University of Ottawa Press (*Can*)
University of Wales Press (*UK*)
The University Press of Kentucky (*US*)
Wallflower Press (*UK*)
Current Affairs
Andrews UK Limited (*UK*)
Aurum Press Ltd (*UK*)
Birlinn Ltd (*UK*)
BlueBridge (*US*)
Central Avenue Publishing (*Can*)
Christian Focus Publications (*UK*)
Constable & Robinson Ltd (*UK*)
Dagda Publishing (*UK*)
Demarche Publishing (*US*)
Demontreville Press, Inc. (*US*)
Divertir Publishing LLC (*US*)
Eleusinian Press (*UK*)
Freelance Writer's Resource (*US*)
Gibson Square Books Ltd (*UK*)
Hay House Publishers (*UK*)
Itoh Press (*US*)
The Lilliput Press (*Ire*)
Luath Press Ltd (*UK*)
Mercier Press (*Ire*)
Methuen Publishing Ltd (*UK*)
New Dawn Publishers Ltd (*UK*)
New Island (*Ire*)
Nortia Press (*US*)
Oneworld Publications (*UK*)
The Orion Publishing Group Limited (*UK*)
Oxford University Press (*UK*)
Pluto Publishing Ltd (*UK*)
Profile Books (*UK*)
Reed Business Information (RBI) (*UK*)
Rivers Oram Press (*UK*)
Seren (*UK*)
Shelfstealers (*US*)

TSO (The Stationery Office) (*UK*)
Tirgearr Publishing (*Ire*)
Tiger of the Stripe (*UK*)
Union Square Publishing (*US*)
University of Ottawa Press (*Can*)
Design
Andrews UK Limited (*UK*)
Betterway Home Books (*US*)
Black Dog Publishing London UK (*UK*)
Booth-Clibborn Editions (*UK*)
Evans Brothers Ltd (*UK*)
Flame Lily Books (*UK*)
Fox Chapel Publishing (*US*)
Gulf Publishing Company (*US*)
Homestead Publishing (*US*)
Frances Lincoln Ltd (*UK*)
Lund Humphries Limited (*UK*)
Medallion Media Group (*US*)
Octopus Publishing Group Limited (*UK*)
The Orion Publishing Group Limited (*UK*)
Phaidon Press Limited (*UK*)
Prestel Publishing Ltd (*UK*)
Quite Specific Media Group (*US*)
Sheldrake Press (*UK*)
Thames and Hudson Ltd (*UK*)
Tiger of the Stripe (*UK*)
ZigZag Education (*UK*)
Drama
Andrews UK Limited (*UK*)
Aurora Metro Press (*UK*)
Belvedere Publishing (*UK*)
Black Coffey Publishing (*UK*)
Bloomsbury Academic (*UK*)
Central Avenue Publishing (*Can*)
Chapultepec Press (*US*)
Colin Smythe Ltd (*UK*)
Cressrelles Publishing Co. Ltd (*UK*)
Dagda Publishing (*UK*)
Demarche Publishing (*US*)
Eleusinian Press (*UK*)
Evans Brothers Ltd (*UK*)
Faber & Faber Ltd (*UK*)
Flame Lily Books (*UK*)
Glass Page Books (*US*)
Glastonbury Publishing (*UK*)
Gomer Press (*UK*)
Itoh Press (*US*)
The Lilliput Press (*Ire*)
Luath Press Ltd (*UK*)
Moose Hide Books (*Can*)
New Dawn Publishers Ltd (*UK*)
New Island (*Ire*)
NeWest Press (*Can*)
The O'Brien Press (*Ire*)
Oberon Books (*UK*)
Open Idea Publishing, LLC (*US*)
Oxford University Press (*UK*)
Pants On Fire Press (*US*)
Parthian Books (*UK*)
Pressgang (*US*)
Quite Specific Media Group (*US*)
SalGad Publishing Group (*UK*)
Seren (*UK*)

Sussex Academic Press (*UK*)
Tirgearr Publishing (*Ire*)
Tiger of the Stripe (*UK*)
ZigZag Education (*UK*)
Entertainment
Andrews UK Limited (*UK*)
Anova Books (*UK*)
Boathook Books (*UK*)
Central Avenue Publishing (*Can*)
Dagda Publishing (*UK*)
Fingerpress UK (*UK*)
Freelance Writer's Resource (*US*)
Indigo Dreams Publishing (*UK*)
Itoh Press (*US*)
Little, Brown Book Group (*UK*)
New Dawn Publishers Ltd (*UK*)
Pants On Fire Press (*US*)
Quite Specific Media Group (*US*)
Ramsay Publishing (*UK*)
Reed Business Information (RBI) (*UK*)
Santa Monica Press (*US*)
Sunberry Books (*UK*)
Tirgearr Publishing (*Ire*)
Tiger of the Stripe (*UK*)
Wallflower Press (*UK*)
Erotic
Andrews UK Limited (*UK*)
Arcturus Publishing Ltd (*UK*)
Artemis Press (*US*)
Belvedere Publishing (*UK*)
bookouture (*UK*)
Central Avenue Publishing (*Can*)
Changeling Press LLC (*US*)
Constable & Robinson Ltd (*UK*)
Erotic Review (ER) Books (*UK*)
Everheart Books (*Can*)
Fingerpress UK (*UK*)
Freya's Bower (*US*)
Glastonbury Publishing (*UK*)
ImaJinn Books (*US*)
Indigo Dreams Publishing (*UK*)
Itoh Press (*US*)
Jupiter Gardens Press (*US*)
Loose Id (*US*)
Mandrake of Oxford (*UK*)
My Pouty Lips (*US*)
Netherworld Books (*UK*)
Open Idea Publishing, LLC (*US*)
Samhain Publishing (*US*)
Tirgearr Publishing (*Ire*)
The Zharmae Publishing Press (*US*)
Fantasy
Allison & Busby Ltd (*UK*)
Andrews UK Limited (*UK*)
Archaia (*US*)
Belvedere Publishing (*UK*)
Black Coffey Publishing (*UK*)
Blind Eye Books (*US*)
bookouture (*UK*)
Brighter Books Publishing House (*Can*)
Central Avenue Publishing (*Can*)
Changeling Press LLC (*US*)
Colin Smythe Ltd (*UK*)

Compelling Books (*UK*)
Constable & Robinson Ltd (*UK*)
Dagda Publishing (*UK*)
Demarche Publishing (*US*)
Divertir Publishing LLC (*US*)
Dragonfairy Press (*US*)
Eleusinian Press (*UK*)
Faery Rose (*US*)
Fingerpress UK (*UK*)
Flame Lily Books (*UK*)
48fourteen (*US*)
Gauthier Publications (*US*)
Glastonbury Publishing (*UK*)
Hadley Rille Books (*US*)
Highland Press (*US*)
ImaJinn Books (*US*)
Indigo Dreams Publishing (*UK*)
Itoh Press (*US*)
Jo Fletcher Books (*UK*)
Jupiter Gardens Press (*US*)
Kane Miller Books (*US*)
Kelly Point Publishing LLC (*US*)
Kitsune Books (*US*)
Knox Robinson Publishing (UK) (*UK*)
Knox Robinson Publishing (US) (*US*)
Little, Brown Book Group (*UK*)
Loose Id (*US*)
Lost Tower Publications (*UK*)
M P Publishing USA (*US*)
Malachite Quills Publishing (*US*)
Medallion Media Group (*US*)
Moonshadow Press (*US*)
Moose Hide Books (*Can*)
New Dawn Publishers Ltd (*UK*)
New Libri (*US*)
Netherworld Books (*UK*)
New Victoria Publishers (*US*)
Open Idea Publishing, LLC (*US*)
The Orion Publishing Group Limited (*UK*)
Pants On Fire Press (*US*)
Quercus Books (*UK*)
Razorbill (*US*)
Shelfstealers (*US*)
Tirgearr Publishing (*Ire*)
Tor/Forge (*US*)
Wizards of the Coast (*US*)
The Zharmae Publishing Press (*US*)
Fiction
Able Muse Press (*US*)
Affluent Publishing Corporation (*US*)
Allison & Busby Ltd (*UK*)
Alma Books Ltd (*UK*)
Ampichellis Ebooks (*US*)
Anarchy Books (*UK*)
Andrews UK Limited (*UK*)
Anova Books (*UK*)
Antarctic Press (*US*)
Arabia Books (*UK*)
Archaia (*US*)
Arcturus Publishing Ltd (*UK*)
Arris Publishing Ltd (*UK*)
Artemis Press (*US*)
AudioGO Ltd (*UK*)

Aunt Lute Books (*US*)
Aurora Metro Press (*UK*)
Aurora Publishing, Inc (*US*)
Award Publications Limited (*UK*)
Azro Press (*US*)
Barefoot Books Ltd (*UK*)
Belvedere Publishing (*UK*)
Birlinn Ltd (*UK*)
Black & White Publishing Ltd (*UK*)
Black Coffey Publishing (*UK*)
Blackstaff Press Ltd (*UK*)
Blind Eye Books (*US*)
Blue Dolphin Publishing (*US*)
Boathook Books (*UK*)
bookouture (*UK*)
Books For All Times (*US*)
Borealis Press (*Can*)
Bottom Dog Press (*US*)
Bracket Books (*US*)
Brighter Books Publishing House (*Can*)
BSTSLLR (*US*)
Canongate Books (*UK*)
Carolrhoda Books, Inc. (*US*)
Cedar Fort (*US*)
Central Avenue Publishing (*Can*)
Changeling Press LLC (*US*)
Chapultepec Press (*US*)
Child's Play (International) Ltd (*UK*)
Christian Focus Publications (*UK*)
City Lights Publishers (*US*)
Coffee House Press (*US*)
Colin Smythe Ltd (*UK*)
Compelling Books (*UK*)
Constable & Robinson Ltd (*UK*)
The Creative Company (*US*)
Cross-Cultural Communications Publications (*US*)
Dedalus Ltd (*UK*)
Demarche Publishing (*US*)
Demontreville Press, Inc. (*US*)
Digital Manga, Inc. (*US*)
Diversion Books (*US*)
Divertir Publishing LLC (*US*)
Down East Books (*US*)
Down The Shore Publishing (*US*)
Dragonfairy Press (*US*)
Duckworth Publishers (*UK*)
Dzanc Books (*US*)
EDCON Publishing Group (*US*)
Egmont UK Ltd (*UK*)
Eleusinian Press (*UK*)
Elliott & Thompson (*UK*)
Emissary Publishing (*UK*)
Enitharmon Press (*UK*)
Erotic Review (ER) Books (*UK*)
Evans Brothers Ltd (*UK*)
Everheart Books (*Can*)
Faber & Faber Ltd (*UK*)
Faery Rose (*US*)
Fingerpress UK (*UK*)
Flame Lily Books (*UK*)
Florida Academic Press (*US*)
Floris Books (*UK*)

48fourteen (*US*)
Four Way Books (*US*)
Freya's Bower (*US*)
Gauthier Publications (*US*)
Geddes & Grosset (*UK*)
Glass Page Books (*US*)
Glastonbury Publishing (*UK*)
Glenbridge Publishing Ltd (*US*)
The Glencannon Press (*US*)
Gomer Press (*UK*)
Grand Canyon Association (*US*)
Gullane Children's Books (*UK*)
Heritage Books, Inc. (*US*)
The Habit of Rainy Nights Press (*US*)
Hachette Children's Books (*UK*)
Hachette UK (*UK*)
Hadley Rille Books (*US*)
Halban Publishers (*UK*)
Headland Publications (*UK*)
High-Lonesome (*US*)
Highland Press (*US*)
Hogs Back Books (*UK*)
Homestead Publishing (*US*)
Honno Welsh Women's Press (*UK*)
Hopewell Publications (*US*)
House of Anansi Press (*Can*)
House of Lochar (*UK*)
Ideals Publications (*US*)
Igloo Books Limited (*UK*)
The Ilium Press (*US*)
Image Comics (*US*)
ImaJinn Books (*US*)
Immedium (*US*)
Impress Books Limited (*UK*)
Indigo Dreams Publishing (*UK*)
Ingalls Publishing Group, Inc. (*US*)
Ion Imagination Entertainment, Inc. (*US*)
Itoh Press (*US*)
Jewish Lights Publishing (*US*)
Jo Fletcher Books (*UK*)
John F. Blair, Publisher (*US*)
John Lynch Digital Publishing House (*Ire*)
Jolly Learning Ltd (*UK*)
Jupiter Gardens Press (*US*)
Just Us Books (*US*)
Kamehameha Publishing (*US*)
Kane Miller Books (*US*)
Kearney Street Books (*US*)
Kelly Point Publishing LLC (*US*)
Kids Can Press (*Can*)
Kitsune Books (*US*)
Knox Robinson Publishing (UK) (*UK*)
Knox Robinson Publishing (US) (*US*)
Legacy Press (*US*)
Leapfrog Press (*US*)
Ledge Hill Publishing (*US*)
Legend Press (*UK*)
Les Figues Press (*US*)
The Lilliput Press (*Ire*)
Frances Lincoln Ltd (*UK*)
Lion Hudson Plc (*UK*)
Little Tiger Press (*UK*)
Little, Brown Book Group (*UK*)

Loose Id (*US*)
Lost Tower Publications (*UK*)
Luath Press Ltd (*UK*)
The Lutterworth Press (*UK*)
M P Publishing USA (*US*)
Macmillan New Writing (*UK*)
Malachite Quills Publishing (*US*)
Mandrake of Oxford (*UK*)
Mango Publishing (*UK*)
Mantra Lingua Ltd (*UK*)
MBooks of BC (Multicultural Books of British
Columbia) (*Can*)
Meadowside Children's Books (*UK*)
Medallion Media Group (*US*)
Mercier Press (*Ire*)
Messianic Jewish Publishers (*US*)
Methuen Publishing Ltd (*UK*)
Monarch Books (*UK*)
Moonshadow Press (*US*)
Moose Hide Books (*Can*)
My Pouty Lips (*US*)
Myriad Editions (*UK*)
Myrmidon Books Ltd (*UK*)
New Dawn Publishers Ltd (*UK*)
New Libri (*US*)
Netherworld Books (*UK*)
New Beacon Books, Ltd (*UK*)
New Island (*Ire*)
New Rivers Press (*US*)
New Victoria Publishers (*US*)
NeWest Press (*Can*)
Nortia Press (*US*)
Nosy Crow (*UK*)
O Books/John Hunt Publishing Ltd (*UK*)
The O'Brien Press (*Ire*)
Octagon Press Ltd (*UK*)
Old Street Publishing Ltd (*UK*)
Oneworld Publications (*UK*)
Onlywomen Press Ltd (*UK*)
Onstream Publications Ltd (*Ire*)
Open Idea Publishing, LLC (*US*)
The Orion Publishing Group Limited (*UK*)
Peter Owen Publishers (*UK*)
Oxford University Press (*UK*)
P&R Publishing (*US*)
Pants On Fire Press (*US*)
PaperBooks Ltd. (*UK*)
Parthian Books (*UK*)
Peachtree Publishers (*US*)
Pen & Sword Books Ltd (*UK*)
Penny-Farthing Press (*US*)
Phoenix Yard Books (*UK*)
Piatkus Books (*UK*)
Piccadilly Press (*UK*)
Poolbeg (*Ire*)
Pressgang (*US*)
PUBSLUSH Press (*US*)
Pureplay Press (*US*)
Quercus Books (*UK*)
Ragged Bears Limited (*UK*)
Ramsay Publishing (*UK*)
Ransom Publishing Ltd (*UK*)
Razorbill (*US*)

Red Moon Press (*US*)
Renaissance House (*US*)
Riverhead Books (*US*)
Robert D. Reed Publishers (*US*)
Robert Hale Publishers (*UK*)
SalGad Publishing Group (*UK*)
Salt Publishing Ltd (*UK*)
Sam's Dot Publishing (*US*)
Samhain Publishing (*US*)
Seafarer Books (*UK*)
Seren (*UK*)
Shelfstealers (*US*)
Short Books (*UK*)
Somerville Press (*Ire*)
Spire Press, Inc. (*US*)
Spout Press (*US*)
Starcherone Books (*US*)
Sunberry Books (*UK*)
Tirgearr Publishing (*Ire*)
Tiger of the Stripe (*UK*)
Tightrope Books (*Can*)
Tilbury House, Publishers (*US*)
Timberline Press Books (*US*)
Tor/Forge (*US*)
Torrey House Press, LLC (*US*)
TouchWood Editions (*Can*)
Tradewind Books (*Can*)
Two Ravens Press Ltd (*UK*)
Unbridled Books (*US*)
Upstart Books (*US*)
Woodbine House (*US*)
Washington Writers' Publishing House (*US*)
White Mane Kids (*US*)
The Wild Rose Press (*US*)
WindRiver Publishing (*US*)
Windswept House Publishers (*US*)
Windward Publishing (*US*)
Wizards of the Coast (*US*)
The Zharmae Publishing Press (*US*)
Film
Andrews UK Limited (*UK*)
Anova Books (*UK*)
Aurum Press Ltd (*UK*)
Bloomsbury Academic (*UK*)
James Currey Publishers (*UK*)
Eleusinian Press (*UK*)
Faber & Faber Ltd (*UK*)
Flame Lily Books (*UK*)
Glenbridge Publishing Ltd (*US*)
Guild of Master Craftsman (GMC) Publications
Ltd (*UK*)
Indigo Dreams Publishing (*UK*)
Itoh Press (*US*)
Methuen Publishing Ltd (*UK*)
Michael Wiese Books (*US*)
Octopus Publishing Group Limited (*UK*)
Phaidon Press Limited (*UK*)
Plexus Publishing Limited (*UK*)
Santa Monica Press (*US*)
Silman-James Press (*US*)
Tirgearr Publishing (*Ire*)
Tiger of the Stripe (*UK*)
The University Press of Kentucky (*US*)

Wallflower Press (*UK*)
Finance
Addicus Books (*US*)
Andrews UK Limited (*UK*)
Birlinn Ltd (*UK*)
Bloomsbury Academic (*UK*)
Bloomsbury Professional (*UK*)
James Currey Publishers (*UK*)
Demarche Publishing (*US*)
Freelance Writer's Resource (*US*)
Glenbridge Publishing Ltd (*US*)
Harriman House Ltd (*UK*)
Hay House Publishers (*UK*)
Humanics Publishing Group (*US*)
Management Books 2000 Ltd (*UK*)
McGraw-Hill Education EMEA (*UK*)
O Books/John Hunt Publishing Ltd (*UK*)
Oxford University Press (*UK*)
Pluto Publishing Ltd (*UK*)
Profile Books (*UK*)
Reed Business Information (RBI) (*UK*)
Robert D. Reed Publishers (*US*)
Sage Publications (*UK*)
Self-Counsel Press (*US*)
Shelfstealers (*US*)
Shepheard-Walwyn (Publishers) Ltd (*UK*)
Square One Publishers, Inc. (*US*)
Sussex Academic Press (*UK*)
Tiger of the Stripe (*UK*)
The Trinity Foundation (*US*)
University of North Carolina Press (*US*)
University of Ottawa Press (*Can*)
The Urban Land Institute (ULI) (*US*)
Which? Books (*UK*)
Wolters Kluwer (UK) Ltd (*UK*)
Woodhead Publishing Ltd (*UK*)
ZigZag Education (*UK*)
Gardening
Andrews UK Limited (*UK*)
Anova Books (*UK*)
Burford Books (*US*)
Constable & Robinson Ltd (*UK*)
Flame Lily Books (*UK*)
Fox Chapel Publishing (*US*)
Fulcrum Publishing (*US*)
Green Books (*UK*)
Guild of Master Craftsman (GMC) Publications Ltd (*UK*)
Frances Lincoln Ltd (*UK*)
Octopus Publishing Group Limited (*UK*)
The Orion Publishing Group Limited (*UK*)
Poolbeg (*Ire*)
Quiller Publishing Ltd (*UK*)
Thames and Hudson Ltd (*UK*)
Tiger of the Stripe (*UK*)
TouchWood Editions (*Can*)
Which? Books (*UK*)
Gothic
Andrews UK Limited (*UK*)
Belvedere Publishing (*UK*)
Central Avenue Publishing (*Can*)
Compelling Books (*UK*)
Dagda Publishing (*UK*)

Fingerpress UK (*UK*)
Glastonbury Publishing (*UK*)
Indigo Dreams Publishing (*UK*)
Itoh Press (*US*)
Lost Tower Publications (*UK*)
M P Publishing USA (*US*)
New Dawn Publishers Ltd (*UK*)
Netherworld Books (*UK*)
Salt Publishing Ltd (*UK*)
Tirgearr Publishing (*Ire*)
Health
Addicus Books (*US*)
Andrews UK Limited (*UK*)
Arcturus Publishing Ltd (*UK*)
Baywood Publishing Company, Inc. (*US*)
Blue Dolphin Publishing (*US*)
Constable & Robinson Ltd (*UK*)
The Creative Company (*US*)
Demarche Publishing (*US*)
Eastland Press (*US*)
Eleusinian Press (*UK*)
EMIS Inc. Medical Publishers (*US*)
Findhorn Press Ltd (*UK*)
Floris Books (*UK*)
Freelance Writer's Resource (*US*)
Grub Street Publishing (*UK*)
Hammersmith Press Ltd (*UK*)
Hay House Publishers (*UK*)
Hinkler Books (*Aus*)
Hodder Education (*UK*)
Jones & Bartlett Learning (*US*)
Lion Hudson Plc (*UK*)
Mandrake of Oxford (*UK*)
Medallion Media Group (*US*)
Mercier Press (*Ire*)
Nicolas Hays Publishers (*US*)
O Books/John Hunt Publishing Ltd (*UK*)
Octopus Publishing Group Limited (*UK*)
The Orion Publishing Group Limited (*UK*)
Pants On Fire Press (*US*)
Pavilion Publishing (*UK*)
Peachtree Publishers (*US*)
Piatkus Books (*UK*)
Radcliffe Publishing Ltd (*UK*)
Robert D. Reed Publishers (*US*)
Rowman & Littlefield Publishing Group (*US*)
Sage Publications (*UK*)
Shelfstealers (*US*)
SLACK Incorporated (*US*)
Square One Publishers, Inc. (*US*)
Tirgearr Publishing (*Ire*)
Tiger of the Stripe (*UK*)
University of Ottawa Press (*Can*)
Vitesse Press (*US*)
Woodbine House (*US*)
Wellness Institute/Self-Help Books, LLC (*US*)
Which? Books (*UK*)
ZigZag Education (*UK*)
Historical
ABC-CLIO / Greenwood (*US*)
Ian Allan Publishing Ltd (*UK*)
Allison & Busby Ltd (*UK*)
Alma Books Ltd (*UK*)

Amberley Publishing (*UK*)
American Atheists (*US*)
Ammonite Press (*UK*)
Andrews UK Limited (*UK*)
Anova Books (*UK*)
Arcturus Publishing Ltd (*UK*)
Arkansas Research, Inc. (*US*)
Arris Publishing Ltd (*UK*)
Ashmolean Museum Publications (*UK*)
Aurum Press Ltd (*UK*)
Behrman House (*US*)
Birlinn Ltd (*UK*)
Blackstaff Press Ltd (*UK*)
Bloomsbury Academic (*UK*)
BlueBridge (*US*)
bookouture (*UK*)
Borealis Press (*Can*)
Canongate Books (*UK*)
Carolrhoda Books, Inc. (*US*)
Cedar Fort (*US*)
Central Avenue Publishing (*Can*)
Chapultepec Press (*US*)
Christian Focus Publications (*UK*)
Clear Light Books (*US*)
Coastal West Publishing (*Can*)
Colin Smythe Ltd (*UK*)
Compelling Books (*UK*)
Constable & Robinson Ltd (*UK*)
The Countryman Press (*US*)
The Creative Company (*US*)
Cross-Cultural Communications Publications (*US*)
James Currey Publishers (*UK*)
Demarche Publishing (*US*)
Demontreville Press, Inc. (*US*)
Divertir Publishing LLC (*US*)
Down East Books (*US*)
Down The Shore Publishing (*US*)
Duckworth Publishers (*UK*)
Eleusinian Press (*UK*)
Elliott & Thompson (*UK*)
ETC Publications (*US*)
Evans Brothers Ltd (*UK*)
Farcountry Press (*US*)
Fifth House Publishers (*Can*)
Fingerpress UK (*UK*)
Flame Lily Books (*UK*)
Florida Academic Press (*US*)
Floris Books (*UK*)
Frontline Books (*UK*)
Fulcrum Publishing (*US*)
Gauthier Publications (*US*)
Geddes & Grosset (*UK*)
Gibson Square Books Ltd (*UK*)
Giles de la Mare Publishers Ltd (*UK*)
Glastonbury Publishing (*UK*)
Glenbridge Publishing Ltd (*US*)
Golden West Books (*US*)
Gomer Press (*UK*)
Grand Canyon Association (*US*)
Grub Street Publishing (*UK*)
Gwasg Carreg Gwalch (*UK*)
Heritage Books, Inc. (*US*)

Hadley Rille Books (*US*)
Halban Publishers (*UK*)
Halsgrove (*UK*)
High-Lonesome (*US*)
Highland Press (*US*)
House of Lochar (*UK*)
The Ilium Press (*US*)
Indigo Dreams Publishing (*UK*)
Ingalls Publishing Group, Inc. (*US*)
Irish Academic Press (*Ire*)
Itoh Press (*US*)
Jewish Lights Publishing (*US*)
John F. Blair, Publisher (*US*)
Kindred Productions (*Can*)
Kamehameha Publishing (*US*)
Kane Miller Books (*US*)
Kelly Point Publishing LLC (*US*)
Knox Robinson Publishing (UK) (*UK*)
Knox Robinson Publishing (US) (*US*)
The Lilliput Press (*Ire*)
Linden Publishing (*US*)
Little, Brown Book Group (*UK*)
Liverpool University Press (*UK*)
Loose Id (*US*)
Luath Press Ltd (*UK*)
Lund Humphries Limited (*UK*)
Mainstream Publishing Co. (Edinburgh) Ltd (*UK*)
Medallion Media Group (*US*)
Mercier Press (*Ire*)
The Merlin Press (*UK*)
Methuen Publishing Ltd (*UK*)
Moose Hide Books (*Can*)
Motor Racing Publications (*UK*)
Mountain Press Publishing Company (*US*)
Neil Wilson Publishing Ltd (*UK*)
New Beacon Books, Ltd (*UK*)
New Island (*Ire*)
NeWest Press (*Can*)
Nicolas Hays Publishers (*US*)
O Books/John Hunt Publishing Ltd (*UK*)
The O'Brien Press (*Ire*)
Michael O'Mara Books Ltd (*UK*)
Octopus Publishing Group Limited (*UK*)
Oneworld Publications (*UK*)
Onstream Publications Ltd (*Ire*)
The Orion Publishing Group Limited (*UK*)
Peter Owen Publishers (*UK*)
Oxford University Press (*UK*)
P&R Publishing (*US*)
Pants On Fire Press (*US*)
Peachtree Publishers (*US*)
Pen & Sword Books Ltd (*UK*)
Phaidon Press Limited (*UK*)
Piatkus Books (*UK*)
Pluto Publishing Ltd (*UK*)
Primordial Traditions (*Aus*)
Profile Books (*UK*)
Pureplay Press (*US*)
Rivers Oram Press (*UK*)
Robert Hale Publishers (*UK*)
Rowman & Littlefield Publishing Group (*US*)
Sage Publications (*UK*)

Santa Monica Press (*US*)
Seafarer Books (*UK*)
Seren (*UK*)
Sheed & Ward (*US*)
Sheldrake Press (*UK*)
Shelfstealers (*US*)
Shepheard-Walwyn (Publishers) Ltd (*UK*)
Society of Genealogists (*UK*)
Sussex Academic Press (*UK*)
Tirgearr Publishing (*Ire*)
Texas Western Press (*US*)
Thames and Hudson Ltd (*UK*)
Tiger of the Stripe (*UK*)
Tilbury House, Publishers (*US*)
Tor/Forge (*US*)
Torrey House Press, LLC (*US*)
TouchWood Editions (*Can*)
The Trinity Foundation (*US*)
Unbridled Books (*US*)
Unicorn Press Ltd (*UK*)
University of North Carolina Press (*US*)
University of Ottawa Press (*Can*)
University of Wales Press (*UK*)
The University Press of Kentucky (*US*)
Wooden Books (*UK*)
Welsh Academic Press (*UK*)
Westholme Publishing (*US*)
White Mane Kids (*US*)
White Mane Publishing Co., Inc. (*US*)
WindRiver Publishing (*US*)
ZigZag Education (*UK*)

Hobbies
Ian Allan Publishing Ltd (*UK*)
Andrews UK Limited (*UK*)
Anova Books (*UK*)
Arcturus Publishing Ltd (*UK*)
Arkansas Research, Inc. (*US*)
Boathook Books (*UK*)
Bristol Publishing Enterprises (*US*)
Cardoza Publishing (*US*)
Carstens Publications, Inc. (*US*)
Colin Smythe Ltd (*UK*)
The Countryman Press (*US*)
The Creative Company (*US*)
Cycle Publishing / Van der Plas Publications (*US*)
Demarche Publishing (*US*)
Divertir Publishing LLC (*US*)
Everyman Chess (*UK*)
Flame Lily Books (*UK*)
Guild of Master Craftsman (GMC) Publications Ltd (*UK*)
High Stakes Publishing (*UK*)
Igloo Books Limited (*UK*)
Indigo Dreams Publishing (*UK*)
Kalmbach Publishing Co. (*US*)
Linden Publishing (*US*)
Methuen Publishing Ltd (*UK*)
O Books/John Hunt Publishing Ltd (*UK*)
Shelfstealers (*US*)
Silman-James Press (*US*)
Tirgearr Publishing (*Ire*)
Tiger of the Stripe (*UK*)

Horror
Andrews UK Limited (*UK*)
Archaia (*US*)
Arcturus Publishing Ltd (*UK*)
Belvedere Publishing (*UK*)
Central Avenue Publishing (*Can*)
Compelling Books (*UK*)
Constable & Robinson Ltd (*UK*)
Dagda Publishing (*UK*)
Demarche Publishing (*US*)
Eleusinian Press (*UK*)
Fingerpress UK (*UK*)
48fourteen (*US*)
Gauthier Publications (*US*)
Glastonbury Publishing (*UK*)
ImaJinn Books (*US*)
Indigo Dreams Publishing (*UK*)
Itoh Press (*US*)
Jo Fletcher Books (*UK*)
Lost Tower Publications (*UK*)
Mandrake of Oxford (*UK*)
Medallion Media Group (*US*)
Moonshadow Press (*US*)
New Dawn Publishers Ltd (*UK*)
Netherworld Books (*UK*)
Pants On Fire Press (*US*)
Pressgang (*US*)
SalGad Publishing Group (*UK*)
Sam's Dot Publishing (*US*)
Samhain Publishing (*US*)
Shelfstealers (*US*)
Tirgearr Publishing (*Ire*)
Tor/Forge (*US*)
The Zharmae Publishing Press (*US*)

How-to
J.A. Allen (*UK*)
American Correctional Association (ACA) (*US*)
Amherst Media (*US*)
Andrews UK Limited (*UK*)
Betterway Home Books (*US*)
Boathook Books (*UK*)
The Bold Strummer Ltd (*US*)
Brighter Books Publishing House (*Can*)
Carstens Publications, Inc. (*US*)
Church Growth Institute (*US*)
The College Board (*US*)
Compelling Books (*UK*)
Demarche Publishing (*US*)
Fingerpress UK (*UK*)
Flame Lily Books (*UK*)
Fox Chapel Publishing (*US*)
Freelance Writer's Resource (*US*)
Gem Guides Book Co. (*US*)
Green Books (*UK*)
Guild of Master Craftsman (GMC) Publications Ltd (*UK*)
Harriman House Ltd (*UK*)
Haynes Publishing (*UK*)
How to Books Ltd (*UK*)
Humanics Publishing Group (*US*)
Impact Books (*US*)
Indigo Dreams Publishing (*UK*)
Kalmbach Publishing Co. (*US*)

Linden Publishing (*US*)
Methuen Publishing Ltd (*UK*)
Michael Wiese Books (*US*)
My Pouty Lips (*US*)
NavPress (*US*)
PennWell Books (*US*)
Seafarer Books (*UK*)
Search Institute Press (*US*)
Shelfstealers (*US*)
Square One Publishers, Inc. (*US*)
Tirgearr Publishing (*Ire*)
Trafalgar Square Books (*US*)
Tiger of the Stripe (*UK*)
Woodbine House (*US*)
WindRiver Publishing (*US*)
Humour
Andrews UK Limited (*UK*)
Anova Books (*UK*)
Arcturus Publishing Ltd (*UK*)
Belvedere Publishing (*UK*)
Birlinn Ltd (*UK*)
Black & White Publishing Ltd (*UK*)
Black Coffey Publishing (*UK*)
Blackstaff Press Ltd (*UK*)
Canongate Books (*UK*)
Central Avenue Publishing (*Can*)
Compelling Books (*UK*)
Constable & Robinson Ltd (*UK*)
Dagda Publishing (*UK*)
Demarche Publishing (*US*)
Divertir Publishing LLC (*US*)
Emissary Publishing (*UK*)
Fingerpress UK (*UK*)
Flame Lily Books (*UK*)
18fourteen (*US*)
Gauthier Publications (*US*)
Geddes & Grosset (*UK*)
Glastonbury Publishing (*UK*)
Glenbridge Publishing Ltd (*US*)
Green Books (*UK*)
Guild of Master Craftsman (GMC) Publications
Ltd (*UK*)
Hinkler Books (*Aus*)
Indigo Dreams Publishing (*UK*)
Ingalls Publishing Group, Inc. (*US*)
Itoh Press (*US*)
Jonathan David Publishers, Inc. (*US*)
Kelly Point Publishing LLC (*US*)
Little, Brown Book Group (*UK*)
Local Gems Poetry Press (*US*)
Mercier Press (*Ire*)
Methuen Publishing Ltd (*UK*)
Moose Hide Books (*Can*)
New Dawn Publishers Ltd (*UK*)
Neil Wilson Publishing Ltd (*UK*)
Netherworld Books (*UK*)
New Island (*Ire*)
New Victoria Publishers (*US*)
O Books/John Hunt Publishing Ltd (*UK*)
The O'Brien Press (*Ire*)
Michael O'Mara Books Ltd (*UK*)
Octopus Publishing Group Limited (*UK*)
Old Street Publishing Ltd (*UK*)

Piatkus Books (*UK*)
Piccadilly Press (*UK*)
Pressgang (*US*)
Profile Books (*UK*)
Quiller Publishing Ltd (*UK*)
Ramsay Publishing (*UK*)
Razorbill (*US*)
Red Rock Press (*US*)
Robert D. Reed Publishers (*US*)
Robert Hale Publishers (*UK*)
Santa Monica Press (*US*)
Shelfstealers (*US*)
Tirgearr Publishing (*Ire*)
Tiger of the Stripe (*UK*)
Trentham Books Limited (*UK*)
The Zharmae Publishing Press (*US*)
Legal
Alexander Hamilton Institute (*US*)
American Atheists (*US*)
Andrews UK Limited (*UK*)
Belvedere Publishing (*UK*)
Birlinn Ltd (*UK*)
Bloomsbury Academic (*UK*)
Bloomsbury Professional (*UK*)
Borealis Press (*Can*)
Chapultepec Press (*US*)
Coastal West Publishing (*Can*)
Eleusinian Press (*UK*)
Freelance Writer's Resource (*US*)
Hart Publishing Ltd (*UK*)
ICSA Information & Training Ltd (*UK*)
Jones & Bartlett Learning (*US*)
Lawyers & Judges Publishing Co (*US*)
Oxford University Press (*UK*)
Pluto Publishing Ltd (*UK*)
Rowman & Littlefield Publishing Group (*US*)
Self-Counsel Press (*US*)
Shelfstealers (*US*)
Tirgearr Publishing (*Ire*)
Tiger of the Stripe (*UK*)
Trentham Books Limited (*UK*)
University of North Carolina Press (*US*)
University of Ottawa Press (*Can*)
Which? Books (*UK*)
Wolters Kluwer (UK) Ltd (*UK*)
ZigZag Education (*UK*)
Leisure
AA Publishing (*UK*)
Andrews UK Limited (*UK*)
Anova Books (*UK*)
Arcturus Publishing Ltd (*UK*)
Burford Books (*US*)
Cardoza Publishing (*US*)
Central Avenue Publishing (*Can*)
Chapultepec Press (*US*)
Constable & Robinson Ltd (*UK*)
The Countryman Press (*US*)
Cycle Publishing / Van der Plas Publications
(*US*)
Demarche Publishing (*US*)
Down East Books (*US*)
Everyman Chess (*UK*)
Flame Lily Books (*UK*)

Freelance Writer's Resource (*US*)
Gomer Press (*UK*)
Grand Canyon Association (*US*)
Haynes Publishing (*UK*)
How to Books Ltd (*UK*)
Indigo Dreams Publishing (*UK*)
Itoh Press (*US*)
Frances Lincoln Ltd (*UK*)
Lost Tower Publications (*UK*)
Luath Press Ltd (*UK*)
Northumbria University Press (*UK*)
Open Idea Publishing, LLC (*US*)
Pocket Mountains (*UK*)
Robert Hale Publishers (*UK*)
Shelfstealers (*US*)
Sunflower Books (*UK*)
Tirgearr Publishing (*Ire*)
Tiger of the Stripe (*UK*)
Vitesse Press (*US*)
Windward Publishing (*US*)
ZigZag Education (*UK*)
Lifestyle
American Atheists (*US*)
Andrews UK Limited (*UK*)
Anova Books (*UK*)
Aurum Press Ltd (*UK*)
Betterway Home Books (*US*)
Blue Dolphin Publishing (*US*)
Central Avenue Publishing (*Can*)
Christian Focus Publications (*UK*)
Constable & Robinson Ltd (*UK*)
The Countryman Press (*US*)
Demarche Publishing (*US*)
Freelance Writer's Resource (*US*)
Glenbridge Publishing Ltd (*US*)
Green Books (*UK*)
Harriman House Ltd (*UK*)
The Harvard Common Press (*US*)
Hay House Publishers (*UK*)
Hinkler Books (*Aus*)
How to Books Ltd (*UK*)
Indigo Dreams Publishing (*UK*)
Inter-Varsity Press (*UK*)
Itoh Press (*US*)
Frances Lincoln Ltd (*UK*)
Lost Tower Publications (*UK*)
Luath Press Ltd (*UK*)
Management Books 2000 Ltd (*UK*)
Mandrake of Oxford (*UK*)
Mercier Press (*Ire*)
NavPress (*US*)
O Books/John Hunt Publishing Ltd (*UK*)
The O'Brien Press (*Ire*)
Octopus Publishing Group Limited (*UK*)
The Orion Publishing Group Limited (*UK*)
P&R Publishing (*US*)
Peachtree Publishers (*US*)
Piatkus Books (*UK*)
Primordial Traditions (*Aus*)
Search Institute Press (*US*)
Shelfstealers (*US*)
Square One Publishers, Inc. (*US*)
Tirgearr Publishing (*Ire*)

Tiger of the Stripe (*UK*)
Which? Books (*UK*)
WindRiver Publishing (*US*)
Literature
Alma Books Ltd (*UK*)
Andrews UK Limited (*UK*)
Bloodaxe Books Ltd (*UK*)
Bloomsbury Academic (*UK*)
Boathook Books (*UK*)
Borealis Press (*Can*)
Carcanet Press Ltd (*UK*)
Central Avenue Publishing (*Can*)
Chapultepec Press (*US*)
Colin Smythe Ltd (*UK*)
Compelling Books (*UK*)
Corwin (*US*)
Cross-Cultural Communications Publications
(*US*)
James Currey Publishers (*UK*)
Dedalus Ltd (*UK*)
Demarche Publishing (*US*)
Dover Publications, Inc. (*US*)
Dzanc Books (*US*)
Eleusinian Press (*UK*)
Erotic Review (ER) Books (*UK*)
Flame Lily Books (*UK*)
Floris Books (*UK*)
Glenbridge Publishing Ltd (*US*)
Gomer Press (*UK*)
Green Books (*UK*)
Halban Publishers (*UK*)
Homestead Publishing (*US*)
House of Lochar (*UK*)
Indigo Dreams Publishing (*UK*)
Irish Academic Press (*Ire*)
Itoh Press (*US*)
Kitsune Books (*US*)
The Lilliput Press (*Ire*)
Little, Brown Book Group (*UK*)
Liverpool University Press (*UK*)
M P Publishing USA (*US*)
Mango Publishing (*UK*)
Methuen Publishing Ltd (*UK*)
New Dawn Publishers Ltd (*UK*)
New Libri (*US*)
New Island (*Ire*)
NeWest Press (*Can*)
The O'Brien Press (*Ire*)
Octagon Press Ltd (*UK*)
Open Gate Press (*UK*)
Open Idea Publishing, LLC (*US*)
The Orion Publishing Group Limited (*UK*)
Peter Owen Publishers (*UK*)
Oxford University Press (*UK*)
Pressgang (*US*)
Red Moon Press (*US*)
Salt Publishing Ltd (*UK*)
Santa Monica Press (*US*)
Shearsman Books (*UK*)
Shelfstealers (*US*)
Sunberry Books (*UK*)
Sussex Academic Press (*UK*)
Tirgearr Publishing (*Ire*)

Texas Western Press (*US*)
Tiger of the Stripe (*UK*)
University of Ottawa Press (*Can*)
University of Wales Press (*UK*)
Upstart Books (*US*)
Media
Andrews UK Limited (*UK*)
Bloomsbury Academic (*UK*)
Booth-Clibborn Editions (*UK*)
Central Avenue Publishing (*Can*)
Coastal West Publishing (*Can*)
Eleusinian Press (*UK*)
Evans Brothers Ltd (*UK*)
Freelance Writer's Resource (*US*)
Indigo Dreams Publishing (*UK*)
Pluto Publishing Ltd (*UK*)
Reed Business Information (RBI) (*UK*)
Sage Publications (*UK*)
Silman-James Press (*US*)
Sussex Academic Press (*UK*)
Tirgearr Publishing (*Ire*)
Tiger of the Stripe (*UK*)
University of Ottawa Press (*Can*)
University of Wales Press (*UK*)
Wallflower Press (*UK*)
ZigZag Education (*UK*)
Medicine
Andrews UK Limited (*UK*)
Birlinn Ltd (*UK*)
Chemical Publishing Company (*US*)
Eastland Press (*US*)
Eleusinian Press (*UK*)
EMIS Inc. Medical Publishers (*US*)
Freelance Writer's Resource (*US*)
Glenbridge Publishing Ltd (*US*)
Hammersmith Press Ltd (*UK*)
Hay House Publishers (*UK*)
Hodder Education (*UK*)
Jones & Bartlett Learning (*US*)
Lawyers & Judges Publishing Co. (*US*)
Medical Group Management Association
(MGMA) (*US*)
O Books/John Hunt Publishing Ltd (*UK*)
Oxford University Press (*UK*)
Portland Press Ltd (*UK*)
Radcliffe Publishing Ltd (*UK*)
Sage Publications (*UK*)
Science Navigation Group (*UK*)
SLACK Incorporated (*US*)
TSO (The Stationery Office) (*UK*)
Tiger of the Stripe (*UK*)
Vitesse Press (*US*)
Wellness Institute/Self-Help Books, LLC (*US*)
Men's Interests
Andrews UK Limited (*UK*)
Belvedere Publishing (*UK*)
Central Avenue Publishing (*Can*)
Eleusinian Press (*UK*)
Fingerpress UK (*UK*)
Glastonbury Publishing (*UK*)
Hay House Publishers (*UK*)
Indigo Dreams Publishing (*UK*)
Jewish Lights Publishing (*US*)

My Pouty Lips (*US*)
Shelfstealers (*US*)
Tirgearr Publishing (*Ire*)
Military
ABC-CLIO / Greenwood (*US*)
Ian Allan Publishing Ltd (*UK*)
Allison & Busby Ltd (*UK*)
Amberley Publishing (*UK*)
Andrews UK Limited (*UK*)
Anova Books (*UK*)
Arcturus Publishing Ltd (*UK*)
Arkansas Research, Inc. (*US*)
Aurum Press Ltd (*UK*)
Belvedere Publishing (*UK*)
Birlinn Ltd (*UK*)
Burford Books (*US*)
Central Avenue Publishing (*Can*)
Constable & Robinson Ltd (*UK*)
Demarche Publishing (*US*)
ETC Publications (*US*)
Fingerpress UK (*UK*)
Flame Lily Books (*UK*)
Freelance Writer's Resource (*US*)
Frontline Books (*UK*)
Gauthier Publications (*US*)
The Glencannon Press (*US*)
Grub Street Publishing (*UK*)
Heritage Books, Inc. (*US*)
Haynes Publishing (*UK*)
Mercier Press (*Ire*)
Methuen Publishing Ltd (*UK*)
The Orion Publishing Group Limited (*UK*)
Pants On Fire Press (*US*)
Pen & Sword Books Ltd (*UK*)
Robert Hale Publishers (*UK*)
Seafarer Books (*UK*)
Shelfstealers (*US*)
Tirgearr Publishing (*Ire*)
Tiger of the Stripe (*UK*)
Ulric Publishing (*UK*)
University of North Carolina Press (*US*)
University of Ottawa Press (*Can*)
The University Press of Kentucky (*US*)
Westholme Publishing (*US*)
White Mane Publishing Co., Inc. (*US*)
Music
Andrews UK Limited (*UK*)
Anova Books (*UK*)
Aurum Press Ltd (*UK*)
Black Dog Publishing London UK (*UK*)
Bloomsbury Academic (*UK*)
The Bold Strummer Ltd (*US*)
Cadence Jazz Books (*US*)
Central Avenue Publishing (*Can*)
Chapultepec Press (*US*)
Consortium Publishing (*US*)
The Creative Company (*US*)
Dover Publications, Inc. (*US*)
Eleusinian Press (*UK*)
Elliott & Thompson (*UK*)
Evans Brothers Ltd (*UK*)
Faber & Faber Ltd (*UK*)
Flame Lily Books (*UK*)

Giles de la Mare Publishers Ltd (*UK*)
Glenbridge Publishing Ltd (*US*)
Gomer Press (*UK*)
Hinkler Books (*Aus*)
The Ilium Press (*US*)
Indigo Dreams Publishing (*UK*)
Itoh Press (*US*)
Kearney Street Books (*US*)
The Lilliput Press (*Ire*)
Liverpool University Press (*UK*)
Kevin Mayhew Publishers (*UK*)
Neil Wilson Publishing Ltd (*UK*)
Northumbria University Press (*UK*)
O Books/John Hunt Publishing Ltd (*UK*)
The O'Brien Press (*Ire*)
Octopus Publishing Group Limited (*UK*)
Omnibus Press (*UK*)
Oxford University Press (*UK*)
Phaidon Press Limited (*UK*)
Plexus Publishing Limited (*UK*)
Quite Specific Media Group (*US*)
Seafarer Books (*UK*)
Seren (*UK*)
Sussex Academic Press (*UK*)
Tiger of the Stripe (*UK*)
ZigZag Education (*UK*)

Mystery
Affluent Publishing Corporation (*US*)
Allison & Busby Ltd (*UK*)
Ampichellis Ebooks (*US*)
Andrews UK Limited (*UK*)
Artemis Press (*US*)
Belvedere Publishing (*UK*)
Black Coffey Publishing (*UK*)
bookouture (*UK*)
Central Avenue Publishing (*Can*)
Compelling Books (*UK*)
The Countryman Press (*US*)
Demarche Publishing (*US*)
Demontreville Press, Inc. (*US*)
Divertir Publishing LLC (*US*)
Flame Lily Books (*UK*)
Gauthier Publications (*US*)
Glastonbury Publishing (*UK*)
Highland Press (*US*)
ImaJinn Books (*US*)
Indigo Dreams Publishing (*UK*)
Ingalls Publishing Group, Inc. (*US*)
Jewish Lights Publishing (*US*)
Kane Miller Books (*US*)
Kelly Point Publishing LLC (*US*)
Loose Id (*US*)
Lost Tower Publications (*UK*)
M P Publishing USA (*US*)
Mandrake of Oxford (*UK*)
Medallion Media Group (*US*)
Moose Hide Books (*Can*)
New Dawn Publishers Ltd (*UK*)
Netherworld Books (*UK*)
New Victoria Publishers (*US*)
Nicolas Hays Publishers (*US*)
Open Idea Publishing, LLC (*US*)
Pressgang (*US*)

SalGad Publishing Group (*UK*)
Shelfstealers (*US*)
Sunberry Books (*UK*)
Tiger of the Stripe (*UK*)
Tor/Forge (*US*)
TouchWood Editions (*Can*)
WindRiver Publishing (*US*)
The Zharmae Publishing Press (*US*)

Nature
Alastair Sawday Publishing Co. Ltd (*UK*)
Andrews UK Limited (*UK*)
Baywood Publishing Company, Inc. (*US*)
Birdsong Books (*US*)
Birlinn Ltd (*UK*)
Black Dog Publishing London UK (*UK*)
Blackstaff Press Ltd (*UK*)
Boathook Books (*UK*)
Burford Books (*US*)
Central Avenue Publishing (*Can*)
Chapultepec Press (*US*)
The Countryman Press (*US*)
The Creative Company (*US*)
Demarche Publishing (*US*)
Demontreville Press, Inc. (*US*)
Down East Books (*US*)
Down The Shore Publishing (*US*)
Farcountry Press (*US*)
Fifth House Publishers (*Can*)
Flame Lily Books (*UK*)
Fountain Press (*UK*)
Fox Chapel Publishing (*US*)
Freelance Writer's Resource (*US*)
Fulcrum Publishing (*US*)
Glenbridge Publishing Ltd (*US*)
Gomer Press (*UK*)
Grand Canyon Association (*US*)
Green Books (*UK*)
Hay House Publishers (*UK*)
Homestead Publishing (*US*)
Indigo Dreams Publishing (*UK*)
The Lilliput Press (*Ire*)
Luath Press Ltd (*UK*)
Mountain Press Publishing Company (*US*)
Neil Wilson Publishing Ltd (*UK*)
NeWest Press (*Can*)
Northumbria University Press (*UK*)
O Books/John Hunt Publishing Ltd (*UK*)
The O'Brien Press (*Ire*)
Open Gate Press (*UK*)
The Orion Publishing Group Limited (*UK*)
Pants On Fire Press (*US*)
Peachtree Publishers (*US*)
Pluto Publishing Ltd (*UK*)
Pocket Mountains (*UK*)
Rowman & Littlefield Publishing Group (*US*)
Shelfstealers (*US*)
Sussex Academic Press (*UK*)
Tirgearr Publishing (*Ire*)
Tiger of the Stripe (*UK*)
Tilbury House, Publishers (*US*)
Torrey House Press, LLC (*US*)
TouchWood Editions (*Can*)
Union Square Publishing (*US*)

University of North Carolina Press (*US*)
University of Wales Press (*UK*)
Whittet Books Ltd (*UK*)
Windward Publishing (*US*)
Woodhead Publishing Ltd (*UK*)
New Age
Andrews UK Limited (*UK*)
Arcturus Publishing Ltd (*UK*)
Belvedere Publishing (*UK*)
Central Avenue Publishing (*Can*)
Findhorn Press Ltd (*UK*)
Gem Guides Book Co. (*US*)
Glastonbury Publishing (*UK*)
Humanics Publishing Group (*US*)
Indigo Dreams Publishing (*UK*)
Itoh Press (*US*)
Jupiter Gardens Press (*US*)
Kitsune Books (*US*)
Netherworld Books (*UK*)
New Victoria Publishers (*US*)
Primordial Traditions (*Aus*)
Tirgearr Publishing (*Ire*)
Nonfiction
AA Publishing (*UK*)
ABC-CLIO / Greenwood (*US*)
Absolute Press (*UK*)
Addicus Books (*US*)
Alastair Sawday Publishing Co. Ltd (*UK*)
Alexander Hamilton Institute (*US*)
Ian Allan Publishing Ltd (*UK*)
J.A. Allen (*UK*)
Allison & Busby Ltd (*UK*)
Alma Books Ltd (*UK*)
Amberley Publishing (*UK*)
American Atheists (*US*)
American Correctional Association (ACA) (*US*)
American Psychological Association (APA)
Books (*US*)
Amherst Media (*US*)
Ammonite Press (*UK*)
Andrews UK Limited (*UK*)
Anova Books (*UK*)
Arcturus Publishing Ltd (*UK*)
Arkansas Research, Inc. (*US*)
The Armchair Traveller at the bookHaus (*UK*)
Arris Publishing Ltd (*UK*)
Ashmolean Museum Publications (*UK*)
Aunt Lute Books (*US*)
Aurora Metro Press (*UK*)
Aurum Press Ltd (*UK*)
Aviation Supplies & Academics, Inc. (*US*)
Award Publications Limited (*UK*)
Azro Press (*US*)
Baywood Publishing Company, Inc. (*US*)
Behrman House (*US*)
Betterway Home Books (*US*)
Birdsong Books (*US*)
Birlinn Ltd (*UK*)
Black & White Publishing Ltd (*UK*)
Black Dog Publishing London UK (*UK*)
Blackline Press (*UK*)
Blackstaff Press Ltd (*UK*)
Bloodaxe Books Ltd (*UK*)

Bloomsbury Academic (*UK*)
Bloomsbury Professional (*UK*)
Blue Dolphin Publishing (*US*)
Blue Guides Limited (*UK*)
BlueBridge (*US*)
Boathook Books (*UK*)
The Bold Strummer Ltd (*US*)
Booth-Clibborn Editions (*UK*)
Borealis Press (*Can*)
Bottom Dog Press (*US*)
Bracket Books (*US*)
Bright Mountain Books, Inc. (*US*)
Brighter Books Publishing House (*Can*)
Bristol Publishing Enterprises (*US*)
Burford Books (*US*)
Cadence Jazz Books (*US*)
Canongate Books (*UK*)
Carcanet Press Ltd (*UK*)
Cardoza Publishing (*US*)
Carolrhoda Books, Inc. (*US*)
Carstens Publications, Inc. (*US*)
Cedar Fort (*US*)
Channel Lake, Inc. (*US*)
Chapultepec Press (*US*)
Chemical Publishing Company (*US*)
Christian Focus Publications (*UK*)
Church Growth Institute (*US*)
City Lights Publishers (*US*)
James Clarke & Co. (*UK*)
Clear Light Books (*US*)
Coastal West Publishing (*Can*)
Coffee House Press (*US*)
Colin Smythe Ltd (*UK*)
The College Board (*US*)
Compelling Books (*UK*)
Consortium Publishing (*US*)
Constable & Robinson Ltd (*UK*)
Corwin (*US*)
The Countryman Press (*US*)
The Creative Company (*US*)
Cressrelles Publishing Co. Ltd (*UK*)
Cross-Cultural Communications Publications
(*US*)
Crossway (*US*)
James Currey Publishers (*UK*)
Cycle Publishing / Van der Plas Publications
(*US*)
Demarche Publishing (*US*)
Demontreville Press, Inc. (*US*)
Diversion Books (*US*)
Divertir Publishing LLC (*US*)
DK Publishing (*US*)
Dover Publications, Inc. (*US*)
Down East Books (*US*)
Down The Shore Publishing (*US*)
Duckworth Publishers (*UK*)
Eastland Press (*US*)
EDCON Publishing Group (*US*)
Edupress, Inc. (*US*)
Eleusinian Press (*UK*)
Elliott & Thompson (*UK*)
EMIS Inc. Medical Publishers (*US*)
Emissary Publishing (*UK*)

Erotic Review (ER) Books (*UK*)
ETC Publications (*US*)
Evans Brothers Ltd (*UK*)
Everyman Chess (*UK*)
Faber & Faber Ltd (*UK*)
Facet Publishing (*UK*)
Farcountry Press (*US*)
Fifth House Publishers (*Can*)
Findhorn Press Ltd (*UK*)
Fingerpress UK (*UK*)
First & Best in Education Ltd (*UK*)
Flame Lily Books (*UK*)
Florida Academic Press (*US*)
Floris Books (*UK*)
Fountain Press (*UK*)
Fox Chapel Publishing (*US*)
Freelance Writer's Resource (*US*)
Frontline Books (*UK*)
Fulcrum Publishing (*US*)
George Ronald Publisher (*UK*)
Galore Park Publishing Ltd (*UK*)
Gauthier Publications (*US*)
Geddes & Grosset (*UK*)
Gem Guides Book Co. (*US*)
Gibson Square Books Ltd (*UK*)
Giles de la Mare Publishers Ltd (*UK*)
Glenbridge Publishing Ltd (*US*)
The Glencannon Press (*US*)
Golden West Books (*US*)
Gomer Press (*UK*)
Grand Canyon Association (*US*)
Green Books (*UK*)
Gresham Books Ltd (*UK*)
Grub Street Publishing (*UK*)
Guild of Master Craftsman (GMC) Publications Ltd (*UK*)
Gulf Publishing Company (*US*)
Gwasg Carreg Gwalch (*UK*)
Heritage Books, Inc. (*US*)
The Habit of Rainy Nights Press (*US*)
Hachette Children's Books (*UK*)
Hachette UK (*UK*)
Halban Publishers (*UK*)
Halsgrove (*UK*)
Hammersmith Press Ltd (*UK*)
Harriman House Ltd (*UK*)
Hart Publishing Ltd (*UK*)
The Harvard Common Press (*US*)
Hay House Publishers (*UK*)
Hayes School Publishing Co., Inc. (*US*)
Haynes Publishing (*UK*)
Headland Publications (*UK*)
High Stakes Publishing (*UK*)
High-Lonesome (*US*)
Highland Press (*US*)
Hilmarton Manor Press (*UK*)
Hinkler Books (*Aus*)
Hodder Education (*UK*)
Homestead Publishing (*US*)
Honno Welsh Women's Press (*UK*)
Hopewell Publications (*US*)
Hopscotch (*UK*)
House of Anansi Press (*Can*)

House of Lochar (*UK*)
How to Books Ltd (*UK*)
Humanics Publishing Group (*US*)
Hyperink (*US*)
ICSA Information & Training Ltd (*UK*)
Ideals Publications (*US*)
Igloo Books Limited (*UK*)
Ignatius Press (*US*)
The Ilium Press (*US*)
Immedium (*US*)
Impact Books (*US*)
Impress Books Limited (*UK*)
Indigo Dreams Publishing (*UK*)
Ingalls Publishing Group, Inc. (*US*)
Inter-Varsity Press (*UK*)
International Press (*US*)
Irish Academic Press (*Ire*)
Itoh Press (*US*)
Jewish Lights Publishing (*US*)
John F. Blair, Publisher (*US*)
Jonathan David Publishers, Inc. (*US*)
Jones & Bartlett Learning (*US*)
Jupiter Gardens Press (*US*)
Just Us Books (*US*)
Kindred Productions (*Can*)
Kalmbach Publishing Co. (*US*)
Kamehameha Publishing (*US*)
Kids Can Press (*Can*)
Jessica Kingsley Publishers (*UK*)
Kitsune Books (*US*)
Legacy Press (*US*)
Lawyers & Judges Publishing Co. (*US*)
Leapfrog Press (*US*)
Ledge Hill Publishing (*US*)
The Lilliput Press (*Ire*)
Frances Lincoln Ltd (*UK*)
Linden Publishing (*US*)
Lion Hudson Plc (*UK*)
Little, Brown Book Group (*UK*)
Liverpool University Press (*UK*)
Luath Press Ltd (*UK*)
Lucent Books (*US*)
Lund Humphries Limited (*UK*)
The Lutterworth Press (*UK*)
M P Publishing USA (*US*)
Magenta Publishing for the Arts (*Can*)
Mainstream Publishing Co. (Edinburgh) Ltd (*UK*)
Management Books 2000 Ltd (*UK*)
Mandrake of Oxford (*UK*)
Mango Publishing (*UK*)
Mantra Lingua Ltd (*UK*)
Master Books (*US*)
Kevin Mayhew Publishers (*UK*)
MBooks of BC (Multicultural Books of British Columbia) (*Can*)
McGraw-Hill Education EMEA (*UK*)
Medallion Media Group (*US*)
Medical Group Management Association (MGMA) (*US*)
Mercier Press (*Ire*)
The Merlin Press (*UK*)
Messianic Jewish Publishers (*US*)

University of Ottawa Press (*Can*)
University of Wales Press (*UK*)
The University Press of Kentucky (*US*)
Upstart Books (*US*)
The Urban Land Institute (ULI) (*US*)
Velazquez Press (*US*)
Vitesse Press (*US*)
Wooden Books (*UK*)
Woodbine House (*US*)
Wallflower Press (*UK*)
Wellness Institute/Self-Help Books, LLC (*US*)
Welsh Academic Press (*UK*)
Westholme Publishing (*US*)
Which? Books (*UK*)
White Mane Publishing Co., Inc. (*US*)
Whittet Books Ltd (*UK*)
William Reed Business Media (*UK*)
WindRiver Publishing (*US*)
Windswept House Publishers (*US*)
Windward Publishing (*US*)
Wolters Kluwer (UK) Ltd (*UK*)
Woodhead Publishing Ltd (*UK*)
Zero to Ten Limited (*UK*)
ZigZag Education (*UK*)
Philosophy
American Atheists (*US*)
Andrews UK Limited (*UK*)
Arcturus Publishing Ltd (*UK*)
Behrman House (*US*)
Bloomsbury Academic (*UK*)
Blue Dolphin Publishing (*US*)
Central Avenue Publishing (*Can*)
Chapultepec Press (*US*)
Clear Light Books (*US*)
Compelling Books (*UK*)
Dagda Publishing (*UK*)
Duckworth Publishers (*UK*)
Eleusinian Press (*UK*)
Floris Books (*UK*)
Gibson Square Books Ltd (*UK*)
Halban Publishers (*UK*)
Hay House Publishers (*UK*)
Itoh Press (*US*)
Jewish Lights Publishing (*US*)
The Lilliput Press (*Ire*)
Mandrake of Oxford (*UK*)
The Merlin Press (*UK*)
Methuen Publishing Ltd (*UK*)
O Books/John Hunt Publishing Ltd (*UK*)
Octagon Press Ltd (*UK*)
Oneworld Publications (*UK*)
Open Court Publishing Company (*US*)
Open Gate Press (*UK*)
Oxford University Press (*UK*)
Primordial Traditions (*Aus*)
Rowman & Littlefield Publishing Group (*US*)
SCM-Canterbury Press (*UK*)
Shelfstealers (*US*)
Shepheard-Walwyn (Publishers) Ltd (*UK*)
Sussex Academic Press (*UK*)
The Trinity Foundation (*US*)
University of Ottawa Press (*Can*)
University of Wales Press (*UK*)

The University Press of Kentucky (*US*)
ZigZag Education (*UK*)
Photography
Amherst Media (*US*)
Ammonite Press (*UK*)
Andrews UK Limited (*UK*)
Anova Books (*UK*)
Aurum Press Ltd (*UK*)
Black Dog Publishing London UK (*UK*)
Booth-Clibborn Editions (*UK*)
Bracket Books (*US*)
Carstens Publications, Inc. (*US*)
Central Avenue Publishing (*Can*)
Chapultepec Press (*US*)
Constable & Robinson Ltd (*UK*)
The Countryman Press (*US*)
Eleusinian Press (*UK*)
Enitharmon Press (*UK*)
Erotic Review (ER) Books (*UK*)
Farcountry Press (*US*)
Fingerpress UK (*UK*)
Fountain Press (*UK*)
Fox Chapel Publishing (*US*)
Gauthier Publications (*US*)
Grand Canyon Association (*US*)
Guild of Master Craftsman (GMC) Publications
Ltd (*UK*)
Halsgrove (*UK*)
Homestead Publishing (*US*)
Indigo Dreams Publishing (*UK*)
The Lilliput Press (*Ire*)
Luath Press Ltd (*UK*)
Magenta Publishing for the Arts (*Can*)
Northumbria University Press (*UK*)
O Books/John Hunt Publishing Ltd (*UK*)
The O'Brien Press (*Ire*)
Phaidon Press Limited (*UK*)
Prestel Publishing Ltd (*UK*)
Santa Monica Press (*US*)
Seren (*UK*)
Texas Western Press (*US*)
Thames and Hudson Ltd (*UK*)
Tiger of the Stripe (*UK*)
Poetry
Able Muse Press (*US*)
Alice James Books (*US*)
Andrews UK Limited (*UK*)
Angoor Press LLC (*US*)
Arctos Press (*US*)
Aunt Lute Books (*US*)
Birlinn Ltd (*UK*)
Blackstaff Press Ltd (*UK*)
Bloodaxe Books Ltd (*UK*)
Blue Dolphin Publishing (*US*)
Borealis Press (*Can*)
Bottom Dog Press (*US*)
Brick Road Poetry Press (*US*)
Bridge Burner's Publishing (*US*)
Carcanet Press Ltd (*UK*)
Central Avenue Publishing (*Can*)
Chapultepec Press (*US*)
City Lights Publishers (*US*)
Coffee House Press (*US*)

Colin Smythe Ltd (*UK*)
Cross-Cultural Communications Publications (*US*)
Dagda Publishing (*UK*)
Divertir Publishing LLC (*US*)
Down The Shore Publishing (*US*)
Eleusinian Press (*UK*)
Enitharmon Press (*UK*)
Evans Brothers Ltd (*UK*)
Everheart Books (*Can*)
Faber & Faber Ltd (*UK*)
Four Way Books (*US*)
Gomer Press (*UK*)
Grey Hen Press (*UK*)
The Habit of Rainy Nights Press (*US*)
Headland Publications (*UK*)
Honno Welsh Women's Press (*UK*)
House of Anansi Press (*Can*)
The Ilium Press (*US*)
Indigo Dreams Publishing (*UK*)
Just Us Books (*US*)
Kitsune Books (*US*)
Leapfrog Press (*US*)
Ledge Hill Publishing (*US*)
Les Figues Press (*US*)
The Lilliput Press (*Ire*)
Local Gems Poetry Press (*US*)
Lost Tower Publications (*UK*)
Luath Press Ltd (*UK*)
Mango Publishing (*UK*)
MBooks of BC (Multicultural Books of British Columbia) (*Can*)
Methuen Publishing Ltd (*UK*)
Moon Tide Press (*US*)
Moose Hide Books (*Can*)
New Beacon Books, Ltd (*UK*)
New Island (*Ire*)
New Native Press (*US*)
New Rivers Press (*US*)
New Victoria Publishers (*US*)
NeWest Press (*Can*)
O Books/John Hunt Publishing Ltd (*UK*)
The O'Brien Press (*Ire*)
Onlywomen Press Ltd (*UK*)
Open Idea Publishing, LLC (*US*)
Oversteps Books (*UK*)
Parthian Books (*UK*)
Perugia Press (*US*)
Phoenix Yard Books (*UK*)
PUBSLUSH Press (*US*)
Pureplay Press (*US*)
Rattapallax Press (*US*)
Red Moon Press (*US*)
Rose Alley Press (*US*)
Sam's Dot Publishing (*US*)
Seren (*UK*)
Shearsman Books (*UK*)
Shepheard-Walwyn (Publishers) Ltd (*UK*)
Spire Press, Inc. (*US*)
Spout Press (*US*)
Tiger of the Stripe (*UK*)
Timberline Press Books (*US*)
Torrey House Press, LLC (*US*)

Tradewind Books (*Can*)
Two Ravens Press Ltd (*UK*)
Washington Writers' Publishing House (*US*)
White Eagle Coffee Store Press (*US*)
Politics
American Atheists (*US*)
Andrews UK Limited (*UK*)
Arris Publishing Ltd (*UK*)
Birlinn Ltd (*UK*)
Blackstaff Press Ltd (*UK*)
Bloomsbury Academic (*UK*)
Blue Dolphin Publishing (*US*)
Borealis Press (*Can*)
Canongate Books (*UK*)
Central Avenue Publishing (*Can*)
Chapultepec Press (*US*)
City Lights Publishers (*US*)
James Currey Publishers (*UK*)
Demarche Publishing (*US*)
Divertir Publishing LLC (*US*)
Eleusinian Press (*UK*)
Faber & Faber Ltd (*UK*)
Florida Academic Press (*US*)
Fulcrum Publishing (*US*)
Gibson Square Books Ltd (*UK*)
Glenbridge Publishing Ltd (*US*)
Green Books (*UK*)
Halban Publishers (*UK*)
Harriman House Ltd (*UK*)
Itoh Press (*US*)
The Lilliput Press (*Ire*)
Liverpool University Press (*UK*)
Luath Press Ltd (*UK*)
Mainstream Publishing Co. (Edinburgh) Ltd (*UK*)
Mercier Press (*Ire*)
The Merlin Press (*UK*)
Methuen Publishing Ltd (*UK*)
Monarch Books (*UK*)
New Beacon Books, Ltd (*UK*)
New Island (*Ire*)
New Victoria Publishers (*US*)
NeWest Press (*Can*)
Nicolas Hays Publishers (*US*)
O Books/John Hunt Publishing Ltd (*UK*)
The O'Brien Press (*Ire*)
Oneworld Publications (*UK*)
Open Gate Press (*UK*)
Oxford University Press (*UK*)
Pluto Publishing Ltd (*UK*)
Primordial Traditions (*Aus*)
Profile Books (*UK*)
Pureplay Press (*US*)
Reed Business Information (RBI) (*UK*)
Rivers Oram Press (*UK*)
Rowman & Littlefield Publishing Group (*US*)
Sage Publications (*UK*)
Seren (*UK*)
Shelfstealers (*US*)
Shepheard-Walwyn (Publishers) Ltd (*UK*)
Sussex Academic Press (*UK*)
Tiger of the Stripe (*UK*)
The Trinity Foundation (*US*)

Union Square Publishing (*US*)
University of Ottawa Press (*Can*)
University of Wales Press (*UK*)
The University Press of Kentucky (*US*)
Welsh Academic Press (*UK*)
WindRiver Publishing (*US*)
ZigZag Education (*UK*)
Psychology
Addicus Books (*US*)
American Psychological Association (APA)
Books (*US*)
Andrews UK Limited (*UK*)
Baywood Publishing Company, Inc. (*US*)
Blue Dolphin Publishing (*US*)
Central Avenue Publishing (*Can*)
Compelling Books (*UK*)
Consortium Publishing (*US*)
Constable & Robinson Ltd (*UK*)
Dagda Publishing (*UK*)
Demarche Publishing (*US*)
Eleusinian Press (*UK*)
EMIS Inc. Medical Publishers (*US*)
Freelance Writer's Resource (*US*)
Gibson Square Books Ltd (*UK*)
Hay House Publishers (*UK*)
Jessica Kingsley Publishers (*UK*)
Monarch Books (*UK*)
Nicolas Hays Publishers (*US*)
O Books/John Hunt Publishing Ltd (*UK*)
Octagon Press Ltd (*UK*)
Octopus Publishing Group Limited (*UK*)
Oneworld Publications (*UK*)
Open Gate Press (*UK*)
Piatkus Books (*UK*)
Profile Books (*UK*)
Psychology Press (*UK*)
Robert D. Reed Publishers (*US*)
Rowman & Littlefield Publishing Group (*US*)
Sage Publications (*UK*)
Shelfstealers (*US*)
Sussex Academic Press (*UK*)
Tiger of the Stripe (*UK*)
University of Ottawa Press (*Can*)
Woodbine House (*US*)
Wellness Institute/Self-Help Books, LLC (*US*)
ZigZag Education (*UK*)
Radio
Andrews UK Limited (*UK*)
Demarche Publishing (*US*)
Tiger of the Stripe (*UK*)
Reference
AA Publishing (*UK*)
ABC-CLIO / Greenwood (*US*)
Ian Allan Publishing Ltd (*UK*)
Andrews UK Limited (*UK*)
Anova Books (*UK*)
Arcturus Publishing Ltd (*UK*)
Award Publications Limited (*UK*)
Birlinn Ltd (*UK*)
Bloomsbury Academic (*UK*)
Bloomsbury Professional (*UK*)
Boathook Books (*UK*)
Cadence Jazz Books (*US*)

Chemical Publishing Company (*US*)
James Clarke & Co. (*UK*)
Constable & Robinson Ltd (*UK*)
Demarche Publishing (*US*)
Eleusinian Press (*UK*)
EMIS Inc. Medical Publishers (*US*)
Facet Publishing (*UK*)
Fox Chapel Publishing (*US*)
Geddes & Grosset (*UK*)
Gomer Press (*UK*)
Guild of Master Craftsman (GMC) Publications
Ltd (*UK*)
Gwasg Carreg Gwalch (*UK*)
Heritage Books, Inc. (*US*)
Hachette Children's Books (*UK*)
Haynes Publishing (*UK*)
Highland Press (*US*)
Hinkler Books (*Aus*)
Hodder Education (*UK*)
How to Books Ltd (*UK*)
ICSA Information & Training Ltd (*UK*)
Igloo Books Limited (*UK*)
Impact Books (*US*)
Inter-Varsity Press (*UK*)
Jonathan David Publishers, Inc. (*US*)
Kalmbach Publishing Co. (*US*)
Lawyers & Judges Publishing Co. (*US*)
The Lilliput Press (*Ire*)
Lion Hudson Plc (*UK*)
My Pouty Lips (*US*)
Myriad Editions (*UK*)
Neil Wilson Publishing Ltd (*UK*)
New Victoria Publishers (*US*)
Nova Press (*US*)
O Books/John Hunt Publishing Ltd (*UK*)
The O'Brien Press (*Ire*)
Octopus Publishing Group Limited (*UK*)
The Orion Publishing Group Limited (*UK*)
Oxford University Press (*UK*)
Pavilion Publishing (*UK*)
PUBSLUSH Press (*US*)
Quiller Publishing Ltd (*UK*)
Robert Hale Publishers (*UK*)
Santa Monica Press (*US*)
SCM-Canterbury Press (*UK*)
Search Institute Press (*US*)
SLACK Incorporated (*US*)
TSO (The Stationery Office) (*UK*)
Trafalgar Square Books (*US*)
Thames and Hudson Ltd (*UK*)
Unicorn Press Ltd (*UK*)
University of Ottawa Press (*Can*)
Velazquez Press (*US*)
Which? Books (*UK*)
William Reed Business Media (*UK*)
Wolters Kluwer (UK) Ltd (*UK*)
Religious
ABC-CLIO / Greenwood (*US*)
Andrews UK Limited (*UK*)
Arcturus Publishing Ltd (*UK*)
Behrman House (*US*)
Blue Dolphin Publishing (*US*)
Cedar Fort (*US*)

Central Avenue Publishing (*Can*)
Christian Focus Publications (*UK*)
Church Growth Institute (*US*)
James Clarke & Co. (*UK*)
Clear Light Books (*US*)
The Creative Company (*US*)
Crossway (*US*)
Demarche Publishing (*US*)
Divertir Publishing LLC (*US*)
ETC Publications (*US*)
Evans Brothers Ltd (*UK*)
Flame Lily Books (*UK*)
Floris Books (*UK*)
George Ronald Publisher (*UK*)
Gauthier Publications (*US*)
Gomer Press (*UK*)
Gresham Books Ltd (*UK*)
Halban Publishers (*UK*)
Hay House Publishers (*UK*)
Humanics Publishing Group (*US*)
Ignatius Press (*US*)
Inter-Varsity Press (*UK*)
Itoh Press (*US*)
Jewish Lights Publishing (*US*)
Jonathan David Publishers, Inc. (*US*)
Kindred Productions (*Can*)
Kelly Point Publishing LLC (*US*)
Jessica Kingsley Publishers (*UK*)
Legacy Press (*US*)
Lion Hudson Plc (*UK*)
The Lutterworth Press (*UK*)
Master Books (*US*)
Kevin Mayhew Publishers (*UK*)
Medallion Media Group (*US*)
Mercier Press (*Ire*)
Messianic Jewish Publishers (*US*)
Monarch Books (*UK*)
NavPress (*US*)
Netherworld Books (*UK*)
New Victoria Publishers (*US*)
Nicolas Hays Publishers (*US*)
O Books/John Hunt Publishing Ltd (*UK*)
The O'Brien Press (*Ire*)
Oneworld Publications (*UK*)
Open Gate Press (*UK*)
Oxford University Press (*UK*)
P&R Publishing (*US*)
Primordial Traditions (*Aus*)
Rowman & Littlefield Publishing Group (*US*)
Sage Publications (*UK*)
Saint Mary's Press (*US*)
SCM-Canterbury Press (*UK*)
Sheed & Ward (*US*)
Sunberry Books (*UK*)
Sussex Academic Press (*UK*)
Thames and Hudson Ltd (*UK*)
Tiger of the Stripe (*UK*)
The Trinity Foundation (*US*)
University of North Carolina Press (*US*)
University of Ottawa Press (*Can*)
University of Wales Press (*UK*)
WindRiver Publishing (*US*)
ZigZag Education (*UK*)

Romance
Affluent Publishing Corporation (*US*)
Andrews UK Limited (*UK*)
Artemis Press (*US*)
Belvedere Publishing (*UK*)
Black & White Publishing Ltd (*UK*)
Blind Eye Books (*US*)
bookouture (*UK*)
Borealis Press (*Can*)
Central Avenue Publishing (*Can*)
Changeling Press LLC (*US*)
Demarche Publishing (*US*)
Divertir Publishing LLC (*US*)
Dragonfairy Press (*US*)
Everheart Books (*Can*)
Faery Rose (*US*)
Flame Lily Books (*UK*)
48fourteen (*US*)
Freya's Bower (*US*)
Gauthier Publications (*US*)
Glastonbury Publishing (*UK*)
Highland Press (*US*)
ImaJinn Books (*US*)
Indigo Dreams Publishing (*UK*)
Ingalls Publishing Group, Inc. (*US*)
Itoh Press (*US*)
John Lynch Digital Publishing House (*Ire*)
Jupiter Gardens Press (*US*)
Kelly Point Publishing LLC (*US*)
Knox Robinson Publishing (UK) (*UK*)
Knox Robinson Publishing (US) (*US*)
Loose Id (*US*)
M P Publishing USA (*US*)
Medallion Media Group (*US*)
My Pouty Lips (*US*)
New Dawn Publishers Ltd (*UK*)
Netherworld Books (*UK*)
New Victoria Publishers (*US*)
Open Idea Publishing, LLC (*US*)
Pants On Fire Press (*US*)
Razorbill (*US*)
SalGad Publishing Group (*UK*)
Samhain Publishing (*US*)
Shelfstealers (*US*)
Tirgearr Publishing (*Ire*)
Tiger of the Stripe (*UK*)
The Wild Rose Press (*US*)
WindRiver Publishing (*US*)
The Zharmae Publishing Press (*US*)
Science
American Psychological Association (APA)
Books (*US*)
Andrews UK Limited (*UK*)
Arcturus Publishing Ltd (*UK*)
Baywood Publishing Company, Inc. (*US*)
Belvedere Publishing (*UK*)
Birdsong Books (*US*)
Canongate Books (*UK*)
Central Avenue Publishing (*Can*)
Chemical Publishing Company (*US*)
Compelling Books (*UK*)
Consortium Publishing (*US*)
Corwin (*US*)

Floris Books (*UK*)
Gauthier Publications (*US*)
Glenbridge Publishing Ltd (*US*)
Hay House Publishers (*UK*)
Hodder Education (*UK*)
How to Books Ltd (*UK*)
Humanics Publishing Group (*US*)
Management Books 2000 Ltd (*UK*)
Mandrake of Oxford (*UK*)
My Pouty Lips (*US*)
Nicolas Hays Publishers (*US*)
O Books/John Hunt Publishing Ltd (*UK*)
Oneworld Publications (*UK*)
Peachtree Publishers (*US*)
Piatkus Books (*UK*)
Red Rock Press (*US*)
Robert D. Reed Publishers (*US*)
Sun Books / Sun Publishing Company (*US*)
Search Institute Press (*US*)
Self-Counsel Press (*US*)
Shelfstealers (*US*)
Square One Publishers, Inc. (*US*)
Tirgearr Publishing (*Ire*)
Tiger of the Stripe (*UK*)
Wellness Institute/Self-Help Books, LLC (*US*)
WindRiver Publishing (*US*)
Short Stories
Allison & Busby Ltd (*UK*)
Andrews UK Limited (*UK*)
Artemis Press (*US*)
Black Coffey Publishing (*UK*)
Blackstaff Press Ltd (*UK*)
Boathook Books (*UK*)
Books For All Times (*US*)
Borealis Press (*Can*)
Bottom Dog Press (*US*)
Cedar Fort (*US*)
Central Avenue Publishing (*Can*)
Chapultepec Press (*US*)
Coastal West Publishing (*Can*)
Coffee House Press (*US*)
Compelling Books (*UK*)
Demarche Publishing (*US*)
Demontreville Press, Inc. (*US*)
Divertir Publishing LLC (*US*)
Down The Shore Publishing (*US*)
Dzanc Books (*US*)
Eleusinian Press (*UK*)
Erotic Review (ER) Books (*UK*)
Flame Lily Books (*UK*)
Four Way Books (*US*)
Freya's Bower (*US*)
Gauthier Publications (*US*)
Glass Page Books (*US*)
Headland Publications (*UK*)
Honno Welsh Women's Press (*UK*)
Jupiter Gardens Press (*US*)
Kelly Point Publishing LLC (*US*)
Kitsune Books (*US*)
Ledge Hill Publishing (*US*)
Les Figues Press (*US*)
M P Publishing USA (*US*)
Mango Publishing (*UK*)

Moose Hide Books (*Can*)
My Pouty Lips (*US*)
New Dawn Publishers Ltd (*UK*)
New Rivers Press (*US*)
New Victoria Publishers (*US*)
Open Idea Publishing, LLC (*US*)
Parthian Books (*UK*)
Pressgang (*US*)
Ramsay Publishing (*UK*)
Sam's Dot Publishing (*US*)
Shelfstealers (*US*)
Spout Press (*US*)
Tiger of the Stripe (*UK*)
Tightrope Books (*Can*)
Upstart Books (*US*)
Sociology
ABC-CLIO / Greenwood (*US*)
Amberley Publishing (*UK*)
American Psychological Association (APA)
Books (*US*)
Ammonite Press (*UK*)
Andrews UK Limited (*UK*)
Baywood Publishing Company, Inc. (*US*)
Birlinn Ltd (*UK*)
Bloomsbury Academic (*UK*)
Blue Dolphin Publishing (*US*)
Central Avenue Publishing (*Can*)
City Lights Publishers (*US*)
The Creative Company (*US*)
James Currey Publishers (*UK*)
Demarche Publishing (*US*)
Eleusinian Press (*UK*)
ETC Publications (*US*)
Evans Brothers Ltd (*UK*)
Florida Academic Press (*US*)
Floris Books (*UK*)
Freelance Writer's Resource (*US*)
Hay House Publishers (*UK*)
Itoh Press (*US*)
Jessica Kingsley Publishers (*UK*)
The Lilliput Press (*Ire*)
Liverpool University Press (*UK*)
Luath Press Ltd (*UK*)
McGraw-Hill Education EMEA (*UK*)
NavPress (*US*)
New Island (*Ire*)
O Books/John Hunt Publishing Ltd (*UK*)
Open Gate Press (*UK*)
Oxford University Press (*UK*)
Pavilion Publishing (*UK*)
Pen & Sword Books Ltd (*UK*)
Pluto Publishing Ltd (*UK*)
Rivers Oram Press (*UK*)
Rowman & Littlefield Publishing Group (*US*)
Sage Publications (*UK*)
Search Institute Press (*US*)
Shelfstealers (*US*)
Sussex Academic Press (*UK*)
Texas Western Press (*US*)
The Policy Press (*UK*)
Trentham Books Limited (*UK*)
Union Square Publishing (*US*)
University of North Carolina Press (*US*)

University of Ottawa Press (*Can*)
University of Wales Press (*UK*)
Wellness Institute/Self-Help Books, LLC (*US*)
ZigZag Education (*UK*)
Spiritual
Andrews UK Limited (*UK*)
Blue Dolphin Publishing (*US*)
BlueBridge (*US*)
Cedar Fort (*US*)
Central Avenue Publishing (*Can*)
Coastal West Publishing (*Can*)
Demarche Publishing (*US*)
Divertir Publishing LLC (*US*)
Eleusinian Press (*UK*)
Findhorn Press Ltd (*UK*)
Floris Books (*UK*)
Freelance Writer's Resource (*US*)
Hay House Publishers (*UK*)
Hinkler Books (*Aus*)
Indigo Dreams Publishing (*UK*)
Itoh Press (*US*)
Jewish Lights Publishing (*US*)
Kelly Point Publishing LLC (*US*)
Lion Hudson Plc (*UK*)
Lost Tower Publications (*UK*)
Mandrake of Oxford (*UK*)
Kevin Mayhew Publishers (*UK*)
Monarch Books (*UK*)
NavPress (*US*)
Netherworld Books (*UK*)
O Books/John Hunt Publishing Ltd (*UK*)
Octopus Publishing Group Limited (*UK*)
Piatkus Books (*UK*)
Primordial Traditions (*Aus*)
Robert D. Reed Publishers (*US*)
Robert Hale Publishers (*UK*)
Saint Mary's Press (*US*)
SCM-Canterbury Press (*UK*)
Sheed & Ward (*US*)
Shelfstealers (*US*)
Wooden Books (*UK*)
Sport
Amberley Publishing (*UK*)
Andrews UK Limited (*UK*)
Anova Books (*UK*)
Arcturus Publishing Ltd (*UK*)
Aurum Press Ltd (*UK*)
Birlinn Ltd (*UK*)
Black & White Publishing Ltd (*UK*)
Blackline Press (*UK*)
Blackstaff Press Ltd (*UK*)
Boathook Books (*UK*)
Burford Books (*US*)
Central Avenue Publishing (*Can*)
Constable & Robinson Ltd (*UK*)
The Creative Company (*US*)
Cycle Publishing / Van der Plas Publications
(*US*)
Demarche Publishing (*US*)
Down East Books (*US*)
Elliott & Thompson (*UK*)
ETC Publications (*US*)
Fox Chapel Publishing (*US*)

Gomer Press (*UK*)
Grand Canyon Association (*US*)
Haynes Publishing (*UK*)
Hinkler Books (*Aus*)
Indigo Dreams Publishing (*UK*)
Jonathan David Publishers, Inc. (*US*)
Kelly Point Publishing LLC (*US*)
The Lilliput Press (*Ire*)
Luath Press Ltd (*UK*)
Mainstream Publishing Co. (Edinburgh) Ltd
(*UK*)
Mercier Press (*Ire*)
Methuen Publishing Ltd (*UK*)
Motor Racing Publications (*UK*)
Northumbria University Press (*UK*)
O Books/John Hunt Publishing Ltd (*UK*)
The O'Brien Press (*Ire*)
Octopus Publishing Group Limited (*UK*)
The Orion Publishing Group Limited (*UK*)
Pants On Fire Press (*US*)
Peachtree Publishers (*US*)
Pennant Books Ltd (*UK*)
Quiller Publishing Ltd (*UK*)
Santa Monica Press (*US*)
Seren (*UK*)
SportsBooks Limited (*UK*)
Vitesse Press (*US*)
Westholme Publishing (*US*)
ZigZag Education (*UK*)
Suspense
Affluent Publishing Corporation (*US*)
Andrews UK Limited (*UK*)
Belvedere Publishing (*UK*)
Black Coffey Publishing (*UK*)
bookouture (*UK*)
Central Avenue Publishing (*Can*)
Dagda Publishing (*UK*)
Demarche Publishing (*US*)
Divertir Publishing LLC (*US*)
Fingerpress UK (*UK*)
Flame Lily Books (*UK*)
Gauthier Publications (*US*)
Glastonbury Publishing (*UK*)
Highland Press (*US*)
Indigo Dreams Publishing (*UK*)
Itoh Press (*US*)
Loose Id (*US*)
Lost Tower Publications (*UK*)
M P Publishing USA (*US*)
Medallion Media Group (*US*)
Moose Hide Books (*Can*)
New Dawn Publishers Ltd (*UK*)
Netherworld Books (*UK*)
Pants On Fire Press (*US*)
Pressgang (*US*)
Razorbill (*US*)
Shelfstealers (*US*)
Tirgearr Publishing (*Ire*)
Tiger of the Stripe (*UK*)
Tor/Forge (*US*)
TouchWood Editions (*Can*)
WindRiver Publishing (*US*)
The Zharmae Publishing Press (*US*)

Technology
Andrews UK Limited (*UK*)
Anova Books (*UK*)
Aviation Supplies & Academics, Inc. (*US*)
Baywood Publishing Company, Inc. (*US*)
Bloomsbury Academic (*UK*)
Central Avenue Publishing (*Can*)
Chemical Publishing Company (*US*)
Compelling Books (*UK*)
Corwin (*US*)
Demarche Publishing (*US*)
Demontreville Press, Inc. (*US*)
Evans Brothers Ltd (*UK*)
Facet Publishing (*UK*)
Fingerpress UK (*UK*)
Flame Lily Books (*UK*)
Freelance Writer's Resource (*US*)
Gulf Publishing Company (*US*)
Haynes Publishing (*UK*)
Jones & Bartlett Learning (*US*)
Morgan Kaufmann Publishers (*US*)
New Libri (*US*)
O Books/John Hunt Publishing Ltd (*UK*)
Pants On Fire Press (*US*)
PennWell Books (*US*)
Que Publishing (*US*)
Rolenta Press (*US*)
Sage Publications (*UK*)
Shelfstealers (*US*)
Tirgearr Publishing (*Ire*)
Tiger of the Stripe (*UK*)
Ulric Publishing (*UK*)
University of Ottawa Press (*Can*)
Which? Books (*UK*)
Woodhead Publishing Ltd (*UK*)
ZigZag Education (*UK*)
Theatre
Andrews UK Limited (*UK*)
Central Avenue Publishing (*Can*)
Colin Smythe Ltd (*UK*)
James Currey Publishers (*UK*)
Eleusinian Press (*UK*)
Faber & Faber Ltd (*UK*)
Glenbridge Publishing Ltd (*US*)
Gomer Press (*UK*)
Indigo Dreams Publishing (*UK*)
Itoh Press (*US*)
Methuen Publishing Ltd (*UK*)
Moose Hide Books (*Can*)
Oberon Books (*UK*)
Open Idea Publishing, LLC (*US*)
Quite Specific Media Group (*US*)
Sussex Academic Press (*UK*)
Tiger of the Stripe (*UK*)
Thrillers
Allison & Busby Ltd (*UK*)
Ampichellis Ebooks (*US*)
Andrews UK Limited (*UK*)
Belvedere Publishing (*UK*)
Black Coffey Publishing (*UK*)
bookouture (*UK*)
Central Avenue Publishing (*Can*)
Demarche Publishing (*US*)

Eleusinian Press (*UK*)
Emissary Publishing (*UK*)
Fingerpress UK (*UK*)
Flame Lily Books (*UK*)
48fourteen (*US*)
Gauthier Publications (*US*)
Glastonbury Publishing (*UK*)
Indigo Dreams Publishing (*UK*)
Little, Brown Book Group (*UK*)
Lost Tower Publications (*UK*)
Luath Press Ltd (*UK*)
M P Publishing USA (*US*)
Medallion Media Group (*US*)
New Dawn Publishers Ltd (*UK*)
Netherworld Books (*UK*)
New Victoria Publishers (*US*)
Old Street Publishing Ltd (*UK*)
Pants On Fire Press (*US*)
Piatkus Books (*UK*)
SalGad Publishing Group (*UK*)
Salt Publishing Ltd (*UK*)
Shelfstealers (*US*)
Tirgearr Publishing (*Ire*)
Tiger of the Stripe (*UK*)
WindRiver Publishing (*US*)
The Zharmae Publishing Press (*US*)
Translations
Andrews UK Limited (*UK*)
Arabia Books (*UK*)
Arris Publishing Ltd (*UK*)
Aurora Metro Press (*UK*)
Aurora Publishing, Inc (*US*)
Canongate Books (*UK*)
Carcanet Press Ltd (*UK*)
Central Avenue Publishing (*Can*)
Chapultepec Press (*US*)
City Lights Publishers (*US*)
Compelling Books (*UK*)
Cross-Cultural Communications Publications
(*US*)
Dedalus Ltd (*UK*)
Duckworth Publishers (*UK*)
Eleusinian Press (*UK*)
Gauthier Publications (*US*)
Indigo Dreams Publishing (*UK*)
Mango Publishing (*US*)
Mantra Lingua Ltd (*UK*)
New Native Press (*US*)
Old Street Publishing Ltd (*UK*)
Peter Owen Publishers (*UK*)
Parthian Books (*UK*)
Primordial Traditions (*Aus*)
Red Moon Press (*US*)
Seren (*UK*)
Shearsman Books (*UK*)
Tiger of the Stripe (*UK*)
University of Ottawa Press (*Can*)
Travel
AA Publishing (*UK*)
Alastair Sawday Publishing Co. Ltd (*UK*)
Ian Allan Publishing Ltd (*UK*)
Allison & Busby Ltd (*UK*)
Amberley Publishing (*UK*)

Andrews UK Limited (*UK*)
Anova Books (*UK*)
The Armchair Traveller at the bookHaus (*UK*)
Arris Publishing Ltd (*UK*)
Aurum Press Ltd (*UK*)
Aviation Supplies & Academics, Inc. (*US*)
Birlinn Ltd (*UK*)
Blackstaff Press Ltd (*UK*)
Blue Guides Limited (*UK*)
BlueBridge (*US*)
Boathook Books (*UK*)
Burford Books (*US*)
Canongate Books (*UK*)
Central Avenue Publishing (*Can*)
Channel Lake, Inc. (*US*)
Constable & Robinson Ltd (*UK*)
The Countryman Press (*US*)
Demontreville Press, Inc. (*US*)
Eleusinian Press (*UK*)
ETC Publications (*US*)
Fingerpress UK (*UK*)
Flame Lily Books (*UK*)
Fox Chapel Publishing (*US*)
Freelance Writer's Resource (*US*)
Gem Guides Book Co. (*US*)
Gibson Square Books Ltd (*UK*)
Giles de la Mare Publishers Ltd (*UK*)
The Glencannon Press (*US*)
Golden West Books (*US*)
Gomer Press (*UK*)
Grand Canyon Association (*US*)
Gwasg Carreg Gwalch (*UK*)
Homestead Publishing (*US*)
House of Lochar (*UK*)
How to Books Ltd (*UK*)
Indigo Dreams Publishing (*UK*)
John F. Blair, Publisher (*US*)
The Lilliput Press (*Ire*)
Frances Lincoln Ltd (*UK*)
Luath Press Ltd (*UK*)
Methuen Publishing Ltd (*UK*)
Neil Wilson Publishing Ltd (*UK*)
New Island (*Ire*)
New Victoria Publishers (*US*)
O Books/John Hunt Publishing Ltd (*UK*)
The O'Brien Press (*Ire*)
Octagon Press Ltd (*UK*)
Octopus Publishing Group Limited (*UK*)
Onstream Publications Ltd (*Ire*)
The Orion Publishing Group Limited (*UK*)
Pen & Sword Books Ltd (*UK*)
Phaidon Press Limited (*UK*)
Pocket Mountains (*UK*)
Poolbeg (*Ire*)
Quiller Publishing Ltd (*UK*)
Reed Business Information (RBI) (*UK*)
Santa Monica Press (*US*)
Seafarer Books (*UK*)
Seren (*UK*)
Sheldrake Press (*UK*)
Shelfstealers (*US*)
Sunflower Books (*UK*)

Thames and Hudson Ltd (*UK*)
Tiger of the Stripe (*UK*)
TouchWood Editions (*Can*)
Ulric Publishing (*UK*)
ZigZag Education (*UK*)

TV

Andrews UK Limited (*UK*)
Guild of Master Craftsman (GMC) Publications Ltd (*UK*)
Itoh Press (*US*)

Westerns

Andrews UK Limited (*UK*)
Belvedere Publishing (*UK*)
Black Coffey Publishing (*UK*)
Central Avenue Publishing (*Can*)
Flame Lily Books (*UK*)
High-Lonesome (*US*)
Indigo Dreams Publishing (*UK*)
Itoh Press (*US*)
Kelly Point Publishing LLC (*US*)
Loose Id (*US*)
New Dawn Publishers Ltd (*UK*)
Pants On Fire Press (*US*)
Robert Hale Publishers (*UK*)
Shelfstealers (*US*)
Tirgearr Publishing (*Ire*)
Westholme Publishing (*US*)

Women's Interests

Allison & Busby Ltd (*UK*)
Andrews UK Limited (*UK*)
Artemis Press (*US*)
Aunt Lute Books (*US*)
Aurora Metro Press (*UK*)
Baywood Publishing Company, Inc. (*US*)
Belvedere Publishing (*UK*)
Blue Dolphin Publishing (*US*)
Central Avenue Publishing (*Can*)
Demarche Publishing (*US*)
Eleusinian Press (*UK*)
Fingerpress UK (*UK*)
48fourteen (*US*)
Glastonbury Publishing (*UK*)
Hay House Publishers (*UK*)
Honno Welsh Women's Press (*UK*)
Indigo Dreams Publishing (*UK*)
Itoh Press (*US*)
Jewish Lights Publishing (*US*)
Kelly Point Publishing LLC (*US*)
Lost Tower Publications (*UK*)
M P Publishing USA (*US*)
My Pouty Lips (*US*)
New Island (*Ire*)
New Victoria Publishers (*US*)
Onlywomen Press Ltd (*UK*)
P&R Publishing (*US*)
Rivers Oram Press (*UK*)
Shelfstealers (*US*)
Sussex Academic Press (*UK*)
Tirgearr Publishing (*Ire*)
Tor/Forge (*US*)
Trentham Books Limited (*UK*)
University of Ottawa Press (*Can*)

US Magazines

For the most up-to-date listings of these and hundreds of other magazines, visit http://www.firstwriter.com/magazines

*To claim your **free** access to the site, please see the back of this book.*

ACP Internist
American College of Physicians
191 North Independence Mall W.
Philadelphia, PA 19106
Tel: +1 (215) 351-2400
Email: acpinternist@acponline.org
Website: http://www.acpinternist.org

Publishes: Articles; News; Nonfiction; *Areas:* Medicine; *Markets:* Professional

Magazine covering internal medicine, aimed at medical professionals. Query with published clips.

ADVANCE for Respiratory Care & Sleep Medicine
Merion Matters
2900 Horizon Drive, Box 61556
King of Prussia, PA 19406-0956
Tel: +1 (800) 355-5627
Email: sgeorge@advanceweb.com
Website: http://respiratory-care-sleep-medicine.advanceweb.com

Publishes: Articles; Nonfiction; *Areas:* Business; Health; Technology; *Markets:* Professional

Editors: Sharlene George

Magazine for healthcare professionals in pulmonary, respiratory care, and sleep. Most contributors are caregivers. No general material.

AeroSafety World Magazine
601 Madison Street, Suite 300
Alexandria, VA 22314
Email: donoghue@flightsafety.org
Website: http://flightsafety.org/aerosafety-world-magazine

Publishes: Articles; Nonfiction; *Areas:* Technology; Travel; *Markets:* Adult; Professional

Editors: J.A. Donoghue

Magazine of aviation safety. Send proposals for articles, technical papers, etc. by post or by email.

Ag Weekly
Lee Agri-Media
PO Box 507
Twin Falls, ID 83303
Tel: +1 (208) 734-9667
Email: mark.conlon@lee.net
Website: http://www.agweekly.com

Publishes: Articles; Interviews; Nonfiction; *Areas:* Nature; Technology; Travel; *Markets:* Professional

Regional agricultural magazine with an emphasis on Idaho.

AKC Gazette
Tel: +1 (800) 533-7323
Email: gazette@akc.org
Website: http://www.akc.org/pubs

Publishes: Articles; Features; Interviews; News; Nonfiction; *Areas:* How-to; Humour; Travel; *Markets:* Professional

Editors: Tilly Grassa

Magazine for pedigree dog fanciers. No fiction or poetry, though runs annual short story contest.

America Magazine
106 West 56th Street
New York, NY 10019-3803
Tel: +1 (212) 581-4640
Fax: +1 (212) 399-3596
Email: articles@americamagazine.org
Website: http://www.americamagazine.org

Publishes: Articles; Nonfiction; Poetry; Reviews; *Areas:* Religious; *Markets:* Adult

Christian magazine published weekly for a largely Roman Catholic audience.

American Cinematographer
American Society of Cinematographers
1782 North Orange Drive
Hollywood, CA 90028
Tel: +1 (323) 969-4333
Fax: +1 (323) 876-4973
Email: newproducts@ascmag.com
Website: http://www.ascmag.com

Publishes: Articles; Interviews; Nonfiction; *Areas:* Film; TV; *Markets:* Professional

Motion picture magazine covering film and TV. Aimed at industry professionals. Query with published clips.

American Hunter
11250 Waples Mill Road
Fairfax, VA 22030-9400
Tel: +1 (703) 267-1336
Fax: +1 (703) 267-3971
Email: americanhunter@nrahq.org
Website: http://www.americanhunter.org

Publishes: Articles; Features; Nonfiction; *Areas:* Hobbies; Nature; Sport; *Markets:* Adult

Hunting magazine. Accepts unsolicited MSS, but prefers queries in the first instance.

The American Spectator
1611 North Kent Street, Suite 901
Arlington, Virginia 22209
Tel: +1 (703) 807-2011
Fax: +1 (703) 807-2013
Email: editor@spectator.org
Website: http://spectator.org

Publishes: Articles; Essays; Features; Nonfiction; *Areas:* Humour; Politics; *Markets:* Adult

Reviews unsolicited mss for online publication. No response unless interested. Send material pasted into an email. See website for full details.

Amulet
PO Box 761495
San Antonio, CA 78245

or

PO Box 884223
San Francisco, CA 94188-4223
Email: amulet20032003@yahoo.com
Website:
https://sites.google.com/site/conceitmagazine/home/amulet

Publishes: Poetry; *Markets:* Adult

Editors: Perry Terrell

Publishes 16 writers each month - both new and established writers. Unsolicited, simultaneous, and previously published manuscripts are welcomed. No reading fee. Submit by post or by email.

Anderbo.com
Email: editors@anderbo.com
Website: http://www.anderbo.com

Publishes: Articles; Essays; Fiction;

Nonfiction; Poetry; *Areas:* Short Stories; *Markets:* Adult; *Treatments:* Literary

Publishes poetry, short fiction, and personal essays / creative nonfiction. Send one piece of prose or up to six poems in the body of an email or as an attachment.

Androids2

Email: mansstory2@aol.com
Website: http://www.androids2.com

Publishes: Fiction; *Areas:* Adventure; Entertainment; Fantasy; Gothic; Horror; Romance; Sci-Fi; Short Stories; Suspense; Thrillers; *Markets:* Adult; Family; *Treatments:* Dark; Mainstream

Editors: Carlos Dunn % C.C. Blake

Strives to re-create the magic of the vintage Sci-Fi pulp-fiction magazines of the 1920s through the mid 1970s.

Anobium

Email: editor@anobiumlit.com
Website: http://www.anobiumlit.com

Publishes: Fiction; *Areas:* Criticism; Current Affairs; Humour; Literature; Media; New Age; Philosophy; Religious; Short Stories; Spiritual; *Markets:* Adult; Professional; *Treatments:* Contemporary; Experimental; Literary; Niche; Satirical

Editors: Mary J. Levine

Esoteric. Psychedlic. Existential. Strange. Fantastic. Surreal.
Sub-real. Agnostic. Insectile.

This magazine is literature. It is a creature, a consciousness, operating in its own realm of meaning and existence. It is a swarm of molecules, amalgamated into an invisible whole (or hole).

Too many literary magazines and reviews forego quality for quantity and content for coherence. With literature, the size of a word matters much less than the way you use it. If brevity is the soul of wit, verbosity is circumlocutory.

Though we are based in Chicago, our values extend beyond borders. Good writing transcends.

Unlike other literary startups, our aim is to produce professionally bound, expertly published, contemporary literature. We want to print literature in a digital world; to rest like a canoe drifting atop the waves in a sea filled with empty submarines. The printed word is permanent (until it reaches 451 degrees, of course).

Of course, we believe in readability, too. We don't want to weigh down anyone's pockets with thick volumes of mediocre writing. Our relatively 'short' volumes (80-100 pages) will read easily, store safely and wear evenly – as a good book should.

Some of our favorite writers fell within the range from John Barth to Vladimir Nabokov to Franz Kakfa to David Foster Wallace to Jonathan Ames to Sam Lipsyte to Blaster Al Ackerman to Haruki Murakami to Jorge Luis Borges to Daniel A.I.U. Higgs to Norman Mailer to Hunter S. Thompson to H.G. Wells to Jose Saramago to Arthur Schopenhauer. Fill in the blanks.

And this is how we feed the woodbeetle.

Antique Trader
700 East State Street
Iola, WI 54990-0001
Tel: +1 (715) 445-2214
Fax: +1 (715) 445-4087
Email: eric.bradley@fwmedia.com
Website: http://www.antiquetrader.com

Publishes: Articles; Features; News; Nonfiction; *Areas:* Antiques; *Markets:* Adult; Professional

Editors: Eric Bradley

Magazine serving the antiques and collectibles community.

Archaeology
36-36 33rd Street
Long Island City, NY 11106
Tel: +1 (718) 472-3050

Fax: +1 (718) 472-3051
Email: editorial@archaeology.org
Website: http://www.archaeology.org

Publishes: Articles; Essays; Features;
Nonfiction; Reviews; *Areas:* Archaeology;
Markets: Adult; Professional

Magazine on archaeology, with a readership
including the general public, amateurs, and
professionals. No unsolicited mss fiction,
poetry, or previously published articles. Send
query up to two pages (500 words) by post or
by email. See website for full details.

Armchair/Shotgun
377 Flatbush Ave., #3
Brooklyn, NY 11238
Email: submissions@armchairshotgun.com
Website:
http://armchairshotgun.wordpress.com

Publishes: Fiction; Nonfiction; Poetry;
Areas: Short Stories; *Markets:* Adult

Founded by writers in January 2009, in the
midst of one of the largest unemployment
crises in American history since the 1930s.
We do not care about your bio. We read all
submissions anonymously, and conceal even
an author's name until a piece has been
selected for publication. We feel that good
writing does not know one MFA program
from another. It does not know a PhD from a
high school drop-out. Good writing does not
know your interstate exit or your subway
stop, and it does not care what you've
written before. Good writing knows only
story. This magazine accepts poetry, fiction,
non-fiction and visual arts submissions for
publication on real honest-to-goodness
paper.

ARMY Magazine
2425 Wilson Blvd.
Arlington, VA 22201
Tel: +1 (703) 841-4300
Email: armymag@ausa.org
Website: http://www.ausa.org

Publishes: Articles; Features; Interviews;
Nonfiction; *Areas:* Historical; Military;
Markets: Adult

Military magazine. Accepts submissions by
post on CD, or by email as a Word
attachment or in the body of the email. See
website for full details.

Arts & Activities Magazine
12345 World Trade Drive
San Diego, CA 92128
Tel: +1 (858) 605-0242
Fax: +1 (858) 605-0247
Email: ed@artsandactivities.com
Website: http://www.artsandactivities.com

Publishes: Articles; Interviews; Nonfiction;
Areas: Arts; Crafts; Historical; How-to;
Philosophy; *Markets:* Professional

Editors: Maryellen Bridge

Magazine for professionals in arts and crafts
education / therapy. See website for detailed
submission guidelines.

Atlanta Parent Magazine
2346 Perimeter Park Drive
Atlanta, GA 30341
Tel: +1 (770) 454-7599
Fax: +1 (770) 454-7699
Email: editor@atlantaparent.com
Website: http://www.atlantaparent.com

Publishes: Articles; Nonfiction; *Areas:*
Lifestyle; *Markets:* Adult

Magazine aimed at parents of children aged
from birth to 18. Prefers submissions by
email. See website for full details.

Authorship
National Writers Association
10940 S. Parker Road, #508,
Parker, CO 80134
Tel: +1 (303) 841-0246
Fax: +1 (303) 841-2607
Email: natlwritersassn@hotmail.com
Website: http://www.nationalwriters.com

Publishes: Articles; Nonfiction; *Markets:*
Adult; Professional

Publishes articles on writing, aimed at
amateur writers to professional authors. Send

query or complete ms. Priority given to members.

AutoInc.
Automotive Service Association
PO Box 929
Bedford, TX 76095
Tel: +1 (800) 272-7467, ext. 216
Email: leonad@asashop.org
Website: http://www.autoinc.org

Publishes: Articles; Nonfiction; *Areas:* How-to; Technology; *Markets:* Professional

Editors: Leona Dalavai Scott

Trade magazine publishing articles on automative repair, etc. Send query with published clips.

Balloons & Parties Magazine
PartiLife Publications, L.L.C.
65 Sussex Street
Hackensack, NJ 07601
Tel: +1 (201) 441-4224
Fax: +1 (201) 342-8118
Email: info@balloonsandparties.com
Website: http://www.balloonsandparties.com

Publishes: Articles; Essays; Features; Interviews; Nonfiction; *Areas:* Crafts; Design; How-to; *Markets:* Professional

Editors: Andrea P. Zettler

Magazine for the balloon, party and event fields. Include SASE with all submissions. See website for full details.

Beauty Store Business
Creative Age Communications, Inc.
7628 Densmore Ave.
Van Nuys, CA 91406
Tel: +1 (818) 782-7328
Fax: +1 (800) 442-5667
Email: mbirenbaum@creativeage.com
Website:
http://www.beautystorebusiness.com

Publishes: Articles; Interviews; Nonfiction; *Areas:* Beauty and Fashion; Business; How-to; *Markets:* Professional

Editors: Marc Birenbaum; Manyesha Batist; Shelley Moench-Kelly

Magazine aimed at beauty store owners, managers, and buyers. Query in first instance.

Better Nutrition Magazine
Active Interest Media
300 North Continental Boulevard, Suite 650
El Segundo, CA 90245
Tel: +1 (800) 443-4974
Email: nbrechka@aimmedia.com
Website: http://www.betternutrition.com

Publishes: Articles; Nonfiction; *Areas:* Health; Lifestyle; *Markets:* Adult; Family; Youth

Editors: Nicole Brechka

Magazine on healthy lifestyles; nutrition; dietary supplements; etc. for men, women, young, and old. Send query by post or email.

Big Fiction
Email: info@bigfictionmagazine.com
Website:
http://www.bigfictionmagazine.com

Publishes: Fiction; *Areas:* Short Stories; *Markets:* Adult; *Treatments:* Literary

Literary magazine devoted to longer short fiction, between 7,500 and 30,000 words. Accepts submissions online via competition ($20 entry fee).

Bike Magazine
PO Box 1028
Dana Point, CA 92629
Tel: +1 (949) 325-6200
Fax: +1 (949) 325-6196
Email: bikemag@sorc.com
Website: http://www.bikemag.com

Publishes: Articles; Features; Interviews; Nonfiction; *Areas:* Humour; Leisure; Sport; Travel; *Markets:* Adult

Mountain biking magazine focusing on

serious mountain bikers rather than beginners. See website for more details.

Birmingham Parent

700 Southgate Drive, Suite C
Pelham, AL 35124
Tel: +1 (205) 987-7700
Fax: +1 (205) 987-7600
Email: carol@biringhamparent.com
Website:
http://birminghamparent.parenthood.com

Publishes: Articles; Features; Interviews; Nonfiction; *Areas:* How-to; Lifestyle; *Markets:* Adult

Editors: Carol Muse Evans

Magazine for parents of children from pre-birth to teens. Stories should be informative, include sources, and have a local slant.

Blue Mesa Review

University of New Mexico Press
1312 Basehart Rd. SE
Albuquerque, NM 87106-4363
Email: bmreditr@unm.edu
Website: http://www.unm.edu/~bluemesa

Publishes: Fiction; Interviews; Nonfiction; Poetry; Reviews; *Areas:* Short Stories; *Markets:* Adult

Submit 3-5 poems or fiction or nonfiction up to 30 pages using the online submission system only.

Blue Ridge Country

3424 Brambleton Avenue
Roanoke, VA 24018
Tel: +1 (800) 877-6026
Email: cmodisett@leisurepublishing.com
Website: http://www.blueridgecountry.com

Publishes: Articles; Features; Nonfiction; *Areas:* Historical; Nature; Travel; *Markets:* Adult

Editors: Cara Ellen Modisett

Regional magazine focusing on the history, heritage, and natural beauty of the Blue Ridge area. See website for submission guidelines.

Boston Magazine

300 Massachusetts Avenue
Boston, MA 02115
Tel: +1 (617) 262-9700
Fax: +1 (617) 262-4925
Email: editor@bostonmagazine.com
Website: http://www.bostonmagazine.com

Publishes: Articles; Interviews; Nonfiction; *Areas:* Culture; Politics; *Markets:* Adult

Magazine publishing material relating to Boston and its environs. Send query by post or by fax. No unsolicited mss.

The Brahman Journal

915 12th Street
Hempstead, Texas 77445
Tel: +1 (979) 826-4347
Email: info@brahmanjournal.com
Website: http://brahmanjournal.com

Publishes: Articles; Interviews; Nonfiction; *Areas:* Historical; Nature; *Markets:* Adult; Professional

Official Publication of the Brahman Breed and the Official Publication of the American Brahman Breeders Association.

The Broadkill Review

104 Federal Street
Milton, DE 19968
Email: the_broadkill_review@earthlink.net
Website:
http://www.thebroadkillreview.blogspot.com

Publishes: Essays; Fiction; Interviews; Nonfiction; Poetry; Reviews; *Areas:* Criticism; Literature; Short Stories; *Markets:* Adult; *Treatments:* Experimental; Literary; Mainstream

Editors: Jamie Brown

Send fiction up to 6,000 words or up to 5 poems, preferably by email, with bio and previous writing credits. For nonfiction, query in first instance.

Broadsheet

Email: broadsheet@broaduniverse.org
Website: http://broaduniverse.org/the-broadsheet-magazine/blog

Publishes: Articles; Interviews; Nonfiction; Reviews; *Areas:* Fantasy; Horror; How-to; Literature; Sci-Fi; Women's Interests; *Markets:* Adult

Editors: Lillian Cohen-Moore

Online magazine covering women writing in science fiction / fantasy / horror. Does not publish any fiction. Considers articles, interviews, book reviews and commentaries as well as general articles on the writing or marketing of sf/f/h. Contributors need not be female, or members. See website for full details.

Canoe & Kayak

236 Avenida Fabricante, Suite 201
San Clemente, CA 92672
Tel: +1 (425) 827-6363
Email: jeff@canoekayak.com
Website: http://www.canoekayak.com

Publishes: Articles; Essays; Features; News; Nonfiction; Reviews; *Areas:* Sport; *Markets:* Adult

Editors: Jeff Moag

Paddlesport magazine covering kayaks, canoes, etc. Send short query by email outlining your idea in first instance. See website for specific interests and contact details of different editors.

Camping Today

Email: D_Johnston01@msn.com
Website: http://www.fcrv.org/Camptoday/campingtoday.php

Publishes: Articles; Interviews; Nonfiction; *Areas:* Humour; Leisure; Technology; Travel; *Markets:* Adult

Editors: DeWayne Johnston

Magazine for camping and RV enthusiasts. Send submissions by email.

Carving Magazine

PO Box 611
Faribault, MN 55021
Tel: +1 (973) 347-6900 x 130
Email: editors@carvingmagazine.com
Website: http://www.carvingmagazine.com

Publishes: Articles; Interviews; Nonfiction; *Areas:* Crafts; Historical; How-to; *Markets:* Adult

Editors: Chris Whillock

Publishes material relating to wood carving. See website for submission guidelines.

The Cattleman

1301 West Seventh Street, Suite 201
Fort Worth, TX 76102
Tel: +1 (800) 242-7820
Fax: +1 (817) 332-5446
Email: lionel@texascattleraisers.org
Website: http://www.thecattlemanmagazine.com

Publishes: Articles; Interviews; News; Nonfiction; *Areas:* Business; Health; How-to; Medicine; Nature; Technology; *Markets:* Professional; *Treatments:* In-depth

Magazine publishing material covering the Texas/Oklahoma beef cattle industry. Send query with published clips.

Charisma

600 Rinehart Road
Lake Mary, FL 32746
Tel: +1 (407) 333-0600
Fax: +1 (407) 333-7100
Email: charisma@charismamedia.com
Website: http://www.charismamag.com

Publishes: Articles; Interviews; Nonfiction; *Areas:* Religious; *Markets:* Adult

Editors: Marcus Yoars

Christian magazine publishing material for members of Pentecostal or independent charismatic churches. Send query in first instance.

Chesapeake Family

929 West Street, Suite 210
Annapolis, MD 21401
Tel: +1 (410) 263-1641
Fax: +1 (410) 280-0255
Email: editor@chesapeakefamily.com
Website: http://www.chesapeakefamily.com

Publishes: Articles; Features; Interviews;
Nonfiction; *Areas:* How-to; Lifestyle;
Markets: Adult

Free monthly magazine aimed at parents in
Anne Arundel, Calvert, Bowie and Upper
Marlboro areas of Prince George's and Kent
Island area in Queen Anne's counties of
Maryland. Aims to publish articles that will
make its readers' lives easier. Will consider
unsolicited mss, but prefers query in first
instance.

Christian Home & School

3350 East Paris Ave. S.E.
Grand Rapids, MI 49512
Tel: +1 (800) 635-8288
Fax: +1 (616) 957-5022
Email: Rheyboer@CSIonline.org

Publishes: Articles; Nonfiction; *Areas:*
Lifestyle; Religious; *Markets:* Adult

Editors: Rachael Heyboer

Magazine for parents who send their children
to Christian schools. Promotes Christian
education and addresses a wide range of
parenting topics. Send complete ms. See
website for full guidelines.

Cigar Aficionado

M. Shanken Communications, Inc.,
387 Park Avenue, South, 8th Floor
New York, NY 10016
Tel: +1 (212) 684-4224
Fax: +1 (212) 684-5424
Website: http://www.cigaraficionado.com

Publishes: Articles; Features; Nonfiction;
Areas: Hobbies; *Markets:* Adult

Magazine covering cigar smoking. Query in
the first instance.

Classic Toy Trains

To the Editor, CLASSIC TOY TRAINS
Kalmbach Publishing Co.
PO Box 1612
21027 Crossroads Cir.
Waukesha, WI 53187-1612
Tel: +1 (262) 796-8776, ext. 524
Fax: +1 (262) 796-1142
Email: manuscripts@classictoytrains.com
Website: http://ctt.trains.com

Publishes: Articles; Nonfiction; *Areas:*
Historical; Hobbies; How-to; *Markets:* Adult

Magazine publishing articles on toy trains:
how-to guides and articles on their history.
Accepts submissions by post and by email -
see website for detailed submission
guidelines.

Club Management

Finan Publishing Co.
107 West Pacific Avenue
St Louis, MO 63119
Tel: +1 (314) 961-6644
Fax: +1 (314) 961-4809
Email: clubs@theYGSgroup.com
Website: http://www.club-mgmt.com

Publishes: Articles; Nonfiction; *Areas:*
Business; Leisure; *Markets:* Professional

Magazine for hospitality industry
professionals, covering the private club
industry and club management. Send query
with published clips.

Coal Hill Review

Autumn House Press
PO 60100, Pittsburgh, PA 15211
Email: reviewcoalhill@gmail.com
Website: http://www.coalhillreview.com

Publishes: Poetry; *Markets:* Adult

Poetry magazine accepting submissions via
its annual poetry contest only ($20 entrance
fee). Enter online.

Colorado Homes & Lifestyles

1777 S. Harrison Street Suite 903
Denver, CO 80210

Tel: +1 (303) 248-2060
Fax: +1 (303) 248-2066
Email: mabel@coloradohomesmag.com
Website:
http://www.coloradohomesmag.com

Publishes: Articles; Nonfiction; *Areas:*
Architecture; Design; Gardening; Lifestyle;
Markets: Adult

Magazine of homes, gardening, and lifestyles
in Colorado. Send query with published clips
in the first instance.

Conceit Magazine
PO Box 761495
San Antonio, CA 78245

or

PO Box 884223
San Francisco, CA 94188-4223
Email: Conceitmagazine2007@yahoo.com
Website:
https://sites.google.com/site/conceitmagazine

Publishes: Articles; Essays; Fiction; News;
Nonfiction; Poetry; *Areas:* Short Stories;
Markets: Adult; *Treatments:* Literary

Editors: Perry Terrell

Publishes poetry, short stories, articles,
essays, and new book and magazine
announcements. Material must be family-
friendly. Submit by post or by email. See
website for more details.

Concrete Homes Magazine
Publications and Communications, Inc.
13581 Pond Springs Road, Suite 450
Austin, TX 78729
Fax: +1 (512) 331-3950
Email: homes@pcinews.com
Website: http://concretehomesmagazine.com

Publishes: Articles; News; Nonfiction;
Areas: Architecture; Design; How-to;
Markets: Adult; Professional

Publishes news and articles on concrete
homes. Aimed at both consumers and

professionals (builders / architects, etc.).
Send query with published clips.

The Conium Review
Portland, OR
Email: coniumreview@gmail.com
Website: http://www.coniumreview.com

Publishes: Fiction; Poetry; *Areas:* Arts;
Culture; Drama; Fantasy; Lifestyle;
Literature; Philosophy; Photography;
Markets: Academic; Adult; *Treatments:*
Contemporary; Experimental; Literary;
Niche; Progressive; Satirical

Editors: James R. Gapinski, Uma Sankaram,
Tristan Beach, and Susan Lynch

A print-based publication. We seek eclectic,
eccentric, and idiosyncratic writing from
new and established, authors. Visit our
website to order an issue, submit your
creative writing, listen to our free podcast, or
read our editorial reviews.

Consumers Digest
Consumers Digest Communications, LLC
520 Lake Cook Road
Suite 500
Deerfield, IL 60015
Email: editor@consumersdigest.com
Website: http://www.consumersdigest.com

Publishes: Articles; Nonfiction; *Areas:*
Finance; Gardening; Health; Leisure;
Lifestyle; Technology; Travel; *Markets:*
Adult

Magazine consumer issues / items of interest
to consumers / new products, etc. Send query
in first instance.

Crain's Detroit Business
Crain Communications, Inc.
1155 Gratiot
Detroit, MI 48207
Tel: +1 (313) 446-0419
Fax: +1 (313) 446-1687
Email: kcrain@crain.com
Website: http://www.crainsdetroit.com

Publishes: Articles; News; Nonfiction;

Areas: Business; *Markets:* Adult; Professional

Editors: Keith Crain

Magazine covering business in the Detroit metropolitan area. Local topics only. Send query with published clips.

Currents

Marine Technology Society
5565 Sterrett Place, Suite 108
Columbia, MD 21044
Email: publications@mtsociety.org
Website:
https://www.mtsociety.org/publications/

Publishes: Articles; News; Nonfiction; *Areas:* Science; Technology; *Markets:* Academic; Professional

Bimonthly newsletter of marine technology. Send query in first instance.

DASH Journal

Department of English and Comparative Literature
California State University Fullerton
800 North State College Boulevard
Fullerton, CA 92831
Email: DASHLiteraryJournal@gmail.com
Website: http://dashliteraryjournal.com

Publishes: Essays; Fiction; Nonfiction; Poetry; *Areas:* Criticism; Short Stories; *Markets:* Adult; *Treatments:* Literary

Submit one piece of prose or up to five poems, between January 1 and March 1 annually. Prefers email submissions. Any submissions not conforming to the guidelines will be immediately discarded. See website for full details.

Delaware Today

3301 Lancaster Pike, Suite 5C
Wilmington, DE 19805
Tel: +1 (302) 656-1809
Email: editors@delawaretoday.com

Publishes: Articles; Features; Interviews; News; Nonfiction; *Areas:* Business; Health;

Historical; *Markets:* Adult

All material must be of genuine interest to residents of Delaware. No national topics dressed up as having a Delaware slant. Send query with published clips.

Diabetes Self-Management

R.A. Rapaport Publishing, Inc.
150 West 22nd Street, Suite 800
New York, NY 10011
Tel: +1 (212) 989-0200
Fax: +1 (212) 989-4786
Email: editor@diabetes-self-mgmt.com
Website:
http://www.diabetesselfmanagement.com

Publishes: Articles; Reviews; *Areas:* Health; Medicine; Self-Help; *Markets:* Adult; *Treatments:* Positive

Magazine for people with diabetes who want to know more about controlling and managing their diabetes. Articles must address the day-to-day and long-term concerns of readers in a positive and upbeat manner. Queries accepted by email. See website for more details.

Discover Maine Magazine

10 Exchange St. Suite 208
Portland, ME 04101
Tel: +1 (800) 753-8684
Email: info@discovermainemagazine.com
Website:
http://www.discovermainemagazine.com

Publishes: Articles; Nonfiction; *Areas:* Historical; Leisure; Nature; Sport; *Markets:* Adult

Regional magazine publishing articles on the history of Maine, as well as its hunting, fishing, and sports. Submit stories via website.

The Doctor T. J. Eckleburg Review

The Johns Hopkins University
1717 Massachusetts Avenue, NW Suite 101
Washington, DC 20036
Tel: +1 (202) 452-1927

Fax: +1 (202) 452-8713
Website:
http://thedoctortjeckleburgreview.com

Publishes: Fiction; Poetry; Reviews; *Areas:*
Arts; Short Stories; *Markets: Treatments:*
Experimental; Literary; Mainstream

Magazine describing itself as eclectic,
literary mainstream to experimental.
Publishes poetry, fiction, creative nonfiction,
and reviews. Submit 1–5 poems or one piece
of prose up to 8,000 words. No multiple
submissions. Simultaneous submissions are
accepted if immediate notification of
publication elsewhere is provided. See
website for full guidelines, and for link to
online submission system.

Draft

Draft Publishing
4742 North 24th Street, Suite 210
Phoenix, AZ 85016
Tel: +1 (888) 806-4677
Email: jessica.daynor@draftmag.com
Website: http://draftmag.com

Publishes: Articles; News; Nonfiction;
Areas: Cookery; Hobbies; Leisure; Sport;
Travel; *Markets:* Adult

Beer magazine, also publishing articles on
food, sports (both professional and leisure),
travel, and many other topics. Beer articles
should concentrate on beer and brewery
news, rather than the technical aspects of
brewing. No pre-written stories. Send query
by email with pitch. See website for full
guidelines.

Earth Mama Magazine

P.O. Box 6141
Asheville, NC 28816
Tel: +1 (828) 242-0526
Email: gennagaea@gmail.com
Website:
http://earthmamapublishing.yolasite.com

Publishes: Articles; Fiction; Interviews;
Nonfiction; Poetry; *Areas:* Adventure; Arts;
Autobiography; Beauty and Fashion;
Biography; Business; Crafts; Culture;
Current Affairs; Design; Drama;

Entertainment; Fantasy; Film; Gardening;
Health; Hobbies; Horror; How-to; Humour;
Leisure; Lifestyle; Literature; Medicine;
Music; Mystery; Nature; New Age;
Philosophy; Sci-Fi; Self-Help; Short Stories;
Spiritual; Suspense; Theatre; Thrillers;
Travel; TV; Women's Interests; *Markets:*
Adult; Family; Youth

Editors: Genevieve Gaea

We are a quarterly journal comprised of
factual articles, fictional short stories, poetry
and graphic comics which address the
complexity embodied in vibrant, strong,
earthy women of all ages and walks of life.

Let it be known, we love credited,
experienced, formally-educated writers.
However, our collective hearts go pitty-pat
when we discovering new talent.
In an effort to celebrate the spirit of the earth
goddess residing inside all of us, we strongly
encourage self-aware previously unpublished
writers to make submissions. Life experience
and authentic voices are what we value in the
writers we select. All high-quality work
aimed at our audience will be seriously
considered for publication

Eclectica Magazine

Email: submissions@eclectica.org
Website: http://www.eclectica.org

Publishes: Essays; Fiction; Interviews;
Nonfiction; Poetry; Reviews; Scripts; *Areas:*
Drama; Film; Humour; Literature; Travel;
Markets: Adult; *Treatments:* Experimental;
Literary; Satirical

Editors: Tom Dooley (fiction); Colleen
Mondor (reviews); Elizabeth P. Glixman
(interviews); Jennifer Finstrom (poetry)

Online magazine. Send a maximum of five
poems or three pieces of fiction per
submission period. Submissions should be
sent by email as plain text or an attachment
in a popular word processing package.
Microsoft Word is preferred. See website for
full details.

EcoHome

Hanley Wood Business Media
One Thomas Circle, NW
Suite 600
Washington, DC 20005
Tel: +1 (202) 452-0800
Fax: +1 (202) 785-1974
Email: cserlin@hanleywood.com
Website: http://www.hanleywood.com

Publishes: Articles; Features; Nonfiction;
Areas: Business; How-to; Technology;
Markets: Professional

Editors: Christine Serlin

Magazine covering environmentally friendly
building practices and trends. Send query
with published clips in first instance.

18 Wheels & Heels

Email: Photos@18wheelsandheels.com
Website:
http://18wheelsandheelsmagazine.com

Publishes: Articles; Interviews; Nonfiction;
Poetry; *Areas:* Beauty and Fashion;
Business; Cookery; Culture; Hobbies; How-
to; Leisure; Lifestyle; Men's Interests;
Music; *Markets:* Adult; Family; *Treatments:*
Contemporary; Niche; Positive

Editors: Tina Foca

Female truckers magazine. Articles and
stories are related to the trucking industry.
Product reviews have to be for products or
services for people on the go. Music reviews
are for driving conditions.

Employee Assistance Report

Impact Publications, Inc.
PO Box 322
Waupaca, WI 54981
Tel: +1 (715) 258-2448
Fax: +1 (715) 258-9048
Email:
mike.jacquart@impacttrainingcenter.net
Website: http://www.impact-
publications.com

Publishes: Articles; Interviews; News;
Nonfiction; *Areas:* How-to; Legal; *Markets:*
Professional

Editors: Mike Jacquart

Monthly newlsetter for employee assistance
professionals. Query in the first instance.

Equus Magazine

656 Quince Orchard Road, Suite 600
Gaithersburg, MD 20878-1409
Fax: +1 (301) 990-9015
Email: EEQEletters@equinetwork.com
Website:
http://www.equisearch.com/magazines/equus
/

Publishes: Articles; News; Nonfiction;
Areas: Business; Hobbies; How-to;
Medicine; Nature; Sport; *Markets:* Adult;
Professional

Magazine covering horse care, behaviour,
treatment, medicine, etc. Send complete MS.

Evidence Technology Magazine

PO Box 555
Kearney, MO 64060
Email: kmayo@evidencemagazine.com
Website: http://www.evidencemagazine.com

Publishes: Articles; News; Nonfiction;
Areas: Crime; Science; Technology;
Markets: Professional

Editors: Kristi Mayo

Magazine publishing news and articles
covering evidence collection, processing,
and preservation. Articles should: be
understandable to every reader with any
level of knowledge and experience; and
provide useful information to every reader
with any level of knowledge and experience.
Send query by email in first instance. See
website for full guidelines.

Faith & Form

47 Grandview Terrace
Essex, CT 06426

Tel: +1 (860) 575-4702
Email: mcrosbie@faithandform.com
Website:
http://www.faithandform.com/magazine

Publishes: Articles; Nonfiction; *Areas:*
Architecture; Arts; Religious; *Markets:*
Adult; Professional

Editors: Michael J. Crosbie, Ph.D., FAIA

Magazine for professionals and lay people
concerned with environments for worship,
and religious arts and architecture. Accepts
electronic submissions only, either by post
on CD or other storage medium, or via form
on website. See website for full submission
guidelines.

FIDO Friendly

PO Box 160
Marsing, ID 83639
Tel: +1 (800) 896-0976
Email: fieldeditor@fidofriendly.com
Website: http://www.fidofriendly.com

Publishes: Articles; Essays; Interviews;
Nonfiction; *Areas:* How-to; Humour; Short
Stories; Travel; *Markets:* Adult

Magazine on travel with your dog. Send
query with published clips.

Fjords Review

Tel: +1 (617) 981-4307
Email: s@fjordsreview.com
Website: http://www.fjordsreview.com

Publishes: Features; Fiction; Poetry;
Reviews; *Areas:* Anthropology; Antiques;
Arts; Beauty and Fashion; Business; Crime;
Criticism; Culture; Drama; Film; Gothic;
Historical; Horror; Humour; Legal;
Lifestyle; Literature; Media; Music;
Mystery; Nature; New Age; Philosophy;
Photography; Psychology; Religious;
Romance; Sci-Fi; Short Stories; Sociology;
Spiritual; Suspense; Theatre; Thrillers;
Translations; *Markets:* Adult; *Treatments:*
Commercial; Contemporary; Cynical; Dark;
Experimental; In-depth; Light; Literary;
Mainstream; Niche; Popular; Positive;
Progressive; Satirical; Serious; Traditional

Editors: John Gosslee

A four-color, 40-60 page, perfect-bound
journal including original photography,
artwork, poetry, short stories and designs. A
bi-annual publication focusing on fine arts
and literature.

We submit poems to the Pushcart Prize and
Best New Poets each year.

We are interested in quality translations and
work from new and established authors.

Query with book reviews before submitting.
Reviews are considered for full-length books
of poetry, prose and short fiction

Focus Magazine of SWFL

Email: info@focusofswfl.com
Website: http://www.focusofswfl.com

Publishes: Articles; Features; Interviews;
News; Nonfiction; Reviews; *Areas:*
Adventure; Antiques; Architecture; Arts;
Beauty and Fashion; Business; Cookery;
Crafts; Culture; Current Affairs; Design;
Drama; Entertainment; Finance; Gardening;
Health; Hobbies; How-to; Leisure; Lifestyle;
Men's Interests; Music; Nature;
Photography; Romance; Self-Help;
Technology; Theatre; Travel; Women's
Interests; *Markets:* Adult; Family; Youth;
Treatments: Contemporary; In-depth; Light;
Mainstream; Popular; Positive; Progressive;
Traditional

Magazine about southwest florida and its
people, in all forms of a subject matter.

Forum

1384 Broadway (38th Street), 11th Floor
New York, NY 10018
Tel: +1 (212) 686-4412
Fax: +1 (212) 686-6821
Email: stunifoo@busjour.com
Website:
http://www.busjour.com/forum.html

Publishes: Articles; Interviews; Nonfiction;
Areas: Beauty and Fashion; Hobbies;
Leisure; Lifestyle; Sport; Travel; *Markets:*
Adult

Fashion and lifestyle magazine for upscale readers. Send query in the first instance.

From A Writer's POV Magazine

Email:
darrylmims@fromawriterspovmagazine.com

Publishes: Articles; Features; Fiction; Interviews; News; Nonfiction; Poetry; Reference; Reviews; *Areas:* Adventure; Autobiography; Beauty and Fashion; Biography; Business; Cookery; Crafts; Crime; Criticism; Culture; Current Affairs; Design; Drama; Entertainment; Erotic; Fantasy; Film; Finance; Gardening; Gothic; Health; Hobbies; Horror; How-to; Humour; Legal; Leisure; Lifestyle; Literature; Media; Medicine; Men's Interests; Music; Mystery; Photography; Politics; Psychology; Radio; Religious; Romance; Science; Sci-Fi; Self-Help; Short Stories; Sociology; Spiritual; Sport; Suspense; Theatre; Thrillers; Travel; TV; Women's Interests; *Markets:* Adult; Children's; Family; Youth; *Treatments:* Commercial; Contemporary; Cynical; Dark; Experimental; In-depth; Literary; Mainstream; Niche; Popular; Positive; Progressive; Serious; Traditional

Editors: Darryl Mims

Created for writers, authors, business owner and readers. It was founded in July 2006. This is a magazine/website that allows writers to display their writings, showcase their work and book as well as network with others for specific services. We allow writers to display their work and advertise their website or links.

We write monthly articles through interviews. highlight the most popular books readers should know about and help get new authors in the light. We look to encourage dedicate writers and help others advance in their writing career through interviews, book reviews, specializing in certain services and we give daily tips and advice for those who need it.

Girls' Life
4529 Harford Road

Baltimore, MD 21214
Email: lizzie@girlslife.com
Website: http://www.girlslife.com

Publishes: Articles; Essays; Features; Interviews; Nonfiction; *Areas:* Beauty and Fashion; How-to; Humour; Sport; Travel; Women's Interests; *Markets:* Children's; Youth

Editors: Katie Abbondanza (Senior Editor)

Magazine for girls aged 9-15. Send query by post with SASE or email providing detailed outline of idea. Postal queries without SASE will be discarded. No poetry or approaches by telephone. Potential contributors are advised to familiarise themselves with the style and content of the magazine before approaching.

Hippocampus Magazine
Email: hippocampusmagazine@gmail.com
Website:
http://www.hippocampusmagazine.com

Publishes: Articles; Essays; Interviews; Nonfiction; Reviews; *Areas:* Autobiography; Crafts; *Markets:* Adult

Editors: Donna Talarico

An exclusively online publication set out to entertain, educate and engage writers and readers of creative non-fiction. Each monthly issue features memoir excerpts, personal essays, reviews, interviews and craft articles. Accepts unsolicited submissions on a rolling basis. View guidelines online. (Nonpaying market.)

Ingram's Magazine
Show-Me Publishing, Inc.
P.O. Box 411356
Kansas City, Missouri 64141-1356
Tel: +1 (816) 842-9994
Fax: +1 (816) 474-1111
Email: editorial@ingramsonline.com
Website: http://www.ingramsonline.com

Publishes: Articles; Interviews; News; Nonfiction; *Areas:* Business; Finance; *Markets:* Adult

Magazine covering business and economics in Kansas City. Local writers familiar with the magazine only. Send query by email.

International Bluegrass

2 Music Circle South, Suite 100
Nashville, TN 37203
Tel: +1 (615) 256-3222
Fax: +1 (615) 256-0450
Email: info@ibma.org
Website: http://ibma.org

Publishes: Articles; Features; News; Nonfiction; *Areas:* Business; Music; *Markets:* Professional

Professional publication of the bluegrass music business. Send query in first instance.

Islands

Bonnier Corporation
460 North Orlando Avenue, Suite 200
Winter Park, FL 32789
Tel: +1 (407) 628-4802
Email: editor@islands.com
Website: http://www.islands.com

Publishes: Articles; Essays; Features; Interviews; News; Nonfiction; *Areas:* Travel; *Markets:* Adult

Publishes material relating to islands. Send complete ms.

Journal of Emergency Medical Services (JEMS)

Elsevier Public Safety
525 B Street, Suite 1900
San Diego, CA 92101
Fax: +1 (619) 699-6396
Email: jems.editor@elsevier.com
Website: http://ees.elsevier.com/jems/

Publishes: Articles; Essays; Interviews; News; Nonfiction; *Areas:* Medicine; *Markets:* Professional

Medical journal for the emergency services. Submit queries via website submission system only.

Journal Plus

654 Osos Street
San Luis Obispo, CA 93401
Email: slojournal@fix.net
Website: http://slojournal.com

Publishes: Articles; Nonfiction; *Areas:* Business; Health; Historical; Leisure; Lifestyle; *Markets:* Adult

Magazine written for and by the local people of the Central Coast, covering people and places, business and leisure, past and present, health and fitness. Send submissions or queries with SASE.

Junior Baseball

JSAN Publishing LLC
14 Woodway Lane
Wilton, CT 06897
Tel: +1 (203) 210-5726
Email: publisher@juniorbaseball.com
Website: http://www.juniorbaseball.com

Publishes: Articles; Features; Interviews; Nonfiction; *Areas:* How-to; Sport; *Markets:* Adult; Children's; Youth

Magazine for baseball players aged 7-17, their coaches and their parents. No fiction, poetry, or first-person articles about your own child. Send query in first instance.

Kalyani Magazine.

Email: info@kalyanimagazine.com
Website: http://kalyanimagazine.com

Publishes: Articles; Essays; Fiction; Nonfiction; Poetry; Scripts; *Areas:* Autobiography; Culture; Short Stories; Women's Interests; *Markets:* Adult; *Treatments:* Experimental; Literary

Editors: Shubha Bala

Publishes work by women of colour. Publishes poetry, prose, lyrical prose, scripts, essays, experimental, flash fiction, investigative reporting, fiction, non-fiction, memoir, and cross-genre. Each issue is on a different theme. See website for next theme and full submission guidelines.

Kids' Ministry Ideas

55 West Oak Ridge Drive
Hagerstown, MD 21740
Email: KidsMin@rhpa.org
Website: http://www.kidsministryideas.com

Publishes: Articles; Features; Nonfiction;
Areas: Religious; *Markets:* Professional

Magazine geared towards those who provide
spiritual nurturing to children in a local
church. Send complete ms by post or email.
See website for full guidelines.

The Ledge Magazine

40 Maple Ave
Bellport, NY 11713
Email: info@theledgemagazine.com
Website: http://www.theledgemagazine.com

Publishes: Fiction; Poetry; *Areas:* Short
Stories; *Markets:* Adult

Editors: Timothy Monaghan

Submit 3-5 poems or one story up to 7,500
words. No email submissions. See website
for more details.

LabTalk

PO Box 1945
Big Bear Lake, CA 92315
Tel: +1 (909) 547-2234
Email: cwalker@jobson.com
Website: http://www.labtalkonline.com

Publishes: Articles; Features; News;
Nonfiction; *Areas:* Business; How-to;
Technology; *Markets:* Professional;
Treatments: In-depth

Editors: Christie Walker

Magazine for optical laboratory managers,
supervisors, and owners.

Lausanne World Pulse (LWP)

PO Box 794
Wheaton, IL 60187
Tel: +1 (630) 752-7158
Fax: +1 (630) 752-7155
Email:

submissions@lausanneworldpulse.com
Website:
http://www.lausanneworldpulse.com

Publishes: Articles; News; Nonfiction;
Areas: Religious; *Markets:* Academic;
Adult; Professional

Evangelical magazine. See website for
complete submission guidelines.
Submissions accepted by email only.

Law Enforcement Technology Magazine

Cygnus Business Media
1233 Janesville Avenue
Fort Atkinson, WI 53538
Tel: +1 (800) 547-7377
Email: officer@corp.officer.com
Website: http://www.officer.com

Publishes: Articles; Features; News;
Nonfiction; *Areas:* Legal; Technology;
Markets: Professional

Magazine aimed at law enforcement
agencies, covering technology and
management.

Literary Juice

Email: srajan@literaryjuice.com
Website: http://www.literaryjuice.com

Publishes: Fiction; Poetry; Reviews; *Areas:*
Adventure; Drama; Fantasy; Horror;
Humour; Mystery; Sci-Fi; Short Stories;
Thrillers; *Markets:* Adult; Family;
Treatments: Literary

Editors: Sara R. Rajan

Actively seeking submissions from talented
and passionate writers in the areas of short
fiction, flash fiction, and poetry. Please do
not send us biographies, non-fiction, or
interviews. It is important all writers review
the submission guidelines before sending
their work.

The Living Church

PO Box 514036
Milwaukee, WI 53203-3436

Tel: +1 (414) 276-5420
Fax: +1 (414) 276-7483
Email: tlc@livingchurch.org
Website: http://www.livingchurch.org

Publishes: Articles; Essays; Features; News; Nonfiction; Reviews; *Areas:* Religious; Spiritual; *Markets:* Adult

Editors: John Schuessler

Publishes material of relevance to the Episcopal Church and the wider Anglican Communion. Send complete ms.

LONE STARS Magazine

4219 Flinthill
San Antonio, TX 78230
Email: lonestarsmagazine@yahoo.com

Publishes: Poetry; *Areas:* Arts; Culture; Current Affairs; Fantasy; Literature; Music; *Markets:* Adult; *Treatments:* Commercial; Contemporary; In-depth; Literary; Mainstream; Popular; Progressive; Serious; Traditional

Editors: Milo Rosebud

8 1/2 x 11, 25+ pages, Saddle stapled. Graphic Art accepted for Cover and Illustration. Authors retain All Rights. Limit 5 poems per submission. Single spaced Camera ready, the way you want to see it in print.

Lummox

c/o PO Box 5301
San Pedro, CA 90733-5301
Email: poetraindog@gmail.com
Website: http://www.lummoxpress.com

Publishes: Articles; Essays; Fiction; Interviews; Nonfiction; Poetry; *Areas:* Biography; Literature; Short Stories; *Markets:* Adult; *Treatments:* Literary

Annual poetry magazine publishing micro and flash fiction; essays on poetics, biographies, and the craft of writing; along with "well written rants", topical articles, and interviews. Submissions will be accepted between March 31 and August 31 each year,

pasted into the body of an email (no attachments), or by snail mail if necessary. See website for full guidelines.

MyBusiness Magazine

600 West Fulton Street, Suite 600
Chicago, IL 60661
Tel: +1 (615) 872-5800
Email: nfib@imaginepub.com
Website: http://www.mybusinessmag.com

Publishes: Articles; Nonfiction; *Areas:* Business; How-to; *Markets:* Professional

Publishes articles of interest to small business owners. Send query with author CV and two published clips in first instance.

Machine Design

1300 East Ninth Street
Cleveland, OH 44114
Tel: +1 (216) 931-9221
Fax: +1 (216) 621-8469
Email: leland.teschler@penton.com
Website: http://machinedesign.com

Publishes: Articles; News; Nonfiction; *Areas:* Design; How-to; Technology, *Markets:* Professional

Editors: Leland Teschler

Magazine covering design engineering of manufactured products. Send complete ms by post or email.

The Maine Sportsman

183 State Street
Augusta, ME 04330
Tel: +1 (207) 622-4242
Fax: +1 (207) 622-4255
Email: info@mainesportsman.com
Website: http://www.mainesportsman.com

Publishes: Articles; Features; News; Nonfiction; *Areas:* Hobbies; Leisure; Nature; Sport; *Markets:* Adult

Monthly outdoors / hunting magazine. Send query or complete ms by email.

Man's Story 2

Email: mansstory2@aol.com
Website: http://www.mansstory2.com

Publishes: Fiction; *Areas:* Adventure;
Crime; Drama; Entertainment; Fantasy;
Gothic; Science; Short Stories; *Markets:*
Adult; Family; *Treatments:* Dark;
Mainstream

Editors: Carlos Dunn C.C. Blake

Strives to recreate the Magic of the Pulp
Fiction Magazines published from the 1920s
through the mid 1970s.

Massage Magazine

5150 Palm Valley Road, Suite 103
Ponte Vedra Beach, FL 32082
Tel: +1 (904) 285-6020
Fax: +1 (904) 285-9944
Email: kmenahan@massagemag.com
Website: http://www.massagemag.com

Publishes: Articles; Features; Interviews;
News; Nonfiction; *Areas:* Health; How-to;
Markets: Professional

Publishes articles of interest to professionals
providing massage and other touch therapies.
Trade magazine not accepting articles aimed
at the general public.

Message of the Open Bible

2020 Bell Avenue
Des Moines, IA 50315-1096
Tel: +1 (515) 288-6761
Email: info@openbible.org
Website: http://www.openbible.org/
publications_message.aspx

Publishes: Articles; Essays; Interviews;
News; Nonfiction; *Areas:* Religious;
Markets: Adult

Religious magazine providing news about
ministries, testimonies of God's miracles and
power, inspirational stories and features, and
biblical insight on contemporary issues. No
sermons. Send complete ms.

Midwest Living

Meredith Corporation
1716 Locust Street
Des Moines, IA 50309
Tel: +1 (515) 284-3000
Fax: +1 (515) 284-3836
Email: midwestliving@meredith.com
Website: http://www.midwestliving.com

Publishes: Articles; Interviews; Nonfiction;
Areas: Historical; Lifestyle; Travel;
Markets: Adult; Family

Lifestyle magazine aimed at Midwest
families. All stories must have direct
relevance to a Midwest audience.

Milwaukee Magazine

126 North Jefferson Street, Suite 100
Milwaukee, WI 53202
Tel: +1 (414) 273-1101
Fax: +1 (414) 287-4373
Email: milmag@milwaukeemagazine.com
Website: http://www.milwaukeemag.com

Publishes: Articles; Essays; Interviews;
News; Nonfiction; *Areas:* Arts; Business;
Current Affairs; Historical; Lifestyle;
Politics; Travel; *Markets:* Adult

Editors: Cristina Daglas

All material must have a strong Milwaukee
or Wisconsin angle. Send query with
published clips.

Model Cars Magazine

2403 Champa Street
Denver, CO 80205
Tel: +1 (303) 296-1600
Email: gregg@modelcarsmag.com
Website: http://www.modelcarsmag.com

Publishes: Articles; Nonfiction; *Areas:*
Hobbies; How-to; *Markets:* Adult

Publishes how-to articles for model car
enthusiasts. Query by post or by email.

Montana Magazine

PO Box 4249
Helena, MT 59604

Tel: +1 (888) 666-8624
Email: editor@montanamagazine.com
Website: http://www.montanamagazine.com

Publishes: Articles; Features; Nonfiction;
Areas: Current Affairs; Historical; Lifestyle;
Nature; Travel; *Markets:* Adult

Editors: Butch Larcombe

Publishes well-written, well-researched
articles and features on issues, interesting
people, and life in Montana. Send query by
post or by email. No queries by phone. See
website for full details.

MSW Management
Forester Media Inc.
PO Box 3100
Santa Barbara, CA 93130
Tel: +1 (805) 682-1300
Fax: +1 (805) 682-0200
Email: jtrotti@forester.net
Website: http://www.mswmanagement.com

Publishes: Articles; Interviews; Nonfiction;
Markets: Professional

Editors: John Trotti

Magazine aimed at municipal solid waste
professionals in the public sector. Query in
first instance.

Native Max
Roth Park
1401 West 85th Avenue
Unit A-103
Federal Heights, CO 80260
Email: talent@native-max.com
Website: http://www.native-max.com

Publishes: Articles; Nonfiction; *Areas:*
Beauty and Fashion; Culture; Men's
Interests; Women's Interests; *Markets:*
Adult; *Treatments:* Contemporary

Fashion magazine geared toward Native
American men and women and non-Native
Americans who want to learn about the
culture.

National Parks Magazine
777 6th Street, NW, Suite 700 Washington,
DC 20001-3723
Tel: +1 (800) 628-7275
Email: npmag@npca.org
Website:
http://www.npca.org/news/magazine/

Publishes: Articles; Features; News;
Nonfiction; *Areas:* Nature; *Markets:* Adult

Publishes articles about areas in the National
Park System, proposed new areas, threats to
parks or park wildlife, scientific discoveries,
legislative issues, and endangered species of
plants or animals relevant to national parks.
No general environmental pieces, fiction,
poetry, or "my trip to" pieces. Query in the
first instance with published clips. See
website for full details.

Necrology Shorts
Isis International
PO Box 510232
Saint Louis, MO 63151
Email: submit@necrologyshorts.com
Website: http://www.necrologyshorts.com

Publishes: Fiction; Nonfiction; Poetry;
Reviews; *Areas:* Biography; Fantasy; Film;
Horror; Sci-Fi; Short Stories; *Markets:*
Adult; *Treatments:* Dark

Editors: John Ferguson

Free online magazine publishing horror and
dark fantasy and science fiction. No
maximum lengths but fiction must be at least
2,000 words. Submit as email attachment or
via form on website, where full submission
guidelines can also be found.

Netsagas.com
Vesturberg 78
Email: netsagas@gmail.com
Website: http://www.netsagas.com

Publishes: Articles; Essays; Fiction;
Nonfiction; Poetry; *Areas:* Adventure;
Anthropology; Antiques; Archaeology;
Architecture; Arts; Autobiography; Beauty
and Fashion; Biography; Business; Cookery;
Crafts; Crime; Criticism; Culture; Current

Affairs; Design; Drama; Entertainment; Fantasy; Film; Finance; Gardening; Gothic; Health; Historical; Hobbies; Horror; How-to; Humour; Legal; Leisure; Lifestyle; Literature; Media; Medicine; Men's Interests; Military; Music; Mystery; Nature; New Age; Philosophy; Photography; Politics; Psychology; Radio; Religious; Romance; Science; Sci-Fi; Self-Help; Short Stories; Sociology; Spiritual; Sport; Suspense; Technology; Theatre; Thrillers; Translations; Travel; TV; Westerns; Women's Interests; *Markets:* Adult; Children's; Family; Youth; *Treatments:* Commercial; Contemporary; Cynical; Dark; Experimental; In-depth; Light; Literary; Mainstream; Niche; Popular; Positive; Progressive; Satirical; Serious; Traditional

Editors: Olithor Eiriks

Publishes free stories, poems, articles, videos, pics and music.

New CollAge

New College of Florida, c/o WRC
5800 Bayshore Road
Sarasota, FL 34243
Tel: +1 (941) 487-4506
Email: newcollagemag@gmail.com
Website:
http://newcollagemag.wordpress.com

Publishes: Fiction; Nonfiction; Poetry; *Areas:* Short Stories; *Markets:* Adult

Editors: Alexis Orgera

Publishes fiction, poetry, and creative nonfiction. Send up to three short pieces by email. See website for full guidelines.

New Jersey Monthly

55 Park Place
PO Box 920
Morristown, NJ 07963-0920
Tel: +1 (973) 539-8230
Fax: +1 (973) 538-2953
Email: kschlager@njmonthly.com
Website: http://njmonthly.com

Publishes: Articles; Essays; Features; Nonfiction; Reviews; *Areas:* Arts; Beauty

and Fashion; Business; Culture; Current Affairs; Gardening; Health; Historical; Leisure; Lifestyle; Music; Nature; Politics; Science; Technology; *Markets:* Adult

Publishes material relating directly to New Jersey only. Send query by email with published clips in first instance. No unsolicited mss. Phone queries are discouraged.

New Madrid

Department of English and Philosophy
Murray State University
7C Faculty Hall
Murray KY 42071-3341
Tel: +1 (270) 809-4730
Email: msu.newmadrid@murraystate.edu
Website: http://www.newmadridjournal.org

Publishes: Fiction; Poetry; *Markets:* Adult; *Treatments:* Literary

Editors: Ann Neelon

Submit one piece of fiction (up to 20 double spaced pages) or up to six poems between January 15 and March 15, or between August 15 and October 15. Use online submission system only. Check website for upcoming themes.

New York

Editorial Submissions
New York Media
75 Varick Street
New York, NY 10013
Email: editorialsubmissions@nymag.com
Website: http://nymag.com

Publishes: Articles; Features; News; Nonfiction; *Areas:* Beauty and Fashion; Design; Entertainment; Lifestyle; Travel; *Markets:* Adult

Magazine covering the New York metropolitan area. Send query by email describing the topic of your email in the first instance.

NextStepU Magazine

Next Step Publishing Inc.

2 W. Main St., Suite 200
Victor, NY 14564
Tel: +1 (800) 771-3117
Email: info@NextStepU.com
Website: http://www.nextstepu.com

Publishes: Articles; Features; Interviews;
Nonfiction; *Areas:* Finance; How-to; Self-
Help; Travel; *Markets:* Youth

Magazine aimed at preparing students for
life after school; covering careers, college,
finance, etc. Send query by email.

The Nocturnal Lyric
Box 542
Astoria, OR 97103
Email: TheNocturnallyric@rocketmail.com
Website:
http://www.angelfire.com/ca/nocturnallyric

Publishes: Fiction; Poetry; *Areas:* Horror;
Short Stories; *Markets:* Adult

Editors: Susan Moon

Publishes bizarre horror fiction and poetry.
Send maximum one story per envelope, or
up to five poems, with SASE. See website
for full guidelines.

North Carolina Literary
Review (NCLR)
English Department
Mailstop 555
East Carolina University
Greenville, NC 27858-4353
Tel: +1 (252) 328-1537
Fax: +1 (252) 328-4889
Email: nclrsubmissions@ecu.edu
Website: http://www.nclr.ecu.edu

Publishes: Articles; Essays; Features;
Fiction; Interviews; Nonfiction; Poetry;
Areas: Criticism; Drama; Historical;
Humour; Literature; Short Stories; Travel;
Markets: Academic; Adult; *Treatments:*
Literary

Annual literary journal publishing interviews
and literary criticism about North Carolina
writers, and poetry, fiction, drama, and
creative nonfiction by North Carolina writers

or set in North Carolina. Prospective
contributors should note upcoming themes
given on website. Accepts fiction through
annual competition only. Submit work using
online submission system. No submissions
by post.

North Dakota Quarterly
Merrifield Hall Room 110
276 Centennial Drive Stop 7209
Grand Forks, ND 58202-7209
Tel: +1 (701) 777-3322
Email: ndq@und.edu
Website: http://arts-sciences.und.edu/north-
dakota-quarterly

Publishes: Essays; Fiction; Nonfiction;
Poetry; *Areas:* Short Stories; *Markets:* Adult

No specific submission guidelines, but aims
to publish the best fiction, poetry, and essays
it can. Simultaneous submissions accepted
for fiction, but not poetry. Hard copy
submissions only. See website for full
details.

Northern Woodlands
1776 Center Road
PO Box 471
Corinth, Vermont 05039
Tel: +1 (802) 439-6292
Fax: +1 (802) 368-1053
Email: mail@northernwoodlands.org
Website: http://northernwoodlands.org

Publishes: Articles; Nonfiction; *Areas:*
Nature; *Markets:* Adult

Publishes nonfiction relating to natural
history, conservation, and forest
management. Send query with published
clips.

Northwest Review
5243 University of Oregon
Eugene, OR 97403-5243
Tel: +1 (541) 346-3957
Fax: +1 (541) 346-0537
Email: nweditor@uoregon.edu
Website: http://nwr.uoregon.edu

Publishes: Articles; Essays; Fiction;

Nonfiction; Poetry; *Areas:* Autobiography; Literature; Short Stories; *Markets:* Adult; *Treatments:* Literary

Publishes creative nonfiction, memoir, literary essays, poetry, and fiction. Not accepting submissions of fiction and poetry at current time. Submissions of nonfiction accepted between October 15 and January 15 only. Submissions accepted by post only, unless authors are based overseas.

Notre Dame Review

840 Flanner Hall
University of Notre Dame
Notre Dame, IN 46556
Email: english.ndreview.1@nd.edu
Website:
http://www.nd.edu/~ndr/submissions.html

Publishes: Fiction; Poetry; *Areas:* Short Stories; *Markets:* Adult

Accepts submissions of poetry and fiction January to March and September to November. Excellence is the only criteria, but is especially interested in fiction and poetry that takes on big issues.

NOVA Science Fiction

17983 Paseo Del Sol
Chino Hills, CA 91709-3947
Website: http://www.novascifi.com

Publishes: Fiction; *Areas:* Religious; Sci-Fi; Short Stories; Markets

Editors: Wesley Kawato

Magazine publishing religious science fiction. No unsolicited MSS. Send query by email outlining your previousl publications or creative writing qualifications (see website for details). Send MS on invitation only.

Now & Then: The Appalachian Magazine

Center for Appalachian Studies and Services
East Tennessee State University
Box 70556
Johnson City, TN 37614-1707

Tel: +1 (423) 439-7994
Fax: +1 (423) 439-7870
Email: nowandthen@etsu.edu
Website:
http://www.etsu.edu/cass/nowandthen

Publishes: Articles; Essays; Features; Fiction; News; Nonfiction; Poetry; *Areas:* Short Stories; *Markets:* Adult

Editors: Jane Woodside

Regional magazine publishing fiction, nonfiction, and poetry relating to Appalachia. All material submitted must relate to Appalachia and the theme of an upcoming issue. Accepts submissions by post and by email, however different email address for poetry submissions. See website for full submission guidelines.

Nuthouse

Twin Rivers Press
P.O. Box 119-W, Ellenton FL 34222
Website: http://www.nuthousemagazine.com

Publishes: Essays; Fiction; Nonfiction; Poetry; *Areas:* Criticism; Humour; Literature; *Markets:* Adult; *Treatments:* Satirical

Publishes humorous prose and poetry. Send complete MS by post only. No email submissions. Send SASE for return (if required) or for response. No response without SASE.

Nuvein Magazine

Email: editor@nuvein.com
Website: http://nuvein.net

Publishes: Essays; Fiction; Nonfiction; Poetry; *Areas:* Literature; Short Stories; *Markets:* Adult; *Treatments:* Experimental; Literary

Online magazine of fiction, poetry, and essays. Accepts queries and submissions by email.

O&A (Oil & Automotive Service) Marketing News

KAL Publications, Inc.
559 South Harbor Boulevard, Suite A
Anaheim, CA 92805-4525
Tel: +1 (714) 563-9300
Fax: +1 (714) 563-9310
Email: kathy@kalpub.com
Website: http://www.kalpub.com

Publishes: Articles; Features; Interviews;
News; Nonfiction; *Areas:* Business;
Markets: Professional

Trade magazine covering the petroleum
marketing industry in the 13 Western states.

Obsidian: Literature in the African Diaspora

North Carolina State University
Department of English, Box 8105
Raleigh, NC 27695-8105
Email: obsidian@gw.ncsu.edu
Website:
http://english.chass.ncsu.edu/obsidian

Publishes: Essays; Fiction; Nonfiction;
Poetry; Reviews; Scripts; *Areas:* Criticism;
Drama; Literature; *Markets:* Adult

Publishes critical essays, fiction, poetry and
creative nonfiction focused on Africa and her
Diaspora. See website for submission
guidelines.

Ohio Teachers Write

Wright State University
470 Millett Hall
Dayton, Ohio 45435
Email: ohioteacherswrite@gmail.com
Website: http://www.octela.org/OTW.html

Publishes: Fiction; Poetry; *Areas:* Short
Stories; *Markets:* Adult

Editors: Dr. Sally Lamping

Publishes the poetry and prose of Ohio
educators. See website for full details.

On the Premises

4323 Gingham Court
Alexandria, VA 22310
Email: Questions@OnThePremises.com

Website: http://www.onthepremises.com

Publishes: Fiction; *Areas:* Short Stories;
Markets: Adult

Publishes the winners of its competitions,
held every three months. Stories up to 5,000
words on a given theme. Submit using online
submission system. No entry fee. See
website for full details.

One

Catholic Near East Welfare Association
1011 First Avenue
New York, NY 10022
Tel: +1 (212) 826-1480
Fax: +1 (212) 838-1344
Email: cnewa@cnewa.org
Website: http://www.cnewa.org

Publishes: Articles; News; Nonfiction;
Areas: Culture; Current Affairs; Politics;
Religious; *Markets:* Adult

Catholic magazine covering political,
cultural, and religious affairs in the Near
East. Send query by fax or by post.

One Less Magazine

6 Village Hill Road
Williamsburg,MA 01096
Email: onelessartontherange@yahoo.com
Website:
http://www.onelessmag.blogspot.com

Publishes: Fiction; Poetry; *Areas:* Short
Stories; *Markets:* Adult; *Treatments:*
Experimental; Literary; Mainstream

Editors: Nikki Widner

Submit 3–5 pages of poetry or 5–10 pages of
prose with cover letter and bio by post or by
email.

Open Spaces

Open Spaces Publications, Inc.
PMB 134
6327 C SW Capitol Hwy.
Portland, OR 97239-1937
Tel: +1 (503) 313-4361
Fax: +1 (503) 227-3401

Email: info@open-spaces.com
Website: http://www.open-spaces.com

Publishes: Essays; Fiction; Nonfiction; Poetry; *Areas:* Arts; Business; Culture; Current Affairs; Legal; Lifestyle; Medicine; Nature; Religious; Science; Short Stories; Sociology; *Markets:* Adult; *Treatments:* Literary

For essays, query with qualifications in first instance. For fiction, send complete MS. For poetry, submit up to three poems (no epics). Include SASE with all submissions. No submissions by email.

Opium Magazine
Email: todd@opiummagazine.com
Website: http://opiummagazine.com

Publishes: Fiction; *Areas:* Humour; Short Stories; *Markets:* Adult; *Treatments:* Experimental; Literary; Satirical; Serious

Editors: Todd Zuniga

Short story magazine focusing mainly on literary humour, but also willing to consider serious pieces. Accepts comics / graphic novels. Submit via website using online submission system.

Overdrive
Randall-Reilly Publishing
3200 Rice Mine Road NE
Tuscaloosa, AL 35406
Tel: +1 (205) 349-2990
Fax: +1 (205) 750-8070
Email: mheine@randallreilly.com
Website: http://www.overdriveonline.com

Publishes: Essays; Features; Interviews; Nonfiction; *Areas:* Business; How-to; Technology; Travel; *Markets:* Professional

Editors: Max Heine, Editorial Director

Magazine for self-employed truck drivers. Send complete ms.

PMS poemmemoirstory
HB 217

1530 3rd Avenue South
Birmingham, AL 35294–1260
Tel: +1 (205) 934-2641
Fax: +1 (205) 975-8125
Email: poememoirstory@gmail.com
Website: http://pms-journal.org

Publishes: Essays; Fiction; Nonfiction; Poetry; *Areas:* Autobiography; Short Stories; Women's Interests; *Markets:* Adult; *Treatments:* Literary

Editors: Kerry Madden

Journal of exclusively women's writing, on any subject. Publishes poetry, fiction, and personal experience. Send up to five poems, or up to 15 pages of prose up to 4,300 words total, between January 1 and March 1 annually. See website for full submission guidelines.

Pulse
International SPA Association
2365 Harrodsburg Road, Suite A325
Lexington, KY 40504
Tel: +1 (859) 226-4326
Fax: +1 (859) 226-4445
Email: mae.manacap-johnson@ispastaff.com
Website: http://www.experienceispa.com/media/pulse-magazine

Publishes: Articles; News; Nonfiction; *Areas:* Business; *Markets:* Professional

Magazine for spa professionals. Send query with published clips.

PRISM Magazine
PO Box 367
Wayne PA 19087
Email: kkomarni@eastern.edu
Website: http://prismmagazine.org

Publishes: Articles; Essays; Features; Interviews; Nonfiction; Reviews; *Areas:* Religious; *Markets:* Adult

Editors: Kristyn Komarnicki

Evangelical magazine. Aims to be a

prophetic, consistently biblical voice in the North American church. Submit by post or by email, with email address or SAE for response. See website for full guidelines.

Pakn Treger

The Yiddish Book Center
Harry and Jeanette Weinberg Building
1021 West Street
Amherst, MA 01002
Tel: +1 (413) 256-4900
Fax: +1 (413) 256-4700
Email: pt@bikher.org
Website: http://www.yiddishbookcenter.org

Publishes: Articles; Essays; Features; Fiction; Interviews; Nonfiction; *Areas:* Culture; Historical; Humour; Literature; Mystery; Religious; Travel; *Markets:* Adult

Publishes fiction and nonfiction for a secular audience interested in Yiddish and Jewish history, literature, and culture. Send query by email in first instance.

Pallet Enterprise

Industrial Reporting, Inc.
10244 Timber Ridge Dr.
Ashland, VA 23005
Tel: +1 (804) 550-0323
Fax: +1 (804) 550-2181
Email: edb@ireporting.com
Website: http://www.palletenterprise.com

Publishes: Articles; Interviews; Nonfiction; *Areas:* Business; How-to; Nature; Technology; *Markets:* Professional

Editors: Edward C. Brindley, Jr., Ph.D.

Describes itself as the leading pallet and sawmill magazine in America. Send query with published clips.

Paradoxism

University of New Mexico
Gallup, NM 87301
Email: smarand@unm.edu
Website: http://fs.gallup.unm.edu
//a/oUTER-aRT.htm

Publishes: Essays; Fiction; Nonfiction;

Poetry; Scripts; *Areas:* Criticism; Drama; Short Stories; *Markets:* Adult; *Treatments:* Experimental; Literary

An avant-garde movement in literature, art, philosophy, science, based on excessive used of antitheses, antinomies, contradictions, parables, odds, anti-clichés, deviations of senses, against-the-grain speech, nonsense, paraphrases, paradoxes, semiparadoxes, etc. in creations.

Passages North

Northern Michigan University
1401 Presque Isle Avenue
Marquette, MI 49855
Tel: +1 (906) 227-2711
Fax: +1 (906) 227-1096
Email: passages@nmu.edu
Website: http://passagesnorth.com

Publishes: Essays; Fiction; Nonfiction; Poetry; *Areas:* Short Stories; *Markets:* Adult; *Treatments:* Literary

Open to submissions between September 1 and April 15 annually. Submit one story or essay, up to three short shorts, or up to five poems, either by post or online submission system. See website for full details.

The Paterson Literary Review

Passaic County Community College
One College Blvd, Paterson, NJ 07505-1179
Tel: +1 (973) 684-6555
Email: mGillan@pccc.edu
Website:
http://www.pccc.edu/home/cultural-affairs/poetry-center/publications

Publishes: Fiction; Poetry; *Areas:* Short Stories; *Markets:* Adult; *Treatments:* Literary

Publishes high quality poetry and fiction; any style, but no formula stories. Send up to five poems or no more than one story with SASE.

The Paumanok Review

Email: submissions@paumanokreview.com
Website: http://www.paumanokreview.com

Publishes: Essays; Fiction; Nonfiction; Poetry; *Areas:* Historical; Horror; Mystery; Politics; Sci-Fi; Short Stories; Westerns; *Markets:* Adult; *Treatments:* Experimental; Mainstream; Satirical

Online English-language magazine, neither US or UK specific. Accepting short short stories up to 1,000 words, short stories between 1,000 and 6,000 words (or over), poetry up to 100 lines (submit up to 5 poems per submission) and essays up to 6,000 words. Submit by email only, with submission(s) as WORD, RTF, HTML, TEXT, or in the body of an email. See website for full details.

The Pedestal Magazine
6815 Honors Court
Charlotte, NC 28210
Tel: +1 (704) 643-0244
Email: pedmagazine@carolina.rr.com
Website:
http://www.thepedestalmagazine.com

Publishes: Fiction; Interviews; Nonfiction; Poetry; Reviews; *Areas:* Short Stories; *Markets:* Adult

Online magazine publishing fiction, poetry, book reviews, and interviews. Previously unpublished material only. All submissions must be sent via the online form. Guidelines change each issue so consult website before submitting.

Pembroke Magazine
P.O. Box 1510
Pembroke, N.C. 28372-1510
Tel: +1 (910) 521-6358
Fax: +1 (910) 775-4092
Email: pembrokemagazine@uncp.edu
Website:
http://www.uncp.edu/pembrokemagazine

Publishes: Essays; Fiction; Interviews; Nonfiction; Poetry; Reviews; *Areas:* Translations; *Markets:* Adult

Accepts unsolicited poetry, fiction, translations, and essays. For book reviews or interviews query in first instance.

Pennsylvania English
Penn State DuBois
College Place
DuBois, PA 15801-3199
Tel: +1 (814) 375-4785
Fax: +1 (814) 375-4785
Email: ajv2@psu.edu
Website: http://www.english.iup.edu/pcea/publications.htm

Publishes: Essays; Fiction; Poetry; *Areas:* Criticism; Literature; Short Stories; *Markets:* Adult; *Treatments:* Contemporary; Literary; Mainstream

Editors: Antonio Vallone

For a complete set of editorial guidelines send SASE by post. No electronic submissions accepted.

Pennsylvania Heritage
The Pennsylvania Heritage Society
Commonwealth Keystone Building
400 North Street
Harrisburg, PA 17120
Tel: +1 (717) 787-2407
Fax: +1 (717) 346-9099
Email: miomalley@state.pa.us
Website: http://www.paheritage.org/pa-magazine.html

Publishes: Articles; Essays; Interviews; Nonfiction; *Areas:* Culture; Historical; *Markets:* Adult

Editors: Michael J. O'Malley III

Publishes material relating to Pennsylvania history and/or culture. Send query by email.

Peregrine
Amherst Writers & Artists Press
PO Box 1076
Amherst, MA 01004
Tel: +1 (413) 253-3307
Fax: +1 (413) 253-7764
Email: peregrinetwo@mac.com
Website:
http://www.amherstwriters.com/awa-press/peregrine/guidelines.html

Publishes: Fiction; Poetry; *Areas:* Short Stories; *Markets:* Adult

Editors: Nancy Rose

Accepts submissions between March 15 and May 15 only. Send one story or 3-5 poems with cover letter and author bio up to 40 words. No inspirational poetry, greeting-card verse, religious tirades, or nostalgia. Shorter stories stand a better chance of acceptance. See website for full guidelines.

Permafrost
University of Alaska Fairbanks
Department of English
P.O. Box 755720
Fairbanks, AK 99775-0640
Tel: +1 (907) 474-5074
Email: editor@permafrostmag.com
Website: http://permafrostmag.com

Publishes: Fiction; Nonfiction; Poetry; *Areas:* Short Stories; *Markets:* Adult; *Treatments:* Literary

Submit by post with SASE or through online submission system ($3 charge per online entry). No submissions directly by email. Submit up to five poems of any length, or prose of up to 8,000 words. See website for more details.

Persimmon Tree
Email: Submissions@persimmontree.org
Website: http://www.persimmontree.org

Publishes: Fiction; Nonfiction; *Areas:* Short Stories; Women's Interests; *Markets:* Adult

Online magazine publishing fiction and nonfiction by women over 60. See website for full details.

Philadelphia Stories
93 Old York Road, Ste 1/#1-753
Jenkintown, PA 19046
Email: christine@philadelphiastories.org
Website: http://www.philadelphiastories.org

Publishes: Essays; Fiction; Nonfiction; Poetry; *Markets:* Adult

Publishes fiction, poetry, and essays by authors living in, or originally from, Pennsylvania, Delaware, or New Jersey. Submit via online submission form only. No postal submissions.

The Photo Review
140 East Richardson Avenue, Suite 301,
Langhorne, PA 19047-2824
Email: info@photoreview.org
Website: http://www.photoreview.org

Publishes: Essays; Interviews; Nonfiction; Reviews; *Areas:* Criticism; Photography; *Markets:* Adult

Photography magazine publishing critical reviews, essays, and interviews. No how-to or technical. Submit complete ms.

Pilgrimage
Box 9110
Pueblo, CO 81008
Email: editor@pilgrimagepress.org

Publishes: Fiction; Nonfiction; Poetry; *Areas:* Short Stories; Spiritual; Translations; *Markets:* Adult; *Treatments:* Literary

Editors: Maria Melendez

Publishes literary nonfiction, poetry, and fiction relating to soul, spirit, place, and social justice. Accepts unsolicited poetry and nonfiction, but fiction by solicitation only. See website for full details.

Pink Chameleon
Email: dpfreda@juno.com
Website: http://www.thepinkchameleon.com

Publishes: Articles; Fiction; Nonfiction; Poetry; *Areas:* Short Stories; *Markets:* Adult; Family; *Treatments:* Positive

Editors: Dorothy Paula Freda

Publishes upbeat stories, touching emotional pieces, short stories, poetry, short anecdotes, articles, and words of wisdom. Any genre as long as the material submitted is in good taste (family orientated) and gives hope for the future, even in sadness. Reading periods are January 1 to April 30, and September 1 to October 31. Send complete MS by email only, pasted into the body of the email. No email attachments or postal submissions. See website for full guidelines.

Pinyon

Languages, Literature and Mass Communication
Colorado Mesa University
1100 North Avenue
Grand Junction, CO 81501-3122
Email: pinyonpoetry@hotmail.com
Website: http://www.coloradomesa.edu/english/publications.html

Publishes: Fiction; Nonfiction; Poetry; *Areas:* Short Stories; *Markets:* Adult; *Treatments:* Literary

Send 3-5 poems, or one piece of fiction or creative nonfiction by post with SASE only. Submissions without an SASE will be recycled without notification. No electronic submissions. Reading period from August 1 to December 1. See website for full guidelines.

Pipeline & Gas Journal

Oildom Publishing Company of Texas, Inc.
PO Box 941669
Houston, TX 77094-8669
Tel: +1 (281) 558-6930, ext. 218
Email: jshare@oildompublishing.com
Website: http://www.pgjonline.com

Publishes: Articles; Features; Nonfiction; *Areas:* Business; Design; Technology; *Markets:* Professional

Editors: Jeff Share

Publishes articles and features relating to the pipeline business: natural gas, crude oil, or products. See website for full submission guidelines.

Pisgah Review

Division of Humanities, Brevard College
400 North Broad Street
Brevard, NC 28712

Tel: +1 (828) 884-8349
Email: tinerjj@brevard.edu
Website: http://www.pisgahreview.com

Publishes: Fiction; Nonfiction; Poetry; *Areas:* Short Stories; *Markets:* Adult; *Treatments:* Literary

Editors: Jubal Tiner

Literary journal publishing short fiction, creative nonfiction, and poetry. Submit via online submission system on website.

Plain Spoke

Amsterdam Press
6199 Steubenville Road SE
Amsterdam, Ohio 43903
Email: plainspoke@gmail.com
Website: http://www.plainspoke.net

Publishes: Fiction; Poetry; *Areas:* Short Stories; *Markets:* Adult; *Treatments:* Literary

Editors: Cindy M. Kelly (poetry); Shaun M. Barcalow (fiction)

Quarterly literary magazine accepting work which can be described as: specific; honest; well-crafted with a strong sense of clarity; wise; quiet; gritty; surprising, true. Prefers email submissions but will also accept submissions by post. No specific reading periods. Material must be unpublished, but may be submitted elsewhere simultaneously provided immediate notification is given of acceptance elsewhere.

Pockets

PO Box 340004
Nashville, TN 37203-0004
Email: pockets@upperroom.org
Website: http://pockets.upperroom.org

Publishes: Articles; Fiction; Nonfiction; Poetry; *Areas:* Cookery; Hobbies; Leisure; Religious; Short Stories; *Markets:* Children's

Magazine for 6 to 12-year-olds, offering wholesome devotional readings that teach about God's love and presence in life. Submissions do not need to be overtly religious, but must support the purpose of the magazine to help children grow in their faith. Welcomes submissions of stories, poems, recipes, puzzles, games, and activities. No email submissions. See website for full guidelines.

Poetry International

Department of English and Comparative Literature
San Diego State University
5500 Campanile Drive
San Diego, CA 92182-6020
Tel: +1 (619) 594-1522
Fax: +1 (619) 594-4998
Email: poetry.international@yahoo.com
Website: http://poetryinternational.sdsu.edu

Publishes: Essays; Nonfiction; Poetry; Reviews; *Areas:* Criticism; Literature; Translations; *Markets:* Adult

Publishes new poetry as well as commentary, criticism, and reviews of poetry. Open to submissions from Autumn 2012.

Pointe Magazine

333 7th Avenue, 11th Floor
New York, NY 10001
Tel: +1 (212) 979-4862
Fax: +1 (646) 459-4848
Email: pointe@dancemedia.com
Website: http://www.pointemagazine.com

Publishes: Articles; Features; Interviews; News; Nonfiction; *Areas:* Drama; Historical; How-to; Music; *Markets:* Adult; Professional

Editors: Amy Cogan, Vice President and Group Publisher

Ballet magazine. Send query with published clips.

Popular Woodworking Magazine

F+W Media, Inc.
8469 Blue Ash Road, Suite 100
Cincinnati, OH 45236
Email: popwood@fwmedia.com

Website:
http://www.popularwoodworking.com

Publishes: Articles; Nonfiction; *Areas:* Crafts; Design; Hobbies; How-to; Humour; Technology; *Markets:* Adult; Professional

Editors: Megan Fitzpatrick

Publishes articles on woodworking as a profession and as a hobby, including how-to and technical guides. Also publishes relevant humour. Does not consider reviews of tools. Send complete ms.

Portland Magazine

165 State
Portland, ME 04101
Tel: +1 (207) 775-4339
Fax: +1 (207) 775-2334
Email: staff@portlandmonthly.com
Website: http://www.portlandmonthly.com

Publishes: Articles; Features; Fiction; Interviews; Nonfiction; *Areas:* Arts; Beauty and Fashion; Business; Cookery; Leisure; Lifestyle; Short Stories; *Markets:* Adult

Editors: Colin Sargent

Regional magazine of Portland / Maine, publishing nonfiction and fiction. Send query by post or by email, with clips and bio if available. See website for full submission guidelines.

The Portland Review

Portland State University
PO Box 347
Portland, OR 97207-0347
Tel: +1 (503) 725-4533
Email: theportlandreview@gmail.com
Website: http://portlandreview.tumblr.com

Publishes: Fiction; Poetry; *Areas:* Short Stories; *Markets:* Adult

Publishes quality fiction, poetry, and art, which is previously unpublished. Submit up to ten poems or one piece of prose via online submission system only.

Post Road

PO Box 600725
Newtown, MA 02460
Email: postroad@bc.edu
Website: http://www.postroadmag.com

Publishes: Essays; Fiction; Interviews;
Nonfiction; Poetry; *Areas:* Criticism;
Literature; Short Stories; Translations;
Markets: Adult; *Treatments:* Literary

Nationally distributed literary magazine
based out of New York and Boston. Submit
online via website.

Potomac Review

Montgomery College
51 Mannakee Street, MT/212
Rockville, MD 20850
Email:
zachary.benavidez@montgomerycollege.edu
Website: http://www.montgomery
college.edu/potomacreview

Publishes: Fiction; Poetry; *Areas:* Short
Stories; *Markets:* Adult; *Treatments:*
Literary

Editors: Zachary Benavidez

Send up to three poems / five pages, or
fiction up to 5,000 words. Submit
electronically via website, or by post with
SASE, brief bio, and email address.
Simultaneous submissions are accepted if
identified as such. See website for more
details.

Prairie Schooner

123 Andrews Hall
University of Nebraska–Lincoln
Lincoln, NE 68588-0334
Tel: +1 (402) 472-0911
Fax: +1 (402) 472-1817
Email: PrairieSchooner@unl.edu
Website: http://prairieschooner.unl.edu

Publishes: Essays; Fiction; Interviews;
Nonfiction; Poetry; Reviews; *Areas:*
Literature; Short Stories; *Markets:* Adult;
Treatments: Literary

Publishes short stories, poems, interviews,

imaginative essays of general interest, and
reviews of current books of poetry and
fiction. Does not publish scholarly articles
requiring footnote references. Submit one
piece of prose or 5-7 poems at a time by post
or using online submission system. See
website for more details.

Prairie Winds

Dakota Wesleyan University
1200 West University Avenue
Box 536
Mitchell, SD 57301
Email: prairiewinds@dwu.edu
Website: http://www.dwu.edu/prairiewinds

Publishes: Essays; Nonfiction; Poetry;
Markets: Adult; *Treatments:* Literary

Welcomes poetry, essay, and photography.
Send complete ms, typed, with SASE, short
biography, and email address (where
available).

Produce Business

5400 Broken Sound Boulevard NW, Suite
400
Boca Raton, FL 33487
Tel: +1 (561) 994-1118
Fax: +1 (561) 994-1610
Email: info@producebusiness.com
Website: http://www.producebusiness.com

Publishes: Nonfiction; *Areas:* Business;
Markets: Professional

Trade magazine concentrating on the buying
end of the produce/floral industry.

Promo

Tel: +1 (203) 899-8442
Email: podell@accessintel.com
Website:
http://www.chiefmarketer.com/promotional-
marketing

Publishes: Articles; Interviews; Nonfiction;
Areas: Business; How-to; *Markets:*
Professional

Editors: Patty Odell, Senior Editor

Magazine for marketing professionals. Send query with published clips.

Provincetown Arts

650 Commercial Street
Provincetown, MA 02657
Tel: +1 (508) 487-3167
Email: cbusa@comcast.net
Website: http://provincetownarts.org

Publishes: Articles; Essays; Features; Fiction; Interviews; Nonfiction; Reviews; *Areas:* Arts; Literature; Short Stories; Theatre; *Markets:* Adult; *Treatments:* Literary

Editors: Christopher Busa

Welcomes unsolicited manuscripts between September and December. Send by email as Word file attachment (no PDFs) with short bio. See website for full submission guidelines.

Pseudopod

Escape Artists, Inc.
PO Box 965609
Marietta, GA 30066
Email: submit@pseudopod.org
Website: http://pseudopod.org

Publishes: Fiction; *Areas:* Crime; Fantasy; Horror; Short Stories; *Markets:* Adult; *Treatments:* Dark; Literary; Mainstream; Popular

Audio podcast, therefore stories must translate well into the spoken word. Seeks dark horror short stories up to 6,000 words, or flash up to 1,500 words. Most material published is not suitable for children. Happy to consider both genre horror and literary horror. Send complete ms by email. Accepts simultaneous submissions but no multiple submissions. See website for full guidelines.

Puckerbrush Review

Email: sanphip@aol.com
Website: http://puckerbrushreview.com

Publishes: Essays; Fiction; Poetry; Reviews; *Areas:* Short Stories; *Markets:* Adult; *Treatments:* Literary

Editors: Sanford Phippen

Publishes poetry, short stories, literary essays and reviews. Submit complete ms by email only. No hard copy submissions.

Quiddity

Benedictine University at Springfield
1500 North Fifth Street
Springfield, IL 62702
Website:
http://www1.ben.edu/springfield/quiddity/

Publishes: Fiction; Nonfiction; Poetry; *Areas:* Short Stories; *Markets:* Adult; *Treatments:* Experimental; Literary; Mainstream

Publishes creative nonfiction and fiction (including novel extracts) up to 5,000 words. Send one piece of prose or up to five poems (up to ten pages maximum) by post with SASE, or via website with $3.50 submission charge. See website for full details.

Quilter's World

306 E PARR RD
BERNE, IN 46711
Email: Editor@QuiltersWorld.com
Website: http://www.quiltersworld.com

Publishes: Articles; Features; Interviews; Nonfiction; *Areas:* Crafts; Hobbies; How-to; *Markets:* Adult

Magazine covering quilting. Send query or manuscript by post or email.

Quite Curious Literature

Email: rp.negrini@gmail.com
Website: http://quite-curious.com

Publishes: Fiction; Poetry; *Areas:* Adventure; Arts; Culture; Fantasy; Literature; Nature; New Age; Short Stories; *Markets:* Professional; *Treatments:* Contemporary; Experimental; In-depth; Light; Literary; Mainstream; Niche; Positive; Progressive; Satirical; Serious; Traditional

Editors: Ryan Negrini

Climbing down the rabbit hole with Lewis Carroll's curious methods, this is a quarterly electronic literary magazine that hopes to publish anything that is creative, unique and, well, curious. If it doesn't fit our theme, then unfortunately, you're just not stepping far enough out of the box. But we trust you all know how to be creative on an epic level. Check out our On Submission page for all the splendid details.

Romance Flash
Email: submissions@romanceflash.com
Website: http://www.romanceflash.com

Publishes: Fiction; *Areas:* Romance; Short Stories; *Markets:* Adult

Editors: Kat de Falla; Rachel Green

Publishes romance flash fiction up to 1,000 words. No heavy erotica or postal submissions. Submit by email or through form on website only.

Radix Magazine
PO Box 4307
Berkeley, CA 94704
Tel: +1 (510) 548-5329
Email: Radixmag@aol.com
Website: http://www.radixmagazine.com

Publishes: Articles; Nonfiction; Poetry; *Areas:* Arts; Culture; Finance; Health; Literature; Media; Religious; *Markets:* Adult; *Treatments:* Contemporary

Christian magazine focusing on the interface between faith and contemporary culture. Submit 1-4 poems at a time, or query with ideas for articles.

The Rag
11901 SW 34th Ave
Portland, OR 97219
Tel: +1 (215) 350-5338
Email: dan@raglitmag.com
Website: http://www.raglitmag.com

Publishes: Fiction; Poetry; Scripts; *Areas:*

Arts; Entertainment; Humour; Literature; Short Stories; *Markets:* Adult; *Treatments:* Cynical; Dark; Literary; Satirical

Editors: Seth Porter

Note: Charges $3 reading fee per submission

A new electronic literary magazine specializing in the publication of short fiction, and is currently accepting poetry and manuscript submissions. Set to debut in fall, 2011, this publication focuses on the grittier genres that tend to fall by the wayside at more traditional literary magazines.

The editors specialize in finding original talent from all over the world, in an effort to produce a unique, entertaining and diverse reading experience, while also providing an income outlet that supports and promotes writers in a way that helps to create a sustainable demand for their work. In other words, we pay our authors for the work we publish. The magazine accepts submissions electronically, all year round.

We see electronic publishing as an opportunity. It lets us distribute our magazine for a reasonable price, while still allowing us to pay our authors for their hard work—in other words, new technology has allowed us to turn back time to an era of affordable distribution and open competition. It's easy for good writing to get lost in the muck of Internet publishing. Many of the existing online magazines aim for quantity over quality. They throw the muck at the wall and hope some sticks. Which is fine and has its place, but that's not the way we operate. The Rag aims to bring a print aesthetic to the digital world. In other words, we have standards. We edit our stories. We design a good-looking magazine. We want publication in to mean something to our authors, and we want our readers to trust that they'll get only the best writing out there.

We like gritty stories, stories that are psychologically believable and stories that have some humor in them, dark or otherwise. We like subtle themes, original characters and sharp wit.

Railroad Evangelist Magazine

PO Box 5026
Vancouver, WA 98668
Email: REA@comcast.net
Website: http://www.railroadevangelist.com

Publishes: Articles; Essays; Fiction;
Interviews; Nonfiction; Poetry; *Areas:*
Historical; Hobbies; Religious; Short Stories;
Travel; *Markets:* Adult; Children's; Youth

Evangelistic magazine the entire railroad
community worldwide, including the railroad
industry, the model railroad hobbyist and the
rail fan enthusiast. All material must be
railroad related. Prose should be between
300 and 800 words. See website for full
details.

RealPoetik

Email: realpoetikblog@gmail.com
Website: http://www.realpoetik.org

Publishes: Poetry; *Markets:* Adult;
Treatments: Contemporary; Experimental;
Literary; Progressive

Editors: Lily Brown; Claire Becker

Send query by email in first instance.

The Red Clay Review

c/o Jim Elledge, Director, MA in
Professional Writing Program
Department of English, Kennesaw State
University
1000 Chastain Road, #2701
Kennesaw, GA 30144-5591
Email: redclay2013@gmail.com
Website: http://redclayreview.com

Publishes: Fiction; Nonfiction; Poetry;
Areas: Short Stories; *Markets:* Adult;
Treatments: Literary

Publishes poetry, fiction, and creative
nonfiction by graduate writing students only.
See website for more details, and to submit
via online submission system.

Red Rock Review

Email: RedRockReview@csn.edu

Website:
http://sites.csn.edu/english/redrockreview/

Publishes: Essays; Fiction; Nonfiction;
Poetry; Reviews; *Areas:* Literature; *Markets:*
Adult; *Treatments:* Contemporary; Literary

Accepts submissions by email only. Send all
submissions as MS Word, RTF, or PDF file
attachments. No postal submissions. Closed
to submissions in June, July, August, and
December. See website for full guidelines.

Redactions: Poetry, Poetics, & Prose

604 North 31st Avenue, Apt. D-2
Hattiesburg, MS 39401
Email: redactionspoetry@yahoo.com
Website: http://www.redactions.com

Publishes: Fiction; Nonfiction; Poetry;
Areas: Short Stories; *Markets:* Adult;
Treatments: Literary

Editors: Tom Holmes

Accepts submissions by email only. Send 3-5
poems, a single piece of fiction or creative
nonfiction up to 2,500 words, or up to three
flash fictions, in a single file as an
attachment, or in the body of an email.

Redivider

Department of Writing, Literature, and
Publishing
Emerson College
120 Boylston Street
Boston, MA 02116
Email: poetry@redividerjournal.org
Website: http://www.redividerjournal.org

Publishes: Fiction; Nonfiction; Poetry;
Areas: Short Stories; *Markets:* Adult;
Treatments: Literary

Publishes fiction, literary nonfiction, poetry,
and visual art. Authors are encouraged to
familiarise themselves with previous copies
of the magazine, and use the online
submission system available on the website.
Hard copy submissions by post will still be
accepted, but no submissions by email.

Reed Magazine

San Jose State University
English Department
One Washington Square
San Jose, CA 95192-0090
Email: reed@email.sjsu.edu
Website: http://www.reedmag.org

Publishes: Essays; Fiction; Nonfiction;
Poetry; *Areas:* Short Stories; *Markets:* Adult;
Treatments: Literary

Submit up to five poems, or as many stories
or essays as you like. Work must be sent as
.doc or .rtf formats. No paper submissions.
Accepts work between June 1 and November
1, only. See website for full submission
guidelines.

Residential Aliens

ResAliens Press
PO Box 780203
Wichita, KS 67278
Email: resaliens@gmail.com
Website: http://www.resaliens.com

Publishes: Fiction; *Areas:* Fantasy; Horror;
Sci-Fi; Thrillers; *Markets:* Adult

Online magazine of speculative fiction. See
website for details of next submission
window.

Rhino Poetry

PO Box 591
Evanston, IL 60204
Email: editors@rhinopoetry.org
Website: http://rhinopoetry.org

Publishes: Fiction; Poetry; *Areas:* Short
Stories; Translations; *Markets:* Adult;
Treatments: Literary

Accepts submissions between April 1 and
October 1 annually. Publishes poetry, poetry
translations, and flash fiction up to 1,000
words. Submissions accepted via online
submissions manager, or by post with SASE.
See website for full guidelines.

Road King

Parthenon Publishing

102 Woodmont Boulevard, Suite 450
Nashville, TN 37205
Website: http://roadking.com

Publishes: Articles; Nonfiction; *Areas:*
Business; Travel; *Markets:* Professional

Magazine publishing articles of interest to
those in the trucking industry. Send query
with published clips.

The Rockford Review

Rockford Writers' Guild
Attn: Connie Kuntz
PO Box 858
Rockford, IL 61105
Email: editor@rockfordwritersguild.com
Website:
http://www.rockfordwritersguild.com

Publishes: Fiction; Poetry; *Areas:* Short
Stories; *Markets:* Adult; *Treatments:*
Literary

Publishes two issues per year: one is open to
submissions from members only, the other is
open to submissions from all writers.
Publishes poetry up to 50 lines and prose up
to 1,300 words which express fresh insights
into the human condition.

RTJ's Creative Catechist

PO Box 6015
New London, CT 06320
Tel: +1 (800) 321-0411
Email:
creativesubs@rtjscreativecatechist.com
Website:
http://www.rtjscreativecatechist.com

Publishes: Articles; Nonfiction; *Areas:*
How-to; Religious; *Markets:* Professional

Magazine for Catholic Directors of Religious
Education. Send complete ms. No response
without SASE.

The Rusty Nail

Email: rustynailmag@gmail.com
Website: http://www.rustynailmag.com

Publishes: Essays; Fiction; Nonfiction;

Poetry; Reviews; *Areas:* Adventure; Arts; Crime; Culture; Horror; Literature; Mystery; Sci-Fi; Short Stories; Suspense; Thrillers; Westerns; *Markets:* Adult; *Treatments:* Contemporary; Cynical; Dark; Literary; Mainstream; Niche; Popular

Our goal is to join the growing community of Internet-based English types who not only love literature and the written word, but are enamored with the future of both. We believe that the Internet has given authors and poets the opportunity to share and get recognition for their work without having to sell their soul to "The Man." This preserves artistic dignity and lets the reader see the writer's thoughts and soul without the often numbing influence of industry "professionals."

We'd love to have you join us on this journey. If you have work to share, visit the Submissions page to learn how to submit your writing. Otherwise, you can help by being a enthusiastic reader and sharing our page with your friends.

Thanks and we hope you enjoy.

RV Business

2901 E. Bristol Street, Suite B
Elkhart, IN 46514
Tel: +1 (800) 831-1076
Fax: +1 (574) 266-7984
Email: bhampson@rvbusiness.com
Website: http://www.rvbusiness.com

Publishes: Articles; News; Nonfiction; *Areas:* Business; Design; Finance; Technology; Travel; *Markets:* Professional

Editors: Bruce Hampson

Magazine for professionals in the recreational vehicle industry. Send query with published clips.

Salmagundi Magazine

Skidmore College
815 North Broadway
Saratoga Springs, NY 12866
Tel: +1 (518) 580-5000
Email: salsubmit@skidmore.edu

Website:
http://cms.skidmore.edu/salmagundi/

Publishes: Essays; Fiction; Nonfiction; Reviews; *Areas:* Criticism; Culture; *Markets:* Adult

Publishes poetry, fiction, personal essays, cultural criticism, and book reviews. Submit five or six poems or up to 12,000 words of prose as an attachment to an email only. Book reviews generally by commission only. No hard copy submissions. See website for dates of reading periods.

Salt Hill Journal

Creative Writing Program, Syracuse University
English Deptartment
401 Hall of Languages, Syracuse University
Syracuse, NY 13244
Email: salthilljournal@gmail.com
Website: http://www.salthilljournal.com

Publishes: Essays; Fiction; Interviews; Nonfiction; Poetry; Reviews; *Areas:* Short Stories; Translations; *Markets:* Adult; *Treatments:* Literary

Reads submissions for the magazine between August 1 and April 1 of each year and for the Poetry Award between May 15 and August 1. Send up to five poems or up to 30 pages of prose. No submissions by email - submit via online submission system.

Salt Water Sportsman

Email: Editor@saltwatersportsman.com
Website:
http://www.saltwatersportsman.com

Publishes: Articles; Nonfiction; *Areas:* Leisure; Sport; *Markets:* Adult

Editors: John Brownlee

Magazine for serious marine sport fishermen. Send articles etc. by email.

Sandy River Review

111 South Street
Farmington, ME 04938

Tel: +1 (207) 778-7000
Fax: +1 (207) 778-7000
Email: SRReview@gmail.com
Website:
http://sandyriverreview.umf.maine.edu

Publishes: Fiction; Nonfiction; Poetry;
Areas: Short Stories; *Markets:* Adult;
Treatments: Literary

Publishes poetry, literary fiction, and
nonfiction. No horror, fantasy, sci-fi, or
romance. Submit up to five poems or up to
three pieces of prose, by email, as Word
attachments. See website for full guidelines.

Santa Clara Review

PO Box 3212
500 El Camino Real
Santa Clara, CA 95053-3212
Tel: +1 (408) 554-4484
Email: santaclarareview@gmail.com
Website: http://www.santaclarareview.com

Publishes: Essays; Fiction; Nonfiction;
Poetry; Scripts; *Areas:* Drama; Short Stories;
Markets: Adult; *Treatments:* Literary

For poetry send up to three poems, up to ten
pages in length. Fiction, nonfiction, and
scripts should be less than 5,000 words.
2,000-4,000 is more normal. Accepts
submissions by post, but prefers electronic
submissions.

Santa Monica Review

Santa Monica College
1900 Pico Boulevard
Santa Monica, CA 90405
Website: http://www2.smc.edu/sm_review

Publishes: Essays; Fiction; Interviews;
Nonfiction; *Areas:* Short Stories; *Markets:*
Adult; *Treatments:* Literary

Publishes literary short stories, essays and
interviews by established and emerging
writers. Makes a special effort to present and
promote writers from Southern California.
Include SASE with submissions.

Saranac Review

CVH, Dept of English
SUNY Plattsburgh
101 Broad Street
Plattsburgh, NY 12901
Email: saranacreview@plattsburgh.edu
Website:
http://research.plattsburgh.edu/saranacreview

Publishes: Essays; Fiction; Nonfiction;
Poetry; *Areas:* Short Stories; Translations;
Markets: Adult; *Treatments:* Literary

Publishes poetry and literary fiction and
nonfiction. Accepts submissions between
September 1 and May 15 each year. Submit
one story or essay, or 3-5 poems by post only
with SASE. No genre fiction (science fiction,
etc.) or light verse. See website for full
submission guidelines.

The Saturday Evening Post

1100 Waterway Boulevard
Indianapolis, IN 46202
Tel: +1 (317) 634-1100
Email: editor@saturdayeveningpost.com
Website:
http://www.saturdayeveningpost.com

Publishes: Articles; Features; Fiction;
Interviews; Nonfiction; *Areas:* Beauty and
Fashion; Entertainment; Finance; Gardening;
Health; How-to; Humour; Lifestyle;
Medicine; Short Stories; Technology;
Travel; *Markets:* Adult; *Treatments:* Light

Publishes articles, features, and new fiction
with a light, humorous touch. Send complete
ms with SASE for return or response. See
website for full details.

Scary Monsters Magazine

Email: Scaremail@aol.com
Website:
http://www.scarymonstersmagazine.com

Publishes: Fiction; *Areas:* Horror; Short
Stories; *Markets:* Adult

Horror magazine focusing on monsters. Send
query in first instance.

School Nurse News

Franklin Communications, Inc.
71 Redner Road
Morristown, NJ 07960
Tel: +1 (973) 644-4003
Fax: +1 (973) 644-4062
Email: editor@schoolnursenews.org
Website: http://www.schoolnursenews.org

Publishes: Articles; Interviews; News;
Nonfiction; *Areas:* Medicine; *Markets:*
Professional

Editors: Deb Ilardi, RN, BSN

Magazine aimed at school nurses and other healthcare professionals serving children. Send query by email.

Scissors and Spackle

516 South Saint Andrews Place #505
Los Angeles, CA 90020
Email: editors@scissorsandspackle.com
Website: http://www.scissorsandspackle.com

Publishes: Essays; Fiction; Interviews;
Nonfiction; Poetry; Scripts; *Areas:*
Criticism; Culture; Current Affairs; Drama;
Erotic; Fantasy; Gothic; Historical; Horror;
Humour; Literature; Music; Mystery;
Nature; Philosophy; Politics; Psychology;
Sci-Fi; Short Stories; Sociology; Theatre;
Thrillers; Women's Interests; *Markets:*
Adult; *Treatments:* Cynical; Dark;
Experimental; Literary; Niche; Progressive;
Satirical; Serious

Editors: Jenny Catlin

We believe in the power and force of the written world. We intend to prove our undying devotion to words, to writers and readers. We release an online and print edition on the 23rd of each month featuring the best writers of today and tomorrow. Its one small step.

There is revolution in the air. Words and language are finally prepared to fight back against the forces that have tried to silence them.

Sea Magazine

17782 Cowan, Suite C
Irvine, CA 92614
Tel: +1 (949) 660-6150
Fax: +1 (949) 660-6172
Email: editorial@seamagazine.com
Website: http://www.seamag.com

Publishes: Articles; Features; Nonfiction;
Areas: How-to; Technology; Travel;
Markets: Adult

Describes itself as "America's western boating magazine". Aims to provide up-to-date information on boating trends, new boat and equipment reports and new product news; electronics, accessory and gear features; maintenance tips and how-to project ideas; anchorages, places to fish, and cruising destinations. Regional editions for California and the Pacific Northwest.

Seek

Standard Publishing
8805 Governor's Hill Drive, Suite 400
Cincinnati, OH 45249
Tel: +1 (800) 543-1353
Email: scck@standardpub.com
Website: http://www.standardpub.com

Publishes: Articles; Fiction; Nonfiction;
Areas: Religious; Short Stories; *Markets:*
Adult

Publishes religious articles and short stories for adults. See website for list of upcoming topics and submit complete ms by email.

Sew News

Creative Crafts Group
741 Corporate Circle, Suite A
Golden, CO 80401
Tel: +1 (303) 215-5600
Fax: +1 (303) 215-5601
Email: sewnews@sewnews.com
Website: http://www.sewnews.com

Publishes: Articles; Features; News;
Nonfiction; *Areas:* Crafts; Hobbies;
Markets: Adult; Professional

Sewing magazine for amateurs and

professionals. Send query with published clips.

The Sewanee Review

University of the South
735 University Avenue
Sewanee, TN 37383-1000
Email: Lcouch@sewanee.edu
Website:
http://www.sewanee.edu/sewanee_review

Publishes: Articles; Essays; Fiction; Nonfiction; Poetry; Reviews; *Areas:* Short Stories; *Markets:* Adult; *Treatments:* Literary

Editors: George Core

For fiction and poetry send complete ms with SASE for response. Stories should be at least 3,500 words. Submit a maximum of six poems per submission. For reviews, query first; for essays a query is acceptable, but the complete ms preferred. No submissions between June 1 and August 31. See website for full guidelines.

Shadows Express

Email:
managingeditor@shadowexpress.com
Website: http://www.shadowexpress.com

Publishes: Articles; Essays; Fiction; Nonfiction; Poetry; *Areas:* Short Stories; *Markets:* Adult; *Treatments:* Literary

Online literary magazine publishing short stories, novel excerpts, poetry, and articles. Submit complete ms by email to specific addresses listed on website if under 2,500 words. For works over 2,500 words, query. See website for full guidelines.

Short Story America

2121 Boundary Street, Suite 204
Beaufort, SC 29902
Tel: +1 (843) 597-3220
Email: editors@shortstoryamerica.com
Website: http://www.shortstoryamerica.com

Publishes: Fiction; *Areas:* Short Stories; *Markets:* Adult; *Treatments:* Literary

Editors: Tim Johnston

Online magazine. Submit short stories and flash fiction using form on website only.

The Sierra Nevada Review

999 Tahoe Boulevard
Incline Village, NV 89451
Tel: +1 (775) 831-1314
Email: sncreview@sierranevada.edu
Website:
http://www.sierranevada.edu/academics/hum
anities-social-sciences/english/the-sierra-
nevada-review/

Publishes: Fiction; Poetry; *Markets:* Adult; *Treatments:* Literary

Submit up to five poems or fiction up to ten pages at a time. Particularly interested in flash fiction. Accepts submissions between September 1 and March 1 annually. Use submission manager on website to submit.

Sign Builder Illustrated

Simmons-Boardman Publishing Corporation
55 Broad Street, 26th floor
New York, NY 10004
Tel: +1 (212) 620-7200
Fax: +1 (212) 633-1863
Email: jwooten@sbpub.com
Website: http://www.signshop.com

Publishes: Articles; Features; Interviews; Nonfiction; *Areas:* Design; How-to; Technology; *Markets:* Professional

Editors: Jeff Wooten

Magazine aimed at professionals in the signage industry. Query in first instance.

Silicon Valley / San Jose Business Journal

125 South Market Street, 11th Floor
San Jose, CA 95113
Tel: +1 (408) 295-3800
Fax: +1 (408) 295-5028
Email: sanjose@bizjournals.com
Website: http://www.bizjournals.com

Publishes: Articles; News; Nonfiction;

Areas: Business; *Markets:* Professional

Business magazine aimed at upper-level management. Query in first instance.

Skin Deep

Associated Skin Care Professionals
25188 Genesee Trail Road, Suite 200
Golden, CO 80401
Tel: +1 (800) 789-0411
Fax: +1 (800) 790-0299
Email: getconnected@ascpskincare.com
Website: http://www.ascpskincare.com

Publishes: Articles; Nonfiction; *Areas:* Beauty and Fashion; Business; Health; *Markets:* Professional

Industry magazine for professional skin care practitioners. Query in first instance.

Smithsonian Magazine

Capital Gallery, Suite 6001
MRC 513, PO Box 37012
Washington, DC 20013
Tel: +1 (202) 275-2000
Email: smithsonianmagazine@si.edu
Website: http://www.smithsonianmag.com

Publishes: Articles; Nonfiction; *Areas:* Anthropology; Archaeology; Arts; Culture; Historical; Lifestyle; Nature; Science; Technology; *Markets:* Adult

Publishes articles on archaeology, arts, different lifestyles, cultures and peoples, nature, science and technology. Submit proposal through online form on website.

Stone Canoe

700 University Avenue, Suite 326
Syracuse, NY 13244-2530
Tel: +1 (315) 443-4165
Fax: +1 (315) 443-4174
Email: stonecanoe@syr.edu
Website: http://www.stonecanoejournal.org

Publishes: Features; Fiction; Nonfiction; Poetry; Scripts; *Areas:* Drama; Literature; Music; Short Stories; Technology; *Markets:* Adult; *Treatments:* Literary

Editors: Robert Colley (Editor); Allison Vincent (Assistant Editor)

Magazine publishing previously unpublished works of short fiction, creative nonfiction, technical writing, short plays, poems, and works of visual art created by people who live or have lived in Upstate New York (not New York City). Submit up to five poems or prose up to 10,000 words. See website for details and for online submission system.

Stone Highway Review

700 Monterey Way Apt. G 1
Lawrence, KS 66049
Email: stonehighwayreview@gmail.com
Website: http://www.stonehighway.com

Publishes: Essays; Fiction; Nonfiction; Poetry; *Areas:* Biography; Criticism; Culture; Current Affairs; Drama; Fantasy; Gothic; Humour; Literature; Media; Mystery; Nature; New Age; Philosophy; Photography; Religious; Short Stories; Suspense; Thrillers; Translations; Travel; Women's Interests; *Markets:* Academic; Adult; Family; *Treatments:* Contemporary; Dark; Experimental; In-depth; Literary; Mainstream; Serious; Traditional

Editors: Mary Stone Dockery and Amanda Hash

We're looking for prose that doesn't belong in other journals, pieces that are evocative, thought-provoking, and have beautiful language.
We like surreal, slipstream -- in other words, genre bending works, in addition to more traditional short prose. We like the gothic tone, but please no werewolf/vampire themes. We prefer shorter works -- around 750 words or so -- but will consider longer pieces as long as they move us. We accept both fiction and nonfiction work.
Simply put, we are looking for amazing poetry that moves us through its specific use of language and images and attention to each individual line.
We want poems that linger, that leave us in wonder. Great poetry should make you have to catch your breath after reading it and that's exactly what we're wanting to find.
We prefer shorter works (2 pages or less) but

will consider longer pieces. We are also very interested in artwork and photography.

Straitjackets Magazine

669 Weir Dr.
Hemet, CA 92545
Tel: +1 (951) 926-6336
Email: jvhitt73@hotmail.com
Website:
http://www.straitjacketsmagazine.com

Publishes: Articles; Essays; Fiction; Interviews; Nonfiction; Poetry; Reviews; *Areas:* Adventure; Arts; Autobiography; Biography; Crime; Criticism; Current Affairs; Entertainment; Fantasy; Film; Gothic; Historical; Horror; Humour; Leisure; Literature; Media; Music; Mystery; Politics; Sci-Fi; Short Stories; Sociology; Suspense; Thrillers; TV; Westerns; *Markets:* Academic; Adult; Family; *Treatments:* Commercial; Contemporary; Dark; Literary; Mainstream; Popular; Satirical; Serious; Traditional

Editors: Lynn Spreen, Jim Hitt, Ray Strait

An on-line literary magazine. We have an eclectic taste, so almost any subject is acceptable except erotica and religion. We are particularly interested in short stories, poetry, essays, novel excerpts, book and film reviews, and personal memoirs. We will also consider photography and photographic essays.

The Tavern's Vault

Email: adam@tavernsvault.com
Website: http://www.tavernsvault.com

Publishes: Fiction; *Areas:* Fantasy; Historical; Short Stories; *Markets:* Adult

Publishes short medieval fiction and fantasy. Send submissions as email attachments with bio in the body of the email.

The Rejected Quarterly

PO Box 1351
Cobb, CA 95426
Email: bplankton@yahoo.com

Website: http://www.rejectedq.com

Publishes: Features; Fiction; Nonfiction; Poetry; Reviews; *Areas:* Humour; Short Stories; *Markets:* Adult

Editors: Daniel Weiss, Jeff Ludecke

Magazine publishing fiction that has been rejected at least 5 times elsewhere, poetry about rejection, plus humour, opinions, and reviews. See website for full submission guidelines.

The Savage Side

Email: nudge@thesavageside.com
Website: http://www.thesavageside.com

Publishes: Articles; Features; Fiction; Interviews; News; Reviews; *Areas:* Entertainment; Fantasy; Music; Photography; Sci-Fi; Short Stories; *Markets:* Adult; *Treatments:* Dark; Experimental; Niche

Editors: Nudge Savage

Online Heavy Metal magazine. We are based out of Denver, and our goal is to promote the local music culture. While our main focus is on local, we also feature acts from around the world, beautiful local models.

The Vehicle

600 Lincoln Avenue
Charleston, IL
Email: vehicleeiu@gmail.com
Website: http://www.thevehiclemagazine.com

Publishes: Essays; Fiction; Interviews; Nonfiction; Poetry; Scripts; *Areas:* Adventure; Arts; Crime; Drama; Fantasy; Gothic; Historical; Horror; Humour; Literature; Mystery; Photography; Romance; Sci-Fi; Short Stories; Suspense; Theatre; Thrillers; Westerns; *Markets:* Adult

Editors: Hannah Green

A biannual literary magazine produced by students. Since 1959, the magazine has been publishing poetry, short stories, creative nonfiction, and artwork by the university's students but now has opened its doors to submissions from anyone, anywhere, and has moved online to facilitate the transition.

Thematic Literary Magazine

PO Box 12321
Casa Grande AZ, 85130
Tel: +1 (510) 375-7113
Website:
http://www.thematicliterarymagazine.com

Publishes: Fiction; Poetry; *Areas:* Crime; Culture; Drama; Entertainment; Erotic; Fantasy; Horror; Humour; Mystery; Politics; Religious; Romance; Sci-Fi; Short Stories; Spiritual; Suspense; Thrillers; *Markets:* Adult; Family; Professional; *Treatments:* Literary

Editors: Tiffany Lewis

Created to help new and amazing writers become professional authors. Anyone who is familiar with the writing career path knows that being published is the only way to become established. We offer a friendly, competitive and helpful environment where writers can become professionals through hard work, networking and accomplishment.

Vampires2

Email: mansstory2@aol.com
Website: http://www.vampires2.com

Publishes: Fiction; *Areas:* Adventure; Crime; Drama; Entertainment; Fantasy; Film; Gothic; Horror; Romance; Sci-Fi; Short Stories; Thrillers; *Markets:* Adult; Family; *Treatments:* Dark; Mainstream

Editors: Carlos Dunn and C.C. Blake

Strives to recreate the Magic of the pulp fiction magazines published from 1920s through the mid 1970s. Strived to deal with the romantic possibilities of Vampirs. Usually but not always, mankind is the bad guy.

Verbatim

PO Box 597302

Chicago, IL 60659
Tel: +1 (800) 897-3006
Email: editor@verbatimmag.com
Website: http://www.verbatimmag.com

Publishes: Articles; Nonfiction; *Areas:* Humour; *Markets:* Adult; *Treatments:* Popular

Publishes articles on English and other languages, focusing on amusing and interesting features of language. Authors are advised to query editor in advance regarding subject matter. No fiction. Submit via online submission system. No hard copy approaches.

Wild Violet

P.O. Box 39706
Philadelphia, PA 19106-9706
Email: wildvioletmagazine@yahoo.com
Website: http://www.wildviolet.net

Publishes: Essays; Fiction; Interviews; Nonfiction; Poetry; Reviews; *Areas:* Culture; Humour; Politics; Short Stories; *Markets:* Adult; *Treatments:* Literary

Quarterly online literary magazine designed to challenge and uplift the reader. Publishes poetry, fiction, and creative nonfiction. See website for full guidelines. Submissions accepted by post or by email.

Wag's Revue

Email: editors@wagsrevue.com
Website: http://www.wagsrevue.com

Publishes: Essays; Fiction; Interviews; Nonfiction; Poetry; *Markets:* Adult

Reading periods run from the beginning of March to the end of May, and from the start of September to the end of November. In addition to these reading periods, accepts submissions via competitions, for which there is a reading fee and a prize of $1,000. See website for full details. All submissions to made via system on website.

The Washington Pastime

Email: paulkaraffa@washingtonpastime.com

Website:
http://www.washingtonpastime.com

Publishes: Articles; Essays; Fiction;
Nonfiction; Poetry; *Areas:* Adventure;
Crime; Drama; Entertainment; Fantasy;
Gothic; Horror; Humour; Literature;
Mystery; Romance; Sci-Fi; Short Stories;
Suspense; Thrillers; Westerns; *Markets:*
Adult; Children's; Family; Professional;
Youth; *Treatments:* Commercial;
Contemporary; Cynical; Dark; Experimental;
In-depth; Light; Literary; Mainstream;
Niche; Popular; Positive; Progressive;
Satirical; Serious; Traditional

Editors: Paul Karaffa, Laura Bolt

In 2010 a study from Central Connecticut
State University found that the Washington
DC area was the most well-read urban city in
the United States. But Washington, DC did
not have a professional literary magazine in
the city representing its stake in
contemporary American literature.

This magazine was founded as an electronic
and print publication based in Washington,
DC committed to publishing the best in
literary and genre fiction. Work featured here
will push literary limitations and take a new
look at antiquated perspectives.

Authors will find a home here from all
around the world, and in turn find
themselves burrowing a place into the hearts
of the readership in the United States, and
specifically the DC metropolitan area.

Water-Stone Review

The Creative Writing Programs at Hamline
University
MS-A1730
1536 Hewitt Avenue
St Paul, MN 55104-1284
Email: water-stone@hamline.edu
Website: http://www.waterstonereview.com

Publishes: Essays; Fiction; Interviews;
Nonfiction; Poetry; Reviews; *Areas:* Short
Stories; *Markets:* Adult; *Treatments:*
Literary

Publishes poetry, fiction, and creative

nonfiction in all genres as well as
essays/reviews and writers' interviews.
Accepts work between October 1 and
December 1 only. No electronic submissions.
See website for full details.

WOW! Women On Writing

Email: submissions@wow-
womenonwriting.com
Website: http://www.wow-
womenonwriting.com

Publishes: Articles; Features; Nonfiction;
Reviews; *Areas:* Women's Interests;
Markets: Adult

Promotes the communication between
women writers, authors, editors, agents,
publishers, and readers. The magazine
provides timely market and industry
information, important interviews, and How
To Columns. Focuses each monthly issue on
a theme. Please see the Editor's Desk for
more information.

Writing that Works

Communications Concepts, Inc.
7481 Huntsman Boulevard #720
Springfield, VA 22153-1648
Tel: +1 (703) 643-2200
Email: concepts@writingthatworks.com
Website: http://www.apexawards.com

Publishes: Articles; Features; Nonfiction;
Areas: Business; How-to; *Markets:*
Professional

Editors: John De Lellis

Newlsetter covering business publication
writing, aimed at professional business
writers. See website for guidelines.

The Yes Factory

169 Rogers Ave #1A
Brooklyn, NY 11216
Tel: +1 (201) 665-3243
Email: submit@theyesfactory.org
Website: http://www.theyesfactory.org

Publishes: Fiction; Poetry; *Areas:*
Adventure; Arts; Crime; Drama;

Entertainment; Fantasy; Gothic; Horror; Humour; Military; Mystery; Philosophy; Photography; Politics; Romance; Science; Sci-Fi; Short Stories; Spiritual; Thrillers; Westerns; *Markets:* Adult; *Treatments:* Contemporary; Experimental; Literary; Positive; Progressive

Editors: Christa Pagliei

Seeks to publish outstanding and innovative poetry, art, and literary fiction. Our aim is to help new, emerging, and established artists reach a wider audience through a variety of mediums: print, online, e-readers, and live events.

The work we're looking to see is thoughtful, positive, sometimes conceptual, and always honest. We strive to answer each submission individually and offer notes whenever we can.

UK Magazines

For the most up-to-date listings of these and hundreds of other magazines, visit http://www.firstwriter.com/magazines

To claim your **free** access to the site, please see the back of this book.

Accountancy Age
Incisive Media
32-34 Broadwick Street
London
W1A 2HG
Tel: +44 (0) 20 7316 9000
Fax: +44 (0) 20 7316 9250
Email: kevin.reed@incisivemedia.com
Website: http://www.accountancyage.com

Publishes: Articles; Features; News; Nonfiction; *Areas:* Business; Finance; *Markets:* Professional

Editors: Kevin Reed

Weekly magazine publishing articles on accountancy, business, and the financial world. Unsolicited MSS welcome; outline ideas in writing.

Agenda
The Wheelwrights
Fletching Street
Mayfield
East Sussex
TN20 6TL
Tel: +44 (0) 1435 873703
Email: submissions@agendapoetry.co.uk
Website: http://www.agendapoetry.co.uk

Publishes: Essays; Poetry; Reviews; *Areas:* Criticism; Literature; *Markets:* Adult; *Treatments:* Literary

Editors: Patricia McCarthy

Publishes poems, critical essays, and reviews. Send up to five poems or up to two essays / reviews with email address, age, and short bio. No previously published material. Submit by email only, with each piece in a separate Word attachment.

AIR International
PO BOX 100
Stamford
PE9 1XQ
Tel: +44 (0) 1780 755131
Fax: +44 (0) 1780 751323
Email: airint@keypublishing.com
Website: http://www.airinternational.com

Publishes: Articles; Features; News; Nonfiction; *Areas:* Design; Military; Technology; *Markets:* Adult

Editors: Mark Ayton

Aviation magazine covering military and civilian aircraft. Unsolicited MSS welcome, but initial query by phone or in writing preferred.

AirForces Monthly
Key Publishing Ltd
PO BOX 100
Stamford

PE9 1XQ
Tel: +44 (0) 1780 755131
Fax: +44 (0) 1780 751323
Email: gary.parsons@keypublishing.com
Website: http://www.airforcesmonthly.com

Publishes: Articles; Features; News;
Nonfiction; *Areas:* Military; *Markets:* Adult

Editors: Gary Parsons

Magazine of modern military aircraft.
Accepts unsolicited submissions but prefers
query in first instance by post, phone, or
email.

Amateur Photographer

Blue Fin Building
110 Southwark Street
London
SE1 0SU
Tel: +44 (0) 20 3148 4138
Email: amateurphotographer@ipcmedia.com
Website:
http://www.amateurphotographer.co.uk

Publishes: Articles; Features; News;
Nonfiction; Reviews; *Areas:* How-to;
Photography; Technology; *Markets:* Adult;
Professional

The world's oldest consumer weekly
photographic magazine, first published in
October 1884. Accepts work from
freelances, but generally requires images to
be provided to accompany the text.

Ambit

AMBIT
17 Priory Gardens
London
N6 5QY
Tel: +44 (0) 20 8340 3566 (Tues, Wed,
Thurs 11am-6pm)
Website: http://ambitmagazine.co.uk

Publishes: Fiction; Poetry; Reviews; *Areas:*
Arts; Short Stories; *Markets:* Adult;
Treatments: Literary

Editors: Martin Bax, JG Ballard, Carol Ann
Duffy, Henry Graham, Geoff Nicholson

An international magazine, funded by the
Arts Council of England. Each issue contains
a 96 page selection of the best new poems,
stories and pictures. We print up and coming
writers alongside the more experimental
work of established writers. The magazine is
eccentric and we advise you read a copy
before submitting work to us. Send 5/6
poems, OR 2/3 stories. Always include an
SAE or endorsed International Reply
Coupons with each submission in order to
get a reply and expect to wait between 2 and
4 months. We do not accept submissions to
our freepost address - this is for subscription
only. We regret that we are unable to give
feedback on work, due to the enormous
amount of material received. We accept
roughly 3% of work submitted. No
submissions by email.

Animals and You

PO Box 305
London
NW1 1TX
Email: animalsandyou@dcthomson.co.uk
Website: http://www.animalsandyou.co.uk

Publishes: Articles; Features; Nonfiction;
Areas: How-to; Nature; *Markets:* Children's

Magazine for girls who love animals. Most
material generated in-house, but will
consider short features with photos or good
illustrations. Send query by email in the first
instance.

Apollo

22 Old Queen Street
London
SW1H 9HP
Tel: +44 (0) 20 7961 0150
Email: editorial@apollomag.com
Website: http://www.apollo-magazine.com

Publishes: Articles; Interviews; Nonfiction;
Reviews; *Areas:* Antiques; Architecture;
Arts; *Markets:* Adult

Editors: Oscar Humphries

Visual arts magazine. Send query by email in
first instance.

Areopagus Magazine

48 Cornwood Road
Plympton
Plymouth
PL7 1AL
Fax: +44 (0) 870 1346384
Email: editor@areopagus.org.uk
Website: http://www.areopagus.org.uk

Publishes: Articles; Fiction; Poetry;
Reviews; *Areas:* Religious; Short Stories;
Markets: Adult

Editors: Julian Barritt

A Christian-based arena for creative writers.
A forum for debate on contemporary issues
relating to Christianity and wider issues. A
chance for new writers to have their work
published for the first time. Writers'
workshop's and market news also help
inform both new and established writers.
This press produce a range of small
publications and have recently produced
their first royalty-paying book. We can only
consider MSS which are submitted by
subscribers to the magazine however.
Subscribers may submit by email.

Areté

8 New College Lane
Oxford
OX1 3BN
Tel: +44 (0) 1865 289193
Fax: +44 (0) 1865 289194
Email: craigraine@aretemagazine.co.uk
Website: http://www.aretemagazine.com

Publishes: Fiction; Poetry; Reviews; *Areas:*
Drama; Short Stories; *Markets:* Adult

Editors: Craig Raine

Arts magazine publishing fiction, poetry,
reportage, and reviews. Previous contributors
have included TS Eliot, William Golding,
Harold Pinter, Ian McEwan, Martin Amis,
Simon Armitage, Rosemary Hill, Ralph
Fiennes, and many more.

Send hard copy only. Unsolicited MSS
should be accompanied by an SAE or email
address for response. No International Reply
Coupons, and no submissions by email.

The Art Newspaper

Third Floor
70 South Lambeth Road
London
SW8 1RL
Tel: +44 (0) 20 3416 9000
Fax: +44 (0) 20 7735 3332
Email: contact@theartnewspaper.com
Website: http://www.theartnewspaper.com

Publishes: Articles; News; Nonfiction;
Areas: Arts; *Markets:* Adult

Editors: Jane Morris

Tabloid-format monthly arts publication. No
unsolicited mss. Send ideas in writing in first
instance.

Assent

c/o Tracey Roberts
Room E701
Kedelston Road
University of Derby
Derby
DE22 1GB
Email: t.roberts@derby.ac.uk
Website:
http://www.nottinghampoetrysociety.co.uk

Publishes: Articles; Nonfiction; Poetry;
Reviews; *Markets:* Adult

Editors: Adrian Buckner

A leading small press magazine with a world
wide circulation and readership.

Autocar

Tel: +44 (0) 20 8267 5630
Email: autocar@haymarket.com
Website: http://www.autocar.co.uk

Publishes: Articles; Features; Interviews;
News; Nonfiction; Reviews; *Areas:*
Technology; Travel; *Markets:* Adult

Weekly car magazine publishing reviews,
news, interviews, etc. Welcomes relevant
contributions.

Awen

Atlantean Publishing
4 Pierrot Steps
71 Kursaal Way
Southend-on-Sea
Essex
SS1 2UY
Email: atlanteanpublishing@hotmail.com
Website: http://atlanteanpublishing.
wikia.com/wiki/Awen

Publishes: Fiction; Poetry; *Areas:* Short
Stories; *Markets:* Adult

Editors: David-John Tyrer

Mostly around four sides in length, this
magazine manages to cram in a surprising
amount of poetry and two or three Vignette
length pieces of prose. Something for
everyone and everyone welcomed!

Email submissions must be pasted into the
body of the email. No attachments.

Bard

Atlantean Publishing
4 Pierrot Steps
71 Kursaal Way
Southend-on-Sea
Essex
SS1 2UY
Email: atlanteanpublishing@hotmail.com
Website: http://atlanteanpublishing.
wikia.com/wiki/Bard

Publishes: Poetry; *Markets:* Adult

Flyer-style broadsheet of poetry released
roughly monthly and available for free to
subscribers of the publisher's magazines.
Occasionally runs themed issues but
generally open to any and all poetry.

Submissions by email must be pasted into
the text of the email. No attachments. See
website for full submission guidelines.

Best of British

The Clock Tower
6 Market Gate
Market Deeping
Lincolnshire

PE6 8DL
Tel: +44 (0) 20 8752 8181
Email:
chris.peachment@bestofbritishmag.co.uk
Website: http://www.bestofbritishmag.co.uk

Publishes: Articles; Nonfiction; *Areas:*
Historical; *Markets:* Adult

Editors: Chris Peachment

Welcomes contributions of articles
celebrating all things British, both past and
present. Emphasis placed on nostalgia and
memories from the 40s, 50s, and 60s, but
will consider things up to the 70s and even
80s. Potential contributors should study a
copy of the magazine before submitting.
Submissions may be sent by email or by
post. See website for more details.

The Big Issue in the North

10 Swan Street
Manchester
M4 5JN
Tel: +44 (0) 1618 315563
Email: kevin.gopal@bigissuenorth.co.uk
Website: http://www.bigissueinthenorth.com

Publishes: Articles; Features; News;
Nonfiction; *Areas:* Arts; Sociology;
Markets: Adult

Publishes general interest articles,
particularly on social issues. Also news and
arts features covering the North of England.
Query with ideas in first instance.

Bird Life Magazine

The RSPB, UK Headquarters
The Lodge
Sandy
SG19 2DL
Tel: +44 (0) 1767 680551
Fax: +44 (0) 1767 683262
Email: derek.niemann@rspb.org.uk

Publishes: Features; News; Nonfiction;
Areas: Nature; *Markets:* Children's

Editors: Derek Niemann

Magazine covering birds, wildlife, and

nature conservation. Welcomes news items but rarely uses unsolicited features. Send query in writing in first instance.

bliss Magazine
Panini UK Ltd
Brockbourne House
77 Mount Ephraim
Tunbridge Wells
Kent
TN4 8BS
Tel: +44 (0) 1892 500100
Fax: +44 (0) 1892 545666
Email: bliss@panini.co.uk
Website: http://www.mybliss.co.uk

Publishes: Articles; Features; News; Nonfiction; *Areas:* Beauty and Fashion; Lifestyle; Women's Interests; *Markets:* Youth

Editors: Leslie Sinoway; Angeli Milburn (Features Editor): amilburn@panini.co.uk

Lifestyle magazine for teenage girls, publishing teenage news articles from around the world up to 200 words, plus true life features and items tackling teenage issues up to 1,500 words. Send query by email and follow up by telephone.

Blueprint
PROGRESSIVE MEDIA PUBLISHING LTD
91 Charterhouse Street
London
EC1M 6HR
Tel: +44 (0) 20 7336 5303
Email: pkelly@blueprintmagazine.co.uk
Website: http://www.blueprintmagazine.co.uk

Publishes: Articles; News; Nonfiction; Reviews; *Areas:* Architecture; Design; *Markets:* Adult

Magazine of design and architecture. Send query by email.

Bowls International
Key Publishing Ltd
PO BOX 100

Stamford
PE9 1XQ
Tel: +44 (0) 1780 755131
Fax: +44 (0) 1780 751323
Email: patrick.hulbert@keypublishing.com
Website: http://www.bowlsinternational.com

Publishes: Articles; Features; News; Nonfiction; *Areas:* Hobbies; Leisure; Sport; *Markets:* Adult

Editors: Patrick Hulbert

Magazine covering the sport of bowls. See website for more information.

British Chess Magazine
The Chess Shop / The Bridge Shop
44 Baker Street
London
W1U 7RT
Tel: +44 (0) 20 7388 2404
Fax: +44 (0) 20 7388 2407
Email: editor@bcmchess.co.uk
Website: http://www.bcmchess.co.uk

Publishes: Articles; Nonfiction; *Areas:* Hobbies; *Markets:* Adult

Magazine covering chess tournaments, history, and related literature. Accepts unsolicited MSS from qualified chess experts only - otherwise submit ideas in writing.

British Woodworking
Freshwood Publishing
The Hope Workshops
Ampney St Peter
Cirencester
Glos
GL7 5SH
Tel: +44 (0) 1285 850481
Email: bw@freshwoodpublishing.com
Website: http://www.britishwoodworking.com

Publishes: Articles; Features; News; Nonfiction; *Areas:* Hobbies; *Markets:* Adult

Magazine publishing articles, features, and news of interest to woodworking hobbyists.

Brittle Star

PO Box 56108
London
E17 0AY
Tel: +44 (0) 20 8802 1507
Email: post@brittlestar.org.uk
Website: http://www.brittlestar.org.uk

Publishes: Fiction; Poetry; *Areas:* Short
Stories; *Markets:* Adult

Editors: Louise Hooper

Publishes original and unpublished poetry
and short stories. Send 1-4 poems or 1-2
stories of up to 2,000 words each. Include
short bio of up to 40 words. No simultaneous
submissions.

Canals, Rivers + Boats

A.E. Morgan Publications Ltd
PO Box 618
Norwich
NR7 0QT
Tel: +44 (0) 1603 708930
Email: chris@themag.fsnet.co.uk
Website: http://www.canalsandrivers.co.uk

Publishes: Articles; Features; News;
Nonfiction; *Areas:* Hobbies; Travel;
Markets: Adult

Editors: Chris Cattrall

Magazine of the inland waterways and
boating. Send articles as PC/Windows
compatible disk or send by email.

Candelabrum Poetry Magazine

The Red Candle Press
Rose Cottage
Main Road Threeholes
WISBECH
PE14 9JR
Email: rcp@poetry7.fsnet.co.uk
Website: http://www.members.tripod.com/
redcandlepress/Magazine.htm

Publishes: Poetry; *Markets:* Adult;
Treatments: Literary; Traditional

Editors: Leonard McCarthy

Poetry: traditionalist metrical and rhymed
preferred, but good quality free verse not
excluded - 5/7/5 haiku accepted. Advise
study of the magazine before submitting
work.

Sexist, racist, ageist matter is not accepted.
CPM is a magazine for people who like their
poetry rhythmic and shapely.

No submissions by email. See website for
full guidelines.

Car Magazine

Bauer Automotive
Media House
Lynchwood
Peterborough
Cambridgeshire
PE2 6EA
Tel: +44 (0) 1733 468485
Fax: +44 (0) 1733 468660
Email: car@bauermedia.co.uk
Website: http://www.carmagazine.co.uk

Publishes: Articles; Features; News;
Nonfiction; *Areas:* Technology; Travel;
Markets: Adult

Car magazine with sister publications around
the world.

Carillon Magazine

19 Godric Drive
Brinsworth
Rotherham
South Yorkshire
S60 5AN
Email: editor@carillonmag.org.uk
Website: http://www.carillonmag.org.uk

Publishes: Articles; Fiction; Nonfiction;
Poetry; Reviews; *Areas:* Adventure; Crime;
Criticism; Drama; Entertainment; Fantasy;
Humour; Literature; Mystery; Sci-Fi; Short
Stories; Suspense; *Markets:* Adult;
Treatments: Contemporary

Editors: Graham Rippon

Perfect-bound paperback,usually with 84
pages.

An eclecic mix of poetry and prose, with a small reward for published pieces.

No "Bad" or discriminatory language.

Accepts email submissions from contributors outside the UK only.

Caterer and Hotelkeeper

Reed Business Information Ltd
Quadrant House
The Quadrant
Sutton
Surrey
SM2 5AS
Tel: +44 (0) 20 8652 3656
Email: info@catererandhotelkeeper.com
Website:
http://www.catererandhotelkeeper.com

Publishes: Articles; Nonfiction; *Areas:* Business; Leisure; Travel; *Markets:* Professional

Editors: Mark Lewis
(mark.lewis@rbi.co.uk)

Magazine for the hotel and catering industries.

Chemist+Druggist

UBM Medica
Ludgate House
245 Blackfriars Road
London
SE1 9UY
Tel: +44 (0) 20 7921 8110 / 8126
Email:
haveyoursay@chemistanddruggist.co.uk
Website:
http://www.chemistanddruggist.co.uk

Publishes: Articles; Features; News; Nonfiction; *Areas:* Medicine; *Markets:* Professional

Magazine aimed at community pharmacists. Query by phone or email with ideas.

Church Times

3rd Floor
Invicta House
108-114 Golden Lane
London
EC1Y 0TG
Tel: +44 (0) 20 7776 1060
Email: editor@churchtimes.co.uk
Website: http://www.churchtimes.co.uk

Publishes: Articles; News; Nonfiction; *Areas:* Religious; *Markets:* Adult

Editors: Paul Handley

Describes itself as the world's leading Anglican newspaper. Publishes news and articles on religious topics. No poetry or fiction.

Classic Rock

ContactFuture Publishing
2 Balcombe Street
London
NW1 6NW
Tel: +44 (0) 20 7042 4000
Fax: +44 (0) 20 7042 4329
Email: classicrock@futurenet.co.uk
Website:
http://www.classicrockmagazine.com

Publishes: Articles; Features; Interviews; News; Nonfiction; *Areas:* Music; *Markets:* Adult

Rock music magazine. Query by email in first instance.

Classical Music

241 Shaftesbury Avenue
London
WC2H 8TF
Tel: +44 (0) 20 7333 1742
Fax: +44 (0) 20 7333 1769
Email: classical.music@rhinegold.co.uk
Website: http://www.rhinegold.co.uk

Publishes: Features; News; *Areas:* Business; Music; *Markets:* Adult; Professional

Editors: Keith Clarke

Magazine for the classical music profession. Focuses on musicians, venue managers, agents, composers, festival directors, and marketing and public relations experts.

Publishes news, previews and features to inform, stimulate and amuse anyone who works in the classical music business in any capacity. Offers music lovers a behind-the-scenes view, which gives them a more realistic take on the business than is offered by consumer magazines and newspapers. Includes job listings in all areas of the music industry including performing, management, teaching and marketing. Most material is commissioned, but ideas from freelances considered. Approach in writing after familiarisation with the magazine's style and content.

Computer Weekly

1st Floor
3-4a Little Portland Street
London
W1W 7JB
Tel: +44 (0) 20 7186 1400
Email: cw-news@computerweekly.com

Publishes: Articles; News; Nonfiction; *Areas:* Technology; *Markets:* Professional

Publishes news and articles relating to IT for business users.

Country Homes & Interiors

Blue Fin Building
110 Southwark Street
London
SE1 0SU
Tel: +44 (0) 20 3148 7190
Email: rhoda_parry@ipcmedia.com
Website: http://www.ipcmedia.com/brands/countryhomes

Publishes: Articles; Features; Interviews; Nonfiction; *Areas:* Design; *Markets:* Adult

Editors: Rhoda Parry

Magazine of modern country decorating style. No unsolicited MSS. Approach in writing with ideas in first instance.

The Countryman

Country Publications Ltd
The Water Mill, Broughton Hall
Skipton

North Yorkshire
BD23 3AG
Tel: +44 (0) 1756 701381
Fax: +44 (0) 1756 701326
Email: editorial@thecountryman.co.uk
Website:
http://www.countrymanmagazine.co.uk

Publishes: Articles; Features; News; Nonfiction; *Areas:* Nature; *Markets:* Adult

Long-running magazine for the countryside. Send news, letters, and feature ideas by email.

Criminal Law & Justice Weekly (Incorporating Justice of the Peace)

Halsbury House
35 Chancery Lane
London
WC2A 1EL
Tel: +44 (0) 20 7400 2828
Email: diana.rose@lexisnexis.co.uk
Website:
http://www.criminallawandjustice.co.uk

Publishes: Articles; Nonfiction; *Areas:* Legal; *Markets:* Professional

Editors: Diana Rose

Weekly magazine covering key developments in criminal law, plus practice and procedure across the whole criminal court system. Includes licensing and the coroners' court. Send complete ms or précis by email. See website for full details.

Crystal Magazine

3 Bowness Avenue
Prenton
Birkenhead
CH43 0SD
Tel: +44 (0) 1516 089736
Email: christinecrystal@hotmail.com
Website:
http://www.christinecrystal.blogspot.com

Publishes: Articles; Fiction; Nonfiction; Poetry; *Areas:* Fantasy; Humour; Literature; Mystery; Nature; Romance; Sci-Fi; Short Stories; Suspense; Thrillers; Travel;

Westerns; *Markets:* Adult; *Treatments:* Light; Literary; Mainstream; Popular; Positive; Traditional

Editors: Mrs C Carr

40-page A4 bi-monthly for creative writers. It is for subscribers only. Contributions required are poems, stories (true and fiction) and articles. Where room permits, work is enhanced with colour photos/graphics. Your submissions can be any length and theme except erotica. You can send your work by email (either in the body of the email or as attachment) or by post. Handwritten material is acceptable. If sent by snail mail, and you wish your work returned, a stamp would be appreciated. Under normal circumstances, you will not have to wait weeks and weeks for a reply.

Usually contains pages and pages of Readers' Letters. The rules are kind comments or none at all. The subscriber mentioned the most times will receive £10.

A regular feature every issue is Wordsmithing; Titters, Tips, Titillations. This is an amusing and informative look into the world of writers and writing. It may possibly inspire you.

Should you have been successful with writing elsewhere, you would be welcome to share your achievements in Subscribers' News.

I also run a free pen-friend service enabling subscribers to get in touch with each other by email.

Subscribers tell me the magazine is good value for money and worth every penny.

Cycling Weekly

IPC Focus Network
Leon House
233 High Street
Croydon
CR9 1HZ
Tel: +44 (0) 20 8726 8453
Email: cycling@ipcmedia.com
Website: http://www.cyclingweekly.co.uk

Publishes: Articles; Features; News; Nonfiction; *Areas:* Sport; *Markets:* Adult

Editors: Robert Garbutt

Publishes news and features on all aspects of cycling sport. Welcomes unsolicited MSS and ideas. Send query in writing in first instance.

Dairy Farmer

PO Box 18
Preston
PR2 9GU
Tel: +44 (0) 1772 799459
Email: FGSupport@farmersguardian.com
Website: http://www.farmersguardian.com

Publishes: Articles; Nonfiction; *Areas:* Business; Nature; *Markets:* Professional; *Treatments:* In-depth

Publishes material of interest to professionals in the dairy industry, including milk marketing and farm management.

Decanto

PO Box 3257
84 Dinsdale Gardens
Littlehampton
BN16 9AF
Email: masque_pub@btinternet.com
Website: http://myweb.tiscali.co.uk/masquepublishing

Publishes: Poetry; *Markets:* Adult

Editors: Lisa Stewart

Send up to six original, unpublished poems by post with SAE or by email in the body of the message (no attachments). Poems of any subject or style are considered.

Delicious

Seven Publishing Group
Sea Container's House
20 Upper Ground
London
SE1 9PD
Tel: +44 (0) 20 7775 7757
Fax: +44 (0) 20 7775 7705

Email: karen.barnes@eyetoeyemedia.co.uk
Website:
http://www.deliciousmagazine.co.uk

Publishes: Articles; Features; Nonfiction;
Areas: Cookery; *Markets:* Adult

Editors: Karen Barnes

Magazine of food and cookery. Publishes
recipes and features on food and its sources.

Devon Life

Archant House
Babbage Road
Totnes
TQ9 5JA
Tel: +44 (0) 1803 860910
Fax: +44 (0) 1803 860922
Email: jane.fitzgerald@archant.co.uk
Website: http://devon.greatbritishlife.co.uk

Publishes: Articles; Nonfiction; *Areas:* Arts;
Cookery; Culture; Historical; Lifestyle;
Nature; Travel; *Markets:* Adult

Editors: Jane Fitzgerald

Magazine publishing articles relating to
Devon. Welcomes ideas.

Director

116 Pall Mall
London
SW1Y 5ED
Tel: +44 (0) 20 7766 8950
Fax: +44 (0) 20 7766 8840
Email: director-ed@iod.com

Publishes: Articles; Features; Nonfiction;
Areas: Business; Finance; Politics; *Markets:*
Professional

Magazine aimed at Directors of businesses.
Send query with outline and writing samples.

DIY Week

Faversham House Ltd
Windsor Court
Wood Street
East Grinstead
West Sussex

RH19 1UZ
Tel: +44 (0) 1342 332000
Website: http://www.diyweek.net

Publishes: Articles; News; Nonfiction;
Areas: Business; *Markets:* Professional

Editors: Fiona Hodge

Magazine providing news and articles of
interest to retailers and suppliers in the home
improvement market.

Dream Catcher

Stairwell Books
161 Lowther Street
York
YO31 7LZ
Tel: +44 (0) 1904 733767
Email: info@dreamcatchermagazine.co.uk
Website:
http://www.dreamcatchermagazine.co.uk

Publishes: Fiction; Interviews; Nonfiction;
Poetry; Reviews; *Areas:* Short Stories;
Translations; *Markets:* Adult; *Treatments:*
Literary

Editors: Paul Sutherland

Send submissions by post, following
guidelines on website.

Early Music

Faculty of Music
University of Cambridge
11 West Road
Cambridge
CB3 9DP
Tel: +44 (0) 1223 335178
Email: earlymusic@oxfordjournals.org
Website: http://em.oxfordjournals.org

Publishes: Articles; Nonfiction; *Areas:*
Music; *Markets:* Academic; Adult;
Professional

Editors: Francis Knights

Magazine covering early music and how it is
being interpreted today. Aimed at scholars,
professional performers, and enthusiasts. An
excessively academic tone should be

avoided. See website for full submission guidelines.

EarthLines Magazine
Email: submissions@earthlines.org.uk
Website:
http://earthlinesmagazine.wordpress.com

Publishes: Articles; Essays; Features; Fiction; Interviews; News; Nonfiction; Poetry; Reviews; *Areas:* Nature; Short Stories; *Markets:* Adult

Magazine publishing features, essays, poetry, and perhaps a little short fiction, exploring nature, place and the environment. Enquire by email in first instance.

The Edge
Unit 138
22 Notting Hill Gate
London
W11 3JE
Tel: +44 (0) 8454 569337
Email: davec@theedge.abelgratis.co.uk
Website:
http://www.theedge.abelgratis.co.uk

Publishes: Features; Fiction; Interviews; Nonfiction; Reviews; *Areas:* Crime; Entertainment; Erotic; Fantasy; Gothic; Horror; Sci-Fi; *Markets:* Adult; *Treatments:* Contemporary; Experimental

Editors: Dave Clark

Send submission by post – do not use a service that requires a signature upon receipt. Publishes fiction, features, interviews, and reviews. Open to all. All material must be previously unpublished (including on websites). No poetry.

Fiction sought has been described by others as modern and borderline gothic horror/fantasy/sf, slipstream, crime fiction or erotica. Often urban themes. Stories should be over 2000 words and should not be whole novels, or sequels to work published in another publication. Send no more than one story at a time.

For all nonfiction contact editor in advance

with sample of writing and SAE. Do not send anything by email.

Consult guidelines on website before submitting or contacting. Always read the guidelines before contacting the editor. The full guidelines are available on the website and are not available by email. No poetry, simultaneous submissions, previously published material, or electronic submissions either on disk or by email.

Electrical Review
St John Patrick Publishers Ltd
6 Laurence Pountney Hill
London
EC4R 0BL
Tel: +44 (0) 20 8319 1807
Email: elinorem@electricalreview.co.uk
Website: http://www.electricalreview.co.uk

Publishes: Articles; Features; News; Nonfiction; *Areas:* Business; Technology; *Markets:* Professional

Electrical journal aimed at electrical engineers, project managers, consultants and electrical contractors, and any other key personnel specifying electrical systems in public/commercial buildings and industry.

Elle Decoration
64 North Row
London
W1K 7LL
Tel: +44 (0) 20 7150 7000
Fax: +44 (0) 20 7150 7671
Email: natalie.evans-harding@hf-uk.com
Website: http://www.elleuk.com

Publishes: Articles; Nonfiction; *Areas:* Design; *Markets:* Adult

Interior design magazine. No unsolicited mss. Send query by email.

Envoi
Meirion House
Glan yr afon
Tanygrisiau
Blaenau Ffestiniog
LL41 3SU

Tel: +44 (0) 1766 832112
Email: jan@envoipoetry.com
Website:
http://www.cinnamonpress.com/envoi

Publishes: Nonfiction; Poetry; Reviews;
Markets: Adult; *Treatments:* Literary

Editors: Dr Jan Fortune-Wood

Magazine of poems, poetry sequences, reviews, and competitions, now more than 50 years old. Submit up to 6 poems up to 40 lines each or one or two longer poems by post or by email (in the body of the email; attachments will not be read).

What others say:

"Probably the best poetry magazine currently available" - The Writers' College

"Without a grant and obviously well read, this poetry magazine excels itself." - Ore

"The policy of giving poets space to show their skills is the right one." - Haiku Quarterly

"Good quality, lots of bounce, poems, comps, reviews, reader comeback" - iota

"If you haven't tried it yet, do so, you'll get your money's worth." - New Hope International

Essentials
IPC Magazines
Blue Fin Building
110 Southwark St
London
SE1 0SU
Tel: +44 (0) 20 3148 7211
Email: goodtoknow@ipcmedia.com
Website: http://www.goodtoknow.co.uk/magazines/Essentials-magazine

Publishes: Articles; Features; Nonfiction; *Areas:* Lifestyle; Women's Interests; *Markets:* Adult

Women's lifestyle magazine. Query by phone or email in first instance.

Eventing
IPC Media Limited
Blue Fin Building
110 Southwark Street
London
SE1 0SU
Tel: +44 (0) 20 3148 4545
Email: julie_harding@ipcmedia.com
Website: http://www.ipcmedia.com/eventing

Publishes: Articles; Essays; Features; News; Nonfiction; *Areas:* How-to; Sport; *Markets:* Adult

Editors: Julie Harding

Magazine covering the sport of horse trials. Includes news, results, features, opinions and instructional articles. Most material is commissioned, but welcomes ideas.

Extastic Magazine
Email: editor@extastic-mag.com
Website: http://www.extastic-mag.com

Publishes: Articles; Interviews; News; Reviews; *Areas:* Arts; Beauty and Fashion; Cookery; Culture; Design; Entertainment; Film; Historical; Hobbies; Humour; Literature; Media; Photography; Romance; Self-Help; Women's Interests; *Markets:* Adult; Youth; *Treatments:* Commercial; Light; Positive

Editors: Bernadette Vong

A fashion and lifestyle magazine for East Asian "Oriental" women who live in the West. Subjects are to investiage and discover their interests, heritage, fashion and social issues in Western countries. How do they see themselves, how to they cope with the working environment, or have they felt any disadvantages being categorised as minor ethnic group? There are a lot of topics to be explored, and we aim to explore these topics with a light-hearted discussion with respect. Along with articles and interviews, we also feature fashion editorials that may interests the modern East Asian women.

Family Tree Magazine
ABM Publishing Limited

61 Great Whyte
Ramsey
Huntingdon
Cambridgeshire
PE26 1HJ
Tel: +44 (0) 1487 814050
Fax: +44 (0) 1487 711361
Email: info@abmpublishing.co.uk
Website: http://www.family-tree.co.uk

Publishes: Articles; Features; News;
Nonfiction; *Areas:* Historical; Military;
Sociology; *Markets:* Adult

Genealogy magazine. Will consider any
articles, news, or features on the subject, but
particularly interested in those that take a
military or social angle, or give an insight
into the research process. Submit ideas in
writing.

Financial Adviser
Financial Times Business
One Southwark Bridge
London
SE1 9HL
Tel: +44 (0) 20 7775 6639
Email: hal.austin@ft.com
Website: http://www.ftadviser.com

Publishes: Articles; Features; News;
Nonfiction; *Areas:* Finance; *Markets:* Adult

Editors: Hal Austin, Senior Editor

Publishes news and features on personal
finance.

Fire
Field Cottage
Old Whitehill
Tackley
Kidlington
Oxon
OX5 3AB
Website: http://www.poetical.org

Publishes: Fiction; Poetry; *Areas:* Short
Stories; *Markets:* Adult; *Treatments:*
Literary

Editors: Jeremy Hilton

A poetry magazine with a big reputation and
represents big value for money. It appears
twice a year (March, October) and each issue
contains 170 pages of poetry (mostly) and
some prose. It is radical, multicultural and
international in outlook, and publishes a
broad range of poetry from around the world.
It tends towards the more alternative end of
the poetry spectrum, and is interested in
poetry with heart, spirit, imagination,
innovation, risk-taking, open-endedness, and
most of all poems that have something to
say. Not neat, tight, closed, clever, cynical,
fashionable poems. This magazine exists to
promote unknown, little-known, new or
unpublished writers and to include features
on young writers and poems by children.
Although the magazine is on email and has a
website (see below), the printed magazine
retains its format. ALL submissions must be
by snailmail, and must include a stamped
addressed envelope. To subscribe (3 issues)
please send a cheque or postal order made
out to FIRE, for £9.00 to the address below.
Single copies cost £5.00. The magazine is
available at some specialist libraries and
bookshops, and at some poetry festivals, but
most copies are sold by mail-order.

Flight International
Reed Business Information
Quadrant House
Sutton
Surrey
SM2 5AS
Tel: +44 (0) 20 8652 3842
Fax: +44 (0) 20 8652 3840
Email: flight.international@flightglobal.com
Website: http://www.flightglobal.com

Publishes: Articles; Features; Interviews;
News; Nonfiction; *Areas:* Design; Military;
Science; Technology; *Markets:* Professional;
Treatments: In-depth

Trade magazine for the aerospace industry,
covering civil, military and space. Publishes
news and in-depth articles. Will consider
unsolicited mss and encourages email
submissions, but prefers queries by phone in
first instance.

FourFourTwo

FREEPOST RSBZ-BKGC-BRLH
PO Box 326
Sittingbourne
Kent
ME9 8FA
Tel: +44 (0) 1795 592979
Email: 442@servicehelpline.co.uk
Website:
http://www.fourfourtwo.magazine.co.uk

Publishes: Articles; Features; Interviews;
Nonfiction; *Areas:* Sport; *Markets:* Adult

Describes itself as the only magazine to truly
reflect football in all its extremes:
spectacular, dramatic, hilarious, opinionated,
authoritative, intelligent, quirky.

Freelance Market News

8-10 Dutton Street
Manchester
M3 1LE
Tel: +44 (0) 161 819 9919
Fax: +44 (0) 161 819 2842
Email: fmn@writersbureau.com
Website:
http://www.freelancemarketnews.com

Publishes: Articles; News; Nonfiction;
Markets: Adult; Professional

Editors: Angela Cox

Publishes well-researched notes for markets
for writers (including the editor's full name
with a complete address, telephone and fax
number, email address and website, and
preferably a quote from the editor or editorial
office giving advice to potential contributors)
and short articles around 700 words (one
page) or 1500 words (two pages). Welcomes
unsolicited MSS.

The Frogmore Papers

21 Mildmay Road
Lewes
East Sussex
BN7 1PJ
Email: j.n.page@sussex.ac.uk
Website: http://www.frogmorepress.co.uk

Publishes: Fiction; Nonfiction; Poetry;

Reviews; *Areas:* Short Stories; *Markets:*
Adult; *Treatments:* Contemporary; Literary

Editors: Jeremy Page

Poetry and prose by new and established
authors. There is no house style but the
extremes of tradition and experiment are
equally unlikely to find favour.

Send between four and six poems, or up to
two prose pieces.

Go Girl Magazine

239 Kensington High Street
Kensington
W8 6SA
Email: gogirlmag@euk.egmont.com
Website: http://www.gogirlmag.co.uk

Publishes: Articles; Features; Interviews;
News; Nonfiction; *Areas:* Beauty and
Fashion; Entertainment; Film; Lifestyle;
Music; *Markets:* Children's

Magazine for girls aged 7-11, covering
beauty, fashion, celebrity news and gossip,
friends, pets, etc.

GamesMaster

Future plc
30 Monmouth Street
Bath
BA1 2BW
Tel: +44 (0) 1225 442244
Fax: +44 (0) 1225 446019
Email: gamesmaster@futurenet.co.uk
Website: http://www.futureplc.com

Publishes: Articles; News; Nonfiction;
Reviews; *Areas:* Entertainment; Leisure;
Technology; *Markets:* Adult; Youth

Editors: Robin Alway

Games magazine, covering all major
formats.

Garbaj

Atlantean Publishing
4 Pierrot Steps
71 Kursaal Way

Southend-on-Sea
Essex
SS1 2UY
Email: atlanteanpublishing@hotmail.com
Website: http://atlanteanpublishing.
wikia.com/wiki/Garbaj

Publishes: Fiction; News; Poetry; *Areas:*
Humour; Politics; Short Stories; *Markets:*
Adult; *Treatments:* Satirical

Editors: David-John Tyrer

Humorous and slightly politically incorrect
paper between four and ten pages long.
Vignette-length fiction and fake news, etc.
Some issues are themed but mostly not too
strictly. Something for everyone who likes to
laugh.

Girl Talk
Media Centre
201 Wood Lane
London
W12 7TQ
Tel: +44 (0) 20 8433 1010
Email: girltalk.magazine@bbc.com
Website: http://www.bbcgirltalk.com

Publishes: Articles; Features; Nonfiction;
Areas: Entertainment; Lifestyle; *Markets:*
Children's

Editors: Sam Robinson

Lifestyle magazine for girls aged 8-12. No
unsolicited mss. Send query with author CV
in first instance.

Golf World
Media House,
Peterborough,
PE2 6EA
Tel: +44 (0) 1733 468243
Fax: +44 (0) 1733 468843
Email: chris.jones@bauermedia.co.uk
Website: http://www.golf-world.co.uk

Publishes: Articles; News; Nonfiction;
Areas: Sport; *Markets:* Adult

Editors: Chris Jones

Golf magazine. No unsolicited mss. Send
ideas in writing.

Greetings Today
1 Churchgates
The Wilderness
Berkhamsted
HP4 2UB
Tel: +44 (0) 1442 289930
Email: tracey@lemapublishing.co.uk
Website: http://www.greetingstoday.co.uk

Publishes: Articles; Features; News;
Nonfiction; Reference; *Areas:* Business;
Markets: Professional

Editors: Tracey Bearton

Trade magazine for the greetings card
industry, publishing articles, features, news,
and a directory for artists seeking publishers.

Guiding Magazine
17–19 Buckingham Palace Road
London
SW1W 0PT
Tel: +44 (0) 20 7834 6242
Fax: +44 (0) 20 7828 8317
Email: guiding@girlguiding.org.uk
Website: http://www.girlguiding.org.uk

Publishes: Articles; Features; News;
Nonfiction; *Areas:* Crafts; Hobbies; Leisure;
Lifestyle; Women's Interests; *Markets:*
Children's; Youth

Magazine of the girl guide movement,
publishing articles, news, and features
relevant to the guiding movement and
women's role in society. Welcomes
unsolicited mss, but query in writing
outlining ideas preferred in first instance.

High Life
Cedar Communications Ltd
85 Strand
London
WC2R 0DW
Tel: +44 (0) 20 7550 8000
Email: high.life@cedarcom.co.uk
Website: http://www.cedarcom.co.uk

Publishes: Articles; Nonfiction; *Areas:* Beauty and Fashion; Business; Entertainment; Lifestyle; Sport; Travel; *Markets:* Adult

Inflight magazine publishing articles up to 2,500 words. No unsolicited mss. Query in writing in first instance.

Heat
Endeavour House
189 Shaftesbury Avenue
London
WC2H 8JG
Email: heatEd@heatmag.com
Website: http://www.heatworld.com

Publishes: Articles; Features; News; Nonfiction; *Areas:* Entertainment; *Markets:* Adult

Publishes news and features on celebrities.

Horse & Hound
IPC Media
Blue Fin Building
110 Southwark Street
SE1 0SU
Tel: +44 (0) 20 3148 4562
Fax: +44 (0) 20 3148 8128
Email: lucy_higginson@ipcmedia.com
Website: http://www.horseandhound.co.uk

Publishes: Articles; News; Nonfiction; *Areas:* Sport; *Markets:* Adult

Editors: Lucy Higginson

Weekly magazine publishing news and articles relating to equestrian sports.

House Beautiful
72 Broadwick Street
London
W1F 9EP
Tel: +44 (0) 20 7439 5000
Fax: +44 (0) 20 7439 5141
Email: houseb.mail@natmags.co.uk
Website:
http://www.allaboutyou.com/housebeautiful

Publishes: Articles; Features; Nonfiction;

Areas: Design; Lifestyle; *Markets:* Adult

Magazine publishing articles and features on interior design and home living.

ICIS Chemical Business Magazine
Reed Business Information
Quadrant House
The Quadrant
Sutton
Surrey
SM2 5AS
Tel: +44 (0) 20 8652 3500
Fax: +44 (0) 20 8652 3375
Email: icbeditorial@icis.com
Website: http://www.icis.com

Publishes: Articles; Features; News; Nonfiction; *Areas:* Business; Science; *Markets:* Professional

Business magazine covering the global chemical markets.

Inclement (Poetry for the Modern Soul)
White Rose House
8 Newmarket Road
Fordham
Ely
Cambs
CB7 5LL
Email:
inclement_poetry_magazine@hotmail.com
Website:
http://inclementpoetrymagazine.webs.com

Publishes: Poetry; *Markets:* Adult

Editors: Michelle Foster

We are a magazine that considers all forms and styles of poetry that are submitted. What is more important is that you believe in your work. Poetry needs a voice, and through several superb publications poets all over the world are finding that voice. Too often, poetry is sidelined as a specialist genre when it should be available to everyone. This is your chance to have your work recognised.

Email submissions are preferred (either in

the body of the email or as a Word file attachment), but postal submissions are also accepted - enclose a stamped, self-addressed envelope. See website for full guidelines.

Intermedia

The International Institute of Communications
2 Printers Yard
90a Broadway
London
SW19 1RD
Tel: +44 (0) 20 8417 0600
Fax: +44 (0) 20 8417 0800
Email: j.grimshaw@iicom.org
Website: http://www.iicom.org/intermedia

Publishes: Articles; Nonfiction; *Areas:* Media; Politics; Science; Technology; *Markets:* Academic; Professional

Editors: Joanne Grimshaw

Journal on media and telecom policy, aimed at regulators and policymakers, academics, lawyers, consultants and service providers around the world. Send query by email.

The Interpreter's House

9 Glenhurst Road
Mannamead
Plymouth
PL3 5LT
Email: simon@simoncurtis.net
Website:
http://www.interpretershouse.org.uk

Publishes: Fiction; Poetry; *Areas:* Literature; Short Stories; *Markets:* Adult; *Treatments:* Contemporary; Experimental; Light; Literary; Popular; Positive; Progressive; Serious; Traditional

Editors: Dr Simon Curtis

While this magazine may tend towards the mainstream, in these days of rap, slams and performance poetry, it hopes nonetheless to welcome inventive and imaginative work, surreal original pieces have been published. It does warm to economical, concise writing, is sympathetic to humour, wit and quirkiness. It seeks the union of simplicity

and mystery which makes writing memorable.

Iota

PO BOX 7721
Matlock
Derbyshire
DE4 9DD
Tel: +44 (0) 1629 582500
Email: info@iotamagazine.co.uk
Website: http://www.iotapoetry.co.uk

Publishes: Essays; Features; Fiction; Interviews; Nonfiction; Poetry; Reviews; *Areas:* Short Stories; Translations; *Markets:* Adult

Editors: Nigel McLoughlin

Poetry magazine now also publishing fiction and nonfiction. Send up to 6 poems by post, or by email after paying a £1 submission charge for electronic submissions. For fiction send stories between 2,000 and 6,000 words by post or by email. For nonfiction send proposals up to 150 words by email. See website for full guidelines and specific email addresses to use.

The Irish Post

Suite A
1 Lindsey Street
Smithfield
London
EC1A 9HP
Tel: +44 (0) 20 8900 4193
Email: editor@irishpost.co.uk
Website: http://www.irishpost.co.uk

Publishes: Articles; News; Nonfiction; *Areas:* Business; Entertainment; Lifestyle; Politics; Sport; Travel; *Markets:* Adult

Editors: Siobhán Breatnach

Magazine aimed at the Irish community in Britain, covering social events, sports, politics, and entertainment.

Jewish Quarterly

ORT House
126 Albert Street

London
NW1 7NE
Tel: +44 (0) 20 7443 5155
Email: editor@jewishquarterly.org
Website: http://www.jewishquarterly.org

Publishes: Fiction; Nonfiction; Poetry;
Areas: Arts; Culture; Current Affairs;
Historical; Literature; Music; Philosophy;
Politics; Religious; Short Stories; *Markets:*
Adult; *Treatments:* Literary

Says of itself it "leads the field in Jewish
writing, covering a wide spectrum of
subjects including art, criticism, fiction, film,
history, Judaism, literature, poetry,
philosophy, politics, theatre, the Shoah,
Zionism and much more". Submissions
welcomed by email or post with SAE.

The Journal
17 High Street
Maryport
Cumbria
CA15 6BQ
Email: smithsssj@aol.com
Website:
http://www.freewebs.com/thesamsmith/

Publishes: Articles; Interviews; Poetry;
Reviews; *Areas:* Translations; *Markets:*
Adult

Editors: Sam Smith

This publication continues to keep up its
Scandinavian connections, especially with
the diaspora. Keen to sustain its international
flavour, I favour dual text publication where
possible. Regards the criteria for acceptance
for those poems written in English, I think it
best to quote from the editorial for issue 1 -
the aim being .... "to publish those poems ...
written with thought to what the poem is
saying and to how it is being said." The
magazine is A4, stapled, about 40 pages
long, a third of the pages given over to
articles and/or reviews.

Email submissions accepted in the body of
the email only, not as attached files. See
website for full details.

Junior
Immediate Media Co. Ltd
(Formerly Magicalia Publishing Ltd)
15-18 White Lion Street
London
N1 9PG

Immediate Media Co.
Vineyard House
44 Brook Green
Hammersmith
W6 7BT
Tel: +44 (0) 20 7150 5000
Email: editorial@juniormagazine.co.uk
Website: http://www.juniormagazine.co.uk

Publishes: Articles; Features; Nonfiction;
Areas: Beauty and Fashion; Cookery;
Entertainment; Health; Lifestyle; Travel;
Markets: Adult; Family

Editors: Catherine O'Dolan

Glossy, family lifestyle magazine aimed at
parents of children 0-8, including
informative features and expert advice on
child development, education and health, as
well as children's fashion, inspirational
interiors and child-friendly travel
suggestions.

Kids Alive!
The Salvation Army
101 Newington Causeway
London
SE1 6BN
Tel: +44 (0) 20 7367 4911
Fax: +44 (0) 20 7367 4710
Email: kidsalive@salvationarmy.org.uk
Website:
http://www.salvationarmy.org.uk/kidsalive

Publishes: Fiction; Nonfiction; *Areas:*
Religious; *Markets:* Children's

Christian children's magazine publishing
puzzles, comic strips, etc.

Lancashire Magazine
Seasiders Way
Blackpool
Lancashire
FY1 6NZ

Tel: +44 (0) 1253 336588
Fax: +44 (0) 1253 336587
Email: website@lancashiremagazine.co.uk
Website: http://thelancashiremagazine.com

Publishes: Articles; Nonfiction; *Areas:* Leisure; Lifestyle; *Markets:* Adult

Publishes articles relating to Lancashire and the North West.

The List
14 High Street
Edinburgh
EH1 1TE
Tel: +44 (0) 1315 503050
Email: newwriters@list.co.uk
Website: http://www.list.co.uk

Publishes: Articles; Features; Nonfiction; *Areas:* Arts; Entertainment; Film; Literature; Music; Theatre; TV; *Markets:* Adult

Magazine intended to publicise and promote arts, events and entertainment taking place in Scotland.

Litro Magazine
Tel: +44 (0) 20 3371 9971
Email: editor@litro.co.uk
Website: http://www.litro.co.uk

Publishes: Fiction; Nonfiction; Poetry; *Areas:* Short Stories; *Markets:* Adult

Independent magazine distributing around 100,000 copies for free, across the UK and France. Publishes fiction and creative nonfiction. See website for upcoming themes. Send submissions by email as Word file attachments with the word "Submission" in the subject line. Also publishes poetry, but no unsolicited poetry submissions accepted.

The London Magazine
11 Queen's Gate
London
SW7 5EL
Tel: +44 (0) 20 7584 5977
Fax: +44 (0) 20 7225 3273
Email: admin@thelondonmagazine.org
Website: http://thelondonmagazine.org

Publishes: Articles; Features; Fiction; Nonfiction; Poetry; Reviews; *Areas:* Arts; Autobiography; Criticism; Literature; Short Stories; *Markets:* Adult; *Treatments:* Literary

Send submissions by post or by email, with the submission in the body of the message as well as an attachment. Does not normally publish science fiction or fantasy writing, or erotica. See website for full guidelines.

London Review of Books
28 Little Russell Street
London
WC1A 2HN
Tel: +44 (0) 20 7209 1101
Fax: +44 (0) 20 7209 1102
Email: edit@lrb.co.uk
Website: http://www.lrb.co.uk

Publishes: Articles; Essays; Nonfiction; Poetry; Reviews; *Areas:* Arts; Culture; Literature; Politics; Science; *Markets:* Adult; *Treatments:* Literary

Editors: Mary-Kay Wilmers

Contact editor in writing in first instance, including SAE. Publishes mainly reviews, essays, and articles, but also publishes poetry. Welcomes unsolicited contributions over 2000 words.

Model Boats
PO Box 9890
Brentwood
Essex
CM13 9EF
Email: Editor@modelboats.co.uk
Website: http://www.modelboats.co.uk

Publishes: Articles; Features; Nonfiction; *Areas:* Hobbies; Technology; *Markets:* Adult

Editors: Paul Freshney

Magazine for model boat enthusiasts.

Macworld
IDG Communications

101 Euston Road
London
NW1 2RA
Tel: +44 (0) 20 7756 2877
Email: karenh@macworld.co.uk
Website: http://www.macworld.co.uk

Publishes: Articles; Features; News;
Nonfiction; *Areas:* How-to; Technology;
Markets: Adult

Editors: Karen Haslam

Magazine covering Apple Mac computers.
Most material is commissioned, but
welcomes ideas for features and articles.

Magma
23 Pine Walk
Carshalton
SM5 4ES
Email: contributions@magmapoetry.com
Website: http://www.magmapoetry.com

Publishes: Nonfiction; Poetry; Reviews;
Areas: Literature; *Markets:* Adult;
Treatments: Literary

Editors: Laurie Smith

Prefers submissions by email. Postal
submissions accepted from the UK only, and
must include SAE. Accepts poems and
artwork. Poems are considered for one issue
only – they are not held over from one issue
to the next. Seeks poems that give a direct
sense of what it is to live today - honest
about feelings, alert about world, sometimes
funny, always well crafted. Strongly prefers
poems to be in the body of the email, rather
than an attachment. If, for formatting
reasons, you feel you must use an attachment
include all the poems you are submitting in
one file. Also publishes reviews of books
and pamphlets of poetry. See website for
details and separate contact details.

Market Newsletter
Bureau of Freelance Photographers
Focus House
497 Green Lanes
London
N13 4BP

Tel: +44 (0) 20 8882 3315
Email: info@thebfp.com
Website: http://www.thebfp.com

Publishes: Articles; News; Nonfiction;
Areas: Photography; *Markets:* Professional

Publishes stories and markets of interest to
freelance photographers.

Media Week
Haymarket Publishing Ltd
174 Hammersmith Road
London
W6 7JP
Tel: +44 (0) 20 8267 8024
Email: arif.durrani@haymarket.com
Website: http://www.mediaweek.co.uk

Publishes: Articles; Features; Interviews;
News; Nonfiction; *Areas:* Business; Media;
Markets: Professional

Editors: Arif Durrani

Online magazine for the media industry.

Metta-Physics Magazine
Dalton House
60 Windsor Avenue
London
SW19 2RR
Email: editor@metta-physics.com
Website: http://www.metta-physics.com

Publishes: Articles; Nonfiction; Reviews;
Areas: Archaeology; Arts; Culture; Current
Affairs; Historical; New Age; Philosophy;
Psychology; Science; Spiritual; *Markets:*
Academic; Adult; Professional; *Treatments:*
Commercial; Contemporary; Literary

Web magazine with aggressive internet
marketing policy through Search engine and
social media optimization. In addition listing
on various news sites. Suits starting authors
looking to build a web portfolio. We are
available on Kindle, although commercial
distribution is a few months off as at June
2011.

We are looking for articles related to the
theme of spirituality and science at their

interface. Please look up magazine to get the feel of content requirements.

Modern Poetry in Translation

The Queens College
Oxford
OX1 4AW
Tel: +44 (0) 1865 244701
Email: submissions@mptmagazine.com
Website: http://www.mptmagazine.com

Publishes: Essays; Nonfiction; Poetry; *Areas:* Literature; Translations; *Markets:* Adult

Editors: David and Helen Constantine, The Editors

Respected poetry series originally founded by prominent poets in the sixties. New Series continues their editorial policy: translation of good poets by translators who are often themselves poets, fluent in the foreign language, and sometimes working with the original poet. See website for submission guidelines.

Modern Language Review

1 Carlton House Terrace
London
SW1Y 5AF
Email: mlr@mhra.org.uk
Website: http://www.mhra.org.uk/Publications/Journals/mlr.html

Publishes: Articles; Reviews; *Areas:* Literature; *Markets:* Academic

Publishes scholarly articles and reviews relating to modern languages. See website for full submission guidelines, including specific email addresses for different languages.

Monkey Kettle

Email: monkeykettle@hotmail.com
Website: http://www.monkeykettle.co.uk

Publishes: Articles; Fiction; Nonfiction; Poetry; *Areas:* Humour; Politics; Short Stories; *Markets:* Adult; *Treatments:* Dark; Satirical

Editors: Matthew Taylor

Send up between five and ten poems at a time, or a short story up to 1,500 words. Favours the funny, surreal, dark, poignant, and political. Not interested "whiny" material about no-one understanding you.

Monomyth

Atlantean Publishing
4 Pierrot Steps
71 Kursaal Way
Southend-on-Sea
Essex
SS1 2UY
Email: atlanteanpublishing@hotmail.com
Website: http://atlanteanpublishing.wikia.com/wiki/Monomyth

Publishes: Fiction; Poetry; *Areas:* Fantasy; Short Stories; *Markets:* Adult

Editors: David-John Tyrer

Publishes longer short stories and long poetry. Submit by post with SASE or by email with your submission in the body of the email (no attachments)

Mountain Biking UK

Future Publishing Ltd
Beauford Court
30 Monmouth Street
Bath
BA1 2BW
Tel: +44 (0) 1225 442244
Fax: +44 (0) 1225 446019
Email: mbuk@futurenet.com
Website: http://magazine.bikeradar.com/category/mountain-biking-uk

Publishes: Articles; Features; News; Nonfiction; Reviews; *Areas:* Leisure; Sport; *Markets:* Adult

Magazine for mountain bike enthusiasts, publishing news, reviews, features, and race coverage.

Mslexia

PO Box 656

Newcastle upon Tyne
NE99 1PZ
Tel: +44 (0) 191 2616656
Fax: +44 (0) 191 2616636
Email: submissions@mslexia.co.uk
Website: http://www.mslexia.co.uk

Publishes: Articles; Essays; Features;
Fiction; Interviews; News; Nonfiction;
Poetry; Reference; Reviews; *Areas:*
Autobiography; Short Stories; Women's
Interests; *Markets:* Adult

Editors: Daneet Steffens

By women, for women who write, who want
to write, who teach creative writing or who
have an interest in womens' literature and
creativity. It is a mixture of original work,
features, news, views, advice and listings.
The UK's only magazine devoted to women
writers and their writing.

See website for themes of upcoming issues /
competitions.

Publishes features, columns, reviews, flash
fiction, and literature listings. Email
submissions for themed new writing from
overseas writers only. Email submissions for
other contributions accepted from anywhere.
See website for full details.

Muscle & Fitness

Weider Publishing
10 Windsor Court
Clarence Drive
Harrogate
North Yorkshire
HG1 2PE
Tel: +44 (0) 1423 504516
Fax: +44 (0) 1423 561494
Website: http://www.muscle-fitness-
europe.com

Publishes: Articles; Nonfiction; *Areas:*
Health; *Markets:* Adult

Magazine on health, fitness, and muscle
development.

Music Teacher

Rhinegold House

20 Rugby Street
London
WC1N 3QZ
Tel: +44 (0) 7785 613145
Fax: +44 (0) 20 7333 1736
Email: music.teacher@rhinegold.co.uk
Website: http://www.rhinegold.co.uk

Publishes: Articles; Nonfiction; Reviews;
Areas: How-to; Music; *Markets:*
Professional

Magazine for both private and school music
teachers.

Neon Highway Poetry Magazine

37 Grinshill Close
Liverpool
L8 8LD
Email: neonhighwaypoetry@yahoo.co.uk
Website:
http://neonhighwaypoetry.webstarts.com

Publishes: Poetry; *Markets:* Adult;
Treatments: Literary

Editors: Alice Lenkiewicz

Avant-garde literary journal publishing
poetry and art. Submissions accepted by post
and by email. See website for details.

.net

30 Monmouth Street
Bath
BA1 2BW
Tel: +44 (0) 1225 442244
Fax: +44 (0) 1225 732295
Email: oliver.lindberg@futurenet.com
Website: http://www.netmagazine.com

Publishes: Articles; Features; News;
Nonfiction; *Areas:* Technology; *Markets:*
Professional

Editors: Oliver Lindberg

Magazine for web designers and developers,
publishing articles, features, and news.

New Law Journal

Halsbury House
35 Chancery Lane
London
WC2A 1EL
Tel: +44 (0) 20 7400 2580
Fax: +44 (0) 20 7400 2583
Email: newlaw.journal@lexisnexis.co.uk
Website: http://www.newlawjournal.co.uk

Publishes: Articles; News; Nonfiction;
Areas: Legal; *Markets:* Professional

Professional magazine for lawyers,
publishing news and articles.

The New Shetlander

Shetland Council of Social Service
Market House
14 Market Street
LERWICK
Shetland
ZE1 0JP
Tel: +44 (0) 1595 743902
Fax: +44 (0) 1595 696787
Email: vas@shetland.org
Website: http://www.shetland-
communities.org.uk/subsites/vas/the-new-
shetlander.htm

Publishes: Articles; Essays; Fiction;
Nonfiction; Poetry; *Areas:* Arts; Criticism;
Historical; Politics; Short Stories; *Markets:*
Adult; *Treatments:* Literary

Editors: Brian Smith; Laureen Johnson

Publishes short stories, poetry, and historical
articles related to Shetland, Scotland, or
Scandinavia. Items should usually be
between 1,000 and 2,000 words, however
longer pieces can be considered.
Contributions and enquiries may be sent by
email.

New Walk Magazine

c/o Nick Everett
School of English
Leicester University
University Road
Leicester
LE1 7RH
Email: newwalkmagazine@gmail.com

Website:
http://newwalkmagazine.wordpress.com

Publishes: Articles; Essays; Features;
Fiction; Interviews; Nonfiction; Poetry;
Reviews; *Areas:* Criticism; Literature; Short
Stories; *Markets:* Adult; *Treatments:*
Experimental; Literary

Editors: Rory Waterman and Nick Everett

Publishes poetry and poetry-related features;
criticism; debate; short fiction; and art. Send
up to six poems or one piece of prose in the
body of an email.

New Welsh Review

PO Box 170
Aberystwyth
SY23 1WZ
Tel: +44 (0) 1970 628410
Email: submissions@newwelshreview.com
Website: http://www.newwelshreview.com

Publishes: Features; Fiction; Nonfiction;
Poetry; Reviews; *Areas:* Short Stories;
Markets: Adult; *Treatments:* Literary

Editors: Kathryn Gray

Focus is on Welsh writing in English, but
has an outlook which is deliberately diverse,
encompassing broader UK and international
contexts. For feature articles, send 300-word
query by email. Submit fiction or up to 6
poems by email or by post with cover letter
and SAE. Full details available on website.

The New Writer

PO Box 60
Cranbrook
Kent
TN17 2ZR
Tel: +44 (0) 1580 212626
Fax: +44 (0) 1580 212041
Email: editor@thenewwriter.com
Website: http://www.thenewwriter.com

Publishes: Articles; Features; Fiction; News;
Nonfiction; Poetry; *Areas:* Short Stories;
Markets: Adult

Editors: Suzanne Ruthven

Short stories by subscribers and prizewinners only – no unsolicited short stories. Poetry welcome from all, but must be previously unpublished. Submit no more than five poems at once. Also publishes articles and features on writing and current editorial practice, but not looking for introspective pieces. See website for full details.

New Writing Scotland
ASLS
Department of Scottish Literature
7 University Gardens
University of Glasgow
Glasgow
G12 8QH
Tel: +44 (0) 1413 305309
Fax: +44 (0) 1413 305309
Email: nws@asls.org.uk
Website: http://www.asls.org.uk

Publishes: Fiction; Poetry; Scripts; *Areas:* Drama; Short Stories; *Markets:* Adult

Editors: Duncan Jones

Publishes short fiction, poetry, and short drama, in any of the languages of Scotland. Contributors must be Scottish by birth or upbringing, or be resident in Scotland. Send no more than one short story and/or four poems. No full-length plays, novels, or submissions by fax or email. Check website for reading period. Include one SAE for receipt and another for return of ms.

Notes from the Underground
23 Sutherland Square
London
SE17 3EQ
Tel: +44 (0) 20 7701 2777
Email: editors@nftu.co.uk
Website:
http://www.notesfromtheunderground.co.uk

Publishes: Articles; Fiction; Nonfiction; *Areas:* Short Stories; *Markets:* Adult

Editors: Christopher Vernon; Tristan Summerscale

Welcomes unsolicited submissions of fiction and nonfiction. Include word count,

description of article or story, and brief personal bio in a short paragraph at the top. Include at least one image or video per 300 words for nonfiction. See website for specific email addresses for submissions.

Now
IPC Media
Blue Fin Building
110 Southwark Street
London
SE1 4SU
Tel: +44 (0) 20 3148 5000
Fax: +44 (0) 20 3148 8110
Email: nowfriends@ipcmedia.com
Website: http://www.nowmagazine.co.uk

Publishes: Articles; Features; News; Nonfiction; *Areas:* Beauty and Fashion; Entertainment; Lifestyle; Media; Women's Interests; *Markets:* Adult

Women's lifestyle magazine, covering celebrity gossip, fashion, news, etc. Most articles are commissioned or originated in-house.

Obsessed with Pipework
Flarestack Publishing
8 Abbot's Way
Pilton
Somerset
BA4 4BN
Tel: +44 (0) 1749 890019
Email: cannula.dementia@virgin.net
Website: http://www.flarestack.co.uk

Publishes: Poetry; *Markets:* Adult; *Treatments:* Experimental; Literary

Editors: Charles Johnson

Submit up to six poems of any length or style. Looking for poems that are original and display an element of creative risk, rather than things that are simply "clever". Nothing predictable or obvious. SAE essential unless submitting by fax or email. Prefers submissions by post, but if you do email your poems send them in the body of an email or in a single attached document.

Old Tractor
Kelsey Publishing Ltd
Cudham Tithe Barn
Berry's Hill
Cudham
Kent
TN16 3AG
Tel: +44 (0) 1959 541444
Fax: +44 (0) 1959 541400
Email: ot.ed@kelsey.co.uk
Website: http://www.oldtractor.co.uk

Publishes: Articles; Features; Interviews;
Nonfiction; *Areas:* Historical; Technology;
Markets: Adult

Editors: Scott Lambert

Tractor magazine aimed at everyone from
enthusiasts and collectors to serious
historians. Looks at the historical aspect of
tractor development through articles,
features, and interviews.

Open Mouse
Email: colin.will@zen.co.uk
Website: http://www.zen39641.zen.co.uk/
ps/openmouse.htm

Publishes: Poetry; *Markets:* Adult

Editors: Colin Will

No frills online poetry magazine, publishing
poetry only - no editorial comment or input.
Selected poems will be posted as submitted
without correspondence. No queries, CVs,
lists of previous publications, etc. or poems
submitted as attachments. Submit poems in
the body of an email only. See website for
full guidelines.

Other Poetry
10 Prospect Bank Road
Edinburgh
EH6 7NR
Email: editors@otherpoetry.com
Website: http://www.otherpoetry.com

Publishes: Poetry; *Markets:* Adult

Send up to five poems by email, or by post if
impossible to send by email. A live email
address must be included for a response. No
correspondence will be entered into by post
and no SAE is required. Submissions should
be sent in the body of the email, rather than
as attachments. Any emails containing
attachments will be deleted unread and
without acknowledgement. Do not submit
more than twice per calendar year, or within
six months of any editorial decision.

Our Dogs
Our Dogs Publishing
1 Lund Street
Trafford Park
Manchester
M16 9EJ
Tel: +44 (0) 844 504 9001
Fax: +44 (0) 844 504 9013
Email: alismith@ourdogs.co.uk
Website: http://www.ourdogs.co.uk

Publishes: Articles; News; Nonfiction;
Areas: Hobbies; How-to; *Markets:* Adult;
Professional

Editors: Alison Smith

Magazine on the showing and breeding of
pedigree dogs.

Pony Magazine
Headley House
Headley Road
Grayshott
Surrey
GU26 6TU
Tel: +44 (0) 1428 601020
Fax: +44 (0) 1428 601030
Email: pony@djmurphy.co.uk
Website: http://www.ponymag.com

Publishes: Articles; Nonfiction; *Areas:*
Hobbies; Nature; Sport; *Markets:* Children's;
Youth

Editors: Janet Rising

Magazine for young horse-lovers aged 8-16.

PC Advisor
101 Euston Road
London

NW1 2RA
Tel: +44 (0) 20 7756 2800
Email: matt_egan@idg.co.uk
Website: http://www.pcadvisor.co.uk

Publishes: Articles; Features; Nonfiction;
Areas: How-to; Technology; *Markets:* Adult

Editors: Matt Egan

PC magazine aimed at proficient users. May
consider unsolicited material.

PC Pro
PC Pro Dennis Technology
30 Cleveland Street
London
W1T 4JD
Tel: +44 (0) 20 7907 6000
Fax: +44 (0) 20 7907 6304
Email: editor@pcpro.co.uk
Website: http://www.pcpro.co.uk

Publishes: Articles; Features; News;
Nonfiction; Reviews; *Areas:* Technology;
Markets: Adult; Professional; *Treatments:*
In-depth

Editors: Barry Collins

IT magazine for professionals in the IT
industry and enthusiasts.

Peace and Freedom
17 Farrow Road
Whaplode Drove
Spalding
Lincs
PE12 0TS
Tel: +44 (0) 1406 330242
Email: p_rance@yahoo.co.uk
Website:
http://pandf.booksmusicfilmstv.com

Publishes: Articles; Fiction; Interviews;
Poetry; Reviews; *Areas:* Nature; Short
Stories; Sociology; *Markets:* Adult;
Treatments: Literary

Editors: Paul Rance

Magazine publishing poetry, fiction, and
articles, with an emphasis on social,

humanitarian and environmental issues. Also
publishes interviews of animal
welfare/environmental/human rights
campaigners, writers, poets, artists, film,
music and TV personalities, up to 1,000
words. Reviews of books / records / events
etc. up to 50 words also considered. Email
submissions accepted for reviews, short
stories, and interviews ONLY. Accepts
submissions from subscribers only.

The Penniless Press
100 Waterloo Road
Ashton
Preston
PR2 1EP
Tel: +44 (0) 1772 736421
Email: editor@pennilesspress.co.uk
Website: http://www.pennilesspress.co.uk

Publishes: Essays; Fiction; Nonfiction;
Poetry; Reviews; *Areas:* Criticism;
Literature; Philosophy; Short Stories;
Translations; *Markets:* Adult; *Treatments:*
Literary

Editors: Alan Dent

Eclectic magazine publishing material on a
diverse range of subjects, as well as fiction,
poetry, criticism, translations, and reviews.
Prose should be restricted to 3,000 words or
less. Send contributions with SAE by post or
by email.

Pennine Platform
Frizingley Hall
Frizinghall Road
Bradford
BD9 4LD
Tel: +44 (0) 1274 541015
Email: nicholas.bielby@virgin.co.uk
Website: http://www.pennineplatform.co.uk

Publishes: Poetry; *Markets:* Adult

Editors: Nicholas Bielby

The pick of poetry from the Pennines and
beyond. Hard copy submissions only.

The People's Friend

80 Kingsway East
Dundee
DD4 8SL
Tel: +44 (0) 1382 223131
Fax: +44 (0) 1382 452491
Email: peoplesfriend@dcthomson.co.uk

Publishes: Articles; Features; Fiction;
Nonfiction; *Areas:* Adventure; Cookery;
Mystery; Romance; Short Stories; Women's
Interests; *Markets:* Adult; Children's; Family

Publishes complete short stories (1,500-
3,000 words) and serials (total 60,000-
70,000 words) focusing on character
development rather than complex plots. Also
considers children's stories and nonfiction on
knitting and cookery. Send request with SAE
for guidelines.

Performance

Mediscript Ltd
1 Mountview Court
310 Friern Barnett Lane
London
Tel: +44 (0) 20 8369 5382
Fax: +44 (0) 20 8446 8898
Email: Fatima@mediscript.ltd.uk
Website: http://www.performancesport
andfitness.co.uk

Publishes: Articles; Features; Interviews;
News; Nonfiction; Reviews; *Areas:* Health;
Sport; *Markets:* Academic; Adult;
Professional; *Treatments:* Commercial;
Contemporary; Popular

Editors: Fatima Patel

A research led magazine for professionals
and sport enthusiasts. It is presented in an
attractive easy to read style, covering a series
of key issues in sport and fitness. These
include training, nutrition, injury and
rehabilitation. There are features on elite
athletes with interviews and commentary on
key research papers by our experts. The
editorial board comprises sport training
professionals and academics.

Period Living

Centaur Special Interest Media

2 Sugar Brook Court
Aston Road
Bromsgrove
Worcestershire
B60 3EX
Tel: +44 (0) 1527 834435
Email: period.living@centaur.co.uk
Website: http://www.periodliving.co.uk

Publishes: Articles; Features; Nonfiction;
Areas: Crafts; Design; Gardening; *Markets:*
Adult

Magazine on renovating and decorating
period homes, or in a period style.

Planet

PO Box 44
Aberystwyth
Ceredigion
SY23 3ZZ
Tel: +44 (0) 1970 611255
Fax: +44 (0) 1970 611197
Email:
planet.enquiries@planetmagazine.org.uk
Website: http://www.planetmagazine.org.uk

Publishes: Articles; Features; Fiction;
Nonfiction; Poetry; Reviews; *Areas:* Arts;
Current Affairs; Literature; Music; Politics;
Short Stories; Theatre; *Markets:* Adult;
Treatments: Literary

Editors: Dr Jasmine Donahaye

Publishes one story and between eight and
ten poems per issue. A range of styles and
themes are accepted, but postal submissions
will not be considered unless adequate return
postage is provided. Submit 4-6 poems or
fiction up to 4,000 words. Submissions are
accepted by email.

Most articles, features, and reviews are
commissioned, however if you have an idea
for a relevant article send a query with brief
synopsis.

Poetic Licence

70 Aveling Close
Purley
Surrey
CR8 4DW

Email: poets@poetsanon.org.uk
Website: http://www.poetsanon.org.uk

Publishes: Poetry; *Markets:* Adult

Editors: Peter L. Evans (co-ordinator)

The editing is rotated through the membership to help ensure that each issue does not get stuck in a rut or 'house style'. Submit up to six poems per issue, by email.

The Poetry Church
Eldwick Crag Farm
High Eldwick
Bingley
Yorkshire
BD16 3BB
Email: reavill@globalnet.co.uk
Website: http://www.waddysweb.freeuk.com

Publishes: Poetry; *Areas:* Religious; *Markets:* Adult

Editors: Tony Reavill

Ecumenical Christian poetry magazine. Features the work of international Christian poets coming from a wide variety of backgrounds in the mainline churches.

Poetry Cornwall / Bardhonyeth Kernow
11a Penryn Street
Redruth
Cornwall/Kernow
TR15 2SP

1 Station Hill
Redruth
Cornwall
TR15 2PP
Tel: +44 (0) 1209 218209
Email: poetrycornwall@yahoo.com
Website:
http://www.poetrycornwall.freeservers.com

Publishes: Poetry; *Markets:* Adult; *Treatments:* Literary

Editors: Les Merton

Publishes poetry from around the world, in

original language (including Kernewek and Cornish dialect) with English translation. Send up to three poems by post with SASE, or (if a subscriber) by email. Non-subscribers may not submit by email.

Poetry Express
Survivors' Poetry
Studio 11, Bickerton House
25-27 Bickerton Road
Archway
London
N19 5JT
Tel: +44 (0) 20 7281 4654
Fax: +44 (0) 20 7281 7894
Email: info@survivorspoetry.org
Website: http://www.survivorspoetry.org
/the-poetry/publications/poetry-express/

Publishes: Articles; News; Nonfiction; Poetry; Reviews; *Areas:* Literature; *Markets:* Adult

Publishes poetry, articles, reviews, and news. Name and contact details on each sheet of submission.

Poetry London
81 Lambeth Walk
London
SE11 6DX
Tel: +44 (0) 20 7735 8880
Fax: +44 (0) 20 7735 8880
Email: colette@poetrylondon.co.uk
Website: http://www.poetrylondon.co.uk

Publishes: Features; Nonfiction; Poetry; Reviews; *Areas:* Translations; *Markets:* Adult; *Treatments:* Contemporary; Literary

Editors: Colette Bryce

Send up to six poems with SASE or adequate return postage, unless you do not require your poems returning, in which case you should make this clear. Considers poems by both new and established poets. Also publishes book reviews. No submissions by email.

Poetry Review
The Poetry Society

22 Betterton Street
London
WC2H 9BX
Tel: +44 (0) 20 7420 9883
Fax: +44 (0) 20 7240 4818
Email: info@poetrysociety.org.uk
Website: http://www.poetrysociety.org.uk

Publishes: Essays; Nonfiction; Poetry;
Reviews; *Markets:* Adult

Editors: Fiona Sampson

Describes itself as "one of the liveliest and
most influential literary magazines in the
world", and has been associated with the rise
of the New Generation of British poets –
Carol Ann Duffy, Simon Armitage, Glyn
Maxwell, Don Paterson... though its scope
extends beyond the UK, with special issues
focusing on poetries from around the world.

Send up to 6 poems with SAE by post only.
No submissions by email.

Poetry Scotland
91-93 Main Street
Callander
FK17 8BQ
Email: sallyevans35@gmail.com
Website: http://www.poetryscotland.co.uk

Publishes: Poetry; *Markets:* Adult

Editors: Sally Evans

Poetry broadsheet with Scottish emphasis.
Considers poetry in English, Gaelic, Scots,
and (on occasions) Welsh. Please see website
for submission guidelines.

Poetry Wales
School of English
Bangor University
Gwynedd
LL57 2DG
Tel: +44 (0) 1656 663018
Email: info@poetrywales.co.uk
Website: http://poetrywales.co.uk

Publishes: Poetry; *Markets:* Adult

Editors: Dr Zoë Skoulding

Send up to six poems with SAE or IRCs for
response / return of MSS. No handwritten or
emailed submissions.

The Police Journal
Vathek Publishing
Bridge House
Dalby
Isle of Man
IM5 3BP
Tel: +44 (0) 1624 844056
Fax: +44 (0) 1624 845043
Email: mlw@vathek.com
Website: http://www.vathek.com

Publishes: Articles; Nonfiction; *Areas:*
Crime; Legal; *Markets:* Professional

Editors: Barry Loveday

Publishes articles aimed at police forces
around the world. Submit using online
submission manager only.

The Political Quarterly
9600 Garsington Road
Oxford
OX4 2DQ
Tel: +44 (0) 1865 776868
Fax: +44 (0) 1865 714591
Website: http://www.wiley.com

Publishes: Articles; Features; Nonfiction;
Areas: Politics; *Markets:* Adult; *Treatments:*
Progressive

Magazine covering national and international
politics. Accepts unsolicited articles.

Practical Wireless
PW Publishing Limited
Tayfield House
38 Poole Road
Westbourne
Bournemouth
BH4 9DW
Tel: +44 (0) 845 803 1979
Email: rob@pwpublishing.ltd.uk
Website: http://www.pwpublishing.ltd.uk

Publishes: Articles; Nonfiction; *Areas:*
How-to; Technology; *Markets:* Adult

Editors: Rob Mannion

Magazine covering amateur radio and communications. Send query by email in first instance.

Premonitions

13 Hazely Combe
Arreton
Isle of Wight
PO30 3AJ
Tel: +44 (0) 1983 865668
Email: mail@pigasuspress.co.uk
Website: http://www.pigasuspress.co.uk

Publishes: Fiction; Poetry; *Areas:* Fantasy; Horror; Sci-Fi; *Markets:* Adult

Editors: Tony Lee

Magazine of cutting edge science fiction and fantasy. Also publishes genre poetry, and horror, however this must have an SF element, and must be psychological rather than simply gory. Send submission with cover letter, bio, and publication credits, with SAE. No supernatural fantasy or swords n' sorcery. Study magazine before submitting.

Presence

90 D Fishergate Hill
Preston
PR1 8JD
Email: haikupresence@gmail.com
Website: http://haiku-presence.50webs.com/

Publishes: Poetry; *Markets:* Adult

Editors: Martin Lucas; Matthew Paul; Ian Storr

The UK's leading forum for the full range of haiku-related genres. Includes haiku of the highest standard from an international list of contributors, backed by insightful reviews and critical prose. Our mission is to encourage dialogue and build a sense of community among haiku poets - and we're definitely getting there!

See website for different submission addresses for specific forms.

Prima Baby & Pregnancy

Hearst Magazines UK
72 Broadwick Street
London
W1F 9EP
Tel: +44 (0) 20 7312 3852
Fax: +44 (0) 20 7312 3744
Email: info@babyexpert.co.uk
Website: http://www.babyexpert.com

Publishes: Articles; Features; News; Nonfiction; *Areas:* Health; How-to; Lifestyle; Women's Interests; *Markets:* Adult

Magazine covering pregnancy, childbirth, and caring for children up to three years of age.

Professional Photographer

Archant House
Oriel Road
Cheltenham
GL50 1BB
Website: http://www.professionalphotographer.co.uk

Publishes: Articles; Nonfiction; *Areas:* Photography; Technology; *Markets:* Professional

Magazine aimed at professional photographers.

Prospect

Prospect Publishing
2 Bloomsbury Place
London
WC1A 2QA
Tel: +44 (0) 20 7255 1281
Fax: +44 (0) 20 7255 1279
Email: submissions@prospect-magazine.co.uk
Website: http://www.prospect-magazine.co.uk

Publishes: Essays; Features; Fiction; Nonfiction; Reviews; *Areas:* Arts; Culture; Current Affairs; Literature; Politics; Short Stories; *Markets:* Adult

Editors: David Goodhart

Intelligent magazine of current affairs and cultural debate. No news features. Almost all articles are commissioned from regular writers, but will consider unsolicited nonfiction submissions if suitable for the magazine, but no unsolicited fiction submissions. Does not publish any poetry. No postal submissions or telephone pitches. Submit by email only.

Pulsar Poetry Magazine

34 Lineacre
Grange Park
Swindon
Wiltshire
SN5 6DA
Tel: +44 (0) 1793 875941
Email: pulsar.ed@btopenworld.com
Website: http://www.pulsarpoetry.com

Publishes: Poetry; *Markets:* Adult

Editors: David Pike

From 2010 a webzine only. We seek interesting and stimulating unpublished work - thoughts, comments and observations, genial or sharp. Prefer hard-hitting work. We welcome poetry and constructive ideas from all areas of the world. Normal time taken to reply is no longer than four weeks, include a stamped addressed return envelope with your submission, (or include International Reply Coupons, if from overseas). Send no more than six poems at a time via conventional post, or three poems via email: note, email file attachments will not be read.

If your work is of a high standard it will be published - may take a few months to appear, though. Poets retain copyright of their poems. Poems which are simultaneously sent to other publications will not be considered.

Pulse

Ludgate House
245 Blackfriars Road
London,
SE1 9UY
Tel: +44 (0) 20 7921 8094
Email: richard.hoey@ubm.com
Website: http://www.pulsetoday.co.uk

Publishes: Articles; Nonfiction; *Areas:* Medicine; *Markets:* Professional

Editors: Richard Hoey

Magazine aimed at GPs.

Quantum Leap

York House
15 Argyle Terrace
Rothesay
Isle of Bute
PA20 0BD
Tel: +44 (0) 1700 505422
Website: http://www.qqpress.co.uk

Publishes: Poetry; *Markets:* Adult

Editors: Alan J. Carter

A poetry magazine only - no short stories please! We have a four-page information leaflet - send SAE or 2 IRCs to 'Guidelines / Competitions' at the address below. We also provide a publication service for collections of people's poetry - send SAE or 2 IRCs to 'Collections' at address below.

We aim to run a 'user-friendly' magazine for our subscribers / contributors, so don't be afraid to ask for advice. We also pay for all poetry we use.

Railway Gazette International

DVV Media UK Ltd
9 Sutton Court Road
Sutton
Surrey
SM1 4SZ
Tel: +44 (0) 20 8652 5200
Fax: +44 (0) 20 8652 5210
Email: editor@railwaygazette.com
Website: http://www.railwaygazette.com

Publishes: Articles; Nonfiction; *Areas:* Business; Technology; Travel; *Markets:* Professional

Magazine for rail industry professionals. No enthusiast articles. Query by phone or email to discuss your ideas in the first instance.

Reach

IDP
132 Hinckley Road
Stoney Stanton
Leicestershire
LE9 4LN
Email: publishing@indigodreams.co.uk
Website:
http://www.indigodreams.co.uk/#/reach-poetry/4536232470

Publishes: Poetry; *Markets:* Adult

Editors: Ronnie Goodyer

Publishes quality poetry from both experienced and new poets. Formal or free verse, haiku.. everything is considered. Subscribers can comment on and vote for poetry from the previous issue, the winner receiving £50, plus regular in-house anthologies and competitions. Receives no external funding and depends entirely on subscriptions.

The Reader

Magazine Submissions
The Reader Organisation
The Friary Centre
Bute Street
LIVERPOOL
L5 3LA
Tel: + 44 (0) 1512 077207
Email: magazine@thereader.org.uk
Website: http://www.thereader.org.uk

Publishes: Articles; Essays; Fiction; Nonfiction; Poetry; Reviews; *Areas:* Literature; Philosophy; Short Stories; *Markets:* Adult; Literary

Publishes poetry, short stories, recommendations for good reading up to 1,000 words, and articles and essays about reading. Accepts literary articles and essays, but not theoretical literary discourses. Approach in writing in first instance.

Reader's Digest

11 Westferry Circus
Canary Wharf
London
E14 4HE
Tel: +44 (0) 20 7715 8000
Fax: +44 (0) 20 7715 8716
Email: theeditor@readersdigest.co.uk
Website: http://www.readersdigest.co.uk

Publishes: Articles; Nonfiction; *Areas:* Cookery; Design; Finance; Gardening; Health; How-to; Humour; Lifestyle; *Markets:* Adult

Popular general interest magazine. Pays £100 for amusing anecdotes up to 150 words.

Real People

Hearst Magazines UK London
72 Broadwick Street
London
W1F 9EP
Email: samm.taylor@hearst.co.uk
Website: http://www.realpeoplemag.co.uk

Publishes: Nonfiction; *Areas:* Lifestyle; Women's Interests; *Markets:* Adult

Editors: Samm Taylor

Publishes real life stories. See website for more details.

Red Magazine

Tel: +44 (0) 20 7150 7641
Email: red@redmagazine.co.uk
Website: http://www.redonline.co.uk

Publishes: Articles; News; Nonfiction; Reviews; *Areas:* Beauty and Fashion; Cookery; Design; Lifestyle; Travel; Women's Interests; *Markets:* Adult

Magazine aimed at women in their thirties. Usually uses regular contributors, but will consider queries for ideas.

Red Pepper

44-48 Shepherdess Walk
London
N1 7JP
Tel: +44 (0) 20 7324 5068
Email: office@redpepper.org.uk
Website: http://www.redpepper.org.uk

Publishes: Articles; Features; News; Nonfiction; Areas: Politics; Markets: Adult

Political magazine aimed at the left and greens.

Red Poets
7 Stryt Gerallt
Wrecsam
LL11 1EH
Email: info@redpoets.org
Website: http://www.redpoets.org

Publishes: Poetry; Areas: Politics; Markets: Adult

Editors: Mike Jenkins; Marc Jones

Magazine of politically left-wing poetry. Submit poems via submission form on website or by email.

The Resurrectionist
Email: editorial@resurrectionreview.com
Website: http://www.resurrectionreview.com

Publishes: Essays; Nonfiction; Poetry; Areas: Arts; Criticism; Humour; Music; Philosophy; Politics; Psychology; Sociology; Markets: Academic; Adult; Treatments: Contemporary; Cynical; Dark; Experimental; Light; Literary; Progressive; Satirical; Traditional

Editors: Kieran Borsden

A biannual poetry journal dedicated to modern formalist poetry. By modern we intend poetry that makes use of contemporary language and grammar, experiments with verse forms or that handles contemporary themes. Submit using online submission system only - no submissions by email.

Right Start Magazine
PO Box 481
Fleet
GU51 9FA
Tel: +44 (0) 7867 574590
Email: lynette@rightstartmagazine.co.uk
Website:

http://www.rightstartmagazine.co.uk

Publishes: Articles; Nonfiction; Areas: Health; Lifestyle; Psychology; Markets: Adult

Editors: Lynette Lowthian

Magazine covering pre-school children's health, lifestyle, development, education, etc.

Sable
SAKS Publications
PO Box 33504
London
E9 7YE
Email: editorial@sablelitmag.org
Website: http://www.sablelitmag.org

Publishes: Essays; Fiction; Nonfiction; Poetry; Reviews; Areas: Autobiography; Short Stories; Translations; Travel; Markets: Adult

Editors: Kadija (George) Sesay

A showcase of new creative work by writers of colour. Not currently accepting unsolicited fiction submissions. Email submission accepted for certain types of material only.

Sarasvati
IDP
132 Hinckley Road
Stoney Stanton
Leicestershire
LE9 4LN
Email: publishing@rocketmail.com
Website: http://www.indigodreams.co.uk

Publishes: Fiction; Poetry; Areas: Short Stories; Markets: Adult

Editors: Ronnie Goodyer; Dawn Bauling

Showcases poetry and prose. Each contributor will have three to four pages available to their poetry, up to 35 lines per page, or prose up to 1,000 words.

The Savage Kick

Murder Slim Press
29 Alpha Road
Gorleston
Norfolk
NR31 0LQ
Email: slim@murderslim.com
Website: http://www.murderslim.com

Publishes: Articles; Fiction; Interviews;
Nonfiction; *Areas:* Crime; Literature;
Military; Westerns; *Markets:* Adult;
Treatments: Niche

Accepts only three or four stories per year.
Publishes work dealing with any
passionately held emotion and/or alternative
viewpoints. Sleazy tales are encouraged.
Prefers real-life stories. No genre fiction or
poetry. See website for full submission
guidelines. Also accepts articles and
interviews relating to authors on the reading
list provided on the website.

The School Librarian

7 Clifton Bank
Rotherham
South Yorkshire
S60 2NA
Email: sleditor@sla.org.uk
Website: http://www.sla.org.uk/the-school-
librarian.php

Publishes: Articles; Nonfiction; *Markets:*
Professional

Editors: Steve Hird

Magazine for professionals working in the
libraries of educational facilities from pre-
school to adult.

Scottish Home and Country Magazine

SWRI Headquarters
42 Heriot Row
Edinburgh
EH3 6ES
Tel: +44 (0) 1312 251724
Fax: +44 (0) 1312 258129
Email: magazine@swri.demon.co.uk
Website: http://www.swri.org.uk

Publishes: Articles; Features; Nonfiction;
Areas: Cookery; Crafts; Health; Historical;
Lifestyle; Sociology; Travel; Women's
Interests; Markets

Publishes articles and features between 500
and 1,000 words on crafts, personal histories,
social history, health, travel, cookery, and
general women's interests. No political or
religious pieces. Send complete MS by post
with SAE or by email. See website for full
guidelines.

Screentrade Magazine

PO Box 144
Orpington
Kent
BR6 6LZ
Email: philip@screentrademagazine.com
Website:
http://www.screentrademagazine.com

Publishes: Articles; Features; Interviews;
News; Nonfiction; Reviews; *Areas:*
Business; Film; *Markets:* Professional

Editors: Philip Turner

Magazine aimed at professionals working in
and running cinemas. Does include some
film reviews, but focuses on cinema
management and related issues. Interviews
of relevant industry figures but no "film star"
interviews. Send query in first instance.

Scribble

Park Publications
14 The Park
Stow on the Wold
Cheltenham
Glos.
GL54 1DX
Tel: +44 (0) 1451 831053
Email: enquiries@parkpublications.co.uk
Website: http://www.parkpublications.co.uk

Publishes: Fiction; *Areas:* Crime; Humour;
Romance; Sci-Fi; Short Stories; *Markets:*
Adult

Editors: David Howarth

Accepts short stories on any subject from

new and experienced writers. If requested, the editor is happy to offer free advice on how a particular story could be improved. Each quarter prizes of £75, £25, and £15 will be awarded for the best three stories in the edition. These competitions are free to annual subscribers. See our website for further details.

Scribbler!

Remus House
Woodston
Peterborough
PE2 9JX
Tel: +44 (0) 1733 890066
Fax: +44 (0) 1733 313524
Email: info@youngwriters.co.uk
Website: http://www.youngwriters.co.uk/Scribbler.html

Publishes: Fiction; Poetry; Reviews; *Areas:* Short Stories; *Markets:* Children's

Editors: Donna Samworth

Magazine for 7–11 year-olds, encouraging them to submit their own poems, stories, and artwork. Email submissions accepted.

Ships Monthly Magazine

Kelsey Publishing Group
Cudham Tithe Barn
Berrys Hill
Cudham
Kent
TN16 3AG
Tel: +44 (0) 1959 541444
Email: ships.monthly@btinternet.com
Website: http://www.shipsmonthly.com

Publishes: Articles; News; Nonfiction; *Areas:* Design; Historical; Technology; Travel; *Markets:* Adult; Professional

Editors: Nicholas Leach

Magazine aimed at ship enthusiasts and maritime professionals. Publishes news and illustrated articles related to all kinds of ships. No yachting. Query by phone or email in first instance.

Sight & Sound

21 Stephen Street
London
W1T 1LN
Website:
http://www.bfi.org.uk/sightandsound

Publishes: Articles; Nonfiction; Reviews; *Areas:* Film; *Markets:* Adult

Describes itself as the international film magazine, publishing articles on international cinema and reviews of film, DVD, and book releases. Send query in writing in first instance.

Somerset Life

Archant House
Babbage Road
Totnes
TQ9 5JA
Website:
http://somerset.greatbritishlife.co.uk

Publishes: Features; Interviews; Nonfiction; *Areas:* Antiques; Arts; Beauty and Fashion; Business; Cookery; Design; Gardening; Health; Historical; Travel; *Markets:* Adult

Regional magazine covering Somerset. Contact through website in first instance.

Stamp Lover

Harvard House
621 London Road
Isleworth
TW7 4ER
Email: stamplover@ukphilately.org.uk
Website:
http://www.ukphilately.org.uk/hmag.htm

Publishes: Articles; News; Nonfiction; *Areas:* Hobbies; *Markets:* Adult

Magazine for stamp collectors, publishing news and articles on stamps past and present and on the hobby in general. Send query by email.

Stand Magazine

School of English
Leeds University

Leeds
LS2 9JT
Tel: +44 (0) 113 233 4794
Fax: +44 (0) 113 233 2791
Email: stand@leeds.ac.uk
Website: http://standmagazine.org

Publishes: Fiction; Poetry; *Areas:* Short
Stories; Translations; *Markets:* Adult;
Treatments: Literary

A well established magazine of poetry and
literary fiction. Has previously published the
work of, among others, Samuel Beckett,
Angela Carter, Seamus Heaney, Geoffrey
Hill, and Andrew Motion. No electronic
submissions. See website for submission
guidelines and alternative US address for
American submissions.

Staple Magazine
114–116 St Stephen's Road
Nottingham
NG2 4JS

Publishes: Articles; Fiction; Nonfiction;
Poetry; Reviews; *Areas:* Short Stories;
Markets: Academic; Adult; *Treatments:*
Literary

Magazine of contemporary international
poetry and short fiction.

The Strad
30 Cannon Street
London
EC4M 6YJ
Email: thestrad@thestrad.com
Website: http://www.thestrad.com

Publishes: Articles; Features; Nonfiction;
Reviews; *Areas:* Music; *Markets:* Adult;
Professional

Magazine for professionals and enthusiasts
interested in string instruments, including
their makers and their players.

The Subterranean Literary Journal
Email: tom@thesubjournal.co.uk
Website: http://www.thesubjournal.co.uk

Publishes: Articles; Essays; Fiction;
Interviews; Nonfiction; Poetry; Reviews;
Scripts; *Areas:* Adventure; Anthropology;
Antiques; Archaeology; Architecture; Arts;
Autobiography; Beauty and Fashion;
Biography; Business; Cookery; Crafts;
Crime; Criticism; Culture; Current Affairs;
Design; Drama; Entertainment; Erotic;
Fantasy; Film; Finance; Gardening; Gothic;
Health; Historical; Hobbies; Horror; How-to;
Humour; Legal; Leisure; Lifestyle;
Literature; Media; Medicine; Men's
Interests; Military; Music; Mystery; Nature;
New Age; Philosophy; Photography;
Politics; Psychology; Radio; Religious;
Romance; Science; Sci-Fi; Self-Help; Short
Stories; Sociology; Spiritual; Sport;
Suspense; Technology; Theatre; Thrillers;
Translations; Travel; TV; Westerns;
Women's Interests; *Markets:* Academic;
Adult; Professional; Youth; *Treatments:*
Commercial; Contemporary; Cynical; Dark;
Experimental; In-depth; Light; Literary;
Mainstream; Niche; Popular; Positive;
Progressive; Satirical; Serious; Traditional

Editors: Liam Kelly

An independent literary journal featuring a
selection of short stories, novellas, essays,
poetry and other writing. The content we
feature is submitted by our readers and our
aim is to create a collection of interesting
literature by underground and undiscovered
writers.

Sugar Magazine
Hachette Filipacchi (UK) Limited
64 North Row
London
W1K 7LL
Tel: +44 (0) 20 7150 7000
Fax: +44 (0) 20 7150 7001
Website: http://www.sugarmagazine.co.uk

Publishes: Articles; Features; Nonfiction;
Areas: Beauty and Fashion; Entertainment;
Film; Lifestyle; Romance; TV; Women's
Interests; *Markets:* Youth

Magazine for teenage girls. No unsolicited
MSS, but will consider ideas for real-life
features. Contact in writing with synopsis in
first instance.

The Tablet

The Tablet Publishing Company Ltd.
1 King Street Cloisters
Clifton Walk
London
W6 0GY
Tel: +44 (0) 20 8748 8484
Fax: +44 (0) 20 8748 1550
Email: thetablet@thetablet.co.uk
Website: http://www.thetablet.co.uk

Publishes: Articles; Nonfiction; *Areas:* Arts;
Literature; Politics; Religious; *Markets:*
Adult

Editors: Catherine Pepinster

Catholic magazine publishing articles by
writers of international standing.

Take a Break

H. Bauer Publishing
Academic House
24-28 Oval Road
London
NW1 7DT
Tel: +44 (0) 20 7241 8000
Fax: +44 (0) 20 7241 8056
Email: tab.features@bauer.co.uk
Website: http://www.takeabreak.co.uk

Publishes: Essays; Features; Fiction; News;
Nonfiction; *Areas:* Beauty and Fashion;
Cookery; Lifestyle; Short Stories; Travel;
Women's Interests; *Markets:* Adult

Editors: John Dale

Approach in writing in first instance.
Women's magazine offering competitions,
puzzles, etc. Publishes features, news, real-
life stories, and sharp, succinct fiction, often
with a twist. See website for online
submission system.

Tatler

Vogue House
Hanover Square
London
W1S 1JU
Tel: +44 (0) 20 7499 9080
Fax: +44 (0) 20 7409 0451
Email: Sara.Mccorquodale@condenast.co.uk
Website: http://www.tatler.co.uk

Publishes: Articles; Features; News;
Nonfiction; Reviews; *Areas:* Beauty and
Fashion; Cookery; Lifestyle; Travel;
Women's Interests; *Markets:* Adult

Editors: Sara McCorquodale (Senior Editor)

Up-market glossy. Unlikely to publish
unsolicited features, but interested writers
should submit a sample of their published or
unpublished output and, if taken up, will ask
writers to work on specific projects.

Tears in the Fence

38 Hod View
Stourpaine
Nr Blandford Forum
Dorset
DT11 8TN
Tel: +44 (0) 1258 456803
Fax: +44 (0) 1258 454026
Website:
http://www.myspace.com/tearsinthefence

Publishes: Essays; Fiction; Interviews;
Nonfiction; Poetry; Reviews; *Areas:* Short
Stories; Translations; *Markets:* Adult

Editors: David Caddy

International literary magazine publishing
both new writing, reviews, and criticism.

Tellus Magazine

Faculty of Classics
University of Cambridge
Sidgwick Avenue
Cambridge
CB3 9DA
Email: poetry@tellusmagazine.co.uk
Website: http://www.tellusmagazine.co.uk

Publishes: Poetry; *Markets:* Adult;
Treatments: Literary

Editors: Ailsa Hunt

Publishes poems interacting with any aspect
of ancient civilisations. Send submissions by
email, in the body of the email or as Word
attachments. See website for more details.

The Cricketer

The Cricketer Publishing Ltd
70 Great Portland Street
London
W1W 7UW
Tel: +44 (0) 20 7460 5200
Email: magazine@thecricketer.com
Website: http://www.thecricketer.com

Publishes: Articles; News; Nonfiction;
Areas: Sport; *Markets:* Adult

Editors: Andrew Miller

The world's biggest-selling cricket
magazine. Query in writing in first instance.

thesnailmagazine

Tel: +44 (0) 1314 415619
Email:
ronfrancis.thesnailmagazine@gmail.com
Website: http://www.thesnailmagazine.com

Publishes: Articles; Essays; Features;
Interviews; Nonfiction; *Areas:* Adventure;
Arts; Business; Criticism; Culture; Current
Affairs; Legal; Literature; Media; Sociology;
Markets: Academic; Adult; Professional;
Treatments: Contemporary; Literary;
Progressive; Serious; Traditional

Editors: Ron Francis

A magazine specialising in longform
narrative journalism. No memoir or family
history. Stories should be fact-based, in-
depth studies of events that will resonate
with the reader. Avoid first-person singular
narrative where possible.

Time Out

Universal House
251 Tottenham Court Road
London
W1T 7AB
Tel: +44 (0) 20 7813 3000
Fax: +44 (0) 20 7813 6001
Website: http://www.timeout.com

Publishes: Articles; Features; News;
Nonfiction; *Areas:* Arts; Design;
Entertainment; Health; Lifestyle; Travel;
Markets: Adult

Material is normally written by staff, or
commissioned, but accepts ideas if
appropriate to the magazine.

Times Educational Supplement (TES) Scotland

Thistle House
21-23 Thistle Street
Edinburgh
EH2 1DF
Tel: +44 (0) 1316 248332
Fax: +44 (0) 1314 678019
Email: scoted@tes.co.uk
Website: http://www.tes.co.uk/scotland

Publishes: Articles; Features; News;
Nonfiction; *Markets:* Professional

News articles and features of interest to
Scottish teachers. Welcomes unsolicited mss.

Tocher

Celtic and Scottish Studies
27 George Square
Edinburgh
EH8 9LD
Tel: +44 (0) 131 650 4167
Fax: +44 (0) 131 650 4163
Email: Celtic@ed.ac.uk
Website:
http://www.celtscot.ed.ac.uk/tocher.htm

Publishes: Articles; Features; Fiction;
Nonfiction; Poetry; *Areas:* Historical; Music;
Short Stories; Translations; *Markets:* Adult;
Treatments: Traditional

Publishes stories, legends, features, songs,
and other material relating to traditional
Scottish life. Gaelic material is translated
into English, and glossaries added to Scots
material where it is deemed appropriate.

Total Flyfisher

2 Stephenson Close
Daventry
Northants
NN11 8RF
Tel: +44 (0) 1327 311999
Fax: +44 (0) 1327 311190
Email: subscriptions@dhpub.co.uk
Website: http://www.totalflyfisher.com

Publishes: Articles; Features; News; Nonfiction; *Areas:* Hobbies; *Markets:* Adult

Instructional magazine publishing news, features, and articles on fly fishing. Approach by email.

Tribune
Woodberry
218 Green Lanes
London
N4 2HB
Tel: +44 (0) 20 8800 4281 ext 244
Email: mail@tribunemagazine.co.uk
Website: http://www.tribunemagazine.co.uk

Publishes: Articles; Features; News; Nonfiction; *Areas:* Arts; Current Affairs; Politics; *Markets:* Adult

Editors: Chris McLaughlin

Independent Labour publication, covering politics, the arts, society, current affairs, trade unions, etc. Approach by phone or by email in first instance.

20x20 magazine
Email: info@20x20magazine.com
Website: http://www.20x20magazine.com

Publishes: Articles; Essays; Fiction; Nonfiction; Poetry; *Areas:* Arts; Culture; Design; Literature; Music; Photography; Short Stories; *Markets:* Academic; Adult; Youth; *Treatments:* Contemporary; Experimental; Literary

Editors: Francesca Ricci & Giovanna Paternò

A square platform for writings, visuals and cross-bred projects. Rather than on a theme, each issue is assembled around meta-words to be interpreted, researched, illustrated according to a loose, wide and multi-angled perspective. The intent is to create homogeneity of spirit within each issue, without the restrictions of a "theme" as such.

The magazine includes 3 sections:

Words – in the shape of fiction, essays, poetry

Visions – drawings, photography and visual projects

The Blender – where words and visions cross paths

Submissions for the three above-mentioned sections are accepted by email only and in response to the meta-words set for the forthcoming issue. These are announced via our website or by joining our e-mailing list.

The Vegan
Donald Watson House
21 Hylton Street
Birmingham
B18 6HJ
Tel: +44 (0) 1215 231730
Email: editor@vegansociety.com
Website: http://www.vegansociety.com

Publishes: Articles; Nonfiction; Health; Lifestyle; *Markets:* Adult

Magazine covering veganism. Welcomes unsolicited articles up to 2,000 words

Wedding Ideas
Herd HQ
Mitre House
Taunton
Somerset
TA1 4BH
Tel: +44 (0) 1823 288344
Email: rachelm@weddingideasmag.com
Website: http://www.weddingideasmag.com

Publishes: Articles; Features; Nonfiction; *Areas:* How-to; Women's Interests; *Markets:* Adult

Editors: Rachel Morgan

Magazine for brides working to a budget. Potential contributors should familiarise themselves with the magazine before sending a query by email.

The War Cry
Salvation Army
101 Newington Causeway
London
SE1 6BN
Email: warcry@salvationarmy.org.uk
Website:
http://www.salvationarmy.org.uk/warcry

Publishes: Articles; Features; News;
Nonfiction; *Areas:* Current Affairs;
Religious; *Markets:* Adult

Editors: Major Nigel Bovey

Magazine of Christian comment. Welcomes
appropriate unsolicited mss. Contact by
email or by phone in first instance. No
fiction or poetry.

Who Do You Think You Are?
Magazine
9th Floor
Tower House
Fairfax Street
Bristol
BS1 3BN
Tel: +44 (0) 1173 147400
Email:
WDYTYAeditorial@immediatemedia.co.uk
Website: http://www.whodoyouthink
youaremagazine.com

Publishes: Articles; Nonfiction; *Areas:*
Historical; Military; Sociology; *Markets:*
Adult

Editors: Sarah Williams

Publishes articles on family history. Send
queries to the editor.

Woman's Weekly
IPC Media Ltd
Blue Fin Building
110 Southwark Street
London
SE1 0SU
Tel: +44 (0) 20 3148 5000
Email:
womansweeklypostbag@ipcmedia.com

Publishes: Features; Fiction; News;

Nonfiction; *Areas:* Short Stories; Women's
Interests; *Markets:* Adult; *Treatments:*
Contemporary

Editors: Diane Kenwood; Sue Pilkington
(Features); Gaynor Davies (Fiction)

Publishes features of interest to women over
forty, plus fiction between 1,000 and 2,000
words and serials of 12,000 words. Only uses
experienced journalists for nonfiction. Send
query by email.

The Woodworker
MyHobbyStore Ltd
PO Box 718
Orpington
BR6 1AP
Tel: +44 (0) 1689 869876
Email: mike.lawrence@myhobbystore.com
Website: http://www.getwoodworking.com

Publishes: Articles; Features; Nonfiction;
Areas: Crafts; Hobbies; How-to; *Markets:*
Adult

Editors: Mike Lawrence

Magazine on woodworking, including
articles on tips, new products, tenchiques,
etc. Welcomes unsolicited MSS, but no
fiction. Query with ideas by writing, phone,
or email.

Words Magazine
PO Box 13574
London
W9 3FX
Email: admin@wordsmag.com
Website: http://www.wordsmag.com

Publishes: Fiction; *Areas:* Short Stories;
Markets: Adult

Not-for-profit magazine donating all
proceeds to a charity for the care of
premature babies. Stories should be typed,
double-spaced, on one side only of A4 paper,
and under 2,000 words. Submit by post or by
email attachment.

Writers' Forum

Select Publisher Services Ltd
PO box 6337
Bournemouth
Dorset
BH9 1EH
Tel: +44 (0) 1202 586848
Email: editorial@writers-forum.com
Website: http://www.writers-forum.com

Publishes: Articles; Nonfiction; *Areas:*
Hobbies; How-to; Literature; *Markets:* Adult

Editors: Carl Styants

Publishes articles on the craft of writing.
Approach editor in writing in first instance.

The Yellow Room

1 Blake Close
Bilton
Rugby
CV22 7LJ
Tel: +44 (0) 1788 334302
Email: jo.derrick@ntlworld.com
Website: http://www.theyellowroom-magazine.co.uk

Publishes: Fiction; *Areas:* Short Stories;
Women's Interests; *Markets:* Adult;
Treatments: Literary

Editors: Jo Derrick

Magazine publishing short stories by UK
women, for women. Accepts submissions by
email with story submitted as a Word file
attachment. No poetry or nonfiction. No
multiple submissions. Simultaneous
submissions accepted if notification given.
See website for full details.

Your Cat

BPG Stamford Ltd
Roebuck House
33 Broad Street
Stamford
Lincolnshire
PE9 1RB
Tel: +44 (0) 1780 766199
Email: sue@yourcat.co.uk
Website: http://www.yourcat.co.uk

Publishes: Articles; Fiction; Nonfiction;
Areas: How-to; Short Stories; *Markets:*
Adult

Editors: Sue Parslow

Practical magazine covering the care of cats
and kittens. No poetry and no articles written
from the cat's viewpoint. Considers fiction
by published novelists only. Send query by
email with outline by post or by email.

Yours

Media House
Peterborough Business Park
Peterborough
PE2 6EA
Tel: +44 (0) 1733 468000
Email: yours@bauermedia.co.uk
Website: http://www.yours.co.uk

Publishes: Articles; Features; Fiction;
Nonfiction; *Areas:* Lifestyle; Short Stories;
Women's Interests; *Markets:* Adult;
Treatments: Positive

Editors: Gemma Toms

Lifestyle magazine aimed at women over 35.
Welcomes nonfiction articles. Uses one or
two pieces of fiction each issue. Send
complete MS with SAE.

Zest

National Magazine House
72 Broadwick Street
London
W1F 9EP
Tel: +44 (0) 20 7439 5000
Fax: +44 (0) 20 7312 3750
Email: zest.mail@natmags.co.uk
Website: http://www.zest.co.uk

Publishes: Articles; Features; Nonfiction;
Areas: Beauty and Fashion; Health;
Lifestyle; Women's Interests; *Markets:*
Adult; *Treatments:* Positive

Editors: Mandie Gower

Approach in writing with ideas in first
instance.

Zoo

Bauer Consumer Media
Mapin House
4 Winsley Street
London
W1W 8HF
Email: info@zootoday.com
Website: http://www.zootoday.com

Publishes: News; Nonfiction; *Areas:* Entertainment; Film; Humour; Lifestyle; Men's Interests; Sport; Technology; *Markets:* Adult

Men's interest magazine featuring girls, sport, humour, movies, showbiz, games, gadgets, cars, etc.

Canadian Magazines

For the most up-to-date listings of these and hundreds of other magazines, visit http://www.firstwriter.com/magazines

*To claim your **free** access to the site, please see the back of this book.*

Alberta Venture
Venture Publishing Inc.
10259 – 105 Street
Edmonton, AB T5J 1E3
Tel: +1 (780) 990-0839
Fax: +1 (780) 425-4921
Email: pmarck@albertaventure.com
Website: http://albertaventure.com

Publishes: Articles; Features; News; Nonfiction; *Areas:* Business; *Markets:* Professional

Magazine for business owners and managers in Alberta. Send query in first instance.

Ascent Aspirations Magazine
1560 Arbutus Drive
Nanoose Bay, BC
C9P 9C8
Email: ascentaspirations@shaw.ca
Website: http://www.ascentaspirations.ca

Publishes: Essays; Fiction; Nonfiction; Poetry; Reviews; *Areas:* Fantasy; Horror; Sci-Fi; Short Stories; *Markets:* Adult; *Treatments:* Dark; Literary

Editors: David Fraser

Originally a quarterly print journal, became a monthly electronic journal in 2009. Publishes poetry, fiction, essays, and reviews. Fiction should be literary, science fiction, fantasy and horror or dark main stream. Poetry can be on any subject. Essays should comment on life, philosophy, mythology and the human condition. Submit by email, with "Poetry/Essay/Short Story Submission" in the query line, as appropriate. See website for full details.

Azure
460 Richmond St. West, Suite 601
Toronto, ON M5V 1Y1
Tel: +1 (416) 203-9674
Fax: +1 (416) 203-9842
Email: azure@azureonline.com
Website: http://www.azuremagazine.com

Publishes: Articles; Features; Nonfiction; *Areas:* Architecture; Design; *Markets:* Adult

Query with details of professional background and clips / writing samples.

BC Outdoors Sport Fishing
OP Publishing
1080 Howe Street, Suite 900
Vancouver, BC V6Z 2T1
Tel: +1 (604) 464-3186
Email: mmitchell@outdoorgroupmedia.com
Website: http://www.bcoutdoorsmagazine.com/sport-fishing

Publishes: Articles; Essays; Nonfiction; Reviews; *Areas:* Adventure; How-to;

Leisure; Nature; Sport; *Markets:* Adult

Editors: Mike Mitchell

Publishes articles on sport fishing and outdoor experiences, relating directly to British Columbia. See website for more details.

Cabling Networking Systems (CNS)

80 Valleybrook Drive
Toronto, ON
M3B 2S9
Tel: +1 (416) 510-6752
Fax: +1 (416) 510-5134
Email: pbarker@cnsmagazine.com
Website: http://www.cnsmagazine.com

Publishes: Articles; Features; Nonfiction; *Areas:* Technology; *Markets:* Professional

Editors: Paul Barker

Magazine aimed at professionals working with and designing cabling and telecommunications products and systems. Send query with published clips.

Canadian Commerce & Industry

Mercury Publications
1740 Wellington Ave
Winnipeg, Manitoba R3H 0E8
Tel: +1 (800) 337-6372 / (204) 954-2085 ext.207
Fax: +1 (204) 954-2057
Email: editorial@mercury.mb.ca
Website: http://www.commerceindustry.ca

Publishes: Articles; News; Nonfiction; *Areas:* Business; *Markets:* Professional

Business magazine. Send query by post, fax, or email, with clippings and details of previous experience.

Canadian Homes and Cottages

2650 Meadowvale Blvd. Unit 4
Mississauga ON L5N 6M5
Tel: +1 (905) 567-1440
Fax: +1 (905) 567-1442
Email: editorial@homesandcottages.com
Website: http://www.homesandcottages.com

Publishes: Articles; Nonfiction; *Areas:* Architecture; Design; Humour; Lifestyle; Technology; *Markets:* Adult

Editors: Oliver Johnson

Magazine on building, renovation and home improvement, aimed at a Canadian audience. Send query in first instance.

Canadian Writer's Journal

Box 1178
New Liskeard, Ontario
P0J 1P0
Tel: +1 (705) 647-5424
Fax: +1 (705) 647-8366
Email: editor@cwj.ca
Website: http://www.cwj.ca

Publishes: Articles; Essays; Features; Nonfiction; Poetry; Reviews; *Areas:* Hobbies; How-to; Literature; *Markets:* Adult; Professional

Magazine aimed at amateur and professional writers, offering how-to articles and publishing poetry. Fiction published via contest only. Also publishes book reviews and opinion pieces. Aims at 90% Canadian material. See website for full details.

Cosmetics Magazine

One Mount Pleasant Road, 8th Floor
Toronto, ON
M4Y 2Y5
Tel: +1 (416) 764-1680
Email: kristen.vinakmens@cosmetics.rogers.com
Website: http://cosmeticsmag.com

Publishes: Articles; Features; Interviews; Nonfiction; *Areas:* Beauty and Fashion; Business; *Markets:* Professional

Editors: Kristen Vinakmens

Magazine for professionals working in the retail sector of the cosmetics industry. Query in first instance.

The Dalhousie Review

Dalhousie University
Halifax
Nova Scotia
B3H 4R2
Tel: +1 (902) 494-2541
Email: dalhousie.review@dal.ca
Website: http://dalhousiereview.dal.ca

Publishes: Articles; Essays; Fiction;
Nonfiction; Poetry; Reviews; *Areas:* Arts;
Autobiography; Criticism; Culture;
Historical; Literature; Philosophy; Politics;
Short Stories; Sociology; *Markets:* Adult

Publishes fiction, poetry, creative nonfiction,
essays, and book reviews. See website for
full submission guidelines. Submit by post
only.

The Fiddlehead

The Fiddlehead
Campus House
11 Garland Court
University of New Brunswick
PO Box 4400
Fredericton NB
E3B 5A3
Email: fiddlehd@unb.ca
Website: http://www.thefiddlehead.ca

Publishes: Fiction; Poetry; *Areas:* Short
Stories; *Markets:* Adult

Submit up to ten poems, or a piece of fiction
up to 6,000 words. Submit only one genre at
a time. All submissions must be original and
unpublished. No submissions by fax or
email. See website for full details.

Geist

Suite 210, 111 West Hastings Street
Vancouver, B.C. V6B 1H4
Tel: +1 (604) 681-9161
Fax: +1 (604) 677-6319
Email: editor@geist.com
Website: http://www.geist.com

Publishes: Essays; Features; Fiction;
Nonfiction; Poetry; Reviews; *Areas:* Arts;
Culture; Historical; Humour; Literature;
Short Stories; *Markets:* Adult; *Treatments:*
Literary

Magazine of culture and ideas publishing
fiction, nonfiction, poetry, photography, art,
reviews, little-known facts of interest,
cartography, and crossword puzzles. Submit
by post or through online submission system.
See website for more details.

Link & Visitor

304 The East Mall
Etobicoke, ON
M9B 6E2
Tel: +1 (416) 651 8967
Email: rsejames@gmail.com
Website:
http://www.baptistwomen.com/link-
visitor/online

Publishes: Articles; Interviews; Nonfiction;
Areas: Religious; Women's Interests;
Markets: Adult

Editors: Renee James

Magazine for Canadian baptist women,
accepting unsolicited mss from Canadian
writers only. Email submissions must be in
the body of the email - no attachments.

The Northern Star

Tel: +1 (250) 640-9455
Email: nspp@shaw.ca
Website: http://www.northernstar-online.com

Publishes: Articles; Features; Fiction; News;
Nonfiction; *Areas:* Adventure;
Anthropology; Antiques; Archaeology; Arts;
Beauty and Fashion; Crime; Current Affairs;
Entertainment; Humour; Media; Mystery;
Nature; Science; *Markets:* Adult; Family;
Youth; *Treatments:* Cynical; Experimental;
Light; Positive; Progressive; Satirical;
Traditional

Editors: Cathie

Magazine designed to entertain, educate and
amuse.

The Oracular Tree

29 Hillyard Street
Chatham ON
N7L 3E1

Email: editor@oraculartree.com
Website: http://www.oraculartree.com

Publishes: Essays; Fiction; Nonfiction;
Poetry; *Areas:* Short Stories; *Markets:* Adult;
Treatments: Literary; Positive

Publishes poetry, stories, essays, and visual
art. Looks for positive transformations of
dysfunctional cultural paradigms.

Pacific Yachting

200 West Esplanade, Suite 500
North Vancouver, BC V7M 1A4
Tel: +1 (604) 998-3310
Email: editor@pacificyachting.com
Website: http://www.pacificyachting.com

Publishes: Articles; Features; Nonfiction;
Areas: How-to; Leisure; Travel; *Markets:*
Adult

Editors: Dale Miller

Magazine for powerboaters and sailors
sharing a common interest in recreational
boating in British Columbia and the Pacific
Northwest. Query by email in first instance.

The Prairie Journal

28 Crowfoot Terrace NW
P.O. Box 68073
Calgary, Alberta
T3G 3N8
Email: prairiejournal@yahoo.com
Website: http://prairiejournal.org

Publishes: Fiction; Interviews; Nonfiction;
Poetry; Reviews; Scripts; *Areas:* Criticism;
Drama; Short Stories; *Markets:* Adult;
Treatments: Literary

Send submissions by post. See website for
detailed requirements. No simultaneous
submissions.

Prairie Messenger

100 College Drive
Box 190
MUENSTER, SK S0K 2Y0
Tel: +1 (306) 682-1772
Fax: +1 (306) 682-5285

Email: pm.canadian@stpeterspress.ca
Website: http://www.prairiemessenger.ca

Publishes: Articles; Features; News;
Nonfiction; Poetry; *Areas:* Current Affairs;
Religious; *Markets:* Adult

Editors: Maureen Weber

16-20-page tabloid newspaper covering
local, national and international religious
news and current affairs. Send complete ms
by post, email, or fax. Responds to postal
submissions only if return Canadian postage
is provided; responds to fax and email
submissions only if interested.

PRISM international

Creative Writing Program, UBC
Buch. E462 – 1866 Main Mall
Vancouver, BC, V6T 1Z1
Tel: +1 (604) 822-2514
Fax: +1 (604) 822-3616
Email: prismfiction@gmail.com
Website: http://prismmagazine.ca

Publishes: Fiction; Nonfiction; Poetry;
Scripts; *Areas:* Drama; Translations;
Markets: Adult; *Treatments:* Literary

Editors: Cara Woodruff (Fiction); Jordan
Abel (Poetry)

Submit one piece of fiction, drama, or
creative nonfiction, or up to 7 poems at a
time. Include cover letter with bio and
publications list, plus email address for
reply, or SASE with Canadian postage or
IRCs. See website for full guidelines.

Queen's Quarterly

144 Barrie Street
Queen's University
Kingston, Ontario K7L 3N6
Tel: +1 (613) 533-2667
Fax: +1 (613) 533-6822
Email: queens.quarterly@queensu.ca
Website: http://www.queensu.ca/quarterly

Publishes: Articles; Essays; Fiction;
Nonfiction; Poetry; Reviews; *Areas:* Short
Stories; Markets

Editors: Boris Castel, Editor (articles, essays and reviews); Joan Harcourt, Literary Editor (fiction and poetry)

Multidisciplinary journal aimed at the general educated reader. Prints unpublished articles, essays, reviews, short stories and poetry. For poetry and fiction, considers up to six poems or two stories. Accepts submissions by post with SASE but encourages email submissions. See website for full guidelines.

Resources for Feminist Research

Ontario Institute for Studies in Education/University of Toronto
252 Bloor Street West
Toronto, Ontario
M5S 1V6
Email: rfrdrf@oise.utoronto.ca
Website: http://legacy.oise.utoronto.ca/rfr

Publishes: Articles; Nonfiction; *Areas:* Women's Interests; *Markets:* Academic

Editors: Philinda Masters

Bilingual (English/French) Canadian scholarly journal, covering Canadian and international feminist research, issues, and debates.

Riddle Fence

Email: contact@riddlefence.com
Website: http://www.riddlefence.com

Publishes: Fiction; Nonfiction; Poetry; *Areas:* Arts; Culture; Short Stories; *Markets:* Adult; *Treatments:* Literary

Newfoundland and Labrador-based journal of arts and culture. Publishes fiction, nonfiction, poetry, and artwork. Submit to appropriate email address listed on website.

Romantic shorts

Email: contactus@romanticshorts.com
Website: http://www.romanticshorts.com

Publishes: Fiction; *Areas:* Romance; Short Stories; *Markets:* Adult; *Treatments:*

Contemporary; Light; Mainstream; Popular

Editors: Alexandra Brown

Online publication looking for romantic short stories (4,500-6,000 words) by new and newer authors. Also runs a writers' competition - deadline March 31st, 2011 - entry fee is $10CAD, prizes range from $250CAD for first place to $10 for 7th place. All winning entries - and quality honourable mentions - will be published. Also accepting unsolicited manuscripts and queries. All submissions made online via email attachment. Entry fees paid via PayPal. Responds to queries within 2 weeks; manuscripts within 4 weeks. Details and guidelines available on our website. Though a new publication - a new concept - our goal is to grow from a stepping stone in a writer's career to a destination, helping as many new and newer writers as we can along the way.

Room Magazine

P.O. Box 46160, Station D
Vancouver, BC
V6J 5G5
Email: submissions@roommagazine.com
Website: http://www.roommagazine.com

Publishes: Fiction; Nonfiction; Poetry; *Areas:* Women's Interests; *Markets:* Adult; *Treatments:* Literary

Publishes fiction, creative nonfiction, and poetry, for, by, and about women. Submit prose up to 3,500 words or up to 5 poems, with cover letter, via online submission system.

Zouch

Email: info@zouchmagazine.com
Website: http://zouchmagazine.com

Publishes: Essays; Fiction; Nonfiction; Poetry; *Areas:* Short Stories; *Markets:* Adult

Publishes poetry of any length or style; essays on any subject up to 2,000 words; fiction on any subject (flash fiction up to 1,000 words; short fiction up to 3,000 words; longer fiction up to 5,000 words). Submit using submission form on website. No postal submissions.

Irish Magazines

For the most up-to-date listings of these and hundreds of other magazines, visit http://www.firstwriter.com/magazines

*To claim your **free** access to the site, please see the back of this book.*

Albedo One

Albedo One
2 Post Road
Lusk
Co Dublin
Email: bobn@yellowbrickroad.ie
Website: http://www.albedo1.com

Publishes: Fiction; Reviews; Areas: Fantasy; Horror; Short Stories; Markets: Adult

Magazine revolving around SF, horror, and fantasy, with broad definitions of these genres – likes to see material that pushes at the boundaries of these definitions. Seeking thoughtfull, well-written fiction. Also publishes interviews, letters, and book reviews.

Send SASE or reply coupon for response. MSS not returned – send disposable copy only. Email submissions accepted but only in the body of the email – no attachments. No previously published material or simultaneous submissions.

Cyphers

3 Selskar Terrace
Ranelagh
Dublin 6
Email: letters@cyphers.ie
Website: http://www.cyphers.ie

Publishes: Fiction; Poetry; Areas: Short

Stories; Translations; Markets: Adult; Treatments: Literary

Publishes poetry and fiction in English and Irish, from Ireland and around the world. Translations are welcome. No unsolicited critical articles. Submissions by post only. Attachments sent by email will be deleted. See website for full guidelines.

The Dublin Review

PO Box 7948
Dublin 1
Website: http://thedublinreview.com

Publishes: Essays; Fiction; Nonfiction; Areas: Criticism; Literature; Short Stories; Markets: Adult

Publishes essays, criticism, reportage, and fiction for a general, intelligent readership. No poetry. Send submissions by post only with SAE and return postage or email address for response.

Irish Arts Review

State Apartments
Dublin Castle
Dublin 2
Tel: +353 1 679 3525
Fax: +353 1 633 4417
Email: editorial@irishartsreview.com
Website: http://www.irishartsreview.com

Publishes: Articles; Nonfiction; Areas: Architecture; Arts; Design; Photography; Markets: Adult

Quarterly review of Irish arts and design, from pre-history to contemporary.

Irish Tatler
Harmonia Ltd
Rosemount House
Dundrum Road
Dublin 14
Email: jcollins@harmonia.ie
Website: http://www.harmonia.ie

Publishes: Articles; Features; Interviews; News; Nonfiction; Areas: Beauty and Fashion; Cookery; Current Affairs; Design; Lifestyle; Women's Interests; Markets: Adult

Women's general interest magazine. Prides itself on supporting Ireland's indigenous fashion industry.

Poetry Ireland Review
Poetry Ireland
32 Kildare Street
Dublin 2
Tel: +353 (0)1 6789815
Fax: +353 (0)1 6789782
Email: info@poetryireland.ie

Website: http://www.poetryireland.ie

Publishes: Articles; Nonfiction; Poetry; Reviews; Areas: Literature; Markets: Adult

Editors: John F Deane

Send up to 6 poems with SASE / IRCs or email address for response. Poetry is accepted from around the world, but must be previously unpublished. No sexism or racism. No submissions by email. Articles and reviews are generally commissioned, however proposals are welcome. No unsolicited reviews or articles.

Southword Journal
The Munster Literature Centre
Frank O'Connor House
84 Douglas Street
Cork
Tel: (353) 021 4312955
Email: munsterlit@eircom.net
Website: http://www.munsterlit.ie

Publishes: Fiction; Nonfiction; Poetry; Reviews; Areas: Literature; Short Stories; Markets: Adult; Treatments: Literary

Send submissions of poetry and fiction by post between January and March 15 or July and September 15. Submit online via website submission system.

Australian Magazines

For the most up-to-date listings of these and hundreds of other magazines, visit http://www.firstwriter.com/magazines

To claim your free access to the site, please see the back of this book.

Beyond the Rainbow
PO Box 2014
NIMBIN 2480
Tel: +61 (0) 2 6689 1182
Email: tamaso@aussieisp.net.au
Website: http://www.nimbinnews.com/beyondtherainbow

Publishes: Essays; Fiction; Nonfiction; Poetry; Reviews; Areas: Adventure; Biography; Crime; Culture; Drama; Erotic; Fantasy; Humour; Literature; New Age; Sci Fi; Short Stories; Spiritual; Suspense; Markets: Adult; Youth; Treatments: Contemporary; Cynical; Light; Literary; Popular; Satirical; Serious; Traditional

Editors: Tamaso Lonsdale

Publishes mostly short stories and poems but is looking for all types of literary creation including extracts from published books and work in progress. We print a photo and short biography of the author.

Cordite Poetry Review
PO BOX 393
Carlton South
3053
Email: cordite@cordite.org.au
Website: http://www.cordite.org.au

Publishes: Essays; Features; Nonfiction; Poetry; Reviews; *Markets:* Adult; *Treatments:* Literary

Online magazine publishing work by writers from Australia and all over the world. Publishes poetry, features, essays, interviews, and audio files. Poetry accepted during specific reading periods only. See website for full guidelines and to submit.

Overland
VU-Footscray Park Campus
PO Box 14428
MELBOURNE VIC 8001
Tel: +61 (0) 3 9919 4163
Fax: +61 (0) 3 9687 7614
Email: overland@vu.edu.au
Website: http://web.overland.org.au

Publishes: Essays; Features; Fiction; Nonfiction; Poetry; Reviews; *Areas:* Autobiography; Culture; Literature; Politics; Short Stories; *Markets:* Adult; *Treatments:* Contemporary

Editors: Jeff Sparrow

Accepts fiction, nonfiction, and poetry from Australian and international writers, but payment available to Australian writers only. Submit using online submission system (see website).

Quadrant Magazine
Suite 2/5 Rosebery Place
Balmain, NSW, 2041
Tel: +61 (0) 2 9818 1155
Fax: +61 (0) 2 8580 4664
Email: keithwindschuttle@quadrant.org.au
Website: http://www.quadrant.org.au

Publishes: Articles; Essays; Fiction;
Nonfiction; Poetry; Reviews; *Areas:*
Historical; Literature; Politics; Short Stories;
Markets: Adult

Editors: Keith Windschuttle

Magazine based on founding principles of
cultural freedom, anti-totalitarianism and
classical liberalism, but open to any well-
written and thoughtful contribution. Accepts
nonfiction submissions by email, but fiction
and poetry by post only. See website for full
details.

Unwind-The Cafe Journal
11 Areca Ct
Narangba Qld 4504
Tel: 0733856304
Email: info@unwindandsmile.com

Publishes: Articles; Fiction; Nonfiction;
Poetry; *Areas:* Adventure; Anthropology;
Antiques; Archaeology; Architecture; Arts;
Autobiography; Beauty and Fashion;
Biography; Business; Cookery; Crafts;
Criticism; Culture; Current Affairs; Design;
Drama; Entertainment; Film; Finance;
Gardening; Gothic; Health; Historical;
Hobbies; How-to; Humour; Legal; Leisure;
Lifestyle; Literature; Media; Medicine;
Men's Interests; Military; Music; Mystery;
Nature; New Age; Philosophy; Photography;
Politics; Psychology; Radio; Religious;
Romance; Science; Sci-Fi; Self-Help; Short
Stories; Sociology; Spiritual; Sport;
Suspense; Technology; Theatre; Thrillers;
Translations; Travel; TV; Westerns;
Markets: Adult; Family

Editors: Sage Lightman

UNIQUE. That is the Journal. With our
delightful columns and informative articles,
it is an enjoyable read while having a cuppa
or just waiting for an appointment. Focuses
on the amusing, uplifting and downright
funny short articles. We now are opening our
doors to authors and poets to aid their quest
for publication. All submitted works must be
AMUSING, and put a smile on the reader's
face.

Magazines Subject Index

This section lists magazines by their subject matter, with directions to the section of the book where the full listing can be found.

You can create your own customised lists of magazines using different combinations of these subject areas, plus over a dozen other criteria, instantly online at http://www.firstwriter.com.

*To claim your **free** access to the site, please see the back of this book.*

Adventure
Androids2 (*US*)
BC Outdoors Sport Fishing (*Can*)
Beyond the Rainbow (*Aus*)
Carillon Magazine (*UK*)
Earth Mama Magazine (*US*)
Focus Magazine of SWFL (*US*)
From A Writer's POV Magazine (*US*)
Literary Juice (*US*)
Man's Story 2 (*US*)
Netsagas.com (*US*)
The Northern Star (*Can*)
The People's Friend (*UK*)
Quite Curious Literature (*US*)
The Rusty Nail (*US*)
Straitjackets Magazine (*US*)
The Subterranean Literary Journal (*UK*)
The Vehicle (*US*)
thesnailmagazine (*UK*)
Unwind-The Cafe Journal (*Aus*)
Vampires2 (*US*)
The Washington Pastime (*US*)
The Yes Factory (*US*)
Anthropology
Fjords Review (*US*)
Netsagas.com (*US*)
The Northern Star (*Can*)
Smithsonian Magazine (*US*)
The Subterranean Literary Journal (*UK*)
Unwind-The Cafe Journal (*Aus*)
Antiques
Antique Trader (*US*)
Apollo (*UK*)
Fjords Review (*US*)

Focus Magazine of SWFL (*US*)
Netsagas.com (*US*)
The Northern Star (*Can*)
Somerset Life (*UK*)
The Subterranean Literary Journal (*UK*)
Unwind-The Cafe Journal (*Aus*)
Archaeology
Archaeology (*US*)
Metta-Physics Magazine (*UK*)
Netsagas.com (*US*)
The Northern Star (*Can*)
Smithsonian Magazine (*US*)
The Subterranean Literary Journal (*UK*)
Unwind-The Cafe Journal (*Aus*)
Architecture
Apollo (*UK*)
Azure (*Can*)
Blueprint (*UK*)
Canadian Homes and Cottages (*Can*)
Colorado Homes & Lifestyles (*US*)
Concrete Homes Magazine (*US*)
Faith & Form (*US*)
Focus Magazine of SWFL (*US*)
Irish Arts Review (*Ire*)
Netsagas.com (*US*)
The Subterranean Literary Journal (*UK*)
Unwind-The Cafe Journal (*Aus*)
Arts
Ambit (*UK*)
Apollo (*UK*)
The Art Newspaper (*UK*)
Arts & Activities Magazine (*US*)
The Big Issue in the North (*UK*)
The Conium Review (*US*)

Fjords Review (*US*)
Focus Magazine of SWFL (*US*)
From A Writer's POV Magazine (*US*)
Greetings Today (*UK*)
High Life (*UK*)
ICIS Chemical Business Magazine (*UK*)
Ingram's Magazine (*US*)
International Bluegrass (*US*)
The Irish Post (*UK*)
Journal Plus (*US*)
LabTalk (*US*)
MyBusiness Magazine (*US*)
Media Week (*UK*)
Milwaukee Magazine (*US*)
Netsagas.com (*US*)
New Jersey Monthly (*US*)
O&A (Oil & Automotive Service) Marketing
News (*US*)
Open Spaces (*US*)
Overdrive (*US*)
Pulse (*US*)
Pallet Enterprise (*US*)
Pipeline & Gas Journal (*US*)
Portland Magazine (*US*)
Produce Business (*US*)
Promo (*US*)
Railway Gazette International (*UK*)
Road King (*US*)
RV Business (*US*)
Screentrade Magazine (*UK*)
Silicon Valley / San Jose Business Journal (*US*)
Skin Deep (*US*)
Somerset Life (*UK*)
The Subterranean Literary Journal (*UK*)
thesnailmagazine (*UK*)
Unwind-The Cafe Journal (*Aus*)
Writing that Works (*US*)
Cookery
Delicious (*UK*)
Devon Life (*UK*)
Draft (*US*)
18 Wheels & Heels (*US*)
Extastic Magazine (*UK*)
Focus Magazine of SWFL (*US*)
From A Writer's POV Magazine (*US*)
Irish Tatler (*Ire*)
Junior (*UK*)
Netsagas.com (*US*)
The People's Friend (*UK*)
Pockets (*US*)
Portland Magazine (*US*)
Reader's Digest (*UK*)
Red Magazine (*UK*)
Scottish Home and Country Magazine (*UK*)
Somerset Life (*UK*)
The Subterranean Literary Journal (*UK*)
Take a Break (*UK*)
Tatler (*UK*)
Unwind-The Cafe Journal (*Aus*)
Crafts
Arts & Activities Magazine (*US*)
Balloons & Parties Magazine (*US*)
Carving Magazine (*US*)

Earth Mama Magazine (*US*)
Focus Magazine of SWFL (*US*)
From A Writer's POV Magazine (*US*)
Guiding Magazine (*UK*)
Hippocampus Magazine (*US*)
Netsagas.com (*US*)
Period Living (*UK*)
Popular Woodworking Magazine (*US*)
Quilter's World (*US*)
Scottish Home and Country Magazine (*UK*)
Sew News (*US*)
The Subterranean Literary Journal (*UK*)
Unwind-The Cafe Journal (*Aus*)
The Woodworker (*UK*)
Crime
Beyond the Rainbow (*Aus*)
Carillon Magazine (*UK*)
The Edge (*UK*)
Evidence Technology Magazine (*US*)
Fjords Review (*US*)
From A Writer's POV Magazine (*US*)
Man's Story 2 (*US*)
Netsagas.com (*US*)
The Northern Star (*Can*)
The Police Journal (*UK*)
Pseudopod (*US*)
The Rusty Nail (*US*)
The Savage Kick (*UK*)
Scribble (*UK*)
Straitjackets Magazine (*US*)
The Subterranean Literary Journal (*UK*)
The Vehicle (*US*)
Thematic Literary Magazine (*US*)
Vampires2 (*US*)
The Washington Pastime (*US*)
The Yes Factory (*US*)
Criticism
Agenda (*UK*)
Anobium (*US*)
The Broadkill Review (*US*)
Carillon Magazine (*UK*)
The Dalhousie Review (*Can*)
DASH Journal (*US*)
The Dublin Review (*Ire*)
Fjords Review (*US*)
From A Writer's POV Magazine (*US*)
The London Magazine (*UK*)
Netsagas.com (*US*)
The New Shetlander (*UK*)
New Walk Magazine (*UK*)
North Carolina Literary Review (NCLR) (*US*)
Nuthouse (*US*)
Obsidian: Literature in the African Diaspora (*US*)
Paradoxism (*US*)
The Penniless Press (*UK*)
Pennsylvania English (*US*)
The Photo Review (*US*)
Poetry International (*US*)
Post Road (*US*)
The Prairie Journal (*Can*)
The Resurrectionist (*UK*)
Salmagundi Magazine (*US*)
Scissors and Spackle (*US*)

The Vehicle (*US*)
Thematic Literary Magazine (*US*)
Tocher (*UK*)
20x20 magazine (*UK*)
Unwind-The Cafe Journal (*Aus*)
Vampires2 (*US*)
Wild Violet (*US*)
Wag's Revue (*US*)
The Washington Pastime (*US*)
Water-Stone Review (*US*)
Woman's Weekly (*UK*)
Words Magazine (*UK*)
The Yellow Room (*UK*)
The Yes Factory (*US*)
Your Cat (*UK*)
Yours (*UK*)
Zouch (*Can*)
Film
American Cinematographer (*US*)
Earth Mama Magazine (*US*)
Eclectica Magazine (*US*)
Extastic Magazine (*UK*)
Fjords Review (*US*)
From A Writer's POV Magazine (*US*)
Go Girl Magazine (*UK*)
The List (*UK*)
Necrology Shorts (*US*)
Netsagas.com (*US*)
Screentrade Magazine (*UK*)
Sight & Sound (*UK*)
Straitjackets Magazine (*US*)
The Subterranean Literary Journal (*UK*)
Sugar Magazine (*UK*)
Unwind-The Cafe Journal (*Aus*)
Zoo (*UK*)
Finance
Accountancy Age (*UK*)
Consumers Digest (*US*)
Director (*UK*)
Financial Adviser (*UK*)
Focus Magazine of SWFL (*US*)
From A Writer's POV Magazine (*US*)
Ingram's Magazine (*US*)
Netsagas.com (*US*)
NextStepU Magazine (*US*)
Radix Magazine (*US*)
Reader's Digest (*UK*)
RV Business (*US*)
The Saturday Evening Post (*US*)
The Subterranean Literary Journal (*UK*)
Unwind-The Cafe Journal (*Aus*)
Gardening
Colorado Homes & Lifestyles (*US*)
Consumers Digest (*US*)
Earth Mama Magazine (*US*)
Focus Magazine of SWFL (*US*)
From A Writer's POV Magazine (*US*)
Netsagas.com (*US*)
New Jersey Monthly (*US*)
Period Living (*UK*)
Reader's Digest (*UK*)
The Saturday Evening Post (*US*)

Somerset Life (*UK*)
The Subterranean Literary Journal (*UK*)
Unwind-The Cafe Journal (*Aus*)
Gothic
Androids2 (*US*)
The Edge (*UK*)
Fjords Review (*US*)
From A Writer's POV Magazine (*US*)
Man's Story 2 (*US*)
Netsagas.com (*US*)
Scissors and Spackle (*US*)
Stone Highway Review (*US*)
Straitjackets Magazine (*US*)
The Subterranean Literary Journal (*UK*)
The Vehicle (*US*)
Unwind-The Cafe Journal (*Aus*)
Vampires2 (*US*)
The Washington Pastime (*US*)
The Yes Factory (*US*)
Health
ADVANCE for Respiratory Care & Sleep
Medicine (*US*)
Better Nutrition Magazine (*US*)
The Cattleman (*US*)
Consumers Digest (*US*)
Delaware Today (*US*)
Diabetes Self-Management (*US*)
Earth Mama Magazine (*US*)
Focus Magazine of SWFL (*US*)
From A Writer's POV Magazine (*US*)
Journal Plus (*US*)
Junior (*UK*)
Massage Magazine (*US*)
Muscle & Fitness (*UK*)
Netsagas.com (*US*)
New Jersey Monthly (*US*)
Performance (*US*)
Prima Baby & Pregnancy (*UK*)
Radix Magazine (*US*)
Reader's Digest (*UK*)
Right Start Magazine (*UK*)
The Saturday Evening Post (*US*)
Scottish Home and Country Magazine (*UK*)
Skin Deep (*US*)
Somerset Life (*UK*)
The Subterranean Literary Journal (*UK*)
Time Out (*UK*)
Unwind-The Cafe Journal (*Aus*)
The Vegan (*UK*)
Zest (*UK*)
Historical
ARMY Magazine (*US*)
Arts & Activities Magazine (*US*)
Best of British (*UK*)
Blue Ridge Country (*US*)
The Brahman Journal (*US*)
Carving Magazine (*US*)
Classic Toy Trains (*US*)
The Dalhousie Review (*Can*)
Delaware Today (*US*)
Devon Life (*UK*)
Discover Maine Magazine (*US*)
Extastic Magazine (*UK*)

Family Tree Magazine (*UK*)
Fjords Review (*US*)
Geist (*Can*)
Jewish Quarterly (*UK*)
Journal Plus (*US*)
Metta-Physics Magazine (*UK*)
Midwest Living (*US*)
Milwaukee Magazine (*US*)
Montana Magazine (*US*)
Netsagas.com (*US*)
New Jersey Monthly (*US*)
The New Shetlander (*UK*)
North Carolina Literary Review (NCLR) (*US*)
Old Tractor (*UK*)
Pakn Treger (*US*)
The Paumanok Review (*US*)
Pennsylvania Heritage (*US*)
Pointe Magazine (*US*)
Quadrant Magazine (*Aus*)
Railroad Evangelist Magazine (*US*)
Scissors and Spackle (*US*)
Scottish Home and Country Magazine (*UK*)
Ships Monthly Magazine (*UK*)
Smithsonian Magazine (*US*)
Somerset Life (*UK*)
Straitjackets Magazine (*US*)
The Subterranean Literary Journal (*UK*)
The Tavern's Vault (*US*)
The Vehicle (*US*)
Tocher (*UK*)
Unwind-The Cafe Journal (*Aus*)
Who Do You Think You Are? Magazine (*UK*)

Hobbies
American Hunter (*US*)
Bowls International (*UK*)
British Chess Magazine (*UK*)
British Woodworking (*UK*)
Canadian Writer's Journal (*Can*)
Canals, Rivers + Boats (*UK*)
Cigar Aficionado (*US*)
Classic Toy Trains (*US*)
Draft (*US*)
Earth Mama Magazine (*US*)
18 Wheels & Heels (*US*)
Equus Magazine (*US*)
Extastic Magazine (*UK*)
Focus Magazine of SWFL (*US*)
Forum (*US*)
From A Writer's POV Magazine (*US*)
Guiding Magazine (*UK*)
Model Boats (*UK*)
The Maine Sportsman (*US*)
Model Cars Magazine (*US*)
Netsagas.com (*US*)
Our Dogs (*UK*)
Pony Magazine (*UK*)
Pockets (*US*)
Popular Woodworking Magazine (*US*)
Quilter's World (*US*)
Railroad Evangelist Magazine (*US*)
Sew News (*US*)
Stamp Lover (*UK*)
The Subterranean Literary Journal (*UK*)

Total Flyfisher (*UK*)
Unwind-The Cafe Journal (*Aus*)
The Woodworker (*UK*)
Writers' Forum (*UK*)

Horror
Albedo One (*Ire*)
Androids2 (*US*)
Ascent Aspirations Magazine (*Can*)
Broadsheet (*US*)
Earth Mama Magazine (*US*)
The Edge (*UK*)
Fjords Review (*US*)
From A Writer's POV Magazine (*US*)
Literary Juice (*US*)
Necrology Shorts (*US*)
Netsagas.com (*US*)
The Nocturnal Lyric (*US*)
The Paumanok Review (*US*)
Premonitions (*UK*)
Pseudopod (*US*)
Residential Aliens (*US*)
The Rusty Nail (*US*)
Scary Monsters Magazine (*US*)
Scissors and Spackle (*US*)
Straitjackets Magazine (*US*)
The Subterranean Literary Journal (*UK*)
The Vehicle (*US*)
Thematic Literary Magazine (*US*)
Vampires2 (*US*)
The Washington Pastime (*US*)
The Yes Factory (*US*)

How-to
AKC Gazette (*US*)
Amateur Photographer (*UK*)
Animals and You (*UK*)
Arts & Activities Magazine (*US*)
AutoInc. (*US*)
Balloons & Parties Magazine (*US*)
BC Outdoors Sport Fishing (*Can*)
Beauty Store Business (*US*)
Birmingham Parent (*US*)
Broadsheet (*US*)
Canadian Writer's Journal (*Can*)
Carving Magazine (*US*)
The Cattleman (*US*)
Chesapeake Family (*US*)
Classic Toy Trains (*US*)
Concrete Homes Magazine (*US*)
Earth Mama Magazine (*US*)
EcoHome (*US*)
18 Wheels & Heels (*US*)
Employee Assistance Report (*US*)
Equus Magazine (*US*)
Eventing (*UK*)
FIDO Friendly (*US*)
Focus Magazine of SWFL (*US*)
From A Writer's POV Magazine (*US*)
Girls' Life (*US*)
Junior Baseball (*US*)
LabTalk (*US*)
MyBusiness Magazine (*US*)
Machine Design (*US*)
Macworld (*UK*)

Massage Magazine (*US*)
Model Cars Magazine (*US*)
Music Teacher (*UK*)
Netsagas.com (*US*)
NextStepU Magazine (*US*)
Our Dogs (*UK*)
Overdrive (*US*)
Pacific Yachting (*Can*)
Pallet Enterprise (*US*)
PC Advisor (*UK*)
Pointe Magazine (*US*)
Popular Woodworking Magazine (*US*)
Practical Wireless (*UK*)
Prima Baby & Pregnancy (*UK*)
Promo (*US*)
Quilter's World (*US*)
Reader's Digest (*UK*)
RTJ's Creative Catechist (*US*)
The Saturday Evening Post (*US*)
Sea Magazine (*US*)
Sign Builder Illustrated (*US*)
The Subterranean Literary Journal (*UK*)
Unwind-The Cafe Journal (*Aus*)
Wedding Ideas (*UK*)
The Woodworker (*UK*)
Writers' Forum (*UK*)
Writing that Works (*US*)
Your Cat (*UK*)
Humour
AKC Gazette (*US*)
The American Spectator (*US*)
Anobium (*US*)
Beyond the Rainbow (*Aus*)
Bike Magazine (*US*)
Camping Today (*US*)
Canadian Homes and Cottages (*Can*)
Carillon Magazine (*UK*)
Crystal Magazine (*UK*)
Earth Mama Magazine (*US*)
Eclectica Magazine (*US*)
Extastic Magazine (*UK*)
FIDO Friendly (*US*)
Fjords Review (*US*)
From A Writer's POV Magazine (*US*)
Garbaj (*UK*)
Geist (*Can*)
Girls' Life (*US*)
Literary Juice (*US*)
Monkey Kettle (*UK*)
Netsagas.com (*US*)
North Carolina Literary Review (NCLR) (*US*)
The Northern Star (*Can*)
Nuthouse (*US*)
Opium Magazine (*US*)
Pakn Treger (*US*)
Popular Woodworking Magazine (*US*)
The Rag (*US*)
Reader's Digest (*UK*)
The Resurrectionist (*UK*)
The Saturday Evening Post (*US*)
Scissors and Spackle (*US*)
Scribble (*UK*)
Stone Highway Review (*US*)

Straitjackets Magazine (*US*)
The Subterranean Literary Journal (*UK*)
The Rejected Quarterly (*US*)
The Vehicle (*US*)
Thematic Literary Magazine (*US*)
Unwind-The Cafe Journal (*Aus*)
Verbatim (*US*)
Wild Violet (*US*)
The Washington Pastime (*US*)
The Yes Factory (*US*)
Zoo (*UK*)
Legal
Criminal Law & Justice Weekly (Incorporating
Justice of the Peace) (*UK*)
Employee Assistance Report (*US*)
Fjords Review (*US*)
From A Writer's POV Magazine (*US*)
Law Enforcement Technology Magazine (*US*)
Netsagas.com (*US*)
New Law Journal (*UK*)
Open Spaces (*US*)
The Police Journal (*UK*)
The Subterranean Literary Journal (*UK*)
thesnailmagazine (*UK*)
Unwind-The Cafe Journal (*Aus*)
Leisure
BC Outdoors Sport Fishing (*Can*)
Bike Magazine (*US*)
Bowls International (*UK*)
Camping Today (*US*)
Caterer and Hotelkeeper (*UK*)
Club Management (*US*)
Consumers Digest (*US*)
Discover Maine Magazine (*US*)
Draft (*US*)
Earth Mama Magazine (*US*)
18 Wheels & Heels (*US*)
Focus Magazine of SWFL (*US*)
Forum (*US*)
From A Writer's POV Magazine (*US*)
GamesMaster (*UK*)
Guiding Magazine (*UK*)
Journal Plus (*US*)
Lancashire Magazine (*UK*)
The Maine Sportsman (*US*)
Mountain Biking UK (*UK*)
Netsagas.com (*US*)
New Jersey Monthly (*US*)
Pacific Yachting (*Can*)
Pockets (*US*)
Portland Magazine (*US*)
Salt Water Sportsman (*US*)
Straitjackets Magazine (*US*)
The Subterranean Literary Journal (*UK*)
Unwind-The Cafe Journal (*Aus*)
Lifestyle
Atlanta Parent Magazine (*US*)
Better Nutrition Magazine (*US*)
Birmingham Parent (*US*)
bliss Magazine (*UK*)
Canadian Homes and Cottages (*Can*)
Chesapeake Family (*US*)
Christian Home & School (*US*)

Colorado Homes & Lifestyles (*US*)
The Conium Review (*US*)
Consumers Digest (*US*)
Devon Life (*UK*)
Earth Mama Magazine (*US*)
18 Wheels & Heels (*US*)
Essentials (*UK*)
Fjords Review (*US*)
Focus Magazine of SWFL (*US*)
Forum (*US*)
From A Writer's POV Magazine (*US*)
Go Girl Magazine (*UK*)
Girl Talk (*UK*)
Guiding Magazine (*UK*)
High Life (*UK*)
House Beautiful (*UK*)
The Irish Post (*UK*)
Irish Tatler (*Ire*)
Journal Plus (*US*)
Junior (*UK*)
Lancashire Magazine (*UK*)
Midwest Living (*US*)
Milwaukee Magazine (*US*)
Montana Magazine (*US*)
Netsagas.com (*US*)
New Jersey Monthly (*US*)
New York (*US*)
Now (*UK*)
Open Spaces (*US*)
Portland Magazine (*US*)
Prima Baby & Pregnancy (*UK*)
Reader's Digest (*UK*)
Real People (*UK*)
Red Magazine (*UK*)
Right Start Magazine (*UK*)
The Saturday Evening Post (*US*)
Scottish Home and Country Magazine (*UK*)
Smithsonian Magazine (*US*)
The Subterranean Literary Journal (*UK*)
Sugar Magazine (*UK*)
Take a Break (*UK*)
Tatler (*UK*)
Time Out (*UK*)
Unwind-The Cafe Journal (*Aus*)
The Vegan (*UK*)
Yours (*UK*)
Zest (*UK*)
Zoo (*UK*)
Literature
Agenda (*UK*)
Anobium (*US*)
Beyond the Rainbow (*Aus*)
The Broadkill Review (*US*)
Broadsheet (*US*)
Canadian Writer's Journal (*Can*)
Carillon Magazine (*UK*)
The Conium Review (*US*)
Crystal Magazine (*UK*)
The Dalhousie Review (*Can*)
The Dublin Review (*Ire*)
Earth Mama Magazine (*US*)
Eclectica Magazine (*US*)
Extastic Magazine (*UK*)

Fjords Review (*US*)
From A Writer's POV Magazine (*US*)
Geist (*Can*)
The Interpreter's House (*UK*)
Jewish Quarterly (*UK*)
The List (*UK*)
The London Magazine (*UK*)
London Review of Books (*UK*)
LONE STARS Magazine (*US*)
Lummox (*US*)
Magma (*UK*)
Modern Poetry in Translation (*UK*)
Modern Language Review (*UK*)
Netsagas.com (*US*)
New Walk Magazine (*UK*)
North Carolina Literary Review (NCLR) (*US*)
Northwest Review (*US*)
Nuthouse (*US*)
Nuvein Magazine (*US*)
Obsidian: Literature in the African Diaspora (*US*)
Overland (*Aus*)
Pakn Treger (*US*)
The Penniless Press (*UK*)
Pennsylvania English (*US*)
Planet (*UK*)
Poetry Express (*UK*)
Poetry International (*US*)
Poetry Ireland Review (*Ire*)
Post Road (*US*)
Prairie Schooner (*US*)
Prospect (*UK*)
Provincetown Arts (*US*)
Quadrant Magazine (*Aus*)
Quite Curious Literature (*US*)
Radix Magazine (*US*)
The Rag (*US*)
The Reader (*UK*)
Red Rock Review (*US*)
The Rusty Nail (*US*)
The Savage Kick (*UK*)
Scissors and Spackle (*US*)
Southword Journal (*Ire*)
Stone Canoe (*US*)
Stone Highway Review (*US*)
Straitjackets Magazine (*US*)
The Subterranean Literary Journal (*UK*)
The Tablet (*UK*)
The Vehicle (*US*)
thesnailmagazine (*UK*)
20x20 magazine (*UK*)
Unwind-The Cafe Journal (*Aus*)
The Washington Pastime (*US*)
Writers' Forum (*UK*)
Media
Anobium (*US*)
Extastic Magazine (*UK*)
Fjords Review (*US*)
From A Writer's POV Magazine (*US*)
Intermedia (*UK*)
Media Week (*UK*)
Netsagas.com (*US*)
The Northern Star (*Can*)
Now (*UK*)

Radix Magazine (*US*)
Stone Highway Review (*US*)
Straitjackets Magazine (*US*)
The Subterranean Literary Journal (*UK*)
thesnailmagazine (*UK*)
Unwind-The Cafe Journal (*Aus*)
Medicine
ACP Internist (*US*)
The Cattleman (*US*)
Chemist+Druggist (*UK*)
Diabetes Self-Management (*US*)
Earth Mama Magazine (*US*)
Equus Magazine (*US*)
From A Writer's POV Magazine (*US*)
Journal of Emergency Medical Services (JEMS)
(*US*)
Netsagas.com (*US*)
Open Spaces (*US*)
Pulse (*UK*)
The Saturday Evening Post (*US*)
School Nurse News (*US*)
The Subterranean Literary Journal (*UK*)
Unwind-The Cafe Journal (*Aus*)
Men's Interests
18 Wheels & Heels (*US*)
Focus Magazine of SWFL (*US*)
From A Writer's POV Magazine (*US*)
Native Max (*US*)
Netsagas.com (*US*)
The Subterranean Literary Journal (*UK*)
Unwind-The Cafe Journal (*Aus*)
Zoo (*UK*)
Military
AIR International (*UK*)
AirForces Monthly (*UK*)
ARMY Magazine (*US*)
Family Tree Magazine (*UK*)
Flight International (*UK*)
Netsagas.com (*US*)
The Savage Kick (*UK*)
The Subterranean Literary Journal (*UK*)
Unwind-The Cafe Journal (*Aus*)
Who Do You Think You Are? Magazine (*UK*)
The Yes Factory (*US*)
Music
Classic Rock (*UK*)
Classical Music (*UK*)
Early Music (*UK*)
Earth Mama Magazine (*US*)
18 Wheels & Heels (*US*)
Fjords Review (*US*)
Focus Magazine of SWFL (*US*)
From A Writer's POV Magazine (*US*)
Go Girl Magazine (*UK*)
International Bluegrass (*US*)
Jewish Quarterly (*UK*)
The List (*UK*)
LONE STARS Magazine (*US*)
Music Teacher (*UK*)
Netsagas.com (*US*)
New Jersey Monthly (*US*)
Planet (*UK*)
Pointe Magazine (*US*)

The Resurrectionist (*UK*)
Scissors and Spackle (*US*)
Stone Canoe (*US*)
The Strad (*UK*)
Straitjackets Magazine (*US*)
The Subterranean Literary Journal (*UK*)
The Savage Side (*US*)
Tocher (*UK*)
20x20 magazine (*UK*)
Unwind-The Cafe Journal (*Aus*)
Mystery
Carillon Magazine (*UK*)
Crystal Magazine (*UK*)
Earth Mama Magazine (*US*)
Fjords Review (*US*)
From A Writer's POV Magazine (*US*)
Literary Juice (*US*)
Netsagas.com (*US*)
The Northern Star (*Can*)
Pakn Treger (*US*)
The Paumanok Review (*US*)
The People's Friend (*UK*)
The Rusty Nail (*US*)
Scissors and Spackle (*US*)
Stone Highway Review (*US*)
Straitjackets Magazine (*US*)
The Subterranean Literary Journal (*UK*)
The Vehicle (*US*)
Thematic Literary Magazine (*US*)
Unwind-The Cafe Journal (*Aus*)
The Washington Pastime (*US*)
The Yes Factory (*US*)
Nature
Ag Weekly (*US*)
American Hunter (*US*)
Animals and You (*UK*)
BC Outdoors Sport Fishing (*Can*)
Bird Life Magazine (*UK*)
Blue Ridge Country (*US*)
The Brahman Journal (*US*)
The Cattleman (*US*)
The Countryman (*UK*)
Crystal Magazine (*UK*)
Dairy Farmer (*UK*)
Devon Life (*UK*)
Discover Maine Magazine (*US*)
Earth Mama Magazine (*US*)
EarthLines Magazine (*UK*)
Equus Magazine (*US*)
Fjords Review (*US*)
Focus Magazine of SWFL (*US*)
The Maine Sportsman (*US*)
Montana Magazine (*US*)
National Parks Magazine (*US*)
Netsagas.com (*US*)
New Jersey Monthly (*US*)
The Northern Star (*Can*)
Northern Woodlands (*US*)
Open Spaces (*US*)
Pony Magazine (*UK*)
Pallet Enterprise (*US*)
Peace and Freedom (*UK*)
Quite Curious Literature (*US*)

Employee Assistance Report (*US*)
Envoi (*UK*)
Equus Magazine (*US*)
Essentials (*UK*)
Eventing (*UK*)
Evidence Technology Magazine (*US*)
Faith & Form (*US*)
Family Tree Magazine (*UK*)
FIDO Friendly (*US*)
Financial Adviser (*UK*)
Flight International (*UK*)
Focus Magazine of SWFL (*US*)
Forum (*US*)
FourFourTwo (*UK*)
Freelance Market News (*UK*)
The Frogmore Papers (*UK*)
From A Writer's POV Magazine (*US*)
Go Girl Magazine (*UK*)
GamesMaster (*UK*)
Geist (*Can*)
Girl Talk (*UK*)
Girls' Life (*US*)
Golf World (*UK*)
Greetings Today (*UK*)
Guiding Magazine (*UK*)
High Life (*UK*)
Heat (*UK*)
Hippocampus Magazine (*US*)
Horse & Hound (*UK*)
House Beautiful (*UK*)
ICIS Chemical Business Magazine (*UK*)
Ingram's Magazine (*US*)
Intermedia (*UK*)
International Bluegrass (*US*)
Iota (*UK*)
Irish Arts Review (*Ire*)
The Irish Post (*UK*)
Irish Tatler (*Ire*)
Islands (*US*)
Jewish Quarterly (*UK*)
Journal of Emergency Medical Services (JEMS) (*US*)
Journal Plus (*US*)
Junior (*UK*)
Junior Baseball (*US*)
Kalyani Magazine. (*US*)
Kids Alive! (*UK*)
Kids' Ministry Ideas (*US*)
Lancashire Magazine (*UK*)
LabTalk (*US*)
Lausanne World Pulse (LWP) (*US*)
Law Enforcement Technology Magazine (*US*)
Link & Visitor (*Can*)
The List (*UK*)
Litro Magazine (*UK*)
The Living Church (*US*)
The London Magazine (*UK*)
London Review of Books (*UK*)
Lummox (*US*)
Model Boats (*UK*)
MyBusiness Magazine (*US*)
Machine Design (*US*)
Macworld (*UK*)

Magma (*UK*)
The Maine Sportsman (*US*)
Market Newsletter (*UK*)
Massage Magazine (*US*)
Media Week (*UK*)
Message of the Open Bible (*US*)
Metta-Physics Magazine (*UK*)
Midwest Living (*US*)
Milwaukee Magazine (*US*)
Model Cars Magazine (*US*)
Modern Poetry in Translation (*UK*)
Monkey Kettle (*UK*)
Montana Magazine (*US*)
Mountain Biking UK (*UK*)
Mslexia (*UK*)
MSW Management (*US*)
Muscle & Fitness (*UK*)
Music Teacher (*UK*)
Native Max (*US*)
National Parks Magazine (*US*)
Necrology Shorts (*US*)
.net (*UK*)
Netsagas.com (*US*)
New CollAge (*US*)
New Jersey Monthly (*US*)
New Law Journal (*UK*)
The New Shetlander (*UK*)
New Walk Magazine (*UK*)
New Welsh Review (*UK*)
The New Writer (*UK*)
New York (*US*)
NextStepU Magazine (*US*)
North Carolina Literary Review (NCLR) (*US*)
North Dakota Quarterly (*US*)
The Northern Star (*Can*)
Northern Woodlands (*US*)
Northwest Review (*US*)
Notes from the Underground (*UK*)
Now (*UK*)
Now & Then: The Appalachian Magazine (*US*)
Nuthouse (*US*)
Nuvein Magazine (*US*)
O&A (Oil & Automotive Service) Marketing News (*US*)
Obsidian: Literature in the African Diaspora (*US*)
Old Tractor (*UK*)
One (*US*)
Open Spaces (*US*)
The Oracular Tree (*Can*)
Our Dogs (*UK*)
Overdrive (*US*)
Overland (*Aus*)
PMS poemmemoirstory (*US*)
Pony Magazine (*UK*)
Pulse (*US*)
PRISM Magazine (*US*)
Pacific Yachting (*Can*)
Pakn Treger (*US*)
Pallet Enterprise (*US*)
Paradoxism (*US*)
Passages North (*US*)
The Paumanok Review (*US*)
PC Advisor (*UK*)

Literary Juice (*US*)
Necrology Shorts (*US*)
Netsagas.com (*US*)
NOVA Science Fiction (*US*)
The Paumanok Review (*US*)
Premonitions (*UK*)
Residential Aliens (*US*)
The Rusty Nail (*US*)
Scissors and Spackle (*US*)
Scribble (*UK*)
Straitjackets Magazine (*US*)
The Subterranean Literary Journal (*UK*)
The Savage Side (*US*)
The Vehicle (*US*)
Thematic Literary Magazine (*US*)
Unwind-The Cafe Journal (*Aus*)
Vampires2 (*US*)
The Washington Pastime (*US*)
The Yes Factory (*US*)
Scripts
Eclectica Magazine (*US*)
Kalyani Magazine. (*US*)
New Writing Scotland (*UK*)
Obsidian: Literature in the African Diaspora (*US*)
Paradoxism (*US*)
The Prairie Journal (*Can*)
PRISM international (*Can*)
The Rag (*US*)
Santa Clara Review (*US*)
Scissors and Spackle (*US*)
Stone Canoe (*US*)
The Subterranean Literary Journal (*UK*)
The Vehicle (*US*)
Self-Help
Diabetes Self-Management (*US*)
Earth Mama Magazine (*US*)
Extastic Magazine (*UK*)
Focus Magazine of SWFL (*US*)
From A Writer's POV Magazine (*US*)
Netsagas.com (*US*)
NextStepU Magazine (*US*)
The Subterranean Literary Journal (*UK*)
Unwind-The Cafe Journal (*Aus*)
Short Stories
Albedo One (*Ire*)
Ambit (*UK*)
Anderbo.com (*US*)
Androids2 (*US*)
Anobium (*US*)
Areopagus Magazine (*UK*)
Areté (*UK*)
Armchair/Shotgun (*US*)
Ascent Aspirations Magazine (*Can*)
Awen (*UK*)
Beyond the Rainbow (*Aus*)
Big Fiction (*US*)
Blue Mesa Review (*US*)
Brittle Star (*UK*)
The Broadkill Review (*US*)
Carillon Magazine (*US*)
Conceit Magazine (*US*)
Crystal Magazine (*UK*)
Cyphers (*Ire*)

The Dalhousie Review (*Can*)
DASH Journal (*US*)
The Doctor T. J. Eckleburg Review (*US*)
Dream Catcher (*UK*)
The Dublin Review (*Ire*)
Earth Mama Magazine (*US*)
EarthLines Magazine (*UK*)
The Fiddlehead (*Can*)
FIDO Friendly (*US*)
Fire (*UK*)
Fjords Review (*US*)
The Frogmore Papers (*UK*)
From A Writer's POV Magazine (*US*)
Garbaj (*UK*)
Geist (*Can*)
The Interpreter's House (*UK*)
Iota (*UK*)
Jewish Quarterly (*UK*)
Kalyani Magazine. (*US*)
The Ledge Magazine (*US*)
Literary Juice (*US*)
Litro Magazine (*UK*)
The London Magazine (*UK*)
Lummox (*US*)
Man's Story 2 (*US*)
Monkey Kettle (*UK*)
Monomyth (*UK*)
Mslexia (*UK*)
Necrology Shorts (*US*)
Netsagas.com (*US*)
New CollAge (*US*)
The New Shetlander (*UK*)
New Walk Magazine (*UK*)
New Welsh Review (*UK*)
The New Writer (*UK*)
New Writing Scotland (*UK*)
The Nocturnal Lyric (*US*)
North Carolina Literary Review (NCLR) (*US*)
North Dakota Quarterly (*US*)
Northwest Review (*US*)
Notes from the Underground (*UK*)
Notre Dame Review (*US*)
NOVA Science Fiction (*US*)
Now & Then: The Appalachian Magazine (*US*)
Nuvein Magazine (*US*)
Ohio Teachers Write (*US*)
On the Premises (*US*)
One Less Magazine (*US*)
Open Spaces (*US*)
Opium Magazine (*US*)
The Oracular Tree (*Can*)
Overland (*Aus*)
PMS poemmemoirstory (*US*)
Paradoxism (*US*)
Passages North (*US*)
The Paterson Literary Review (*US*)
The Paumanok Review (*US*)
Peace and Freedom (*UK*)
The Pedestal Magazine (*US*)
The Penniless Press (*UK*)
Pennsylvania English (*US*)
The People's Friend (*UK*)
Peregrine (*US*)

Permafrost (*US*)
Persimmon Tree (*US*)
Pilgrimage (*US*)
Pink Chameleon (*US*)
Pinyon (*US*)
Pisgah Review (*US*)
Plain Spoke (*US*)
Planet (*UK*)
Pockets (*US*)
Portland Magazine (*US*)
The Portland Review (*US*)
Post Road (*US*)
Potomac Review (*US*)
The Prairie Journal (*Can*)
Prairie Schooner (*US*)
Prospect (*UK*)
Provincetown Arts (*US*)
Pseudopod (*US*)
Puckerbrush Review (*US*)
Quadrant Magazine (*Aus*)
Queen's Quarterly (*Can*)
Quiddity (*US*)
Quite Curious Literature (*US*)
Romance Flash (*US*)
The Rag (*US*)
Railroad Evangelist Magazine (*US*)
The Reader (*UK*)
The Red Clay Review (*US*)
Redactions: Poetry, Poetics, & Prose (*US*)
Redivider (*US*)
Reed Magazine (*US*)
Rhino Poetry (*US*)
Riddle Fence (*Can*)
The Rockford Review (*US*)
Romantic shorts (*Can*)
The Rusty Nail (*US*)
Sable (*UK*)
Salt Hill Journal (*US*)
Sandy River Review (*US*)
Santa Clara Review (*US*)
Santa Monica Review (*US*)
Saranac Review (*US*)
Sarasvati (*UK*)
The Saturday Evening Post (*US*)
Scary Monsters Magazine (*US*)
Scissors and Spackle (*US*)
Scribble (*UK*)
Scribbler! (*UK*)
Seek (*US*)
The Sewanee Review (*US*)
Shadows Express (*US*)
Short Story America (*US*)
Southword Journal (*Ire*)
Stand Magazine (*UK*)
Staple Magazine (*UK*)
Stone Canoe (*US*)
Stone Highway Review (*US*)
Straitjackets Magazine (*US*)
The Subterranean Literary Journal (*UK*)
Takahe (*NZ*)
Take a Break (*UK*)
The Tavern's Vault (*US*)
Tears in the Fence (*UK*)

The Rejected Quarterly (*US*)
The Savage Side (*US*)
The Vehicle (*US*)
Thematic Literary Magazine (*US*)
Tocher (*UK*)
20x20 magazine (*UK*)
Unwind-The Cafe Journal (*Aus*)
Vampires2 (*US*)
Wild Violet (*US*)
The Washington Pastime (*US*)
Water-Stone Review (*US*)
Woman's Weekly (*UK*)
Words Magazine (*UK*)
The Yellow Room (*UK*)
The Yes Factory (*US*)
Your Cat (*UK*)
Yours (*UK*)
Zouch (*Can*)

Sociology
The Big Issue in the North (*UK*)
The Dalhousie Review (*Can*)
Family Tree Magazine (*UK*)
Fjords Review (*US*)
From A Writer's POV Magazine (*US*)
Netsagas.com (*US*)
Open Spaces (*US*)
Peace and Freedom (*UK*)
The Resurrectionist (*UK*)
Scissors and Spackle (*US*)
Scottish Home and Country Magazine (*UK*)
Straitjackets Magazine (*US*)
The Subterranean Literary Journal (*UK*)
thesnailmagazine (*UK*)
Unwind-The Cafe Journal (*Aus*)
Who Do You Think You Are? Magazine (*UK*)

Spiritual
Anobium (*US*)
Beyond the Rainbow (*Aus*)
Earth Mama Magazine (*US*)
Fjords Review (*US*)
From A Writer's POV Magazine (*US*)
The Living Church (*US*)
Metta-Physics Magazine (*UK*)
Netsagas.com (*US*)
Pilgrimage (*US*)
The Subterranean Literary Journal (*UK*)
Thematic Literary Magazine (*US*)
Unwind-The Cafe Journal (*Aus*)
The Yes Factory (*US*)

Sport
American Hunter (*US*)
BC Outdoors Sport Fishing (*Can*)
Bike Magazine (*US*)
Bowls International (*UK*)
Canoe & Kayak (*US*)
Cycling Weekly (*UK*)
Discover Maine Magazine (*US*)
Draft (*US*)
Equus Magazine (*US*)
Eventing (*UK*)
Forum (*US*)
FourFourTwo (*UK*)
From A Writer's POV Magazine (*US*)

Pembroke Magazine (*US*)
The Penniless Press (*UK*)
Pilgrimage (*US*)
Poetry International (*US*)
Poetry London (*UK*)
Post Road (*US*)
PRISM international (*Can*)
Rhino Poetry (*US*)
Sable (*UK*)
Salt Hill Journal (*US*)
Saranac Review (*US*)
Stand Magazine (*UK*)
Stone Highway Review (*US*)
The Subterranean Literary Journal (*UK*)
Tears in the Fence (*UK*)
Tocher (*UK*)
Unwind-The Cafe Journal (*Aus*)
Travel
AeroSafety World Magazine (*US*)
Ag Weekly (*US*)
AKC Gazette (*US*)
Autocar (*UK*)
Bike Magazine (*US*)
Blue Ridge Country (*US*)
Camping Today (*US*)
Canals, Rivers + Boats (*UK*)
Car Magazine (*UK*)
Caterer and Hotelkeeper (*UK*)
Consumers Digest (*US*)
Crystal Magazine (*UK*)
Devon Life (*UK*)
Draft (*US*)
Earth Mama Magazine (*US*)
Eclectica Magazine (*US*)
FIDO Friendly (*US*)
Focus Magazine of SWFL (*US*)
Forum (*US*)
From A Writer's POV Magazine (*US*)
Girls' Life (*US*)
High Life (*UK*)
The Irish Post (*UK*)
Islands (*US*)
Junior (*UK*)
Midwest Living (*US*)
Milwaukee Magazine (*US*)
Montana Magazine (*US*)
Netsagas.com (*US*)
New York (*US*)
NextStepU Magazine (*US*)
North Carolina Literary Review (NCLR) (*US*)
Overdrive (*US*)
Pacific Yachting (*Can*)
Pakn Treger (*US*)
Railroad Evangelist Magazine (*US*)
Railway Gazette International (*UK*)
Red Magazine (*UK*)
Road King (*US*)
RV Business (*US*)
Sable (*UK*)
The Saturday Evening Post (*US*)
Scottish Home and Country Magazine (*UK*)
Sea Magazine (*US*)
Ships Monthly Magazine (*UK*)

Somerset Life (*UK*)
Stone Highway Review (*US*)
The Subterranean Literary Journal (*UK*)
Take a Break (*UK*)
Tatler (*UK*)
Time Out (*UK*)
Unwind-The Cafe Journal (*Aus*)
TV
American Cinematographer (*US*)
Earth Mama Magazine (*US*)
From A Writer's POV Magazine (*US*)
The List (*UK*)
Netsagas.com (*US*)
Straitjackets Magazine (*US*)
The Subterranean Literary Journal (*UK*)
Sugar Magazine (*UK*)
Unwind-The Cafe Journal (*Aus*)
Westerns
Crystal Magazine (*UK*)
Netsagas.com (*US*)
The Paumanok Review (*US*)
The Rusty Nail (*US*)
The Savage Kick (*UK*)
Straitjackets Magazine (*US*)
The Subterranean Literary Journal (*UK*)
The Vehicle (*US*)
Unwind-The Cafe Journal (*Aus*)
The Washington Pastime (*US*)
The Yes Factory (*US*)
Women's Interests
bliss Magazine (*UK*)
Broadsheet (*US*)
Earth Mama Magazine (*US*)
Essentials (*UK*)
Extastic Magazine (*UK*)
Focus Magazine of SWFL (*US*)
From A Writer's POV Magazine (*US*)
Girls' Life (*US*)
Guiding Magazine (*UK*)
Irish Tatler (*Ire*)
Kalyani Magazine. (*US*)
Link & Visitor (*Can*)
Mslexia (*UK*)
Native Max (*US*)
Netsagas.com (*US*)
Now (*UK*)
PMS poemmemoirstory (*US*)
The People's Friend (*UK*)
Persimmon Tree (*US*)
Prima Baby & Pregnancy (*UK*)
Real People (*UK*)
Red Magazine (*UK*)
Resources for Feminist Research (*Can*)
Room Magazine (*Can*)
Scissors and Spackle (*US*)
Scottish Home and Country Magazine (*UK*)
Stone Highway Review (*US*)
The Subterranean Literary Journal (*UK*)
Sugar Magazine (*UK*)
Take a Break (*UK*)
Tatler (*UK*)
Wedding Ideas (*UK*)
Woman's Weekly (*UK*)

WOW! Women On Writing (*US*)
The Yellow Room (*UK*)

Yours (*UK*)
Zest (*UK*)

Get Free Access to the firstwriter.com Website

To claim your free access to the **firstwriter.com** website simply send an email to free.access@firstwriter.com, including the following details:

- Your full name
- Your full postal address
- Your email address
- Promotional code: **LK72**

You should receive a response within two working days.

If you need any assistance please email support@firstwriter.com.

If you have found this book useful, please consider leaving a review on the website where you bought it!

What you get

Once you have set up access to ths site you will be able to benefit from all the following features:

Databases

All our databases are updated almost every day, and include powerful search facilities to help you find exactly what you need. Searches that used to take you hours or even days in print books or on search engines can now be done in seconds, and produce more accurate and up-to-date information. Our agents database also includes independent reports from at least three separate sources, showing you which are the top agencies and helping you avoid the scams that are all over the internet. You can try out any of our databases before you subscribe:

- Search **over 850 literary agencies**
- Search **over 1,400 book publishers**
- Search **over 1,500 magazines**
- Search between **100** and **250 current competitions**

PLUS advanced features to help you with your search:

- Save searches and save time – set up to 15 search parameters specific to your work, save them, and then access the search results with a single click whenever you log

Printed in Great Britain
by Amazon.co.uk, Ltd.,
Marston Gate.